THE
LAW OF CORPORATIONS
AND OTHER BUSINESS
ORGANIZATIONS

SIXTH EDITION

THE
LAW OF CORPORATIONS
AND OTHER BUSINESS
ORGANIZATIONS

SIXTH EDITION

ANGELA SCHNEEMAN

DELMAR
CENGAGE Learning·

Australia • Brazil • Japan • Korea • Mexico • Singapore • Spain • United Kingdom • United States

**The Law of Corporations
and Other Business
Organizations, Sixth Edition**
Angela Schneeman

Vice President, Editorial: Dave Garza

Director of Learning Solutions:
Sandy Clark

Senior Acquisitions Editor:
Shelley Esposito

Managing Editor: Larry Main

Product Manager: Anne Orgren

Editorial Assistant: Diane Chrysler

Vice President, Marketing:
Jennifer Baker

Marketing Director:
Deborah S. Yarnell

Senior Marketing Manager:
Mark Linton

Marketing Coordinator:
Erin DeAngelo

Senior Production Director:
Wendy Troeger

Production Manager: Mark Bernard

Senior Content Project Manager:
Betty Dickson

For product information and technology assistance, contact us at
Cengage Learning Customer & Sales Support, 1-800-354-9706

For permission to use material from this text or product,
submit all requests online at **www.cengage.com/permissions**.
Further permissions questions can be e-mailed to
permissionrequest@cengage.com

Library of Congress Control Number: 2012931336

ISBN-13: 978-1-133-01914-5

ISBN-10: 1-133-01914-5

Delmar
5 Maxwell Drive
Clifton Park, NY 12065-2919
USA

Cengage Learning is a leading provider of customized learning solutions with office locations around the globe, including Singapore, the United Kingdom, Australia, Mexico, Brazil, and Japan. Locate your local office at:
international.cengage.com/region

Cengage Learning products are represented in Canada by Nelson Education, Ltd.

To learn more about Delmar, visit **www.cengage.com/delmar**

Purchase any of our products at your local college store or at our preferred online store **www.cengagebrain.com**

Notice to the Reader

Printed in the United States of America
1 2 3 4 5 6 7 16 15 14 13 12

Dedication

IN MEMORY OF MY MOTHER,
ANNA LUTTERMAN

Brief Contents

CHAPTER 4 Limited Partnerships. . . . 119

CHAPTER 5 Limited Liability Partnerships and Limited Liability Limited Partnerships. 168

CHAPTER 14 Corporate Dissolution . . 604

CHAPTER 15 Employee Benefit Plans and Employment Agreements 639

Detailed Contents

CHAPTER 2

Sole Proprietorships. 32

CHAPTER 3

General Partnerships 56

CHAPTER 4

Limited Partnerships 119

CHAPTER 5

Limited Liability Partnerships and Limited Liability Limited Partnerships 168

CHAPTER 6

Limited Liability Companies 208

CHAPTER 7

Corporations 259

CHAPTER 8

Incorporations. 294

CHAPTER 9

The Corporate Organization. 351

CHAPTER 10

The Corporate Financial Structure 415

CHAPTER 11

Public Corporations and
Securities Regulations 457

CHAPTER 13

Foreign Corporation Qualification 575

CHAPTER 14

Corporate Dissolution 604

Preface

The Law of Corporations and Other Business Organizations is an in-depth introduction to the law of business organizations for paralegal students. This text focuses on corporations, sole proprietorships, partnerships, limited partnerships, and limited liability entities. An overview of the law and theory behind the law are provided for each type of business organization, as well as practical information that the paralegal can use on the job.

Relying on my own experience as a corporate paralegal, and input from several other paralegals, I have included in this text practical information that paralegals need to succeed on the job—without sacrificing content concerning the law. Paralegals need to know the law, but they also need to know how to get things done. Each chapter of the text includes a discussion of the law, as well as a section entitled "The Paralegal's Role," which focuses on procedures and includes several valuable resources. Paralegal profiles in each chapter give students some insight as to how working paralegals put what they have learned to use.

Because most law concerning corporations is based on state law and can vary among the states, this text focuses on the Model Business Corporation Act as revised through 2010, which is the basis for most of the state business corporation acts in the country. Discussions in the partnership and limited liability company chapters focus on the pertinent uniform laws. State charts are included where practical, as well as cites for state statutes. The CourseMate website for this text includes excerpts from the Model Business Corporation Act, as well as links to the uniform laws and the pertinent statutes of each state. In addition, examples, sample documents, sample paragraphs, and practical advice are included for the paralegal student within the text and on CourseMate, providing information and resources the corporate paralegal can use on the job. This is the text students will want to take from the classroom to the office.

TEXT ORGANIZATION

Each chapter begins with a discussion of the law and ends with procedural information specifically for paralegals. A typical chapter of this text includes the following:

- An in-depth discussion of the law, with a general focus on the pertinent model and uniform acts and how the law may differ among the states
- Current charts and statistics pertinent to the subject
- Tables including citations for pertinent state law
- Sidebars, disbursed through each chapter, providing relevant and interesting facts, statistics, and quotations
- Edited cases illustrating some of the more important points made in the chapter
- Sample documents and document paragraphs
- The Paralegal's Role section with a general discussion of the paralegal's role in working with the particular subject of the chapter, checklists, and resources
- A profile of a paralegal who works in the subject area of law
- An Ethical Consideration feature providing a discussion of one of the basic rules of legal ethics from the paralegal's perspective
- Resources
- Section summaries
- Chapter Summary
- Review Questions
- Exercise in Critical Thinking
- Practical Problems
- Workplace Scenario

NEW TO THE SIXTH EDITION

This edition brings new and up-to-date information on the laws and trends affecting limited liability entities and corporations. Following is an outline of some of the more important changes made to this sixth edition:

- Updated statistics and sidebars have been added throughout this edition, adding interesting and up-to-date facts and bits of information to keep students engaged.
- A new In Summation feature in each chapter provides a quick review of the highlights of each section to help students fully comprehend the material in each chapter.
- New and updated Paralegal Profiles throughout the text introduce students to paralegals who work in the corporate law area and give insight into the actual work being done by corporate paralegals.

- New Exercise in Critical Thinking questions ask the students to think beyond the materials they have learned and consider the reasons for certain corporate and business organization laws and established procedures as well as their possible flaws.
- A brief Portfolio Reminder section following the Workplace Scenario assignment in each chapter helps students track their class assignments to create their own portfolios of the sample documents they have created.

ANCILLARY MATERIALS

- The CourseMate website to accompany *The Law of Corporations and Other Business Organizations* includes:

  — An interactive e-book, with highlighting, note-taking, and search capabilities

  — Interactive learning tools, including:

  – Quizzes

  – Flash cards

  – Case Studies

  – Online Resources for the Corporate Paralegal

  – And more!

  — Go to http://www.cengagebrain.com to access these resources, and look for this icon to find resources related to this text in CourseMate.

- **WebTutor on Blackboard and Angel**—The WebTutor™ supplement to accompany *The Law of Corporations and Other Business Organizations* allows you to extend your reach beyond the classroom. This online courseware is designed to complement the text and helps students and instructors to better manage time, prepare for exams, organize notes, and more.

INSTRUCTOR
RESOURCES

- With Delmar Cengage Learning's Instructor Resources to accompany *The Law of Corporations and Other Business Organizations*, preparing for class and evaluating students have never been easier! Access these resources— anywhere, anytime, online—through Single Sign-On (SSO) and on CD-ROM:

  — Written by the author of the text, the **Instructor's Manual** contains outlines, suggested approaches, case briefs of the cases in the text, additional review questions and exercises, and a test bank.

  — The **Computerized Testbank** (available in ExamView®, Blackboard, WebCT and rich-text format) makes generating tests and quizzes a snap. With different question styles to choose from, you can create customized assessments for your students with the click of a button. Add your own unique questions and print rationales for easy class preparation.

  — Customizable **PowerPoint**® presentations focus on key points for each chapter. PowerPoint® is a registered trademark of the Microsoft Corporation.

ACKNOWLEDGMENTS

I would like to express my gratitude to several people for the assistance they have given me on this project, especially Shelley Esposito, Senior Acquisitions Editor; Anne Orgren, Product Manager; Diane Chrysler, Editorial Assistant; and Betty Dickson, Senior Content Project Manager.

I would like to acknowledge the contributions of Daniel Oran, author of *Dictionary of the Law*, and William Statsky, author of *West's Legal Thesaurus/Dictionary*, for providing many of the glossary definitions throughout this text.

I would also like to thank my family, friends, and coworkers for their advice and encouragement. And very special thanks go to my husband Greg and our children Alex and Katherine for their patience and support.

Last, I acknowledge the contributions of the following reviewers, whose suggestions and insights have helped me enormously.

Kristen Brown
Guildford Technical Community College
Jamestown, NC

Stacie J. Brunet, Esq.

Jay Strike Carlin
Grantham University
Kansas City, MO

Kathy Chew
Attorney at Law

Russell R. Clark
George Washington University
Washington, DC

Wm Bruce Davis
University at Cincinnati Clermont College
Batavia, OH

Tangela S. King, J.D.
Central Georgia Technical College
Macon, GA

Laura Rosenthal, J.D.
Empire College of Business
Santa Rosa, CA

Sean D. K. Scott, J.D.
St. Petersburg College
St. Petersburg, FL

Annette Whitby
Park University
Parkville, MO

ABOUT THE AUTHOR

Angela Schneeman is a freelance paralegal who specializes in the corporate area of law. She has been a paralegal since receiving her legal assistant certificate from the University of Minnesota in 1984. She also earned her Bachelor of Science degree in Business and Legal Studies from the University of Minnesota. Angela has worked as a paralegal for law firms, the legal department of publicly held corporations, and a major accounting firm. She currently offers her services to attorneys in Minneapolis, St. Paul, and White Bear Lake, Minnesota. Angela is the author of five textbooks for paralegals.

Table of Cases

Introduction

This text concerns not just corporations, but all of the most important business organizations in the United States. The business organizations discussed include:

- Corporations
- S Corporations
- Sole proprietorships
- Partnerships
- Limited partnerships
- Limited liability partnerships
- Limited liability limited partnerships
- Limited liability companies

The individual or group wanting to begin business in the United States has an interesting and important decision to make. Never before have there been so many types of business organizations to choose from. In the not too distant past, business organizations included sole proprietorships, partnerships, and corporations. The addition of several new types of business entities has made the selection more appealing, but possibly overwhelming. Each of the newer business entities was designed to fill a void or to meet a need in the business community. For example, the limited liability company was designed for those individuals who wanted both the tax status of a partnership and the limited liability of a corporation.

It is important to know the major characteristics of each type of available business entity, and to keep up to date on new developments. In Chapter 8, Exhibit 8-1 sets forth some of the more important characteristics of the business organizations discussed in this text. Keep in mind that some of these factors vary by state, and the law of the entity's state of organization is the final authority for defining the business enterprise.

As you proceed through this text, you may want to refer to Exhibit 8-1 to make a quick comparison of the various business organizations.

INTRODUCTION TO AGENCY AND BUSINESS ORGANIZATIONS

CHAPTER OUTLINE

INTRODUCTION

When one person acts on behalf of another, an agency relationship is formed. The agency relationship is very important to all business organizations and to the transaction of business worldwide. Without the ability of one person to act for another person or business organization, the transaction of modern business would be impossible. Employees, partners, and corporate officers and directors all act as agents.

Agency law establishes the rights and liabilities created when one person acts for another. The action of the agent on behalf of the principal is considered an act of the principal. Most often, disputes concerning agency relationships are resolved under contract law or the common law of the state where the agency was created.

Because agency relationships are so important to the function of all business organizations, this first chapter is a brief introduction to the agency relationship. First we define some terms and concepts associated with agencies, including those used for the various parties to the agency relationship. Then we look at the elements of the agency relationship and how that relationship is created. After examining the nature of the agency relationship and termination of the agency, we will conclude with a closer look at how agency relationships permit business organizations to transact business.

§ 1.1 AGENCY CONCEPTS AND DEFINITIONS

AGENCY

A relationship in which one person acts for or represents another by the latter's authority.

An **agency** is a legal relationship in which one person (the agent) acts for or represents another (the principal) by the latter's authority. More specifically, agency is "A fiduciary relationship created by express or implied contract or by law, in which one party (the agent) may act on behalf of another party (the principal) and bind that other party by words or actions."[1]

AGENT

AGENT

A person authorized (requested or permitted) by another person to act for him or her; a person entrusted with another's business.

In an agency relationship, the **agent** is the person authorized by the principal to act with third parties on the principal's behalf. The agent represents the principal and acquires authority from the principal. There are two kinds of agents—general agents and special agents.

General Agent

GENERAL AGENT

One who is authorized to act for his or her principal in all matters concerning a particular business or employment of a particular nature.

A **general agent** is an agent authorized to transact all business of the principal, all business of a particular kind, all business at a particular place, or all acts connected with a particular employment or business. For example, if a small business owner decides to travel abroad for a year, the business owner may enlist a trusted employee as general agent to take care of all business and financial affairs in the business owner's absence.

Special Agent

SPECIAL AGENT

One employed to conduct a particular transaction or piece of business for his or her principal or authorized to perform a specified act.

A **special agent** is authorized to do one or more specific acts in accordance with instructions from the principal. Using the previous example, if the business owner who is going abroad decides to sell her yacht, she could enlist the services of a yacht broker to see to the sale in her absence. The yacht broker would be a special agent with the authority to negotiate a price and handle the sale of the business owner's yacht. The special agent would not, however, have authority to take other actions on behalf of the business owner with regard to other business or financial affairs.

PRINCIPAL

In an agency relationship, the **principal** is the party for whom the agent acts and from whom the agent derives authority to act. Under the law of agency, the principal acts through the agent. "As a general rule, a person may properly appoint an agent to do the same acts and achieve the same legal consequences as if he or she had acted personally."[2] The principal has some degree of control over the acts of the agent.

PRINCIPAL
An employer or anyone else who has another person (an agent) do things for him or her.

MASTER AND SERVANT

The terms "master" and "servant" may seem rather antiquated, but they are still used from time to time to describe certain concepts of agency law. In agency law, the master is the employer who acts as principal by employing the servant (employee) to perform services. The master retains control over the manner of the servant's performance. It is important to distinguish this relationship from that of an individual or business who hires an independent contractor.

INDEPENDENT CONTRACTOR

An **independent contractor** is an individual hired by another to perform some specific task or function, but not in a representative capacity. The independent contractor contracts with an employer for specific results; the employer does not control how the independent contractor achieves those results. The employer retains no right of control over the independent contractor.

INDEPENDENT CONTRACTOR
A person who contracts with an "employer" to do a particular piece of work by his or her own methods and under his or her own control.

The key determiner as to whether an individual is an employee or an independent contractor is whether the principal (employer) has the right to control the manner of the employee or independent contractor's performance. The distinction between employee status and independent contractor status can be a very important one. Under certain circumstances, an employer may be liable for the **torts** of an employee, but not those of an independent contractor.

TORT
A civil (as opposed to a criminal) wrong, other than a breach of contract. For an act to be a tort, there must be: a legal duty owed by one person to another, a breach (breaking) of that duty, and harm done as a direct result of the action. Examples of torts are negligence, battery, and libel.

The following factors are often considered in determining whether an individual is an employee or an independent contractor:

- How much control does the employer have over the individual? If the employer has the right to control the actions of the individual, the individual would most likely be considered an employee.

- Is the individual engaged in a distinct occupation or business? If a restaurant owner hires an established painter to paint his or her restaurant, the painter would probably be considered an independent contractor.

- Is the type of service being performed customarily performed by an employee under the supervision of an employer, or by an independent contractor without supervision? If a golf course owner hires a full-time groundskeeper, an individual who would customarily be supervised, it is much more likely that the groundskeeper would be considered an employee than an independent contractor.

POWER OF ATTORNEY
A document authorizing a person to act as attorney in fact for the person signing the document.

ATTORNEY IN FACT
Any person who acts formally for another person.

SPECIAL POWER OF ATTORNEY
A power of attorney authorizing the attorney in fact to act for the principal with regard to a specific action or a specific transaction.

- Who supplies the tools and place of work for the services rendered? If a hotel manager hires an individual to handle the laundry for the hotel, using the hotel's washers and dryers, it is much more likely that that person would be considered an employee than if the hotel hires someone with his or her own equipment to pick up the laundry and use his or her own equipment to perform the service.

- How long is the individual employed? An individual who is hired to perform services for years is much more likely to be considered an employee than one who is hired to perform services on a one-time basis for a few days.

- How is the individual paid? An individual who submits an invoice on a per-project basis upon the completion of a task is much more likely to be considered an independent contractor than an individual who gets paid by the hour on a weekly basis.

- Is the work performed part of the regular business of the employer? A dishwasher is much more likely to be considered an employee of a caterer than an individual who shampoos the carpet at the caterer's shop.

- What is the understanding between the parties? Important consideration will be given to any agreement between the employer and the individual hired with regard to the hired person's status.

SIDEBAR

Paralegals who work on a temporary or contract basis may be considered independent contractors rather than employees, especially if they work for more than one client (attorney or law firm), pay their own business expenses, set their own hours, and prioritize their own work assignments.

POWER OF ATTORNEY

GENERAL POWER OF ATTORNEY
A power of attorney authorizing the attorney in fact to act on behalf of the principal in all matters.

DURABLE POWER OF ATTORNEY
A power of attorney that lasts as long as a person remains incapable of making decisions, usually about health care.

A **power of attorney** is a special type of agency created by a written instrument that authorizes another to act as one's agent. The agent named in the power of attorney is referred to as the **attorney in fact**. A power of attorney may be a **special power of attorney**, authorizing the attorney in fact to act for the principal with regard to specific transactions; or, it may be a **general power of attorney**, authorizing the agent to act on behalf of the principal in all matters. As a general rule, a written power of attorney is required to allow an agent to transfer real estate on behalf of the principal. See Exhibit 1-1 for an example of a special power of attorney and Exhibit 1-2 for an example of a general power of attorney.

A **durable power of attorney** is a special type of power of attorney that is designed to continue for certain purposes even after the illness or incapacity of the principal. See Exhibit 1-3.

EXHIBIT 1-1   SPECIAL POWER OF ATTORNEY FORM

I, _____ *[name of principal]*, the undersigned, of _____
_____ *[address]*, hereby make, constitute, and appoint _____
_____ *[agent]*, of _____ *[address]*, to be my
attorney in fact to act in my place and stead with regard to the following:

[Specific transactions or type of transactions]

The rights, powers, and authority hereby given to my attorney in fact to act on my
behalf shall commence and be in full force and effect on _____
[date], and shall remain in full force and effect until _____
[date], or unless specifically extended or rescinded earlier by either party.

Dated:

_____
[Signature]
[Acknowledgment]

West/a Thomson Reuters Business

EXHIBIT 1-2   GENERAL POWER OF ATTORNEY FORM

I, *[name of principal]*, the undersigned, of *[address of principal]*, do now make,
constitute, and appoint *[name of agent]*, of *[address of agent]*, my true and lawful attorney in fact, in my name, place, and stead, giving my attorney in fact full
power to do and perform all and every act that I may legally do through an attorney
in fact, and every proper power necessary to carry out the purposes for which this
power is granted, with full power of substitution, revocation, ratifying and affirming
that which attorney in fact or a substitute shall lawfully do or cause to be done by
an attorney in fact or a substitute lawfully designated.

[OPTIONAL: This power ends at [time of termination] on [date of termination].]
Dated: *[date of execution]*

[Name of principal]

[Acknowledgment]

From AM. JUR. Legal Forms, § 14:161 (May 2011z).
Reprinted with permission from *American Jurisprudence Legal Forms 2d*. © 2008 West Group.

EXHIBIT 1-3 SAMPLE DURABLE POWER OF ATTORNEY

I, GARY HARDING, of 4785 Elm Street, Maplewood, Maine, appoint BRANDON HARDING, my brother, of 875 Elizabeth Avenue, Baldwin, Maine, my attorney in fact, in my name, place, and stead, and for my use and benefit to act on my behalf to do every act that I may legally do through an attorney in fact.

This durable power of attorney shall not be affected by any disability on my part, except as provided by the statutes of Maine. The power conferred on my attorney in fact by this instrument shall be exercisable from May 14, 2012, notwithstanding a later disability or incapacity on my part, unless otherwise provided by the statutes of Maine.

All acts done by my attorney in fact pursuant to the power conferred by this durable power of attorney during any period of my disability or incompetence shall have the same effect and inure to the benefit of and bind me or my heirs, devisees, and personal representatives as if I were competent and not disabled.

This durable power of attorney shall be nondelegable and shall be valid until such time as I revoke this power.

Dated: May 14, 2012

_____

Gary Harding
[Acknowledgment]

IN SUMMATION

- An agency is a legal relationship in which the agent acts for the principal on the principal's authority.
- A general agent has broad authority to transact business on behalf of the principal.
- A special agent has authority only to conduct one or more specific acts on behalf of the principal.
- The terms "master" and "servant" are sometimes used in agency law to refer to the employer and employee.
- An employee works under the control of an employer, unlike an independent contractor, who does not work under the control of an employer.
- An employer may be held responsible for torts committed by an employee during his or her employment. The employer will typically not be responsible for torts committed by an independent contractor.
- A power of attorney is a written grant of authority to an agent.
- A power of attorney is usually required for an agent to transfer real estate on behalf of a principal.

§ 1.2 AGENCY CREATION

At times, it can be important to establish whether an agency relationship exists. Did that individual really have the authority to sign a contract on behalf of the band you want to hire for your wedding reception? In this section, we look at the elements of an agency relationship that courts consider to determine whether an actual agency exists. We also discuss the different means for creating the agency relationship.

ELEMENTS OF AN AGENCY RELATIONSHIP

A valid **contract** is an agreement between two or more parties, with capacity to act, to do, or refrain from doing, some lawful act. An agency relationship is a contractual relationship, with a few deviations. The following elements determine the existence of an agency relationship and distinguish it from other forms of contracts:

- Consent of the parties
- Capacity of the parties to act
- No written agreement required
- No exchange of **consideration** required
- Proper purpose

CONTRACT

An agreement that affects or creates legal relationships between two or more persons. To be a contract, an agreement must involve: at least one promise, consideration (something of value promised or given), persons legally capable of making binding agreements, and a reasonable certainty about the meaning of the terms.

CONSIDERATION

The reason or main cause for a person to make a contract; something of value received or promised to induce (convince) a person to make a deal.

Consent of the Parties

The agency relationship is consensual. Both the principal and agent must consent to the agency relationship. An individual becomes an agent only if the principal in some way indicates that the agent may act on the principal's behalf and the agent agrees to do so.

Capacity of the Parties to Act

Both the principal and the agent must have the capacity to act in their respective roles. Certain individuals may lack capacity to act on their own behalf or appoint an agent to act on their behalf, including minors and insane or legally incompetent persons. For example, a minor cannot appoint another to act as the minor's agent, except to the extent required to contract for the minor's necessities of life. The principal who has capacity to act in a certain manner has the capacity to appoint an agent to act in the principal's place. The agent appointed, on the other hand, need not have such capacity. The agent's power to act on behalf of the principal is limited only by the agent's physical or mental ability to act. A minor, or an individual who is considered legally incompetent, could be appointed as an agent, so long as that individual is capable of performing the necessary duties as agent. For example, the 16-year-old clerk at the convenience store acts as an agent of the store's owner to sell goods on the owner's behalf. The agent must have the capacity to act in any specific manner required by the agency agreement.

No Written Agreement Required

Like several forms of contracts, most agency agreements need not be in writing. With a few exceptions, an oral agreement between the principal and agent usually suffices to create an agency relationship.

No Exchange of Consideration Required

Unlike most forms of contracts, the exchange of consideration is not required for an agency relationship to exist. An agent may act on behalf of the principal without any consideration being exchanged. For example, if your elderly aunt asks you to sell several household items for her, you could act as her agent to negotiate prices and complete the sales on her behalf. You may do this as a favor to your aunt, without any compensation from her. The agreements you make would be binding on the purchasers and on your aunt as the principal.

Proper Purpose

The purpose of the agency relationship must be legal, and the acts delegated to the agent by the principal must be acts that are delegable under the law.

The appointment of an agent to do an act is illegal if the act itself would be criminal, **tortious**, or otherwise opposed to public policy. If an agent performs an illegal act under the direction of a principal, the principal may be responsible—both criminally and civilly.

Some acts are illegal if performed by agents. For example, a licensed pharmacist may not direct an unlicensed individual to dispense prescription medications in the pharmacist's place. The performance of certain personal services is not delegable to agents under contract and under law. A concert pianist who has a contract to perform cannot delegate that duty to another. Public policy also prevents the delegation of certain acts. For example, the right to vote in a public election may not be delegated to an agent. Before the 2008 presidential election, a 19-year-old University of Minnesota student was arrested for felony bribery when he tried to sell his vote to the highest bidder on eBay.

TORTIOUS
Wrongful. A civil (as opposed to a criminal) wrong (tort), other than a breach of contract. For an act to be a tort, there must be: a legal duty owed by one person to another, a breach (breaking) of that duty, and harm done as a direct result of the action. Examples of torts are negligence, battery, and libel.

CREATING THE AGENCY RELATIONSHIP

The agency relationship can be created by a variety of means, including:

- Express agreement
- Implied agreement
- Conduct of the principal/agent
- Ratification
- Estoppel

Express Agreement

An agency by agreement must be formed by some **express** indication (1) by the principal, either verbal or written, that the principal consents to have the agent act on the principal's behalf and (2) by the agent, that the agent is so willing to act.

Most agency agreements can be made orally; however, there are certain types of agency relationships that must be evidenced in writing, or transactions that cannot be performed by the agent without written authorization from the principal. For example, under most circumstances, if the agent is given the authority to execute contracts for the sale of land, that authority must be in writing. In some states, whenever the agent is authorized by the principal to enter into contracts that must be in writing, that authority must be in writing. If the principal fails to confer authority to the agent in writing when required by law, the contract executed by the agent is unenforceable against the principal. It is voidable at the option of the principal rather than the other party to the contract. Therefore, under certain circumstances, it is very important to require the agent to produce written proof of authority when dealing with an agent who is signing a contract on behalf of another.

Typically, no special form of appointment of an agent is required, and the authority to act as an agent may be conferred orally.

EXPRESS
Clear, definite, direct, or actual (as opposed to implied); known by explicit words.

Implied Agreement

The existence of an agency often depends not on the express agreement of the parties, but rather the parties' intent and actions. Agency may be **implied** from the words or conduct of the parties and the circumstances of the situation. An implied agency is as much an actual agency as if it were created expressly.

IMPLIED
Known indirectly. Known by analyzing surrounding circumstances or the actions of the persons involved.

Conduct of the Principal/Agent

When the principal intentionally or negligently causes a third party to reasonably believe that another individual is acting as the principal's agent, and the third party relies on that belief, an **apparent** agency may exist. An apparent agency cannot be created by the actions of an apparent agent alone; the third party must be reasonably relying on the actions of the principal.

APPARENT
Easily seen; superficially true.

Ratification

An agency may be created by **ratification** when the principal accepts the benefits derived from the agent acting on his or her behalf or otherwise affirms the conduct of an individual acting on the principal's behalf. For example, if an individual purporting to represent an antique dealer sells an antique chair to a third party, and the dealer later accepts the check and deposits it in her account, the dealer has acted as a principal and ratified the acts of her agent.

A principal cannot partially ratify the acts of an agent and refuse to affirm the rest. If the principal ratifies some aspect of the agent's actions, the principal ratifies the entire transaction.

RATIFICATION
Confirmation and acceptance of a previous act done by you or by another person.

Estoppel

An agency by **estoppel** may be created to prevent a loss by innocent persons. The term *estoppel* merely means "stopped" or "blocked" or "not allowed." When used in agency law, it means that due to his or her own actions, the principal or agent is stopped from denying the existence of an agency, even when there is no actual agreement between the principal and agent. If an individual misrepresents himself or herself as an agent on behalf of another, with the knowledge of the purported principal, the principal is estopped from denying the agency when third parties act in reliance on that information.

The so-called principal may also be estopped from denying that an agency exists if the principal wrongly represents that another is his or her agent with the intent to mislead, and this action causes injury to a third party who was acting in good faith. For example, suppose that a sales agent offers to sell to an auto dealer a rare automobile owned by a collector. The dealer asks the collector whether the agent is authorized to act on the collector's behalf and the collector either intentionally or negligently misleads the dealer into thinking that the agent has that authority. If the sales agent negotiates the sale of the automobile and the dealer sells another automobile to raise the funds for its purchase, the collector would be estopped from denying the agency relationship. The collector would be obligated to sell the automobile to the dealer who has acted in reliance on the belief the agent was negotiating on behalf of the collector. Even though the agent had no actual authority to act on behalf of the collector, the fact that the collector misled the dealer and the dealer relied on that information to the dealer's detriment is sufficient to invoke an estoppel against the collector.

IN SUMMATION

- Elements of an agency relationship include:
  - Consent of the principal and agent
  - Capacity of the parties to act
  - Proper purpose
- Unlike other forms of contract, an agency agreement does not necessarily include:
  - A written agreement
  - Exchange of consideration
- An agency agreement may be created by:
  - Express agreement
  - Implied agreement
  - Conduct of the principal/agent
  - Ratification
  - Estoppel

§ 1.3 AGENCY RELATIONSHIP

The agency relationship is a special kind of contract because an agent is a fiduciary subject to the principal's direction.[3] Both the agent and the principal have the duties set forth in any contract they enter into, in addition to those established by law. In this section, we look at the agent's authority to act on behalf of the principal and the duties the agent and principal owe to each other.

AGENT AUTHORITY

The agent's authority is the agent's power to act on behalf of the principal in accordance with the principal's consent. The authority of the agent is the very essence of the principal and agent relationship.[4] The source of the agent's authority is always the principal. The agent's authority to act is dependent on the principal's consent and the principal's will.

The authority of a general agent includes all delegable powers of the principal. The special agent's authority is limited to the particular business entrusted to the agent and by any accompanying limitations and private instructions given by the principal. In general, the actions of the agent on the principal's behalf are binding on the principal, so long as the agent acts within the scope of his or her authority. There are two basic kinds of authority, actual authority and apparent authority.

Actual Authority

Actual authority is that authority a principal intentionally confers upon the agent and certain incidental powers that are either necessary or customary. Authority that the principal causes or permits the agent to believe the agent possesses is also actual authority. Actual authority may be granted either expressly or impliedly.

Express Authority

Express authority is actual authority that is expressly granted or conferred to the agent by the principal, either in writing or verbally. A power of attorney grants written express authority. If the principal tells the agent "Purchase the artwork for the hotel," the agent has express authority to do so.

Implied Authority

Implied authority is actual authority given implicitly by the principal to his or her agent.[5] It may be implied from the words and conduct of the principal and agent and the facts and circumstances of the transaction in question. Implied authority exists when the agent reasonably believes, because of the principal's conduct, that the principal desires the agent to act on the principal's behalf. For example, assume that Dan oversees management of four hotels for Simon. If Dan has had the authority to purchase equipment and furnishings for the hotels, he would have implied authority to purchase furnishings for a fifth hotel Simon has asked him to manage.

ACTUAL AUTHORITY
In the law of agency, the right and power to act that a principal (often an employer) intentionally gives to an agent (often an employee) or at least allows the agent to believe he or she has been given.

EXPRESS AUTHORITY
Authority delegated to an agent by words that expressly authorize him to do a delegable act. Authority that is directly granted to or conferred upon agent in express terms. That authority which principal intentionally confers upon his or her agent by manifestations to him or her.

IMPLIED AUTHORITY
The authority one person gives to another to do a job, even if the authority is not given directly.

Implied authority may arise incidental to express authority, and it may be implied from the principal's conduct, by custom, or due to an emergency.

Incidental to Express Authority

To achieve the principal's objectives an agent will, at times, require powers in addition to those expressly granted. Those powers that are incidental to those expressly granted will be implied powers if (1) they are necessary to carry into effect the express powers and (2) if they are powers ordinarily required in the line of business the agent is conducting on behalf of the principal. Incidental authority is granted with nearly every grant of express authority. For example, if an individual is hired to manage a bakery, she may be given express authority to oversee the bakery personnel, to purchase supplies, and to sell food items. Authority to donate day-old bread to a local food pantry may be incidental to express authority if that is customary for similar businesses in the area.

Implied Because of Emergency

An agent may possess implied authority to act on behalf of a principal because of an emergency. If it is necessary for an agent to quickly perform some act without the possibility of communicating with the principal to save the principal's property or other interests, the agent will have implied authority to so act. For example, suppose while you are out of the country you have asked a neighbor to keep an eye on your house for you. If a storm comes through town and damages your roof, your neighbor would have the implied authority to have your roof repaired to prevent water damage in your home, even if you can't be reached for permission. In this emergency situation, your neighbor would have the implied authority to act as an agent on your behalf to fix your roof and prevent further damage to your home's interior and furnishings.

Apparent Authority

APPARENT AUTHORITY
The authority an agent seems to have, judged by the words or actions of the person who gave the authority or by the agent's own words or actions.

Apparent authority to do a specific act can be created by the actions of the principal—either by written or spoken word, or by the principal's conduct. Apparent authority to do an act is created as to a third party when the principal's conduct causes the third party to reasonably believe that the principal consents to having the agent act on the principal's behalf. If, for example, an individual who has organized a fashion show for a new designer contracts for the sale of several garments to a buyer while in the presence of the designer, the fashion show organizer would have apparent authority to sell garments made by the fashion designer unless the designer were to speak up and object.

Apparent authority, also known as ostensible authority, is that authority that the principal represents the agent as possessing. An agent's apparent authority is determined by the actions of the principal, not the agent.

The elements of apparent agency include:

1. Acts or conduct of the principal. The conduct of the principal must indicate the individual is acting as his or her agent. The actions of the agent alone will not suffice.
2. Reliance by a third person. A third person must deal with the agent, reasonably relying on his or her belief that the agent was acting for the principal.

3. Change of position by third person to his or her detriment. The third party must have relied on the agent's apparent authority and taken action based on that belief to his or her detriment.

Although apparent authority is not actual authority, in regard to third persons dealing with the agent in good faith, the agent's apparent powers are the agent's real powers. An innocent party may rely on the apparent authority of an agent. However, if a third party acts with an agent, knowing that the agent has no actual authority or has exceeded the bounds of that actual authority, the third party cannot hold the principal liable for the act of the agent.

Inherent Agency Authority

An agent may have **inherent** authority to act on behalf of a principal based solely on their relationship. For example, an employee will have inherent authority to act on behalf of an employer as is customary, even though that employee may not have actual authority or apparent authority. A receptionist will sign for a package delivered for the executive she works for, even if she does not have actual authority to do so. It is inherent in her position.

See Exhibit 1-4 for an overview of agent authority.

INHERENT
Derived from and inseparable from the thing itself.

EXHIBIT 1-4	SOURCES OF AGENT AUTHORITY			
Actual Authority	**Apparent Authority**	**Authority by Estoppel**	**Authority by Ratification**	**Inherent Authority**
The authority that a principal intentionally confers upon the agent. Includes certain incidental powers. May be granted either expressly or impliedly.	The authority created as to third parties when the conduct of the principal would cause the third party to reasonably believe that the principal consents to having the agent act on the principal's behalf.	The authority created when an innocent third party relies on the actions of the so-called principal, indicating that an agency actually exists. The principal is estopped from denying the agency.	The authority that is given after an action takes place whereby the principal ratifies the actions of another acting on the principal's behalf.	The authority derived solely from the relationship between the principal and agent—such as an employer/ employee relationship.
Express Authority				
Actual authority that is expressly granted to the agent by the principal either in writing or verbally.				
Implied Authority				
Actual authority that may be implied from the words and conduct of the principal and agent and the facts and circumstances of the transaction in question.				

© Cengage Learning 2013

AGENT'S DUTIES TO THE PRINCIPAL

In any agency relationship, the agent owes certain duties to the principal. Some of those duties include the duty to perform and the duty to act with reasonable care. Above all, the agent owes a fiduciary duty to the principal.

Duty to Perform

An agent who is compensated owes a duty to perform to the principal. A compensated agent who does not perform may be held liable for breach of contract. An uncompensated agent generally does not owe a duty to perform, but once the uncompensated agent undertakes to perform, the agent may be subject to tort liability for underperformance.

A gratuitous agent who performs in a negligent or careless manner generally will not be liable for breach of contract, as there is no contractual agreement between the principal and agent. However, a gratuitous agent who acts negligently or carelessly on behalf of the principal, causing harm to the principal or a third party, may be subject to tort liability.

Reasonable Care

The agent's duty to perform is a duty to perform with reasonable care and to obey reasonable direction from the principal. An agent who performs in a careless or negligent manner, causing harm to the principal, may be liable for the tort of negligence, as well as for breach of contract.

Fiduciary Duty

FIDUCIARY

1. A person who manages money or property for another person and in whom that other person has a right to place great trust.
2. A relationship like that in definition (no. 1).
3. Any relationship between persons in which one person acts for another in a position of trust, for example, lawyer and client or parent and child.

The agent is a **fiduciary**. As such, the agent must act with the utmost good faith and loyalty to further the principal's interests. The agent is required to place the principal's interests first. Acts contrary to the fiduciary duty of the agent are considered fraudulent and voidable. As a fiduciary, the agent owes the principal the duty to notify and the duty of loyalty.

Duty to Notify

The agent has a fiduciary duty to notify the principal of information learned that affects the subject of the agency, including all material facts of which the agent has knowledge. The agent is required to make a full, fair, and prompt disclosure of all facts that are currently, or may in the future, be material to the matter for which the agent is employed, if that information might affect the principal's rights and interests or if that knowledge may affect the principal's actions. Outsiders dealing with the agent have the right to assume that important and relevant information they give to the agent will be given to the principal. For example, suppose that a retiring farmer has hired an agent to sell off 100 acres of his farmland. The agent has been working with some potential buyers who are willing to offer $3,000 per acre for the land. Before the offer is written, the agent learns that the farmer's neighbor has just sold similar property for $4,000 per acre. The agent has the duty to relay this information to the farmer, as it could affect the farmer's decision to sell at $3,000 per acre.

Duty of Loyalty

The agent owes a duty of loyalty, good faith, and fair dealing to the principal. An agent has a duty to faithfully and honestly represent the principal, and to act in the best interest, and not to the detriment, of the principal.[6] The agent must conduct himself or herself with loyalty and fidelity to the subject of the agency, placing the interests of the agency before the agent's own interest. The agent's duty of loyalty requires the agent to avoid any **conflict of interest**. The agent must not act in competition with the principal, or act for those who are in competition with the principal. The agent may not take a position adverse to that of the principal without the principal's consent. For example, suppose that a wealthy art dealer has hired a manager for one of her galleries to sell the dealer's artwork. The gallery manager may not sell her own artwork at the gallery—at least not without the gallery owner's permission.

CONFLICT OF INTEREST
Being in a position where your own needs and desires could possibly lead you to violate your duty to a person who has a right to depend on you, or being in a position where you try to serve competing masters or clients.

Remedies Available to Principal

If an agent breaches his or her duty of loyalty to the principal, the agent is liable to the principal for any loss that breach may cause. If the agent has failed to perform under the agency contract, the principal may bring an action for breach of contract. If the agent has committed a tort, causing harm to the principal, the principal may bring a suit to recover any damages sustained.

Unless authorized, an agent may not use the principal's money or other assets for the agent's own advantage. If the agent does so, the principal may demand the return of the profits wrongfully earned by the agent.

PRINCIPAL'S DUTIES TO THE AGENT

The principal owes the agent the duties established by the terms of the agency agreement, as well as those established by law. The principal also has an obligation to use good faith with the agent. In addition to compensating the agent as agreed, the principal has the duty to reimburse the agent for most agency-related expenses, the duty to cooperate with the agent, and the duty of care when dealing with the agent.

Duty to Compensate

Unless the agency is to be gratuitous, the principal has the duty to compensate the agent as agreed. If the principal is an employer of the agent, specific duties to compensate may be established by law—such as the duty to pay overtime. In general, a nonemployee agent who performs services for a principal is not entitled to compensation unless the principal requests the services and agrees to compensate the agent. The principal also has the duty to reimburse the agent for costs incurred on the principal's behalf.

Duty to Cooperate

The principal must cooperate with the agent in the agent's performance of responsibilities. The principal must not act in any manner that hinders the agent's fulfillment of responsibilities.

Duty of Care

In general, a principal has the obligation to exercise reasonable care to avoid placing the agent in harm's way in the course of carrying out the agency. The principal has the duty to use care to inform the agent of any danger of physical harm or risks to life or property of which the principal is aware. If the principal is the agent's employer, the principal may have a special duty of care with regard to the agent, such as the duty to furnish safe working conditions.

See Exhibit 1-5 for an overview of the duties principals and agents owe each other.

INDEMNIFICATION

INDEMNIFICATION

The act of compensating or promising to compensate a person who has suffered a loss or may suffer a future loss.

Under most circumstances, unless otherwise provided in an agency agreement, the agent is entitled to **indemnification** and reimbursement by the principal for any damages incurred in the course of acting as agent. The agent must be reimbursed for expenses incurred on behalf of the agency, including any expenses relating to property the agent is holding on behalf of the agency. For example, if the agent pays property taxes on property the agent is holding on behalf of the principal subject to an agency agreement, the agent is entitled to reimbursement.

EXHIBIT 1-5	AGENT AND PRINCIPAL DUTIES TO EACH OTHER
Agent's Duties to Principal	**Principal's Duties to Agent**
Duty to perform	Duty to compensate
Reasonable care	Duty to cooperate
Fiduciary duty, including:	Duty of care
• Duty to notify	
• Duty of loyalty	

© Cengage Learning 2013

IN SUMMATION

- An agent is considered a fiduciary subject to the principal's direction.
- The agent's authority is his or her power to act on behalf of the principal in accordance with the principal's consent.
- An agent may possess:
  - Actual authority—authority a principal intentionally confers upon the agent.
  - Express authority—actual authority expressly granted either in writing or verbally.
  - Implied authority—actual authority given implicitly.

- An agent's implied authority may be incidental to express authority, and it may be implied from the principal's conduct, by custom, or due to an emergency.
- An agent may have inherent authority to act on behalf of a principal based solely on their relationship.
- An agency relationship may be created by:
  - Conduct of the principal and agent
  - Ratification of the agent's actions on behalf of the principal
  - Estoppel to prevent a loss by innocent persons
- An agent owes the principal several duties, including:
  - Duty to perform (if compensated)
  - Duty to act with reasonable care
  - Fiduciary duty
  - Duty to notify
  - Duty of loyalty
- Principals owe several duties to the agent, including:
  - Duty to compensate (if and as agreed)
  - Duty to cooperate
  - Duty of care
  - Duty to indemnify the agent

§ 1.4 PRINCIPAL'S LIABILITY TO THIRD PARTIES

Because an authorized agent acts in place of the principal, the principal will usually be liable for the acts of the agent. The principal will be liable for the terms of contracts entered into by his or her agent as if the principal had personally entered into the contract. Under certain conditions, the principal may also be liable for the torts or even crimes committed by the agent.

PRINCIPAL'S LIABILITY UNDER CONTRACTS

The principal is liable under a contract made on his or her behalf by an agent acting within the agent's authority as if the principal had entered into the contract. This rule holds true whether the agent was authorized or apparently authorized by the principal. A principal will generally not be liable for unauthorized acts of an agent. A person dealing with an agent he or she knows is acting outside the agent's limitations cannot enforce the contract against the principal.

PRINCIPAL'S LIABILITY FOR TORTS OF THE AGENT

Agents are personally liable for the torts they commit. Whether or not the principal will also be responsible for the agent's torts depends on a number of circumstances.

Respondeat Superior

A master (employer) is subject to liability for the torts of his or her servants (employees), but only if those acts are committed while acting in the scope of their employment. Under the doctrine of **respondeat superior**, an employer who retains control over the manner in which the agent (employee) performs his or her duties will be responsible for the torts committed by that employee. Respondeat superior applies if (1) the agent is an actual employee and not an independent contractor, and (2) the employee is acting within the scope of the employer's business. Respondeat superior is a form of vicarious liability, as the employer is held accountable for the acts of his or her employee.

RESPONDEAT SUPERIOR

(Latin) "Let the master answer." Describes the principle that an employer is responsible for most harm caused by an employee acting within the scope of employment. In such a case, the employer is said to have vicarious liability.

Acts Intended by the Principal

A principal is generally liable for torts committed by an agent that result from the principal's directions as if it were the principal's own conduct, if the principal intended the conduct or intended its consequences. An individual causing and intending an act or result is as responsible as if that individual had personally performed the act or produced the result.[7] If a principal directs his or her agent to do a particular act, and the agent acts as directed, the principal is subject to liability if the act constitutes a tort.

For example, if a nightclub owner directs her manager to seal off exits to the club because people are sneaking in without paying, and three people are injured when a fire breaks out in the club and they cannot escape because of the sealed doors, the owner is subject to liability to those who were injured.

Negligence or Recklessness by the Principal

The principal will also be subject to liability for harm resulting from the acts of his or her agent if the principal is negligent or reckless:

- In the employment of an improper agent to perform work involving risk of harm to others
- In supervising the activity
- In giving improper or ambiguous instructions and orders
- In permitting or failing to prevent negligent or tortious conduct upon premises or under conditions within the principal's control

The employment of an unqualified individual to perform a task that may cause harm to another may cause the principal to be liable for the torts of those employees. For example, if the owner of a day care center hires an inexperienced bus driver with a poor driving record to take the children on field trips, and the bus is involved in an accident due to the driver's negligence, the owner of the day care could be found liable (in addition to the driver).

Employers have a certain duty to supervise their employees. Failure to properly supervise an employee can cause an employer to be liable for the employee's torts. For example, if a law firm administrator hires a bookkeeper, the administrator or other appropriate individuals in the law firm have the responsibility to make sure the bookkeeper has appropriate supervision and that proper checks and balances are in place. If the bookkeeper is given little or no supervision, and her work is not checked, the law firm would be liable if the bookkeeper were to embezzle client funds.

Principals may be liable for the acts of the agents they hire when they neglect to give proper instructions or orders. If, for example, a construction company hired an individual to operate heavy equipment, but failed to properly train or instruct the equipment operator on how to safely use the equipment, the construction company would be liable for any damages caused by the operator's negligent use of the equipment.

A principal may also be liable for the torts of the agent if the principal fails to prevent negligent or tortious conduct under the principal's control. For example, if the foreman of a manufacturing plant observes negligent behavior, such as smoking in an unsafe area, but doesn't put a stop to it, the foreman and the company may be liable for any damages caused by the negligent behavior.

See Exhibit 1-6 for an overview of conditions under which a principal may be liable for torts of an agent.

EXHIBIT 1-6	CONDITIONS UNDER WHICH PRINCIPAL MAY BE LIABLE FOR TORTS OF AGENTS

- The tort is committed by employee (agent) acting in the scope of his or her employment by the principal (respondeat superior).
- The tort was committed by the agent pursuant to instructions given by the principal.
- The principal is negligent or reckless in the employment of an improper agent to perform work involving risk of harm to others.
- The principal is negligent or reckless in the supervision of the activity.
- The principal gives improper or ambiguous instructions or orders to the agent.
- The principal is negligent or reckless in permitting or failing to prevent negligent or tortious conduct of the agent upon the principal's premises or under the principal's control.

© Cengage Learning 2013

IN SUMMATION

- The principal is usually liable for the acts of his or her agent.
- The principal is liable for any contracts entered into by the agent while acting on the principal's behalf.
- The principal is generally not liable for unauthorized acts of the agent.
- Both the agent and principal are responsible for torts committed by the agent if those acts are committed while the agent is acting in the scope of his or her employment.
- Respondeat superior is a form of vicarious liability whereby an employer who controls the actions of his or her employee is responsible for torts committed by that employee.

§ 1.5 AGENT'S LIABILITY TO THIRD PARTIES

An authorized agent is not acting on his or her own behalf; the agent is acting on behalf of the principal. The agent is, therefore, usually not liable for contracts entered into on behalf of the principal. However, it is difficult for an individual to escape personal liability for his or her own wrongdoing and, in addition to the principal, agents are usually liable to third parties for torts committed by them.

AGENT'S LIABILITY TO THIRD PARTIES UNDER CONTRACTS

In general, a duly-authorized agent is not liable on contracts made on behalf of a disclosed principal. For example, an officer or director acting as agent for a corporation is not personally liable for contracts entered into on behalf of the corporation. There are, however, certain circumstances under which an agent may be personally liable, such as when the agent enters into a contract without authorization from the principal, or when the agent enters into a contract without disclosing the existence of a principal. An agent is personally liable for contracts entered into outside the scope of the agency for which the agent has not been authorized by the principal.

When an agent enters into a contract with a third party on behalf of a principal, without disclosing the identity or even existence of that principal, the agent will be personally liable with regard to the agent's dealings with that third party. This rule is in fairness to the third party who does not realize that the agent is not the individual he or she is dealing with.

AGENT'S LIABILITY FOR TORTS AND CRIMES

An agent is liable for his or her crimes and torts, even when the act is within the scope of the agent's authority and done at the instruction of the principal. The principal may also be held responsible for the same act.

The agent's liability to third parties for tortious acts is founded on the common-law principle that every person must act in a manner so as not to injure another, and is independent of the agency relationship.[8]

SIDEBAR

Some common torts include:

- Fraud
- Negligence
- Assault
- Battery
- Nuisance
- Trespass

IN SUMMATION

- An agent is typically not liable for contracts entered into on behalf of the principal.
- The agent will be responsible for torts committed by him or her.
- The agent may be responsible under certain circumstances for contracts entered into beyond the agent's authority.
- The agent may be liable under a contract if the agent does not disclose the existence of the principal.

§ 1.6 AGENCY TERMINATION

The agency relationship may be an ongoing relationship, or it may be established for a limited purpose or duration. Once the agency relationship has been established, it will continue until terminated by an act or agreement of the principal and agent, or by law.

If no term is specified for the duration of the agency, the agency will be considered to exist for a reasonable time. The definition of "reasonable time" will depend on the circumstances, including the nature and purpose of the agency.

After termination of the agency agreement, the former agent has no authority to act on behalf of the principal. Actions taken by the agent on behalf of the principal after the agency has terminated are not binding on the principal.

The agency may be terminated pursuant to the agency contract, the fulfillment of the agency purpose, by the death or bankruptcy of either the principal or agent, or by the act of the principal and agent or either one of them.

Most written agency agreements include clauses that provide for the agency being terminated on notice given by either party.

EXPIRATION OF AGENCY TERM

An express agreement between the principal and agent, either written or verbal, may include a duration for the agency. For example, the agency agreement could provide that the agent will act on behalf of the principal for the term of one year. When such a term is provided for in the agency contract, the agency will terminate upon the conclusion of the specified term unless action is taken by the parties to continue the agency. An agency that was established without a defined duration is considered an **agency at will**.

FULFILLMENT OF AGENCY PURPOSE

An agency that is created for a specific purpose terminates upon the completion of that purpose. For example, if a local realtor is hired to sell your home, that realtor will act as your agent with regard to the sale of your home only until your home is sold. The realtor will no longer act as your agent once your home is sold and the agent's business is concluded.

AGENCY AT WILL
Agency relationship that exists at the will of both parties and may be canceled by either the principal or agent at any time.

DEATH OR INCAPACITY OF PRINCIPAL OR AGENT

Generally, the death or incapacity of either the principal or agent terminates the agency relationship. The death of the principal generally results in the immediate and absolute revocation of the agent's authority or power, unless the agency is coupled with an interest. An exception to this rule is the durable power of attorney, a written instrument provided for by the laws of most states. The durable power of attorney, which is often used as an estate planning tool, may provide that the agency will remain effective even after the incapacity of the principal. For example, an elderly woman may give a durable power of attorney to a grown son, giving that son the power to act on her behalf should she become incapacitated and unable to handle her own affairs.

CHANGE IN CIRCUMSTANCES—IMPOSSIBILITY OF PERFORMANCE

Generally, the loss or destruction of the subject of the agency will terminate the agency. Other changes in circumstances that make performance of the agency impossible may also terminate the agency.

ACT OR AGREEMENT OF THE PARTIES

The agency relationship must be consensual. If at any time either the principal or agent does not consent to continue the agency relationship, the agency may be terminated. However, if the termination is in breach of the contract between the two parties, the party wrongfully terminating the agency may be liable to the other party for any damages caused by the termination.

A contract for agency may provide that either the principal or agent may discontinue the agency upon notification to the other party. See Exhibit 1-7 for a sample termination of agency notice.

Renunciation by Agent

The agent has the right to renounce the agency relationship, although at times the agent may be liable for breach of contract in so doing.

Revocation of Authority by Principal

In general, the principal has the power to revoke the agent's authority at any time. Under certain circumstances, such as when the principal revokes the agent's authority contrary to a written contract or without giving proper notice, the principal may be liable for breach of contract.

Although the principal always has the power to revoke the agent's authority, the principal may not always have the right to do so. The principal does not have the right to breach the agency contract.

Termination of Apparent Authority

Whenever a principal represents to a third party that another is acting as agent on the principal's behalf, the agent has apparent authority to act. The agent's apparent authority will continue until the third party receives notice to the contrary.

When an agent has apparent authority to act on behalf of the principal, the principal must notify third parties to effectively terminate that authority. Third parties who have dealt directly with the agent in the past must be notified of the agency termination.

EXHIBIT 1-7	SAMPLE TERMINATION OF AGENCY NOTICE FROM PRINCIPAL TO AGENT

To: Nathan Thompson

From: Gabrielle Ruiz

Section 14 of our agency agreement, executed the 23rd day of November, 2007, provides that the agreement shall continue in full force until terminated. Our agreement further provides that it may be terminated upon not less than 60 days' written notice from one party to the other.

Pursuant to the provisions of our agreement, I hereby terminate our agreement, effective May 25, 2012. As of May 25, 2012, you will no longer be authorized to act as my agent.

Dated: March 25, 2012.

_____

Gabrielle Ruiz

© Cengage Learning 2013

IN SUMMATION

- An agency relationship may be terminated pursuant to the terms of the contract between the principal and agent or by agreement of the principal and agent.

- Either principal or agent may terminate the agency relationship at any time, but doing so contrary to an agreement of the parties may cause the terminating party to be liable for any damages the termination causes.

- An agency for a specific purpose terminates when that purpose is fulfilled or no longer exists. Under most circumstances, the death or incapacity of either the principal or agent terminates the agency relationship.

- A change in circumstances that makes performance of the agency agreement impossible terminates the agreement.

- When an agent has apparent authority, the principal must notify third parties who deal with the agent to effectively terminate that authority.

§ 1.7 AGENCY AND BUSINESS ORGANIZATIONS

Business in the United States and throughout the world is conducted through a variety of business organizations—from the simplest sole proprietorship to the more complex public corporation. The type of organization selected to conduct business will depend on a number of factors, including:

- The number of individuals who will own and manage the business
- The income tax implications
- The necessity of raising capital to operate the business
- The most desired management structure for the business
- The importance of limited liability for the owners and managers of the business
- The applicable taxation rules
- The cost and formalities associated with forming the business organization

With the possible exception of the sole proprietor who has no employees, all business organizations operate through agents.

BUSINESS ORGANIZATIONS AS ENTITIES

Some business organizations, especially corporations, are considered separate entities, with their own distinct identities. As a separate entity, these business organizations must, by necessity, operate through their officers, directors, partners, members, and employees who act as agents on behalf of the business organization. While the exact nature of the relationship may vary somewhat from the individual agents and principals as discussed through this chapter, the same basic principles apply to business organizations and the agents who act for them.

SOLE PROPRIETORSHIPS

SOLE PROPRIETORSHIP
An unincorporated business owned by one person.

Sole proprietorships are the simplest form of business organization. As the name implies, this type of business organization is owned and operated by one individual—the sole proprietor. The sole proprietor may, however, hire any number of employees to act on behalf of the sole proprietorship. These employees serve as agents of the sole proprietor. Sole proprietorships are discussed in detail in Chapter 2 of this text.

GENERAL PARTNERSHIP
A typical partnership in which all partners are general partners.

GENERAL PARTNERSHIPS AND LIMITED LIABILITY PARTNERSHIPS

LIMITED LIABILITY PARTNERSHIP
A partnership in which the partners have less than full liability for the actions of other partners, but full liability for their own actions.

Partnerships are a slightly more complex form of business organization, necessarily involving two or more partners. These partners act as agents, not only for the partnership itself, but also for each other.

General partnerships and **limited liability partnerships** are discussed in Chapters 3 and 5 of this text, respectively.

LIMITED PARTNERSHIPS AND LIMITED LIABILITY LIMITED PARTNERSHIPS

Limited partnerships and **limited liability limited partnerships** vary from general partnerships in that they have at least one limited partner who acts more as an investor than a partner. Limited partners are not personally liable for the debts and obligations of the limited partnership. In most jurisdictions they do not have the right to participate in the management of the limited partnership. Limited partnerships are managed by the general partner, or general partners, who serve as agents for the limited partnership and the limited partners. General partners have apparent authority to bind the partnership to contracts. Limited partners do not. Limited partnerships and limited liability limited partnerships are discussed in Chapters 4 and 5 of this text, respectively.

LIMITED LIABILITY COMPANIES

Limited liability companies (LLCs) are a unique type of business organization that has similarities to both corporations and partnerships. LLCs may be managed by their members (owners), or the members may appoint managers to oversee the management. If an LLC is member managed, the members each serve as agents for the LLC for the purpose of carrying on the business of the company in the usual way. If the LLC is manager managed, that authority is reserved for the managers of the LLC.

CORPORATIONS

Corporations are separate and distinct entities, apart from their individual owners. The owners of a corporation (shareholders) elect a board of directors to oversee the operation of the corporation's business. The directors, in turn, appoint officers to oversee the day-to-day business of the corporation. In smaller corporations, the shareholders, directors, and officers may all be the same individuals. The officers and directors of the corporation serve as agents to the corporation. Corporations and their officers and directors are discussed in more detail in Chapters 6 and 8 of this text.

LIMITED PARTNERSHIP

A partnership formed by general partners (who run the business and have liability for all partnership debts) and limited partners (who partly or fully finance the business, take no part in running it, and have no liability for partnership debts beyond the money they put in or promise to put in).

LIMITED LIABILITY LIMITED PARTNERSHIP

A type of limited partnership permissible in some states in which the general partners have less than full liability for the actions of other general partners.

LIMITED LIABILITY COMPANY

A cross between a partnership and a corporation owned by members who may manage the company directly or delegate to officers or managers who are similar to a corporation's directors. Governing documents are usually publicly filed articles of organization and a private operating agreement. Members are not usually liable for company debts, and company income and losses are usually divided among and taxed to the members individually according to share.

CORPORATION

An organization that is formed under state or federal law and exists, for legal purposes, as a separate being or an "artificial person."

SIDEBAR

Corporations often hire **registered agents** to act on their behalf to accept service of process and perform other administrative duties in states where the corporation does not have an office or physical presence.

REGISTERED AGENT
Individual appointed by a corporation to receive service of process on behalf of the corporation and perform such other duties as may be necessary. Registered agents may be required in the corporation's state of domicile and in each state.

IN SUMMATION

- All business organizations act through agents.
- Employees hired by a sole proprietor act as the sole proprietor's agent.
- All partners are agents of each other and the general partnership.
- General partners act as agents of the limited partnership and limited partners.
- Limited partners do not typically act as agents of the limited partnership.
- Managers act as agents of the manager-managed limited liability company.
- All members are agents of the member-managed limited liability company.
- The corporation's board of directors, officers, and the employees they hire act as agents of the corporation.

§ 1.8 THE PARALEGAL'S ROLE

According to the U.S. Department of Labor,[9] there were approximately 263,800 paralegals in the United States in the year 2008. It is expected that the number of paralegal jobs in the United States will increase by approximately 28 percent between 2008 and 2016, at a much faster than average rate. Roughly 71 percent of all paralegals work in law firms. Many paralegals employed by law firms specialize in work that involves corporations and other business organizations. In addition, approximately 20 percent of all paralegals are employed by corporations or other business organizations.

Throughout this text we will be looking at the paralegal's role as it relates to the topics covered in each chapter. The paralegal profiles included in each chapter feature working corporate paralegals and illustrate the variety of positions and responsibilities corporate paralegals may have. They also provide an understanding of how you may be called on to put to use the information discussed in each chapter.

CORPORATE PARALEGAL PROFILE
Elizabeth Miner

I like working on such a variety of projects across the world. I may be forming an entity in South America and changing officers in Singapore while participating in a complex tax reorganization crossing multiple jurisdictions.

NAME Elizabeth Miner
LOCATION Worcester, Massachusetts
TITLE Paralegal
SPECIALTY Corporate
EDUCATION Paralegal Certificate—Colorado University, San Pueblo
EXPERIENCE 18 years

continues

CORPORATE PARALEGAL PROFILE
Elizabeth Miner (continued)

Elizabeth Miner is a paralegal who has worked in a variety of settings and with a variety of business organizations. She began her paralegal career in the corporate setting, working in insurance defense for a large, privately held company. She has also worked for small law firms and sole proprietors. One attorney she worked for was also a professor who worked on highly visible cases, usually at the Supreme Court or circuit court level. Elizabeth assisted that attorney, who worked out of his home, and backed up his law school assistant as needed. She reports that the position was the most fascinating small firm experience she has had to date.

According to Elizabeth, the major difference she found between small firm and corporate settings is the number of hats one might need to wear at any given time. While a corporate setting may allow you to concentrate more on the actual legal work and to specialize, a smaller firm usually requires you to accomplish many tasks, some that may be more administrative in nature and take away from your ability to focus solely on the legal aspects of your duties.

Elizabeth has worked with all types of business organizations and experienced firsthand how those organizations work through their agents. She has been responsible for assisting with sole proprietorship formalities, and the formation of new limited liability companies and corporations. When forming business organizations, Elizabeth has worked with the agents of those entities—the limited liability company's members and the corporation's board of directors.

Elizabeth currently works for Thermo Fisher Scientific Inc., where she specializes in corporate governance and reports to the Associate General Counsel. Thermo Fisher Scientific is a biotechnology company with approximately 34,000 employees and clients located all over the world. Elizabeth is responsible for corporate record maintenance and compliance for Thermo Fisher Scientific's subsidiaries worldwide. She spends a lot of her time drafting resolutions for the subsidiary board of directors and stockholders and overseeing the company's registered agent annual report filings.

Elizabeth reports that she enjoys working on such a variety of projects across the world. She may be forming an entity in South America the same day she is changing officers of a subsidiary in Singapore. She finds the merger and acquisition work she does to be interesting, especially the acquisition of multinational companies, which can present very unique challenges.

Elizabeth is an active member of the Massachusetts Paralegal Association, where she is part of the Mentor Group. She is also a member of the National Association of Legal Assistants.

Elizabeth's advice to new paralegals?

My advice is to find a mentor, join paralegal associations, and constantly update and expand your knowledge base in your specialty. Read any and all relevant news stories, blogs, and group discussions to keep abreast of the constantly changing environment of law.

For more information on careers for corporate paralegals, log in to http://www.cengagebrain.com to access the CourseMate website that accompanies this text; then see the Corporate Careers Section.

Agency is a very broad concept. A basic understanding of agency law will benefit paralegals who work in nearly every area of law. It can help you to understand contracts and litigation that clients may be involved in. Some specific tasks related to agency law that may be assigned to corporate paralegals include reviewing and drafting powers of attorney, employment agreements, and other contracts that may involve an agency relationship.

ETHICAL CONSIDERATION

Does your supervising attorney need to review all of the work you do for a sole proprietor? When is it okay to release a corporate client's financial information? Is it okay to give legal advice to partnership clients on routine matters? These are all questions of ethics, the type of ethical dilemmas often faced by paralegals who work with all types of business organizations.

The rules of ethics applicable to attorneys generally apply to the paralegals who work for them as well. In addition, the National Association of Legal Assistants (NALA) and the National Federation of Paralegal Associations (NFPA) have both established codes of ethics for their members. Every day paralegals must make important ethical decisions. Their decisions can affect not only their employers and clients, but also the public.

In addition to costing the paralegal his or her job, unethical behavior may cause the paralegal's supervising attorney to be disciplined—possibly even disbarred. In some instances, a civil lawsuit or even criminal prosecution may result.

The rules of ethics as they apply to paralegals who work for corporations and other business organizations will be discussed briefly throughout this text. For more information on ethics for corporate paralegals, including links to the NALA and NFPA codes of ethics, log in to http://www.cengagebrain.com to access the CourseMate website that accompanies this text; then see the Ethics Section.

§ 1.9 RESOURCES

The concepts of agency law are found throughout federal and state statutes. Disputes concerning agency law are settled by the rules of the state where the agency contract was entered into or where the agency relationship was conducted. The basic concepts of agency law have been defined by case law and authoritative treatises.

AGENCY TREATISES

More information on agency law can be found in the following treatises:

The **Restatement of the Law—Agency 3d** is considered the most comprehensive treatise on agency law. Copies of this treatise may be found in law libraries and on Westlaw.

American Jurisprudence 2d (AmJur) is a multivolume encyclopedia of U.S. law, both state and federal. The current edition has more than 140 volumes that are updated with replacement volumes and annual pocket supplements. See AmJur Agency §1, et seq. AmJur can be found in law libraries and on Westlaw.

Corpus Juris Secondum (CJS) is an encyclopedia of U.S. law that contains an alphabetical arrangement of legal topics as developed by U.S. federal and state cases. See CJS Agency § 1, et seq. CJS can be found in law libraries and on Westlaw.

SUMMARY

- An agency is a legal relationship whereby one person (the agent) acts for or represents another (the principal) by the principal's authority.
- The agent is the person authorized to act with third parties on behalf of the principal.
- The principal is the party for whom the agent acts.
- A power of attorney is a special type of agency that is created by a written instrument, authorizing an attorney in fact to act for the principal.
- For an agency relationship to exist, both the principal and agent must consent to the arrangement.
- No written agreement is required to create most agency relationships.
- No consideration is required for an agency relationship to exist.
- An agency relationship can be created by express or implied agreement.
- Apparent authority to do a specific act can be created by the action of the principal—either by written or spoken word, or by the conduct of the principal.
- Apparent authority is created by (1) the act or conduct of the principal, (2) reliance on the principal's action by a third person who deals with the agent, and (3) a change in position by the third person to his or her detriment.
- An agent owes the principal the duty to perform, the duty to act with reasonable care, and the fiduciary duties of notification and loyalty.
- The principal owes the agent the duty to compensate (under most circumstances), the duty to cooperate, and the duty of care.
- The principal is liable under contracts entered into on his or her behalf by a duly authorized agent.
- The agent, and under certain circumstances the principal, may be liable for torts committed by the agent.

- Under the doctrine of respondeat superior, an employer who retains control over the manner in which an employee performs his or her duties will be responsible for the torts committed by the employee.
- The agency relationship may be terminated pursuant to the agency contract, the fulfillment of the agency purpose, by the death or bankruptcy of either the principal or agent, or by the act of the principal and agent or either one of them.
- Business organizations operate through their agents, who may be officers, directors, partners, or employees.

REVIEW QUESTIONS

1. What is the difference between a general agent and a special agent?

2. Suppose you give your friend some cash and ask her to pick up a video for you at the video rental store. Has an agency relationship been created? Discuss each of the elements of an agency relationship as they relate to this situation.

3. Can an agency relationship be created without a written agreement? What if the agent is asked to sell a parcel of land for the principal?

4. Can an agency relationship be created if the principal does not pay the agent to act on his or her behalf?

5. Suppose that before a horse race, the owner of one of the horses, along with the trainer and a racehorse investor, are all having a conversation. The trainer offers to sell the racehorse to the investor for $10,000 (in the owner's presence, and without her objection). The investor agrees and gives the owner a $500 check to show his good faith. He also makes a deal to sell one of his other investments to raise the additional $9,500. When the horse in question wins the next race the owner refuses to sell, stating that the trainer was not acting on her behalf and had no authority to sell the horse. Is the owner correct? What type of authority, if any, does the trainer have? Does the investor have any right to purchase the horse?

6. What duties does an agent owe the principal?

7. Under what circumstances may a principal be liable for torts committed by his or her agent?

8. What is *respondeat superior*?

9. Who are the agents for a general partnership?

10. Who are the agents for a corporation?

PRACTICAL PROBLEMS

Assume that you will be leaving the country for at least six months to study in Spain. You would like to give a power of attorney to your brother to handle your affairs while you are gone. Using the resources in this chapter, draft a sample power of attorney to your fictitious brother. This power of attorney should be a general power of attorney.

EXERCISE IN CRITICAL THINKING

Attorneys often prepare power of attorneys as a matter of convenience for their clients. What are some considerations to be given by clients and their attorneys before granting a power of attorney to another individual? What consideration must be given concerning the individual named as attorney in fact? What consideration must be given concerning the scope of powers granted in the power of attorney?

◾ WORKPLACE SCENARIO

Assume that you are a paralegal for a small, general practice law firm. You and Belinda Murphy, one of the attorneys you work for, have just come out of a meeting with a new client, Bradley Harris. Mr. Harris has just started a computer-consulting and repair business and he has come to Belinda Murphy seeking advice.

You and Ms. Murphy will be helping Mr. Harris with several of the formalities associated with starting and operating a new business, but first Mr. Harris has other matters to attend to. He will be going into the hospital for surgery in two days and he needs someone to look after the affairs of his business. He has been negotiating some significant contracts and he is afraid he will lose the business if there is no one to act on his behalf while he is in the hospital. Mr. Harris has asked his friend, Cynthia Ann Lund, who is familiar with his business and his circumstances, to negotiate and sign contracts on his behalf and just, in general, to operate his business for him while he is recovering from surgery.

Mr. Harris would like to give Cynthia Ann Lund a special power of attorney to act on his behalf on matters related to his computer repair and consulting business, which he refers to as Cutting Edge Computer Repair, for 30 days.

Using the Client Information Sheet provided in Appendix B-1 to this text, and forms found in this text or online, prepare a special power of attorney from Mr. Harris to Cynthia Ann Lund, granting Ms. Lund the power and authority to act on behalf of Mr. Harris while he is incapacitated.

Portfolio Reminder
Save the documents prepared for the Workplace Scenario exercises in each chapter, either in hard copy or electronically, to build a portfolio of documents to be used for job interviews or as sample documents on the job.

◾ ENDNOTES

1. *Black's Law Dictionary*, (7th ed., West 1999).
2. CJS Agency § 1 (March 2011).
3. CJS Agency § 240 (March 2011).
4. AmJur 2d Agency § 68 (November 2010).
5. CJS Agency § 136 (March 2011).
6. CJS Agency § 244 (March 2011).
7. Restatement of the Law 2nd—Agency § 140 (August 2007).
8. CJS Agency § 370 (March 2011)
9. U.S. Department of Labor, Bureau of Labor Statistics Occupational Outlook Handbook, http://www.BLS.gov (December 2009).

◾ CourseMate

To access additional course materials, including CourseMate, please visit http://www.cengagebrain.com. At the CengageBrain home page, search for the ISBN of your title (from the back cover of your book) using the search box at the top of the page. This will take you to the product page where these resources can be found. The CourseMate resources for this text include Web links, downloadable forms, flash cards, and more.

CHAPTER

2

SOLE PROPRIETORSHIPS

INTRODUCTION

Before we begin our in-depth discussion of corporations in this text, we investigate the characteristics of some simpler forms of business organizations and determine how those business organizations compare to corporations.

This chapter focuses on sole proprietorships, the most prevalent form of business in the United States. We begin by defining the term **sole proprietorship** and taking a look at the role of sole proprietorships in the United States. We then consider the advantages and disadvantages of doing business as a sole proprietorship in contrast to the other types of business organizations. Next we focus on what it takes to operate a sole proprietorship, the role of paralegals working with sole proprietorships, and the resources that are available to paralegals whose work involves sole proprietorships.

§ 2.1 SOLE PROPRIETORSHIP DEFINED

A sole proprietorship is an unincorporated business owned by one person. It is the simplest type of business organization. A **sole proprietor** is the sole owner of all the assets of the business and is solely liable for all debts and obligations of the business.

Unlike a corporation, the sole proprietorship is not considered a separate entity. Rather, it is considered an extension of the sole proprietor. No action need be taken to form a sole proprietorship. Whenever an individual begins operating business without forming another type of business organization, that individual is a sole proprietor and the business is a sole proprietorship. The sole proprietor is personally responsible for all legal debts and obligations of the business and is entitled to all of the profits of the business.

The sole proprietor may delegate decisions and management of the business to agents, but all authority to make decisions must come directly from the sole proprietor who is responsible for all business-related acts of employees.

SOLE PROPRIETORSHIP
An unincorporated business owned by one person.

SOLE PROPRIETOR
The owner of a sole proprietorship.

IN SUMMATION

- A sole proprietorship is an unincorporated business owned by one individual.
- The sole proprietorship is considered to be an extension of the sole proprietor—not a separate entity.
- An individual who begins doing business without incorporating or forming another type of business organization is considered a sole proprietor.

§ 2.2 SOLE PROPRIETORSHIPS IN THE UNITED STATES

The small business owned by a sole proprietor is the most common form of business in the United States. Although sole proprietorships make up the majority of business enterprises in this country, they account for a much smaller portion of gross business receipts than corporations do. For example, income tax returns for 2008 indicated that there were more than 22 million sole proprietorships in the United States and over 5.8 million corporations. However, those 5.8 million corporations showed business receipts for the year of nearly $25 trillion, while the sole proprietorships accounted for receipts of approximately $1.3 trillion.[1,2] See Exhibit 2-1.

Sole proprietors have always been a driving force in our economy and culture. In years past, the term *sole proprietor* would often bring to mind the man or woman who owned and operated the local corner store or barbershop. In the twenty-first century, sole proprietors have taken on a new identity, being more likely to run a

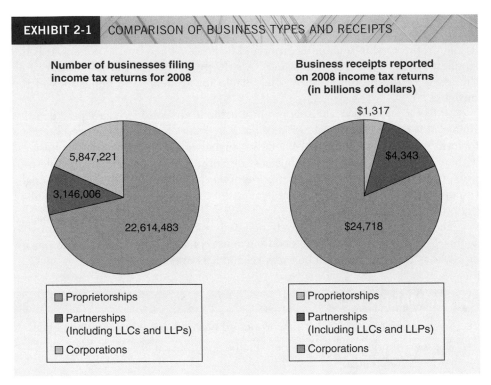

| EXHIBIT 2-1 | COMPARISON OF BUSINESS TYPES AND RECEIPTS |

Number of businesses filing income tax returns for 2008

5,847,221

3,146,006

22,614,483

☐ Proprietorships

■ Partnerships
(Including LLCs and LLPs)

☐ Corporations

Business receipts reported on 2008 income tax returns (in billions of dollars)

$1,317

$4,343

$24,718

☐ Proprietorships

■ Partnerships
(Including LLCs and LLPs)

☐ Corporations

From 2008 Tax Stats, Internal Revenue Service, http://www.irs.gov.

professional services or technology-based business from a home office. According to income tax returns filed for the year 2008,[3] the largest number of sole proprietors owned businesses that provided professional, scientific, and technical services. See Exhibit 2-2.

IN SUMMATION

- Sole proprietorships are the most common form of business in the United States.
- Total business receipts of U.S. corporations are much higher than those of sole proprietorships.

EXHIBIT 2-2 MOST POPULAR TYPES OF BUSINESSES OPERATED BY SOLE PROPRIETORS IN 2008

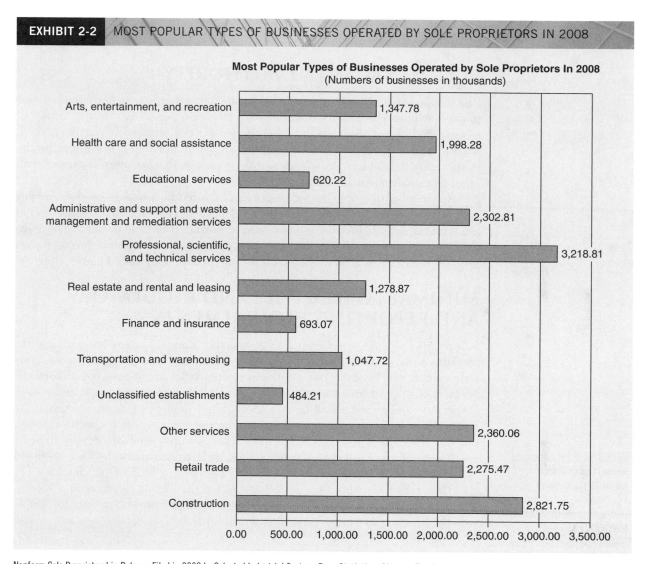

Most Popular Types of Businesses Operated by Sole Proprietors In 2008
(Numbers of businesses in thousands)

Type of Business	Number (thousands)
Arts, entertainment, and recreation	1,347.78
Health care and social assistance	1,998.28
Educational services	620.22
Administrative and support and waste management and remediation services	2,302.81
Professional, scientific, and technical services	3,218.81
Real estate and rental and leasing	1,278.87
Finance and insurance	693.07
Transportation and warehousing	1,047.72
Unclassified establishments	484.21
Other services	2,360.06
Retail trade	2,275.47
Construction	2,821.75

Nonfarm Sole Proprietorship Returns Filed in 2008 by Selected Industrial Sectors. From Statistics of Income Tax Stats., Internal Revenue Service, http://www.irs.gov.

§ 2.3 ADVANTAGES OF DOING BUSINESS AS A SOLE PROPRIETOR

The small businessperson can find several advantages in doing business as a sole proprietor. This section focuses on some of the more important advantages of operating as a sole proprietorship in contrast to operating as a corporation or limited liability company. These advantages include the sole proprietor's full management authority of the business, the minimal formalities and reporting requirements associated with sole proprietorships, the low cost of organizing sole proprietorships, the income tax benefits offered by sole proprietorships, and the relative ease with which a sole proprietor's business can be discontinued.

FULL MANAGEMENT AUTHORITY

The sole proprietor has the advantage of having full authority to manage the business in any way he or she sees fit, without having to obtain permission from a partner or a board of directors. Because the sole proprietor is not required to document decisions or obtain permission from others, the sole proprietorship is not subject to the bureaucracy and delays in the decision-making process that are often associated with other types of business organizations.

Any number of employees or agents may be hired by a sole proprietor, and any authority the sole proprietor chooses may be delegated. However, as the only owner of the business, the sole proprietor is always in command. If the sole owner of a business chooses to grant an ownership interest to an employee in exchange for the employee's services, the business is no longer a sole proprietorship, but rather a partnership.

MINIMAL FORMALITIES AND REGULATORY AND REPORTING REQUIREMENTS

CERTIFICATE OF ASSUMED NAME, TRADE NAME, OR FICTITIOUS NAME
A certificate issued by the proper state authority to an individual or an entity that grants the right to use an assumed or fictitious name for the transaction of business in that state.

Sole proprietorships are not created or governed by statute, so there are relatively few formalities that must be followed by a sole proprietor. A sole proprietor must, however, comply with licensing and taxation regulations that are imposed on all forms of business. A sole proprietor must be aware of and obtain any necessary licenses, sales tax permits, and tax identification numbers before commencing business. Also, if the business is transacted under a name other than the sole proprietor's personal name, the state where the business is transacted will probably require that an application for **certificate of assumed name, trade name, or fictitious name** be filed. Assumed names, trade names, and fictitious names are discussed in § 2.5 of this chapter.

There are no qualification requirements for transacting business in a foreign state as a sole proprietorship. The sole proprietor must, however, be sure to comply with the licensing and taxation requirements of that foreign state.

LOW COST OF ORGANIZATION

Formalities and regulatory requirements for beginning and operating a sole proprietorship are minimal. As a result, the costs for starting and maintaining a sole proprietorship are relatively low. There are no minimum capital restrictions and few, if any, state filing fees. Some possible startup expenses include attorneys' fees for legal advice, license fees, and filing and publishing fees for a certificate of assumed name, trade name, or fictitious name.

INCOME TAX BENEFITS

The income of the sole proprietorship is reported on Schedule C to the sole proprietor's individual income tax return. The profit or loss of the business is added to the sole proprietor's other income, if any, and taxed at the individual rate of the taxpayer. This can be particularly advantageous for new businesses, which often incur a loss in the first year or so. If a sole proprietorship experiences a net loss during a particular year, the sole proprietor can use that loss to offset other income.

For example, suppose that the manager of your favorite restaurant decides to open a catering business on the side. Initial expenses for the catering business, including a van and food preparation equipment, may be rather high and he may lose money on the venture the first year. If he experienced a $10,000 loss from the catering business his first year, he could use that $10,000 loss to offset his restaurant manager income that same year.

Another income tax benefit to the sole proprietor is that there is no double taxation, which is often a drawback to corporate ownership. Double taxation refers to a situation whereby the income of the business is taxed twice—income taxes are paid once at the corporate level and again as the income flows through to the individual shareholders in the form of a salary or dividend.

EASE OF DISCONTINUING BUSINESS

The sole proprietor has the freedom to discontinue his or her business at will, without having to seek approval from a partner or from shareholders. If, for example, the sole proprietor decides to retire, he may simply pay his business debts, fulfill any pending contracts, and stop transacting business. Because the sole proprietorship is not a separate entity, there are no formalities that must be complied with to discontinue the business. The sole proprietor will remain personally responsible for the outstanding debts and liabilities of the business.

SIDEBAR

Advances in technology have given an increasing number of sole proprietors the opportunity to operate their businesses from their own homes. According to a survey by the Bureau of Labor Statistics, more than one-third of self-employed workers worked from home on an average workday in 2009.[5]

IN SUMMATION

Some of the advantages of doing business as a sole proprietor compared to other types of businesses include:

- Full management authority
- Few formalities and reporting requirements
- Low cost of organization
- Beneficial taxation
- Ease of discontinuing the business

§ 2.4 DISADVANTAGES OF DOING BUSINESS AS A SOLE PROPRIETOR

Along with the advantages of doing business as a sole proprietor, there are several disadvantages. Operating as a sole proprietorship can significantly restrict the growth of the business. It is not uncommon for sole proprietors to eventually incorporate to achieve their business's full growth potential.

The disadvantages discussed in this section include the unlimited liability of the sole proprietor, the sole proprietorship's lack of business continuity, the fact that there is no diversity in the management of a sole proprietorship, and the difficulty a sole proprietor may have in attracting highly qualified employees. We also examine the difficulty in transferring the proprietary interest of a sole proprietorship and the limitations on raising capital for a sole proprietorship. All of these disadvantages must be weighed against potential advantages before a sound business decision can be made as to the best business format. See Exhibit 2-3.

UNLIMITED LIABILITY

One of the most significant disadvantages of doing business as a sole proprietor is the unlimited liability faced by the owner of the business. The owner is solely responsible for all debts and obligations of the business, as well as any torts committed personally by the sole proprietor or by employees acting within the scope of their employment, without any protection of the sole proprietor's personal assets. Creditors may look to both the business and personal assets of the sole proprietor to satisfy their claims.

For example, suppose that a sole proprietor owns a messenger service and hires a college student to work as a driver for him during the summer. If the student hits

EXHIBIT 2-3	ADVANTAGES AND DISADVANTAGES OF DOING BUSINESS AS A SOLE PROPRIETORSHIP

Advantages	Disadvantages
• Full management authority	• Unlimited liability
• Minimal formalities	• Lack of business continuity
• Ease of formation	• No diversity in management
• Low cost of organization	• Difficulty in transferring proprietary interest
• No double taxation	• Limited ability to attract high-caliber employees
• Ease of business termination	• Restricted ability to raise capital

© Cengage Learning 2013

a pedestrian and seriously injures him, the sole proprietor would be responsible for the damages sustained by the injured pedestrian. If the sole proprietor does not have adequate insurance, the injured pedestrian could bring a suit against the sole proprietor personally. The sole proprietor would be personally responsible for any damages awarded to the injured pedestrian and might even be forced to sell personal assets to compensate the injured pedestrian.

Insurance can help to prevent a personal catastrophe to the sole proprietor. Sole proprietors may purchase general and product liability insurance, as well as business interruption insurance and malpractice insurance. However, insurance is not available to cover every potential type of liability. Individuals who operate businesses that have a high, uninsurable liability risk will almost always do best to incorporate or form a limited liability company.

LACK OF BUSINESS CONTINUITY

Because the sole proprietorship is in many ways merely an extension of the individual, when the individual owner dies or ceases to do business, the business itself usually terminates. Although the sole proprietor may have employed several employees or agents, the agency relationship terminates upon the death of the sole proprietor. In most states, the personal representative of a deceased sole proprietors's estate may oversee the continuance of the business until the estate has been settled and the business is passed to the **heirs**. However, if the business depended on the sole proprietor for its management and direction, it may be difficult to maintain the business. The decision as to whether to continue the business may be left to an heir who has little or no interest in it. If all of the assets of the business are transferred to another individual and the business is kept intact, another sole proprietorship is formed.

HEIR
A person who inherits property, a person who has a right to inherit property, or a person who has a right to inherit property only if another person dies without leaving a valid, complete will. [pronounce: air]

No Diversity in Management

Although it may be very appealing to an entrepreneur to be able to make all the business decisions, there are many instances in which diversity in management can be advantageous. The sole proprietor does not have the experience and expertise of partners, directors, shareholders, or others who have a financial stake in the business to rely on.

LIMITED ABILITY TO ATTRACT HIGHLY QUALIFIED EMPLOYEES

Sole proprietors often find they are limited in their ability to attract and hire high-caliber employees. Employees with significant experience, knowledge, and talent may demand a partnership or an ownership interest in the business for which they choose to work.

DIFFICULTY IN TRANSFERRING PROPRIETARY INTEREST

When it comes time to sell the business, transferring the full interest of a sole proprietorship may be difficult. Because the business is linked closely with the identity of the owner, the business may be worth much less when broken down by tangible assets. The sole proprietor may be the key to the success of the business. If no buyer is available for the business, the sole proprietor may have to take a loss by selling off the individual assets of the business.

It can be expensive to sell the business of a sole proprietorship. Unlike the shareholder of a publicly traded corporation who can sell shares of stock on an exchange for a small broker's fee, selling a sole proprietorship can be a difficult, time-consuming, and expensive ordeal. Many sales require extensive appraisals of the assets of the business. It may be difficult to place a fair dollar value on several assets of the business, including the **goodwill** and name of the business.

GOODWILL
The reputation and patronage of a company. The monetary worth of a company's goodwill is roughly what a company would sell for over the value of its physical property, money owed to it, and other assets.

LIMITED ABILITY TO RAISE CAPITAL

A wealthy entrepreneur starting a second or third business may not have a problem with lack of capital to start a sole proprietorship. However, for most individuals, a barrier is created by the limitations of their own financial wealth. The funds they are able to borrow based on their personal assets and their business plan may not be sufficient to fund the type of business they desire to run.

IN SUMMATION

Some of the disadvantages of doing business as a sole proprietor compared to other types of businesses include:

- Unlimited liability for the sole proprietor
- Lack of business continuity
- No diversity in management
- Limited ability to attract employees
- Difficulty in transferring ownership
- Limited ability to raise capital

ASSUMED NAME
Alias that may be used to transact business. Usually requires filing or notification at the state or local level. Same as fictitious name.

TRADE NAME
The name of a business. It will usually be legally protected in the area where the company operates and for the types of products in which it deals.

FICTITIOUS NAME
Alias that may be used to transact business. Usually requires filing or notification at the state or local level. Same as assumed name.

§ 2.5 OPERATION OF THE SOLE PROPRIETORSHIP

There are few formalities to follow before an individual commences business as a sole proprietorship. Because a sole proprietorship is not considered to be a separate entity, but rather an extension of the individual owner, one need do nothing to "form" the sole proprietorship. The formalities that must be followed are not unique to sole proprietorships, but are required of all types of business organizations. These may include filing a certificate of assumed name, trade name, or fictitious name; applying for tax identification numbers, sales tax permits, and licenses; and registering any pertinent trademarks, copyrights, or patents.

USING AN ASSUMED NAME, TRADE NAME, OR FICTITIOUS NAME

Most states allow a sole proprietor to transact business under a name other than his or her own name, an **assumed name**, **trade name**, or **fictitious name**, provided that the purpose for doing so is not a fraudulent design or with the intent to injure others.[6] The statutes of most states set forth certain requirements that must be followed before an individual may transact business under an assumed name, trade name, or fictitious name, as it may variously be called.

As indicated in *Thomas v. Colvin*, the following case, operating under a fictitious or assumed name does not change the nature of the sole proprietorship, nor does it limit the liability of the sole proprietor in any way.

CONVERSION
Any act that deprives an owner of property without that owner's permission and without just cause. For example, it is conversion to refuse to return a borrowed book.

DEMURRER
A legal pleading that says, in effect, "even if, for the sake of argument, the facts presented by the other side are correct, those facts do not give the other side a legal argument that can possibly stand up in court." The demurrer has been replaced in many courts by a motion to dismiss.

NOMENCLATURE
Designation, title, or name of something.

CASE

Johnnie E. THOMAS, Appellee, v. Bennie J. COLVIN, and R. A. Coker, d/b/a Sherwood Motors, Appellants. NO. 50209. Court of Appeals of Oklahoma, Division No. 1. Jan. 16, 1979. Rehearing Denied Feb. 27, 1979. Appeal from the District Court of Oklahoma County; William S. Myers, judge.

REYNOLDS, Judge:

Does an individual who does business as a sole proprietor under one or several names remain one person, personally liable for all his obligations?

Jury returned verdict in **conversion** action against defendant-appellant, R. A. Coker, d/b/a Sherwood Motors, for $1,625 actual damages and $17,500 punitive. Defendant appeals, contending that trial court erred in overruling his **demurrer** to plaintiff's evidence.

Plaintiff's action was premised on defendant's wrongful repossession of plaintiff's automobile. The car had been purchased from defendant on a credit plan, and the resulting security agreement and promissory note were assigned to B.F.T.C. Finance

Corporation, of which Coker is president. Evidence established that Coker called Bennie Colvin in Oklahoma City and hired him to repossess the car. This was done even though plaintiff was not in default on the note.

Defendant argues that trial court erred since evidence failed to establish that Colvin was the agent of "R. A. Coker, d/b/a Sherwood Motors." Defendant treats this **nomenclature** as a separate entity arguing that since Coker was not acting on behalf of Sherwood Motors when he hired Colvin and directed him to convert plaintiff's car, he is not liable. Coker argues that since he was not sued "individually" he is not responsible for any

CASE *(continued)*

Johnnie E. THOMAS, Appellee, v. Bennie J. COLVIN, and R. A. Coker, d/b/a Sherwood Motors, Appellants.

individual actions apart from the operation of Sherwood Motors. Plaintiff argues correctly that even though Colvin may not have been the agent of "Sherwood Motors" in repossessing the car, Coker's participation in the commission of this tort as an individual and as agent of B.F.T.C. makes him liable. . . .

Defendant treats this case as if the use of the "d/b/a" designation limited the capacity in which he could be liable. No authority is cited to support this contention that a separate entity is created by this nomenclature. The Oklahoma Supreme Court decided in National Surety Co. v. Oklahoma Presbyterian College for Girls, 38 Okl. 429, 132 P. 652 (1913), that naming a sole proprietor defendant under his trade name was the same as naming the defendant individually.

This same result has been reached elsewhere. In Duval v. Midwest Auto City, Inc., 425 F.Supp. 1381 (D.Neb.1977), the court noted:

The designation "d/b/a" means "doing business as" but is merely descriptive of the person or corporation who does business under some other name. Doing business under another name does not create an entity distinct from the person operating the business. The individual who does business as a sole proprietor under one or several names remains one person, personally liable for all his obligations.

. . . R. A. Coker was before the trial court as a defendant individually liable for his actions whether performed on behalf of B.F.T.C. Finance Corporation or as operator of his other business.

Plaintiff presented sufficient evidence to support a finding that defendant participated in the commission of a tort in Oklahoma. There being no absence of proof, trial court properly overruled defendant's demurrer. . . .

AFFIRMED.

ROMANG, P. J., and BOX, J., concur.

Note that in this case the sole proprietor defendant could not escape personal liability merely by operating under an assumed name.

Case material reprinted from Westlaw, with permission.

Typically, if the proposed name is available and otherwise complies with state statutes, an application for certificate of assumed name, trade name, or fictitious name, or similar document, is filed with the secretary of state of the state in which the sole proprietor intends to do business. State statutes often require publication of a notice of intent to transact business under an assumed name. The intent of these statutes is to protect the public by giving notice or information as to the persons with whom they deal and to afford protection against fraud and deceit.[7]

The appropriate state statutes should be carefully reviewed to ascertain the state requirements for assumed names, trade names, or fictitious names, and the secretary of state or other appropriate state official should be contacted. Often the secretary of state's office will provide its own forms to be completed to apply for a certificate of assumed name. Exhibit 2-4 shows a fictitious or assumed name certificate that may be used by a sole proprietor.

EXHIBIT 2-4	APPLICATION FOR CONDUCT OF BUSINESS UNDER FICTITIOUS OR ASSUMED NAME FORM

From 13C Am. Jur. Legal Forms 2d Name § 182:5 (May 2011)

APPLICATION—CONDUCT OF BUSINESS UNDER FICTITIOUS OR ASSUMED NAME—GENERAL FORM

Application

To: _____ *[Secretary of State of* _____ *(state) or other public official]* _____ *[address]*

Pursuant to _____ *[cite statute]*, relating to the conduct of business under _____ *[a fictitious or an assumed]* name, the undersigned _____ *[person or persons or partnership or corporation]* who _____ *[is or are]*, or will be, carrying on business in _____ *[state]* under _____ *[a fictitious or an assumed]* name, presents for filing the following application in the office of _____ *[the secretary of state or other public official]*:

1. The _____ *[fictitious or assumed]* name under which the business is, or will be, carried on is: _____.
2. The real name and address of each person owning or interested in the business is: _____.
3. The nature of the business is: _____.
4. The business will be conducted at _____ *[address]*, _____ *[city]*, _____ County, _____ *[state]*, _____ *[zip code]*.

[If applicable, add:]

5. The name of the agent through whom the business is, or will be, carried on is _____, whose address is _____ *[address]*, _____ *[city]*, _____ County, _____ *[state]* _____ *(zip code)*.

Dated: _____

_____

[Signature]
[Acknowledgment]

Reprinted with permission from American Jurisprudence Legal Forms 2d © 2008 Thomson Reuters/West.

HIRING EMPLOYEES AND USING TAX IDENTIFICATION NUMBERS

If a sole proprietor will be hiring employees, a federal employer identification number (EIN) must be obtained. This number is obtained by completing and filing with the Internal Revenue Service (IRS) an Application for Employer Identification

INTELLECTUAL PROPERTY

1. A copyright, patent, trademark, trade secret, or similar intangible right in an original tangible or perceivable work.
2. The works themselves in (no. 1).
3. The right to obtain a copyright, patent, etc., for the works in no. 1.

PATENT
An exclusive right granted by the federal government to a person for a limited number of years (usually 20) for the manufacture and sale of something that person has discovered or invented.

Number (Form SS-4). See Exhibit 2-5. The Form SS-4 may be completed online from the IRS website. Forms may also be downloaded from the IRS's website for completion and mailing to the IRS, or they may be obtained by calling the IRS at 1-800-829-1040.

SIDEBAR

Whenever a form is completed online on behalf of a client, it is important to retain a hard copy of the form, signed by the client, in the client's file.

Some states require employers to have a state tax identification number separate from the federal tax identification number. The appropriate state authority should be contacted to ensure that the sole proprietor is in compliance with all requirements for tax identification numbers.

Sole proprietors with employees must also be aware of and comply with all requirements concerning state and federal withholding and unemployment taxes.

TRADEMARK
A distinctive mark, brand name, motto, or symbol used by a company to identify or advertise the products it makes or sells. Trademarks (and service marks) can be federally registered and protected against use by other companies if the marks meet certain criteria. A federally registered mark bears the symbol ©.

SALES TAX PERMITS

Most states require businesses to obtain a sales tax permit before sales are made. Again, the appropriate state authority must be contacted to ensure that the proper procedures are followed.

LICENSING

Many types of businesses are regulated by state or local law and are required to obtain licenses of one form or another. The proper city and state authorities must be contacted to ascertain whether a license is required for the type of business that the sole proprietor proposes to commence.

COPYRIGHT
The right to control the copying, distributing, performing, displaying, and adapting of works (including paintings, music, books, and movies). The right belongs to the creator, or to persons employing the creator, or to persons who buy the right from the creator. The right is created, regulated, and limited by the Federal Copyright Act of 1976 and by the Constitution. The symbol for copyright is ©. The legal life (duration) of a copyright is the author's life plus 50 years, or 75 years from publication date, or 100 years from creation, depending on the circumstances.

REGISTERING INTELLECTUAL PROPERTY

When a sole proprietor forms a new business, the business may involve **intellectual property**, including inventions, the unique use of words and symbols that represent the business or product, and creative material prepared by the sole proprietor. The registration of **patents**, **trademarks**, or **copyrights** will protect the sole proprietor's exclusive rights and make it illegal for anyone else to use that material. Patents and trademarks are protected at the federal level by registering with the United States Patent and Trademark Office. Copyrights are protected by the United States Copyright Office. It may also be possible to protect the sole proprietor's trademark at the state level by filing the proper documentation with the secretary of state or other designated state official.

EXHIBIT 2-5 APPLICATION FOR EMPLOYER IDENTIFICATION NUMBER

Form **SS-4**
(Rev. January 2010)
Department of the Treasury
Internal Revenue Service

Application for Employer Identification Number

(For use by employers, corporations, partnerships, trusts, estates, churches, government agencies, Indian tribal entities, certain individuals, and others.)

▶ See separate instructions for each line.   ▶ Keep a copy for your records.

OMB No. 1545-0003

EIN

Type or print clearly.

1 Legal name of entity (or individual) for whom the EIN is being requested	

2 Trade name of business (if different from name on line 1)	**3** Executor, administrator, trustee, "care of" name

4a Mailing address (room, apt., suite no. and street, or P.O. box)	**5a** Street address (if different) (Do not enter a P.O. box.)

4b City, state, and ZIP code (if foreign, see instructions)	**5b** City, state, and ZIP code (if foreign, see instructions)

6 County and state where principal business is located

7a Name of responsible party	**7b** SSN, ITIN, or EIN

8a Is this application for a limited liability company (LLC) (or a foreign equivalent)?   ☐ Yes   ☐ No   **8b** If 8a is "Yes," enter the number of LLC members . . . . ▶

8c If 8a is "Yes," was the LLC organized in the United States?   ☐ Yes   ☐ No

9a **Type of entity** (check only one box). **Caution.** If 8a is "Yes," see the instructions for the correct box to check.

☐ Sole proprietor (SSN) _____
☐ Partnership
☐ Corporation (enter form number to be filed) ▶ _____
☐ Personal service corporation
☐ Church or church-controlled organization
☐ Other nonprofit organization (specify) ▶ _____
☐ Other (specify) ▶

☐ Estate (SSN of decedent) _____
☐ Plan administrator (TIN) _____
☐ Trust (TIN of grantor) _____
☐ National Guard   ☐ State/local government
☐ Farmers' cooperative   ☐ Federal government/military
☐ REMIC   ☐ Indian tribal governments/enterprises
Group Exemption Number (GEN) if any ▶

9b If a corporation, name the state or foreign country (if applicable) where incorporated

State	Foreign country

10 **Reason for applying** (check only one box)

☐ Started new business (specify type) ▶ _____
☐ Hired employees (Check the box and see line 13.)
☐ Compliance with IRS withholding regulations
☐ Other (specify) ▶

☐ Banking purpose (specify purpose) ▶ _____
☐ Changed type of organization (specify new type) ▶ _____
☐ Purchased going business
☐ Created a trust (specify type) ▶ _____
☐ Created a pension plan (specify type) ▶ _____

11 Date business started or acquired (month, day, year). See instructions.

12 Closing month of accounting year

13 Highest number of employees expected in the next 12 months (enter -0- if none).

If no employees expected, skip line 14.

Agricultural	Household	Other

14 If you expect your employment tax liability to be $1,000 or less in a full calendar year **and** want to file Form 944 annually instead of Forms 941 quarterly, check here. (Your employment tax liability generally will be $1,000 or less if you expect to pay $4,000 or less in total wages.) If you do not check this box, you must file Form 941 for every quarter. ☐

15 First date wages or annuities were paid (month, day, year). **Note.** If applicant is a withholding agent, enter date income will first be paid to nonresident alien (month, day, year) . . . . ▶

16 Check **one** box that best describes the principal activity of your business.

☐ Construction   ☐ Rental & leasing   ☐ Transportation & warehousing   ☐ Health care & social assistance   ☐ Wholesale-agent/broker
☐ Real estate   ☐ Manufacturing   ☐ Finance & insurance   ☐ Accommodation & food service   ☐ Wholesale-other   ☐ Retail
☐ Other (specify)

17 Indicate principal line of merchandise sold, specific construction work done, products produced, or services provided.

18 Has the applicant entity shown on line 1 ever applied for and received an EIN?   ☐ Yes   ☐ No
If "Yes," write previous EIN here ▶

Third Party Designee	Complete this section **only** if you want to authorize the named individual to receive the entity's EIN and answer questions about the completion of this form.	
	Designee's name	Designee's telephone number (include area code) ( )
	Address and ZIP code	Designee's fax number (include area code) ( )

Under penalties of perjury, I declare that I have examined this application, and to the best of my knowledge and belief, it is true, correct, and complete.

Name and title (type or print clearly) ▶

Applicant's telephone number (include area code) ( )

Signature ▶   Date ▶

Applicant's fax number (include area code) ( )

For Privacy Act and Paperwork Reduction Act Notice, see separate instructions.   Cat. No. 16055N   Form **SS-4** (Rev. 1-2010)

IN SUMMATION

- Because the sole proprietorship is not considered a separate entity, nothing needs to be done to form the sole proprietorship.

- If a sole proprietor does business under a name other than his or her own name, a certificate of assumed name, trade name, or fictitious name, or some similar document, must be filed at the state level.

- Publication of a notice of the use of an assumed name, trade name, or fictitious name may be required to put the public on notice.

- Any sole proprietor who hires employees must comply with certain federal, state and local requirements, including obtaining tax identification numbers for the sole proprietorship and following requirements for withholding income tax.

- Sole proprietors may be required to obtain sales tax permits before sales are made.

- Certain types of businesses operated by a sole proprietorship may require licensing at the state or local level.

- Sole proprietors may need to take steps to register patents, trademarks, or copyrights to protect their intellectual property.

§ 2.6 THE PARALEGAL'S ROLE

Paralegals who work with attorneys representing sole proprietorships can get very involved with that client representation. If the client is an experienced business-person who perhaps has started a business before, he or she may need little legal assistance from the attorney or the paralegal. Legal services may be confined to legal advice given by the attorney to the sole proprietor. An experienced business-person may decide to personally handle all formalities connected with the sole proprietorship.

Other clients, however, because of inexperience or lack of time, may decide to ask more assistance of the attorney and the paralegal. The attorney may meet with the client to give legal advice as requested, and then ask the paralegal to directly assist the client by seeing that all of the necessary formalities are complied with.

The paralegal may prepare for the client, or assist the client in preparing, all necessary documents, including tax identification number applications and an application for a certificate of assumed name. For this reason, it is important for paralegals to be familiar with state and local requirements and procedures that must be followed to organize and operate a sole proprietorship.

The checklist in Exhibit 2-6 can be used to ensure that the client is given all the necessary information and assistance to begin his or her own sole proprietorship.

EXHIBIT 2-6   CHECKLIST FOR STARTING A SOLE PROPRIETORSHIP

- Contact proper state and federal agencies to request information regarding taxation, unemployment insurance, workers' compensation insurance, and so forth. (The law firm may keep extra state and federal information and forms on hand for clients.)

- Complete and file necessary applications for employer identification numbers—both federal and state, if necessary.

- File application for certificate of assumed name, trade name, or fictitious name with secretary of state or other appropriate state agency, if necessary.

- Publish notice of transacting business under assumed name in local newspaper, if necessary.

- Secure necessary business licenses and permits—state and local.

- Obtain sales tax permits, if necessary.

- Ascertain whether the sole proprietor has any intellectual property rights that must be protected through application for a patent, trademark, or copyright.

© Cengage Learning 2013

CORPORATE PARALEGAL PROFILE
Jamie L. Burud

My coworkers are great and we can work as a team if necessary to get a project done.

NAME Jamie L. Burud
LOCATION Edina, Minnesota
TITLE Legal Assistant
SPECIALTY Corporate Law
EDUCATION Legal Office Certificate from Rasmussen College; Additional Paralegal Coursework North Hennepin Community College
EXPERIENCE 6 years

Jamie Burud is a legal assistant with Hellmuth & Johnson, PLLC, a law firm with 42 attorneys, 22 legal assistants, and 7 paralegals. Hellmuth & Johnson employs both paralegals and legal assistants, although much of their work is interchangeable. Jamie reports to two attorneys and she specializes in corporate law.

One of Jamie's primary tasks is the formation of business entities. She often works with entrepreneurs and sole proprietors who have decided to take their business to the next level and incorporate or form a one-person limited liability company. Jamie assists in the formation and registration of those entities.

She has the primary responsibility to correspond with clients and collect the necessary information for the entity formation. She then prepares and files the articles of organization or articles of incorporation, as applicable, with the Minnesota secretary of state. Jamie is often responsible for creating the first draft of the limited liability company operating agreement, member control agreement, and/or corporate bylaws for the managing

continues

CORPORATE PARALEGAL PROFILE
Jamie L. Burud (continued)

attorney's approval. She also requests tax identification numbers and files certificates of assumed names on behalf of clients, whether they are sole proprietors or a new entity she is helping to form.

In addition to forming business entities, Jamie is responsible for assisting with their maintenance. At the beginning of each year, she prepares fiscal-year-end minutes and files annual renewals with the secretary of state's office for over 100 corporate clients represented by Hellmuth & Johnson.

One thing Jamie likes about her job is the variety—every day is very different. While her firm assists clients with corporate formations throughout the year, at the beginning of the year she typically spends more time on annual filings and fiscal-year-end minutes. One day she might be in crunch and crisis mode, and the next could be a catch-up day, dealing with paperwork and filing.

From time to time, Jamie finds herself working on a totally unexpected project. Several years ago, when an up-and-coming consumer-products company (with many high-profile shareholders) brought its corporate records to the firm, Jamie was tasked with helping to organize them. According to Jamie, the corporate records were a mess. But she stuck with it and organized the records and over 400 stock certificates. Working on such a big project from beginning to end made it one of the most satisfying projects Jamie has worked on.

Years later, she is still issuing, cancelling, and transferring stock and stock certificates for that company.

From Jamie's perspective, one of the best aspects of her job is the people she works with. She likes working with smart attorneys in a prestigious law firm and likes that her coworkers are great. They can always work as a team to get a project done. Jamie also likes having the opportunity to learn new things all the time.

While she admits that some parts of her position can be repetitious day after day, Jamie feels that that repetition has allowed her to feel quite confident, both about the accuracy of her work and the quality of the work product.

With a new baby at home, Jamie has not had a lot of time for involvement in the local paralegal association, but her employers report that she is a great mentor and role model to new employees at their firm.

Jamie's advice to new paralegals?

Go above and beyond what you are asked to do; and it is very important to pay attention to detail. Also, look for a job in an area of law that interests you and that will keep you thinking and challenging yourself. Also, find a firm/ job that suits your lifestyle. If you have a family and need more flexibility, look for a firm that is willing to offer that flexibility.

For more information on careers for corporate paralegals, log in to http://cengagebrain.com to access the CourseMate website that accompanies this text; then see the Corporate Careers Section.

ETHICAL CONSIDERATION

Attorneys have an ethical duty to provide their clients with competent, diligent representation. Generally, competent representation means that the attorney must demonstrate the following at a reasonable level:

- Legal knowledge

- Skill

- Thoroughness

- Preparation

As part of the legal representation team, paralegals also have an ethical duty to perform their jobs with competence and diligence. Because paralegals are not regulated by law in most states, it is not always clear exactly what makes a paralegal competent and diligent. However, it is generally agreed that competent paralegals have a basic knowledge of the legal system in the jurisdiction in which they work, and possess skill in the following areas:

- Organization and management

- Communication

- Critical thinking

- Computers

- Legal research and investigation

- Interpersonal

Corporate paralegals must have a good understanding of the corporate laws in their state. If they work for public corporations, they should also be familiar with the pertinent securities laws and regulations.

Both the National Association of Legal Assistants (NALA) and the National Federation of Paralegal Associations (NFPA) have designed tests for their members to prove their competence as paralegals. Paralegals can take NALA's Certified Paralegal exam to become a Certified Paralegal, or they may take the NFPA's Paralegal Advanced Competency Exam (PACE) to become a PACE Registered Paralegal. These tests are not required by law; they are merely a means for paralegals to demonstrate their competence.

For more information on ethics for corporate paralegals, including links to the NALA and NFPA codes of ethics, log in to http://cengagebrain.com to access the CourseMate website that accompanies this text; then see the Ethics Section.

§ 2.7 RESOURCES

Many resources are available to paralegals who work with sole proprietorships. Much of this information is published by the government and is free for the asking. Some of the most valuable resources include United States Small Business Administration publications and publications and information available from state and local government offices, state statutes, and the secretary of state's offices.

UNITED STATES SMALL BUSINESS ADMINISTRATION

The United States Small Business Administration (SBA) has offices in nearly every major city in the country. Local SBA offices provide a wide variety of free information on requirements for forming and operating small businesses, including sole proprietorships. The SBA's website provides information on starting a business, including start-up basics, financing, hiring employees, and legal aspects.

STATE AND LOCAL GOVERNMENT OFFICES

Licensing and taxation requirements vary by state and locality, and it is important that the appropriate authorities be contacted to obtain information relating to all state and local licensing and taxation matters, including unemployment insurance, withholding for employee income taxation, and sales tax permits and licenses. Again, the information obtainable from your local SBA office can help direct you to the appropriate offices that must be contacted. Many state and local agencies have helpful websites.

STATE STATUTES

The appropriate state statutes must be consulted for information regarding use of assumed names, trade names, or fictitious names, if applicable, as well as for any requirements or regulations related to sole proprietorships. Exhibit 2-7 is a list of state statute citations concerning assumed names.

SECRETARY OF STATE OFFICES

The secretary of state or other appropriate state authority should be contacted for procedural information regarding filing of an application for use of an assumed or fictitious name, if applicable. The appropriate secretary of state's office may also be able to advise you on the procedures for registering a trademark at the state level.

EXHIBIT 2-7	LIST OF STATE STATUTES CONCERNING ASSUMED, FICTITIOUS, OR TRADE NAMES
Arizona	Ariz. Rev. Stat. Ann. §§ 44-1236, 44-1460
Arkansas	Ark. Code Ann. § 4-27-404
California	Cal. Bus. & Prof. Code § 17910 et seq.
Colorado	Colo. Rev. Stat. § 7-71-101
Connecticut	Conn. Gen. Stat. Ann. § 35-1
Delaware	Del. Code Ann. tit. 6 § 3101
Florida	Fla. Stat. Ann. § 865.09
Georgia	Ga. Code Ann. § 10-1-490
Idaho	Idaho Code § 53-504
Illinois	805 ILCS 5/4.15
Indiana	Ind. Code Ann. §§ 23-15-1-1, 23-15-1-3
Iowa	Iowa Code Ann. § 547.1
Kentucky	Ky. Rev. Stat. Ann. § 365.015
Louisiana	La. Rev. Stat. Ann. § 51:281, et seq.
Maine	10 M.R.S.A. § 1521, 13-C M.R.S.A. § 404.
Maryland	Md. Corps. & Assns. § 1-401 et seq.
Massachusetts	Mass. Ann. Laws ch. 110, §§ 4; 5
Michigan	Mich. Comp. Laws Ann. § 445.1 et seq.
Minnesota	Minn. Stat. § 333.01–333.11
Missouri	Mo. Rev. Stat. § 417.200 et seq.
Montana	Mont. Code Ann. § 30-13-201 et seq.
Nebraska	Neb. Rev. Stat. § 87-208 et seq.
Nevada	Nev. Rev. Stat. § 602.010 et seq.
New Hampshire	N.H. Rev. Stat. Ann. § 349:1 et seq.
New Jersey	N.J. Rev. Stat. § 14A:2-2.1
New York	N.Y. Gen. Bus. Law §§ 130, 133
North Carolina	N.C. Gen. Stat. §§ 66–68
North Dakota	N.D. Stat. Ann. § 47-25-01 et seq.
Ohio	Ohio Rev. Code Ann. §§ 1329.01–1329.06
Oklahoma	Okla. Stat. Ann. tit. 18 § 1140 et seq.
Oregon	Or. Rev. Stat. § 648.005 et seq.
Pennsylvania	54 Pa. Cons. Stat. § 301 et seq.
Rhode Island	R.I. Gen. Laws § 6-1-1
South Carolina	S.C. Code Ann. § 33-42-45
South Dakota	S.D. Codified Laws Ann. § 37-11-1 et seq.
Tennessee	Tenn. Code Ann. §§48-14-102, 48-207-101
Texas	Tex. Bus & Com. § 36.10 et seq.
Utah	Utah Code Ann. § 42-2-5 et seq.

continues

EXHIBIT 2-7	*(continued)*
Vermont	Vt. Stat. Ann. tit. 11 § 1621
Virginia	Va. Code Ann. § 59.1-69 et seq.
Washington	Wash. Rev. Code § 19.80.001 et seq.
West Virginia	W. Va. Code § 47-8-2 et seq.
Wisconsin	Wis. Stat. § 134.17
Wyoming	Wyo. Stat. §§ 40-2-101 to 40-2-109

© Cengage Learning 2013

Typically, a division of the secretary of state's office is designated to accept filings for corporations and all other business organizations. That division may be referred to as the Division of Corporations, Business Registration Division, or it may have some similar name. In some states, business organization filings are handled by a separate department, such as the Arizona Corporation Commission, or the Michigan Department of Commerce. This will also be the office where applications for assumed or fictitious name certificates are filed. Throughout this text, we refer to these state offices as the secretary of state offices for ease of explanation. In any event, it will be important for you to determine the correct office to accept business organization filings in your state. Appendix A to this text is a directory of secretary of state offices.

INTERNAL REVENUE SERVICE AND STATE TAX INFORMATION

In addition to providing the Form SS-4 to apply for an employer identification number, the Internal Revenue Service provides a variety of important information concerning sole proprietorships. The IRS Small Business/Self-Employed website includes downloadable information on taxation for sole proprietors and other small business owners, as well as an online classroom with a series of self-directed workshops on a variety of topics for small business owners. In addition, this site provides links to state government websites with important information for businesses. Paralegals will find it useful to review the requirements for sole proprietorships here. They may also refer sole proprietor clients to the IRS website.

If the sole proprietor hires employees, a state employer identification number may be required. The website of the Federation of Tax Administrators provides links to the state tax agency of each state.

U.S. PATENT AND TRADEMARK OFFICE

The U.S. Patent and Trademark Office provides information concerning the registration of trademarks and patents at the federal level. The Patent and Trademark Office may be contacted by calling (800) 786-9199, or by visiting its website.

SUMMARY

- The sole proprietorship is the simplest, most common form of business ownership in the United States.
- The sole proprietor is the sole owner of all assets of the sole proprietorship. He or she is personally responsible for all debts and liabilities of the business.
- Sole proprietors may hire employees to act on their behalf, but they retain full authority and responsibility.
- Sole proprietorships may conduct their businesses under assumed names, trade names, or fictitious names by filing the appropriate documentation with state authorities.
- Some of the advantages to conducting business as a sole proprietorship include (1) the full management authority possessed by the sole proprietor, (2) the minimal formalities and regulatory reporting requirements to form and maintain a sole proprietorship, (3) the low cost of organization, (4) income tax benefits, and (5) the relative ease with which a sole proprietorship can be discontinued.
- Some of the disadvantages to conducting business as a sole proprietorship include (1) the sole proprietor's unlimited liability for debts and obligations of the business, (2) the lack of business continuity, (3) the lack of diversity in management, (4) the difficulty sole proprietors may face in attracting highly qualified employees, (5) the difficulty in transferring the proprietary interest of the sole proprietorship, and (6) the sole proprietor's limited ability to raise capital.

REVIEW QUESTIONS

1. What form of business ownership is the most prevalent in the United States? What form of business organization generates the most income?

2. Explain why doing business as a sole proprietor instead of as a corporation can be an income tax advantage for some individuals.

3. Suppose that the Johnson Grocery Store is a sole proprietorship owned by Jill Johnson. If Jill's store manager, Ben, in the ordinary course of business, orders too many tomatoes, can Jill Johnson refuse to pay for the order, claiming it's "not her fault"? Why or why not?

4. Explain why an individual with limited financial resources might choose to incorporate rather than operate a sole proprietorship.

5. Jim is contemplating going into business for himself as a general contractor specializing in apartment complexes. For what reasons may Jim choose to operate as a sole proprietorship? What factors may cause him to consider incorporating or forming a limited liability company?

6. If Lucy decides to start a tailoring business from her home, what must she do before she begins advertising under the name of Lucy's Alterations?

7. Would a student who operates a lawn service, working afternoons and weekends to help pay tuition, be considered a sole proprietor? Why or why not?

■ PRACTICAL PROBLEMS

1. What are the requirements for filing a certificate of assumed name in your state? Find the pertinent statutes in your state, or contact your secretary of state's office or other appropriate state office, to answer the following questions:

   a. What is the document called in your state?

   b. What is the filing fee for filing the certificate of assumed name in your state?

   c. How long does the assumed name, or fictitious name, remain active?

   d. What is the procedure for filing the certificate of assumed name?

2. Is a state tax identification number required for sole proprietors who hire employees in your state?

   a. What are the procedures for requesting such a number?

   b. Whom must be contacted?

   c. What forms must be completed?

■ EXERCISE IN CRITICAL THINKING

It is estimated that at least 30 percent of small businesses fail within the first year. Even with that high failure rate, some sole proprietors enjoy great success. What do you think are some of the common characteristics and traits possessed by successful sole proprietors?

■ WORKPLACE SCENARIO _____ DE home state

Assume that you are a paralegal working in the same scenario as discussed in Chapter 1. Your new client, Bradley Harris, has made it through surgery just fine and he is ready to get back to business. Mr. Harris has come to your law firm seeking advice as to any formalities he must comply with to operate his business within the law as a sole proprietorship. Mr. Harris operates out of his home under the name of Cutting Edge Computer Repair. He has one employee, who works as his secretary/assistant.

Using the Client Information Sheet provided in Appendix B-1 to this text, prepare the necessary documents for Mr. Harris. You may create your own documents using the sample forms in this chapter, or you may obtain the forms from the appropriate state and federal offices. Several of these forms are available for downloading from the secretary of state websites. Form SS-4 is available for downloading on the Internal Revenue Service website.

Your documents should be prepared with cover letters to the appropriate state and federal authorities, making mention of the appropriate filing fee. The necessary documents may include:

1. Application for certificate of assumed name (or similar document as required in your state).

2. Application for federal employer identification number.

3. Application for state employer identification number (if required in your state).

Portfolio Reminder

Save the documents prepared for the Workplace Scenario exercises in each chapter, either in hard copy or electronically, to build a portfolio of documents to be used for job interviews or as

sample documents on the job. At this point, your portfolio should include the following:

1. Power of attorney
2. Application for assumed name
3. Application for federal employer identification number
4. Application for state employer identification number

ENDNOTES

1. Department of the Treasury, Internal Revenue Service. Sole Proprietorship Returns, 2008, 2010, Figure A. http://www.irs.gov.

2. Department of the Treasury, Internal Revenue Service. 2008 Statistics of Income, Corporate Income Tax Returns, 2011, Table 1. http://www.irs.gov.

3. Department of the Treasury, Internal Revenue Service. Sole Proprietorship Returns, 2008, 2010, Table 1. http://www.irs.gov.

4. U.S. Department of Labor, Bureau of Labor Statistics, "American Time Use Survey," Center for Women's Business Research, The Economic Impact of Women-Owned Businesses in the United States, October 2009, http://www.womensbusinessresearch.org.

5. U.S. Department of Labor, Bureau of Labor Statistics, "American Time Use Survey" as summarized in "Issues in Labor Statistics," March 2009, http://www.bls.gov/opub/ils/pdf/opbils72.pdf.

6. 57 AM. JUR. 2d Name § 66 (November 2010).

7. Id. § 68.

CourseMate

To access additional course materials including CourseMate, please visit http://www.cengagebrain.com. At the CengageBrain home page, search for the ISBN of your title (from the back cover of your book) using the search box at the top of the page. This will take you to the product page where the resources can be found. The CourseMate resources for this text include Web links to the resources discussed earlier, including several resources for sole proprietors and small businesses, downloadable forms, flash cards, and more.

3

GENERAL PARTNERSHIPS

CHAPTER OUTLINE

INTRODUCTION

Although **partnerships** are not as prevalent as sole proprietorships or corporations, they are a common form of business organization. Partnerships involve two or more people and are naturally somewhat more complex than sole proprietorships. However, for many of the reasons discussed in this chapter, the formation of a partnership is often a viable alternative to incorporating or forming a limited liability company.

In this chapter, we define the term *partnership* and take a look at the legal relationships between partners and others and among the partners. We then investigate the specific advantages and disadvantages of doing business as a general partnership. Next we examine the organization and management of the partnership, including the partnership agreement. We then focus on the financial structure of a partnership and the dissolution, dissociation, winding up, and termination of the partnership. The chapter concludes with a discussion of the role of the paralegal working with partnerships and the resources available to assist in that area.

PARTNERSHIP

An association of two or more persons to carry on as co-owners of a business for profit.

§ 3.1 AN INTRODUCTION TO GENERAL PARTNERSHIPS

The **general partnership** is a type of business organization that creates a unique relationship among its members. In this section, we define *partnership*, discuss the role of partnerships in the United States, and review the law that governs partnerships. We conclude with a look at the aggregate and entity theories of partnerships.

GENERAL PARTNERSHIP

A typical partnership in which all partners are general partners.

Elements of Partnership
- Association of two or more persons
- Carry on
- Co-ownership
- Business
- For profit

PARTNERSHIP DEFINED

A partnership is an "association of two or more persons to carry on as co-owners a business for profit."[1] The essential elements of the partnership definition are "association of two or more persons," "carry on," "co-owners," "business," and "for profit." This definition is found in the Uniform Partnership Act (1914), discussed later in this chapter.

The "association of two or more persons" element differentiates the partnership from the sole proprietorship. The word "persons," as used in this definition, includes "individuals, partnerships, corporations, and other associations."[2] Generally, any individual or entity with the capacity to enter into a contract can be a partner.

The "carry on" element implies that the partners must actively carry on the partnership business together.

The "co-ownership" element refers to ownership of the business of the partnership and requires that the business be a single business entity owned by more than one person. Co-ownership also means that the partners have a right to participate in the management of the partnership and to share in the profits (and losses) of the partnership.

The "business" element of the definition includes "every trade, occupation, or profession."[3]

The "for profit" element refers to the intention of the partnership. Obviously, not every partnership earns a profit, but earning a profit must be an objective of the partnership. Nonprofit organizations may not be partnerships.

SIDEBAR

Elements of Partnership:
- Association of two or more persons
- Carry on
- Co-ownership
- Business
- For profit

Although most states base their definition of partnership on the Uniform Partnership Act (1914), the courts are sometimes called on to interpret that law to establish whether or not a partnership exists. In the following case in New York, a state that has adopted the Uniform Partnership Act (1914) definition of partnership, the court found that, "Among the factors to be considered in determining whether a partnership was created are the intent of the parties (express or implied), whether there was joint control and management of the business, whether there was a sharing of the profits as well as a sharing of the losses, and whether there was a combination of property, skill or knowledge." In this case, the court found that those elements did not exist and that there was no partnership between the parties.

CASE

Supreme Court, Appellate Division, Third Department, New York. Jennifer Cleland, Appellant, v. Christian Thiron, Respondent, et al., Defendant. 268 A.D.2d 842, 704 N.Y.S.2d 316, 2000 N.Y. Slip Op. 00477 Jan. 20, 2000.

. . . Plaintiff and defendant Christian Thirion (hereinafter defendant) were lovers for slightly less than three years, beginning in mid-1993. During that period, they resided together in plaintiff's residence. When the relationship commenced, defendant was already established as an artisan glassblower, doing business under the trade name of Glassart, and had recently purchased a building which he intended to convert into a studio and personal living quarters. It is undisputed that during the parties' relationship, plaintiff accompanied defendant to craft shows, assisted with various tasks, installed a computer system in the studio and paid various expenses of the business.

In August 1994, plaintiff drafted and the parties executed a one-page document (hereinafter the agreement) which, by its terms, was intended to establish the parties' "financial and personal relationship . . . for the purpose of reducing [plaintiff's] personal financial liability for debts incrued [sic] in her name in the course of the construction of [the studio]." The agreement identified three revolving credit accounts that had been established

in plaintiff's name, which "have been and will continue to be used exclusively for expenses related to the construction and establishment of [the studio], and for operating expenses associated with the Glassart business," and provided that "[i]n the event of [defendant's] death or disability . . . the assets of the Glassart business . . . should be used to pay the debts which exist in these accounts, as well as to pay [a $6,000 loan to defendant from plaintiff's parents]." Finally, and of primary interest here, the agreement provided:

This document is also to acknowledge that [defendant is] separated from his wife . . . and that he and [plaintiff] have been living as domestic partners since August of 1993. [Defendant and plaintiff] *have also agreed to become partners in the Glassart company business* (emphasis supplied).

Plaintiff commenced this action in May 1997, seeking a declaration that the agreement "constitutes a partnership agreement for ownership and operation of [the Glassart business]" (second cause of action), damages for breach of the agreement (first cause of action), an accounting of the profits, losses and assets of Glassart from April 1, 1993 (third cause of action), and imposition of a constructive trust upon the assets of Glassart and its real property and payment to plaintiff of not less than $60,000 therefrom (fourth cause of action).... Supreme Court found that the parties never entered into a partnership, that to the extent that the agreement might be viewed as contemplating the parties' future partnership it was unenforceable due to the absence of any material terms.... Plaintiff appeals.

We affirm. First, we agree with the Supreme Court's conclusion that no partnership existed as a matter of law. "Among the factors to be considered in determining whether a partnership was created are the intent of the parties (express or implied), whether there was joint control and management of the business, whether there was a sharing of the profits as well as a sharing of the losses, and whether there was a combination of property, skill or knowledge". . . the evidence adduced on the summary judgment motion fails to raise a genuine question of fact concerning the existence of any of those factors.

The record establishes that the studio property was owned solely by defendant and that plaintiff made no contribution to its purchase and neither made nor assumed responsibility for the mortgage payments thereon. Further, it is undisputed that plaintiff's name was never placed on a certificate of doing business as partners, no partnership tax returns were ever filed and there never was any sharing of profits or losses. Although there is no question that plaintiff made some financial contributions to defendant's business, both the agreement and plaintiff herself would characterize those contributions as loans, the very antithesis of a partnership relationship. Similarly, although plaintiff apparently performed some services for the business, by seeking compensation in the form of wages she would portray herself as a mere employee. In sum, our review of the record reveals not a scintilla of evidence supporting plaintiff's claim of the existence of a partnership.

Plaintiff's remaining contentions have been considered and found to be also unavailing.

ORDERED that the order is affirmed, with costs.

PETERS, SPAIN, GRAFFEO and MUGGLIN, JJ., concur.

Case material reprinted from Westlaw, with permission.

PARTNERSHIPS IN THE UNITED STATES

Approximately 669,601 general partnerships filed tax returns with the Internal Revenue Service (IRS) for the year 2008, with net income totaling $80.5 billion.[4] The number of general partnerships filing returns in the United States has been declining somewhat in the past decade, due to the growing popularity of other types of partnerships and limited liability companies, which are taxed like partnerships.

U.S. partnerships are formed for a variety of business purposes. For the year 2008, 238,586 general partnership returns were filed in the real estate, rental, and leasing category, which is by far the largest category of partnerships in the United States. The finance and insurance category ranked second with 74,185 partnership returns filed, and the retail trade category ranked third with 64,675 returns.[5] (See Exhibit 3-1.)

EXHIBIT 3-1 NUMBER OF GENERAL PARTNERSHIP RETURNS FILED FOR THE YEAR 2008 BY INDUSTRY

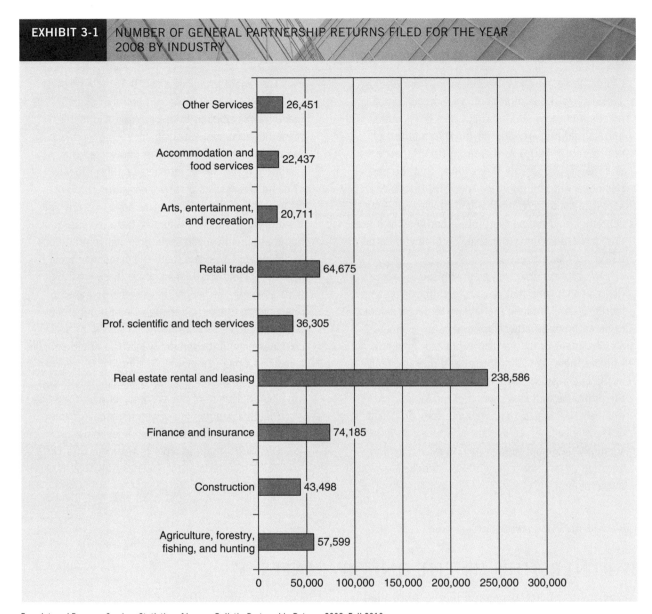

From Internal Revenue Service, *Statistics of Income Bulletin,* Partnership Returns 2008, Fall 2010.

LAW GOVERNING PARTNERSHIPS

Prior to 1914, partnerships were governed by state statutes that codified **common law** and **civil law**. In 1914 the **Commission on Uniform State Laws** approved the Uniform Partnership Act (1914) (UPA [1914]), which was designed to codify existing statutory and common law, and recommended it for adoption by all state legislatures. The American Bar Association approved the UPA in 1915. It was subsequently adopted by nearly every state in the country.

In 1987, work began on revising the UPA (1914). Amendments were made to the act in both 1992 and 1993. In 1994 a revised version was approved by the American Bar Association House of Delegates and became the Uniform Partnership Act (1994).

Again in 1996 and 1997, major changes came about in partnership law. The Uniform Partnership Act was amended to include provisions for the election of limited liability partnerships. These amendments were largely reactive changes—an attempt to codify and provide a uniform model for changes that had already been made by several states. By 1996 over 40 states had already adopted limited liability provisions in their general partnership acts. This newer version is commonly referred to as the Uniform Partnership Act (1997) (UPA [1997]). Limited liability partnerships are discussed in Chapter 5 of this text.

Adoption of a uniform law by the Commission on Uniform State Laws does not constitute the passing of a law. Rather, uniform laws are laws that are recommended for adoption by each state in the country. State legislatures may adopt uniform laws in whole or in part, or they may choose not to adopt them at all. As of 2011, every state in the country except Louisiana had adopted the UPA (1914) or the UPA (1997). For that reason, our focus in this chapter is on those two acts. It is always important to consult the state statutes for specific information on partnerships in the state in which you are working. A list of state partnership statutes and their origin is included in § 3.12 of this chapter. The full text of the Uniform Partnership Act (1997) can be found on the website of the Uniform Law Commission.

COMMON LAW
1. Judge-made law (based on ancient customs, mores, usages, and principles handed down through the ages) in the absence of controlling statutory or other enacted law.
2. All the statutory and case law of England and the American colonies before the American Revolution.

CIVIL LAW
1. Law that originated from ancient Rome rather than from the common law or from canon law.
2. The law governing private rights and remedies as opposed to criminal law, military law, international law, natural law, etc.

COMMISSION ON UNIFORM STATE LAWS
An organization that, along with the American Law Institute, proposes various Model Acts and Uniform Acts for adoption by the states.

SIDEBAR

The National Conference of Commissioners on Uniform State Laws (NCCUSL) is a nonprofit unincorporated association that has been in existence since 1892. The NCCUSL is comprised of more than 300 state commissioners on uniform laws who are attorneys appointed by each state to study and review the law of the states to determine which areas of law should be uniform. They then work to draft uniform laws that may be adopted by each state.

Partnerships are governed mainly by the provisions of the UPA (1914) or the UPA (1997), as modified by the state of domicile, but also by the partnership agreement and common law. The partnership agreement is often considered to be the law of the partnership. Partnerships are governed by the provisions of the partnership agreement so long as those provisions are permissible under the state's partnership law. The UPA (1914) or UPA (1997), as modified by the state of domicile, governs on all issues for which the partnership agreement is silent. Because the partnership agreement is a form of contract, partnerships are subject to contract law. Exhibit 3-2 summarizes the history of partnership law in the United States.

EXHIBIT 3-2	HISTORY OF PARTNERSHIP LAW IN THE UNITED STATES
Prior to 1914	Partnerships were governed by state statutes based on common law and civil law.
1914	The Commission on Uniform Sate Laws approved the Uniform Partnership Act (1914) and recommended it for adoption by all state legislatures.
1915	The American Bar Association approved the Uniform Partnership Act (1914).
1994	The Revised Uniform Partnership Act was approved by the American Bar Association.
By 1996	Over 40 states had adopted limited liability provisions in their general partnership acts.
1996 and 1997	Revisions were made to the Revised Uniform Partnership Act to add provisions for the election of limited liability partnerships, resulting in the Uniform Partnership Act (1997).
2012	Every state except Louisiana has adopted the Uniform Partnership Act (1914) or the Uniform Partnership Act (1997).

© Cengage Learning 2013

AGGREGATE THEORY

Theory regarding partnerships suggesting that a partnership is the totality of the partners rather than a separate entity.

ENTITY THEORY

Theory suggesting that a partnership is an entity separate from its partners, much like a corporation.

FIDUCIARY

1. A person who manages money or property for another person and in whom that other person has a right to place great trust.
2. A relationship like that in definition no. 1.
3. Any relationship between persons in which one person acts for another in a position of trust, for example, lawyer and client or parent and child.

THE PARTNERSHIP AS A SEPARATE ENTITY

Whereas the sole proprietor's business is considered an extension of the individual, and the corporation is considered to be a separate entity, the exact nature of the partnership is not so readily defined. There are arguments to support both the **aggregate theory**, which suggests that a partnership is the totality of persons engaged in a business rather than an entity in itself, and the **entity theory**. Under common law the partnership was not considered to be a separate entity, but rather an extension of its partners.

The UPA (1914) recognized a partnership as a separate entity for certain purposes. For example, there are specific provisions in the UPA (1914) for property ownership and transfer in the name of the partnership, and for the continuance of the partnership after the assignment of a partner's interest. Also, under the UPA (1914), partners are charged with a **fiduciary** duty to the partnership itself, in addition to their fiduciary duty to each other. Partnerships are also considered legal entities for purposes of taxation, attachment, licensing, garnishment, liability for tortious injury to third parties, and enforcement of judgments against partnership property.[6]

The aggregate theory applies in many sections of the UPA (1914) relating to substantive liabilities and duties of the partners. Most important, the act provides that partners are jointly and severally liable on certain obligations.

Unlike its predecessor, the UPA (1997) specifically states that, "[a] partnership is an entity distinct from its partners."[7] This appears to be the modern view, as noted in several recent court cases. As a separate entity, the partnership can own property in its own name, enter into contracts, and sue and be sued in court. For example, if an individual enters into a contract with a partnership that fails to perform under the contract, the individual can bring an action against the partnership for monetary damages. If the individual wins a judgment against the partnership, the partnership must satisfy the judgment from the assets of the partnership. If, however, the partnership assets are insufficient to satisfy the judgment, the individual partners will be personally liable for the amount owed.

It is important to note that both the UPA (1914) and the UPA (1997) serve only as models for the states that have adopted them. State statutes and common law are the final authority on whether a partnership is considered a separate entity or an aggregate of its partners in a particular state.

IN SUMMATION

- A partnership is:
  - An association of two or more persons
  - Formed to carry on some form of business
  - Co-owned by the partners
  - Intended to earn a profit
- The number of general partnerships in the United States has been declining in recent years due to the growing popularity of limited liability business organizations that may be taxed like a partnership.
- Partnerships are governed mainly by state laws derived from either the Uniform Partnership Act (1914) or the Uniform Partnership Act (1997), as amended.
- Under the aggregate theory, partnerships are considered a totality of the partners themselves and not a separate entity.
- Under the entity theory, the partnership is considered a separate entity, apart from its partners.

§ 3.2 THE RELATIONSHIP BETWEEN PARTNERS AND OTHERS

Whether the partnership is viewed as an aggregate of its partners or as a separate entity, it must act through its partners when dealing with outside parties. This section examines the unique legal relationship partners have with others when acting on behalf of the partnership and the other partners. First we look at how partners act as agents for the partnership and the statement of authority or denial that may be filed to give notice of each partner's authority (or lack thereof) to act on behalf of the partnership. Then we discuss the personal liability of partners.

With a few exceptions, each partner may act on behalf of the partnership when dealing with others concerning partnership business. Each partner has actual authority to bind the partnership to contractual relationships with third parties. That authority may be express, stemming from the partnership agreement, or it may be implied, based on the nature of the partnership relationship. In addition, each partner has apparent authority to bind the partnership in a contractual relationship so long as the partner appears to be acting as an agent of the partnership in accordance with the usual partnership business.

PARTNERS AS AGENTS

Partnership law has always considered partners to be agents of the other partners and of the partnership. Acts of any one partner are binding on the partnership so long as the partner's act is apparently undertaken for the purpose of carrying on the ordinary course of the partnership business or businesses of the kind carried on by the partnership. For example, a partner of a partnership formed to own and operate an automobile dealership has apparent authority to enter into contracts to receive delivery of cars from manufacturers and to sell them to customers.

The act of one partner is usually sufficient to bind the partnership, even if that partner is not acting in good faith. The signature of one partner is sufficient to execute any instrument in the name of the partnership, so long as the instrument is executed for the apparent purpose of carrying on, in the usual way, the business of the partnership. For example, suppose that four partners of a retail clothing store consider entering into a contract with a wholesaler to carry a new line of clothing in their shop. The partners decide the new line does not fit well with their existing merchandise and agree not to enter into the contract. If one of the partners later changes his mind, he could go behind the backs of his other partners and enter into the contract with the wholesaler. If it appears to the wholesaler that the one contracting partner was acting on behalf of the entire partnership, the contract would be binding on the partnership. Outsiders dealing with a partnership may reasonably assume that a partner has the authority to enter the partnership into a contractual agreement that appears to be in line with the usual business of the partnership.

ACTS REQUIRING UNANIMOUS CONSENT OF THE PARTNERS

Certain acts, specifically those that are not within the normal course of business, require unanimous consent of the partners. Ideally, the partnership agreement will outline the types of transactions that require the unanimous consent of the partners. For example, if one partner of a partnership formed to own and operate a bicycle shop were to sell its entire inventory of bicycles to a competitor, the action would require the unanimous consent of all partners. If one partner sold the inventory without the knowledge of the other partners, the sale would not be binding on the partnership.

State statutes set forth important exceptions to the rule that acts of any partner are binding on the partnership. Under the UPA (1914), the following acts are not binding on the partnership unless all partners have approved the act:

1. Acts undertaken with a third party who has knowledge that the act is not authorized[8]
2. Acts not apparently for the carrying on of the business of the partnership in the usual way[9]
3. Acts to assign the partnership property in trust for creditors or the assignee's promise to pay the debts of the partnership[10]
4. Acts to dispose of the goodwill of the business[11]

5. Acts that would make it impossible to carry on the ordinary business of a partnership[12]
6. Acts to confess a judgment on behalf of the partnership[13]
7. Acts submitting a partnership claim or liability to arbitration or reference[14]
8. Acts admitting new partners to the partnership[15]

There is some room for discretion in determining which acts of the partnership require the consent of all partners, and at times such decisions are made in the courts. The UPA (1997) leaves even more room for discretion, as it relies more heavily on the partnership agreement that is signed by all partners. The partnership agreement will usually set forth exactly what issues must be agreed on by all partners.

Under the UPA (1997), the following actions must have the unanimous consent of all partners to be binding on the partnership:

1. Acts undertaken with a third party who has knowledge, or has received notification, that the act is not authorized[16]
2. Acts apparently not undertaken for the purpose of carrying on in the ordinary course of the partnership business[17]

Amending the partnership agreement and adopting limited liability partnership status usually require unanimous consent of the partners also, unless otherwise specified in the partnership agreement.

Often, when a partnership enters into an agreement with an outside party, the agreement will include provisions indicating certain limitations on the authority of the individual partners. Such an agreement may also provide that the outside party will be notified by the partnership of any changes or additional restrictions placed on the authority of individual partners. An agreement entered into by one partner exceeding such authority will not be binding on the partnership. For example, suppose the agreement of a partnership formed to own and operate a chain of electronics stores limits the spending authority of each partner to $250,000 unless that partner has the approval of all partners, and that all of the partnership's vendors have been given notice of the limitation. A contract between one partner and a vendor to purchase $350,000 worth of computers for the partnership would not be binding on the partnership if the vendor had prior knowledge of the partner's lack of authority.

Any one partner can generally transfer partnership property to third parties by an instrument of transfer executed in the partnership name. However, under the UPA (1997), transfers contrary to a certified copy of a filed statement of partnership authority recorded in the office for recording transfers of that real estate are not binding on the partnership.[18]

STATEMENT OF PARTNERSHIP AUTHORITY

The UPA (1997) provides that partners have the option of filing a **statement of authority** with the secretary of state or other appropriate state official. The statement of authority gives public notice of the authority granted or denied certain partners. Pursuant to § 303 of the UPA (1997), the statement of authority must include:

STATEMENT OF AUTHORITY
A statement filed for public record by the partners of a partnership to expand or limit the agency authority of a partner, to deny the authority or status of a partner, or to give notice of certain events such as the dissociation of a partner or the dissolution of the partnership.

- The name of the partnership.
- The street address of its chief executive office and of one office in this state, if there is one.
- The names and mailing addresses of all of the partners or of an agent appointed and maintained by the partnership.
- The names of the partners authorized to execute an instrument transferring real property held in the name of the partnership.

In addition, the statement of authority may set forth the authority, or limitations on the authority, of some or all of the partners to enter into other transactions on behalf of the partnership and any other matter.

A statement of authority that is in full force and effect supplements the authority of a partner to enter into transactions on behalf of the partnership as follows:[19]

1. Except for real estate transfers, a grant of authority in the statement of authority is conclusive in favor of a person who gives value without knowledge to the contrary, so long as and to the extent that a limitation on that authority is not then contained in another filed statement.
2. A grant of authority to transfer real estate held in the name of the partnership contained in a certified copy of a filed statement of partnership authority recorded in the office for recording transfers of that real estate is conclusive in favor of a person who gives value without knowledge to the contrary.

In general, outside parties may rely on the authority granted by a valid statement of authority as binding on the partnership. However, persons transacting business with the partnership are not deemed to know of a limitation on the authority of a partner merely because the limitation is contained in the filed statement.

Although the filing of a statement of authority is optional, partnerships that routinely transact business such as buying and selling real estate may be required to file a statement by those who wish to transact business with the partnership.

Exhibit 3-3 is a sample of a Statement of Partnership Authority form. This form is from the state of Tennessee and is similar in content to forms used in other states.

STATEMENT OF DENIAL

In addition to the statement of authority, in most states a **statement of denial** may be filed. A statement of denial can be filed by a partner or other interested party to contradict the information included in a statement of authority. For example, a withdrawing partner may file a denial of his or her status as a partner.

LIABILITY OF PARTNERS

In states that follow the UPA (1997) in this regard, partners have **joint and several** liability for all obligations of the partnership unless otherwise agreed by the claimant or provided by law.[20] This means that any claimant or creditor of the partnership can sue the partners either individually or together, and any partner can be held liable for the entire amount of the damages or obligation.

STATEMENT OF DENIAL
A statement filed for public record by a partner or other interested party to contradict the information included in a statement of authority.

JOINT AND SEVERAL
Both together and individually. For example, a liability or debt is joint and several if the creditor may sue the debtors either together as a group (with the result that the debtors would have to split the loss) or individually (with the result that one debtor might have to pay the whole thing).

EXHIBIT 3-3	SAMPLE STATEMENT OF PARTNERSHIP AUTHORITY FORM

State of Tennessee

Department of State
Corporate Filings
312 Eighth Avenue North
6th Floor, William R. Snodgrass Tower
Nashville, TN 37243

GENERAL PARTNERSHIP
(Statement of Partnership Authority)

For Office Use Only

1. The name of the general partnership (as recorded with the Secretary of State) is:
    _____

2. The *street* address of its chief executive office is:
    _____

3. The *street* address of one of its offices in Tennessee (if any) is:
    _____

4. The names of the partners authorized to execute an instrument transferring real property held in the name of the partnership are:

    _____   _____
    _____   _____
    _____   _____
    _____   _____

5. If applicable, state the authority, or limitations of authority, of some or all partners to enter into other transactions on behalf of the partnership (attach separate sheet if necessary):
    _____
    _____
    _____

The execution of this statement constitutes an affirmation under the penalties of perjury that the undersigned has/have the authority to file this statement and that the contents of the statement are accurate.

Signed and dated this _____ day of _____, _____

_____   _____
        Signature   **Printed Name**

_____   _____
        Signature   **Printed Name**

Notes:
*   A document filed by a partnership must be executed by at least two partners. Other documents must be executed by a partner or other person authorized by the Revised Uniform Partnership Act.
*   This statement is cancelled by operation of law five years after the date on which the statement, or the most recent amendment, is filed with the Secretary of State.

SS-4514   Filing Fee: $20   RDA pending

http://www.tn.gov/sos/bus_svc/forms.htm

The partnership's creditors or claimants can look to the individual partners for payment after the partnership's assets have been exhausted. If the debts of a partnership exceed its assets, the creditors of the partnership can collect from the personal assets of all or any one of the partners until their claim has been satisfied. If only one partner has substantial personal assets, that partner can be held responsible for the entire obligation of the partnership, even if the obligation arose from the wrongdoing of another partner. Joint and several liability for the partners of all partnership obligations is one of the biggest drawbacks to forming a general partnership.

There are a few exceptions to the rule that partners are personally liable for the obligations of the partnership in all instances. For example, newer partners are generally not personally liable for obligations arising from action taken prior to their admission to the partnership.

IN SUMMATION

- In most instances, any partner may act on behalf of the partnership and has the authority to enter the partnership into a contract with third parties.

- In a general partnership, each partner acts as an agent of the partnership concerning most matters transacted in the ordinary course of business.

- Extraordinary acts of the partnership that are not undertaken in the ordinary course of business may require the unanimous consent of all partners under. state statutes or the partnership agreement.

- A statement of authority filed with the proper state or local authority gives public notice of the authority granted or denied to certain partners.

- A statement of authority may be required to transfer real estate to or from the partnership.

- A statement of denial may be filed with the proper state or local authority to contradict information filed in a statement of authority.

§ 3.3 THE RELATIONSHIP AMONG PARTNERS AND BETWEEN PARTNERS AND THE PARTNERSHIP

TENANCY IN PARTNERSHIP
Form of ownership provided for under the Uniform Partnership Act whereby all partners are co-owners with the other partners. Each partner has an equal right to possess the property for partnership purposes, but has no right to possess the property for any other purpose without the consent of the other partners.

Partners have a unique relationship both among themselves and with the partnership. This section examines the rights of partners with regard to the partnership property and the rights and duties partners owe to each other and to the partnership.

PARTNERS' RIGHTS IN PARTNERSHIP ASSETS

Under the UPA (1914), each partner was considered a co-owner with the other partners of specific partnership property. Partnership property was held in a **tenancy in partnership**. Each partner had an equal right to possess specific partnership property for partnership purposes, but had no right to possess such property for any other purpose without the consent of the other partners.[21]

The UPA (1997) treats partnerships as separate entities. It does not recognize the concept of tenancy in partnership. Rather, the partnership property is considered to be owned by the partnership itself, as an entity separate from the partners. The UPA (1997) states specifically that a partner "is not a co-owner of partnership property and has no interest in partnership property which can be transferred, either voluntarily or involuntarily."[22] This restriction on transfers refers only to the partnership property itself, not to each partner's right to receive income or profits and losses from the partnership property.

Because partnership property is owned by the partnership rather than the individual partners, in states that follow the UPA (1997), partners cannot transfer their entire right to the partnership property. They can, however, transfer their rights to receive income, or profits and losses, from the partnership. For example, assume that Andy, Barbara, and Chet are partners in a partnership that owns a $300,000 rental property. Pursuant to the partnership agreement, each partner is entitled to receive $1,000 in rent from the partnership each month. Under the UPA (1997), Barbara could transfer her right to receive $1,000 to her sister to cover a debt. She could not, however, transfer any right to co-own the building itself. She could not transfer a one-third interest in the building to repay a $100,000 debt.

A partner's right in specific partnership property is not assignable except in connection with the assignment of rights of all the partners in the same property, nor is the right in specific partnership property subject to attachment or execution, except on a claim against the partnership. For example, if Barbara defaulted on the loan to her sister, her sister would have no legal right to the partnership's rental property. She could not force the partnership to sell the property to collect what she is entitled to from Barbara. The rental property could not be assigned or sold to Barbara's sister unless Andy and Chet agreed that it would be in their best interests to sell or assign the rights of the entire partnership in the rental property to her.

Not all states have adopted this view of partnership property. As always, it is important that the pertinent state statutes be consulted.

PARTNERSHIP PROPERTY

Typically, whenever partners contribute real or personal property to the partnership or acquire property with funds of the partnership, it is considered partnership property and not property of the individual partners.

Acquisitions of significant partnership property should be approved by unanimous written consent of the partners to alleviate any possible future problems. Following is § 204 of the UPA (1997), which discusses when property is partnership property:

204. When Property Is Partnership Property

(a) Property is partnership property if acquired in the name of:
   (1) the partnership; or
   (2) one or more partners with an indication in the instrument transferring title to the property of the person's capacity as

EXHIBIT 3-4   PARTNERSHIP PROPERTY

Characteristics under the UPA (1914)	Characteristics under the UPA (1997)
• Each partner is considered a co-owner with the other partners of specific partnership property.	• Partnership property is owned by the partnership itself.
• Property is held in a tenancy in partnership.	• Partners are not considered co-owners of the property.
• Each partner has equal right to possess specific partnership property for partnership purposes, but no right to possess for any other purpose without consent of other partners.	• Individual partners have no interest in the partnership property itself that can be transferred, either voluntarily or involuntarily.

© Cengage Learning 2013

a partner or of the existence of a partnership but without an indication of the name of the partnership.

(b) Property is acquired in the name of the partnership by a transfer to:
   (1) the partnership in its name; or
   (2) one or more partners in their capacity as partners in the partnership, if the name of the partnership is indicated in the instrument transferring title to the property.

(c) Property is presumed to be partnership property if purchased with partnership assets, even if not acquired in the name of the partnership or of one or more partners with an indication in the instrument transferring title to the property of the person's capacity as a partner of the existence of a partnership.

(d) Property acquired in the name of one or more of the partners, without an indication in the instrument transferring title to the property of the person's capacity as a partner or of the existence of a partnership and without use of partnership assets, is presumed to be separate property, even if used for partnership purposes.

Exhibit 3-4 summarizes the characteristics of partnership property under the UPA (1914) and the UPA (1997).

PARTNERS' RIGHTS IN DEALING WITH EACH OTHER

Many rights are granted to partners by state statute. These rights vary by state, and many can be waived or expanded on in the partnership agreement. Some cannot be waived—not even by agreement. To avoid any potential conflicts, the partnership agreement should be carefully drafted to address any desired deviations from the applicable statutes regarding the partners' rights in dealing with each other. Following is a list of typical rights granted to partners by state statute. But remember, these rights vary by state, and many of them can be modified by the partnership agreement.

1. The right to have a separate account that reflects each partner's contributions, share of the gains, and share of the losses in the partnership assets
2. The right to an equal share of the partnership profits
3. The right to be repaid contributions and share equally in the surplus remaining after partnership liabilities are satisfied
4. The right to reimbursement for certain money spent by a partner on behalf of the partnership
5. The right of each partner to share equally in the management and conduct of the business
6. The right of access to the books and records of the partnership
7. The right to reasonable compensation for services rendered in winding up the partnership affairs
8. The right to have one's partnership interest purchased by remaining partners after a permissible dissociation from the partnership

Partners' Rights to a Separate Account

Under the UPA (1997), each partner is deemed to have a separate account in an amount equal to the partner's contributions and share of the partnership profits, less the partner's distributions received and the partner's share of partnership losses.[23] This is generally the manner for accounting for each partner's interest in the partnership in states following either the UPA (1914) or the UPA (1997), although more details or a different method may be set forth in the partnership agreement.

Partners' Rights to an Equal Share of Partnership Profits

Under the UPA (1997), each partner is entitled to an equal share of the partnership's profits and is responsible for a share of the partnership losses in proportion to his or her share of the profits. This rule is substantially the same as the rule established under the UPA (1914). It is important to note, however, that this is a right that can be—and often is—revised in a partnership agreement. To offer the partnership maximum flexibility, it is common for partners to make contributions to the partnership in unequal amounts. In that event, profits and losses are usually not shared equally among all partners, but rather in proportion to their contributions. Any arrangements that suit the partners with regard to sharing the profits and losses of the partnership can be made in the partnership agreement.

Partners' Rights to Reimbursement

Certain partners may be called on to spend their own money on behalf of the partnership. In almost every instance those partners have the right to be reimbursed for their expenditures. Most of these expenditures are considered to be loans to the partnership made by the partner and must be repaid with interest, which accrues from the date of payment or advance. The default rules under state statutes generally provide for reimbursement when partners put forth their own money for payments made (1) in the ordinary course of business of the partnership or for the preservation of its business or property, or (2) as an advance to the partnership beyond the amount of the partner's agreed contribution.[24] Details regarding repayment of loans made to the partnership by a partner generally are set forth in the partnership agreement, but state law typically makes it clear that repayment must be made with interest.

Partners' Rights to Participate in Management

Each partner is granted by statute the right to participate in the management of the partnership. However, because full management participation by every partner is often not practical or desirable, the partnership agreement may appoint a managing partner or a managing partnership committee. Note that the right to participate in the management of the partnership must be specifically waived by any partner giving up that right.

Partners' Rights to Access Books and Records

Unless otherwise specified in the partnership agreement, the partnership must keep its books and records, if any, at its principal place of business or chief executive office, and these books and records must be available to each partner and each partner's agents and attorneys, within reason.

Partners' Rights to Wind Up Partnership Business

WIND UP
Finish current business, settle accounts, and turn property into cash in order to end a corporation or a partnership and split up the assets.

Both the UPA (1914) and the UPA (1997) provide that partners who have not caused a wrongful dissolution or dissociation of the partnership have the right to **wind up** the partnership business. Any partner may also petition for a court-supervised winding up if he or she feels it necessary.

Whereas partners are not usually entitled to receive payment for their services rendered to the partnership, when a partnership dissolves, any partner who is charged with the duty of winding up the affairs of the partnership is entitled to receive fair compensation for that service. Partnership dissolution and winding up is discussed in more detail in § 3.9 of this chapter.

Exhibit 3-5 lists the rights of partners under the UPA (1914) and the UPA (1997). Note that some rights can be altered in the partnership agreement, and others cannot.

PARTNERS' DUTIES IN DEALING WITH EACH OTHER

Partners' duties are also prescribed by statute. Although many of the prescribed duties cannot be amended by the partnership agreement, they can be clarified by it. Following is a list of duties typically required by statute or by partnership agreement:

1. The duty of partners to contribute toward losses sustained by the partnership according to each partner's share in the profits

EXHIBIT 3-5 RIGHTS OF PARTNERS

Under the UPA (1914)	Under the UPA (1997)
• The right of access to the books and records of the partnership.	• The right of access to the books and records of the partnership.
• The right to formal account as to partnership affairs (under certain circumstances).	• The right to dissociate from the partnership upon giving proper notice.
• The right to co-own specific partnership property as a tenant in partnership.	

Rights under the UPA (1914) Unless Altered in the Partnership Agreement	Rights under the UPA (1997) Unless Altered in the Partnership Agreement
• The right to be repaid contributions made to the partnership after the liabilities of the partnership have been paid.	• The right to have a separate account reflecting the partners' contributions, share of the gains, and share of the losses in partnership assets.
• The right to an equal share of the partnership profits.	• The right to an equal share of the partnership profits.
• The right to reimbursement for certain money spent by the partner on behalf of the partnership.	• The right to reimbursement for certain money spent by the partner on behalf of the partnership.
• The right to share equally in the management and conduct of the business.	• The right to share equally in the management and conduct of the business.
• The right to repayment of loans made to the partnership, with interest.	• The right to repayment of loans made to the partnership, with interest.
• The right to reasonable compensation for services rendered in winding up the partnership affairs.	• The right to reasonable compensation for services rendered in winding up the partnership affairs.
• The right to wind up the affairs of the partnership on dissolution.	• The right to wind up the affairs of the partnership on dissolution.
• The right to be repaid contributions made to the partnership, after the liabilities of the partnership have been paid.	• The right to have the partner's interest purchased by remaining partners after a permissible dissociation from the partnership.

© Cengage Learning 2013

2. The duty of partners to work for the partnership without remuneration
3. The duty of partners to submit to a vote of the majority of the partners when differences arise among the partners as to any ordinary matters connected with the partnership affairs
4. The duty of partners to provide information concerning the partnership to the other partners
5. The fiduciary duty to all partners and the partnership

Partners' Duties to Contribute to Partnership Losses

Unless the partnership agreement specifically states otherwise, each partner has the duty to contribute equally to any losses and liabilities incurred by the partnership.

Partners' Duties to Work without Remuneration

Partners are not entitled to remuneration for services performed for the partnership, except for reasonable compensation for services rendered in winding up the partnership business. This stipulation can, of course, be revised in the partnership agreement in the event that the participation of the partners is unequal. Often one partner contributes only capital or other resources to the partnership whereas another may devote his or her full-time services to the business. In such an event, the partnership agreement could be worded so that the working partner receives compensation from the partnership business.

Partners' Duties to Submit to a Vote of the Majority

Unless the partnership agreement states otherwise, the vote of the majority of the partners will be the deciding factor in resolving a disagreement among the partners.

Partners' Duties to Render Information

For partners to protect their rights in the partnership, it is important that they be kept informed of all important matters concerning the partnership business. Both the UPA (1914) and the UPA (1997) provide that each partner has a duty to the other partners to provide true and full information in all things concerning the partnership so as to enable the partners to exercise their rights and duties under the partnership agreement or state statute.

Partners' Fiduciary Duties to Partnership and Other Partners

Under the UPA (1914) and common law, partners have always owed a fiduciary duty to each other. Courts have held that partners owe one another the duty of the finest loyalty. Many forms of conduct permissible in the workaday world for those acting at arm's length are forbidden to those bound by fiduciary ties. " Every partner is bound to act in a manner not to obtain any advantage over his or her co-partner in the partnership affairs by the slightest misrepresentation, concealment, threat, or adverse pressure of any kind."[25] For example, suppose one partner of a real estate management partnership receives an offer for the partnership to manage a high-rise apartment building. That partner has a duty to present the offer to the other partners for their consideration and cannot accept the offer personally to become the sole manager of the high rise. To do so would be a breach of the partner's fiduciary duty.

Section 404 of the UPA (1997) states specifically that the fiduciary duty partners owe to the partnership and other partners includes the duty of loyalty and the duty of care. In general, a duty of loyalty means that partners must be loyal to the partnership and other partners and not engage in outside activities that compete with or are detrimental to the partnership. A duty of care means that partners must not behave in a manner that is considered negligent or reckless and must not engage in intentional misconduct or knowingly commit a violation of the law when conducting partnership business.

These duties may be further defined or expanded on in the partnership agreement, but they cannot be diminished or eliminated.

IN SUMMATION

- Under the Uniform Partnership Act (1914), property was held in a tenancy in partnership and each partner was considered a co-owner with the other partners of specific partnership property.
- Under the Uniform Partnership Act (1997), partnership property is owned by the partnership itself.
- Several rights are granted to partners under state statute. Some of those rights can be altered by the partnership agreement, others cannot.
- Typical partner rights include:
  - The right to a separate account
  - The right to an equal share of the partnership profits
  - The right to be repaid contributions and share in the surplus remaining after partnership liabilities are paid
  - The right to reimbursement for certain partnership expenses
  - The right to share equally in the management of the partnership and operation of its business
  - The right to access the partnership books and records
  - The right to wind up the partnership business
  - The right to have partnership interest purchased by remaining partners after a dissociation from the partnership
- Partners are subject to several duties to the partnership and the other partners under state statute. Some of those duties can be altered by the partnership agreement, others cannot.

continues

IN SUMMATION *(continued)*

- Some of the duties partners owe to the partnership and the other partners include:
  - The duty to contribute toward partnership losses according to each partner's share
  - The duty to work for the partnership without remuneration
  - The duty to submit to a vote of the majority of the partners
  - The duty to provide information concerning the partnership to the other partners
  - The fiduciary duty to all partners and the partnership

§ 3.4 ADVANTAGES OF DOING BUSINESS AS A GENERAL PARTNERSHIP

Doing business as a partnership offers some unique advantages. In this section, we discuss some of those advantages, including the flexibility of the management of the partnership, the minimal formalities and regulatory and reporting requirements, and the relatively low cost of organizing a partnership. We also examine the unique income tax benefits available to partners and the expanded base from which capital may be raised for the partnership.

PARTICIPATION AND FLEXIBILITY IN MANAGEMENT

Unless one or more partners waive their rights, every partner has equal power and authority to manage the partnership affairs. Partners of smaller partnerships may find this appealing if they have varied backgrounds and areas of expertise and all wish to actively participate. All partners are allowed to act freely on behalf of the partnership, with few restrictions.

Larger partnerships, on the other hand, are allowed the flexibility of putting the management of the partnership into the hands of the best individual or group of individuals for the job, with the consent of all partners.

MINIMAL FORMALITIES AND REGULATORY AND REPORTING REQUIREMENTS

Although partnerships are governed by statute, the required statutory formalities are few. A concise written partnership agreement is a good investment in almost any circumstance. However, it is not required, and a partnership may be formed by a verbal agreement between two or more people and can be implied by behavior.

State statutes vary with regard to partnership filing requirements and other formalities, and the pertinent state statutes must always be reviewed and complied with. Most states do not require partnership registration with the secretary of state or other state official before commencing business. However, a certificate of assumed name or similar document is usually required when the partnership will be transacting business under an assumed name, trade name, or fictitious name. If the partnership name consists of the names of the partners, it usually is not considered a fictitious name requiring registration. However, some state statutes provide that the name of a partner followed by "& Co." or "Co." may require the filing of an application for certificate of assumed name, trade name, or fictitious name, or other similar document.[26]

A number of states require the registration of every partnership with the appropriate state official, regardless of whether the partnership is using a fictitious name. Typically, a certificate setting forth the name of the partnership, its principal place of business, and the names of all partners is filed with the secretary of state or the county clerk of the county in which the partnership's principal place of business is located.

A partnership transacting business in any state other than its state of domicile may be required to register with the secretary of state of the foreign state as a foreign partnership. Again, a thorough review of the pertinent statutes must be made to ensure that all statutory requirements with regard to fictitious name filings, partnership registrations, and qualification of foreign partnerships are complied with.

Although it is an option rather than a requirement, partnerships in states that closely follow the UPA (1997) may find it advantageous to file a statement of partnership authority with the secretary of state specifying which partners are authorized to execute real estate transfer documents, and any other information concerning the authority of individual partners to act on behalf of the partnership.

Any business carried on by a partnership that requires licensing must be licensed by the partnership or by the individual partners. Typically, no special licensing requirements are imposed on a partnership because it is a partnership; rather, the licensing requirements are imposed because of the nature of the business transacted by the partnership.

Partnerships are required to file a United States Partnership Return of Income, which reports the partnership's income and distributions to the partners. A tax return also may be required at the state level.

LOW COST OF ORGANIZATION

There are no minimum capital requirements for starting a partnership, and the startup costs, including any required state filing fees, tend to be lower than those for corporations.

INCOME TAX BENEFITS

The partners of a general partnership are taxed in much the same way as sole proprietors. The net income or loss of the partnership is passed through to the partners, according to the partnership agreement or statute. The partnership is required to file a Partnership Return (Form 1065) annually with the Internal Revenue Service (IRS), but no income tax is owed by the partnership itself. Rather, the partnership's return indicates the income earned by the partnership and allocated to the individual partners. The individual partners must report their allocation of the partnership income on a Schedule K-1 filed with their personal tax returns and they must pay income tax at their personal income tax rates. The principal tax benefit to the partners over doing business as a corporation is that a corporation is subject to a first tax on its income, and then a second tax is paid by the shareholders when corporate after-tax income is distributed to them. A partnership, on the other hand, is not taxable as a separate entity, so that only a single tax is paid by the partners on income derived from the partnership.

SIDEBAR

The IRS estimates that more than 4.7 million partnership returns will be filed for the year 2016. That figure includes partnership returns filed by limited partnerships and limited liability companies.

(IRS, Projections of Federal Tax Return Filings: Calendar Years 2008–2016, http://www.irs.gov)

Also, because the income of the partnership flows through to the individual partners, if the partnership experiences a net loss, each partner's share of that loss may be written off on the partner's individual income tax return, offsetting any other income. The partnership allocation of profits and losses must, however, comply with the substantial economic effect requirements of the IRS that provide that allocations must reflect the partners' actual economic circumstances and not be designed merely to shift income to reduce taxes.

DIVERSIFIED CAPITAL RESOURCES

Although partnership capital is generally limited by the personal capital of the partners and the capital that they are able to borrow based on their personal wealth, the partnership does have an advantage over the sole proprietorship in that there is a broader base from which to obtain capital. Simply put, more than one person is contributing to the business; therefore, more is potentially available.

IN SUMMATION

- There are several advantages to doing business as a partnership, including:
  - Flexibility in management
  - Relatively few formalities and regulatory and reporting requirements
  - Relatively low cost of organization
  - Income tax benefits
  - Diversified capital resources

§ 3.5 DISADVANTAGES OF DOING BUSINESS AS A GENERAL PARTNERSHIP

Some of the same partnership characteristics that present advantages to the partners in certain circumstances can be considered disadvantages under other circumstances. This section discusses the disadvantages of doing business as a partnership. We start with the partnership characteristic that is often considered to be the most significant disadvantage—the unlimited liability exposure of the partners. Next, we look at the loosely structured management of the partnership, the partnership's lack of business continuity, and the difficulty in transferring a proprietary interest in a partnership. We also investigate the possible hardships in raising capital for a partnership and the legal and organizational expenses. This section concludes with an examination of the potential income tax disadvantages to partners.

UNLIMITED LIABILITY

One of the strongest arguments against doing business as a general partnership is the unlimited liability characteristic of the partnership. Partners are personally liable for the debts, obligations, and torts committed by or on behalf of the partnership. This disadvantage is compounded by the fact that all partners are liable for the acts of any one partner who is acting on behalf of the partnership. For example, suppose that one partner were to unwisely invest the partnership's cash without the knowledge of the other partners. If the partnership is unable to meet its obligations because of the poor investment, unless otherwise provided for in a partnership agreement, all partners must contribute equally to pay the partnership's bills—even the partners who did not know about, or disapproved of, the investment. Wealthy partners may be at a disadvantage when the liabilities of the partnership exceed the partnership assets and creditors turn to the individual partners for payment.

There are ways to reduce the probability that the partners will have to personally cover the debts and liabilities of the partnership. The partnership may, for instance, purchase insurance to cover many potential liabilities, and third parties may agree in their contracts with the partnership to limit their recovery to partnership assets. However, not all liabilities are insurable, and lenders may not work with a partnership without the personal guarantees of the partners.

LOOSELY STRUCTURED MANAGEMENT

Although the loosely structured management of a partnership may be an advantage under certain circumstances, it may also work as a disadvantage to other partnerships. The number and personalities of the partners can greatly affect the success, or failure, of the loosely structured management prescribed for partnerships by statute. Because the majority rules, in the event of disagreement regarding management decisions, a stalemate can result if the partnership consists of an even number of partners. This, in turn, can lead to the partnership's inability to act. The fact that each partner can act on behalf of the partnership can also cause problems when partners disagree on fundamental issues.

A carefully constructed partnership agreement that delegates the authority to make management decisions can alleviate some of these problems when there is disagreement among the partners, but it is difficult to craft a partnership agreement to account for all possible contingencies.

LACK OF BUSINESS CONTINUITY

Under the UPA (1914), unless otherwise specified in the partnership agreement or other written agreement among the partners, the partnership dissolves whenever one partner ceases to be a partner, for whatever reason. This can be a definite disadvantage for an ongoing concern, as the dissolution may be untimely and costly to the remaining partners.

Upon the death of a partner, the deceased partner's right to specific partnership property will pass to the remaining partners, who have the right to possess the property for partnership purposes. However, the deceased partner's financial interests in the partnership pass to the deceased partner's heirs. Unless addressed in a carefully worded agreement, the remaining partners may have to liquidate the partnership assets to distribute the deceased partner's interest to his or her heirs.

Under the UPA (1997) it is much easier for the partnership to continue after the death or withdrawal of one partner. However, if the partnership is a partnership at will, it may be dissolved whenever one of the partners decides to withdraw and dissolve the partnership.

DIFFICULTY IN TRANSFERRING PARTNERSHIP INTEREST

Unlike corporate shareholders who may sell their shares of stock without restriction, a partner's entire right to the partnership is not freely transferable. Although a partner may sell or assign his or her rights to receive profits and losses from the partnership business, the right to specific partnership property may not be sold or assigned unless sold or assigned by all partners. In addition, a partner's right to participate in the management of the partnership is not assignable. Therefore, a partner's share of the partnership may not simply be sold to another individual who will become a partner.

LIMITED ABILITY TO RAISE CAPITAL

Unlike a corporation, a partnership may not sell shares of stock to raise capital to run its business. The capital of the partnership usually consists of contributions from the partners and any loans obtained based on the partners' personal wealth and the partnership assets. This can be a great deterrent to businesses that have substantial initial capital requirements.

LEGAL AND ORGANIZATIONAL EXPENSES

Although the legal and organizational expenses involved in forming and operating a partnership are usually less than those involved in forming and operating a corporation, these costs can still be substantial. In addition to possible state filing fees for the partnership certificate and a certificate of assumed or fictitious name, there are typically significant legal fees associated with drafting a partnership agreement. Because of the diverse nature of partnerships, a good partnership agreement will usually require significant and specific drafting, and the initial legal fees can be considerable.

TAX DISADVANTAGES

As previously discussed, partnership income flows through to the partners, to be taxed at each partner's personal income tax rate. The individual partners are responsible for the income tax on their share of the profits of the partnership, even if those profits are retained in the partnership business and not distributed to the partners. Under this scenario, it is possible that partners will be required to pay more in income tax than they receive from the partnership in a given year.

Exhibit 3-6 lists the advantages and disadvantages of doing business as a partnership.

EXHIBIT 3-6	ADVANTAGES AND DISADVANTAGES OF DOING BUSINESS AS A PARTNERSHIP
Advantages	**Disadvantages**
• All partners are entitled to manage the partnership.	• Under most circumstances partners may be held personally responsible for the debts and obligations of the partnership.
• Maximum flexibility in management.	• Lack of business continuity.
• Minimal formalities and regulatory and reporting requirements.	• Difficulty in transferring interest in partnership.
• Low cost of organization.	• Limited ability to raise capital for the partnership business.
• No double taxation.	• Significant legal and organizational expenses.
• Diversified pool of capital resources.	• Partnership taxation may not be beneficial for all partners under all circumstances.

© Cengage Learning 2013

IN SUMMATION

- There can be certain disadvantages to doing business as a general partnership, including:
  - Unlimited personal liability for the partners
  - Loosely structured management
  - Lack of business continuity
  - Difficulty in transferring partnership interest
  - Limits on ability to raise capital for the partnership business
  - Significant legal and organizational expenses
  - Partnership taxation—for certain partners in certain circumstances

§ 3.6 MANGEMENT AND CONTROL OF A GENERAL PARTNERSHIP

The organization and management of partnerships vary significantly depending on the number and identity of the individual partners and the nature of the partnership business. The parameters for the organization and management of partnerships are outlined by state statute and may be expanded on and clarified in the partnership agreement.

This section focuses on the management and control of the partnership and how partnership decisions are made.

MANAGEMENT AND CONTROL

Although all partners have an equal right to manage the partnership, that is not always a practical or desirable method of management, and those rights may be altered in an agreement among the partners. Especially with larger partnerships, the partners often delegate the management to one or more partners. This delegation of the right to manage must be granted by all partners, and no partner can be denied the right to manage the partnership unless that right is waived.

When one partner is delegated to oversee the management of the partnership, that partner is usually referred to as the managing partner. Management also may be delegated to a management committee or one or more other partners named in the partnership agreement.

Often, the partners each agree to be responsible for a different area of partnership management. For example, one partner may be in charge of the partnership accounting, while another takes care of public relations and promotion. Regardless of the style of management decided upon by the partners, it is highly desirable that the management duties of each partner be fully described in the partnership agreement.

The general rule regarding a dispute in the internal management affairs of the partnership is that the decision is made by a majority of the partners.[27] The partnership agreement may also provide an alternate method for resolving disputes among the partners. For instance, the managing partner or partners may be given authority to make the final decision in the event of a disagreement among the partners. The partnership agreement may prescribe mediation or arbitration for certain disagreements among the partners.

References to a majority of the partners generally do not take into account the disproportionate percentages of interest that the partners may hold. The partnership agreement may contain provisions fixing a different method for determining what is the majority of the partners, such as the contributors of a majority of the partnership capital. Acts taken outside of the ordinary course of business of the partnership require the unanimous consent of all partners, as do acts not in accordance with the partnership agreement and acts amending the partnership agreement.

Managing partners and other partners who are required to spend a significant amount of their time managing the business and assets of the partnership are usually compensated by way of a salary and expense reimbursement paid by the partnership. This salary is over and above any profits to which the managing partner is entitled. Any salaries paid to partners for their management of the partnership should be specifically designated as such on the books and records of the partnership. However the partners agree to manage the partnership, those terms should be set forth in detail in the partnership agreement to avoid future disagreements.

IN SUMMATION

- By law, all partners have the right to participate in the management of the partnership business, but the partners may agree to manage by a different means.
- The partnership may be managed by a designated managing partner or by management committees.
- In the event of a dispute, the decision is made by a majority of the partners unless some other method of resolving the dispute is agreed on.

§ 3.7 GENERAL PARTNERSHIP AGREEMENT

Partnerships are formed by agreement between the partners. While it is possible to form a partnership by oral agreement, in almost all circumstances a written partnership agreement setting forth the agreement of the partners is recommended. In this section, we will take a brief look at the requirements for an oral partnership agreement, then move on to a detailed look at that very important document, the partnership agreement.

ORAL PARTNERSHIP AGREEMENTS

Although the partnership agreement is fundamental to the partnership, the agreement may be oral, or a partnership may exist with no express agreement between the parties whatsoever, so long as all the elements of a partnership are present. Although an oral partnership agreement may be legal and binding, it is inadvisable, because it is difficult to prove the terms of an oral partnership agreement—or even that a partnership exists—when there is no written agreement. Attorneys almost always advise their clients to put their agreement into a formal, written contract to avoid future disputes.

In *The Autobiography*, Benjamin Franklin wrote:

Partnerships often finish in quarrels, but I was happy in this, that mine were all carried on and ended amicably, owing, I think, a good deal to the precaution of having very explicitly settled in our articles everything to be done by or expected from each partner, so that there was nothing to dispute—which precaution I would therefore recommend to all who enter partnerships, for whatever esteem partners may have for and confidence in each other at the time of the contract, little jealousies and disgusts may arise, with ideas of inequality in the care and burden of the business, etc., which are often attended with breach of friendship and of the connection, perhaps with lawsuits and other disagreeable consequences.

WRITTEN PARTNERSHIP AGREEMENTS

The partnership agreement, or partnership articles, as that document is sometimes referred to, is the contract entered into by all partners setting forth the agreed-upon terms of the partnership. The partnership agreement is considered the "law of the partnership" and will be enforced as such, unless any of the terms of the partnership agreement are contrary to law. The partnership agreement is a contract among the partners and thus is subject to contract law.

Following is a discussion of some of the various matters that should be contained in a partnership agreement. The sample paragraphs used here are only a small representation of the types of clauses that may be included in a partnership agreement. See § 3.11 of this chapter for a checklist of items to be considered when drafting a partnership agreement, and Appendix C for a partnership agreement form.

Names and Addresses of Partners

The full name and address of each partner should be included in the first section of the partnership agreement.

Name of Partnership

The partnership agreement should set forth the full name of the partnership. The name of the partnership may, but need not, include any or all of the names of the partners, or it may be a totally fictitious name. If a fictitious name is used, a certificate of assumed or fictitious name may be required.[28]

Purpose of Partnership

A specific purpose may be set forth in the agreement, or a general purpose, such as the one shown in the following example, may be stated. This section may also set limitations on business activities and on partners' competitive business activities.

EXAMPLE: Partnership Purpose

The partnership shall have a general business purpose and may exercise all powers now or hereafter conferred by the laws of the State of ___ to partnerships.

Address of Principal Place of Doing Business

In addition to setting forth the address of the partnership's principal place of business, the partnership agreement may also contain a provision designating the governing law under which the terms of the partnership agreement must be applied and construed.

Term of Partnership

The partnership agreement may designate a date upon which the partnership will terminate, such as in the following example, or it may designate a condition upon which such termination shall occur. For instance, if a partnership is formed for the development and sale of several specific pieces of real estate, the partnership agreement may state that the partnership will terminate when all of the designated real estate has been sold.

A partnership that is formed without designating a date for termination, or without stating a condition under which the partnership will terminate, is a **partnership at will**. This type of partnership continues as long as the parties give their mutual consent. The partnership at will may be terminated when agreed to by the partners, or upon the withdrawal of any one partner.

When a partnership for a fixed term or particular undertaking is continued after the termination of such term or particular undertaking without any express agreement, the partnership continues as if it were a partnership at will.

PARTNERSHIP AT WILL
Partnership formed for an indefinite period of time, without a designated date for termination.

EXAMPLE: Duration of Partnership

The partnership shall exist for a term of ___ years, commencing on ___, and terminating on ___, unless terminated sooner by mutual consent of the partners or by operation of this agreement.

Contribution of Partners

The section of the partnership agreement that addresses partner contributions should be drafted with care because it may be crucial to the division of the profits and losses of the partnership and the distribution of assets upon the partnership's termination. This section may include the amount of contribution made by each partner, the date each contribution is made to the partnership, the form of contribution, and valuation of contributions other than cash. In addition, provisions for any interest to be paid on contributions, adjustments in contributions required from each partner, and provisions for loans to the partnership by the partners may be included in this section.

EXAMPLE: Contribution to Partnership Capital—Cash

The initial capital contribution to the partnership shall be $_____ *[dollar amount of initial capital contribution]*, which shall consist of $_____ *[dollar amount of initial cash contribution of partner 1]* in cash contributed by _____ *[name of partner 1]*, for a _____% *[percentage interest of partner 1]* interest in the partnership, and $_____ *[dollar amount of initial cash contribution of partner 2]* in cash contributed by _____ *[name of partner 2]*, for a _____% *[percentage interest of partner 2]* interest in the partnership.

All initial capital contributions shall be made to the partnership capital account at _____ *[name of bank]*, located at _____ *[address of bank]*, on or before _____ *[date of contribution]*. A failure by one partner to contribute the specified capital by that date shall result in an immediate return to the contributing partner or partners of any capital contributed to date.[29]

Additional Contribution Requirements

The partnership agreement should include the procedure for establishing the necessity of additional capital contributions, the amount of those contributions required from each partner, the notification requirements for additional contributions, and the redistribution of partnership interest for nonproportional contributions.

Assets of Partnership

The asset section of the partnership agreement should identify the assets of the partnership, including a valuation of the assets, the manner for handling the control of assets and accountability therefore, and the distribution of assets. Following is an example of a paragraph that may be used with an attached schedule that may be updated from time to time.

EXAMPLE: Description of Assets by Attached List

All property, both personal and real, specifically set forth in Exhibit _____ attached to this agreement and made a part of it, is deemed by the partners to be partnership property and shall be and constitute the assets of the partnership as of the date of this agreement. The items of partnership property set forth in the attached Exhibit _____ are set forth by way of specification and not by way of limitation, and may be added to subsequently at the discretion of the partners.[30]

Goodwill Evaluation to Be Considered on Distribution of Assets

The goodwill of a partnership may be considered a sizable asset to a continuing business. However, it may be no asset at all to a partnership that is discontinuing its business. This section should set forth the conditions under which the goodwill of the partnership will be considered as a part of the evaluation of the assets of the partnership, and set forth the formula to be used in that evaluation of goodwill when applicable.

Liability

The partnership agreement may restate and amend many of the provisions for partner liability found in the statutes. It may also be used to address more specific conditions regarding liability among the partners. It should address the partners' liability to one another, the partners' liability to third parties, and the liability of the partnership. The partners cannot limit their personal liability in the agreement beyond what is allowed by statute.

Distribution of Profits and Losses

Provisions for the distribution of profits and losses are very important to the partnership agreement. Those provisions should address all matters regarding distribution of the profits and losses of the partnership, including how the division of profits and losses is to be made.

Following are examples of paragraphs that may be used when equal distribution among all partners is desired or when proportional distribution is desired, respectively:

EXAMPLE: Equal Distribution of Profits and Losses

Each partner shall be entitled to an equal share of the net profits of the business. All losses occurring in the course of business shall be borne equally unless the losses are due to the willful neglect or default, and not the mere mistake or error, of any of the partners, in which case the loss so incurred shall be borne solely by the partner or partners whose neglect or default caused the loss. Distribution of profits shall be made on the _____ day of _____ each year.

EXAMPLE: Proportionate Distribution of Profits and Losses

_____ has contributed $_____ to the capital of the partnership, which is equal to _____% of the partnership interest, and _____ has contributed $_____ to the capital of the partnership, which is equal to _____% of the partnership interest. Each partner shall be entitled to a share of the partnership net profits or shall be assessed for the partner's share of the partnership losses in direct proportion to the partner's partnership interest.[31]

Indemnity Provisions

This section should set forth the partners' agreement for indemnification of their obligations on behalf of the partnership.

EXAMPLE: Indemnity by Partnership—Obligation of Existing Partners

Each partner shall be indemnified by the partnership on all obligations incurred by that partner in the normal course of conducting partnership business. The partners are limited by the provisions of Section _____ of this agreement in the scope of obligations they shall incur on behalf of the partnership.[32]

Duties of Partners

The duties of the partners should be set forth in the partnership agreement in as much detail as practical, addressing the specific responsibilities of each partner and the approximate amount of time required of each partner.

Powers of Partners and Limitations Thereon

The partnership agreement should set forth the powers of the partners and any limitations on those powers. It should also address the scope of partnership business, partnership employee policies, contractual rights and limitations, and patents and trade secrets.

Compensation and Benefits for Partners

The compensation section of the partnership agreement may address any compensation and benefits that will be given to the partners in any form, including salaries, drawing accounts, vacations, holidays, retirement, and other benefits.

EXAMPLE: Salary—In General

In consideration for the services performed on behalf of the partnership, _____ shall receive a salary of $_____ per month, and _____ shall receive a salary of $_____ per month. These salaries shall be considered an expense of the partnership, and shall be payable whether or not the partnership earns a profit. These salaries shall not affect any other distributions payable to _____ and _____ under this agreement.

EXAMPLE: Drawing Account—Partner Entitled to Weekly Draw to Meet Personal Expenses

Each partner shall be authorized to draw $_____ *[dollar amount of weekly draw]* per week from the funds of the partnership to meet that partner's personal expenses. Any draw shall be chargeable against that partner's share of partnership net profits, and the total amount of draw taken by each partner during the fiscal year shall be deducted from the partner's share of the net profits prior to distribution of net profits.[33]

Management and Control of Business

The management and control section of the partnership agreement should set forth all partnership policies for the management and control of the business. It should appoint any desired managing partner or committee and should specify the management rights and duties of each partner, to the extent practical.

EXAMPLE: Management and Control—Each Partner Has Equal Role

Each partner shall have an equal role in the management and conduct of the partnership business. All decisions affecting the policy and management of the partnership, including compensation of partners and personnel policies, may be made on behalf of the partnership by any active partner. In the event of a disagreement among the partners, a decision by the majority of them shall be binding on the partnership. All partners shall be authorized to sign checks and to make, deliver, accept, or indorse any commercial paper in connection with the business and affairs of the partnership.

The partners shall conduct a _____ *[weekly/monthly]* meeting at the principal office of the partnership to discuss matters of general interest to the partnership. A vote of partners representing _____%[*percentage of interest*] of the partnership interest shall be necessary to implement any policy or procedure introduced at a partnership meeting, except for any change in this partnership agreement, which shall require a unanimous vote.[34]

EXAMPLE: Management and Control—By All Partners

All partners shall have an equal share in the management of the partnership's business activities. The partners shall freely and informally consult with each other regarding the establishment, maintenance, and alterations in any management policies. If any disputes shall arise, the vote of partners holding a *[percentage of interest]*% interest in the partnership shall be controlling. If the required vote cannot be obtained, either for or against a proposal, the issue shall be submitted to arbitration as provided in Section *[number of section]* of this agreement.[35]

Partnership Accounting and Financial Management

The partnership agreement should set forth all accounting methods and financial management policies of the partnership, including the accounting period and fiscal year of the partnership, the frequency and types of reports to be completed, details regarding the books of accounts, audit provisions, and provision for examination of books. All matters concerning the expenses of the partners and the partnership should also be addressed. The partnership agreement should designate a depository for the partnership funds, name the party responsible for controlling income and distribution, designate the authorized signatures on checks and drafts, and authorize partners to negotiate loans. In addition, it should set forth a method and time for disbursing payments on indebtedness and set limitations on indebtedness of partners.

Changes in Partners

One restriction that is an essential characteristic of the partnership is that no person can become a member of a partnership without the consent of all of the partners, unless there is a contrary provision in the partnership agreement. The partnership agreement should set forth the partners' wishes regarding the admission of new partners and provisions for the redistribution of assets. This section should also address all matters concerning withdrawing partners, including requirements for the consent of the other partners, notice requirements, valuation of the withdrawing partner's share of the partnership, the option of the remaining partners to purchase the interest, and the assignment of the withdrawing partner's interest to a third party. It should describe the conditions for expulsion of a partner, including notice requirements, and all other matters concerning the expulsion.

The partnership's policy regarding a retiring partner should also be addressed in this section, including the reorganization of partnership rights and duties.

EXAMPLE: Withdrawing Partner—Option of Remaining Partners to Purchase Interest

Any partner desiring to withdraw from the partnership prior to termination or dissolution of the partnership shall be allowed to do so only with the consent of the remaining partners. Prior to granting or denying approval of a partner's request to withdraw, the remaining partners shall have the option to purchase a proportionate share of the partner's interest in the partnership. On their election to exercise the option, the withdrawing partner shall immediately be paid the appraised value of the partner's share, and the remaining partners' interests shall be proportionately increased.

If any of the remaining partners approve of the withdrawal of the partner, but do not desire to purchase a portion of the partner's share, the other remaining partners may purchase the additional segment and thereby obtain a larger proportionate share in the partnership.[36]

EXAMPLE: Retirement of Partner—Sale of Retiring Partner's Interest

A partner shall retire from the partnership after attaining age _____ *[age of retirement]*, after the partner has given _____ *[number of days]* days' notice of the partner's intention to retire. At the time of giving notice of retirement, the partner shall offer the partner's share in the partnership for sale to the remaining partners on a proportionate basis to their partnership interest at the time of the partner's retirement. If the remaining partners desire the interest, they shall purchase it for cash and their interest in the partnership shall be increased proportionately. If the remaining partners do not desire to purchase the retiring partner's share, the partner may sell the partner's share to any purchaser the partner desires.[37]

Death of Partner

The section of the partnership agreement dealing with the death of any partner should address all aspects of the purchase of the deceased partner's interest, including the valuation of the deceased partner's share, the dissolution of the partnership, and any desired provision for the estate of the deceased to act as a partner.

EXAMPLE: Termination of Partnership on Death of Partner—At Conclusion of Fiscal Year

The partnership shall terminate at the close of the current partnership fiscal year on the death of any partner during that fiscal year. The estate of the deceased partner shall be paid the full share to which the deceased partner shall be entitled, at the time of distribution of partnership assets, _____ days after winding up the partnership business.[38]

EXAMPLE: Partnership to Continue after Death of Partner—Estate to Continue as Partner

On the death of any partner the partnership shall not terminate, but the legal representative of the deceased partner's estate shall immediately be substituted as a partner under this agreement, with all rights, powers, and duties of a partner as provided in this agreement. The legal representative shall execute a supplemental agreement with the surviving partners, agreeing to be bound by all terms and conditions of this partnership agreement.[39]

Sale or Purchase of Partnership Interest

The partnership agreement may set forth all desired provisions regarding the potential sale or purchase of the partnership interest, including conditions for right of first refusal in remaining partners, limitations on purchase of interest, terms of sale, and the reorganization of the partnership.

EXAMPLE: Sale of Interest to Remaining Partners— Other Partner Given First Refusal

Neither partner shall, during the partner's lifetime, sell, assign, encumber, transfer, or otherwise dispose of all or any part of the partner's interest in the partnership without complying with the following procedure:

If one of the partners wishes to dispose of that partner's interest voluntarily, the partner shall first offer in writing to sell the partner's interest to the other partner at the price determined in accordance with the provisions of Section _____. If the other partner wishes to purchase the partnership interest, that partner shall notify the offering partner of the partner's decision in writing within _____ days after receipt of the offer and shall pay for the partnership interest in any case within _____ days after giving notice of the partner's acceptance. In the event the offer to sell has not been accepted within such _____-day period, the offering partner shall have the right to take legal steps to dissolve the partnership.[40]

Arbitration of Differences

The partners may provide in their partnership agreement that certain differences between the partners will be settled by arbitration, upon the terms and conditions set forth in the agreement.

Termination of Partnership

The partnership agreement should set forth the agreement of the partners concerning the termination of the partnership, including the set date of termination, if there is one, events requiring termination, and procedures for terminating the partnership.

Dissolution and Winding Up

The partnership agreement should set forth all of the agreed-upon terms of the partnership for dissolving and winding up the partnership. It should include provisions for an individual or committee who will be responsible for winding up the partnership business, and compensation for that individual or committee.

EXAMPLE: Dissolution—By Unanimous Agreement of Partners

The partnership shall not be dissolved prior to the termination date set forth in Section _____ of this agreement, except by the unanimous consent of all partners to this agreement at least _____ days prior to the intended date of dissolution.

The unanimous consent shall be obtained at a duly constituted business meeting of the partnership, and the proceedings of the meeting shall be properly and accurately recorded.[41]

EXAMPLE: Winding Up—Appointment of Committee

In the event of the dissolution of the partnership, a management committee shall be selected, with the approval of partners owning _____% of the partnership interest, to consist of _____ partners, who shall have the right to wind up the partnership business and dispose of or liquidate the partnership's assets. In the event of liquidation, the committee members are appointed as liquidating partners.

Members of the committee shall each be entitled to receive $_____ per month as compensation for services during the duration of the committee.[42]

Date of Agreement and Signature of Partners

The partnership agreement must be dated and signed by all partners.

IN SUMMATION

- While it is possible to form a partnership by oral agreement, a written partnership agreement is almost always recommended.
- The partnership agreement is often considered the "law of the partnership."
- Several provisions of state partnership law can be altered by the partnership agreement.
- A written partnership agreement is typically several pages long and addresses the full agreement of the partners to the extent practical.
- The partnership agreement must be signed by all partners.

§ 3.8 FINANCIAL STRUCTURE OF A GENERAL PARTNERSHIP

Partnerships have a unique financial structure that can be tailored to suit the needs of the partners. This section discusses the capital of the partnership and the allocation and distribution of profits and losses.

PARTNERSHIP CAPITAL

The partnership capital, which consists of all the assets of the partnership, includes contributions from the partners and the undistributed income earned by the partnership.

Capital Contributions

There are no minimum capital requirements for partnerships under the UPA (1914) or the UPA (1997). The partnership capital is usually contributed by the partners, and it may be in the form of cash, real property, or personal property. The partnership agreement should state the required capital contribution of each partner and the form of that contribution. In addition to the initial capital contribution, the partnership agreement may require each partner to contribute additional capital to the partnership as needed for the continuance of the partnership business.

Generally, no withdrawal of capital from the partnership is permitted until the partnership is dissolved. If this is not desirable, the appropriate provisions should be made in the partnership agreement for the withdrawal of capital prior to dissolution of the partnership.

Partner Loans and Advances

In addition to the capital contribution, partners may provide capital to the partnership in the form of a loan or an advance to be repaid with interest on terms provided for in the partnership agreement, or on terms agreed to by the loaning partner and the remaining partners.

Partners' Right to Accounting

Under the UPA (1914), every partner is entitled to a formal accounting as to the partnership's financial affairs. This right may be exercised whenever a partner is wrongfully excluded from the partnership business or possession of its property by the co-partners; whenever such rights exist under the partnership agreement or other agreement; whenever appropriate because of the fiduciary nature of each partner to the partnership; or whenever other circumstances render it just and reasonable.[43] The statutory language concerning the partners' rights to a formal account is quite broad, so these rights should be more clearly defined in the partnership agreement.

While the UPA (1997) is silent on the right of a partner to a formal accounting, it does provide for broad rights of inspection of the books and records of the partnership by the partners, their agents, and their attorneys.

Partnership Records

Unless otherwise provided for in the partnership agreement, the partnership books must be kept at the partnership's executive office and are subject to inspection by any partner at any time. The duty to keep the books of the partnership usually falls to the managing partner or another partner, as appointed in the partnership agreement or by oral agreement between the partners.

PROFITS AND LOSSES

Another of the more important characteristics of a partnership is a sharing of the profits and losses among the partners. By default, under both model laws, the partners share the profits and losses of the partnership equally, regardless of each partner's capital contribution to the partnership. The partners may, however, set their own formula for sharing in the profits and losses of the partnership, which may be based on several factors, including (1) the amount of the initial capital contribution by each partner, (2) additional capital contributions, and (3) services rendered on behalf of the partnership by each partner. If the partners' contributions to the partnership are unequal, their shares of the profits and losses may be unequal as well. For example, suppose that a father and son want to start a roofing business. The father provides most of the capital and equipment to start the business. The partnership agreement could provide that the father would receive a much higher proportion of the partnership profits until he has recouped his initial investment.

The Internal Revenue Service (IRS) generally recognizes a profit and loss allocation that is agreed to by all partners, so long as it has "substantial economic effect." If the IRS determines that the profit and loss allocation set forth in the partnership agreement has no economic effect, but has been drafted merely as a means to avoid paying income taxes, the IRS will allocate profits and losses pursuant to each partner's ownership interest in the partnership.

In any event, if it is not desirable for all partners to share all profits and all losses equally, it is crucial that this matter be addressed in the written partnership agreement.

IN SUMMATION

- The financial structure of the partnership can be tailored to meet the needs of the partners.
- The partnership capital consists of all assets of the partnership, including partner contributions and the undistributed income earned by the partnership.
- Generally, no withdrawals are made of the partnership capital until the partnership is dissolved.
- State statutes generally provide that the partners are entitled to a formal account of the partnership business or full inspection of the partnership books and records.
- Under state partnership acts, the profits and losses of the partnership are shared equally. The equal sharing of profits and losses may be amended, however, by the partnership agreement.
- Partners pay income tax on the amount of partnership profit that is allocated to them each year.

§ 3.9 DISSOLUTION, DISSOCIATION, WINDING UP, AND TERMINATION OF THE GENERAL PARTNERSHIP

The dissolution of a partnership is more of a process than an event. This section first examines the definition of the terms *dissociation, dissolution*, and *winding up* of a partnership. Next, it discusses the events that cause partnership dissociation and the effects of partnership dissociation, causes and effects of partnership dissolution, the continuation of a partnership after dissolution, wrongful dissociation of a partnership, and the use of a dissolution agreement. This section concludes with a look at giving notice to third parties of a partnership dissolution, winding up the partnership, and distributing partnership assets.

DISSOCIATION, DISSOLUTION, AND WINDING UP

DISSOCIATION

The event that occurs when a partner withdraws or otherwise ceases to be associated with the carrying on of the partnership business.

DISSOLUTION

The termination of a corporation, partnership, or other business entity's existence.

The term **dissociation** is a term new to the UPA (1997). It is distinctly different from dissolution. Under the UPA (1914), whenever one partner ceased being a partner for any reason, the partnership was considered to be dissolved. Under the UPA (1997), one or more partners may be dissociated from a partnership without causing its dissolution. The term *dissociation* denotes the change in the relationship caused by a partner's ceasing to be associated in the carrying on of the business.

The term **dissolution** refers to the commencement of the winding-up process. Upon dissolution, the partnership relationship terminates with respect to all future transactions and the authority of all partners to act on behalf of the partnership and on behalf of each other terminates, except to the extent necessary for winding up the partnership. The partnership will cease to exist upon completion of the winding-up process—the disposition of all liabilities and assets of the partnership. See Exhibit 3-7 for a list of possible outcomes when a partner withdraws from a partnership.

EVENTS CAUSING PARTNER'S DISSOCIATION

A partner's dissociation can be caused by agreement, by statute, or wrongfully. The UPA (1997) sets forth the following acts that can cause a partner's dissociation:[44]

1. The partner giving notice to the partnership of his or her express will to withdraw as a partner on some specific date
2. The occurrence of an event agreed to in the partnership agreement as causing the partner's dissociation
3. The partner's expulsion pursuant to the partnership agreement
4. The partner's expulsion by the unanimous vote of the other partners if:
   a. It is unlawful to carry on the partnership business with that partner
   b. The partner transfers all or substantially all of his or her transferable interest in the partnership
   c. The partner is a corporation that has filed a certificate of dissolution, had its charter revoked, or had its right to conduct business suspended
   d. The partner is a partnership that has been dissolved and its business is being wound up

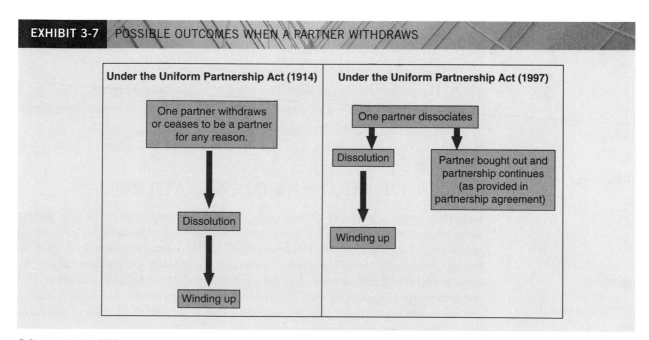

EXHIBIT 3-7   POSSIBLE OUTCOMES WHEN A PARTNER WITHDRAWS

Under the Uniform Partnership Act (1914)

One partner withdraws or ceases to be a partner for any reason.

↓

Dissolution

↓

Winding up

Under the Uniform Partnership Act (1997)

One partner dissociates

Dissolution

↓

Winding up

Partner bought out and partnership continues (as provided in partnership agreement)

© Cengage Learning 2013

5. Judicial determination, based on an application by the partnership or another partner because:
   a. The partner engaged in wrongful conduct that adversely and materially affected the partnership
   b. The appointment of a trustee, receiver, or liquidator of the partner's property
6. The partner's death
7. Appointment of a guardian or general conservator for the partner
8. A judicial determination that the partner has otherwise become incapable of performing the partner's duties under the partnership agreement
9. If the partner is a trust, distribution of the trust's entire transferable interest in the partnership
10. If the partner is an estate, distribution of the estate's entire transferable interest in the partnership
11. Termination of a partner who is not an individual, corporation, trust, or estate

WRONGFUL DISSOCIATION

Under the UPA (1997), partners always have the power to dissociate from the partnership, although, under some circumstances, the dissociation may be considered a wrongful dissociation. A partner's dissociation will be considered wrongful if it is contrary to the partnership agreement. The partner's dissociation will also be considered wrongful if the dissociation occurs prior to the expiration of any set term for the partnership or prior to the completion of any preestablished task, and if one of the following events occurs:

- The partner withdraws of his or her express will, unless the withdrawal follows within 90 days the dissociation of another party
- The partner is expelled from the partnership by the court
- The partner is dissociated by becoming a debtor in bankruptcy
- The partner is a trust or estate that becomes willfully dissolved or terminated

A partner who is wrongfully dissociated from a partnership is liable to the partnership and the other partners for damages caused by the wrongful dissociation.

EFFECT OF PARTNER'S DISSOCIATION

Generally, upon a partner's dissociation, the partner's rights to participate in the management and conduct of the partnership business terminate. The dissociated partner will no longer be able to act on behalf of the partnership except to wind up the affairs of a dissolving partnership. Likewise, the dissociated partner will not be liable for any obligations incurred by the partnership after his or her dissociation. The partner's duty of loyalty and duty of care continue only with regard to matters arising and events occurring before the partner's dissociation, unless the partner participates in winding up the partnership's business.

The effect a partner's dissociation will have upon the partner and upon the partnership depends on whether the dissociation causes the dissolution and winding up of the partnership and whether the partner's dissociation was wrongful.

Effect of Partner's Dissociation When Partnership Continues

In most instances, a dissociating partner has the right to have his or her interest in the partnership purchased for a buyout price as set forth in the partnership agreement or by statute. The UPA (1997) defines the buyout price of a dissociated partner's interest as "the amount that would have been distributable to the dissociating partner under Section 807(b) if, on the date of dissociation, the assets of the partnership were sold at a price equal to the greater of the liquidation value or the value based on a sale of the entire business as a going concern without the dissociated partner and the partnership were wound up as of that date."[45]

In the case of a wrongful dissociation, the damages caused by that dissociation can be used to offset the buyout price paid to the dissociated partner.

The buyout of a dissociated partner is a new concept under the UPA (1997). Previously, whenever a partner dissociated, the partnership would be dissolved.

In the event of the death of a partner, the deceased partner is considered to be dissociated, and the partner's transferable interest in the partnership will pass to his or her estate. The remaining partners or the partnership typically will then buy out that interest from the estate and continue the partnership business.

STATEMENT OF DISSOCIATION

In states where the UPA (1997) has been adopted, either the dissociated partner or the partnership may file with the appropriate state authority a statement of dissociation stating that the partner is dissociated from the partnership. The statement of dissociation is a public notice of the dissociated partner's limitation of authority and liability with regard to partnership matters.

EVENTS CAUSING DISSOLUTION AND WINDING UP OF PARTNERSHIP BUSINESS

Exactly what precipitates the dissolution and winding up of a partnership will be dictated by state statute. Pursuant to § 31 of the UPA (1914), the following acts cause dissolution:

- The expiration of the term or completion of a particular undertaking specified in the partnership agreement
- The express will of any partner when no definite term or particular undertaking is specified
- The express will of all the partners who have not assigned their interests in the partnership

- The expulsion of any partner from the business pursuant to the partnership agreement
- The express will of any partner at any time if contrary to the agreement when circumstances do not permit a dissolution under any other statutory provision
- Any event that makes it unlawful for the business of the partnership to be carried on
- The death of any partner
- The bankruptcy of any partner or the partnership
- The order of a court

Regardless of this provision, it is not uncommon for partnerships governed under the UPA (1914) to continue to operate after the withdrawal of one or more partners. If the partners who have not caused the wrongful dissolution so desire, they can continue the business in the same name, either by themselves or with others, during the agreed term for the partnership. The partnership will continue to possess the partnership property, with an obligation to pay the dissolving partner his or her fair share, less damages caused by the wrongful dissolution, when the partnership is liquidated. A court-approved bond must secure payment to the partner who dissolved the partnership.

In states that have adopted the UPA (1997), only the following events cause a dissolution and winding up of the partnership business:

1. In a partnership at will, the partnership receiving notice from a partner of that partner's express will to withdraw as a partner
2. In a partnership for a definite term or particular undertaking:
    a. The expiration of a 90-day period after a partner's dissociation by death or otherwise or through wrongful dissociation, unless a majority of the remaining partners agree to continue the partnership
    b. The express will of all of the partners to wind up the partnership business
    c. The expiration of the term or the completion of the undertaking
3. An event agreed to in the partnership agreement as being sufficient to cause the winding up of the partnership business
4. An event that makes it unlawful for the partnership business to be continued
5. A judicial determination based on an application by a partner that one of the following conditions prevails:
    a. The economic purpose of the partnership is likely to be unreasonably frustrated
    b. Another partner has engaged in conduct that makes it not reasonably practicable to carry on the business in partnership with that partner
    c. It is not reasonably practicable to carry on the partnership business in conformity with the partnership agreement
6. A judicial determination based on an application by a transferee of a partner's transferable interest that the term for the partnership has expired or the undertaking has been completed, or at any time if the partnership was a partnership at will at the time of transfer

Most of the foregoing provisions can be amended by the partnership agreement. For example, the partnership agreement can provide that the partnership will continue after the dissociation of one or more partners.

When it is the desire of the partners to plan for the continuation of the partnership after the death of one or more of the partners, life insurance on the life of each partner is often purchased by the partnership or by the partners to fund the buyout of a deceased partner.

Exhibit 3-8 lists the causes of dissolution as set forth by the UPA (1914) and the UPA (1997).

DISSOLUTION AGREEMENT

A written dissolution agreement among the partners of a dissolving partnership can help alleviate disputes as to the method and timing of the dissolution, as well as any disputes that may arise subsequent to the winding up of the partnership due to unforeseen circumstances. In the dissolution agreement, the partners who have the right to wind up the partnership generally appoint a liquidating partner or partners and delegate the authority to liquidate the partnership and settle the partnership affairs.

EXHIBIT 3-8 CAUSES OF PARTNERSHIP DISSOLUTION	
Under the UPA (1914)	**Under the UPA (1997)**
• Expiration of the term established for the partnership pursuant to the partnership agreement.	• Any partner giving notice to partnership of his or her withdrawal (in a partnership at will).
• Completion of undertaking by partnership formed for specific undertaking.	• Expiration of 90-day period after death or wrongful dissociation of a partner (unless a majority of remaining partners agree to continue partnership).
• Express will of all partners.	• Express will of all partners to wind up business.
• Expulsion of any partner pursuant to partnership agreement.	• Expiration of term of partnership for definite term.
• Express will of a partner that is contrary to the partnership agreement when the circumstances do not permit a dissolution under another provision.	• Completion of task of partnership formed for particular task.

(*continues*)

EXHIBIT 3-8 *(continued)*

Under the UPA (1914)	Under the UPA (1997)
• The happening of any event that makes it unlawful to carry on the partnership.	• Any event resulting in winding up of partnership business pursuant to partnership agreement.
• The death of any partner.	• Happening of event that makes it unlawful to continue partnership.
• The bankruptcy of any partner or the partnership.	• Judicial determination.
• By decree of a court upon application by or for a partner.	

© Cengage Learning 2013

NOTICE TO THIRD PARTIES

Notice of the partnership dissolution or withdrawal of a partner must be given to parties who have previously dealt with the partnership. Creditors who are not given notice and do not know of the dissolution may be entitled to hold former partners liable for obligations incurred after the dissolution as if the dissolution never occurred.

The statutes of some states provide for an optional filing of a statement of dissolution by any partner of a dissolving partnership who has not wrongfully dissociated. The statement of dissolution cancels any statement of partnership authority that may have been filed on behalf of the partnership.

WINDING UP

Winding up is the process by which the accounts of the partnership are settled and the assets are liquidated to make distribution of the net assets of the partnership to the partners and dissolve the partnership. This may include the performance of existing contracts, the collection of debts or claims due to the partnership, and the payment of the partnership debts.

DISTRIBUTION OF ASSETS

The partnership agreement will typically set forth guidelines for the distribution of assets on dissolution of the partnership—including the proportionate share of assets to be received and losses to be covered by each partner. Unless otherwise specified in the partnership agreement, the rules for distribution of the partnership assets are set by statute. In general terms, the partnership assets will be liquidated and used to pay the debts and obligations of the partnership, and the surplus will be distributed to the partners. If there are not enough partnership assets to pay the creditors of the partnership, the partners must contribute a sufficient amount.

In states that follow the UPA (1914) with regard to the rules for distribution of assets on dissolution, the assets of the partnership are used to pay the liabilities of the partnership in the order set forth as follows:

1. Those owing to creditors other than partners
2. Those owing to partners other than for capital and profits
3. Those owing to partners in respect of capital
4. Those owing to partners in respect of profits

The assets of the partnership include the partnership property as well as any contributions required by statute or partnership agreement for the payment of all liabilities of the partnership. Partners are entitled to receive their distribution in cash.

The partners must contribute to the assets of the partnership to the extent necessary to pay the liabilities of the partnership. The partners will all contribute equally unless otherwise provided for in the partnership agreement.

The procedures for distributing partnership assets on winding up the partnership are very similar in states that follow the UPA (1997). Again, the procedures for liquidating and distributing the assets may be set forth in the partnership agreement so long as the partnership agreement does not violate the statutes.

Unlike the UPA (1914), the UPA (1997) provisions do not give preference to creditors who are not partners. Therefore, the assets of the partnership must be first applied to discharge the partnership obligations to creditors, including partners who are creditors.

Also, the UPA (1997) provides that each partner is entitled to a settlement of all partnership accounts upon winding up. In settling the accounts of the partnership, the partnership property is first used to pay the creditors of the partnership. If the partnership property is insufficient to cover all of the partnership liabilities, then the partners are required to make contributions to cover the liabilities. If there is a surplus of assets after all creditors are paid, the surplus is paid to the partners.

Each partner is entitled to receive a share of the assets as determined by the partnership agreement. If the partnership agreement is silent on distribution of assets upon winding up, each partner is entitled to a share in the same proportion as the proportion of profits and losses that he or she is entitled to receive either under the partnership agreement or under law.

State law generally provides that if any, but not all, of the partners are insolvent, or otherwise unable or unwilling to contribute to the payment of the liabilities, the liabilities of the partnership must be paid by the remaining partners in the same proportion as their share of the profits of the partnership. Any partner, or the legal representative of any partner, who is required to pay in excess of his or her fair share of the liabilities to settle the affairs of the partnership has the right to enforce the contributions of the other partners pursuant to statute and the partnership agreement, to the extent of the amount paid in excess of his or her share of the liability.

The exact method of asset distribution should be set forth clearly in the partnership agreement. Generally, the partners are entitled to a distribution of the assets in the same percentage as their contribution of capital to the partnership, with adjustments made for subsequent contributions in the form of capital contributions and services rendered on behalf of the partnership. If partners' contributions to the partnership are unequal, their shares of the profits and losses may be unequal as well, so long as the appropriate provision is made in the partnership agreement.

Exhibit 3-9 lists the UPA (1914) and UPA (1997) requirements as to distribution of partnership assets upon dissolution.

EXHIBIT 3-9	DISTRIBUTION OF PARTNERSHIP ASSETS UPON DISSOLUTION UNDER THE UPA (1914) AND THE UPA (1997)

UPA (1914)	UPA (1997)
• Partnership assets must be liquidated and used to pay all outstanding debts and obligations of the partnership. Nonpartnership creditors are given priority over those partners who are creditors of the partnership.	• Partnership assets must be liquidated and used to pay all outstanding debts and obligations of the partnership. Partners who are creditors of the partnership are treated the same as nonpartnership creditors.
• Debts and obligations owing to partners other than for capital and profits are paid.	• Partners are entitled to a separate accounting of the partnership assets. Any gain or loss due to the liquidation of assets of the partnership is credited to a separate account for each partner, either equally or pursuant to the partnership agreement.
• Capital owing to partners is paid to partners.	• Any partner with a negative balance in his or her account must pay in an amount equal to the negative balance.
• Profits owing to partners are paid to partners.	• Any partner with a positive balance in his or her account is entitled to receive an amount equal to the balance.
• If necessary and unless otherwise established in the partnership agreement, partners must contribute equally to pay the liabilities of the partnership, including capital owing to partners.	

© Cengage Learning 2013

IN SUMMATION

- Under the UPA (1914), whenever one partner ceases being a partner for any reason, the partnership is considered dissolved.

- Under the UPA (1997), one or more partners may be dissociated from the partnership without causing its dissolution.

- The term *dissolution* refers to the commencement of the winding-up process.

- Some of the more common events that can cause a partner's dissociation include:
  - The partner's voluntary withdrawal after giving notice
  - The occurrence of an event designated in the partnership agreement to cause a dissociation
  - The transfer by a partner of all his or her interest in the partnership
  - The partner's death

- If a partner's dissociation is contrary to provisions of the partnership agreement, it will be considered a wrongful dissociation.

- Dissociating partners generally have the right to have their interest in the partnership bought out by the partnership and remaining partners on terms agreed to in the partnership agreement.

- Several different events may cause the dissolution and winding up of the partnership business. Some of those events include:
  - The expiration of the term of the partnership per the partnership agreement
  - The express will of any partner when no definite term has been established
  - An event that causes the continuation of the partnership to be illegal
  - The death of any partner
  - The bankruptcy of any partner
  - The order of a court

- Partners of a dissolving partnership will often enter into a dissolution agreement to set forth their full understanding regarding the dissolution process.

- Notice of partnership dissolution must be given to creditors and other parties who have previously dealt with the partnership.

- Winding up is the process by which the accounts of the partnership are settled and assets liquidated to make distribution to the partnership's creditors and partners.

- Procedures for distributing the final assets of the partnership are established by state statute, but in general, creditors must be paid before partners receive their final distribution.

§ 3.10 OTHER TYPES OF PARTNERSHIPS

In addition to general partnerships, state statutes provide for other forms of partnerships or quasi-partnerships.

LIMITED PARTNERSHIPS

LIMITED PARTNERSHIP

A partnership formed by general partners (who run the business and have liability for all partnership debts) and limited partners (who partly or fully finance the business, take no part in running it, and have no liability for partnership debts beyond the money they put in or promise to put in).

Limited partnerships differ from general partnerships in that the limited partnership has at least one limited partner, as well as one or more **general partners**. Unlike general partners, limited partners do not have unlimited personal liability. Limited partners risk no more than their investment in the partnership. Limited partnerships are discussed in detail in Chapter 4 of this text.

LIMITED LIABILITY PARTNERSHIPS

GENERAL PARTNER

Synonymous with partner. A partner in a general partnership, or limited partnership, who typically has unlimited personal liability for the debts and liabilities of the partnership.

Since the mid-1990s, statutes of most states have provided for the formation of **limited liability partnerships** (LLPs). These entities are very similar to general partnerships, with one important distinction. Under most circumstances, partners of a general partnership are personally liable for the debts and obligations of the partnership—partners of an LLP are not. LLPs are generally provided for as an election under the partnership act adopted by each state. Typically, an LLP must be registered with the secretary of state to be formed. You cannot form a limited liability partnership by oral agreement. Limited liability partnerships are discussed in detail in Chapter 5 of this text.

LIMITED LIABILITY PARTNERSHIP

A partnership in which the partners have less than full liability for the actions of other partners, but full liability for their own actions.

JOINT VENTURES

JOINT VENTURE

Sometimes referred to as a joint adventure; the relationship created when two or more persons combine jointly in a business enterprise with the understanding that they will share in the profits or losses and that each will have a voice in its management. Although a joint venture is a form of partnership, it customarily involves a single business project rather than an ongoing business relationship.

Joint ventures and partnerships are similar, but not identical. The primary difference is that a joint venture is more narrow in scope and purpose and is usually formed for a single transaction or isolated enterprise, whereas a partnership is formed to operate an ongoing concern. Joint ventures and partnerships are governed by the same basic legal principles, and a joint venture that meets the definition of a partnership may be considered a partnership when determining its rights and obligations. Joint ventures can be formed by individuals, corporations, or other entities.

IN SUMMATION

- Limited partnerships have at least one limited partner with limited liability who risks no more than his or her investment in the partnership.
- Limited liability partnerships are general partnerships that have adopted limited liability provisions to limit the liability of all partners of the partnership.
- Joint ventures are similar to partnerships, with the difference that they are typically formed for one particular transaction or an isolated enterprise.

§ 3.11 THE PARALEGAL'S ROLE

As with sole proprietorships, the bulk of legal services performed for partnerships is usually in the form of legal advice given by the attorney. Paralegals who work in the partnership law area may, however, be asked to assist with any number of tasks involving researching, forming, operating, and dissolving partnerships, including:

- Research state partnership law
- Research state requirements for filing partnership-related documents with the proper state or local authorities
- Research possible licensing requirements for partnership business
- Draft statement of partnership authority
- Draft statement of denial of partnership authority
- Draft written consents of the partners for certain acts of the partnership
- Request federal tax identification number
- Request state tax identification number
- File certificate of assumed or fictitious name for partnership name
- Assist with drafting partnership agreement
- Organize and establish a method for retaining partnership records
- Assist with drafting minutes of partnership meetings
- Assist with preparation of partnership tax returns and schedules of partner's share of income (Schedule K-1)
- Assist with winding up and dissolution of partnership

Paralegals are often instrumental in drafting the partnership agreement. Most law firms that represent partnerships have partnership agreement forms integrated into their word-processing systems. The paralegal is often responsible for the revising and drafting required to make each agreement fit the unique circumstances of each new partnership.

Form books commonly found online and in law libraries may help with the drafting of unique language, as will samples of previous work done by the paralegal or others in the law firm.

Following is a checklist of items that should be considered when drafting a partnership agreement.

Partnership Agreement Checklist

☐ Names and addresses of partners

☐ Name of partnership

☐ Purpose of partnership

- ☐ Limited liability status
- ☐ Address of principal place of doing business
- ☐ Term of partnership agreement
- ☐ Partner contributions
- ☐ Requirements for additional contributions
- ☐ Partnership assets
- ☐ Goodwill evaluation on distribution of assets
- ☐ Partners' and partnership liability
- ☐ Distribution of profits and losses
- ☐ Partner indemnification
- ☐ Partners' duties
- ☐ Partners' powers and limitations thereon
- ☐ Partner compensation and benefits
- ☐ Partner and partnership expenses
- ☐ Management and control of business
- ☐ Life insurance on lives of partners
- ☐ Accounting procedures and record keeping
- ☐ Changes in partners
- ☐ Death of partner
- ☐ Sale or purchase of partnership interest
- ☐ Arbitration of differences among partners
- ☐ Partnership termination
- ☐ Dissolution and winding up
- ☐ Date of agreement
- ☐ Signatures of all partners

CORPORATE PARALEGAL PROFILE
Arlene L. Morris

My job as a paralegal is to anticipate what needs to be done on an assignment and complete the assignment before the deadline.

NAME Arlene L. Morris
LOCATION Indianapolis, Indiana
TITLE Paralegal
SPECIALTY Probate/Tax and Corporate Law
EDUCATION State of Indiana Medicaid Fraud Unit on-the-job training; additional Continuing Legal Education
EXPERIENCE 19 years

Arlene Morris is a paralegal with Lewis & Kappes, a 30-attorney law firm located in Indianapolis, Indiana. As one of just four paralegals, Arlene is asked to work in a number of areas of law, including, but not limited to, corporate law. In addition to her responsibilities as a corporate paralegal, Arlene specializes in probate/tax and litigation work.

Arlene's varied experience includes working with partnerships. At times, she is asked to prepare partnership agreements and amendments thereto. She has also drafted security agreements and purchase agreements and prepared tax returns for partnerships. Arlene often takes responsibility for obtaining tax identification numbers for partnerships and other types of business organizations.

Arlene spends a significant amount of her time working with corporations and limited liability companies. She assists with the formation of corporations by preparing articles of incorporation, by-laws, and subscription agreements. With regard to limited liability companies, Arlene prepares drafts of the articles of organization and operating agreements for attorney review.

Arlene finds that each area of law she works in requires different skills and draws on different areas of expertise. While she enjoys the challenge of working with clients on their corporate matters, Arlene also finds it rewarding to work in the probate area from time to time, helping families who have recently suffered a great loss.

Arlene enjoys the freedom she has to work independently at her job and in scheduling and planning her own day. While she is a meticulous planner, Arlene admits that at times she will arrive at work in the morning only to find that a client needs something immediately and her plans for the day will have to be put on hold.

Indiana has a very active paralegal association, and Arlene is cochair of the probate/tax section, attending all monthly meetings and seminars. She is also a paralegal member of the Indianapolis Bar Association.

Arlene's advice to new paralegals?

Never give up! I felt like I was in over my head when I first became a paralegal because it seemed that everything was thrown at me at once; but, believe it or not, as the weeks, months, and years went by, things got much easier, and I now feel a sense of worth for helping someone. Never stop learning; stay on top of changes in the law. More times than not, you are the first source that your attorneys will come to for answers on procedures.

For more information on careers for corporate paralegals, log in to http://www.cengagebrain.com to access the CourseMate website that accompanies this text; then see the Corporate Careers Section.

ETHICAL CONSIDERATION

If you are a paralegal who works with partnerships, you may become familiar with your clients' personal and financial affairs. It is not uncommon for paralegals to assist in preparing financial documents for the partnership, as well as employment agreements and other agreements, the nature of which must be kept strictly confidential.

The rules of ethics provide that, with certain exceptions, attorneys and paralegals have an ethical duty to keep all information learned from clients confidential. The client-lawyer relationship is based on loyalty and requires that the lawyer, and any paralegals involved, maintain confidentiality of information relating to the representation. The confidential relationship between the client and attorney encourages the client to communicate fully and frankly with the attorney, even with regard to matters that may be damaging or embarrassing to the client.

Most law firms have strict policies regarding the divulgence of client information to the press or any outsider. Typically, all requests for information regarding a client should be directed to the attorney who is responsible for the client's affairs, and no one else will be permitted to pass on any information regarding a client without permission, even information that may seem quite inconsequential.

Here are some tips for keeping client information and documents confidential:

- Be sure you never meet with clients in a part of the office where your conversation could be overheard.

- Keep office conversations concerning clients on a need-to-know basis—forego idle gossip.

- Be sure client meetings held outside the office take place in a location where your conversation cannot be overheard.

- Double-check addresses of all correspondence leaving the office—including e-mail.

- Double-check any e-mail attachments you send out to make sure you don't send out the wrong document in error.

- Check all fax numbers and dial carefully.

- When holding meetings in your office, make sure no confidential information is visible, on your desk, cabinet, or computer screen.

ETHICAL CONSIDERATION
(continued)

- Do not talk to the press.

- Lock all files in fireproof file cabinets at the end of the day.

- Shred confidential materials you are disposing of.

- When dealing with outside photocopy, billing, file storage, or similar services, make sure you are dealing with reputable services. Get signed confidentiality agreements when necessary.

There are several exceptions to the rules of confidentiality. For example, confidential client information may be released when requested by the client or when ordered by a court. If you are in doubt as to whether to divulge any information that may be considered confidential, always be sure to ask your supervising attorney or an experienced paralegal first.

Excerpt from the National Federation of Paralegal Association's (NFPA's) Model Code of Ethics and Professional Responsibility:

A paralegal shall preserve all confidential information provided by the client or acquired from other sources before, during, and after the course of the professional relationship.

Excerpt from the National Association of Legal Assistant's (NALA's) Code of Ethics and Professional Responsibility:

A legal assistant must protect the confidences of a client and must not violate any rule or statute now in effect or hereafter enacted controlling the doctrine of privileged communications between a client and an attorney.

For more information on ethics for corporate paralegals, including links to the NALA and NFPA codes of ethics, log in to cengagebrain.com to access the CourseMate website that accompanies this text; then see the Ethics Section.

§ 3.12 RESOURCES

The paralegal has many resources available for researching statutory requirements for partnerships and drafting partnership agreements. For state and local formalities concerning partnerships, the secretary of state and other state and local government offices should be contacted.

STATE STATUTES

When working with partnerships, your most important resource will be the Uniform Partnership Act as adopted by your state. Exhibit 3-10 lists the statutory citations of the UPA (1914) or UPA (1997) as adopted by each state.

EXHIBIT 3-10	UNIFORM PARTNERSHIP ACTS ADOPTED BY STATE AS OF 2011	

STATE	CODE	VERSION OF UNIFORM ACT ADOPTED
Alabama	Ala. Code §§ 10-8A-101 to 10-8A-1109	UPA (1997)
Alaska	Alaska Stat. §§ 32.06.201 to 32.06.997	UPA (1997)
Arizona	Ariz. Rev. Stat. Ann. §§ 29-1001 to 29-1111.	UPA (1997)
Arkansas	Ark. Code Ann. §§ 4-46-101 to 4-46-1207	UPA (1997)
California	Cal. Corp. Code §§16100 to 16962	UPA (1997)
Colorado	Colo. Rev. Stat. §§ 7-64-101 to 7-64-1206	UPA (1997)
Connecticut	Conn. Gen. Stat. §§ 34-300 to 34-434	UPA (1997)
Delaware	Del. Code Ann. Tit. 6 §§ 15-101 to 15-1210	UPA (1997)
District of Columbia	DC Official Code §§ 33-101.01 to 33-1112.04	UPA (1997)
Florida	Fla. Stat. §§ 620.81001 to 620.9902	UPA (1997)
Georgia	Ga. Code §§ 14-8-1 to 14-8-61	UPA (1914)
Hawaii	Haw. Rev. Stat. §§ 425-101 to 425-145	UPA (1997)
Idaho	Idaho Code §§ 33-101 to 53-3-1205	UPA (1997)
Illinois	805 Ill Comp. Stat. §§ 206/100 to 206/1208	UPA (1997)
Indiana	Ind. Code §§ 23-4-1-1 to 23-4-1-54	UPA (1914)
Iowa	Iowa Code § 486A.101 to 486A.1302	UPA (1997)
Kansas	Kan. Stat. Ann. § 56a-101 to 56-1305	UPA (1997)
Kentucky	Ky. Rev. Stat. Ann. Ch. 362.1-101 to 362.1-1205	UPA (1997)
Louisiana	La. Rev. Stat. Ann. § 9:3401 et seq.	Not an adaptation of either the UPA (1914) or the UPA (1997)
Maine	Me. Rev. Stat. Ann. tit. 31, ch 17 §§ 1001 to 1105	UPA (1997)
Maryland	Md. Code Ann., Corps. & Ass'ns §§ 9A-101 to 9A-1205	UPA (1997)
Massachusetts	Mass. Gen. L. ch. 108A §§ 1 to 49	UPA (1914)

EXHIBIT 3-10 *(continued)*

STATE	CODE	VERSION OF UNIFORM ACT ADOPTED
Michigan	Mich. Comp. Laws §§ 449.1 to 449.48	UPA (1914)
Minnesota	Minn. Stat. Ann. § 323.0101 to 323A.1203	UPA (1997)
Mississippi	Miss. Code Ann. §§ 79-13-101 to 79-13-1206	UPA (1997)
Missouri	Mo. Rev. Stat. §§ 358.010 to 358.520	UPA (1914)
Montana	Mont. Rev. Stat. §§ 35-10-101 to 79-13-1206	UPA (1997)
Nebraska	Neb. Rev. Stat. §§ 67-401 to 67-467	UPA (1997)
Nevada	Nev. Rev. Stat. §§ 87.4301 to 87.4357	UPA (1997)
New Hampshire	N.H. Rev. Stat. Ann. §§ 304-A:1 to 304-A:62	UPA (1914)
New Jersey	N.J. Stat. Ann. § 42:1A-1 to 42:1A-56	UPA (1997)
New Mexico	N.M. Rev. Stat. §§ 54-1-47, 54-1A-101 to 54-1A-1206	UPA (1997)
New York	N.Y. Partnership Law §§ 1 to 74, 121-1500 to 121-1507	UPA (1914)
North Carolina	N.C. Gen. Stat. §§ 59-31 to 59-73	UPA (1914)
North Dakota	N.D. Cent. Code §§ 45-13-01 to 45-21-08	UPA (1997)
Ohio	Ohio Rev. Code Ann. §§ 1776.01 to 1776.96	UPA (1997)
Oklahoma	Okla. Stat. tit. 54, §§ 1-100 to 1-1207	UPA (1997)
Oregon	Or. Rev. Stat. §§ 67.005 to 67.815	UPA (1997)
Pennsylvania	15 Pa. Cons. Stat. Ann. § § 8301 to 8365	UPA (1914)
Rhode Island	Gen. Laws 1956, § § 7-12-12 to 7-12-59	UPA (1914)
South Carolina	S.C. Code Ann. §§ 33-41-10 to 33-41-1220	UPA (1914)
South Dakota	S.D. Codified Laws Ann. §§ 48-7A-101 to 48-7A-1208	UPA (1997)
Tennessee	Tenn Code Ann. §§ 61-1-101 to 61-1-1208	UPA (1997)
Texas	Tex. Rev. Civ. Stat. Ann. art. 6132b-101 to 6132b-11.05	UPA (1997)
U.S. Virgin Islands	V.I. Code Ann. Tit. 26 § 1 to 274	UPA (1997)
Utah	Utah Code Ann. §§ 48-1-1 to 48-1-48	UPA (1914)
Vermont	Vt. Stat. Ann. tit. 11, §§ 3201 to 3313	UPA (1997)
Virginia	Va. Code Ann. §§ 50-73.79 to 50-73.150	UPA (1997)
Washington	Wash. Rev. Code §§ 25.05.005 to 25.05.907	UPA (1997)
West Virginia	W. Va. Code §§ 47B-1-1 to 47B-11-5	UPA (1997)
Wisconsin	Wis. Stat. §§ 178.01 to 178.53	UPA (1914)
Wyoming	Wyo. Stat. Ann. §§ 17-21-101 to 17-21-1003	UPA (1997)

UNIFORM PARTNERSHIP ACT (1914) AND UNIFORM PARTNERSHIP ACT (1997)

The website of the **National Conference of Commissioners on Uniform State Law (NCCUSL)** provides links to drafts and final versions of uniform state laws, including the Uniform Partnership Act (1914) and Uniform Partnership Act (1997).

LEGAL FORM BOOKS AND PARTNERSHIP FORMS

Legal form books such as *Am. Jur. Legal Forms 2d., Nichols Cyclopedia of Legal Forms Annotated, Rabkin & Johnson Current Legal Forms,* and *West's Legal Forms Second Edition* are good sources for general information and for obtaining sample paragraphs for drafting partnership agreements and other documents related to the formation and operation of partnerships.

Forms for partnership agreements and other partnership-related documents can be found online from several different sources. Before any of these forms are used, they must be carefully reviewed and edited to be certain that they meet the statutory requirements of your state and that they fulfill the needs of the proposed partnership. Some sites charge a fee for downloading certain forms.

SECRETARY OF STATE OFFICES

The secretary of state or other appropriate state authority must be contacted to determine if there are any requirements for partnership registration with the state. The secretary of state offices provide a wealth of online information concerning any requirements they have for filing partnership documents. The secretary of state should also be consulted for procedural information regarding filing of an application for a certificate of assumed name, trade name, or fictitious name, if applicable. Most states provide downloadable forms as well. Appendix A to this text is a directory of secretary of state offices. Links to the secretary of state office websites may be accessed from the CourseMate website.

FEDERAL AND STATE TAX INFORMATION

Questions concerning requirements for filing federal partnership returns can be answered by contacting the Internal Revenue Service or visiting its website. For information on state taxation for partnerships, see the websites of the state tax authorities.

Links to several of the websites discussed in this section can be accessed through CourseMate.

SUMMARY

- A partnership is an association of two or more persons to carry on as co-owners of a business for profit.

- All the partners of a general partnership are general partners.

- Most states have adopted a version of either the Uniform Partnership Act (1914) or the Uniform Partnership Act (1997).

- The partnership is considered a separate entity for most purposes and an aggregate of its partners for other purposes.

- Each partner typically has the right to act on behalf of the partnership when dealing with others concerning partnership business.

- Unless otherwise agreed to in the partnership agreement, each partner has an equal right to manage the partnership business.

- Unless otherwise agreed to in the partnership agreement, each partner has the right to receive an equal share of the profits and the responsibility to pay an equal share of the losses of the partnership.

- Certain acts outside the ordinary course of business require the unanimous consent of all partners. Acts requiring the unanimous consent of partners may be prescribed by statute or by the partnership agreement.

- Partners may file a statement of authority to give public notice of the authority granted or denied certain partners.

- In states that follow the UPA (1914), partnership property is held in tenancy of partnership.

- In states that follow the UPA (1997), partnership property is owned by the partnership itself.

- Partners owe a fiduciary duty to each other and to the partnership. That duty may be expanded on and detailed in the partnership agreement, but the fiduciary duty of partners cannot be diminished under the partnership agreement.

- The partnership agreement is considered the law of the partnership for most purposes. The terms of the partnership agreement govern the partnership unless they are contrary to the laws of the state.

- Under the UPA (1914), the withdrawal of any partner causes a dissolution of the partnership.

- Under the UPA (1997), partners may be dissociated from the partnership without dissolving the partnership.

- Winding up is the process by which the accounts of the partnership are settled and the assets are liquidated in order to make final distributions to the partners and dissolve the partnership.

- In general, the liabilities of the partnership must be paid before final distributions can be made to the partners of a dissolving partnership.

■ REVIEW QUESTIONS

1. What five elements are necessary to form a partnership?

2. In what ways are partnerships similar to sole proprietorships? In what ways do they differ from sole proprietorships?

3. Suppose that John, Megan, and Alex form a partnership to operate a restaurant in a state that follows the UPA (1997). John decides to buy hamburger buns from the Fresh Bread Bakery. He enters into a contract with the owner of the Fresh Bread Bakery, on behalf of the partnership, for the delivery of 500 hamburger buns each week, for the price of $70 per week. If Megan and Alex disagree with this decision because they prefer another baker, is the partnership still liable for this contract? Must the Fresh Bread Bakery be paid out of the partnership funds?

4. Suppose again that John, Megan, and Alex form a partnership, and John has contributed 50 percent of the capital, Megan has contributed 30 percent of the capital, and Alex has contributed 20 percent of the capital. Who has the right to manage the partnership under the UPA (1997), assuming the partnership agreement has no contrary provisions? How will decisions be made in the event of a disagreement?

5. In a state that follows the UPA (1914), how is partnership property owned? How is that different from property owned by a partnership in a state that follows the UPA (1997)?

6. Kara, Tim, and Anna have formed a partnership to purchase and renovate old homes. Kara and Tim have contributed the bulk of the capital for the corporation, and Anna's main contribution has been her services. All partners agree that either Kara or Tim should have the authority to sign documents transferring real estate on behalf of the partnership and that Anna should not have that authority. If the partnership is formed in a state that follows the UPA (1997), what steps must they take to give notice to those dealing with their partnership of their agreement with regard to the authority to transfer real estate?

7. Janet is a partner in a 10-partner partnership located in a state that follows the UPA (1997). If Janet decides to withdraw from the partnership before its duration lapses, what are the possible outcomes to the partnership and the remaining partners? What if the partnership is located in a state that follows the UPA (1914)?

8. Suppose that three retirees form a partnership to own and operate a horse ranch. They all plan to work at the ranch and board horses to supplement their retirement income. If the business does not go as planned, and the retirees earn no income from the ranch, do they still have a valid partnership? Why or why not?

9. Suppose that Ken, Bill, and Mary form a partnership to build and lease a strip mall. The partners agree that Ken will be responsible for securing the location on which to build the mall. Ken selects a site that turns out to have poor soil quality, and the project suffers several setbacks before they finally decide it is not feasible and the partners decide to go their separate ways. If the partnership funds have all been exhausted, and the partnership still owes $20,000 to an environmental engineering firm that Ken hired, who must pay? What if Ken and Mary have no substantial personal assets, but Bill has $30,000 in the bank?

10. Suppose that the three partners of a partnership have a falling out, and two of them stop communicating, leaving the third partner to wind up and dissolve the partnership. The third partner claims she is entitled to compensation for her time spent winding up the partnership, but the other partners claim that, unless agreed to in a partnership agreement, partners are not entitled to compensation for their time spent on partnership business. Assuming that their partnership agreement is silent on the matter, who is right? Why?

PRACTICAL PROBLEMS

1. Locate and cite the partnership act in your state to answer the following questions.

   a. Is your state's partnership act based on the UPA (1914) or the UPA (1997)?

   b. When was your state's current act adopted?

2. Do the statutes of your state provide for the filing of a statement of authority? Where is that document filed?

3. What are the basic steps for dissolving a partnership under the statutes of your state?

EXERCISE IN CRITICAL THINKING

While it is possible to make all management decisions of small- to medium-sized partnerships by consensus of all partners, what are some possible drawbacks to operating the partnership in that manner? Under what circumstances might such a management structure work?

WORKPLACE SCENARIO

Assume that you and the attorney you work for have just met with your new client, Bradley Harris, from previous chapters of this text. Instead of operating as a sole proprietor, Mr. Harris has entered into a general partnership with his friend and former colleague, Cynthia Lund. Bradley and Cynthia have decided they would like to lease some office space from which to operate their business. Bradley will be traveling extensively, and both partners have agreed that Cynthia should have the authority to sign a lease on behalf of the partnership.

Using the earlier information and the information provided in Appendices B-1 and B-2 of this text, prepare for filing in your state a statement of authority, or similarly titled document, to meet Bradley's and Cynthia's objectives. You may create your own form that conforms to the statutes in your state, or you can download a form from the appropriate state office for completion. If the statutes in your state do not provide for the filing of a statement of authority, assume for purposes of this assignment that your state has elected the pertinent sections of the UPA (1997).

In addition to the statement of authority, prepare a cover letter filing the form with the appropriate state authority, along with any required filing fee.

check IRS for filing fees

Portfolio Reminder

Save the documents prepared for the Workplace Scenario exercises in each chapter, either in hard copy or electronically, to build a portfolio of documents to be used for job interviews or as sample documents on the job. At this point, your portfolio should include the following:

- Power of attorney
- Application for assumed name
- Application for federal employer identification number
- Application for state employer identification number
- Partnership statement of authority

END NOTES

1. Uniform Partnership Act (1914) § 6.
2. Uniform Partnership Act (1914) § 2.
3. Uniform Partnership Act (1914) § 3.
4. Department of the Treasury, Internal Revenue Service. Partnership Returns 2008. *Statistics of Income Bulletin*, 2010, http://www.irs.gov.

5. Id.

6. 59A Am. Jur. 2d Partnership § 7 (2010).

7. Uniform Partnership Act (1997) § 201.

8. Uniform Partnership Act (1914) § 9(1).

9. Id. § 9(2).

10. Id. § 9(3)(a).

11. Id. § 9(3)(b).

12. Id. § 9(3)(c).

13. Id. § 9(3)(d).

14. Id. § 9(3)(e).

15. Id. § 18(e).

16. Uniform Partnership Act (1997) § 301(1).

17. Id. § 302(2).

18. Id. § 303(d)(2).

19. Id. § 303(d).

20. Id. § 306(a).

21. Uniform Partnership Act (1914) § 25(2)(a).

22. Uniform Partnership Act (1997) § 501.

23. Id. § 401(a).

24. Uniform Partnership Act (1914)§ 18(b),
    Uniform Partnership Act (1997) § 401(c).

25. *Meinhard v. Salmon, et al.*, 164 NE 545
    (NY Ct. App. 1928).

26. See § 2.5 of this text.

27. Uniform Partnership Act (1997)§ 401(j),
    Uniform Partnership Act (1914)§ 18(h).

28. See § 2.5 of this text.

29. 14 AM. JUR. Legal Forms 2d (May 2008)
    § 194:115. Reprinted with permission from
    American Jurisprudence Legal Forms 2d.
    © 2011 West Group.

30. Id. § 194:157.

31. Id. § 194:278.

32. Id. § 194:211.

33. Id. § 194:309.

34. Id. § 194:344.

35. Id. § 194:355

36. Id. § 194:430.

37. Id. § 194:460.

38. Id. § 194:465.

39. Id. § 194:499.

40. Id. § 194:515.

41. Id. § 194:545.

42. Id. § 194:568.

43. Uniform Partnership Act (1914) § 22.

44. Uniform Partnership Act (1997) § 801.

45. Id. § 701(b).

CourseMate

To access additional course materials, including CourseMate, please visit http://www.cengagebrain .com. At the CengageBrain home page, search for the ISBN of your title (from the back cover of your book) using the search box at the top of the page.

This will take you to the product page where the resources can be found. The CourseMate resources for this text include Web links to the resources discussed earlier, downloadable partnership forms and other forms, flash cards, and more.

4

LIMITED PARTNERSHIPS

CHAPTER OUTLINE

INTRODUCTION

Limited partnerships are a special type of partnership that offers certain partners limited liability. This business organization shares many of the characteristics of general partnerships, with a few important differences. Those differences are highlighted in this chapter.

First, we define the characteristics of a limited partnership. We then discuss the rights and responsibilities of the general and limited partners and the advantages and disadvantages of doing business as a limited partnership. We then look at the organization and management of a limited partnership, including the contents of a limited partnership agreement. Next, we investigate the financial structure of limited partnerships and their dissolution. After a brief discussion of derivative actions,

LIMITED PARTNERSHIP

A partnership formed by general partners (who run the business and have liability for all partnership debts) and limited partners (who partly or fully finance the business, take no part in running it, and have no liability for partnership debts beyond the money they put in or promise to put in).

GENERAL PARTNER

1. Synonymous with partner. A partner in a general partnership, or limited partnership, who typically has unlimited personal liability for the debts and liabilities of the partnership.
2. A member of a general or limited partnership who shares in the profits and losses of the partnership and may participate fully in the management of the partnership. General partners are usually personally liable for the debts and obligations of the partnership.

LIMITED PARTNER

A partner who invests in a limited partnership, but does not assume personal liability for the debts and obligations of the partnership. Limited partners may not participate in the management of the limited partnership in most states.

LIMITED LIABILITY LIMITED PARTNERSHIP

A type of limited partnership permissible in some states in which the general partners have less than full liability for the actions of other general partners.

we will take a look at a special kind of limited partnership—the family limited partnership. This chapter then concludes with a discussion of the role of paralegals who work with limited partnerships, and resources available to aid the paralegal.

§ 4.1 AN INTRODUCTION TO LIMITED PARTNERSHIPS

This section begins by defining the terms *limited partnership* and *limited liability limited partnership*. Next, the role of limited partnerships in the United States, the laws governing limited partnerships, and the separate-entity nature of limited partnerships are discussed.

LIMITED PARTNERSHIP DEFINED

A **limited partnership** is a partnership created by statute with one or more **general partners** and one or more **limited partners**. The status of the general partners in a limited partnership is very similar to that of the partners in general partnerships, and they have many of the same rights, duties, and obligations. Limited partners, on the other hand, are in many ways more like investors than partners, as they risk only the amount of their contribution to the limited partnership, and they are generally not entitled to manage the partnership business.

As with a general partnership, a partner to a limited partnership may be a "natural person, partnership, limited partnership (domestic or foreign), trust, estate, association, or corporation."[1]

Limited Liability Limited Partnerships

Some jurisdictions have adopted statutes providing for the formation of **limited liability limited partnerships** (LLLPs). This relatively new type of limited partnership provides limited liability for both the general and limited partners of the LLLP. The amount of protection offered to both the general and limited partners of LLLPs varies by state. LLLPs are discussed in Chapter 5 of this text.

LIMITED PARTNERSHIPS IN THE UNITED STATES

The popularity of limited partnerships in the United States has been attributed mainly to the unique tax advantages they offer. Because the limited partnership is usually not taxed as a separate entity, profits and losses may be passed directly to the partners (within certain limitations). For that reason, and because limited partners are not personally liable for the debts and obligations of the partnership, the limited partnership has been a favored entity for investments in this country, particularly in the area of real estate.

Of the limited partnerships filing income tax returns for the year 2008, 246,760 (more than half) of the limited partnerships indicated they were part of the real estate and rental and leasing industry.

In recent years, both the general partnership and limited partnership entities have seen increasing competition from limited liability companies (discussed in Chapter 6 of this text). Limited liability companies offer both limited liability for all owners and partnership taxation treatment. The number of limited partnerships filing tax returns has been declining slightly each year since 2006. See Exhibit 4-1.

EXHIBIT 4-1 NUMBER OF LIMITED AND GENERAL PARTNERSHIPS IN THE UNITED STATES

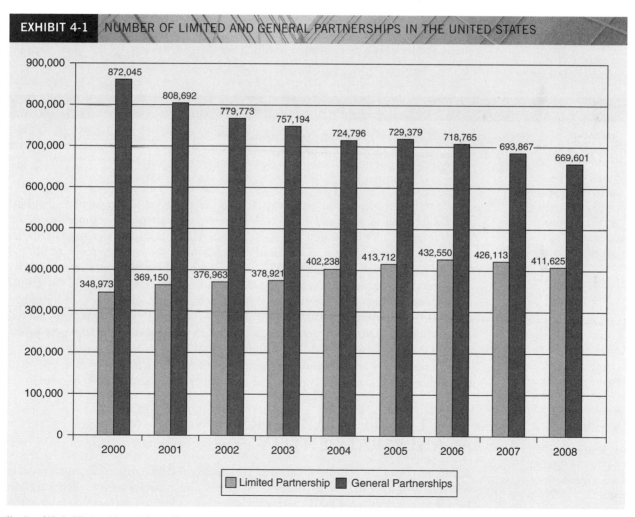

Number of Limited Partnerships and General Partnerships Filing Partnership Returns in the United States 2000 through 2008. Business Tax Statistics 2000–2008, Internal Revenue Service, http://www.irs.gov.

LAW GOVERNING LIMITED PARTNERSHIPS

The first uniform law concerning limited partnerships in the United States was the Uniform Limited Partnership Act of 1916 (ULPA), which was adopted by the vast majority of the states. In 1976, the Revised Uniform Limited Partnership Act was introduced and in 1985 substantial changes were made to that act. Nearly every state has adopted the 1976 Revised Uniform Limited Partnership act (RULPA) with 1985 amendments. Some states, however, have amended their limited partnership acts to include provisions for the limited liability limited partnership, which is discussed in Chapter 5 of this text. A few states have recently adopted their own versions of a new uniform act—the Uniform Limited Partnership Act 2001 (ULPA 2001). The full text of the Uniform Limited Partnership Act 2001 can be found on the website of the National Conference of Commissioners on Uniform State Law. Exhibit 4-8 in the Resources section of this chapter is a list of state limited partnership statute citations, along with an indication of which version of Uniform Act has been adopted by each state.

SIDEBAR

While the Revised Uniform Limited Partnership Act with 1985 amendments is often referred to as RULPA, the act as amended in 2001 is sometimes referred to as Re-RULPA.

The Uniform Limited Partnership Act 2001 is a new act that recognizes that limited liability partnerships and limited liability companies are now meeting many of the needs formerly met by limited partnerships. The ULPA 2001 was designed to fill the needs of two types of enterprises the drafters felt were "beyond the scope of limited liability partnerships and limited liability companies."[2] The two types of enterprises are (i) certain sophisticated manager-entrenched commercial deals, and (ii) family limited partnerships used for estate planning arrangements. As of 2011, 15 states had adopted the ULPA 2001. This chapter will focus on the Revised Uniform Limited Partnership Act with 1985 amendments (RULPA). Comparison with the new provisions in the Uniform Limited Partnership Act 2001 will be made where relevant.

Uniform laws are not always adopted verbatim, and it is very important when researching limited partnership law that the proper state's statutes be consulted.

THE LIMITED PARTNERSHIP AS A SEPARATE ENTITY

A limited partnership is usually treated as a separate entity, especially when dealing with matters such as real estate ownership and the capacity to sue. The Uniform Limited Partnership Act 2001 specifically states that a limited partnership is an entity separate from its partners.[3] Under some circumstances, however, especially those dealing with substantive liabilities and duties of the partners, the limited partnership is considered an aggregate of the individual partners. Although limited partnerships are required to file partnership income returns with the Internal Revenue Service each year, they are not subject to federal income taxation as separate entities.

Exhibit 4-2 provides a comparison of the principal features of general and limited partnerships.

EXHIBIT 4-2	LIMITED PARTNERSHIPS v. GENERAL PARTNERSHIPS

General Partnerships	Limited Partnerships
• All partners are general partners.	• The limited partnership must have at least one general partner and may have any number of limited partners.
• All partners are personally liable for the debts and obligations of the partnership.	• The general partners are personally responsible for the debts and obligations of the limited partnership. Limited partners risk only their investment in the limited partnership.
• Unless otherwise provided in the partnership agreement, all partners have an equal right to manage the partnership business.	• In most states limited partners may not participate in the control and management of the limited partnership or they will lose their limited liability status.
• In most instances, a general partnership may be formed without filing any documentation at the state level.	• State statutes provide for the formation of limited partnerships. A limited partnership certificate must be filed at the state level before the entity exists.
• The partnership is considered an entity separate from its partners for most purposes.	• The limited partnership is considered an entity separate from its partners for most purposes.

© Cengage Learning 2013

IN SUMMATION

- A limited partnership is a partnership with one or more general partners and one or more limited partners.
- The status of the general partners of a limited partnership is very similar to that of partners of a general partnerships.
- Limited partners enjoy limited personal liability, but may not be entitled to participate in the management of the partnership business.
- Some jurisdictions have adopted laws that provide for limited liability limited partnerships, a type of limited partnership whereby all partners have limited personal liability, at least to a certain extent.

continues

IN SUMMATION (*continued*)

- There are far fewer limited partnerships in the United States than general partnerships.
- The number of active limited partnerships has started declining in recent years due to the popularity of the limited liability company and other types of limited liability entities that offer limited liability to all owners.
- Limited liability partnerships are governed by state laws, most of which are based on the Revised Uniform Limited Partnership Act.
- Some states have adopted a version of the newer Uniform Limited Partnership Act 2001.
- For most purposes, limited partnerships are considered entities separate from their partners.

§ 4.2 PARTNERS' RIGHTS AND RESPONSIBILITIES

Limited partnerships have two types of partners, and those partners are subject to different statutory rights and responsibilities. This section examines the rights and responsibilities unique to general partners and those unique to limited partners, and concludes with a discussion of the relationship between general partners and limited partners.

GENERAL PARTNERS' RIGHTS AND RESPONSIBILITIES

Except as otherwise provided by statute and the limited partnership agreement, the rights and responsibilities of a general partner in a limited partnership are the same as the rights and responsibilities of those of a partner in a general partnership. Unlike limited partners, general partners are personally responsible for the debts and obligations of the limited partnership.

LIMITED PARTNERS' RIGHTS AND RESPONSIBILITIES

The limited partner is often seen as more of an investor than an actual partner in the partnership. The limited partner has few of the rights granted to partners in a general partnership, and correspondingly few of the responsibilities. One of the most important characteristics of limited partners is that they have limited liability. The risk of a limited partner is limited to the amount of that partner's investment in the limited partnership. Creditors of the limited partnership may not look to the personal assets of limited partners when trying to collect on a debt owed by the limited partnership.

The interest of a limited partner in a partnership is considered to be personal property, even if the partnership assets include or consist solely of land. The limited partner holds no title to the assets of the partnership, but has only his or her interest in the partnership.[4]

Unlike the partners in a general partnership, in most states limited partners have no right to participate in the management of the partnership, and may actually be in danger of losing their limited liability status if they do participate in the control of the partnership business. In that event, the limited partner may be held personally liable for the debts and obligations of the limited partnership. Under the RULPA, a limited partner who participates in control of the business is liable only to persons who transact business with the limited partnership reasonably believing, based upon the limited partner's conduct, that the limited partner is a general partner.[5]

Exactly what constitutes "taking part in control" of the business has been the subject of many a court case and is still subject to debate. However, under the RULPA, some guidance is given by way of a list of "safe harbor" activities. The RULPA states:

A limited partner does not participate in the control of the business ... Solely by doing one or more of the following:

1. being a contractor for or an agent or employee of the limited partnership or of a general partner or being an officer, director, or shareholder of a general partner that is a corporation;
2. consulting with and advising a general partner with respect to the business of the limited partnership;
3. acting as surety for the limited partnership or guaranteeing or assuming one or more specific obligations of the limited partnership;
4. taking any action required or permitted by law to bring or pursue a derivative action in the right of the limited partnership;
5. requesting or attending a meeting of partners;
6. proposing, approving, or disapproving, by voting or otherwise, one or more of the following matters:
   i. the dissolution and winding up of the limited partnership;
   ii. the sale, exchange, lease, mortgage, pledge, or other transfer of all or substantially all of the assets of the limited partnership;
   iii. the incurrence of indebtedness by the limited partnership other than in the ordinary course of its business;
   iv. a change in the nature of the business;
   v. the admission or removal of a general partner;
   vi. the admission or removal of a limited partner;
   vii. a transaction involving an actual or potential conflict of interest between a general partner and the limited partnership or the limited partners;
   viii. an amendment to the partnership agreement or certificate of limited partnership; or

      ix. matters related to the business of the limited partnership not otherwise enumerated in this subsection (b), which the partnership agreement states in writing may be subject to the approval or disapproval of limited partners;

  7. winding up the limited partnership... or

  8. exercising any right or power permitted to limited partners under this Act and not specifically enumerated in this subsection (b).[6]

The RULPA further states that the possession or exercise of any powers not included in the preceding list does not necessarily constitute participation of the limited partner in the partnership business.

The newer Uniform Limited Partnership Act 2001 differs substantially from the RULPA where limited partnership participation is concerned. Under the Uniform Limited Partnership Act 2001, limited partners are not personally liable for obligations of the limited partnership "even if the limited partner participates in the management and control of the limited partnership."[7]

All limited partners are granted certain rights by statute, including the statutory right to information regarding the partnership business. Limited partners are generally entitled to inspect the limited partnership records at any reasonable time.[8]

The limited partnership agreement may also grant certain rights to limited partners. The right to vote on certain extraordinary matters affecting the limited partnership is one such right that is often granted in the limited partnership agreement.

THE RELATIONSHIP BETWEEN GENERAL PARTNERS AND LIMITED PARTNERS

Because limited partners are typically prohibited from participating in the control of the business, the relationship between general partners and limited partners differs significantly from the relationship among partners in a general partnership. General partners owe a fiduciary duty to limited partners, and the sole general partner of a limited partnership owes an even greater duty than that normally imposed on partners, especially when the general partner holds a majority interest.[9] The duty of a general partner, acting in complete control, has been compared both to the fiduciary duty of a trustee to the beneficiaries of a trust, and to the fiduciary relationship of a corporate director to a shareholder.

One person may be both a general partner and a limited partner in the same partnership. In that event, the partner will have all of the rights and responsibilities of a general partner. However, his or her contribution to the partnership as a limited partner will be protected in the same manner as the contribution of any other limited partner.

IN SUMMATION

- Unlike limited partners, general partners are personally responsible for the debts and obligations of the limited partnership.
- The personal risk of a limited partner is limited to his or her investment in the limited partnership.
- The interest of a limited partner is considered to be personal property.
- In most states, limited partners who take part in the control of the limited partnership business risk losing their limited liability status.
- In states that follow the ULPA 2001 in this regard, limited partners are not personally liable for obligations of the limited partnership even if they participate in the management and control of the limited partnership.
- General partners owe a fiduciary duty to the limited partners of the limited partnership.

---

§ 4.3 ADVANTAGES OF DOING BUSINESS AS A LIMITED PARTNERSHIP

Limited partnerships have several unique advantages to offer both general and limited partners. In this section, we look at some of the more important advantages of doing business as a limited partnership, including the limited liability available to limited partners, potential income tax benefits, the relative transferability of partnership interests and continuity of business as compared to general partnerships, and the availability of diversified capital resources.

LIMITED LIABILITY FOR LIMITED PARTNERS

One of the most attractive features of a limited partnership is the limited liability offered to its limited partners. Limited partners can invest money without becoming personally liable for the debts of the firm as long as they do not participate in the control of the business or hold themselves out to be general partners.

In *Commonwealth of Pennsylvania, Department of Revenue for the Bureau of Accounts Settlement v. McKelvey,* a schoolteacher who invested in a bicycle business protected his personal liability by acting as a limited partner. When the business failed to pay its taxes, the court determined that a tax lien could not be placed on the property of the limited partner, and that the partner could not be held personally responsible for taxes owed by the limited partnership.

CASE

Limited Partnerships Supreme Court of Pennsylvania. Commonwealth of Pennsylvania, Department of Revenue for the Bureau of Accounts Settlement, Appellee, v. Patrick J. Mckelvey, Peter Bradley T/A Different Spokes. Appeal of Peter Bradley T/A Different Spokes. No. 81 E.D. Appeal 1990. Argued Jan. 15, 1991. Decided March 7, 1991.

Opinion of the Court
LARSEN, Justice.

The issues raised by this appeal are whether appellant, Peter Bradley, received actual notice of a tax assessment against the business in which he was a limited partner, and whether appellant, as a limited partner, was liable for a partnership debt under the Uniform Limited Partnership Act.

Appellant is a school teacher who was requested by Patrick McKelvey to provide the financial backing for a retail bicycle business. The two men entered into a limited partnership agreement, and appellant provided an $18,000.00 loan to the business. As a limited partner, appellant took no part in the operation or management of the bicycle shop. McKelvey, as general partner, handled all of the purchases, sales, and financial aspects of the business. Identifying himself as the partnership's "principal" partner (we interpret this as meaning the partnership's general partner), McKelvey filed an application for sales, use, and hotel occupancy license with the Department of Revenue of the Commonwealth of Pennsylvania, and designated appellant as a limited partner in the business, which was known as "Different Spokes."

On October 10, 1985, appellee, Commonwealth of Pennsylvania, Department of Revenue for the Bureau of Accounts Settlement, mailed a notice of sales and use tax assessment to the business address of Different Spokes for a series of tax periods beginning July 1, 1983, and ending June 30, 1985, in the amount of $17,636.86. The total assessment amounted to $27,974.21

with penalties and interest. No challenge was made to this assessment nor was the assessment paid.

In April of 1986, appellee issued liens in the amount of $27,974.21 against the business and its general and limited partners. Appellant, who had not been individually notified of the assessment by the appellee, did not discover the lien that had been filed against properties he owned until he was conducting a title search several months thereafter during a routine application for a mortgage. Appellant promptly filed a Petition to Strike Tax Lien in the Court of Common Pleas of Delaware County. That court determined that its jurisdiction was limited to the question of whether or not appellant had received notice of the assessment. The common pleas court then held that notice to the partnership constituted notice to the appellant, and thus, that the appellant had received notice of the assessment. Accordingly, appellant's petition to strike tax lien was denied.

Appellant filed an appeal to Commonwealth Court which affirmed, holding that the notice of tax assessment sent to the limited partnership was "sufficient to support the lien entered against [appellant] as a limited partner.". . . We granted appellant's petition for allowance of appeal, and we now reverse.

The trial court erred in holding that notice to a partnership constitutes notice to a limited partner. The trial court also erred in holding by implication that the personal assets of a limited partner can be liened to satisfy the debt of a limited partnership.

continues

CASE *(continued)*
Limited Partnerships Supreme Court of Pennsylvania. Commonwealth of Pennsylvania, Department of Revenue

As a matter of law, notice to a limited partnership can never constitute notice to a limited partner. A limited partner has no role in the exercise, control or management of the limited partnership business. Limited partners, by statutory definition, do not take part in the control or management of partnership business.

Section 521 of the Uniform Limited Partnership Act which was in effect at the time of the events giving rise to this litigation provided as follows:

A limited partner shall not become liable as a general partner unless, in addition to the exercise of his rights and powers as a limited partner, he takes part in the control of the business. 59 Pa.C.S.A. § 521 (now repealed).

Appellant was a limited partner and did not take part in the control or management of Different Spokes; accordingly, the notice received by the partnership of the tax assessment did not constitute actual notice to appellant . . . .

Finally, it is the law of this Commonwealth that a limited partner is not liable for the obligations of the limited partnership. . . . Thus, assuming proper notice to appellant, his liability would be limited.

Accordingly, we reverse the decision of the commonwealth court, and we remand to the court of common pleas of Delaware County for the entry of an order granting appellant's petition to strike tax lien.

Note: In this case, the court made it clear that the limited partner who did not take part in the control of the business was not personally liable for the tax obligations of the limited partnership.

Case material reprinted from Westlaw, with permission.

INCOME TAX BENEFITS

A limited partnership is usually not taxed as a separate tax entity for federal income tax purposes. Therefore, limited partnerships can offer attractive tax advantages to both general and limited partners. The ability of the limited partnership to pass tax profits and losses directly to the limited partners, without the limited partners risking anything more than their investment, can be a significant advantage over the corporate and general partnership tax structures. There are, however, limits to the amount of loss partners can claim on their income tax returns. All partners are subject to limits established by the Internal Revenue Service on losses that can be claimed, based on the amount of the partners' investment in the partnership and the amount for which the partner is actually considered at risk. In addition, limited partners may be subject to limits on the losses they may claim under rules that apply to income derived from passive activities. Although limited partnerships generally are not subject to federal income taxation, they are subject to state income taxation in many states.

TRANSFERABILITY OF PARTNERSHIP INTEREST

Although a partner's interest in a limited partnership is not as easily transferred as a corporate interest, the limited partner's interest is generally assignable with fewer restrictions than those imposed on the partners of a general partnership. The assignment of a limited partner's interest in a limited partnership does not cause a dissolution of the limited partnership. In some situations, the entire interest of the limited partner may be assigned, with the assignee becoming a substitute limited partner. An assignment that has the effect of admitting new limited partners to the limited partnership must be permissible under the limited partnership agreement, or it must be approved by the unanimous consent of all partners.

General partners also have certain rights to assign their interests in the limited partnership. A general partner may have all of the same rights of assignability as a limited partner, if permitted in the limited partnership agreement. In any event, the limited partnership offers much more flexibility with regard to the transfer of partnership interests than the general partnership.

BUSINESS CONTINUITY

The limited partnership does not enjoy the continuity of business to the same extent as a corporation, but it is not always necessary for a limited partnership to dissolve upon the death, retirement, or withdrawal of a partner.

A limited partner's death or incompetency does not dissolve the limited partnership. Instead, the deceased or incompetent partner's legal representative will continue to have that partner's right to withdraw from the limited partnership and to be compensated for the partnership interest.

The limited partnership will not necessarily dissolve upon the death or withdrawal of a general partner if at the time (1) there is at least one other general partner, (2) the written provisions of the partnership agreement permit the business of the limited partnership to be carried on by the remaining general partner, and (3) that partner does so. In any event, the limited partnership need not be dissolved and is not required to be wound up by reason of any event of withdrawal if, "within 90 days after the withdrawal, all partners agree in writing to continue the business of the limited partnership and to the appointment of one or more additional general partners if necessary or desired."[10]

DIVERSIFIED CAPITAL RESOURCES

In addition to the capital resources that are typically available to the general partnership, the limited partnership has the ability to raise cash by attracting passive investors. The limited partnership may raise additional capital when required by adding new limited partners.

Even with the increasing popularity of newer forms of business organizations, limited liability partnerships are still a popular choice for new business formations. During 2009, the state of Delaware formed 5,488 new limited partnerships.

IN SUMMATION

- There are several advantages to forming a limited partnership instead of a general partnership or other form of business organization, including:
  - Limited liability for limited partners
  - Income tax benefits
  - Relative ease of transferring interest in limited partnership
  - Continuity of business
  - Opportunity for diversified capital resources

§ 4.4 DISADVANTAGES OF DOING BUSINESS AS A LIMITED PARTNERSHIP

Although there are several advantages to doing business as a limited partnership, this type of entity also has some serious disadvantages. This section explains the disadvantages associated with operating as a limited partnership due to the unlimited liability of the general partners, the prohibition on control of the business by limited partners, the formalities and regulatory and reporting requirements, and the associated legal and organizational expenses.

UNLIMITED LIABILITY

Because limited partners put at risk only their investment in the limited partnership, a limited partnership cannot exist without at least one general partner who has unlimited liability for the debts and obligations of the limited partnership. As discussed in previous chapters, there are ways to decrease the impact of unlimited personal liability. However, because personal liability of the general partners cannot be totally eliminated, it is a serious drawback to doing business as a limited partnership.

PROHIBITION ON CONTROL OF BUSINESS

Although every partner is entitled to an equal share of the management of a general partnership, in states that follow the RULPA, limited partners must relinquish all control over partnership matters in order to maintain their status and enjoy limited liability. Limited partners must place their full trust in the general partners for the successful management and control of the business.

FORMALITIES AND REGULATORY AND REPORTING REQUIREMENTS

The limited partnership is a creature of statute and, as such, must be "created" by documentation filed with the proper state authority. A **limited partnership certificate** must be executed and filed before the limited partnership's existence begins. Therefore, more formalities are associated with the creation of a limited partnership than with a sole proprietorship or a general partnership. Limited partnerships are also subject to many of the same reporting requirements as corporations, including annual reporting with the secretary of state.

Limited partnerships may be required to register or qualify to do business as a foreign limited partnership in any state, other than their states of domicile, in which they propose to transact business. The registration or qualification requirements are set by the statutes of the state where the foreign limited partnership is proposing to transact business, and are often the same or similar to the requirements for foreign corporations transacting business in that state.[11] These requirements vary greatly from state to state, so the appropriate statutes must be consulted whenever a limited partnership is considering transacting business in a state other than its state of domicile. Foreign business organization qualification is discussed in Chapter 13 of this text.

In addition, limited partnerships are required to file annual tax returns to report any income or loss, and they are required to distribute annual schedules to each partner to report their distributive share of the limited partnership's income or loss.

LEGAL AND ORGANIZATIONAL EXPENSES

Compared with the sole proprietorship or general partnership, the legal and organizational expenses of a limited partnership can be quite substantial. In addition to the capital required for the ordinary expenses incurred in operating the limited partnership business, the founders of a limited partnership will usually incur significant legal fees for preparation of a limited partnership agreement and certificate, filing fees for the certificate of limited partnership, and possibly for filing a certificate of assumed name.

Exhibit 4-3 provides a comparison of the advantages and disadvantages of doing business as a limited partnership.

EXHIBIT 4-3	ADVANTAGES AND DISADVANTAGES OF DOING BUSINESS AS A LIMITED PARTNERSHIP

Advantages	Disadvantages
• *Limited Liability for Limited Partners.* Limited partners have no personal liability for the debts and obligations of the limited partnership.	• *General Partners Do Not Usually Have Limited Liability.* Every limited partnership must have at least one general partner who is personally liable for the debts and obligations of the limited partnership.
• *Income Tax Benefits.* Limited partnerships are not subject to federal income taxation. Income "flows through" to the partners.	• *Limited Partnerships May Be Subject to State Income Taxation in Some States.*
• *Transferability of Partnership Interest.* Compared with general partnerships, limited partners have much more freedom to transfer their interests in the limited partnership.	• *Prohibition on Control of Business.* Under most circumstances, limited partners cannot be involved in the management of the limited partnership.
• *Business Continuity.* In contrast to the general partnership or sole proprietorship, the limited partnership offers much more continuity of business.	• *Formalities and Regulatory and Reporting Requirements.* Limited partnerships cannot exist until the proper documentation is filed at the state level. In addition, limited partnerships may be subject to various reporting requirements that are not imposed on sole proprietorships and general partnerships.
• *Diversified Capital Resources.* Unlike sole proprietorships and general partnerships, limited partnerships have the ability to attract passive investors who accept no personal liability for the debts and obligations of the limited partnership.	• *Legal and Organizational Expense.* The legal and organizational expenses associated with forming and maintaining a limited partnership are typically considerably greater than those associated with partnerships and sole proprietorships.

IN SUMMATION

- There can be disadvantages to forming a limited partnership compared to other types of business organizations, including:
  - Unlimited personal liability for the general partners
  - Prohibition on limited partner management in some states
  - Several formalities and reporting requirements must be followed to form and operate a limited partnership
  - Legal and organizational expenses for forming a limited partnership can be substantial

§ 4.5 ORGANIZATION AND MANAGEMENT OF A LIMITED PARTNERSHIP

The organization and management of a limited partnership are unlike that of any other type of entity. This section discusses the management and control of the limited partnership by the general partners, the preparation and filing of the limited partnership certificate, and the contents of the limited partnership agreement.

MANAGEMENT AND CONTROL

The management and control of a limited partnership are similar to that of a general partnership, with one important distinction: in states that follow the RULPA, only the general partners of the limited partnership have control of the partnership business.

LIMITED PARTNERSHIP CERTIFICATE

The document that is filed with the secretary of state or other designated state authority to form the limited partnership is called the limited partnership certificate. This document may include the entire agreement between the partners, but more commonly it contains the minimum amount of information required by state statute, with the full agreement of the partners contained in a limited partnership agreement or in other documents that are not filed for public record.

Under the RULPA, many of the provisions concerning the management of the limited partnership may be included in the limited partnership agreement or records kept by the limited partnership. They need not be made public in the limited partnership certificate. In states that have adopted the RULPA, the certificate of limited partnership must include the following:

1. The name of the limited partnership
2. The office address and the name and address of the agent for service of process

3. The name and business address of each general partner
4. The latest date upon which the limited partnership is to dissolve
5. Any other matters the general partners desire to include in the certificate[12]

In states that follow the ULPA (2001), a statement in the limited partnership certificate concerning the latest date upon which the limited partnership is to dissolve is optional. Limited partnerships formed under the ULPA (2001) have a perpetual duration unless otherwise stated. Also, in states that follow the ULPA (2001), the certificate of limited partnership must indicate whether the limited partnership is a limited liability partnership.

The limited partnership certificate must be signed by the general partner(s) of the limited partnership and it must be filed with the appropriate state authority along with the required filing fee to be effective. In addition, any other filing requirements set forth in the state statutes must be complied with.

The limited partnership certificate in Exhibit 4-4 is an example of a limited partnership certificate that could be filed in a state that closely follows the RULPA. Exhibit 4-5 is a Certificate of Limited Partnership form that could be completed and filed in the state of Delaware.

EXHIBIT 4-4   LIMITED PARTNERSHIP CERTIFICATE

1. The name of the limited partnership is _____.

2. The office address of the principal place of business of the limited partnership is: _____.

3. The name and office address of the agent for service of process are: _____
   _____

4. The name and business address of each general partner are as follows:
   Name   Address

   _____   _____

   _____   _____

   _____   _____

5. The latest date upon which the limited partnership is to dissolve is
   _____, _____.

   Signed this _____ day of _____, _____.

   GENERAL PARTNERS:

   _____

EXHIBIT 4-5 CERTIFICATE OF LIMITED PARTNERSHIP FROM THE STATE OF DELAWARE

STATE OF DELAWARE
CERTIFICATE OF LIMITED PARTNERSHIP

- **The Undersigned,** desiring to form a limited partnership pursuant to the Delaware Revised Uniform Limited Partnership Act, 6 Delaware Code, Chapter 17, do hereby certify as follows:

- **First:** The name of the limited partnership is _____

  _____.

- **Second:** The address of its registered office in the State of Delaware is _____

  _____ in the city of _____.

  Zip code_____. The name of the Registered Agent at such address is

  _____.

- **Third:** The name and mailing address of each general partner is as follows:

- **In Witness Whereof,** the undersigned has executed this Certificate of Limited Partnership as of _____ day of _____, A.D. _____ .

  By:_____
  General Partner

  Name: _____
  (type or print name)

Delaware Division of Corporations

AMENDMENT TO LIMITED PARTNERSHIP CERTIFICATE

The RULPA sets forth events that necessitate the filing of an amendment to the limited partnership certificate and the requirements for the certificate of amendment itself.[13] In general, when any significant information that is included in the limited partnership certificate changes or when an error in the information on the limited partnership certificate is detected, an amendment must be filed. Under most circumstances, amendments to the limited partnership certificate must be approved and executed by all partners—both general and limited.

RECORDS REQUIRED BY STATUTE

Partly because so little information is required to be filed for the limited partnership certificate, state statutes typically require that certain records and documents be maintained for the inspection of limited partners. The following records are usually required to be kept at a designated partnership office:

1. A current list of the names and business addresses of all partners; this list must identify the general partners, in alphabetical order, and separately list, in alphabetical order, the limited partners
2. A copy of the certificate of limited partnership and all certificates of amendment thereto, together with executed copies of any powers of attorney pursuant to which any certificate has been executed
3. Copies of the limited partnership's federal, state, and local income tax returns and reports, if any, for the three most recent years
4. Copies of any effective written partnership agreements
5. Copies of any financial statements of the limited partnership for the three most recent years[14]

The following information must be set forth in documents kept at the partnership office, unless it is contained in the limited partnership agreement:

1. The amount of cash and a description and statement of the agreed value of any other property or services contributed by each partner and that each partner has agreed to contribute
2. The times at which, or events on the happening of which, any additional contributions agreed to be made by each partner are to be made
3. Any rights of partners to receive, or of a general partner to make, distributions, which include a return of all or any part of the partner's contribution
4. Any events upon the happening of which the limited partnership is to be dissolved and its affairs wound up[15]

These records must be kept and are subject to inspection and copying at the reasonable request and at the expense of any partner during ordinary business hours.

LIMITED PARTNERSHIP AGREEMENT

The limited partnership agreement should encompass the entire agreement among all partners. This document usually goes into much more detail than the limited partnership certificate because it is not a document of public record, and because it is more easily amended than the limited partnership certificate.

Following is a discussion of some of the various matters that should be contained in a limited partnership agreement. The examples used in the following sections are only a small representation of the type of paragraphs and clauses that may be included in a limited partnership agreement. See Appendix D of this text for a limited partnership agreement form.

Name of Limited Partnership

The full name of the limited partnership should be set forth in the limited partnership agreement. Special consideration must be given to the name of a limited partnership, for several reasons. First, the name chosen for the limited partnership must be available. The availability of a proposed name can usually be verified by checking the secretary of state's website or by calling the secretary of state's office. (See Appendix A of this text for a secretary of state directory.)

Second, state statutes may require that the name of the limited partnership contain the words "limited partnership," the abbreviation "L.P.," or other specific language. Finally, the inclusion of a limited partner's name in the name of the limited partnership may be prohibited in some states. The appropriate state statutes must be consulted to be certain that all requirements regarding the name of the limited partnership are complied with.

Names and Addresses of Partners and Designation of Partnership Status

The partnership agreement should contain the names and addresses of all partners and, most important, the designation as to which partners are general partners, which partners are limited partners, and which partners (if any) are both.

Purpose of Partnership

There are few statutory restrictions on the nature of business that may be carried on by a limited partnership. The RULPA provides that a limited partnership may carry on any business that can be transacted by a general partnership.[16] However, the statutes of some states may prohibit certain regulated industries, such as insurance or banking, from transacting business as a limited partnership.

This section of the limited partnership agreement should set forth the purpose of the limited partnership, without being restrictively specific.

EXAMPLE: Partnership Purpose—Generally

This limited partnership is formed for the purpose of _____ and all lawful purposes and activities incidental to that purpose. This purpose shall not be construed as limiting or restricting in any manner the limited partnership from conducting any other purposes or powers authorized under the laws of the State of _____ concerning limited partnerships.

Principal Place of Business

The address of the partnership's principal place of business should be set forth in the limited partnership agreement. This is important because certain documents are required by law to be kept at the principal place of business of the limited partnership.

Duration of Limited Partnership

The limited partnership agreement should include the intended duration of the limited partnership, as well as certain conditions that may cause the termination of the partnership.

Limited partnerships formed in states that follow the ULPA (2001) will have a perpetual duration unless otherwise indicated in the limited partnership certificate or agreement. In states following the RULPA, the latest date upon which the limited partnership is to dissolve must be set forth in the limited partnership certificate filed with the secretary of state.

EXAMPLE: Duration of Limited Partnership

The limited partnership shall commence on _____, 20____, and shall continue for a period of five (5) years ending on _____, 20____. The duration of the limited partnership may be continued upon the written agreement of all partners for such extended period of time as the partners may agree.

The limited partnership may be terminated prior to the end of such prescribed period of time by _____ months' notice in writing from any partner desiring to withdraw from the limited partnership and requesting the partnership's termination. All partnership obligations shall be discharged during the notice period and prior to the effective date of the limited partnership termination.

Contributions of Both General and Limited Partners

This very important section of the agreement should set forth the partners' agreement regarding all contributions to the limited partnership, including the form of each contribution, any interest to be paid on contributions, any adjustment provisions for contributions, any additional contribution requirements, and the time when contributions are to be returned to limited partners. This section should also set forth any rights of partners to demand property in lieu of cash for a return of contribution.

EXAMPLE: Capital Contribution of General Partner

General partner shall contribute $____ to the original capital of the partnership. The contribution of general partner shall be made on or before [date]. If general partner does not make [his or her] entire contribution to the capital of the partnership on or before that date, this agreement shall be void. Any contributions to the capital of the partnership made at that time shall be returned to the partners who have made the contributions.[17]

EXAMPLE: Capital Contributions of Limited Partners

The capital contributions of limited partners shall be as follows:

Name	Amount
_____	$_____
_____	$_____
_____	$_____

Receipt of the capital contribution from each limited partner as specified above is acknowledged by the partnership. No limited partner has agreed to contribute any additional cash or property as capital for use of the partnership.[18]

Assets of Limited Partnership

Important information regarding the assets of the limited partnership should be included in the limited partnership agreement, including identification, valuation, control, and distribution of assets, and accountability therefor.

EXAMPLE: Distribution of Assets—Return of Contribution Plus Increment on Dissolution

The contribution of each limited partner, increased by any gains and not withdrawn or decreased by losses, is to be returned on the termination of the partnership in accordance with the terms of Section _____, or on any earlier dissolution of the partnership if caused by the death, retirement, or insanity of a general partner, provided, however, that at any such time all liabilities of the partnership, except liabilities to general partners and to limited partners on account of their contributions, shall have been paid, and that there shall then remain property of the partnership sufficient to make such return.[19]

EXAMPLE: Distribution of Assets—Proration if Assets Insufficient

If the property remaining following the payment of all liabilities of the partnership is not sufficient to repay in full all the partners' (general and limited) contributions adjusted to reflect accumulated gains or losses, then each of the partners shall receive such proportion of the remaining property as his, her, or their respective contribution as adjusted shall bear to the aggregate of all such adjusted partnership contributions that have not been repaid. In such event, limited partners shall not have any further claim against the partners for the return of the balance of their contributions or credited gains.[20]

Liability

This section of the agreement should contain all provisions regarding the liability of general and limited partners to one another and to third parties.

EXAMPLE: Liability to Third Party—Limitation of Liability

Notwithstanding any other provision contained in this agreement, except to have a limited partner's capital account charged for losses to be borne by the limited partner as provided in this agreement, no limited partner shall have any personal responsibility whatever for or on account of any losses or liabilities of the partnership. To the extent that losses and liabilities of the partnership exceed its assets, the losses shall be borne solely by the general partners.[21]

Distribution of Profits and Losses to General and Limited Partners

The terms and conditions for distributions from the partnership, including restrictions on distributions and distributions made to various classes of partners, should be documented in the limited partnership agreement.

EXAMPLE: Profit and Loss Sharing by Limited Partners

The limited partners shall receive the following shares of the net profits of the partnership:

Name   Amount

_____   _____

_____   _____

_____   _____

Each limited partner shall bear a share of the losses of the partnership equal to the share of the profits to which the partner is entitled. The share of the losses of each limited partner shall be charged against the partner's contribution to the capital of the partnership.

No limited partner shall at any time become liable to any obligations or losses of the partnership beyond the amount of the partner's respective capital contribution.[22]

Indemnity

The partners' agreement for indemnification of their expenses on behalf of the partnership should be set forth in the limited partnership agreement.

Duties of General Partners

The limited partnership agreement should establish the duties of each general partner in as much detail as practical.

EXAMPLE: Duties of General Partners

The general partners shall at all times during the continuance of this partnership diligently and exclusively devote themselves to the business of the partnership to the utmost of their skills and abilities, and on a full-time basis. The general partners shall not engage, either directly or indirectly, in any business similar to the business of the partnership at any time during the term of this agreement without obtaining the written approval of all other parties.

Duties of Limited Partners

This section of the limited partnership agreement should set forth the duties of the limited partners, with careful attention given to the duties of any limited partners who are employees of the limited partnership. This section should be carefully drafted so that no misunderstanding arises regarding the inability of limited partners to control the partnership business in states where limited partner management participation is prohibited.

Limited Partners' Rights of Substitution

The limited partnership agreement should include the desired rights of partners to substitution, including the right to admit additional limited partners and priorities of certain limited partners over others.

EXAMPLE: Powers of Partners—Assignment of Limited Partner's Interest

A limited partner's interest shall be assignable in whole or in part. A limited partner may confer the rights of a substituted limited partner upon the assignee of his or her interests.

Compensation and Benefits for Partners

All matters concerning the compensation of and benefits for general partners, including salaries, bonuses, retirement benefits, health and other insurance, and so forth, should be set forth in the limited partnership agreement.

EXAMPLE: Salary of General Partner

General partner shall be entitled to a monthly salary of $_____ for the services rendered. The salary shall commence on [date], and be payable on the _____ day of each month. The salary shall be treated as a partnership expense and shall be payable whether or not the partnership is operating at a profit.

Management and Control of Business by General Partners

The management and control section of the limited partnership agreement should document the management policies of the limited partnership.

EXAMPLE: Limited Partners' Participation in Control of the Limited Partnership

No limited partner shall have any right to participate in the control of the limited partnership business, or have the power to bind the limited partnership in any contract, agreement, promise, or undertaking.

Limited Partnership Business Policies

Any policies that the partners desire to set forth in a written agreement may be set forth in the limited partnership agreement, along with the limited partnership's policy with regard to the limited partners' rights to review the business policies of the partnership.

Accounting Practices and Procedures

The accounting methods, practices, and policies of the partnership, including the accounting period and fiscal year of the partnership, the frequency and types of reports to be completed, details regarding the books of accounts, audit provisions, and provisions for examination of books, should all be set forth in the limited partnership agreement.

Changes in General or Limited Partners by Withdrawal, Expulsion, Retirement, or Death

The partners should set forth their desires regarding the admission of new general and limited partners, their acceptance requirements, and the redistribution of assets in the limited partnership agreement. This section should also address all matters concerning withdrawing partners, including the necessity of the consent of the other partners, notice requirements, valuation of the withdrawing partner's share of the partnership, the option of the remaining partners to purchase the interest, and the assignment of the withdrawing partner's interest to a third party. Partners may also want to include conditions and procedures for expulsion of a partner, including notice requirements.

The partnership's policy regarding a retiring partner should likewise be addressed in this section, including the reorganization of partnership rights and duties.

EXAMPLE: New Limited Partner

Amendments to the certificate of limited partnership of the partnership for the purpose of substituting a limited partner will be validly made if signed only by the general partners and by the person to be substituted and by the assigning limited partner. If any one or all general partners resign or are expelled or otherwise cease to be a general partner under the provision of this agreement, and pursuant to this agreement a new general partner or partners are elected, the amendment to the certificate to make the change will be validly made if signed only by the remaining general partner and the new general partner or by the new general partners.[23]

EXAMPLE: Expulsion of Partner by Vote of Limited Partners

On the vote of limited partners holding a majority in interest of the partnership, a general partner may be expelled as a general partner of the partnership and a new general partner may be elected by the same vote.[24]

Sale or Purchase of Limited Partnership Interest

The limited partnership agreement should set forth the partners' agreement with regard to the sale of new limited partners' interests, either to replace a withdrawing limited partner or to add new limited partners to raise additional capital for the partnership. Provisions for the purchase of a withdrawing limited partner's interest by the limited partnership should also be included.

Termination of Limited Partnership

Provisions for the termination of the limited partnership should be included in the limited partnership agreement.

Dissolution and Winding Up

The limited partnership agreement should include provisions for the dissolution and winding up of the limited partnership, including the settlement and distribution of partnership assets.

EXAMPLE: Winding Up—Distribution of Assets

On the dissolution or termination of the partnership, after the liabilities shall have been paid, payment shall be made to the partners in the following order: (1) to the limited partners the sums to which they are entitled by way of interest on their capital contributions and their share of profits; (2) to the limited partners the amount of their capital contributions; (3) to the general partners such sums as may be due, if any other than for capital and profits; (4) to the general partners the amount they are entitled to receive as interest on their capital contributions and as profits; and (5) to the general partners for their capital contributions.[25]

Date of Agreement and Signatures

The limited partnership agreement should be dated and signed by all partners, both general and limited.

IN SUMMATION

- A limited partnership certificate setting forth certain details must be filed with the secretary of state or other designated state authority to form a limited partnership.
- State statues generally require certain documents and information to be maintained at the designated partnership office for inspection by any partner.
- The limited partnership agreement includes the full agreement among the limited partnership partners—both general and limited.
- The limited partnership agreement should be dated, signed by all partners, and kept on file with the limited partnership records.
- The limited partnership agreement need not be filed with any state authority.

§ 4.6 CHANGES IN THE LIMITED PARTNERSHIP

Changes in the limited partnership can affect its continuance. This section examines the effects of common changes on the limited partnership, including the admission of new general partners, the admission of new limited partners, and the withdrawal of both general and limited partners.

ADMISSION OF NEW GENERAL PARTNERS

The requirements for admitting new general partners vary from state to state. In most states, general partners may be admitted with the written consent of all partners, or by another means set forth in the limited partnership agreement.

ADMISSION OF NEW LIMITED PARTNERS

In states following the RULPA, an additional limited partner may be admitted in compliance with the provisions of the limited partnership agreement. If such an event is not provided for in the limited partnership agreement, an additional limited partner may be admitted by the written consent of all partners.[26] Amendment of the limited partnership certificate is not necessary because the names of the limited partners are not required to be set forth in the limited partnership certificate. The assignee of a limited partner's interest in a limited partnership may become a limited partner to the extent that the assignor gives the assignee that right, and if all other partners consent.

WITHDRAWAL OF GENERAL PARTNERS

As with the general partnership, the death or withdrawal of a general partner generally causes the dissolution of a limited partnership. However, the limited partnership may continue after the death or withdrawal of a general partner if, at the time of the withdrawal, there is at least one other general partner and the written provisions of the partnership agreement permit the continuance of the limited partnership under the circumstances.

A general partner may withdraw from a limited partnership at any time by giving written notice to the other partners. However, if a general partner withdraws from the partnership in violation of the terms of the limited partnership agreement, the limited partnership may recover damages from the withdrawing partner for breach of the partnership agreement, and those damages may be used to offset any distribution to which the withdrawing general partner is otherwise entitled.

WITHDRAWAL OF LIMITED PARTNERS

The limited partnership is not dissolved upon the death or withdrawal of a limited partner. In the event of the death of a limited partner, the executor, representative, or administrator of the deceased limited partner's estate succeeds to all of the decedent's rights for the purpose of settling the estate.

Unless otherwise indicated in the limited partnership agreement, a limited partner may generally withdraw from the limited partnership at any time with six months' notice to each general partner.[27]

The withdrawing partner is entitled to receive the distribution as set forth in the limited partnership agreement. Pursuant to the RULPA, if the amount of distribution is not provided for in the limited partnership agreement, the withdrawing partner is entitled to receive the fair value of his or her interest in the limited partnership based upon his or her right to share in distributions from the limited partnership.[28]

The distribution to which each partner is entitled under the partnership agreement will be in cash, unless otherwise indicated in the partnership agreement.

IN SUMMATION

- In most states, unless the limited partnership agreement provides otherwise, new general partners may be admitted with the written consent of all partners.

- The limited partnership agreement typically provides for the admission of additional limited partners with the written consent of all partners.

- While the death or withdrawal of a general partner may cause the dissolution of a limited partnership, the limited partnership may continue if there is at least one other general partner and the partnership agreement provides for the continuance under the circumstances.

- The death or withdrawal of a limited partner does not dissolve the limited partnership.

§ 4.7 FINANCIAL STRUCTURE OF A LIMITED PARTNERSHIP

The financial structure of a limited partnership is typically more complex than that of either a sole proprietorship or a general partnership. This section focuses on the capital of the limited partnership, limited partnership profits and losses, and distributions from the limited partnership.

PARTNERSHIP CAPITAL CONTRIBUTIONS

A basic concept of the limited partnership is that a limited partner must "make a stated contribution to the partnership and place it at risk."[29] The limited partners' contribution may be in the form of cash, property, or services. In addition, the RULPA specifically states that the contributions may be in the form of a "promissory note or other obligation to contribute cash or property or perform services."[30] Any promise made by a limited partner to contribute to the limited partnership must be in writing to be enforceable.

LIMITED PARTNERSHIP PROFITS AND LOSSES

The profits and losses of the limited partnership derived from the contributions and efforts of the partners are shared among the partners pursuant to the partnership agreement or certificate. Section 503 of the RULPA provides that the profits and losses of a limited partnership shall be allocated among the partners in the manner provided in writing in the partnership agreement. If the partnership agreement does not specify a manner for allocation, profits and losses will be allocated on the basis of the value, as stated in the partnership records, of the contributions made by each partner.

LIMITED PARTNERSHIP DISTRIBUTIONS

The profits of the limited partnership are reinvested in the limited partnership or disbursed to the limited partners and general partners as specified in the limited partnership agreement. The agreement may provide for mandatory distributions to the limited partners, or it may give very broad discretion to the general partners to determine if and when profits will be disbursed. However, there are certain statutory restrictions on the withdrawal of contributions. Under the RULPA, distributions to partners are forbidden to the extent that, after the distributions are made, the partnership liabilities exceed the fair value of the partnership assets. This law prohibits the limited partnership from making distributions to the partners in priority of outside creditors. The limited partnership may not distribute all of its assets to its partners if there is not enough cash to meet its liabilities. For example, if the limited partnership had assets of $10,000 and liabilities of $6,000, distributions to the partners may not be made in excess of $4,000.

The partners will owe income tax on the amount allocated to them, whether that amount was actually distributed to them or reinvested in the limited partnership. Often, the limited partnership agreement will be drafted to provide that all partners will receive an annual distribution from the limited partnership that is at least equal to their income tax liability generated by allocations to them from the limited partnership. This minimum distribution will ensure that partners will have the ability to meet their limited partnership income tax liability each year. As discussed previously in this chapter, if a loss from the limited partnership is allocated to the partners, the partners may use that loss to offset other income and reduce their personal income tax liability.

Income Tax Reporting

The limited partnership's income is reported to the Internal Revenue Service on a Form 1065 Partnership Return in the same manner that a general partnership's income is reported. The limited partnership itself is not subject to income taxation at the federal level. Rather, the general and limited partners pay income tax on their allocation of the limited partnership's income, as reported on the Schedule K-1 filed with their personal income tax returns. A blank Schedule K-1 is shown as Exhibit 4-6.

IN SUMMATION

- Limited partners must make a contribution to the limited partnership and put it at risk.

- Partnership profits and losses are allocated to the partners pursuant to the limited partnership agreement.

- Distributions of profit may be made to the partners so long as there is enough cash to meet the partnership's obligations to outside creditors.

- The limited partnership must report its income to the Internal Revenue Service on a Form 1065 Partnership Return.

- General and limited partners must pay income tax on the limited partnership income that is allocated to them as reported on their Schedule K-1s.

§ 4.8 LIMITED PARTNERSHIP DISSOLUTION, WINDING UP, AND TERMINATION

The process of terminating a limited partnership involves several steps. This section investigates the termination process, including the distinction between limited partnership dissolution and winding up, the causes of dissolution, cancellation of the limited partnership certificate, winding up the affairs of the limited partnership, and settlement and distribution of the assets of the limited partnership.

EXHIBIT 4-6 SCHEDULE K-1

651110

☐ Final K-1   ☐ Amended K-1   OMB No. 1545-0099

**Schedule K-1
(Form 1065)**

2010

Department of the Treasury
Internal Revenue Service

For calendar year 2010, or tax
year beginning _____, 2010
ending _____, 20 _____

**Partner's Share of Income, Deductions,
Credits, etc.**   ▶ See back of form and separate instructions.

Part I   Information About the Partnership

A   Partnership's employer identification number

B   Partnership's name, address, city, state, and ZIP code

C   IRS Center where partnership filed return

D   ☐ Check if this is a publicly traded partnership (PTP)

Part II   Information About the Partner

E   Partner's identifying number

F   Partner's name, address, city, state, and ZIP code

G   ☐ General partner or LLC   ☐ Limited partner or other LLC
      member-manager   member

H   ☐ Domestic partner   ☐ Foreign partner

I   What type of entity is this partner? _____

J   Partner's share of profit, loss, and capital (see instructions):

	Beginning	Ending
Profit	%	%
Loss	%	%
Capital	%	%

K   Partner's share of liabilities at year end:
     Nonrecourse . . . . $ _____
     Qualified nonrecourse financing . $ _____
     Recourse . . . . $ _____

L   Partner's capital account analysis:
     Beginning capital account . . . $ _____
     Capital contributed during the year $ _____
     Current year increase (decrease) . $ _____
     Withdrawals & distributions . . . $ (_____)
     Ending capital account . . . . . $ _____

     ☐ Tax basis   ☐ GAAP   ☐ Section 704(b) book
     ☐ Other (explain)

M   Did the partner contribute property with a built-in gain or loss?
     ☐ Yes   ☐ No
        If "Yes", attach statement (see instructions)

**Part III   Partner's Share of Current Year Income,
Deductions, Credits, and Other Items**

1	Ordinary business income (loss)	15	Credits
2	Net rental real estate income (loss)		
3	Other net rental income (loss)	16	Foreign transactions
4	Guaranteed payments		
5	Interest income		
6a	Ordinary dividends		
6b	Qualified dividends		
7	Royalties		
8	Net short-term capital gain (loss)		
9a	Net long-term capital gain (loss)	17	Alternative minimum tax (AMT) items
9b	Collectibles (28%) gain (loss)		
9c	Unrecaptured section 1250 gain		
10	Net section 1231 gain (loss)	18	Tax-exempt income and nondeductible expenses
11	Other income (loss)		
12	Section 179 deduction	19	Distributions
13	Other deductions	20	Other information
14	Self-employment earnings (loss)		

*See attached statement for additional information.

For IRS Use Only

For Paperwork Reduction Act Notice, see Instructions for Form 1065.   Cat. No. 11394R   Schedule K-1 (Form 1065) 2010

DISSOLUTION VERSUS WINDING UP

As with the general partnership, once a limited partnership has been dissolved, the partnership does not terminate until the affairs of the limited partnership have been wound up.

CAUSES OF DISSOLUTION

In states following the RULPA, a limited partnership is dissolved, and its affairs must be wound up, when one of the following events first occurs:

1. The time period specified in the certificate expires.
2. Specific events documented in the certificate occur.
3. All the partners consent in writing to dissolve the partnership.
4. An event of withdrawal of a general partner occurs.
5. A decree of judicial dissolution is entered.[31]

An event of withdrawal, as that term is used in the RULPA, refers to:

1. The general partner's voluntary withdrawal
2. Assignment of the general partner's interest
3. Removal of the general partner in accordance with the partnership agreement
4. Certain transactions evidencing the general partner's insolvency (unless otherwise provided in the certificate of limited partnership)
5. In the case of a general partner who is an individual, the partner's death or an adjudication that the partner is incompetent to manage his or her person or estate
6. In the case of a general partner acting as such by virtue of being the trustee of a trust, the termination of the trust
7. In the case of a general partner that is a separate partnership, its dissolution and the commencement of its winding up
8. In the case of a general partner that is a corporation, the filing of a certificate of its dissolution (or the equivalent) or the revocation of its charter
9. In the case of an estate, the distribution by the fiduciary of the estate's entire interest in the partnership[32]

An event of withdrawal does not cause dissolution if there is at least one other general partner and the certificate of limited partnership allows continuation under the circumstances, or if within 90 days after such an event, all partners agree in writing to continue the business. If all partners agree to continue the business, they may appoint one or more additional general partners, if necessary or desirable.

State statutes usually provide that a limited partner may apply for a court decree to dissolve a limited partnership whenever it is not reasonably practical to carry on the business of the limited partnership in conformity with the partnership agreement.

CANCELLATION OF CERTIFICATE OF LIMITED PARTNERSHIP

Because a limited partnership is created by a certificate of limited partnership that is filed with the secretary of state or other state authority, the certificate must be canceled to terminate the limited partnership. The certificate of limited partnership is canceled upon the dissolution of the limited partnership and the commencement of its winding up, or at any other time that there are no limited partners. The certificate is canceled by means of a certificate of cancellation, which is filed with the secretary of state and must contain:

1. The name of the limited partnership
2. The date of filing of the certificate of limited partnership
3. The reason for filing the certificate of cancellation
4. The effective date of cancellation, if not effective upon filing the certificate
5. Any other information determined by the general partners filing the certificate[33]

The certificate must be signed by all general partners.

Exhibit 4-7 is a sample of a form that may be filed in the state of Delaware to cancel a limited partnership certificate.

WINDING UP

Under the RULPA, "the general partners who have not wrongfully dissolved a limited partnership or, if none, the limited partners, may wind up the limited partnership's affairs."[34] Any partner or any partner's legal representative or assignee may also make application to an appropriate court to wind up the limited partnership's affairs.

SETTLEMENT AND DISTRIBUTION OF ASSETS

State statutes provide the means for distributing the assets of the limited partnership upon dissolution. In most states, assets of a dissolving limited partnership are paid out until they are exhausted, in the following order:

1. To the creditors, including any partners who are creditors, to satisfy liabilities of the limited partnership (other than liabilities for distributions to partners)
2. To partners to satisfy any distributions due to them under the partnership agreement
3. To partners as a return of their contributions
4. To partners as a return of their partnership interest in the same proportions in which the partners share distributions

Partners (except partners who are creditors of the limited partnership) will not receive a distribution from the partnership unless the limited partnership's assets are sufficient to pay all creditors.

EXHIBIT 4-7 CERTIFICATE OF CANCELLATION

STATE OF DELAWARE
CERTIFICATE OF CANCELLATION OF
CERTIFICATE OF LIMITED PARTNERSHIP

The limited partnership organized under the Delaware Revised Uniform Limited Partnership Act (the "Act"), for the purpose of canceling the Certificate of Limited Partnership pursuant to Section 17-203 of the Act, hereby certifies that:

1. The name of the limited partnership is _____
_____ (the "Partnership").

2. The Certificate of Limited Partnership was filed in the   Office of the Secretary of State of the State of Delaware on_____.

3. This Certificate of Cancellation shall become effective_____.

IN WITNESS WHEREOF, the undersigned, constituting the general partner(s) of the partnership has executed this Certificate of Cancellation as of the _____ day of _____, A.D._____.

By:_____
General Partner(s)
or
Liquidating Trustee(s)

Name:_____
Print or Type

Delaware Division of Corporations

IN SUMMATION

- State statutes, the limited partnership certificate, or the limited partnership agreement may specify when the dissolution of the limited partnership will occur.
- Because the limited partnership is formed by filing a certificate with the secretary of state's office, that certificate must be cancelled or withdrawn when the limited partnership dissolves.
- The affairs of the limited partnership may be wound up by any general partner not wrongfully causing the dissolution of the limited partnership.
- The assets of a dissolving limited partnership must be paid out in the following priority:
  - To creditors
  - To partners to satisfy any distributions due to them under the limited partnership agreement
  - To partners as a return of their contribution
  - To partners as a return of their partnership interest in the same proportions in which the partners share distributions

§ 4.9 DERIVATIVE ACTIONS

DERIVATIVE ACTION

With regard to a limited partnership, a derivative action is a lawsuit by a limited partner against another person or entity to enforce claims the limited partner thinks the limited partnership has against that person. Limited partners may bring derivative actions in some states if the general partner(s) refuse to bring the action. Derivative actions by limited partnerships are not allowed in all states.

A derivative action is a type of lawsuit usually brought by a shareholder to enforce a claim of the corporation. A **derivative action** may also be brought by a limited partner in the right of a limited partnership to recover a judgment in its favor. The RULPA expressly grants limited partners the right to bring an action on behalf of the limited partnership if the general partners with authority have refused to bring an action or if an effort to cause those general partners to bring the action is not likely to succeed. A derivative action may be needed when the general partner to the partnership has a conflict of interest that would prevent or discourage the general partner from bringing an action on behalf of the limited partnership.

In states where such suits are permitted, an interested limited partner may pursue a derivative action on behalf of the limited partnership when the injury is primarily to the limited partnership and only indirectly to the limited partners. The cause of action accrues to the limited partnership. For example, suppose that a limited partnership is formed for the purpose of purchasing a property and developing it into a shopping mall. If the contractor hired by the general partner acts fraudulently, causing the limited partnership to sustain a loss, a limited partner could bring a derivative action on behalf of the limited partnership if the general partner refuses to bring suit against the contractor he hired. The limited partnership itself has sustained damages through loss of income. The limited partner bringing the suit has been injured because of that loss.

Derivative actions are not accepted or permitted in all states. The statutes of a few jurisdictions hold that only a general partner may maintain an action on behalf of the partnership, leaving the limited partner to pursue redress of any wrong through dissolution or individual action against the wrongdoer.

IN SUMMATION

- A derivative action is a type of lawsuit brought by a limited partner on behalf of the limited partnership.

- Requirements for bringing a derivative action on behalf of a limited partnership are specifically set forth in the statutes of some states.

- Derivative actions on behalf of limited partnerships are not permitted in all states.

§ 4.10 FAMILY LIMITED PARTNERSHIPS

A family limited partnership is just what the name implies—a limited partnership owned and operated by a family. Most often, the family limited partnership is established by individuals who are concerned about protecting their assets and transferring them to their children with the least amount of income and estate tax liability. Typically, the parents will establish the limited partnership as both general and limited partners. They will fund the family limited partnership with assets of a family business or family investments. The parents then give their children gifts of the interests in the limited partnership as limited partners. As general partners, the parents retain the exclusive right to manage the limited partnership.

Assets held in a family limited partnership can be protected from the claims of creditors and others. A partner's interest in a limited partnership is considered to be personal property. The partnership property is owned by the family limited partnership, not by the individual partners. Creditors who have a judgment against a limited partner may seize cash or assets that have been distributed out of the partnership to the limited partner. However, creditors may not take family limited partnership property to fulfill an obligation to them unless the partnership is dissolved. Typically, the dissolution of the family limited partnership requires the unanimous consent of all partners.

The family limited partnership allows parents the flexibility to manage the business or their assets by retaining control as general partners, while gradually transferring the responsibilities and ownership to their children. In addition, parents who are general partners of the family limited partnership can give their children the benefit of owning a piece of the business, while still ensuring that their interests will not be transferred to others outside the family—at least not until after their deaths. The family limited partnership can be established to provide that new limited partners can only be admitted with the unanimous consent of all partners.

The family limited partnership can be used to reduce the amount of estate taxes paid when transferring wealth from one generation to the next. By gifting shares in the limited partnership equal to the annual gift tax exclusion to each child each year, parents can reduce the size of their estates on their deaths, while gradually transferring the limited partnership to their children.

SIDEBAR

State statutes do not provide for "family limited partnerships." A family limited partnership (FLP) is simply a limited partnership formed under state statute by a family.

IN SUMMATION

- A family limited partnership is a limited partnership that is typically formed to move wealth or a family business from one generation to the next.

§ 4.11 THE PARALEGAL'S ROLE

The role of the paralegal in working with limited partnerships is similar to that in working with general partnerships, with a few additions. Paralegals are often responsible for drafting and filing limited partnership documents, for researching limited partnership law, and for assisting limited partnership clients to comply with other formalities for forming and operating their businesses. Specifically, paralegals are often asked to perform or assist with the following tasks related to limited partnerships:

- Research state law concerning requirements for forming a limited partnership
- Research possible licensing requirements for the limited partnership business
- Research state law concerning the role of limited partners and restrictions on their participation in the management of the limited partnership
- Prepare limited partnership certificate
- Assist with drafting the limited partnership agreement
- Request federal tax identification number and state tax identification number (if required)
- Prepare and file a certificate of assumed or fictitious name for limited partnership (if applicable)
- Establish and organize a method for retaining limited partnership records
- Assist with drafting minutes of limited partnership meetings
- Prepare any required amendments to the limited partnership certificate and agreement
- Assist with preparation of the limited partnership's income tax return and schedule K-1s for the partners
- Assist with winding up and dissolution of the limited partnership

Paralegals are often asked to help draft the limited partnership agreement, usually with the aid of office forms and examples of previously drafted limited partnership agreements. Following is a checklist of items to be considered when drafting a limited partnership agreement.

Limited Partnership Agreement Checklist

- ☐ Name and address of each limited partner and each general partner and a designation of partnership status

- ☐ Name of the limited partnership

- ☐ Purpose of the limited partnership

- ☐ Address of principal place of business of the limited partnership

- ☐ Duration of limited partnership

- ☐ Contributions of both general partners and limited partners

- ☐ Limited partnership assets

- ☐ Liability of general partners and limited partners to each other and third parties

- ☐ Distribution of profits and losses to general and limited partners

- ☐ Indemnification of partners

- ☐ Duties of general partners

- ☐ Duties of limited partners

- ☐ Limited partners' rights of substitution

- ☐ Limitations on limited partners' rights to participate in the control of management of the partnership business

- ☐ General partner compensation

- ☐ Partnership expenses

- ☐ Management and control of business by general partners

- ☐ Limited partners' rights in review of business policies

- ☐ Business policies

- ☐ Accounting practices and procedures

- ☐ Changes in general or limited partners by withdrawal, expulsion, retirement, or death

- ☐ Sale or purchase of limited partnership interest

- ☐ Arbitration provisions

- ☐ Termination of limited partnership

- ☐ Dissolution and winding up

- ☐ Date of agreement

- ☐ Signatures of all general and limited partners

The paralegal may also be responsible for filing the limited partnership certificate pursuant to state statutes. If there are any publication or county recording requirements for the limited partnership certificate, it is often the paralegal's responsibility to see that those requirements are complied with as well.

The paralegal must be well acquainted with the state statutory requirements for limited partnerships, as well as the procedural requirements at the state level. In addition, the paralegal must be aware of any requirements for qualifying the limited partnership as a foreign limited partnership in other states in which the limited partnership intends to transact business.

CORPORATE PARALEGAL PROFILE
Patricia E. Rodgers

I thoroughly enjoy working with clients and the challenge of always learning about new law-related topics.

NAME Patricia E. Rodgers
LOCATION Hartford, Connecticut
TITLE Corporate Paralegal
SPECIALTY Corporate
EDUCATION Associate Degree from Bryant University
EXPERIENCE 33 Years

Patricia Rodgers is a corporate paralegal who has worked extensively with limited partnerships over the years. Limited partnership law is one of her specialties at Murtha Cullina LLP, a large law firm with offices in Hartford, New Haven, and Stamford, Connecticut; Boston and Woburn, Massachusetts; and Bedford, New Hampshire.

Murtha Cullina LLP has acted as local counsel to a large New York real estate syndicate that formed hundreds of limited partnerships in Connecticut. Patricia has been responsible for assisting with all aspects of the formation of the limited partnerships, as well as preparing voting rights and financing opinions and restructuring the entities.

continues

CORPORATE PARALEGAL PROFILE
Patricia E. Rodgers (continued)

In addition to limited partnerships, Patricia works with entities of all types, including corporations, limited liability companies, and limited liability partnerships. Her responsibilities include the formation and dissolution of business entities, mergers and acquisitions, corporate financings, qualifications of foreign entities, formation of nonstock corporations, and preparation of state and federal tax forms. She reports to the chairman of Murtha Cullina's Corporate Department.

Patricia enjoys working with clients and the challenge of learning about new law-related topics. One of Patricia's favorite areas is mergers and acquisitions, which sometimes involves travel and long, hard days of work (including weekends and all-nighters). To Patricia, the satisfaction and rewards associated with the successful completion of a transaction make all the hard work worthwhile.

Although Patricia enjoys a challenge, she admits that working for several different attorneys and clients can sometimes be frustrating. She does not enjoy being torn in many different directions at the same time. Planning her day can be challenging, when one of the lawyers or a client has a need requiring her immediate attention.

Patricia has used her corporate expertise to provide some pro bono services to the National Kidney Foundation of Connecticut, and Connecticut Self-Advocates for Mental Health, Inc. Patricia was recognized by both organizations for her outstanding service. She has also assisted with the formation of Avon Education Association, Inc. Patricia was one of the founders of the Central Connecticut Association of Legal Assistants (now known as Central Connecticut Paralegal Association, Inc.) in 1982, and she has been very active since its incorporation. She has served as vice president, chair of the Constitution and Bylaws Committee, Public Relations Chair, Connecticut Alliance Chair, Legislative Committee Chair, and NFPA Primary and Secondary Representative. She has been a member of the Central Connecticut Paralegal Association's NFPA National Affairs Committee for approximately 26 years.

Patricia's advice to new paralegals?

Work hard; be open to suggestions; do not turn down work if at all possible; try to be pleasant at all times; do not be afraid to admit that you have made a mistake; and most of all—be a team player.

For more information on careers for corporate paralegals, log in to http://cengagebrain.com to access the CourseMate website that accompanies this text; then see the Corporate Careers Section.

ETHICAL CONSIDERATION

The attorney-client privilege, which is found in evidence law, is closely related to the ethical rules of confidentiality. The attorney-client privilege provides that an attorney may not be called on to testify concerning confidential information learned during the representation of a client. The attorney-client

continues

ETHICAL CONSIDERATION
(continued)

privilege will apply to communications between the client and the attorney or between the client and the attorney's agents (including paralegals). Communications subject to the attorney-client privilege must be made in a confidential setting for the purpose of securing legal advice or assistance. Again, the purpose of the attorney-client privilege is to encourage free and open communication between the client and the attorney without the client having to worry that information given in confidence can later be used against him or her.

To protect the attorney-client privilege, you will want to be sure that all confidential conversations take place in a private setting where those conversations cannot be overheard by a third party.

The work-product rule also protects confidential client information. This rule most often comes into play during discovery. Discovery is the exchange of information between the parties to a lawsuit prior to trial. The work-product rule provides that the attorney's work product in preparation of a possible trial is not subject to discovery. The attorney need not turn over his or her personal notes or pre-trial work during the discovery process. Those documents are subject to the work-product rule.

Paralegals, including corporate paralegals, are sometimes charged with the responsibility of responding to requests for discovery. This may mean producing photocopies of numerous documents on behalf of a client. If you are given that responsibility, you must be sure that you do not turn over documents that fall under the work-product rule. You will always want to carefully review any documents that are produced during discovery to ensure that no documents subject to the work-product rule are inadvertently produced. In fact, courts have found that if confidential documents are not handled with proper care, the work-product rule may not apply.

For more information on ethics for corporate paralegals, including links to the NALA and NFPA codes of ethics, log in to http://cengagebrain.com to access the CourseMate website that accompanies this text; then see the Ethics Section.

§ 4.12 RESOURCES

Numerous resources are available to the paralegal working with limited partnerships. This section lists some of the more important resources, including state statutes, legal form books, and information available from the office of the secretary of state, state and local government offices, and the Internal Revenue Service.

STATE STATUTES

It is always important to be familiar with the state statutes of the limited partnership's state of domicile. Exhibit 4-8 is a list of the statutory citations of the limited partnership acts that have been adopted in each state. Links to those statutes may also be found at the CourseMate website that accompanies this text.

EXHIBIT 4-8	STATUTORY CITATIONS OF THE LIMITED PARTNERSHIP ACTS BY STATE	

State	Code	Version of Uniform Act Adopted
Alabama	Ala. Code §§ 10A-9-1.01 through 10A-9-12.08	ULPA (2001)
Alaska	Alaska Stat. §§32.11.010 through 32.11.990	RULPA
Arizona	Ariz. Rev. Stat. Ann. §§29-301 through 29-376	RULPA
Arkansas	Ark. Code Ann. §§ 4-47-101 through 4-47-1302	ULPA (2001)
California	Cal. Corp. Code §§ 159000 through 15912.07	ULPA (2001)
Colorado	Colo. Rev. Stat §§7-62-101 through 7-62-1201	RULPA
Connecticut	Conn. Gen. Stat. §§ 34-9 through 34-38u	RULPA
Delaware	Del. Code Ann. Tit. 6, §§ 17-101 through 17-1111	RULPA
District of Columbia	D.C. Code §§ 33-201.01 through 33-211.07	RULPA
Florida	Fla. Stat. Ann. §§ 620.1101 through 620.2205	ULPA (2001)
Georgia	Ga. Code Ann. §§14-9-100 through 14-9-1204	RULPA
Hawaii	Haw. Rev. Stat. §§ 425E-101 through 425E-1206	ULPA (2001)
Idaho	Idaho Code §§ 53-2-101 through 53-2-1205	ULPA (2001)
Illinois	805 ILCS §§ 215/0.01 through 215/1402	ULPA (2001)
Indiana	Ind. Code §§ 23-16-1-1 through 23-16-12-6	RULPA
Iowa	Iowa Code §§ 488.101 through 488.1207	ULPA (2001)
Kansas	Kan. Stat. Ann. §§ 56-1a101 through 56-1a610	RULPA
Kentucky	Ky. Rev. Stat. Ann §§ 362.2-102 through 362.2-1207	ULPA (2001)
Louisiana	La. Rev. Stat. Ann §§ 9:3401 through 9:3410	Neither
Maine	Me. Rev. Stat. Ann. Tit. 31, §§ 1301 through 1461	ULPA (2001)
Maryland	Md. Corps. & Ass'ns §§ 10-101 through 10-1105	RULPA
Massachusetts	Mass. Gen. L. ch. 109 §§ 1 through 66	RULPA
Michigan	Mich. Comp. Laws §§ 449.1101 through 449.2108	RULPA
Minnesota	Minn. Stat. §§321.0101 through 321.1208	ULPA (2001)

continues

EXHIBIT 4-8 *(continued)*

State	Code	Version of Uniform Act Adopted
Mississippi	Miss. Code Ann. §§79-14-101 through 79-14-1107	RULPA
Missouri	Mo. Rev. Stat. §§ 359.011 through 359.691	RULPA
Montana	Mont. Code Ann. §§ 35-12-501 through 35-12-1404	RULPA
Nebraska	Neb. Rev. Stat. §§ 67-233 through 67-296	RULPA
Nevada	Nev. Rev. Stat §§ 87A.010 through 87A.700	ULPA (2001)
New Hampshire	N.H. Rev. Stat. Ann. §§ 304-B:1 through 304-B:64	RULPA
New Jersey	J.J. Ann. Stat. §§ 42:2A-1 through 42:2A-73	RULPA
New Mexico	N.M. Ann. Stat. §§ 54-2A-101 through 54-2A-1206	ULPA (2001)
New York	McKinney's Partnership Law, §§ 121-101 through 121-1300	RULPA
North Carolina	N.C. Gen Stat. §§ 59-101 through 59-1107	RULPA

© Cengage Learning 2013

UNIFORM LIMITED PARTNERSHIP ACT, REVISED UNIFORM LIMITED PARTNERSHIP ACT, AND UNIFORM LIMITED PARTNERSHIP ACT (2001)

The website of the National Conference of Commissioners on Uniform State Law (NCCUSL) provides links to drafts and final versions of uniform state laws, including the Uniform Limited Partnership Acts.

LIMITED PARTNERSHIP FORMS

Because a limited partnership is formed only by the filing of a certificate of limited partnership, the drafting of a suitable certificate and the limited partnership agreement are vital. In addition to limited partnership certificates and agreements previously drafted by the law firm and those provided by the secretary of state's office, legal form books such as *Am. Jur. Legal Forms 2d, Nichols Cyclopedia of Legal Forms Annotated, Rabkin & Johnson Current Legal Forms*, and *West's Legal Forms, Second Edition* can be excellent resources for finding appropriate forms and optional language to use in limited partnership documents. State-specific continuing legal education (CLE) materials are also an excellent resource for forms and information to assist with drafting limited partnership documents. Forms for limited partnership agreements and other partnership-related documents can be found online from several different sources. Before any of these forms are used, they must be carefully reviewed and edited to be certain that they meet the statutory requirements of your state and that they fulfill the needs of the proposed partnership.

SECRETARY OF STATE OFFICES

For information on requirements for filing the Certificate of Limited Partnership and any other limited partnership documents at the state level, visit the website for the secretary of state. The secretary of state offices provide a wealth of online information concerning any requirements they have for filing limited partnership documents. Most states provide downloadable forms as well. Appendix A to this text is a directory of secretary of state offices. Links to those secretary of state offices may be found at the CourseMate website that accompanies this text.

STATE AND FEDERAL TAX OFFICES

As when working with a general partnership, it is important that the appropriate state offices be contacted regarding state income taxation matters. Information on federal taxation requirements is available from the Internal Revenue Service.

SUMMARY

- A limited partnership is a special type of partnership that offers limited liability to certain of its partners (limited partners).
- Limited partnerships must have at least one general partner and one limited partner.
- Any individual or entity may be a general partner or limited partner of a limited partnership.
- An individual or entity may be both a general and limited partner of a limited partnership.
- General partners in limited partnerships have personal liability for the debts and obligations of the limited partnership.
- Limited partners have no personal liability for the debts and obligations of the limited partnership.
- In most states, limited partners are prohibited from participating in the management of the limited partnership.
- General partners owe a fiduciary duty to limited partners.
- Most states have adopted a version of the Revised Uniform Limited Partnership Act or the Uniform Limited Partnership Act (2001) for their own limited partnership act.

- The limited partnership is created when a limited partnership certificate or similar document is filed with the proper state authority, typically the secretary of state.

- The limited partnership certificate that is filed with the state usually sets forth the minimum information required by statute. A limited partnership agreement should set forth the full agreement of the partners.

- Limited partnerships are treated as separate entities for most purposes.

- The income of the limited partnership is allocated to the general and limited partners pursuant to the terms of the limited partnership agreement.

- General and limited partners pay income tax on the amount of income that is allocated to them each year.

- In some states a limited partner may bring a derivative action on behalf of the limited partnership if the general partners refuse to bring the action.

- The death or withdrawal of a limited partner will usually not cause a dissolution of the limited partnership.

- The death or withdrawal of a general partner causes a dissolution of the limited partnership unless the limited partnership agreement provides otherwise and there remains at least one general partner.

▪ REVIEW QUESTIONS

1. Is a limited partnership treated as a separate entity for all purposes? If not, give an example of an instance in which a limited partnership is treated as an aggregate of its partners.

2. Why is the fiduciary duty between the general partner and limited partners even greater than the fiduciary duty between partners in a general partnership?

3. Suppose that Beth Henderson is a limited partner of the ABC Limited Partnership, a limited partnership formed for the purpose of purchasing and developing real estate. Beth wanted to be a limited partner because she has considerable personal assets that she wants to protect. Soon after the formation of the limited partnership, Beth becomes concerned about its management by the general partners. She starts attending the general partners' meetings and participating in all major decisions concerning the limited partnership. However, the partnership becomes insolvent anyway. Creditors are left with thousands of dollars' worth of unpaid bills. The limited partnership and the general partners have no substantial cash or other assets. If the partnership is in a state that follows RULPA, might creditors prevail in a lawsuit against Beth Henderson personally to recover their losses? Why or why not?

4. Brian, Jeanne, and William have formed OakRidge Limited Partnership, a limited partnership for shopping center development and management. William is the general partner and Brian and Jeanne are limited partners. The limited partnership is about to enter into an agreement to purchase a new shopping center; however, the bank that

is lending them the money wants personal guarantees from each partner. If the limited partnership is governed by the laws of a state that follows the Revised Uniform Limited Partnership Act, would Brian and Jeanne be able to guarantee the obligation of the OakRidge Limited Partnership without risking their limited liability status?

5. Suppose that Jake, Bryan, and Jill decide to form a limited partnership for the purpose of owning and operating a liquor store. They are all concerned about their personal liability, so they decide that they will all be limited partners. Would this be possible? Why or why not? What if Jill agreed to be both a general partner and a limited partner?

6. Why might a limited partnership want to put only the minimum required information in the limited partnership certificate and go into more detail in the limited partnership agreement or other documents?

7. What is one advantage the limited partnership has over the general partnership with regard to raising capital for the business?

8. Who may initiate a derivative action?

9. Suppose that Katherine, Brianna, and Paige have formed a limited partnership to operate a video arcade. Katherine is the general partner. She has contributed $2,000 and her time to get the operation running. Brianna and Paige, the limited partners, have each contributed $3,000. After one year of operation, the arcade has debts of $10,000 and assets of $20,000, but the three partners decide to discontinue their business and the limited partnership. Brianna and Paige want their investment returned to them. Who should Katherine, who is winding up the business, pay first, Brianna and Paige, or the creditors? How much will Brianna and Paige receive? How about Katherine?

10. Suppose a limited partnership has just one general partner, who suddenly dies. Will the partnership dissolve? Could a limited partnership continue if one of three general partners suddenly dies? If yes, under what circumstances?

■ PRACTICAL PROBLEMS

1. Locate and cite the limited partnership act in your state to answer the following questions.

   a. When was your state's current act adopted?

   b. After which uniform act is the limited partnership act of your state modeled?

   c. What is the name of the document that must be filed in your state to form a limited partnership?

   d. What must be included in that document?

   e. Where is that document filed?

■ CRITICAL THINKING EXERCISE

In general partnerships, every partner has the statutory right to participate in the management of the partnership. Why do you think limited partners are prohibited from participating in the management of the limited partnership in some states?

Why do you think some states have adopted statutes that specifically provide that limited partners do not lose their limited liability status just because they participate in the partnership's management?

■ WORKPLACE SCENARIO

Assume the same set of facts as in the Workplace Scenario from Chapter 3 of this text, except now Bradley Harris and Cynthia Lund want to form a limited partnership. Bradley Harris will be the general partner. Cynthia Lund will be the limited partner.

Using the earlier information and the information provided in Appendices B-1 and B-2 of this text, prepare a limited partnership certificate in your state. You may create your own form that conforms to the statutes of your state, or you can download a form from the appropriate state office.

Also prepare a cover letter to the appropriate state authority filing the limited partnership certificate and enclosing the appropriate filing fee.

Portfolio Reminder

Save the documents prepared for the Workplace Scenario exercises in each chapter, either in hard copy or electronically, to build a portfolio of documents to be used for job interviews or as sample documents on the job. At this point, your portfolio should include the following:

- Power of attorney
- Application for assumed name
- Application for federal employer identification number
- Application for state employer identification number
- Partnership statement of authority
- Limited partnership certificate

■ ENDNOTES

1. Revised Uniform Limited Partnership Act § 101(11).

2. Uniform Limited Partnership Act 2001, Prefatory Note.

3. Id. § 104.

4. 59A Am Jur. 2d Partnership § 863 (March 2011).

5. Revised Uniform Limited Partnership Act § 303(a).

6. Id. § 303(b).

7. Uniform Limited Partnership Act 2001 § 303.

8. Revised Uniform Limited Partnership Act § 105.

9. 59A Am. Jur. 2d Partnership § 853 (March 2011).

10. Revised Uniform Limited Partnership Act § 201.

11. See Chapter 13 of this text.

12. Revised Uniform Limited Partnership Act § 201.

13. Id. § 202.

14. Id. § 105.

15. Id.

16. Id. § 106.

17. 14A Am. Jur. Legal Forms 2d Partnership § 194:727 (November 2010). Reprinted with permission from American Jurisprudence Legal Forms 2d. © 2011 West Group.

18. Id. Reprinted with permission from American Jurisprudence Legal Forms 2d. © 2011 West Group.

19. Id. § 194:760. Reprinted with permission from American Jurisprudence Legal Forms 2d. © 2011 West Group.

20. Id. § 194:761. Reprinted with permission from American Jurisprudence Legal Forms 2d. © 2011 West Group.

21. Id. § 194:768. Reprinted with permission from American Jurisprudence Legal Forms 2d. © 2011 West Group.

22. Id. § 194:796. Reprinted with permission from American Jurisprudence Legal Forms 2d. © 2011 West Group.

23. Id. § 194:823. Reprinted with permission from American Jurisprudence Legal Forms 2d. © 2011 West Group.

24. Id. § 194:829. Reprinted with permission from American Jurisprudence Legal Forms 2d. © 2011 West Group.

25. Id. § 194:853. Reprinted with permission from American Jurisprudence Legal Forms 2d. © 2011 West Group.

26. Revised Uniform Limited Partnership Act § 704.28.

27. Revised Uniform Limited Partnership Act § 603.

28. Id. § 604.

29. 59A Am. Jur. 2d Partnership § 868 (March 2011).

30. Revised Uniform Limited Partnership Act § 501.

31. Revised Uniform Limited Partnership Act § 801.

32. Id. § 203.

33. Id. § 803.

34. Id. § 1001.

CourseMate

To access additional course materials, including CourseMate, please visit http://www.cengagebrain.com, At the CengageBrain home page, search for the ISBN of your title (from the back cover of your book) using the search box at the top of the page. This will take you to the product page where the resources can be found. The CourseMate resources for this text include Web links to the resources discussed earlier, downloadable limited partnership forms, flash cards, and more.

5

LIMITED LIABILITY PARTNERSHIPS AND LIMITED LIABILITY LIMITED PARTNERSHIPS

CHAPTER OUTLINE

INTRODUCTION

In the mid-1990s, several states introduced legislation to allow the formation of a new form of partnership, the **limited liability partnership** (LLP). A few years later, many states began recognizing another form of business organization, the

limited liability limited partnership (LLLP). As the names of these two entities imply, these business organizations are very similar to the general partnerships discussed in Chapter 3 of this text, and the limited partnerships discussed in Chapter 4. The defining characteristic of these two newer forms of business organizations is the limited personal liability they offer to all partners. In this chapter, we will look at both of these types of business organizations, focusing on the differences between them and general partnerships and limited partnerships.

LIMITED LIABILITY PARTNERSHIP
A partnership in which the partners have less than full liability for the actions of other partners, but full liability for their own actions.

LIMITED LIABILITY LIMITED PARTNERSHIP
A limited partnership in which the general partners have less than full liability for the actions of other general partners.

§ 5.1 INTRODUCTION TO LIMITED LIABILITY PARTNERSHIPS

The first state law in the United States authorizing the formation of the limited liability partnership (LLP) was adopted in Texas in 1991. A decade later, every state in the country had passed legislation recognizing this new form of business entity. The initial motivation for the inception of the LLP was a strong desire to limit the personal liability exposure of professionals (especially accountants and lawyers) who have traditionally done business as partnerships. Some states still limit the formation of limited liability partnerships to professionals. See Exhibit 5-10 in the Resources section of this chapter for a list of those states. The benefits of transacting business as an LLP (sometimes referred to as a "registered limited liability partnership") soon became evident to those beyond the professions, and the LLP quickly became an important alternative for existing partnerships and those forming new business enterprises. In most states, any general partnership can become an LLP by filing a statement of qualification with the secretary of state.

SIDEBAR

One reason for the development of the LLP was that a growing number of national professional firms needed a partnership-like organization that could operate across state lines but not impose vicarious liability on its owners.

Since the Internal Revenue Service began tracking the number of LLPs filing partnership returns in the United States, that number has grown at an impressive rate. Between 1998 and 2008, the number of LLPs in the United States has more than tripled. See Exhibit 5-1.

LAW GOVERNING LIMITED LIABILITY PARTNERSHIPS

LLPs are governed mainly by the statutes of the state in which the entity is formed, more specifically by special provisions within the Uniform Partnership Act as adopted in each state. Most states have amended their partnership acts by adding special

EXHIBIT 5-1 LIMITED LIABILITY PARTNERSHIPS IN THE UNITED STATES

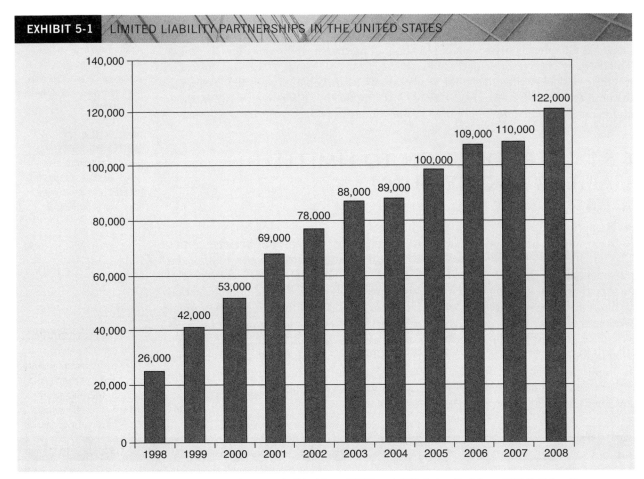

Number of Limited Liability Partnerships Filing Partnership Returns in the United States 1998 through 2008. Partnership Returns, 2008, Statistics of Income, Internal Revenue Service, http://www.irs.gov.

provisions that deal with limited liability partnerships. Those provisions generally address the following:

- The nature and extent of the personal liability of the partners
- Voting requirements to elect limited liability partnership status
- Requirements for filing a statement of qualification to become a limited liability partnership
- The annual reporting requirements for limited liability partnerships
- Liability insurance or segregated funds requirements (in certain states)

See Exhibit 5-10 in the Resources section of this chapter for a list of limited liability partnership provisions within the state partnership acts.

The partners of an LLP are also governed by their Partnership Agreement. The partnership agreement adopted by the LLP will govern the LLP on any matter that is not addressed in the partnership act of the LLP's state of domicile.

IN SUMMATION

- Texas passed the first laws providing for limited liability partnerships in 1991.
- All states now have some type of limited liability partnership laws.
- Some states limit the formation of limited liability partnerships to professionals.
- Most limited liability partnership law is found within state partnership acts.

§ 5.2 LIMITATIONS ON PERSONAL LIABILITY

The distinguishing feature of limited liability partnerships is that, unlike general partnerships, LLPs offer their partners at least a degree of protection from personal liability for partnership obligations. The amount of protection offered to partners varies from state to state. State statutes that dictate how much personal liability protection partners have are generally referred to as either **partial shield statutes** or **full shield statutes**. Those statutes shield the partners from personal liability for the debts and obligations of the partnership.

PARTIAL SHIELD STATUTES

As discussed in Chapter 3 of this text, one of the major drawbacks to doing business as a partnership is that the partners have **joint and several** liability for the debts and obligations of the partnership. This means that creditors and claimants of the partnership can look to the partners either as a group or individually to fulfill partnership obligations. Each partner can be held personally responsible for partnership obligations—even those incurred by another partner on behalf of the partnership. In effect, any partner can be held personally liable for the bad business decisions or even negligence and wrongdoing of any other partner.

Generally, partners of LLPs in states with partial shield LLP laws do not have personal liability for partnership obligations arising from the wrongdoing of other partners; however, they remain personally liable for all other partnership obligations. For example, suppose that Jack, Karen, and Lisa are all partners of the JKL Limited Liability Partnership, a limited liability partnership formed in a state with partial shield laws. If there are insufficient partnership assets to repay a partnership obligation incurred in the ordinary course of business, Jack, Karen, and Lisa would all be personally responsible for the repayment of the debt. If, however, the partnership debt was incurred due to Jack's misconduct, Karen and Lisa would be shielded from personal liability. Jack would be solely responsible for the debt incurred by his own wrongdoing. Section 362.220 from the Kentucky Revised Statutes, shown below, is

PARTIAL SHIELD STATUTES
Laws designed to protect individual partners from incurring personal liability for partnership debts and obligations arising specifically from the negligence and wrongdoing of other partners.

FULL SHIELD STATUTES
Laws that provide that obligations of the partnership belong solely to the partnership and that partners are not personally liable for any partnership obligations.

JOINT AND SEVERAL
Both together and individually. For example, a liability or debt is joint and several if the creditor may sue the debtors either together as a group (with the result that the debtors would have to split the loss) or individually (with the result that one debtor might have to pay the whole thing).

one example of a partial shield provision. Subsection (2) of that statute specifically exempts partners from liability for partnership obligations "arising from negligence, malpractice, wrongful acts, or misconduct committed while the partnership is a registered limited liability partnership." Subsection (3) further states that that exemption does not apply to the partners for obligations arising from their own negligence, wrongful acts, or misconduct.

362.220 Nature of Partner's Liability

(1) Except as provided in subsection (2) of this section, all partners shall be liable:

    (a) Jointly and severally for everything chargeable to the partnership under KRS 362.210 and 362.215; and

    (b) Jointly for all other debts and obligations of the partnership; but any partner may enter into a separate obligation to perform a partnership contract.

(2) Subject to subsection (3) of this section and subject to any agreement among the partners, a partner in a registered limited liability partnership shall not be liable directly or indirectly, including by way of indemnification, contribution, assessment or otherwise, for debts, obligations, and liabilities of or chargeable to the partnership, whether arising in tort, contract, or otherwise, arising from negligence, malpractice, wrongful acts, or misconduct committed while the partnership is a registered limited liability partnership and in the course of the partnership business by another partner or an employee, agent, or representative of the partnership.

(3) Subsection (2) of this section shall not affect the liability of a partner in a registered limited liability partnership for his own negligence, wrongful acts, or misconduct.

FULL SHIELD STATUTES

The Uniform Partnership Act of 1997 (UPA [1997]) and a majority of the states follow the full shield approach for LLPs. These statutes provide that obligations of the partnership belong solely to the partnership. Partners are not personally liable, solely by reason of being a partner, for any obligation of the partnership incurred while the partnership is an LLP. Partners usually remain liable for obligations arising in whole or in part due to their own negligence, wrongful acts, errors, or omissions. The exact nature of that personal liability of partners for their own wrongdoing varies by state. For example, suppose JKL Limited Liability Partnership from our previous example is an LLP formed in a state with full shield laws. If there are insufficient partnership assets to repay a partnership obligation incurred in the ordinary course of business, Jack, Karen, and Lisa would all be shielded from personal liability for the repayment of the debt. The debt belongs only to the partnership. If, however, the partnership debt was incurred due to Jack's misconduct, Karen and Lisa would still be shielded from personal liability, but Jack would be responsible for the debt incurred by his own wrongdoing.

EXHIBIT 5-2	CHART COMPARING THE PERSONAL LIABILITY OF PARTNERS IN PARTIAL SHIELD AND FULL SHIELD STATES	
	Partial Shield State	**Full Shield State**
For most debts and obligations of the partnership	• The partnership • The partners	• The partnership
For debts and obligations arising from the wrongdoing of any one partner	• The wrongdoing partner	• The wrongdoing partner

*State statutory provisions for limited liability partnerships are not uniform—always check the statutes of the state you are concerned with.

Section 306(c) of the UPA (1997), which follows, makes it clear that debts and obligations of a limited liability partnership belong solely to the partnership, and that the partners are not personally liable.

> (c) An obligation of a partnership incurred while the partnership is a limited liability partnership, whether arising in contract, tort, or otherwise, is solely the obligation of the partnership. A partner is not personally liable, directly or indirectly, by way of contribution or otherwise, for such an obligation solely by reason of being or so acting as a partner. This subsection applies notwithstanding anything inconsistent in the partnership agreement that existed immediately before the vote required to become a limited liability partnership under Section 1001(b).

Exhibit 5-2 is a chart comparing the personal liability of partners in partial shield and full shield states.

INSURANCE/SEGREGATED FUNDS REQUIREMENTS

Because the personal liability of LLP partners is limited, several states require that LLPs carry liability insurance covering the partnership for errors, omissions, negligence, wrongful acts, misconduct, and malpractice. This requirement ensures that third parties who are wronged by the LLP will have some type of recourse if the LLP itself has limited assets. In lieu of a liability insurance policy, the LLP may segregate funds in an amount required by law in a trust, escrow, or similar arrangement, to provide for the payment of such partnership obligations. Following is an example of such a statute from the state of New Mexico:

> A. A registered limited liability partnership shall carry at least five hundred thousand dollars ($500,000) per occurrence and one million dollars ($1,000,000) in the aggregate per year of liability insurance, beyond the

amount of any applicable deductible, covering the partnership for errors, omissions, negligence, wrongful acts, misconduct and malpractice for which the liability of partners is limited by Section 54-1A-306 NMSA 1978. Such an insurance policy may contain reasonable provisions with respect to policy periods, deductibles, territory, claims, conditions, exclusions and other usual matters.

B. If a registered limited liability partnership is in substantial compliance with the requirements of Subsection A of this section, the requirements of this section shall not be admissible or in any way be made known to a jury in determining an issue of liability for or extent of the debt or obligation or damages in question.

C. A registered limited liability partnership is considered to be in substantial compliance with Subsection A of this section if the partnership provides an amount of funds equal to the amount of insurance required by that sub-section specifically designated and segregated for the satisfaction of judg-ments against the partnership or its partners based on errors, omissions, negligence, wrongful acts, misconduct and malpractice for which liability is limited by Section 54-1A-306 NMSA 1978 as follows:

(1) A deposit in trust or bank escrow or cash, bank certificates of deposit, or United States treasury obligations

(2) A bank letter of credit or insurance company surety bond

LLPs that provide professional services may be required to maintain professional malpractice insurance under the state's partnership laws, or under other statutes governing the profession. This requirement is not uniform among the states. The proper state statutes must be consulted when electing LLP status to ensure that any requirements regarding liability insurance or segregated funds are complied with. Exhibit 5-10 in the Resources section of this chapter indicates which states require LLPs to maintain liability insurance or segregated funds as of 2010.

IN SUMMATION

- In states that have adopted partial shield limited liability partnership provi-sions, partners are shielded from personal liability for obligations arising from the wrongdoing of other partners.

- In states that have adopted full shield limited liability partnership provisions, partners are shielded from personal liability for all partnership obligations except those arising from their own wrongdoing.

- There is generally no protection from personal liability for a partner for obligations arising from his or her own wrongdoing.

- In some states, limited liability partnerships must carry liability insurance covering the partnership for errors, omissions, negligence, wrongful acts, misconduct, and malpractice.

§ 5.3 LIMITED LIABILITY PARTNERSHIP FORMATION AND OPERATION

LLPs are formed pursuant to the requirements of state statutes. LLPs are generally treated as an election made by an existing general partnership. However, the formation of the partnership and its election of limited liability status may be done simultaneously. Generally, the formation of an LLP involves a vote of all partners and is valid only after filing a **statement of qualification** with the secretary of state (or other designated state official). Another important aspect of the formation of any type of partnership is the adoption of the partnership agreement, which will govern the LLP on all matters that either are not addressed by state statute, or that are addressed in the statutes but may be amended in a valid partnership agreement.

STATEMENT OF QUALIFICATION
With regard to limited liability partnerships, this is the document filed by general partnerships to elect limited liability partnership status.
   With regard to limited liability limited partnerships, this is the document filed by limited partnerships to elect limited liability limited partnership status.

VOTING

Under the UPA (1997) and the laws of most states, the same number of partners required to approve an amendment to the partnership agreement must vote to approve the limited liability partnership election. In most instances, a unanimous vote of the partners will be required, although the number may be less if the partnership agreement so provides. It is important to consult the pertinent provisions of the state partnership act and the partnership agreement to ensure that the LLP election is made properly.

The statutes of most states follow the provisions set forth in § 1001(b) of the UPA (1997), as follows:

> (b) The terms and conditions on which a partnership becomes a limited liability partnership must be approved by the vote necessary to amend the partnership agreement except, in the case of a partnership agreement that expressly considers obligations to contribute to the partnership, the vote necessary to amend those provisions.

STATEMENT OF QUALIFICATION

In most states, a limited liability partnership is formed when a statement of qualification (or similarly named document) is filed with the secretary of state or other appropriate state official with the required filing fee. The statement of qualification generally states that the partnership has elected to become a limited liability partnership pursuant to the relevant state statutes, and it sets forth the information required by statute. In states that follow the requirements of the UPA (1997),[1] the statement of qualification must set forth:

1. The name of the partnership
2. The street address of the partnership's chief executive office and, if different, the street address of an office in this state, if any

3. If the partnership does not have an office in the state, the name and street address of the partnership's agent for service of process
4. A statement that the partnership elects to be a limited liability partnership
5. A deferred effective date, if any

Name

The name of the limited liability partnership is generally required by law to indicate in some fashion that it is, in fact, a limited liability partnership. Usually, state statutes require that the name of the limited liability partnership include the words "limited liability partnership," "registered limited liability partnership," or the abbreviations "LLP" or "RLLP."

Chief Executive Office Address

The statement of qualification will generally designate a chief executive office. This is important, as it is the office where service of process can be made, where notifications by the secretary of state may be sent, and where certain required partnership documents must be kept.

Designated Agent for Service of Process

If the LLP does not maintain a chief executive office in the state in which the statement of qualification is filed, the LLP will be required to appoint an agent who has an office with a street address in the state to receive service of process on behalf of the LLP.

Statement Regarding Limited Liability Status

The statement of qualification will include a statement that the partners of the LLP desire to adopt limited liability partnership status. A statement indicating that limited liability partnership status was approved by the unanimous vote of the partners pursuant to state statute will typically be included.

EXAMPLE: Statement Regarding Limited Liability Status

This partnership has elected to become a limited liability partnership by a vote of the partners and pursuant to Section _____ of the Uniform Partnership Act of the State of _____.

Effective Date of the Election

The statement of qualification will indicate the date that the LLP status is to be effective. The effective date will generally be the date of filing with the secretary of state, or some later date (if allowed by state statute). Exhibit 5-3 is a sample Statement of Qualification for the state of Kansas.

EXHIBIT 5-3 LIMITED LIABILITY PARTNERSHIP STATEMENT OF QUALIFICATION—KANSAS

Contact Information
Kansas Secretary of State
Ron Thornburgh
Memorial Hall, 1st Floor
120 S.W. 10th Avenue
Topeka, KS 66612-1594
(785) 296-4564
kssos@kssos.org
www.kssos.org

KANSAS SECRETARY OF STATE
Limited Liability Partnership Statement of Qualification
QLLP
51

All information must be completed or this document will not be accepted for filing.

Do not write in this space

1. Name of the limited liability partnership:

2. Partnership's principal address:
Address must be a street address. A post office box is unacceptable.

Street address

City   State   Zip

3. If different from above, the address of any partnership office in Kansas:

Street address   City   State   Zip

4. If there is no office in Kansas, give the name and street address of the partnership's agent for service of process. The agent must be an individual resident or person authorized to do business in this state.

Name

Street address   City   State   Zip

5. The future effective date of qualification, if not effective upon filing:

6. The above-named partnership elects to be *(check one)*:

or
☐ a foreign limited liability partnership from _____
   Home state
☐ a Kansas limited liability partnership

We declare under penalty of perjury under the laws of the state of Kansas that the foregoing is true and correct.

Executed on the _____ of _____ , _____ by two partners.
            Day   Month   Year

_____   _____
Signature   Signature

Page 1 of 2

Kansas Secretary of State's Office

Annual Reporting Requirements

The laws of most states follow the example set forth in the Uniform Partnership Act[2] and require that all limited liability partnerships file an annual report in the office of the secretary of state that sets forth:

1. The name of the limited liability partnership
2. The state or other jurisdiction under whose laws the limited liability partnership is formed
3. The street address of the partnership's chief executive office or the street address of an office of the partnership within the state

An annual registration fee, which can be quite significant in some states, is required to be filed with the annual statement. Filing these statements in a timely manner can be important to the continued limited liability status of the partnership. Exhibit 5-4 is a sample Limited Liability Partnership Annual Report for the state of Kansas.

LIMITED LIABILITY PARTNERSHIP AGREEMENT

A carefully drafted partnership agreement can be crucial to the success of the limited liability partnership. Partnership agreements for LLPs will generally be no different than those for general partnerships discussed in Chapter 3 of this text, with the exception of added language to clearly indicate that the partnership is an LLP, and to further define the limits on personal liability of the partners. Following is sample language that may be used in an LLP agreement to denote its LLP status:

EXAMPLE: Qualification as a Limited Liability Partnership

Agreement to Qualify. The Partnership shall be a limited liability partnership as that term is described in the Act, and the Managing Partners are authorized to execute a statement of qualification of a limited liability partnership or such other documents as may be required in order to qualify the Partnership in any jurisdiction which the Managing Partners deem appropriate.

Authorization to Execute Statements. The Managing Partners are authorized to execute any statement of authority, annual report, statement of foreign qualification, revocation of a statement of qualification as a limited liability partnership, or other filing required or authorized to be filed by the Act, and pay appropriate fees therefore necessary or convenient to the Partnership's status as a limited liability partnership.[3]

EXHIBIT 5-4 LIMITED LIABILITY PARTNERSHIP ANNUAL REPORT FOR THE STATE OF KANSAS

Contact Information
Kansas Secretary of State
Ron Thornburgh
Memorial Hall, 1st Floor
120 S.W. 10th Avenue
Topeka, KS 66612-1594
(785) 296-4564
kssos@kssos.org
www.kssos.org

KANSAS SECRETARY OF STATE
Limited Liability Partnership Annual Report

LLP

50

All information must be completed and the required fee submitted or this document will not be accepted for filing. **Please read all instructions before completing this document.**

1. Business Entity ID Number: _____
   (This is not the FEIN)

2. Partnership name: _____

   _____
   (Name must match the name on record with the Secretary of State)

3. Mailing address (this address will be used to send official mail from the Secretary of State's Office):

   _____
   Address

   _____
   City   State   Zip

Do not write in this space

4. Tax closing date: _____
   Month   Day   Year

5. State of organization: _____

6. Federal Employer ID Number (FEIN): _____

7. Partners who own 5% or more of capital (**Kansas limited liability partnerships only**):

Name	Address	City	State	Zip

8. I declare under penalty of perjury pursuant to the laws of the state of Kansas that the foregoing is true and correct and that I have remitted the required fee. (Do not leave blank.)

_____
Signature of partner

_____
Date (month, day, year)

_____
Name of signer (printed or typed)

_____
Phone number

Rev. 12/1/07 nr

K.S.A. 56a-1201, 56a-1202
1/2

Kansas Secretary of State's Office

FOREIGN LIMITED LIABILITY PARTNERSHIPS

The limited liability partnership will be considered a foreign LLP in any state other than its state of domicile (the state in which its statement of qualification is filed). If the LLP is to transact business in any state where it is considered a foreign LLP, it must first file a statement of foreign qualification (or similarly named document) with the secretary of state or other designated state official of the foreign state. Exhibit 5-5 is a sample form that can be filed in the state of Idaho to qualify to do business in the state as a foreign limited liability partnership.

Foreign LLPs are also required to file annual reports in most states in which they are qualified. Filing fees will be required for both the qualification statement and annual reports. Generally, the same laws that apply to foreign corporations and foreign limited partnerships will apply to foreign LLPs. Qualification of foreign corporations and other business organizations is discussed further in Chapter 13 of this text.

DISSOLVING THE LIMITED LIABILITY PARTNERSHIP

Limited liability partnerships are dissolved pursuant to the partnership act of the state of domicile and the LLP's partnership agreement. Because a statement of qualification is filed with the secretary of state, giving notice of the formation of the limited liability partnership, a statement of cancellation must be filed with that same office when the LLP dissolves.

IN SUMMATION

- A general partnership may elect to become a limited liability partnership when the partnership is formed or after the partnership has been organized.
- The election to become a limited liability partnership must be approved by a vote of the partners—unanimous approval is usually required.
- A statement of qualification or some similar document is filed with the secretary of state to adopt limited liability partnership status.
- Limited liability partnerships are subject to simple annual registration or reporting requirements in most states.
- Limited liability partnerships are typically governed by a partnership agreement very similar to the general partnership agreement.
- A limited liability partnership is required to register as a foreign business entity in most states in which it does business other than its state of domicile.
- Limited liability partnerships are dissolved pursuant to state statutes in the same manner as general partnerships.

EXHIBIT 5-5 STATEMENT OF FOREIGN QUALIFICATION LIMITED LIABILITY PARTNERSHIP FOR THE STATE OF IDAHO

STATEMENT OF FOREIGN QUALIFICATION
LIMITED LIABILITY PARTNERSHIP
(Instructions on back of application)

The undersigned partnership hereby files a statement of foreign qualification of Limited Liability Partnership, and submits the following information to the Secretary of State pursuant to Idaho Code § 53-3-1102.

1. The name of the foreign limited liability partnership is:

   _____

2. The name under which the foreign limited liability partnership will do business in Idaho is:

   _____

3. The street address of the partnership's chief executive office is:

   _____

4. The mailing address for future correspondence, if different than the address in line 3:

   _____

5. The name and street address of the registered agent is:

   _____

6. Effective date of filing:(optional): _____

7. The domestic state of organization is: _____

8. Signature of at least two partners.

   1)_____
   Typed Name_____
   2)_____
   Typed Name_____
   3)_____
   Typed Name_____

   g:\corp\forms\sxqualfllp.p65 Revised 06/2004

   Secretary of State use only

continues

EXHIBIT 5-5 *(continued)*

INSTRUCTIONS

Optional: If the document is incorrect where can you be reached for questions? _____

Note: Complete and submit the application in duplicate.

1. Line 1 - Enter the name of the limited liability partnership as it is filed in the domestic state.

2. Line 2 - If the name of the limited liability partnership does not end with the words Registered Limited Liability Partnership, Limited Liability Partnership or the abbreviation R.L.L.P., L.L.P. or LLP it must designate a name to use in Idaho which satisfy's the above requirements of Idaho Code § 53-3-1102. Add one of the required terms at the end of the company name on line 2.

3. Line 3 - Enter the street address of its chief executive office (not a PO Box or Personal Mail Box)

4. Line 4 - Enter the mailing address for the LLP, if different from the address in line 3.

5. Line 5 - Enter the name and street address of the registered agent in Idaho (not a PO Box or Personal Mail Box). The registered agent is the person designated to receive service of process in the event of litigation. This person must be located in Idaho at a street address.

6. Line 6 - Deferred effective date (optional)

7. Line 7 - Enter the domestic state of organization.

8. Line 8 - Requires the signature of at least 2 partners of the limited liability partnership. The partners must be identified by typing his/her name beneath the signature.

9. Enclose the appropriate fee:
   a. If the application is typed the fee is $100.00.
   b. If the application is not typed or a non standard form is used, the fee is $120.00.
   c. If expedited service is requested, add $20.00 to the filing fee.
   d. If the fees are to be paid from the filing party's pre-paid customer account, conspicuously indicate the customer account number in the cover letter or transmittal document.
   Pursuant to Idaho Code § 67-910(6), the Secretary of State's Office may delete a business entity filing from our database if payment for the filing is not completed.

10. Mail or deliver to:
    Office of the Secretary of State
    700 West Jefferson
    PO Box 83720
    Boise ID 83720-0080

11. If you have questions or need help, call the Secretary of State's Office at (208) 334-2301.

http://www.sos.idaho.gov

§ 5.4 ADVANTAGES AND DISADVANTAGES OF DOING BUSINESS AS A LIMITED LIABILITY PARTNERSHIP

As with any type of business organization, the LLP offers both advantages and disadvantages. Because of the significant differences in the LLP statutes among the states, it is important to consult the pertinent state statutes before choosing an LLP over another form of business organization.

ADVANTAGES

The LLP offers most of the same advantages to doing business as a general partnership. They both offer management flexibility, partnership taxation, and a diversified pool of capital resources (all of these advantages are discussed in Chapter 3). In addition, the LLP offers the distinct advantage of limited liability.

Limited Liability

The most important and most obvious advantage to doing business as a limited liability partnership is the limited liability offered to all partners. Although not without limits, the protection from personal liability for the negligence and wrongdoing of other partners gives LLPs a distinct advantage over general partnerships.

The following case, *Kus v. Irving*, shows what a distinct advantage limited liability can be to partners of a law firm operating as a limited liability partnership. In this case, it was held that two partners were not responsible for any damages caused by the alleged negligence, wrongful acts, and misconduct of a third partner.

CASE
Superior Court of Connecticut, Judicial District of New London.
Margaret KUS v. Charles J. IRVING et al. No. Cv990549519s. June 10, 1999.

HURLEY, Judge Trial Referee.
The two defendants, attorneys Narcy Z. Dubicki and Garon Camassar, claim in their motion for summary judgment that there is no genuine issue of material fact as to their liability and request, as a matter of law, that the motion be granted. The law firm is a limited liability partnership.

The plaintiff, Margaret Kus, claims that a third defendant, attorney Charles J. Irving, a partner in the firm of Irving, Dubicki and Camassar, induced her to sign a fee agreement to pay him a fee of 25 percent of what he collected on the life insurance policy of the husband of the plaintiff before suit was filed and 33 percent of any proceeds after

continues

suit was brought. The policy had a death benefit of $400,000. She claims that Irving had already received the $400,000, but nevertheless filed suit to collect the larger fee of 33 percent. Irving then paid the plaintiff $270,692.26 and took a fee of $135,365.63, which the plaintiff claims was $33,841.41 too high. The plaintiff sued all three partners in the firm.

Both Dubicki and Camassar have filed affidavits stating that they had no personal knowledge of the case or the dealings between Irving and the plaintiff until November 24, 1998, which was several days after the matter between the plaintiff and Irving was concluded. They claim that under General Statutes § 34-327, they are protected from liability for any actions by their partner, Irving.

Section 34-327 provides in pertinent part: "(c) . . . a partner in a registered limited liability partnership is not liable directly or indirectly . . . for any debts, obligations and liabilities . . . chargeable to the partnership or another partner or partners . . . arising in the course of the partnership business while the partnership is a registered limited liability partnership. "(d) The provisions of subsection (c) . . . shall not affect the liability of a partner . . . for his own negligence, wrongful acts or misconduct, or that of any person under his direct supervision or control."

In their affidavits, Dubicki and Camassar state that they had no personal knowledge of the dealings between the plaintiff and Irving, nor did they have any supervision or control of Irving. Furthermore, they state that under the partnership

agreement, Irving retains all fees for his activities and does not share any of them with the other partners.

The plaintiff claims that the two defendants are guilty of negligence, wrongful acts and misconduct. She produced no affidavit or other documents, however, to support this claim. The court must, therefore, find that there is no genuine issue of material fact in this regard.

The plaintiff then claims that the two defendants violated various sections of the Rules of Professional Conduct. The court, however, cannot treat her mere assertions as evidence that they violated rule 5.1 of those rules. She claims they admitted knowledge of what happened and did not attempt to rectify it. All they admitted was knowledge after the transaction was concluded. Again, the plaintiff's claims are made without supporting affidavits.

Even if there were evidence of a violation of rule 5.1(a) and (c) of the Rules of Professional Conduct, the court finds § 34-327(d) supersedes both subsections of the rule except where the other person is under the partners' "direct supervision or control." Here, the sworn affidavits deny that this was the case. Accordingly, since the two defendants shared no benefit, did not have direct supervision or control over Irving and did not know about the matter until nine days after the funds were distributed, the court finds that they are protected from liability by § 34-327(c).

The motion for summary judgment by defendants Dubicki and Camassar is granted.

DISADVANTAGES

The disadvantages to doing business as an LLP include most of the disadvantages of doing business as a general partnership. The LLP does not offer a uniform or simple means of business continuity and the LLP interests are relatively difficult to transfer. The LLP may find that it has a limited capacity to raise capital for the partnership business. LLPs also have a disadvantage when it comes to being subject to several, sometimes costly, formalities that do not apply to sole proprietorships and general partnerships.

Organization and Management Formalities

Unlike a general partnership, an LLP doesn't exist until the proper documentation is filed with the secretary of state, along with a filing fee. As discussed earlier in this chapter, LLPs are also subject to annual reporting requirements, and they must register in any foreign state in which they transact business. Exhibit 5-6 is a summary of the advantages and disadvantages of doing business as a limited liability partnership.

EXHIBIT 5-6 ADVANTAGES AND DISADVANTAGES OF DOING BUSINESS AS A LIMITED LIABILITY PARTNERSHIP

Advantages	Disadvantages
• *Limited Liability for All Partners.* Each partner is protected from personal liability for partnership debts and obligations incurred due to the wrongdoing of other partners (partial shield states).	• *Personal Liability for Certain Obligations.* Partners are personally responsible for partnership obligations incurred due to their own wrongdoing.
• *Limited Liability for All Partners.* Each partner is protected from personal liability for partnership debts and obligations, unless the partnership obligations was incurred due to his or her own wrongdoing (full shield states).	• *Lack of Business Continuity.* Like any general partnership, the partnership may discontinue on the death or disability of one of the partners.
• *Income Tax Benefits.* Limited liability partnerships are not subject to federal income taxation. Income "flows through" to the partners.	• *Difficulty in Transferring Interest in Partnership.* A partner's interest in a limited liability partnership is not freely transferable.

continues

EXHIBIT 5-6 *(continued)*

Advantages	Disadvantages
• *Diversified Capital Resources.* Unlike sole proprietorships and general partnerships, limited liability partnerships have the ability to attract investors who accept no personal liability.	• *Formalities and Regulatory and Reporting Requirements.* Limited liability partnerships cannot exist until the proper election is made and the proper documentation is filed at the state level. In addition, limited liability partnerships may be subject to various reporting requirements that are not imposed on proprietorships and general partnerships.
	• *Legal and Organizational Expense.* There are more legal and organizational expenses associated with forming and maintaining a limited liability partnership than with partnerships and sole proprietorships.
	• *Lack of Uniform Case Law and State* Law. Because limited liability partnerships are a relatively new form of business organization, there is little case law involving limited liability partnerships. Also, there are significant differences among state limited liability partnership statutes, making interpretation of state statutes somewhat uncertain.

© Cengage Learning 2013

IN SUMMATION

- In addition to the advantages offered by all general partnerships, limited liability partnerships offer the added advantage of providing limited personal liability to all partners.
- The limited liability partnership also provides some unique disadvantages as a form of business organization, including:
  - There are additional formalities to conducting business as a limited liability partnership (compared to a general partnership). Documentation must be filed at the state level to form a limited liability partnership.
  - The lack of uniformity in state limited liability partnership law provides uncertainty for limited liability partnerships that may transact business in more than one state.

§ 5.5 INTRODUCTION TO LIMITED LIABILITY LIMITED PARTNERSHIPS

The limited liability limited partnership (LLLP, pronounced "triple L P") is a newer form of limited partnership that offers protection from personal liability to both general and limited partners. As of 2011, over half of the states had adopted statutes approving the formation of domestic LLLPs. These provisions are usually within the state's limited partnership act. Because there is little uniformity among LLLP statutes, our attention in this chapter will be given to LLLPs in general terms, and the differences between LLLPs and limited partnerships.

LAW GOVERNING LIMITED LIABILITY LIMITED PARTNERSHIPS

LLLPs are governed by the statutes of the state where they are formed. Some states include provisions for LLLPs in their partnership acts along with provisions for LLPs, but most of the states that recognize this new form of limited partnership provide for it in their limited partnership acts. The Uniform Limited Partnership Act 2001, which had been adopted by several states as of 2011, does not presume that a limited partnership will be an LLLP, but it does make it relatively simple to adopt limited liability limited partnership status. Exhibit 5-11 in the Resources section is a list of states that have adopted LLLP legislation, along with cites to the limited partnership acts that include LLLP provisions.

LIMITED LIABILITY LIMITED PARTNERSHIPS IN THE UNITED STATES

In 2011, the use of LLLPs was growing, but still relatively limited. Existing limited partnerships are electing LLLP status in states where it is available to provide their general partners with limited liability. At least one study has found that the LLLP entity is formed primarily for ventures that are expected to have a termination date, as opposed to long-term, ongoing ventures with an indefinite life.[4] As of 2011, the number of limited liability limited partnerships in the United States was not being tracked by the Internal Revenue Service or any other public agency. Whatever the exact number of LLLPs, it is sure to grow as more states adopt legislation providing for the new entity.

IN SUMMATION

- As of 2011, more than half of the states had adopted legislation approving the limited liability limited partnership.
- Limited liability limited partnerships are governed by state law—typically provisions within the state's limited partnership act.

§ 5.6 PARTNER LIABILITY

Pursuant to the Uniform Limited Partnership Act 2001 § 404(c), the general partners of an LLLP have the same full liability shield granted to partners in an LLP:

> (c) An obligation of a limited partnership incurred while the limited partnership is a limited liability limited partnership, whether arising in contract, tort, or otherwise, is solely the obligation of the limited partnership. A general partner is not personally liable, directly or indirectly, by way of contribution or otherwise, for such an obligation solely by reason of being or acting as a general partner. This subsection applies despite anything inconsistent in the partnership agreement that existed immediately before the consent required to become a limited liability limited partnership under Section 406(b)(2).

As with LLPs, a general partner has no shield from liability for LLLP obligations arising due to his or her own wrongdoing.

Limited partners of a LLLP will have protection from personal liability much like the limited partners of a regular limited partnership. Limited partners of an LLLP may be allowed to participate in the management of the LLLP, depending on state statute. Under the Uniform Limited Partnership Act 2001, limited partners have no personal liability for the debts of the entity, regardless of whether the entity is a limited partnership or an LLLP, and regardless of whether the limited partner participates in the management of the limited partnership business. Exhibit 5-7 is a chart depicting the limits on liability offered by the various forms of partnerships.

EXHIBIT 5-7	PARTNERSHIP LIABILITY COMPARISON			
	General Partnership	**Limited Partnership**	**Limited Liability Partnership**	**Limited Liability Limited Partnership**
Most States	No partner is protected from personal liability for partnership debts and obligations.	In most states, limited partners who do not participate in the management of the partnership business are protected from personal liability for partnership debts and obligations. In some states, limited partners are protected from personal liability even if they do participate in the management of the partnership business.		Both limited and general partners are protected from personal liability for partnership debts and obligations unless the obligation was incurred due to a partner's own wrongdoing. Limited partners may be allowed to participate in the management of the partnership business in some states.

continues

EXHIBIT 5-7 *(continued)*

	General Partnership	Limited Partnership	Limited Liability Partnership	Limited Liability Limited Partnership
Partial Shield Statute States			Each partner is protected from personal liability only for partnership debts and obligations incurred due to the wrongdoing of other partners.	
Full Shield Statute States			Each partner is protected from personal liability for all partnership debts and obligations, unless the partnership obligation was incurred due to his or her own wrongdoing.	

© Cengage Learning 2013

IN SUMMATION

- In most instances, general partners of a limited liability limited partnership have the same protection from personal liability granted to partners in a limited liability partnership.
- Limited partners in a limited liability limited partnership have the same protection from personal liability as limited partners in a regular limited partnership.
- In some states, limited partners do not put their protection from personal liability at risk by participating in the management of the limited liability limited partnership.

§ 5.7 LIMITED LIABILITY LIMITED PARTNERSHIP FORMATION AND OPERATION

Requirements for forming and operating a limited liability limited partnership are very similar to the requirements for a limited partnership. In addition, an election to be treated as a limited liability limited partnership must be approved by the vote of the partners of a limited partnership and the proper documentation must be filed at the state level.

LLLP ELECTION AND FORMATION

LLLPs are formed pursuant to state statutes. In states that provide for the formation of limited liability limited partnerships, that entity is usually formed when a limited partnership that complies with all other requirements affecting limited partnerships files an additional election to become a limited liability limited partnership with the secretary of state or other state authority. Exhibit 5-8 is a statement of qualification to elect to become an LLLP in the state of Delaware.

In states that follow the ULPA 2001, every limited partnership certificate that is filed must state whether the limited partnership is a limited liability limited partnership.

VOTING

The voting requirements for a limited partnership to approve an LLLP election vary by state. Typically, the election of LLLP status will require the affirmative vote of the

EXHIBIT 5-8	STATE OF DELAWARE STATEMENT OF QUALIFICATION

STATE OF DELAWARE STATEMENT OF QUALIFICATION

1. The name of the limited liability limited partnership is _____ _____

2. The address of its registered office in the State of Delaware is

```
┌─────────────────────────────────────────────┐
│                                               │
│                                               │
│                                               │
│                                               │
│                                               │
│                                               │
└─────────────────────────────────────────────┘
```

The name and address of the registered agent is _____ _____

3. The number of partners of the limited liability limited partnership is

_____

4. The partnership elects to be a limited liability limited partnership.

IN WITNESS WHEREOF, the undersigned have executed this Statement of Qualification this _____ day of _____ _____ A.D.

Name _____

Delaware Division of Corporations

same partners required to amend the limited partnership agreement. A statement of the manner of approval for the election may be required for inclusion in the document filed with the secretary of state. Section 1107 of the Tennessee Code Annotated sets forth typical voting requirements as follows:

§ 1107. Limited Liability Limited Partnership

(a) A limited partnership may become a limited liability limited partnership by:

(1) obtaining approval of the terms and conditions of the limited partnership becoming a limited liability limited partnership by the vote necessary to amend the limited partnership agreement except, in the case of a limited partnership agreement that expressly considers contribution obligations, the vote necessary to amend those provisions.

ANNUAL REPORTING REQUIREMENTS

Limited liability limited partnerships are generally subject to the same annual reporting requirements as limited partnerships.

LIMITED LIABILITY LIMITED PARTNERSHIP AGREEMENT

A carefully drafted limited partnership agreement is very important to the limited liability limited partnership. LLLP agreements will generally be no different than those for limited partnerships, with the exception of added language to clearly indicate that the partnership is an LLLP, and possibly to further define the limits on personal liability of both the limited and general partners. Following is sample language that may be used in an LLLP agreement to denote its LLLP status:

EXAMPLE: Qualification as a Limited Liability Limited Partnership

The partners hereby agree that this limited partnership shall be a limited liability limited partnership as that term is described in the Act, and the general partners and limited partners shall have the maximum protection from personal liability provided under § _____ of _____ Statutes.

Any general partner is hereby authorized to execute any statement of authority, annual report, statement of foreign qualification, revocation of a statement of qualification as a limited liability limited partnership, or other filing required or authorized to be filed by the Act, and pay appropriate fees therefore necessary or convenient to the Partnership's status as a limited liability limited partnership.

FOREIGN LIMITED LIABILITY LIMITED PARTNERSHIPS

Foreign limited liability limited partnerships are subject to the same state requirements as foreign limited partnerships for qualifying to do business and filing annual reports.

DISSOLVING THE LIMITED LIABILITY LIMITED PARTNERSHIP

Limited liability limited partnerships are dissolved pursuant to the limited partnership act of the state of domicile and the LLLP's partnership agreement in the same manner that limited partnerships are dissolved.

IN SUMMATION

- Requirements for creating a limited liability limited partnership are very similar to the requirements for forming a limited liability partnership or a limited partnership.

- An election to adopt limited liability limited partnership status must be filed with the proper state authority.

- The election to adopt limited liability limited partnership status generally must be approved by a vote of all partners—both general and limited, unless another manner for approval is set forth in the limited partnership agreement.

- Limited liability limited partnerships are generally subject to the same reporting and registration requirements applicable to limited partnerships.

- Limited liability limited partnerships are typically governed by a partnership agreement very similar to the limited partnership agreement.

- A limited liability limited partnership is required to register as a foreign business entity in most states in which it does business other than its state of domicile.

- Limited liability limited partnerships are dissolved pursuant to state statutes in the same manner as limited partnerships.

§ 5.8 ADVANTAGES AND DISADVANTAGES OF DOING BUSINESS AS A LIMITED LIABILITY LIMITED PARTNERSHIP

The advantages and disadvantages to doing business as a limited liability limited partnership are much the same as those of a limited partnership. LLLPs offer the same advantageous income tax benefits, relative transferability of partnership interest and business continuity, and diversified capital resources as limited partnerships. LLLPs offer the added advantage of limited liability for both general and limited partners.

The same disadvantages to doing business as a limited partnership, including formalities and regulatory and reporting requirements as well as legal and organizational expenses, apply to limited liability limited partnerships. The restrictions on management participation by limited partners apply to LLLPs in some states, but not all. See Exhibit 5-9 for an overview of the advantages and disadvantages of doing business as an LLLP.

EXHIBIT 5-9	ADVANTAGES AND DISADVANTAGES OF DOING BUSINESS AS A LIMITED LIABILITY LIMITED PARTNERSHIP

Advantages	Disadvantages
• *Limited Liability for Limited Partners*—Limited partners have no personal liability for the debts and obligations of the limited liability limited partnership.	• *Personal Liability for Certain Obligations*—General partners are personally responsible for partnership obligations incurred due to their own wrongdoing.
• *Limited Liability for All Partners*—Each partner is protected from personal liability for partnership debts and obligations incurred due to the wrongdoing of other partners (partial shield states).	• *Limited liability limited partnership may be subject to state income taxation in some states.*
• *Limited Liability for All Partners*—Each partner is protected from personal liability for partnership debts and obligations, unless the partnership obligation was incurred due to his or her own wrongdoing (full shield states).	• *Prohibition on Control of Business*—Limited partners cannot be involved in the management and control of the limited liability limited partnership in all states.
• *Income Tax Benefits*—Limited liability limited partnerships are not subject to federal income taxation. Income "flows through" to the partners.	• *Formalities and Regulatory and Reporting Requirements*—Limited liability limited partnerships cannot exist until the proper election is made and the proper documentation is filed at the state level. In addition, limited liability limited partnerships may be subject to various reporting requirements that are not imposed on sole proprietorships and general partnerships.
• *Transferability of Partnership Interest*—Compared with general partnerships and limited liability partnerships, limited partners have much more freedom to transfer their interests in the limited liability limited partnership.	• *Legal and Organizational Expense*—The legal and organizational expenses associated with forming and maintaining a limited liability limited partnership are typically considerably greater than those associated with general partnerships and sole proprietorships.
• *Business Continuity*—In contrast to the general partnership or sole proprietorship, the limited liability limited partnership offers more continuity of business.	• *Lack of Case Law and Uniform State Law*—The lack of case law and uniformity of state laws may mean some uncertainty with this newer type of entity.
• *Diversified Capital Resources*—Unlike sole proprietorships and general partnerships, limited liability limited partnerships have the ability to attract passive investors who accept no personal liability.	

IN SUMMATION

- In addition to the advantages offered by all limited partnerships, limited liability limited partnerships offer the added advantage of providing limited personal liability to all partners.
- The limited liability limited partnership also provides some unique disadvantages as a form of business organization, including:
  - There are additional formalities to conducting business as a limited liability limited partnership (compared to a limited partnership). An election must be filed at the state level to form a limited liability partnership.
  - The lack of uniformity in state limited liability limited partnership law provides uncertainty for limited liability limited partnerships that may transact business in more than one state.

§ 5.9 THE PARALEGAL'S ROLE

The paralegal's role in working with LLPs and LLLPs will likely involve conducting research, assisting with forming the appropriate entity, and tracking ongoing formalities.

State law concerning limited liability partnerships, especially limited liability limited partnerships, is relatively new in most states. Not all attorneys are familiar with these newer forms of business organizations and their requirements. Paralegals who work for law firms that advise clients regarding business enterprises may be asked to research these new laws and track new legislation involving these entities. They may be asked to determine the level of protection from personal liability available from each type of limited liability entity, and to determine the filing fees for the initial limited liability election and annual reports.

Paralegals also assist with the filings required at the secretary of state's office to form LLPs and LLLPs and to maintain their good standing. Following is a checklist of items that may require attention to form a new LLP or LLLP:

- Research state statutes to determine requirements for forming an LLP or an LLLP
- Draft documentation evidencing the vote of partners to elect limited liability status
- Draft a statement of qualification or certificate of limited partnership
- Draft LLP or LLLP agreements

CORPORATE PARALEGAL PROFILE
Joanne Zern

I enjoy the variety of work that I experience on a daily basis as well as the ongoing interaction and contact with other corporate departments, government agencies, and outside counsel and paralegals.

NAME Joanne Zern
LOCATION Phoenix, Arizona
TITLE Paralegal Supervisor/Licensing Manager
SPECIALTY Corporate/Restaurant Licensing and Regulation
EDUCATION BA University of California Irvine; Paralegal Certificate, UCLA Extension Program, Attorney Assistant Training Program
EXPERIENCE 30 years

Joanne Zern is a paralegal with P. F. Chang's China Bistro, Inc., a publicly traded corporation, and Pei Wei Asian Diner, Inc., a wholly owned subsidiary. The companies operate two restaurant concepts: P. F. Chang's China Bistro and Pei Wei Asian Diner. All together the companies own and operate more than 375 restaurants throughout the United States and 12 international locations.

Joanne works with four in-house attorneys, as well as three other paralegals, a lease coordinator, and a department assistant. She was promoted to the position of supervisor/manager after being with the company for two years. Joanne reports to the secretary and chief legal officer of P. F. Chang's, and she is responsible for the management of two of the paralegals and the department assistant.

Much of Joanne's work is centered on the regulation and licensing requirements restaurants must adhere to. She researches state and local licensing, zoning, health, tax, corporate, and architectural requirements for the restaurants owned by P. F. Chang's and Pei Wei Asian Diner, and works to obtain the licenses required to open and operate new restaurants throughout the United States as well as to maintain current licenses in existing markets. Her work often includes coordination with government agencies, construction and restaurant personnel, and sometimes outside local counsel.

Because many of the subsidiaries and affiliates of P. F. Chang's China Bistro, Inc. and Pei Wei Asian Diner, Inc. are organized as limited liability partnerships for business operations purposes, Joanne has become very familiar with the requirements for forming and maintaining limited liability partnerships in several states. She is responsible for preparing and filing annual limited liability partnership registrations throughout the country and preparing partnership and corporate resolutions. She has been involved with internal corporate, partnership, and LLC reviews that have resulted in the merger, termination, cancellation, and withdrawal of various partnerships, corporations, and LLCs, and she is knowledgeable as to the documentation and process for accomplishing these tasks. Joanne is also responsible for maintaining current lists of the officers and directors for P. F. Chang's and its subsidiaries and affiliates, as well as a chart of all entities that provides entity detail and current status.

continues

CORPORATE PARALEGAL PROFILE (continued)
Joanne Zern

Joanne loves the challenge of her position, reporting that it challenges her in a different way each day. For Joanne, each day is busy and full and she enjoys the variety of her work. She likes the training and teaching time that she spends with those in her department and is still enjoying learning what responsibilities go with her position as a manager, as well as learning the management skills and putting them to work.

One of the most interesting projects Joanne has worked on involved the opening of more than 20 restaurants over about a year's time span. Her involvement started with the licensing due diligence research, then moved to working with lease counsel regarding liquor-licensing requirements and contingencies, purchasing liquor licenses for certain locations, and obtaining direct issue licenses from government agencies for other locations. She prepared all of the license applications required by the various states, cities, and counties for liquor licenses as well as for business licenses, tax licenses, health permits, and other licenses required to operate each restaurant. Joanne found that coordinating the timing and working with local counsel, government agencies, and restaurant field personnel for all of the different locations was interesting, exciting, and definitely challenging.

Joanne lives in Phoenix with her significant other and two miniature schnauzers. When she is not working, she enjoys traveling, cooking, movies, music, reading, exercising, spending time with friends and family, and trying new things she has never done before. She is a member of the CT Corporation Corporate Paralegal Group, and a founding member, former treasurer, and current board member of the National Association of Licensing and Compliance Professionals.

Joanne's advice to new paralegals?

Be patient, trust yourself, develop confidence, choose good mentors, and listen and learn as much as possible. Accept new projects in different areas and get a taste for all different practice areas, but in time develop an area of expertise. Don't be afraid to challenge yourself, to ask questions. It is important to not fear making mistakes. If you do make a mistake, acknowledge it quickly and learn what you can from the experience.

For more information on careers for corporate paralegals, log in to http://www.cengagebrain.com to access the CourseMate website that accompanies this text; then see the Corporate Careers Section.

ETHICAL CONSIDERATION

Both corporate paralegals who work for law firms and those who work in corporate legal departments often take on a tremendous amount of responsibility. Experienced paralegals can be given very important tasks to complete with very little supervision.

continues

As an important member of the legal services team, it is important for paralegals to assume as much responsibility as they are competent to handle and feel comfortable with. However, it is also important for all paralegals to be aware of the limitations imposed on them by the rules prohibiting the **unauthorized practice of law.**

As set forth in Rule 5.3 of the **Rules of Professional Conduct** and similar rules in each state, attorneys are responsible for the conduct of their non-attorney employees, and they may be held accountable for the unethical actions of their employees. Licensed attorneys must responsibly supervise the actions of any employees or agents to assure that they are not engaging in the unauthorized practice of law or they will be in violation of the pertinent rules or statutes concerning the unauthorized practice of law.

Paralegals who work for corporations must be aware of their legal and ethical boundaries. A corporation may not designate a non-attorney to represent it in matters of a legal nature. Again, if you work under the direct supervision of attorneys in a legal department, you probably need not be too concerned. However, if you find you are working on legal matters with very little or no attorney supervision, you must consider the possibility that the work you are performing could be considered the unauthorized practice of law.

Defining exactly what constitutes the practice of law can be problematic. The term has been defined differently by state statutes and by the courts. The practice of law generally includes the following activities:

1. Setting fees for legal work.

2. Giving legal advice.

3. Preparing or signing legal documents.

4. Representing another before a court or other tribunal.

Following are some suggestions for avoiding the unauthorized practice of law:

*   Always disclose your status as a paralegal, including on letterhead and business cards.

*   Get the approval and signature of your supervising attorney for any legal documents and any correspondence prepared by you that may express a legal opinion.

*   Communicate important issues concerning each case or legal matter with your supervising attorney concerning matters on which you are working.

continues

RULES OF PROFESSIONAL CONDUCT
American Bar Association rules stating and explaining what lawyers must do, must not do, should do, and should not do. They cover the field of legal ethics (a lawyer's obligations to clients, courts, other lawyers, and the public) and have been adopted in modified forms by most of the states.

- Never give legal advice.

- Never discuss the merits of a case with opposing counsel.

- Never agree to represent a client on behalf of an attorney.

- Never represent a client at a deposition, in a court of law, or before an administrative board (unless specifically authorized by the court's rules or agency regulations).

SIDEBAR

From the Model Rules of Professional Conduct 5.5, Unauthorized practice of law: A lawyer shall not

(a) practice law in a jurisdiction where doing so violates the regulation of the legal profession in that jurisdiction; or

(b) assist a person who is not a member of the bar in the performance of activity that constitutes the unauthorized practice of law.

For more information on ethics for corporate paralegals, including links to the NALA and NFPA codes of ethics, log in to http://cengagebrain.com to access the CourseMate website that accompanies this text; then see the Ethics Section.

§ 5.10 RESOURCES

Because the limited liability partnership and the limited liability limited partnership are relatively new entities, new resources are continually being introduced. It is important when working with these entities to make sure that you are using up-to-date resources and information. Some of the more important resources for LLPs and LLLPs are state statutes, continuing education courses and materials, and various Internet resources.

STATE STATUTES

The most important resource to assist with LLP or LLLP matters will be the pertinent state statutes and information available from the secretary of state or other appropriate state office. Exhibit 5-10 is a list of partnership acts that include LLP provisions, and Exhibit 5-11 is a list of limited partnership acts that include limited liability limited partnership provisions. If your state is not on the list for LLLP statutes, you may want to check the limited partnership laws of your state to see if new legislation provides for this entity. Links to these statutes may be accessed from CourseMate.

| EXHIBIT 5-10 | STATE PARTNERSHIP ACTS WITH FULL AND PARTIAL LIMITED LIABILITY PARTNERSHIP PROVISIONS |

State	LLP Provision within State Partnership Act	Type of Personal Liability Protection	Restrictions
Alabama	Ala. Code §§10-8A-1001 through 10-8A-1010	Full Shield	
Alaska	Alaska Uniform Partnership Act §§ 32.06.911 through 32.06.913	Full Shield	
Arizona	Arizona Revised Uniform Partnership Act, Ariz. Rev. Stat. Ann. §§ 29-1101 through 29-1109	Full Shield	
Arkansas	Arkansas Uniform Limited Partnership Act (2001), Ark. Code Ann. §§ 4-47-101 through 4-47-130	Full Shield	
California	Cal. Corp. Code §§ 16951 through 16962	Full Shield	Professional Partnerships Only/Liability Insurance Required or Segregated Funds for Satisfaction of Judgment Required
Colorado	Colorado Uniform Partnership Act 1997, Colo. Rev. Stat. §§7-64-1001 through 7-64-1010	Full Shield	
Connecticut	Uniform Partnership Act, Conn. Gen. Stat. §§ 34-406 though 34-434	Full Shield	Liability Insurance Required for Professional Limited Liability Partnerships
Delaware	Delaware Revised Uniform Partnership Act, Del. Code Ann. Tit. 6 §§ 15-1001 through 15-1004	Full Shield	
District of Columbia	District of Columbia Uniform Partnerships, D.C. Official Code §§ 33-110.01 through 33-110.04	Full Shield	
Florida	Florida Revised Uniform Partnership Act of 1995, Fla. Stat. §§ 620.9001 through 620.90032	Full Shield	

continues

EXHIBIT 5-10 *(continued)*

State	LLP Provision within State Partnership Act	Type of Personal Liability Protection	Restrictions
Georgia	Georgia Uniform Partnership Act, Ga. Code Ann. §§14-8-62 through 14-8-64	Full Shield	
Hawaii	Hawaii Uniform Partnership Act, Haw. Rev. Stat. Ch. 425-151 through 425-173	Full Shield	
Idaho	Idaho Uniform Partnership Act, Idaho Code §§ 53-3-1001 through 53-3-1003	Full Shield	
Illinois	Illinois Uniform Partnership Act (1997), 805 Ill. Comp. Stat. §§ 206/1001 through 206/1003	Full Shield	
Indiana	Indiana Uniform Partnership Act, Ind. Code § 23-4-1-15 and §§ 23-4-1-44 through 23-4-1-53	Full Shield	
Iowa	Iowa Uniform Partnership Act, Iowa Code §§ 486A.101 through 486A.1001	Full Shield	
Kansas	Kansas Uniform Partnership Act, Kan. Stat. Ann.§§ 56a-306 and 56a-1001 through 56a-1004	Full Shield	
Kentucky	Kentucky Revised Uniform Partnership Act (2006), Ky. Rev. Stat. Ann. Ch. 362.1-101 through 362.1-1205 (limited liability partnership provisions throughout)	Full Shield	
Louisiana	La. Civil Code, Arts 2801 through 2835	Full Shield	
Maine	Maine Uniform Limited Liability Partnership Act, Me. Rev. Stat. Ann. tit 31, ch 15 §§ 801 through 876	Full Shield	

continues

EXHIBIT 5-10 *(continued)*

State	LLP Provision within State Partnership Act	Type of Personal Liability Protection	Restrictions
Maryland	Md. Corps. & Ass'ns §§ 9A-1001 through 9A-1016	Full Shield	
Massachusetts	Mass. Gen. L. ch. 108A, §§ 45 through 47	Full Shield	Liability Insurance Required for Professional Limited Liability Partnerships
Michigan	Michigan Uniform Partnership Act, Mich. Comp. Laws §§ 449.44 through 449.48	Partial Shield	
Minnesota	Uniform Partnership Act of 1994; Minn. Stat. Ann. §§ 323.1001 through 323A.1003	Full Shield	
Mississippi	Mississippi Uniform Partnership Act (1997); Miss. Code Ann. §§ 79-13-1001 through 79-13-1002	Full Shield	
Missouri	Mo. Rev. Stat. §§ 358.450 through 358.500	Full Shield	
Montana	Uniform Partnership Act; Mont. Rev. Stat. §§ 35-10-701 through 35-10-710	Full Shield	
Nebraska	Nebraska Uniform Partnership Act 1998, Neb. Rev. Stat. §§ 67-454 through 65-455 and 67-465	Full Shield	
Nevada	Uniform Partnership Act (1997); Nev. Rev. Stat. §§ 87.440 through 87.540	Partial Shield	Professional Partnerships Only
New Hampshire	Uniform Partnership Act, N.H. Rev. Stat. Ann. §§ 304-A:1 through 304-A:62	Partial Shield	
New Jersey	Uniform Partnership Act (1996), N.J. Stat. Ann. §§ 42:1A-1 through 42:1A-56	Full Shield	

continues

EXHIBIT 5-10 *(continued)*

State	LLP Provision within State Partnership Act	Type of Personal Liability Protection	Restrictions
New Mexico	Uniform Partnership Act (1994),N.M. Stat. Ann. §§ 54-1A-1001 through 54-1A-1003	Full Shield	Liability Insurance or Segregated Funds for Satisfaction of Judgment Required
New York	N.Y. Partnership Law §§121-1500 through 121-1507	Full Shield	Professional Partnerships Only
North Carolina	N.C. Gen Stat. §§ 59-84.2 through 59-84.4	Full Shield	
North Dakota	Limited Liability Partnerships, N.D. Cent. Code §§ 45-22-01 through 45-22-27	Full Shield	
Ohio	Ohio Uniform Partnership Act, Ohio Rev. Code Ann. §§ 1776.81 through 1776.84	Full Shield	
Oklahoma	Oklahoma Revised Uniform Partnership Act, Okla. Stat. tit. 54, §§ 1-1001 through 1-1002	Full Shield	Professional Partnerships Only
Oregon	Oregon Revised Partnership Act, Or. Rev. Stat. §§ 67.500 through 67.680	Full Shield	Professional Partnerships Only
Pennsylvania	Registered Limited Liability Partnerships, Pa. Cons. Stat. Ann. §§ 8201 through 8221	Partial Shield	
Rhode Island	Uniform Partnership Act, Gen. Laws 1956, §§ 7-12-56 through 7-12-59	Full Shield	Liability Insurance or Segregated Funds for Satisfaction of Judgment Required
South Carolina	Uniform Partnership Act, S.C. Code Ann. §§ 33-41-1110 through 33-41-1220	Partial Shield	Liability Insurance or Segregated Funds for Satisfaction of Judgment Required

continues

EXHIBIT 5-10 (*continued*)

State	LLP Provision within State Partnership Act	Type of Personal Liability Protection	Restrictions
South Dakota	Uniform Partnership Act, S.D. Codified Laws Ann. §§ 48-7A-101 through 48-7A-1004.1	Full	
Tennessee	Tennessee Revised Uniform Partnership Act, Tenn Code Ann. §§ 61-1-100 through 61-1-1006	Partial Shield	
Texas	Tex. Partnership Law, Texas Stats. §§ 152.801 through 152.805	Full Shield	Liability Insurance or Segregated Funds for Satisfaction of Judgment Required
Utah	Utah Code Ann. §§ 48-1-41 through 48-1-48	Partial Shield	
Vermont	Partnerships, Vt. Stat. Ann. tit. 11, §§ 3291 through 3293	Full Shield	
Virginia	Va. Code Ann. §§ 50-73.132 through 50-73.143	Full Shield	
Washington	Washington Revised Uniform Partnership Act, Wash. Rev. Code §§ 25.05.500 through 25.05.536	Full Shield	
West Virginia	Uniform Partnership Act, W. Va. Code §§ 47B-10-1 through 47B-10-5	Partial Shield	Liability Insurance or Segregated Funds for Satisfaction of Judgment Required
Wisconsin	Uniform Partnership Act, Wis. Stat. §§ 178.40 through 178.44	Partial Shield	
Wyoming	Uniform Partnership Act, Wyo. Stat. Ann. §§ 17-21-1101 through 17-21-1107	Full Shield	

© Cengage Learning 2013

EXHIBIT 5-11 STATE LIMITED PARTNERSHIP STATUTES INCLUDING LIMITED LIABILITY LIMITED PARTNERSHIP PROVISIONS

State	State LLP Statutes that Include LLLP Provisions	Version of Uniform Act Adopted
Alabama	Ala. Code §§ 10A-9-1.01 through 10A-9-12.08	ULPA (2001)
Arkansas	Ark. Code Ann. §§ 4-47-101 through 4-47-1302	ULPA (2001)
California	Cal. Corp. Code §§ 159000 through 15912.07	ULPA (2001)
Delaware	Del. Code Ann. Tit. 6, §§ 17-101 through 17-1111	RULPA
District of Columbia	D.C. Code §§ 33-201.01 through 33-211.07	RULPA
Florida	Fla. Stat. Ann. §§ 620.1101 through 620.2205	ULPA (2001)
Hawaii	Haw. Rev. Stat. §§ 425E-101 through 425E-1206	ULPA (2001)
Idaho	Idaho Code §§ 53-2-101 through 53-2-1205	ULPA (2001)
Illinois	805 ILCS §§ 215/0.01 through 215/1402	ULPA (2001)
Iowa	Iowa Code §§ 488.101 through 488.1207	ULPA (2001)
Kentucky	Ky. Rev. Stat. Ann §§ 362.2-102 through 362.2-1207	ULPA (2001)
Maine	Me. Rev. Stat. Ann. Tit. 31, §§ 1301 through 1461	ULPA (2001)
Maryland	Md. Corps. & Ass'ns §§ 10-101 through 10-1105	RULPA
Minnesota	Minn. Stat. §§321.0101 through 321.1208	ULPA (2001)
Missouri	Mo. Rev. Stat. §§ 359.011 through 359.691	RULPA
Nevada	Nev. Rev. Stat 87A.010 through 87A.700	ULPA (2001)
New Mexico	N.M. Ann. Stat. §§ 54-2A-101 through 54-2A-1206	ULPA (2001)
North Carolina	N.C. Gen Stat. §§ 59-101 through 59-1107	RULPA
North Dakota	N.C. Cent. Code §§ 45-10.2-01 through 45-10.2-117	ULPA (2001)
Oklahoma	Okla. Stat. Ann. Tit. 54, §§ 500-101A through 1207A	ULPA (2001)
South Dakota	S.D. Codified Laws Ann. §§ 48-7-101 through 48-7-1106	RULPA
Texas	Texas Bus Org. Code §§ 153.001 through 153.555	RULPA
Washington	Wash. Rev. Code §§ 25.10.006 through 25.10.926	ULPA (2001)
Wyoming	Wyo. Stat. §§ 17-14-201 through 17-14-1104	RULPA

© Cengage Learning 2013

SECRETARY OF STATE OFFICES

For information on procedural requirements for adopting limited liability partnership or limited liability limited partnership status, visit the website for the secretary of state. The secretary of state websites provide information concerning their requirements for filing limited liability partnership documents. Most states provide downloadable forms as well. Appendix A to this text is a directory of secretary of state offices. Links to those secretary of state offices may be found at the CourseMate website that accompanies this text.

INCOME TAX INFORMATION FOR LLPS AND LLLPS

Information on federal taxation requirements is available from the Internal Revenue Service.

Information concerning any state requirements for filing limited liability partnership returns can usually be obtained from the appropriate state tax agency or the secretary of state's office.

CONTINUING EDUCATION

Because LLPs and LLLPs are relatively new, these entities are likely topics for continuing education courses offered throughout the country. Continuing education classes, and the materials distributed in the classes, are usually very up to date and informative. Continuing education classes are often offered by state and local bar associations, as well as national organizations.

SUMMARY

- Limited liability partnerships were first introduced into state legislation in the mid-1990s.
- Limited liability partnerships were first designed for professionals who provided services as partnerships.
- Limited liability partnerships are governed by state statute—typically provisions found within the Uniform Partnership Act as adopted by each state.
- Partial shield statutes protect partners from personal liability for the negligence and wrongdoing of other partners.
- Full shield statutes protect partners from personal liability for all debts and obligations of the partnership, although a partner may still be personally liable for his or her own wrongdoing.
- Some states require limited liability partnerships to carry liability insurance or segregate funds for the payment of judgments against the partnership.
- As of 2011, more than half the states had passed laws approving LLLPs.
- The general partners of an LLLP are protected from personal liability to the extent provided for by state statute or the limited partnership agreement (in compliance with state statute).
- LLPs and LLLPs are subject to annual reporting requirements in their states of domicile and in states where they transact business as a foreign partnership.

REVIEW QUESTIONS

1. How do limited liability partnerships differ from general partnerships?

2. Where in the state statutes is law governing limited liability partnerships generally found?

3. In states that follow the UPA (1997), what information must be included in a statement of qualification to elect limited liability partnership statutes?

4. Why do some states require limited liability partnerships to maintain liability insurance?

5. What is the difference between partial shield statutes and full shield statutes?

6. If a partnership formed in a partial shield state has a judgment filed against it for a $10,000 debt arising from the embezzlement of funds by one partner, who will be responsible for paying the partnership debt once the partnership assets have been exhausted?

7. Why might a limited liability limited partnership be a poor choice of entity for a business that operates in several states?

8. In states that follow the ULPA 2001, how is an election made to form a limited liability limited partnership?

PRACTICAL PROBLEMS

1. Locate the limited liability partnership statute provisions within the statutes of your state. Is your state a partial shield or full shield state? What statute section defines whether your state is a full or partial shield state?

2. Are limited liability limited partnerships provided for under the statutes of your state? If yes, what is the citation for the statute that allows the formation of limited liability limited partnerships in your state?

CRITICAL THINKING EXERCISE

Law firms have traditionally operated as general partnerships. Why might a limited liability partnership be a good choice of entity for a law firm partnership? What are some possible drawbacks?

WORKPLACE SCENARIO

Assume the facts given in the Workplace Scenario at the end of Chapter 3 of this text. Bradley Harris and Cynthia Lund have formed their partnership, and they are operating as Cutting Edge partners. Mr. Harris and Ms. Lund would like to elect limited liability partnership status.

Using the earlier information and the information provided in Appendices B-1 and B-2 of this text, prepare for filing in your state a statement of qualification, or similarly titled document. You may create your own form that conforms to the statutes of your state, or you can download a form from the appropriate

state office. Some statement of qualification forms for specific states are also available for downloading on CourseMate.

In addition to the statement of qualification, prepare a cover letter filing the form with the appropriate state authority, along with any required filing fee.

Portfolio Reminder
Save the documents prepared for the Workplace Scenario exercises in each chapter, either in hard copy or electronically, to build a portfolio

of documents to be used for job interviews or as sample documents on the job. At this point, your portfolio should include the following:

- Power of attorney
- Application for assumed name
- Application for federal employer identification number

- Application for state employer identification number
- Partnership statement of authority
- Limited partnership certificate
- Limited liability partnership statement of qualification

ENDNOTES

1. Uniform Partnership Act (1997) § 1001.
2. Uniform Partnership Act (1997) § 1003.
3. Adapted from the "Prototype Partnership Agreement for a Limited Liability Partnership Formed under the Uniform Partnership Act" (1997), by the subcommittee on the

   Prototype Limited Liability Partnership Agreement, *Business Lawyer*, Feb. 2003.
4. "Reforming Corporate Governance: What History Can Teach Us," *Berkeley Bus. L.J.* 1, 33, 2004.

CourseMate

To access additional course materials including CourseMate, please visit http://www.cengagebrain .com At the CengageBrain home page, search for the ISBN of your title (from the back cover of your book) using the search box at the top of the page.

This will take you to the product page where these resources can be found. The CourseMate resources for this text include Web links to further information on LLPs and LLLPs, downloadable forms, flash cards, and more."

6

LIMITED LIABILITY COMPANIES

CHAPTER OUTLINE

INTRODUCTION

In recent years, several new limited liability entities have been introduced in the United States, including the limited liability partnerships discussed in Chapter 5 and the limited liability company, which is the focus of this chapter.

In this chapter, we define the term "limited liability company," look at the unique characteristics of limited liability companies, and examine the history and status of that entity in the United States. Our discussion then turns to the law governing limited liability companies and the advantages and disadvantages of doing business as a limited liability company. Next, we focus on the rights and powers limited liability companies possess, the members' rights and responsibilities, and the organization and management of the limited liability company. After a discussion of the limited liability company's financial structure, limited liability company lawsuits, and the dissolution of limited liability companies, we will briefly explore foreign limited liability companies and conclude with a look at the role of paralegals working with limited liability companies.

§ 6.1 AN INTRODUCTION TO LIMITED LIABILITY COMPANIES

The **limited liability company** (LLC) is a type of business organization that offers many of the benefits of both partnerships and corporations. The LLC is the most prevalent type of noncorporate entity in the United States. In recent years, the number of new limited liability companies has surpassed the number of new corporations being formed in most states.

LIMITED LIABILITY COMPANY DEFINED

The limited liability company is a noncorporate entity that offers limited personal liability to its owners. It is somewhat of a cross between a partnership and a corporation. The LLC is owned by **members** who either manage the company directly or delegate that responsibility to managers or officers. Like a corporation, the owners of a limited liability company are usually not liable for company debts and obligations. Like a partnership, the LLC's income and losses are allocated to the owners, who then pay tax on their allocated share.

LIMITED LIABILITY COMPANY CHARACTERISTICS

The limited liability company is an unincorporated entity based on the concept of freedom of contract. It is a legal entity distinct from its owners.

The characteristics of any limited liability company will depend on its members' objectives and the statutes of the state in which it is formed. However, most limited liability companies have common characteristics, including limited liability, flexible management, continuity of life, restricted transferability of interest, unrestricted ownership, certain formalities for formation, and partnership taxation status.

Limited Liability

Like a corporation, the owners of a limited liability company typically have no personal liability for the debts and obligations of the company.

LIMITED LIABILITY COMPANY
A cross between a partnership and a corporation owned by members who may manage the company directly or delegate to officers or managers who are similar to a corporation's directors. Governing documents are usually publicly filed.

MEMBER
An owner of a limited liability company.

SIDEBAR

The limited liability shield provided by the LLC statutes will not protect limited liability members from personal liability for their own crimes and wrongdoing.

Management

Management of the limited liability company is very flexible. All members of the limited liability company are granted the right to manage the LLC's business unless otherwise provided for in the limited liability company's **articles of organization**.

State statutes typically permit the owners of a limited liability company to allocate management authority among the LLC's members in any manner they choose. They may decide to be managed by one individual, by committee, or by the majority of the owners. Most limited liability companies appoint a **board of managers**, similar to a corporation's board of directors. A written agreement among the members, referred to as an **operating agreement**, sets forth the details concerning the management of the limited liability company.

Major decisions of a limited liability company are usually made by the members holding a majority of the limited liability company interest, unless otherwise provided for in the operating agreement or by statute.

Continuity of Life

The statutes of most states provide that a limited liability company may be designed for continuity. Unless the articles of organization provide that the limited liability company will be a term company that will dissolve on a certain future date or event, the limited liability company will be an **entity at will**, meaning that it exists indefinitely, until the members dissolve it.

The death or dissociation of one or more of the members of a limited liability company does not necessarily cause the dissolution of the LLC. The statutes of some states provide that the members of a limited liability company must give six months' notice of their intent to dissociate from the company.

Transferability of Interest

State statutes place restrictions on the transfer of the ownership interest of limited liability companies. Many statutory restrictions may be modified by the company's operating agreement.

Members of a limited liability company are not considered to be co-owners of the company's property. Limited liability company property is owned by the company itself. A member may usually transfer or assign his or her right to receive distributions to another person. This transfer does not necessarily make the new owner of the distribution rights a member of the limited liability company. The **transferee** of a member's financial rights to a limited liability company does not have the same rights to participate in the management and operation of the company that members do.

ARTICLES OF ORGANIZATION
Document required to be filed with the proper state authority to form a limited liability company.

BOARD OF MANAGERS
Group of individuals elected by the members of a limited liability company to manage the limited liability company. Similar to a corporation's board of directors.

OPERATING AGREEMENT
Document that governs the limited liability company. Similar to a corporation's bylaws.

ENTITY AT WILL
Entity that may be dissolved at the wish of one or more members or owners.

TRANSFEREE
A person to whom a transfer is made.

A person may become a member of a limited liability company only if he or she is substituted, or admitted, to the limited liability company as provided by the company's articles of organization.

Ownership

There are very few restrictions on the number or type of owners who may own limited liability companies. Most state statutes provide that a limited liability company may be formed by one or more persons. That definition of persons usually includes corporations, partnerships, trusts, and other entities. Larger corporations may form subsidiary LLCs of which the corporation is the sole shareholder.

Formalities of Organization

The limited liability company is formed in much the same way that the limited partnership or business corporation is formed. Articles of organization are filed with the secretary of state or other appropriate state authority. In addition, a limited liability company may be subject to annual reporting requirements imposed by the state in which it was organized.

Taxation

One of the most important benefits to forming a limited liability company is the partnership taxation status, which is preferable to corporate taxation for most members.

In 1997, the Internal Revenue Service adopted Check the Box regulations,[1] which make it simple for a limited liability company to be taxed as a partnership. When the members of a limited liability company file an income tax return for the LLC, it is classified, by default, as a partnership. If the members prefer, they can simply check the box on an election form and elect to be taxed as a corporation. Single-member limited liability companies are disregarded as entities separate from

EXHIBIT 6-1	LIMITED LIABILITY COMPANY CHARACTERISTICS SIMILAR TO CORPORATIONS AND SIMILAR TO PARTNERSHIPS
Characteristics Similar to Corporations	**Characteristics Similar to Partnership**
• Formed by filing articles with secretary of state (or similar official)	• Not incorporated
• Legal entity distinct from its members	• Flexible management by owners
• Limited personal liability for owners	• Restricted transferability of interest
	• Partnership taxation status

their owners for federal income taxation purposes unless the sole member elects for the LLC to be taxed as a corporation.

Most states follow the federal scheme for limited liability company income taxation. However, some states, especially those that do not have a personal state income tax, may either treat limited liability companies as corporations for income taxation purposes, or they may assess special taxes on limited liability companies. Exhibit 6-1 lists the particular characteristics of a limited liability company.

IN SUMMATION

- The limited liability company has the following characteristics:
  - Limited liability for owners—not personally responsible for the LLC's debts and obligations
  - Flexible management—may be centralized or decentralized
  - Continuity of life—may continue indefinitely in most states
  - Transferability of interest—may be restricted
  - Ownership—very few restrictions on ownership
  - Formalities—certain formalities must be followed to organize
  - Taxes—taxed like a partnership under most circumstances

§ 6.2 LIMITED LIABILITY COMPANIES IN THE UNITED STATES

Limited liability companies were one of the first new entities to be introduced in the United States in several decades. While similar business organizations have existed in other countries for several years, the first state legislation adopting limited liability companies was not passed in this country until 1977. This first state, Wyoming, was followed by Florida in 1982. These statutes did not receive much national attention until a 1988 IRS Revenue Ruling[2] classified a Wyoming limited liability company as a partnership for federal tax purposes—a decided advantage for many business owners. At this time, every state in the country and the District of Columbia has adopted legislation approving the limited liability company. The number of limited liability companies formed each year has grown dramatically since their inception. See Exhibit 6-2.

Limited liability companies have become "the dominant form for newly created small businesses in a clear majority of the states,"[3] rivaling corporations. For the first time in 2002, the number of limited liability companies filing federal income tax returns exceeded the number of any other entity filing such noncorporate returns, including general and limited partnerships. In 2008, 1,898,178 limited liability companies filed income tax returns.[4] During that same year, 669,601 general partnerships filed returns.[5] Exhibit 6-3 shows the increase in the number of limited liability companies in the United States since 1998 compared to general and limited partnerships.

EXHIBIT 6-2	NUMBER OF LIMITED LIABILITY COMPANIES FILING TAX RETURNS FROM 1999 TO 2008.

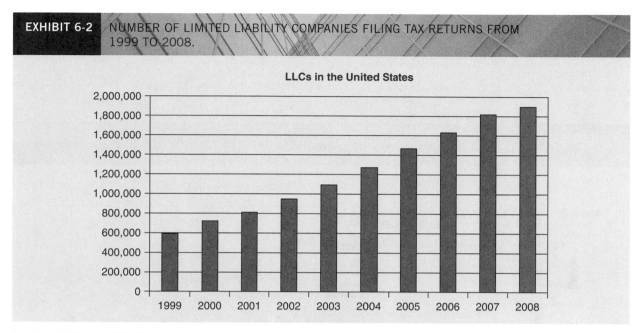

From Income Tax Returns, 1999–2008 Internal Revenue Service.

EXHIBIT 6-3	NUMBER OF LIMITED LIABILITY COMPANIES FILING PARTNERSHIP RETURNS EACH YEAR COMPARED TO PARTNERSHIPS AND LIMITED PARTNERSHIPS

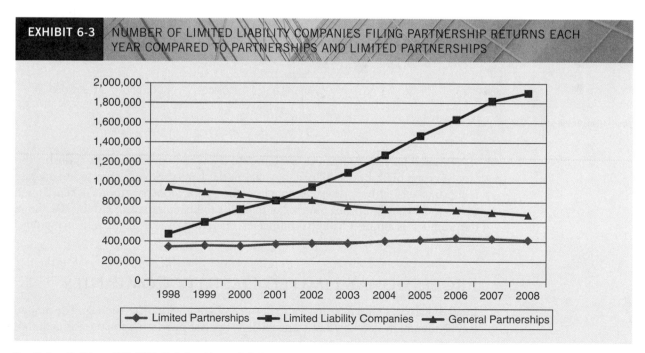

From Partnership Returns 1998–2008, Statistics of Income Bulletins, Internal Revenue Service.

SIDEBAR

More than half of all 2008 partnership returns filed with the Internal Revenue Service were filed by limited liability companies.

EXHIBIT 6-4   NUMBER OF LIMITED LIABILITY COMPANIES FILING TAX RETURNS IN 2008 BY INDUSTRY GROUP

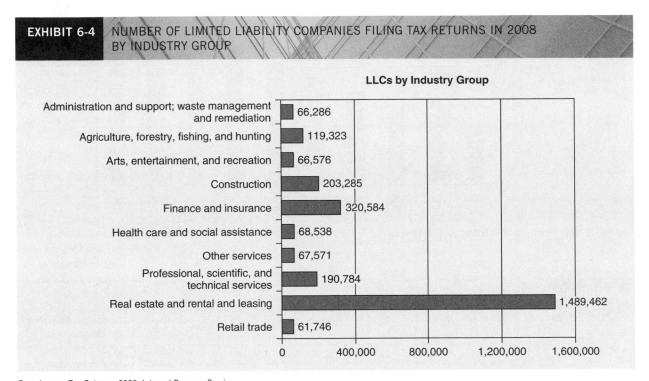

From Income Tax Returns, 2008, Internal Revenue Service.

Limited liability companies are formed for a variety of reasons. By industry, the largest group of limited liability companies in the United States is formed to operate real-estate-related businesses, although all the major industry groups in the United States include a significant number of limited liability companies. Exhibit 6-4 shows the number of limited liability companies operating in the major industry groups in 2008.

PROFESSIONAL LIMITED LIABILITY COMPANIES

Limited liability companies have also become popular with professionals. The limited liability company acts of most states include special provisions for the formation of professional limited liability companies (PLLCs) by doctors, lawyers, and other professionals. The requirements for PLLCs are generally very similar to those of other limited liability companies, with a few distinctions. Following are some of the typical requirements unique to professional limited liability companies:

- Membership in professional limited liability companies may be restricted to licensed professionals of a single profession.
- The members who are professionals are personally liable for any acts of malpractice.
- The name of the company must include the words "professional limited liability company" or the initials "PLLC."

LOW-PROFIT LIMITED LIABILITY COMPANIES

Since 2008, a few states have adopted provisions in their LLC laws that provide for a new subcategory of limited liability company, the **low-profit limited liability company**. The low-profit limited liability company, or "L3C" as it may be referred to, is a special type of entity that may only be formed by companies that have a charitable or educational purpose.

IN SUMMATION

- In many states, more limited liability companies are being formed than any other business entity.
- Professional limited liability companies may be formed by members of a single licensed profession in most states.
- A few states have adopted provisions in their limited liability company acts to provide for low-profit limited liability companies that may be formed for certain nonprofit purposes.

§ 6.3 LAW GOVERNING LIMITED LIABILITY COMPANIES

Limited liability companies are governed by the statutes of the state in which the LLC is formed. Many of the state limited liability company acts resemble the **Uniform Limited Liability Company Act** or the **Revised Uniform Limited Liability Company Act**. In addition, limited liability companies may be subject to the **Securities Act of 1933** and the **Securities Exchange Act of 1934**.

STATE LAW AND THE UNIFORM LIMITED LIABILITY COMPANY ACT

In the early 1990s, state legislatures were quick to adopt limited liability company acts, and the statutes were very diverse. The differences between state acts created

LOW-PROFIT LIMITED LIABILITY COMPANY
A subcategory of limited liability company that may be formed in a few states by certain entities that have a charitable or educational purpose.

UNIFORM LIMITED LIABILITY COMPANY ACT
Uniform Act adopted by the National Conference of Commissioners on Uniform State Laws In 1994 and amended In 1995 to give states guidance when drafting limited liability company statutes.

REVISED UNIFORM LIMITED LIABILITY COMPANY ACT
Uniform Act adopted by the National Conference of Commissioners on Uniform State Laws in 2006 to address numerous questions that had arisen concerning limited liability company law.

SECURITIES ACT OF 1933
Federal securities act requiring the registration of securities that are to be sold to the public and the disclosure of complete information to potential buyers.

SECURITIES EXCHANGE ACT OF 1934
Federal securities act that regulates stock exchanges and over-the-counter stock sales.

difficulties for limited liability companies that transact business in more than one state. To compound that problem, little case law existed to interpret state statutes because the limited liability company entity was relatively new.

In 1994, the National Conference of Commissioners on Uniform State Laws adopted the Uniform Limited Liability Company Act, which was amended in 1995. The purpose of the Uniform Limited Liability Company Act was to give state legislatures some uniform guidelines for drafting state legislation. The Uniform Limited Liability Company Act encompasses many of the provisions that had already been adopted by individual states, but it allows for maximum flexibility.

In 2006, the Uniform Law Commission drafted a new, revised act, referred to as the Revised Uniform Limited Liability Company Act, which was approved by the American Bar Association. This newer version of the act was drafted to address numerous questions that had arisen concerning limited liability company law, and to address changes made to tax regulations applicable to limited liability companies. The new act is intended to preserve the best elements of the original Uniform Limited Liability Company Act; address questions that have arisen in practice and in litigation; and offer a modern, updated, "second generation" Uniform Limited Liability Company Act.[6]

As of late 2011, only eight states[7] and the Virgin Islands had adopted the original Uniform Limited Liability Company Act, and four states[8] had adopted the Revised Uniform Limited Liability Company Act (2006). Because it is impossible to discuss the laws of each state individually in one chapter, this chapter focuses on the provisions of the Uniform Limited Liability Company Act. This act most closely resembles the limited liability company acts currently followed by most states. The Uniform Limited Liability Company Act and the Revised Uniform Limited Liability Company Act may be found online on the Uniform Law Commission website. It is important to remember, however, that the limited liability company act of your state may vary significantly from the Uniform Act, and state law must always be consulted. Exhibit 6-12 in the Resources section of this chapter includes a list of state limited liability company statutes as of late 2011.

SECURITIES LAWS

Most limited liability companies have a small number of members who all participate in the company's business to a certain extent. Compliance with state and federal securities acts, which are designed primarily to protect inactive investors in larger corporations and other entities, is of little concern to such companies.

However, the applicability of state and federal securities laws to some limited liability company interests is still an open question in many respects. If a member's interest is determined to be an **investment contract** under the Securities Exchange Act, then the interest is considered a **security** subject to state and federal securities laws. For purposes of determining the existence of an investment contract as defined in federal securities law, the investment must have the following three elements: It must be (1) an investment (2) in a common enterprise (3) with an expectation of profits to be derived solely from the efforts of others.

INVESTMENT CONTRACT
Under federal law, any agreement that involves an investment of money pooled with others' money to gain profits solely from the efforts of others.

SECURITY
A share of stock, a bond, a note, or one of many different kinds of documents showing a share in a company or a debt owed by a company or a government. The U.S. Supreme Court has defined a security as any investment in a common enterprise from which the investor is "led to expect profits solely from the efforts of a promoter or a third party."

A membership interest in a limited liability company will include these first two elements. It is the third element, requiring an expectation of profits to be derived solely from the efforts of others, that will determine whether a member's interest is considered a security. In a limited liability company where all members play an active role in the operation of the business, the limited liability company will not be considered a security, whereas the interest of a member in a limited liability company with very centralized management may be considered a security.

In several court cases in the late 1990s the courts held that membership interests in wireless cable limited liability companies were considered investment contracts. In one case, it was determined that the limited liability company interests sold were securities because (1) they were sold by the defendant to over 700 individual investors in 43 states, (2) members were required to purchase at least two $5,000 "units," and (3) the defendant "exercised near-total control" over the management of the limited liability company.[9]

More recent cases have gone both ways. In *Robinson v. Glynn*,[10] an investor in an LLC doing business in the telecommunications field brought a securities fraud action against the LLC and its former chairman. The plaintiff alleged that he purchased his LLC membership interest by relying on misrepresentations made to him by the former chairman. The defendant LLC in this case was member-managed, and the LLC interests were determined not to be securities, partly because the plaintiff had the power to participate in the management of the LLC and to appoint members to management positions.

In another case heard recently, *KFC Ventures, L.L.C. v. Metaire Medical Leasing Corp.*, it was ruled that the LLC interests were securities, partly because the member of the manager-managed LLC did not have the ability to exercise any management control of the LLC.[11]

Some states have attempted to answer the question by passing laws that include interests in limited liability companies in their list of securities subject to regulation. However, not all states have taken this step, and even those that have list exceptions to the rule. For example, an interest in a small limited liability company in which all members actively participate is almost never considered a security. An interest in a limited liability company that is determined to be a security is subject to both federal securities laws and state blue sky laws, which are discussed in Chapter 11 of this text.

IN SUMMATION

- Limited liability companies are subject to state limited liability company law, which may be based on the Uniform Limited Liability Company Act or the Revised Uniform Limited Liability Company Act.
- Some larger limited liability companies where members are investors with little or no control over their investments may be subject to state and federal securities laws.

§ 6.4 ADVANTAGES OF DOING BUSINESS AS A LIMITED LIABILITY COMPANY

There can be several advantages to doing business as a limited liability company. Some of the most important advantages include the limited personal liability offered to owners of the company, the beneficial tax treatment received by the owners, and the flexible management structure available to the limited liability company.

LIMITED LIABILITY FOR ALL OWNERS

The fact that the owners of the limited liability company are not subject to personal liability for the debts and obligations of the company is probably the most significant advantage to doing business as a limited liability company as opposed to doing business as a limited partnership, general partnership, or sole proprietorship. Whereas sole proprietors and general partners may be held personally liable for the debts and other obligations of their businesses, owners of a limited liability company may not. The owners of a limited liability company generally have the same protection from personal liability that is granted to shareholders of a corporation.

Although members of a limited liability company, especially a startup company, may find it necessary to give personal guarantees to secure financing for their business, members of a limited liability company cannot be held personally liable for the company's debts and obligations merely because of their status in the company.

In *Addy v. Myers*, the case that follows in this chapter, two members of a limited liability company borrowed funds from a bank on behalf of the company and gave personal guarantees. When the business of the limited liability company failed and the bank loans became due, the two members who gave personal guarantees for the funds were found to be responsible for the loans. Because the members of a limited liability company are not personally liable for the debts of the company, the court determined that members who did not give personal guarantees for the loans could not be held responsible.

UNRESTRICTIVE OWNERSHIP

Unlike the S Corporation, a somewhat similar organization discussed in Chapter 7 of this text, there are very few, if any, restrictions placed on the number or identity of the owners of limited liability companies. A limited liability company may have any number of members, and those members may include corporations or other entities. For example, the members of an LLC may include a corporation and one or more individuals.

ABILITY TO RAISE CAPITAL FOR THE BUSINESS

Membership interests in the limited liability company offer maximum flexibility to investors. In general, the details of the membership interests sold in the limited liability company are up to the company's members. Unlike S Corporations, investors in a limited liability company may include corporate or foreign investors.

Limiting the personal liability of business owners increases the number of potential investors.

BENEFICIAL TAX TREATMENT

By default, the owners of a limited liability company will be taxed as a partnership by the Internal Revenue Service. Or, in the case of a single-owner limited liability company, the entity is disregarded for federal income tax purposes and the owner is taxed in the same manner as a sole proprietor. This gives the limited liability company a decided tax advantage over the corporation. When a limited liability company is treated like a partnership for federal income tax purposes, the income earned by the limited liability company flows through to the owners of the company and is added to their personal income. The limited liability company's income is taxed once at the income tax rate of the individual owners. Corporate income, on the other hand, may be subject to double taxation—once at the corporate level when the income is earned by the corporation, and once at the shareholder level when dividends are received.

FLEXIBILITY OF MANAGEMENT

In comparison with other forms of business, there are generally few statutory restrictions placed on the management of a limited liability company. Unlike the limited partnership, for example, all members of the limited liability company are free to contribute to the management of the company without the threat of losing their limited liability status. In addition, limited liability companies are not subject to the requirements for holding shareholder meetings to which corporations must adhere.

CASE

Supreme Court of North Dakota. Boyd ADDY and Tom Hutchens, dba the M.A.H.D. Group, L.L.C., Plaintiffs and Appellants, v. Guy MYERS, Defendant, and Nancy Myers, individually and as part of M.A.H.D., L.L.C., Defendants and Appellees. No. 990387. Aug. 31, 2000.

VANDE WALLE, Chief Justice.
Boyd Addy and Tom Hutchens appealed from a judgment dismissing their action against Guy and Nancy Myers . . .

I

In June 1995, the M.A.H.D. Group was formed . . . to establish a restaurant in Bismarck named Ed Foo Yungs. . . . Each of the named owners of the M.A.H.D. Group contributed $32,500 and owned 25 percent of the company.

Although they were not all formally named in the M.A.H.D. Group organizational papers, the company informally consisted of four

continues

CASE *(continued)*

Supreme Court of North Dakota. Boyd ADDY and Tom Hutchens, dba the M.A.H.D. Group, L.L.C., Plaintiffs and Appellants, v. Guy MYERS, Defendant, and Nancy Myers, individually and as part of M.A.H.D., L.L.C., Defendants and Appellees.

families: Guy and Nancy Myers, Boyd and Deb Addy, Tom and Kathy Hutchens, and Lance and Lori Doerr.

Ed Foo Yungs opened in February 1996 and in a short time began experiencing financial difficulties. The minutes of a May 15, 1996 meeting for the M.A.H.D. Group state "[i]t was agreed that a $30,000.00 line of credit be set up at BNC National Bank." According to Boyd Addy and Tom Hutchens, they personally signed for what they described as a $15,000 line of credit for Ed Foo Yungs in May 1996 and for another $15,000 line of credit in July 1996. Boyd Addy and Tom Hutchens testified they loaned the $30,000 to the M.A.H.D. Group and it was to repay BNC National Bank with proceeds from the business.

In November 1996, Ed Foo Yungs was still experiencing financial difficulties. On November 7, 1996, Boyd Addy, Tom Hutchens, Lance and Lori Doerr, and Guy and Nancy Myers attended a company meeting at the Myers's home. According to Nancy Myers, she was told Ed Foo Yungs needed another $15,000 line of credit, the money would be borrowed by the M.A.H.D. Group, and it would repay the loan. . . . On November 8, 1996, Boyd Addy and Tom Hutchens personally signed for the $15,000 line of credit.

Ed Foo Yungs continued to experience financial difficulties, and the minutes of a February 13, 1997 meeting state the owners decided to close the business on February 16, 1997. The minutes of a March 26, 1997 meeting state: "[i]t was agreed that the $45,000.00 due BNC National

would be assumed equally by the Addys, Myers, and Hutchens, to be assumed by the 15th of April." Boyd Addy testified Nancy Myers objected at that meeting to paying $15,000. Guy and Nancy Myers subsequently retained an attorney, who wrote a letter to Lori Doerr requesting the minutes of the March 26 meeting be revised to reflect the Myers had not agreed to assume any personal liability for the $15,000.

Boyd Addy and Tom Hutchens sued Guy and Nancy Myers. The trial court granted summary judgment for Guy Myers, concluding he was not personally obligated for the $15,000 loan because he was not listed as a capital contributor, an owner, a manager, a governor, or an officer of the company. After a bench trial, the court decided Nancy Myers had not guaranteed repayment of the $15,000 loan because there was no written guaranty signed by her. The court decided the $15,000 loan signed for by Boyd Addy and Tom Hutchens in November 1996 was for the M.A.H.D. Group; however, the company's articles of organization specifically stated its members were not liable for its debt, obligation, or liability and Nancy Myers did not intend to assume any personal liability for the $15,000 loan. . . . The M.A.H.D. Group was established as a limited liability company under N.D.C.C. ch. 10–32, which was enacted in 1993 N.D Sess. Laws. ch. 92. A limited liability company combines the flow-through income tax advantages and capital structure of a partnership with the limited liability and governance structure of a corporation. . . . Limited

CASE *(continued)*
Supreme Court of North Dakota. Boyd ADDY and Tom Hutchens, dba the M.A.H.D. Group, L.L.C., Plaintiffs and Appellants, v. Guy MYERS, Defendant, and Nancy Myers, individually and as part of M.A.H.D., L.L.C., Defendants and Appellees.

liability companies are taxed like partnerships, but are like corporations in that members have limited liability like corporate shareholders. . . . A limited liability company is a separate business entity and its owners or members are not exposed to personal liability for the entity's debts unless there are personal guarantees. . . . Owners or members of a limited liability company can participate in management of the company without becoming personally liable for the entity's debt.

Although a majority of members and owners of the M.A.H.D. Group could take action on its behalf to render it liable for its debt. . ., there is a difference between the company itself being liable for its debt and individual owners of the company being personally liable for its debt. Under N.D.C.C. § 10-32-29 and the articles of organization of the M.A.H.D. Group, owners and members of the limited liability company generally are not, merely because of that status, personally liable for a judgment, decree or order of a court, or in any other manner for a debt, obligation or liability of the company. . . .

To the extent the additional $15,000 loan constituted debt for the company, the owners or members of the company are not, merely because of that status, personally liable for the company debt under N.D.C.C. § 10-32-29 and the company's articles of organization. . . .

The trial court found Nancy Myers did not intend or agree to assume any personal liability for the debt. . . . Although there is some evidence Nancy Myers believed she might be personally liable for one-fourth of the $15,000 loan, her belief was apparently based on her erroneous assumption that owners were personally liable for the debt of a limited liability company. Nancy Myers' mistaken belief does not constitute an agreement to be personally liable for any part of the $15,000 loan. On this record, we are not left with a definite and firm conviction the trial court made a mistake in finding Nancy Myers did not intend or agree to assume any personal liability for the loan. We therefore conclude the trial court's finding is not clearly erroneous under N.D.R.Civ.P. 52(a).

We affirm the judgment.

Case material reprinted from Westlaw, with permission.

IN SUMMATION

- Advantages to doing business as a limited liability company include:
  - Limited liability for all owners
  - Unrestrictive ownership
  - Ability to raise capital by selling interests in the LLC
  - Partnership taxation status
  - Flexible management

§ 6.5 DISADVANTAGES OF DOING BUSINESS AS A LIMITED LIABILITY COMPANY

The advantages to doing business as a limited liability company must be weighed against the potential disadvantages. One disadvantage is the limitation on transferring the ownership interest of a limited liability company. Other disadvantages include the uncertainties associated with piercing the veil of the limited liability company, the lack of uniformity in limited liability law among the states, and the formalities and reporting requirements associated with limited liability companies.

LIMITED TRANSFERABILITY OF OWNERSHIP

There may be several restrictions placed on the transfer of ownership of a limited liability company. As discussed previously in this chapter, a member of a limited liability company may not merely transfer his or her interest to another individual who will then become a new member. While a member may transfer his or her financial rights to a limited liability company, the transferee may only become a new member of the limited liability company pursuant to the provisions of state statutes and the company's operating agreement.

POSSIBILITY OF PIERCING THE LIMITED LIABILITY COMPANY VEIL

A limited liability company does not protect its members from personal liability in every instance. Under certain circumstances, such as when the members of a limited liability company have used the company to defraud creditors or investors, members may be found personally liable for the debts and obligations of the limited liability company. Disregarding the limited liability entity and looking to the members personally is referred to as "piercing the limited liability company veil."

Similar rules for piercing the corporate veil of a corporation and holding shareholders personally liable for certain debts and obligations of the corporation are widely accepted and established by case law. Under the statutes and case law of several states, it has been established that many of the conditions and circumstances under which the corporate veil may be pierced also apply to limited liability companies. Piercing the corporate veil is discussed further in Chapter 7.

LACK OF UNIFORMITY IN STATE LAWS

Although the Uniform Limited Liability Company Act was drafted to bring uniformity to state law, as of late 2011, only eight states had adopted the act and four states had adopted the newer Uniform Limited Liability Company Act (2006). Thus, there is a certain lack of uniformity in state limited liability company law. This can present challenges for limited liability companies that transact business in several states.

EXHIBIT 6-5	ADVANTAGES AND DISADVANTAGES OF DOING BUSINESS AS A LIMITED LIABILITY COMPANY

Advantages	Disadvantages
• Limited liability for all owners	• Limited transferability of ownership
• Unrestrictive ownership	• Possibility of piercing the LLC veil
• Ability to raise capital for business	• Lack of uniformity in state LLC law
• Beneficial tax treatment	• Formalities and reporting requirements
• Flexibility of management	

© Cengage Learning 2013

LIMITED LIABILITY COMPANY FORMALITIES AND REPORTING REQUIREMENTS

Compared to sole proprietorships and partnerships, there are several formalities that must be followed to form and operate a limited liability company. The limited liability company must be formed by filing articles of organization with the appropriate state authority, and annual registration with the secretary of state is usually required. Also, a limited liability company must qualify to do business in any state other than its state of domicile in which it transacts business.

Exhibit 6-5 lists the advantages and disadvantages of doing business as a limited liability company.

IN SUMMATION

- Disadvantages to doing business as a limited liability company include:
  - Limited transferability of ownership
  - Possibility of piercing the limited liability company veil
  - Lack of uniform state law
  - Formalities and reporting requirements

§ 6.6 LIMITED LIABILITY COMPANY POWERS

Much like a partnership or corporation, the limited liability company is granted certain powers by statute and by its articles of organization. In states that follow § 112 of the Uniform Limited Liability Company Act, limited liability companies have the same powers as individuals to do all things necessary or convenient to carry on business, including the following powers to:

- Sue and be sued, and defend in the name of the limited liability company
- Purchase, receive, lease, or otherwise acquire and own real or personal property

- Sell, convey, mortgage, grant a security interest in, lease, exchange, or otherwise encumber or dispose of all or any parts of its property
- Purchase, receive, or otherwise acquire and own shares or other interest in any other entity
- Sell, mortgage, grant a security interest in, or otherwise dispose of and deal in and with shares or other interest of any other entity
- Make contracts and other obligations, which may be convertible into or include the option to purchase other securities of the limited liability company
- Secure any of its obligations by a mortgage on, or a security interest in, any of its property, franchises, or income
- Lend money, invest and reinvest funds, and receive and hold real and personal property as security for repayment
- Be a promoter, partner, member, associate, or manager of any partnership, joint venture, trust, or other entity
- Conduct its business, locate offices, and exercise the powers granted by the act within or without this state
- Elect managers and appoint officers, employees, and agents of the limited liability company, define their duties, fix their compensation, and lend them money and credit
- Pay pensions and establish pension plans, pension trusts, profit sharing plans, and any other type of employee benefit plan for any or all of its current or former members, managers, officers, employees, and agents
- Make charitable donations
- Make payments or donations, or perform any other act, not inconsistent with law, that furthers the business of the limited liability company

Many state statutes provide a similar list of powers. Others simply state that a limited liability company has all powers necessary to transact business in that state.

IN SUMMATION

- State statutes and the articles of organization of the limited liability company grant the company certain powers that are necessary to transact business.

§ 6.7 MEMBERS' RIGHTS AND RESPONSIBILITIES

There are few restrictions on the membership of a limited liability company. Members may include corporations, trusts, and other entities, as well as individuals. Like partners and shareholders, members have certain rights and responsibilities prescribed by statute and by the entity's governing documents.

MEMBERS' RIGHTS

State statutes grant several different rights to members of the limited liability company. Many of those rights may be amended in the limited liability company's articles of organization or operating agreement. Following is a list of rights typically granted to members of limited liability companies:

- Each member has an equal right to manage the limited liability company or to appoint managers to manage the company.
- Members have the right to be reimbursed for liabilities they incur in the ordinary course of the business of the company or for the preservation of its business or property.
- Each member has the right to receive an equal share of any distribution made by the limited liability company before its dissolution and winding up.
- Members have the right to access the records of the limited liability company at the company's principal office or other reasonable location specified in the operating agreement.
- Members have the right to certain information concerning the company's business or affairs.
- Members have the right to receive a copy of the company's written operating agreement.
- Members have the right to maintain an action against a limited liability company or other member to enforce the operating agreement and other rights.
- Members have the right to dissociate from a limited liability company and have their shares purchased by the limited liability company.
- Members generally have the right to wind up the business of the limited liability company.

The vast majority of member rights will be provided for in the limited liability company's operating agreement.

MEMBERS AS AGENTS

If a limited liability company has no designated manager, its members are considered to be agents of the limited liability company in much the same way as partners may act on behalf of a partnership. Each member has the authority to bind the limited liability company in actions that are apparently aimed at carrying on the ordinary course of the limited liability company's business. The act of a member that is not apparently aimed at carrying on the ordinary course of the company's business does not bind the company unless such act is authorized by the other members. The authority of members to act on behalf of the limited liability company is a matter that may be dictated by statute and amended by the LLC's operating agreement. For example, under Delaware law, each member of the LLC has the power to bind the LLC unless otherwise provided in an LLC agreement.

IN SUMMATION

- Limited liability company members are granted certain rights by state statute and by the company's operating agreement.
- The company's operating agreement may amend certain rights granted by state statute—but not all rights may be amended.
- All members of a member-managed LLC are considered agents of the company.
- Only managers are considered agents of a manager-managed limited liability company.

§ 6.8 LIMITED LIABILITY COMPANY FORMATION

A limited liability company is formed when the articles of organization are filed with the secretary of state or other appropriate state authority. The limited liability company is then given its life by the proper state authority. A limited liability company generally can be formed for any lawful business purpose. State statutes may restrict the formation of not-for-profit limited liability companies or professional limited liability companies.

ORGANIZERS OF THE LIMITED LIABILITY COMPANY

The Uniform Limited Liability Company Act, and the statutes of most states, provides that any one or more persons may form a limited liability company. In most states, the organizer of the limited liability company must be an adult individual.

ARTICLES OF ORGANIZATION

The articles of organization must contain the information prescribed by the statutes of the state in which the limited liability company is formed. Typically, the articles of organization will include:

- The name of the limited liability company
- The address of the initial designated office
- The name and address of the initial agent for service of process
- The name and address of each organizer
- The duration of the existence of the limited liability company or a statement that the limited liability company will exist perpetually
- The name and address of the limited liability company's initial managers if the limited liability company is to be managed by managers
- Information concerning the members' liability for any debts, obligations, and liabilities of the limited liability company

Tips for drafting articles of organization are given in Exhibit 6-6.

EXHIBIT 6-6   TIPS FOR DRAFTING ARTICLES OF ORGANIZATION

- Always begin by checking state statutes for requirements.
- Make sure the name being used for the limited liability company is available and that it conforms to state requirements.
- Do not use a post office box for the address of the agent for service of process.
- Be sure the articles are signed by the proper individual or individuals.
- Information not required to be included in the articles of organization by state statute may be included in the operating agreement, which is not filed for public record.

© Cengage Learning 2013

Name of The Limited Liability Company

There are two types of limited liability company name requirements set by state statute:

1. The name must contain language specifying that the entity is a limited liability company.
2. The name must be available for use in the state in question.

The name of a limited liability company must include certain words or abbreviations required by state statute. For example, the names of limited liability companies in states following the Uniform Limited Liability Company Act must include the words "limited liability company" or "limited company" or the abbreviation "LLC" or "LC." "Limited" may also be abbreviated as "Ltd.," and "company" may be abbreviated as "Co."

The name of a limited liability company must be distinguishable upon the records of the secretary of state from the names of other limited liability companies, corporations, partnerships, and limited partnerships. State statutes set forth the exact standards to which the names of limited liability companies must adhere.

A paralegal who is responsible for filing articles of organization must first determine that the proposed name is available for use in the state of organization. To do this, the secretary of state's office or other appropriate office must be contacted. Typically, the office of the secretary of state will grant a preliminary approval of a name on its website or over the telephone, but not guarantee the availability until the articles of organization are filed or until the name is formally reserved pursuant to state statutes. In some states, name availability may be reserved on the secretary of state's website. See Appendix A of this text for a directory of secretary of state offices. Exhibit 6-7 lists tips for checking name availability.

EXHIBIT 6-7	TIPS FOR CHECKING LIMITED LIABILITY COMPANY NAME AVAILABILITY

- Make sure the name you are checking complies with state statutes for inclusion of the words *limited liability company* or similar words or abbreviations.
- Before you place a call or log on to the secretary of state's website, have one or two alternate names ready to check.
- Search the secretary of state's website or call the secretary of state's office to determine if the proposed name is available for use in your state—see the secretary of state directory in Appendix A of this text.
- If you choose to call, remember that secretary of state phone lines tend to be very busy—be patient.
- If articles of organization will not be filed very shortly after name availability is checked, the name should be reserved with the secretary of state.
- Clients should be advised not to use their new name until (1) articles of organization have been accepted for filing, or (2) the name has been reserved.

© Cengage Learning 2013

Not only must the name set forth in the articles of organization include words that indicate the entity is a limited liability company, but the company must be sure that the full name with such an indication is used in all correspondence, stationery, checks, and other materials that the company uses to conduct its business. It is important that the company establishes itself as a limited liability company with those with whom the company transacts business. In fact, if the company does not use those specific words in its name when it transacts business, and individuals doing business with the limited liability company are deceived into thinking they are dealing with a partnership, the members of the limited liability company may be held personally accountable for any debts or obligations to such individuals who were so deceived.

Address of the Limited Liability Company's Initial Office

The articles of organization must set forth the complete address of the limited liability company's initial office.

Registered Agent for Service of Process

Within the articles of organization, a limited liability company must designate the name and address of an agent who is located within the state of organization and who is authorized to accept service of process on behalf of the limited liability company. The address set forth in this section may not be a post office box. It must be a physical location where service of process may be made in person.

Names and Addresses of the Organizers of the Limited Liability Company

The full names and addresses of the organizers of the limited liability company, who may or may not be the original members, must be set forth in the articles of organization.

Duration of the Limited Liability Company

Most state statutes permit perpetual existence for limited liability companies. However, in some states the articles of organization must state the duration of the limited liability company.

Names and Addresses of the Managers of the Limited Liability Company

If the limited liability company is formed as a manager-managed limited liability company, the names and addresses of the initial manager or managers must be set forth in the articles of organization.

Information Concerning Personal Liability of the Limited Liability Company's Members

Pursuant to the Uniform Limited Liability Company Act, no member or manager of the limited liability company is personally liable for the debts, obligations, or liabilities of the limited liability company. If, however, the organizers of a limited liability company feel that it is in the best interests of the company for certain managers or members to be held personally liable for certain types of debts, obligations, or liabilities of the company, they can so provide by setting forth those exceptions in the articles of organization. No member or manager can be held personally liable for any debts, obligations, or liabilities of a limited liability company unless he or she agrees to be held personally liable in a written agreement with the company.

Statutory Requirements

Several other requirements for articles of organization are set by state statutes. Some of the more common requirements for inclusion in the articles of organization are:

- Powers of the limited liability company
- Terms and conditions for new members
- Rights of members to continue business after death or withdrawal of one or more members
- Rights of members to withdraw
- Rights of members upon dissolution

Exhibit 6-8 shows a sample articles of organization form for a limited liability company.

EXHIBIT 6-8 SAMPLE ARTICLES OF ORGANIZATION

ARTICLES OF ORGANIZATION OF _____, **LLC**

Limited Liability Company Act § _____

State of _____

ARTICLE ONE

NAME OF COMPANY

The name of the Company is _____.

ARTICLE TWO

DESIGNATED OFFICE

The address of the initial designated office of the Company is:

_____

_____.

ARTICLE THREE

AGENT FOR SERVICE OF PROCESS

The name and street address of the registered agent to receive service of process for the Company is:

_____

_____.

ARTICLE FOUR

ORGANIZERS

The name and street address of the organizers of the Company are:

_____

_____.

Date:_____

_____

Organizer

_____

Organizer

IN SUMMATION

- In most states, a limited liability company may be formed by any one adult individual acting as the organizer.
- A limited liability company is formed when the proper document, usually articles of organization, is filed with the secretary of state or other designated state authority.
- Articles of organization typically include:
  - Name of LLC (available in state and acceptable under state statutes)
  - LLC address
  - Name and address of initial agent for service of process
  - Name and address of organizers
  - Statement concerning duration of company
  - Statement concerning management status—manager managed or member managed
  - Statement concerning the limited liability status of members
  - Date and signatures of organizers

§ 6.9 LIMITED LIABILITY COMPANY OPERATION AND MANAGEMENT

The management of a limited liability company is generally very flexible. Most details concerning the operation and management of the limited liability company may be set forth in the operating agreement. The limited liability company may be either member managed or manager managed.

MEMBER-MANAGED LIMITED LIABILITY COMPANIES

In a **member-managed limited liability company**, each member has equal rights in the management of the limited liability company's business. Each member has the right to act on behalf of the limited liability company with regard to most matters. Decisions relating to the business of the company are made by a majority of the members.

Much like partners in a general partnership, members of a member-managed limited liability company owe a fiduciary duty to one another. In states that follow the Uniform Limited Liability Company Act in this regard, the members owe each other a duty of loyalty and a duty of care, as prescribed by statute.

MEMBER-MANAGED LIMITED LIABILITY COMPANY
A limited liability company in which the members have elected to share the managing of the company's affairs.

MANAGER-MANAGED LIMITED LIABILITY COMPANIES

The organizers of a limited liability company may decide to elect a board of managers to manage the business of the company. In that event, the limited liability company is referred to as a **manager-managed limited liability company**. Such managers are typically named in the company's articles of organization, which must be amended if the managers change. If the limited liability company is manager-managed, the managers are

MANAGER-MANAGED LIMITED LIABILITY COMPANY
A limited liability company in which the members have agreed to have the company's affairs managed by one or more managers.

agents of the limited liability company and other members are not. Non-managers lack the authority to act on behalf of the limited liability company in most instances. The acts of a limited liability company manager generally bind the limited liability company unless:

1. The manager has no authority to act for the company in that particular matter and the individual with whom the manager was dealing knew or had notice that the manager lacked authority.
2. The act of the manager was not apparently aimed at carrying on the ordinary course of the company's business or the business of the kind carried on by the company, and the members of the limited liability company did not authorize such act.

Because managers are given the authority to act on behalf of the other members of the limited liability company, they owe a fiduciary duty to the other members. In states that follow the Uniform Limited Liability Company Act, the managers owe members the duty of loyalty and duty of care. They also have the obligation to act with good faith and fair dealing. Under the statutes of some states, managers are required to perform their duties "in good faith, in a manner the manager reasonably believes to be in the best interests of the limited liability company, and with the care an ordinarily prudent person in a like position would exercise under similar circumstances."[12]

SIDEBAR

One of the key decisions made by the organizers of an LLC is whether the LLC will have centralized management (manager managed), or whether it will have decentralized management (member managed).

MATTERS REQUIRING CONSENT OF ALL MEMBERS

Certain matters provided for in state statutes or the limited liability company's articles of organization or operating agreement require the consent of all members. Actions that often require unanimous consent of the members include:

- Amendments to the articles of organization
- Amendment of the limited liability company's operating agreement
- Approval of acts or transactions by certain members or managers that would otherwise violate their duty of loyalty
- The compromise of an obligation to make a contribution
- The making of interim distributions
- The admission of a new member
- The use of the company's property to redeem an interest subject to a charging order
- The merger of the limited liability company with another entity
- Dissolution of the company
- A waiver of the right to have the company's business wound up and the company terminated

- The sale, lease, exchange, or other disposal of all, or substantially all, of the company's property with or without goodwill

The above matters require the consent of all members, regardless of whether the limited liability company is member managed or manager managed.

When the act of a limited liability company requires the consent of all members, the act may be approved at a meeting of the members or by a written consent signed by all members.

MEETINGS OF THE LLC MEMBERS OR MANAGERS

It is important that decisions concerning the management of the LLC are properly documented. If meetings of the managers or members of the LLC are held, minutes documenting any decisions made at those meetings should be prepared. If no formal meeting is held, decisions of the members or managers may be documented in a written consent of the members or managers. Written consents set forth the agreement among the members or managers and must be signed by everyone who was responsible for the decision. Any meeting minutes or written consents of the members and managers should be kept in an LLC record book along with the articles of organization, operating agreement, and other important documents concerning the formation and operation of the LLC.

THE OPERATING AGREEMENT

Operating agreements set forth the agreement of the members of the limited liability company concerning the management and operation of the company. Because the operating agreement is not filed for public record, information that may be contained in either the articles of organization or the operating agreement is often contained in the operating agreement. The items included in an operating agreement will vary depending on the pertinent state statutes and the particular circumstances. Following is a sample checklist of items that often are included in an operating agreement.

Operating Agreement Checklist

- ☐ Formation and Term
- ☐ Nature of Business
- ☐ Accounting and Records
- ☐ Names and Addresses of Members
- ☐ Rights and Duties of Members
- ☐ Meetings of Members
- ☐ Managing Members

- ☐ Contributions and Capital Accounts
- ☐ Allocations and Distributions
- ☐ Taxes
- ☐ Disposition of Membership Interests
  - ☐ Dissociation of a Member
  - ☐ Additional and Substitute Members
  - ☐ Dissolution and Winding Up
  - ☐ Amendment
  - ☐ Miscellaneous Provisions

See Appendix E for a sample Limited Liability Company Operating Agreement.

Most state statutes allow for maximum flexibility concerning the contents of the operating agreement, but there are limitations. Some rights and duties may not be amended or eliminated, even in the limited liability company's operating agreement. Section 103(b) of the Uniform Limited Liability Act provides:

(b) The operating agreement may not:

1. unreasonably restrict a right to information or access to records under Section 408;

2. eliminate the duty of loyalty under Section 409(b) or 603(b)(3), but the agreement may:

   i. identify specific types or categories of activities that do not violate the duty of loyalty, if not manifestly unreasonable; and

   ii. specify the number or percentage of members or disinterested managers that may authorize or ratify, after full disclosure of all material facts, a specific act or transaction that otherwise would violate the duty of loyalty;

3. unreasonably reduce the duty of care under Section 409(c) or 603(b)(3);

4. eliminate the obligation of good faith and fair dealing under Section 409(d), but the operating agreement may determine the standards by which the performance of the obligation is to be measured, if the standards are not manifestly unreasonable;

5. vary the right to expel a member in an event specified in Section 601(5);

6. vary the requirement to wind up the limited liability company's business in a case specified in Section 801(3); or

7. restrict rights of a person, other than a manager, a member, or a transferee of a member's distributional interest, under this [Act].

The operating agreement is similar to both the partnership agreement and corporate bylaws, but it includes unique features for LLCs.

ANNUAL REPORTING REQUIREMENTS

Like corporations, limited liability companies in most states are subject to annual reporting requirements with the secretary of state or other appropriate state authority. The statutes of the limited liability company's state of organization must be checked carefully to be sure that all annual reporting requirements are complied with. Typically, annual reports containing the following information must be filed:

- Name of the limited liability company
- State or country where limited liability company is organized
- Name and address of agent within state for service of process
- Address of the limited liability company's principal office
- Names and addresses of any managers

In some states, failure to file an annual report can cause the limited liability company to be dissolved by the state—usually after several notices from the state. Exhibit 6-9 is a sample Limited Liability Company Annual Report for the state of Minnesota.

IN SUMMATION

- In a member-managed limited liability company, each member has the authority to act on behalf of the LLC.
- In a manager-managed limited liability company, the managers, who are typically named in the articles of organization, have full management authority with regard to most matters.
- The managers of a manager-managed limited liability company owe a fiduciary duty to other members.
- Certain matters that affect the future of the limited liability company require the consent of all members, whether the LLC is member managed or manager managed.
- The limited liability company operating agreement sets forth the agreement of the members of the limited liability company concerning the company's management.
- While the operating agreement sets forth the agreement of the members, it cannot limit member rights contrary to state statutes. Limited liability companies must file annual reports in most states with the secretary of state or other designated state authority.

EXHIBIT 6-9 LIMITED LIABILITY COMPANY ANNUAL REPORT FORM FROM THE STATE OF MINNESOTA

**STATE OF RHODE ISLAND
AND PROVIDENCE PLANTATIONS**
Office of the Secretary of State

Matthew A. Brown, Secretary of State
Corporations Division
100 North Main Street, Providence, RI 02903-1335
401.222.3040

LIMITED LIABILITY COMPANY ANNUAL REPORT FOR THE YEAR _____

Filing Period: September 1 - November 1 ● *Filing Fee: $50.00*
(FORM MUST BE TYPED OR PRINTED IN BLACK)

1. ID No.	2. Exact name of the limited liabilty company

3. State of Formation	4. Brief description of the character of the business which is actually conducted in Rhode Island

5. Principal office address	City	State	Zip

6. MAILING ADDRESS OF LIMITED LIABILITY COMPANY AND NAME OR TITLE OF CONTACT PERSON:

Contact Name	Contact Title		
Street Address	City	State	Zip

7. NAME AND ADDRESS OF EACH MANAGER OF THE LIMITED LIABILITY COMPANY, IF APPLICABLE
FILL IN SPACES BEFORE USING ATTACHMENTS ("X" BOX FOR ATTACHMENT) ☐
ANY MODIFICATIONS TO MANAGERS REQUIRES FILING OF AMENDMENT. R.I.G.L 7-16-12 (a) (2) / 7-16-52

Manager Name			Manager Name		
Street Address			Street Address		
City	State	Zip	City	State	Zip
Manager Name			Manager Name		
Street Address			Street Address		
City	State	Zip	City	State	Zip

8. RESIDENT AGENT IN RHODE ISLAND *-DO NOT ALTER-* **Changes require filing of Form 642** - R.I.G.L. 7-16-11

Agent Name	Address	
Address	City	Zip
fg		

This report must be **signed in ink** by an authorized person pursuant to 7-16-66.

Under penalty of perjury, I declare and affirm that I have examined this report, including any accompanying schedules and statements, and that all statements contained herein are true and correct.

File Date _____

Check No. _____

By: _____

FOR SECRETARY OF STATE USE ONLY

Signature of Authorized Person _____ Date _____

Print or Type Name of Authorized Person _____

Form 632 Rev. 6/02

Minnesota Secretary of State's Office

§ 6.10 FINANCIAL STRUCTURE OF A LIMITED LIABILITY COMPANY

The financial structure of a limited liability company resembles that of a partnership in many ways. Financing generally comes from member contributions. Members who spend money on behalf of the limited liability company are entitled to reimbursement for expenditures they make on behalf of the company, and members are entitled to receive distributions pursuant to statute and the limited liability company's operating agreement.

MEMBER CONTRIBUTIONS

The initial assets of the limited liability company typically consist of the contributions of members. Limited liability company members will be required to make certain contributions to the company as provided for in the company's operating agreement, articles of organization, and agreement of the members. Unless otherwise prohibited by statute or by the limited liability company's articles of organization or operating agreement, member contributions may be in the form of cash or tangible or intangible property, including services. For example, if a limited liability company formed for the purposes of developing a piece of property is in need of the services of a general contractor, the members of the company may decide to grant membership to a general contractor in return for his or her services. Other new members may be required to make cash contributions.

Member interests are sometimes sold to raise funds for the limited liability company. Certificates may be issued to evidence the interest owned by the members. Although such interests are similar in many respects to the shares of stock that are issued by corporations, the term "stock" is usually used exclusively for corporations.

MEMBER REIMBURSEMENT

From time to time, certain members who are involved in the operation of the limited liability company may make expenditures on behalf of the company. These members are entitled to reimbursement of certain expenses made by them on behalf of the limited liability company, as provided by state statute and the company's operating agreement.

DISTRIBUTIONS TO MEMBERS

Details concerning potential distributions made to members of the limited liability company should be set forth in the operating agreement of the company. Unless otherwise provided for in the operating agreement or articles of organization, any distributions made by the limited liability company must be made pursuant to state statute. Most state statutes provide that any distributions must be made to the members in equal shares. This, however, can be amended in the operating agreement of the organization. Members who contribute more to the company are usually entitled to receive larger distributions.

Distributions may be prohibited by statute under certain circumstances, such as when the distribution would deplete the limited liability company's cash so that the LLC would not be able to pay its debts when they are due in the ordinary course of business.

As with partnerships, the income or loss of the limited liability company is allocated among the members, who include their share on their personal income tax returns. The income of the limited liability company is reported on the Form 1065 Partnership Return.

IN SUMMATION

- Financing for most new limited liability companies generally comes from member contributions.

- Members are usually entitled to reimbursement for expenditures they make on behalf of the limited liability company.

- Details concerning distributions to be made from the limited liability company are typically set forth in the company's operating agreement.

- Most state statutes dictate that distributions must be made in equal shares to members unless otherwise provided for in the company's articles of organization or operating agreement.

- Distributions from the LLC may be prohibited by state statute if the limited liability company is unable to pay its debts after the distribution.

---

§ 6.11 LIMITED LIABILITY COMPANY LAWSUITS

Limited liability companies are considered separate entities and, as separate entities, they may sue or be sued in the company's name, much the same as an individual. Under § 112 of the Uniform Limited Liability Company Act, unless otherwise provided in its articles of organization, a limited liability company has the same powers as an individual to do all things necessary or convenient to carry out its business or affairs, including the power to sue and to be sued and to defend in its name.

If the LLC is a member-managed company, a vote of the majority of the members will probably be required to bring or defend a lawsuit in the name of the LLC. In a manager-managed LLC, the managers will probably have the authority to bring a suit on behalf of the LLC. More specific provisions as to who has the power to bring suit on behalf of the LLC may be prescribed by state statute or by the LLC's operating agreement.

DERIVATIVE SUITS

Derivative lawsuits may be brought by a member on behalf of the limited liability company to recover damages sustained by the LLC. Where the limited liability company is a manager-managed company and one or more managers refuse to bring a suit on behalf of the LLC because they are personally interested, a derivative suit brought by a member may be appropriate. Specific requirements for bringing derivative lawsuits are usually set forth in the state limited liability company statutes. The Uniform Limited Liability Company Act provides for derivative lawsuits in § 1101, which follows:

1101. Right of Action

A member of a limited liability company may maintain an action in the right of the company if the members or managers having authority to do so have refused to commence the action or an effort to cause those members or managers to commence the action is not likely to succeed.

ACTIONS BY MEMBERS

If the cause of action belongs not to the limited liability company, but to an individual member or class of members, a lawsuit may be brought against the limited liability company or against individual members. Members may bring suits to enforce or protect their rights and interests under the operating agreement or under law. Again, the limited liability company statutes of most states include specific provisions for actions by members. The Uniform Limited Liability Company Act addresses actions by members in § 410(a):

410. Actions by Members

(a) A member may maintain an action against a limited liability company or another member for legal or equitable relief, with or without an accounting as to the company's business, to enforce:
   1. the member's rights under the operating agreement;
   2. the member's rights under this [Act]; and
   3. the rights and otherwise protect the interests of the member, including rights and interests arising independently of the member's relationship to the company.

IN SUMMATION

- As separate entities, limited liability companies have the power to bring and defend lawsuits.
- Derivative suits are lawsuits brought by a member of the limited liability company on behalf of the limited liability company.
- Derivative lawsuits are specifically authorized by the statutes of most states
- Limited liability company members may bring lawsuits against the company or other members for equitable relief to enforce the members' rights.

§ 6.12 LIMITED LIABILITY COMPANY DISSOLUTION

The dissolution of a limited liability company may be prompted either by the end of its planned and stated duration or by some other event that triggers a dissolution. One or more members may be dissociated from the limited liability company without causing a dissolution of the company.

MEMBER'S DISSOCIATION

In states that follow the Uniform Limited Liability Company Act[13] in this regard, dissociation may be caused by several events, including a member's withdrawal (with written notice), death, bankruptcy, or appointment of a guardian for the member. Members may also become dissociated from the limited liability company upon the occurrence of an event agreed to in the operating agreement to cause the dissociation of a member, upon the transfer of all of a member's interest in the limited liability company, or by unanimous vote of the other members under certain circumstances, such as when it is unlawful to carry on the company's business with the member.

Wrongful Dissociation

A member's dissociation may be wrongful, as in instances where the dissociation is in breach of an express provision of the operating agreement, or, under certain circumstances, when the dissociation is before the expiration of the term of a company that has a definite term. If a member wrongfully dissociates from a limited liability company, he or she may be liable to the company and the remaining members for damages caused by his or her wrongful dissociation.

Effect of Dissociation of a Member

Upon a member's dissociation from a limited liability company:

- The member loses all right to participate in the management of the company's business.
- The member's duty of loyalty and duty of care continue only with regard to events occurring before the dissociation, unless the member participates in winding up the company's business.

Purchase of the Dissociated Member's Interest

State statutes and the limited liability company's operating agreement typically will provide specific terms and conditions for the purchase of a dissociating member's interest in the limited liability company. Members who dissociate from a limited liability company at will are usually entitled to have their interest purchased shortly after their dissociation.

When the member's dissociation results in the dissolution of the limited liability company, the dissociating member is generally entitled to a final distribution when the business of the company is wound up.

DISSOLUTION OF THE LIMITED LIABILITY COMPANY

The events that cause the dissolution of a limited liability company are provided for by the limited liability company's articles of organization, operating agreement, and by state statute. In states that follow the Uniform Limited Liability Company Act,[14] the following events cause a dissolution and winding up of the limited liability company business:

1. An event specified in the operating agreement
2. Consent of the members, as specified in the operating agreement
3. An event that makes it unlawful for the business to continue, if such illegality is not cured within 90 days after notice is given to the company of the event
4. Entry of a judicial decree, upon the application by a member, that:
    i. the economic purpose of the company is likely to be unreasonably frustrated;
    ii. another member has engaged in conduct relating to the company's business that makes it not reasonably practicable to carry on the company's business with that member;
    iii. it is not otherwise reasonably practicable to carry on the company's business in conformity with the articles of organization and the operating agreement;
    iv. the company failed to purchase the petitioner's distributional interest as required by statute;
    v. actions of the managers or members in control of the company are, or have been, illegal, oppressive, fraudulent, or unfairly prejudicial to the petitioner
5. A judicial determination, based on application by a transferee of a member's interest, that it is equitable to wind up the company's business:
    i. after the expiration of a specified term; or
    ii. at any time, if the company is a company at will.

After the limited liability company has been dissolved, it continues only for the purpose of winding up its business.

WINDING UP THE LIMITED LIABILITY COMPANY

After a decision has been made to dissolve a limited liability company, its business must be wound up. Any member who has not wrongfully dissociated from the limited liability company may participate in winding up its business. Judicial supervision of the winding up may be ordered upon the application of any member of the company for good cause.

DISTRIBUTION OF ASSETS

The rules for distribution of the assets of the limited liability company may be set by the articles of organization, or the company's operating agreement. However, state statutes have provisions regarding distribution of the limited liability company's assets that may not be superseded. These rules may provide that the property of the limited liability company must first be used to pay the debts and obligations of the limited liability company, before the members receive distributions.

ARTICLES OF TERMINATION

ARTICLES OF TERMINATION
Document filed with proper state authority to dissolve a limited liability company. Same as articles of dissolution.

Because the articles of organization are filed with the secretary of state or other state authority to give notice of the company's existence, notice of the company's dissolution must also be filed at the state level. In states that follow the Uniform Limited Liability Company Act,[15] this involves filing **articles of termination** or articles of dissolution with the secretary of state.

Articles of termination typically include the following information:

1. The name of the company
2. The date of the company's dissolution
3. A statement that the company's business has been wound up and the legal existence of the company has been terminated

The existence of the limited liability company is terminated when the articles of termination are filed, or on a later date specified in the document. Exhibit 6-10 is a sample Articles of Dissolution Form that may be filed in the state of Florida.

IN SUMMATION

- Member dissociation occurs when a member withdraws from the limited liability company, dies, declares bankruptcy, or has a guardian appointed for him or her.

- Under certain circumstances, a member's dissociation may be considered wrongful dissociation, such as when it is in breach of a provision of the operating agreement or before the termination of the limited liability company.

- The limited liability company does not necessarily dissolve when one or more members dissociates.

- State statutes or the limited liability company's operating agreement typically provide for the purchase of a dissociating member's interest in the limited liability company by the company or remaining members.

- A limited liability company may be dissolved when an event specified in the operating agreement or articles of organization occurs, by member consent, or when dictated by statute or judicial decree.

- The business of a dissolving limited liability company may be wound up by any member who has not wrongfully dissociated from the company.

- Rules for distributing the assets of a dissolving limited liability company may be set by the company's articles of organization or operating agreement, as long as those rules are not contrary to state statute.

- Articles of termination or a similar document are filed with the secretary of state to terminate the existence of the limited liability company.

EXHIBIT 6-10   ARTICLES OF DISSOLUTION FOR A LIMITED LIABILITY COMPANY

ARTICLES OF DISSOLUTION
FOR
A LIMITED LIABILITY COMPANY

1.   The name of a limited liability company is

_____

2. The Articles of Organization were filed on _____ and assigned document number

_____.

3. The date the dissolution was approved: _____.

4. A description of occurrence that resulted in the limited liability company's dissolution pursuant to section 608.441, Florida Statutes, (copy 608.441 on back cover letter).

_____

_____

_____

_____

5. **CHECK ONE:**

☐ All debts, obligations and liabilities of the limited liability company have been paid or discharged.
-OR-
☐ Adequate provision has been made for the debts, obligations and liabilities pursuant to s. 608.4421.

6. All remaining property and assets have been distributed among its members in accordance with their respective rights and interests.

7. **CHECK ONE:**

☐ There are no suits pending against the company in any court.
-OR-
☐ Adequate provision has been made for the satisfaction of any judgment, order or decree which may be entered against it in any pending suit.

Signatures of the members having the same percentage of membership interests necessary to approve the dissolution:

Signature   Printed Name

_____   _____

_____   _____

_____   _____

_____   _____

FILING FEE: $25.00

Florida Secretary of State's Office

§ 6.13 TRANSACTING BUSINESS AS A FOREIGN LIMITED LIABILITY COMPANY

FOREIGN LIMITED LIABILITY COMPANY

A limited liability company that is transacting business in any state other than the state of its organization.

CERTIFICATE OF AUTHORITY

Certificate issued by the secretary of state, or other appropriate state official, to a foreign business entity to allow that entity to transact business in that state.

In every state in which a limited liability company transacts business, other than its state of organization, it is considered a **foreign limited liability company**. A foreign limited liability company must be granted a **certificate of authority** (or similar document) before it begins transacting business in any state other than its state of organization.

A foreign limited liability company subjects itself to the jurisdiction of the courts of each state in which it transacts business. For that reason, foreign limited liability companies must comply with state statutes that pertain to the transaction of business in the foreign state, and they must comply with statutory formalities regarding foreign limited liability companies.

When the owners of a limited liability company organize or expand their business, they must decide what their legal obligations are with regard to states with which the company comes in contact, other than the company's state of organization. First, it must be determined whether the limited liability company is actually transacting business within the foreign state, as defined by the statutes of the foreign state. If the limited liability company is in fact transacting business in the foreign state, or if it plans to in the future, the limited liability company must obtain a certificate of authority from the secretary of state of the foreign state and appoint an agent for service of process who is located within the foreign state.

The statutes of each state in which the limited liability company wishes to transact business must be carefully reviewed before the company begins transacting business in that state.

TRANSACTING BUSINESS AS A FOREIGN LIMITED LIABILITY COMPANY

At times, there is no question whether a limited liability company is transacting business in another state—for instance, if the expansion of a limited liability company into another state involves the construction of a factory in that state and hiring employees from that state to work in the factory. In other instances, however, such as when a salesperson occasionally crosses state borders to make a sale, the question requires a closer look at state statutes.

The statutes of most states address the matter either by giving a general definition of what constitutes transacting business in their state or by providing a list of activities that do not constitute the transaction of business. State statutes concerning what constitutes doing business and the requirements for qualifying as a foreign limited liability company entity are usually identical or very similar to the statutes concerning qualification of foreign corporations. For more information on qualifying as a foreign corporation or limited liability company, see Chapter 13 of this text.

NAME REGISTRATION

One important factor for the organizers of a limited liability company to consider is the company's name, and its name availability in other states. If a limited liability company plans to expand its business into several states in the future, the organizers must make sure that its name will be available for use in each state. For example, suppose a limited liability company is organized under the laws of Iowa as Peterson Engineering Limited Liability Company. The organizers plan to build their business on the reputation of its founders and expand it into the entire Midwest region. If their state-by-state expansion begins in three years, they may have a problem if the name Peterson Engineering Limited Liability Company is not available for use in any of the surrounding states.

One way around this problem is foreign name registration. In states that follow the Uniform Limited Liability Company Act in this regard, a limited liability company may register its name in a foreign state, provided that name meets with the state's requirements. Names of foreign limited liability companies are typically registered for a one-year period. A registered name will be reserved for future use for the limited liability company if the limited liability company decides to transact business in that state in the future.

IN SUMMATION

- When a limited liability company transacts business in a state other than its state of formation, it is considered a foreign LLC and must qualify to transact business in that state.

- State requirements for foreign limited liability company qualification are very similar to those for foreign corporation qualification.

- Limited liability companies may register their names in states where they are considered a foreign LLC to reserve their names for use in those states.

§ 6.14 THE PARALEGAL'S ROLE

Paralegals can perform a variety of functions to assist with the formation, maintenance, and dissolution of limited liability companies. Many of the services to be performed on behalf of a limited liability company will be procedural in nature and can easily be performed by an experienced paralegal with the proper resources. Most of the functions performed by paralegals will involve drafting appropriate legal documentation and performing research. Specifically, paralegals are often asked to perform or assist with the following tasks related to limited liability companies:

- Research state limited liability company law.
- Research securities law issues with regard to limited liability companies.
- Check name availability with secretary of state.
- File name reservation with secretary of state.
- Draft and file articles of organization with secretary of state.

- Draft operating agreement.
- Draft minutes of meetings of the members and/or managers of the limited liability company.
- Draft articles of termination of the limited liability company.
- Draft application for certificate of authority to transact business as a foreign limited liability company.

LIMITED LIABILITY COMPANY RESEARCH

Because limited liability company law varies between states, there may be a need for legal research in this area. Most research will include state statutes, case law, the Internal Revenue Code and Revenue Rulings, and Securities Acts.

DRAFTING LIMITED LIABILITY DOCUMENTATION

Paralegals, with the use of current forms and form books, may be responsible for drafting virtually all documents associated with the limited liability company. These documents may include the articles of organization, operating agreement, applications for certificates of authority to transact business as a foreign limited liability company, and others.

The paralegal may be responsible for attending an initial client meeting to collect information concerning the formation of a limited liability company. With the use of a customized checklist, the paralegal can collect all of the information required to prepare drafts of the organization documents. The paralegal may also become the client contact to assist with future needs of the limited liability company client.

Exhibit 6-11 provides a checklist for drafting articles of organization.

EXHIBIT 6-11	CHECKLIST FOR DRAFTING ARTICLES OF ORGANIZATION

The following items must be considered for inclusion in the articles of organization for a limited liability company:

☐ Name of the limited liability company; it must contain the words "limited liability company," "LLC," or "L.L.C."

☐ The address of the principal place of business within the state.

☐ The purpose of the limited liability company.

☐ The name of the limited liability company's registered agent and the address of its registered office (not a P.O. box).

☐ The names and business addresses of the initial manager or managers, if any.

☐ The names and addresses of the initial members of the limited liability company.

☐ The duration of the limited liability company.

EXHIBIT 6-11 (*continued*)

- ☐ The names and addresses of all organizers, who need not be members of the limited liability company.

- ☐ The effective date of the limited liability company.

- ☐ Any other provisions required by the statutes of the state or organization or desired by the members of the limited liability company.

© Cengage Learning 2013

IN SUMMATION

- Paralegals who work with limited liability companies are often responsible for:
  - Researching limited liability company law
  - Drafting limited liability documentation
  - Maintaining a limited liability record book

PARALEGAL PROFILE
Christine Springer

It's fun to help business owners find the right solutions to their legal issues.

NAME Christine Springer
LOCATION Phoenix, Arizona
TITLE Legal Consultant/Former Certified Legal-Document Preparer
SPECIALTY Formation of limited liability companies, corporations, and partnerships
EDUCATION Associate in Paralegal Studies, Sanford Brown College; Bachelor of Science in Management, Louis University; Master of Arts in International Affairs, Washington University
EXPERIENCE 12 years

Christine Springer has a background full of rich and varied experiences, including time spent in the U.S. Army, where she was trained as a firefighter. Christine earned several firefighter

certifications and an Army Achievement Medal for her efforts to save a home from a fire.

After her discharge from the military, Christine continued her education, earning an Associate of Arts in paralegal studies, a Bachelor of Science in management, and a Master of Arts in international affairs.

Christine began her paralegal career working for a law firm in St. Louis, specializing in corporate law in the firm's transactional/corporate group. After several years' experience as a corporate paralegal and completion of her master's degree, Christine moved to Phoenix, Arizona, and began her own company, Desert Edge Legal Services, LLC.

Arizona is one of a few states that recognizes specially qualified paralegals as certified legal-document preparers. According to Arizona statutes,

continues

PARALEGAL PROFILE (continued)
Christine Springer

to prepare legal documents for the public you must be an attorney, supervised by an attorney, or become licensed as a certified legal-document preparer. A certified legal-document preparer is barred by law from giving legal advice, but can explain the differences between the options and let clients make a determination as to their needs.

Christine provided her services to laypeople who wanted to form limited liability companies and other types of business organizations in Arizona. For clients who wished to form limited liability companies, Chrstine prepared the articles of organization, handled the publication requirement, prepared initial minutes and resolutions, obtained the employer identification number (EIN), and provided the client with a basic operating agreement. She also referred clients to attorneys when they needed one, and served as a general resource for the public on navigating the sometimes confusing legal process.

Christine also prepared resolutions, consents, minutes, agreements, withdrawals, qualifications, and other legal documents required for corporate entities, as well as wills, family law documents, and many other legal documents.

According to Christine, the best thing about her work is that she controls her schedule and has the opportunity to create her perfect work situation. She is not punching a time clock, which can be an issue for many paralegals. Christine also likes that she no longer faces the "hourly vs. salary" issue that paralegals in law firms deal with.

As the owner of her own business, Christine is responsible for new business development, which she considers fun, but also challenging. To bring in new business, Christine is committed to networking, public speaking, and using social media to reach new clients. Business building can be time consuming. Not only does she have to bring in the clients, Christine has to do the work too. Setting your own hours does not necessarily mean working fewer hours.

Christine's business has brought her into contact with some interesting clients and some interesting assignments. One client from New York develops and manufactures a line of luxury skin-care products. This client had no idea whether her company was in compliance with New York law. She hired Christine to make sure her corporate house was in order. Upon investigating, Christine learned that her client had not complied with the New York publication requirements and that it would cost a lot of money to bring her into compliance with that requirement. Her client decided to form a new Delaware limited liability company instead. Christine handled the entire matter for her.

Christine's advice to paralegal students?

Network, network, network! Meet all the other paralegals and attorneys you can. Attend networking events outside of the legal field and meet professionals in other industries. There is a huge demand from the public for legal services that do not require an attorney and you might find that you stumble onto an opportunity to work for yourself. As I was building my business, there were hardly ever any attorneys, which meant that when people had a legal issue, they called me because they did not know an attorney.

It has been an amazing experience and I do not ever see myself going back to being an employee.

For more information on careers for corporate paralegals, log in to http://www.cengagebrain.com to access the CourseMate website that accompanies this text; then see the Corporate Careers Section.

ETHICAL CONSIDERATION

All attorneys and paralegals owe a duty of loyalty to their clients, including corporate clients. When the interests of one client conflict with the interests of another current or past client of the attorney, the attorney has a potential conflict of interest. This can happen when a potential client is or has been involved in a lawsuit with another current or past client. If the representation of a new client presents a possible conflict of interest, the attorney must turn down the new representation or obtain consent of both parties. An attorney with a conflict of interest may be disqualified and prohibited from representing that client by the proper court.

Because it is assumed that attorneys within a law firm may share confidences, under the rule of imputed disqualification, all members of a law firm may be disqualified from representing a potential client if one member of the firm is disqualified because of a conflict of interest. At times, the representation may be permitted if the attorney with the conflict does not participate in the matter and the law firm screens the affected attorney from any and all confidential material concerning the representation of the client who presents the conflict. This is referred to as "erecting an ethical (or Chinese) wall."

The rules concerning conflicts of interest, including imputed disqualification, can also be applied to paralegals. In fact if you, as a paralegal, have a conflict of interest with a potential client, the entire firm you work for may be disqualified from representing that client unless the matter is handled correctly.

Undisclosed conflicts of interest can have serious consequences for the paralegal, the attorney, and the entire law firm or legal department. You must be sure to keep current with your firm's or department's conflict of interest procedures. Law firms commonly circulate weekly lists of new clients and new matters that the firm is representing. You should carefully review these lists to make sure you have no potential conflict of interest.

Above all, if you have any questions concerning conflicts of interest, immediately discuss the matter with a supervising attorney or consult the rules of your paralegal association and the rules applicable to attorneys in your jurisdiction. Specific rules concerning conflicts of interest are included in the rules of ethics for attorneys in every state, as well as in the Model Rules of Ethics of the National Federation of Paralegal Associations and the National Association of Legal Assistants.

For more information on ethics for corporate paralegals, including links to the NALA and NFPA codes of ethics, log in to http://www.cengagebrain.com to access the CourseMate website that accompanies this text; then see the Ethics Section.

§ 6.15 RESOURCES

The main resources paralegals will use when working with limited liability companies are the state statutes, state authorities, the Internal Revenue Code, and form books and treatises.

STATE STATUTES

The main source for answering questions concerning limited liability companies is the statutes of the state of organization. State statutes will include all basic information regarding the formation, operation, and dissolution of a limited liability company within that state. In addition, state statutes also contain information concerning foreign limited liability companies doing business within that state. See Exhibit 6-12 for a list of state limited liability company statutes. Links to those statutes may also be found at the CourseMate website that accompanies this text.

UNIFORM LIMITED LIABILITY COMPANY ACT

The website of the National Conference of Commissioners on Uniform State Law (NCCUSL) provides drafts and final versions of Uniform State Laws, including the Uniform Limited Liability Company Act.

SECRETARY OF STATE OFFICES

At times, the quickest way to find an answer concerning requirements for forming or operating a limited liability company (especially procedural questions regarding state filings) may be to check the website or call the office of the secretary of state or other appropriate state official. The secretary of state's website will often provide the following forms to use for filing in its office:

- Articles of organization
- Name reservation
- Annual reports
- Name registration
- Application for certificate of authority to transact business as a foreign limited liability company

In addition, the office of the secretary of state provides filing fee schedules and instructions for filing procedures. A directory of secretary of state offices is included as Appendix A to this text. Links to those secretary of state offices may be found at the CourseMate website that accompanies this text.

IRS AND STATE TAX AGENCIES

Questions concerning the taxation of a limited liability company may be answered by researching the Internal Revenue Code (IRC), Treasury Regulations, and Revenue Rulings and Procedures. Information on the taxation of limited liability companies can also be found online.

EXHIBIT 6-12 STATE LIMITED LIABILITY COMPANY STATUES

State	Limited Liability Company Act
Alabama	Alabama Limited Liability Company Act, Ala. Code §§ 10A-5-1.01 through 10A-5-9.06
Alaska	Alaska Limited Liability Company Act, Alaska Stat. §§ 10.50.010 through 10.50.995.
Arizona	Arizona Limited Liability Company Act, Ariz Rev. Stat. Ann. §§ 29-601 through 29-857
Arkansas	Arkansas Small Business Entity Tax Pass Through Act, Ark. Code Ann. §§ 4-47-101 through 4-47-1401
California	California Beverly-Killea Limited Liability Company Act, Cal. Corp. Code §§ 17000 through 17656
Colorado	Colorado Limited Liability Company Act, Colo. Rev. Stat. §§ 7-80-101 through 7-80-1101
Connecticut	Connecticut Limited Liability Company Act, Conn. Gen. Stat. §§ 34-100 through 34-242
Delaware	Limited Liability Company Act, Del. Code Ann. Tit. 6 §§ 18-101 through 18-1101
District of Columbia	District of Columbia Limited Liability Companies, D.C. Official Code §§ 29-1001 through 29-1075
Florida	Florida Limited Liability Company Act, Fla. Stat. Ann. Ch. 608.401 through 608.705
Georgia	Georgia Limited Liability Company Act, Ga. Code Ann. §§ 14-11-100 through 14-11-1109
Hawaii	Hawaii Uniform Limited Liability Company Act, Haw. Rev. Stat. Ch. 428-101 through 425-1306
Idaho	Idaho Uniform Limited Liability Company Act, Idaho Code §§ 30-6-101 through 30-6-1104
Illinois	Illinois Limited Liability Company Act, 805 Ill. Comp. Stat. §§ 180/1-1 through 180/60-1
Indiana	Indiana Business Flexibility Act, Ind. Code §§ 23-18-1-1 through 23-19-13-1
Iowa	Iowa Limited Liability Company Act, Iowa Code §§ 490A.100 through 490A.1601
Kentucky	Kentucky Limited Liability Company Act, Ky. Rev. Sta. Ann §§ 275.001 through 275.455

continues

EXHIBIT 6-12 *(continued)*

State	Limited Liability Company Act
Louisiana	Louisiana Limited Liability Company Law, La. Stat. Ann. §§ 12:1301 through 1369
Maine	Maine Limited Liability Company Act, Me. Rev. Stat. Ann. Tit. 31 §§ 1501 through 1693
Maryland	Maryland Limited Liability Company Act, Md. Code Ann., Corps., & Ass'ns §§ 4A-101 through 4A1103
Massachusetts	Massachusetts Limited Liability Company Act, Mass. Gen. Laws ch. 156C, §§ 1 through 68
Michigan	Michigan Limited Liability Company Act, Mich. Comp. Laws §§ 450.4101 through 450.5200
Minnesota	Minnesota Limited Liability Company Act, Minn. Stat. Ann. §§ 322B.01 through 322B.960
Mississippi	Revised Mississippi Limited Liability Company Act, Miss. Code Ann. §§ 79-29-101 through 79-29-1317
Missouri	Missouri Limited Liability Company Act, Mo. Rev. Stat. §§ 347.010 through 347.187
Montana	Montana Limited Liability Company Act, Mont. Code Ann. §§ 35-8-101 through 35-8-1309
Nebraska	Nebraska Limited Liability Company Act, Neb. Rev. Stat. §§ 21-2601 through 21-2653
Nevada	Nevada Limited Liability Company Act, Nev. Rev. Stat. §§ 86.010 through 86.590
New Hampshire	New Hampshire Limited Liability Company Act, N.H. Rev. Stat. Ann. §§ 304-C:1 through 304-C:85New Hampshire Professional Limited Liability Companies, 304-D:1 through 304-D:20.
New Jersey	New Jersey Limited Liability Company Act, N.J. Stat. Ann. §§ 42:2B-1 through 42:2B-70
New Mexico	New Mexico Limited Liability Company Act, N.M. Stat. Ann. §§ 53-19-1 through 53-19-74.
New York	New York Limited Liability Company Act, N.C. Gen. Stat. §§ 57C-1-101 through 1403.
North Carolina	North Carolina Limited Liability Company Act, N.C. Gen Stat. §§ 57C-1 through 53-19-74

EXHIBIT 6-12 (*continued*)

State	Limited Liability Company Act
North Dakota	North Dakota Limited Liability Act, N.D. Cent. Code §§ 10-32-01 through 10-32-155
Ohio	Ohio Limited Liability Company Act, Ohio Rev. Code Ann. §§ 1705.01 through 1705.61
Oklahoma	Oklahoma Limited Liability Company Act, Okla. Stat. Ann. Tit. 18 §§ 2000 through 2060
Oregon	Oregon Limited Liability Company Act, Or. Rev. Stat. §§ 63.001 through 63.990
Pennsylvania	Pennsylvania Limited Liability Company Act of 1994, 15 Pa. Cons. Stat. §§ 8901 through 8998
Rhode Island	Rhode Island Limited Liability Company Act, R.I. Gen Laws §§ 7-16-1 through 7-16-75
South Carolina	South Carolina Uniform Limited Liability Company Act of 1996, S.C. Code Ann. §§ 34-44-101 through 33-44-1208
South Dakota	South Dakota Limited Liability Company Act, S.D. Codified Laws §§ 47-34A-101 through 47-34A-1201
Tennessee	Tennessee Revised Limited Liability Company Act, Tenn. Code Ann. §§ 48-249-101 through 48-248-116
Texas	Texas Limited Liability Company Act, Tex. Stats. §§ 101.001 through 101.621
Utah	Utah Revised Limited Liability Company Act, Utah Code Ann. §§ 48-2c-101 through 48-2c-1902
Vermont	Vermont Limited Liability Company Act, Vt. Stat. Ann. Tit 11, §§ 3001 through 3162
Virginia	Virginia Limited Liability Company Act, Va. Code Ann §§ 13.1-1000 through 13.1-1121
Washington	Washington Limited Liability Company Act, Wash. Rev. Code §§ 25.15.005 through 25.15.902
West Virginia	West Virginia Limited Liability Company Act, Va. Code §§ 31B-1-101 through 31B-13-1306
Wisconsin	Wyoming Limited Liability Company Act, Wyo. Stat. Ann. §§ 17-29-101 through17-29-1105
Wyoming	Wyoming Limited Liability Company Act, Wyo. Stat. §§ 17-14-201 through 17-14-1104

The **Internal Revenue Service** website provides downloadable partnership tax return forms (filed by LLCs) and general information on taxation of limited liability companies.

The website of the **Federation of Tax Administrators** provides state tax forms and links to the state tax agencies of each state.

LLC FORMS

Generic forms for limited liability company operating agreements and other LLC-related documents can be found online from several different sources. Before any of these forms are used, they must be carefully reviewed and edited to be certain that they meet the statutory requirements of your state and that they fulfill the needs of the proposed LLC.

ONLINE LIMITED LIABILITY COMPANY INFORMATION

In recent years, numerous periodical articles and treatises on the topic of limited liability companies have been published online. One popular online resource for limited liability company research is the *Limited Liability Companies Reporter*, a resource for attorneys, CPAs, and business planners that provides cutting-edge information on the developing and rapidly changing unincorporated business association.

SUMMARY

- The limited liability company is a type of business entity that has some characteristics of both partnerships and corporations.
- All states in the United States and the District of Columbia now have statutes providing for limited liability companies.
- The owners of a limited liability company are referred to as its members.
- The members of a limited liability company typically have no personal liability for the debts and obligations of the limited liability company.
- A limited liability company may be member managed or manager managed.
- The limited liability company is formed when articles of organization or some similar document is filed with the secretary of state or appropriate state authority.
- The limited liability company is one of the fastest-growing types of business entities in the United States.
- Few states have adopted the Uniform Limited Liability Company Act.
- The members of a limited liability company may choose to be taxed as a partnership or as a corporation.

- Single-member limited liability companies are disregarded as separate entities for federal income tax purposes, unless the single member chooses to be taxed as a corporation.

- Members of a member-managed limited liability company act as agents for the limited liability company.

- Certain limited liability company actions require the approval of all members, regardless of whether the company is member managed or manager managed.

- The managers of a manager-managed limited liability company act as its agents—the members who are not managers do not.

- The limited liability company operating agreement sets forth the agreement of all members in much more detail than the articles of organization. The operating agreement is similar to both the partnership agreement and the corporate bylaws.

- The provisions of the limited liability company's operating agreement govern the limited liability company, so long as those provisions are not contrary to the pertinent state statutes.

- The limited liability company existence is ended when articles of termination or articles of dissolution are filed with the secretary of state.

- Limited liability companies must apply for a certificate of authority to transact business in any state other than the state of domicile in which the company does business.

REVIEW QUESTIONS

1. In what ways are limited liability companies different from general partnerships?

2. If Sandy owes Mike $5,000 that she is unable to repay, can she assign to him her rights as a limited liability company member to receive payments as set forth in the company's operating agreement? Can Sandy assign her entire rights in the limited liability company to Mike, making him a new member with the right to manage the business?

3. Katherine is a member of a member-managed limited liability company, K & A Software Ltd. Liability Company, that designs software. Can she enter the company into a contract for the design of new educational software for a local college? What if the K & A Software Ltd. Liability Company is manager managed?

4. Are the members of a limited liability company always protected from personal liability for the debts and obligations of the company? What are some circumstances under which members of a limited liability company may be personally liable for the company's debts and obligations?

5. Suppose that you are forming a limited liability company that will own and operate auto dealerships. Your company will only operate one dealership in Missouri to start with, but you want to expand into Illinois, Texas, and Arizona. What steps might you take during the organization process to plan for your future expansion?

6. If you are a family practice physician going into business with three other doctors, why might a professional limited liability company be an attractive option?

7. Why is it important to designate in the articles of organization whether a limited liability company will be member managed or manager managed?

8. Why might an investor prefer to become a member of an LLC rather than a limited partner of a limited partnership?

9. Suppose that Dan decides to form a limited liability company to operate a grocery delivery service with his two sons, Tom and Bob. Tom and Bob are each contributing $10,000, but Dan's initial contribution is $20,000. Can the LLC's operating agreement provide for Dan to receive distributions that are twice the amount of the distribution that Tom and Bob each receive? If the operating agreement is silent on the subject of distributions, how would a $6,000 distribution be divided among the three members?

10. Suppose that you have formed a limited liability company in your state to operate a sporting goods franchise. Your business has become very successful and you and your members would like to expand. One of your members, who will be managing the new store, lives in a neighboring state and would like to open a store in his hometown. Would it be necessary to form a new limited liability company, or can your limited liability company own and operate a store in a neighboring state? What formalities may be required?

PRACTICAL PROBLEMS

1. Locate the limited liability company act from your state to answer the following questions:
   a. What is the cite for your state's limited liability company act?
   b. When was your state's act adopted? Are the limited liability companies in your state either member managed or manager managed by default?

2. Locate the pertinent section of your state's limited liability company act or contact the appropriate state office to answer the following questions:
   a. What is the title of the document for forming limited liability companies in your state?
   b. Where is this document filed?
   c. What is the filing fee for filing the document to organize a limited liability company?
   d. Are there any additional documents that must be filed with the organization document in your state? If so, what are they?

EXERCISE IN CRITICAL THINKING

Why might an investor want to become a member of a manager-managed LLC when the investor would have no authority to manage the company? What can a member of a manager-managed LLC do to influence the direction of the LLC?

WORKPLACE SCENARIO

Assume that our fictional clients, Bradley Harris and Cynthia Lund, want to form a limited liability company in your state for their business, Cutting Edge Computer Repair. Bradley and Cynthia will each invest an equal amount in the limited liability company, which will be member managed.

Using the information provided in Appendices B-1 and B-2 of this text, prepare for filing articles of organization for a limited liability company in your state. You may create your own form that conforms to the statutes of your state, or you can download and complete a form from the appropriate state office. The CourseMate resources for this text include articles of organization forms. If your state requires the filing of any other documentation to form a limited liability company, prepare that documentation also.

Then prepare a cover letter to the appropriate state authority filing the articles of organization and enclosing the appropriate filing fee and any other documentation required by the secretary of state.

Portfolio Reminder

Save the documents prepared for the Workplace Scenario exercises in each chapter, either in hard copy or electronically, to build a portfolio of documents to be used for job interviews or as sample documents on the job. At this point, your portfolio should include the following:

- Power of attorney
- Application for assumed name
- Application for federal employer identification number
- Application for state employer identification number
- Partnership statement of authority
- Limited partnership certificate
- Limited liability partnership statement of qualification
- Articles of organization

ENDNOTES

1. Treas. Reg. § 301.7701–3 (1997).

2. Rev. Rul. 88–76.

3. Friedman, Howard. "The Silent LLC Revolution—The Social Cost of Academic Neglect," *38 Creighton L. Rev.* 35, Dec. 2004.

4. Internal Revenue Service, "Partnership Returns, 2008," *Statistics of Income Bulletin*, Fall 2010, http://www.irs.gov, 2011.

5. Id.

6. National Conference of Commissioners on Uniform State Laws, July 13, 2006, News Release: New Act Updates the Rules on Limited Liability Companies.

7. As of late 2010, the states of Alabama, Hawaii, Illinois, Montana, South Carolina, South Dakota, Vermont, and West Virginia had adopted the original Uniform Limited Liability Company Act.

8. As of late 2010, Idaho, Iowa, Nebraska, and Wyoming had adopted the Revised Uniform Limited Liability Company Act.

9. *SEC v. Parkersburg Wireless*, 991 F.Supp. 6 (D.C. 1997).

10. *Robinson v. Glynn*, 349 F.3d 166 (4th Cir. 2003).

11. *KFC Ventures, L.L. C. v. Metaire Medical Leasing Corp.*, 2000 WL 726877 (ED La 2000).

12. Minn. Stat. § 322B.69. Colorado, Iowa, and Rhode Island have similar statutory provisions.

13. Uniform Limited Liability Company Act § 601.

14. Uniform Limited Liability Company Act § 801.

15. Uniform Limited Liability Company Act § 805.

CourseMate

To access additional course materials including CourseMate, please visit www.cengagebrain.com. At the CengageBrain.com home page, search for the ISBN of your title (from the back cover of your book) using the search box at the top of the page. This will take you to the product page where the resources can be found. The CourseMate resources for this text include web links to the resources discussed above, including several resources for sole proprietors and small businesses, downloadable forms, flash cards and more. In addition to the statement of authority, prepare a cover letter filing the form with the appropriate state authority, along with any required filing fee.

CORPORATIONS

INTRODUCTION

The corporation is one of the most complex forms of business organization. Although there are several other types and classifications of corporations, this chapter and the rest of this book focus on the business corporation, unless otherwise noted. First we look at the unique characteristics of business corporations and discuss the role of corporations in the United States. Next, we examine the rights and powers of a corporation and consider both the advantages and disadvantages of doing business as a corporation compared to other types of business organizations. Our focus then moves on to what can happen when shareholders lose the legal protection of the corporate entity—piercing the corporate veil.

This chapter concludes with a discussion of other types and classifications of corporations, a look at the role of the paralegal working in the corporate law area, and coverage of the resources available to assist them.

§ 7.1 AN INTRODUCTION TO CORPORATIONS

The **corporation** shares many characteristics of the limited liability entities discussed previously in this text, but it is still an entity like no other. Almost without exception, the corporation is considered a separate legal entity governed by state statute, as well as federal law and local ordinances.

CORPORATION DEFINED

An early Supreme Court decision defined the corporation as "an artificial being, invisible, intangible, and existing only in contemplation of law."[1] This definition has been used frequently by the courts over the years. More simply put, a corporation is an organization that is formed under state or federal law and exists, for legal purposes, as a separate being or an "artificial person."[2] Whatever the exact definition, the corporation possesses four characteristics that distinguish it from other types of business organizations:

1. The corporation is an artificial entity created by law.
2. The corporation is an entity separate from its owners or managers.
3. The corporation has certain rights and powers, which it exercises through its agents.
4. The corporation has the capacity to exist perpetually.

THE CORPORATION AS A SEPARATE LEGAL ENTITY

In contrast to the sole proprietorship and general partnership, which are considered extensions of the individual owner or owners, the corporation is considered a "legal entity with an identity or personality separate and distinct from that of its owners or shareholders and must be thought of without reference to the members who compose it."[3] In many respects, corporations are treated as artificial persons under law, unless the law provides otherwise. As an artificial person, a corporation is subject to many of the same rights and obligations under law as a natural person. The courts have found on several occasions that while all statutes that speak of persons cannot be construed to include corporations, the term "person" may include a corporation. It is the intent behind the statute that must be considered.

Because the corporation is a separate entity, the corporation itself is liable for any debts and obligations it incurs. The shareholders, directors, and officers of a corporation are generally not personally liable for the corporation's debts and obligations merely by virtue of their interest in the corporation.

LAW GOVERNING CORPORATIONS

As a separate entity, the corporation must at all times be in compliance with all relevant laws. The sources of most laws to which corporations are subject are state statutes, common law, case law, federal statutes, and local ordinances.

STATE STATUTES

Corporations are created by and generally governed by the statutes of the state of **domicile** (the state in which the corporation is incorporated). A corporation that is qualified to do business in a foreign state, however, subjects itself to the statutes of that state for certain purposes.

> **DOMICILE**
>
> A person's permanent home, legal home, or main residence. The words "abode," "citizenship," "habitancy," and "residence" sometimes mean the same as *domicile* and sometimes not. A corporate domicile is the corporation's legal home (usually where its headquarters is located); an elected domicile is the place the persons who make a contract specify as their legal homes in the contract.

The corporate statutes of every state in the country are derived, at least in part, from the Model Business Corporation Act (MBCA), first published in 1950, or the 1984 Revised Model Business Corporation Act. These acts were drafted by the American Bar Association Section of Corporation, Banking and Business Law. The 1984 Revised Model Business Corporation Act continues to be revised through the date of this publication. As of December 2007, 30 states have business corporation acts that are an adoption of all, or substantially all, of the Model Business Corporation Act (1984),[4] as amended. In this text, all references to the "Model Business Corporation Act" are to the 1984 Revised Model Business Corporation Act, as amended through December 2009. See also Exhibit 7-8 for a list of state business corporation acts.

Unlike the Uniform Partnership and Limited Partnership Acts, the model corporation acts are just model acts, not uniform acts. The model acts serve as an aid to the state legislatures in drafting their own statutes, and corporate laws still vary significantly from state to state. The laws of the state of Delaware, the state often referred to as the "incorporation state," have also served as a model to the legislatures of other states.

Common Law and Case Law

Corporations are created and governed by statute. Therefore, common and case law play a less significant role in governing corporations. However, the number of corporate issues decided in court illustrates that case law is relevant in interpreting the law governing corporations and in ruling on matters not covered by the statutes. Because Delaware has such a disproportionately high number of domestic corporations, much of today's corporate law has been derived from the decisions of the courts of Delaware.

Federal Statutes

Federal law also governs corporations. For instance, securities of publicly held corporations are subject to federal statutes and regulations, as well as the statutes of the state of incorporation. The Securities Exchange Act of 1934, the Securities Act of 1933, and the Sarbanes-Oxley Act of 2002, concerning corporate financial and accounting disclosures, are the major federal laws governing corporations that sell shares of stock or other securities publicly. Corporations are also subject to federal legislation in other areas, including bankruptcy, intellectual property, antitrust, interstate commerce, and taxation.

IN SUMMATION

- A corporation is an organization formed under law that is considered an entity separate from its owners.
- Corporations have certain rights and powers and the capacity to exist perpetually.
- Corporations are subject to:
  - State law
  - Federal statutes
  - Common law and case law
  - Local ordinances

§ 7.2 CORPORATIONS IN THE UNITED STATES

This text focuses on the law of corporations; therefore, a full analysis of the influence of corporations on our society is beyond its scope. However, it is important to recognize the magnitude of the role that corporations play in the U.S. economy and in each of our lives. During 2008, U.S. corporations reported more than $24.7 trillion in business receipts,[5] compared to just over $3.8 trillion for partnerships,[6] and $1.3 billion for sole proprietorships.[7] In 2008, corporate income tax returns filed with the Internal Revenue Service indicated that corporations in the United States had a total net worth of more than $25.4 trillion.[8]

Exhibit 7-1 provides a chart of corporate net worth in the United States from 2003 to 2008.

A growing number of Americans become corporate shareholders each year, either individually or through their retirement plans. According to the U.S. Census Bureau, during the year 2007, more than half of the households in the United States owned shares of stock or mutual funds.[9]

SIDEBAR

With revenues of more than $408 billion for 2010, Wal-Mart was the number one corporation on the 2010 Fortune 500 list.

IN SUMMATION

- With business receipts of several trillion dollars each year, large corporations play a very important role in the economy of the United States.
- In 2007, more than half of the households in the United States owned shares of stock or mutual funds.

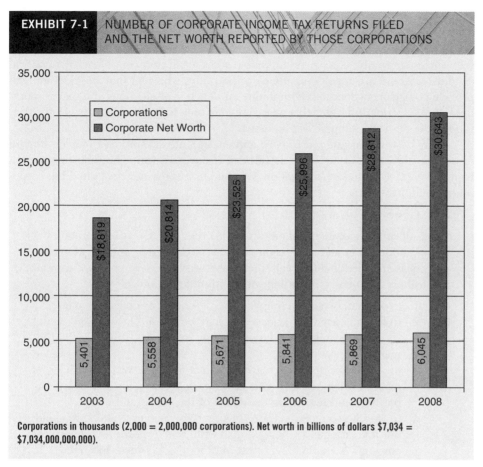

EXHIBIT 7-1   NUMBER OF CORPORATE INCOME TAX RETURNS FILED AND THE NET WORTH REPORTED BY THOSE CORPORATIONS

Corporations in thousands (2,000 = 2,000,000 corporations). Net worth in billions of dollars $7,034 = $7,034,000,000,000).

Statistics from the 2011 *Statistical Abstract* §752 and Corporate Income Tax Returns, 2008, *Statistics of Income Bulletin*, Internal Revenue Service.

§ 7.3 CORPORATE RIGHTS AND POWERS

As a separate entity, the corporation enjoys certain rights and powers apart from those of its shareholders, directors, or officers. Corporations, as artificial persons, are entitled to many of the same rights as natural persons, including many of the same constitutional rights. There is currently a debate in the United States concerning the issue of "corporate personhood." The debate concerns the question of what subset of rights should be granted to corporations—under what circumstances should corporations be considered "persons" under the law and the Constitution of the United States. Historically, the courts have not treated corporations as persons for certain purposes. For instance, the Fourteenth Amendment to the Constitution, which guarantees liberty, and the Fifth Amendment, which protects persons from self-incrimination, apply to natural persons only. In 2010, the U.S. Supreme

Court issued a controversial opinion, *Citizens United v. Federal Election Commission* (2010), in which it held that corporations have a right to free speech and that a corporation's political spending is protected by the First Amendment. This ruling, in effect, allows corporations to spend unlimited sums in support (or defeat) of a political candidate. There are many opponents to the ruling who feel that the decision will provide powerful corporations with undue influence over elections and that corporations are being granted rights that were intended only for individuals. As of late 2011, the full effect of this ruling is yet unknown.

Many powers are granted to corporations by state statute, and may be limited or enhanced by the corporation's **articles of incorporation**. The following section from the Model Business Corporation Act enumerates the powers granted to corporations under the act:

3.02 General Powers

Unless its articles of incorporation provide otherwise, every corporation has perpetual duration and succession in its corporate name and has the same powers as an individual to do all things necessary or convenient to carry out its business and affairs, including without limitation power:

1. to sue and be sued, complain and defend in its corporate name;
2. to have a corporate seal, which may be altered at will, and to use it, or a facsimile of it, by impressing or affixing it or in any other manner reproducing it;
3. to make and amend bylaws, not inconsistent with its articles of incorporation or with the laws of this state, for managing the business and regulating the affairs of the corporation;
4. to purchase, receive, lease, or otherwise acquire, and own, hold, improve, use, and otherwise deal with, real or personal property, or any legal or equitable interest in property, wherever located;
5. to sell, convey, mortgage, pledge, lease, exchange, and otherwise dispose of all or any part of its property;
6. to purchase, receive, subscribe for, or otherwise acquire; own, hold, vote, use, sell, mortgage, lend, pledge, or otherwise dispose of; and deal in and with shares or other interests in, or obligations of, any other entity;
7. to make contracts and guarantees, incur liabilities, borrow money, issue its notes, bonds, and other obligations (which may be convertible into or include the option to purchase other securities of the corporation), and secure any of its obligations by mortgage or pledge of any of its property, franchises, or income;
8. to lend money, invest and reinvest its funds, and receive and hold real and personal property as security for repayment;
9. to be a promoter, partner, member, associate, or manager of any partnership, joint venture, trust or other entity;
10. to conduct its business, locate offices, and exercise the powers granted by this Act within or without this state;

ARTICLES OF INCORPORATION

The document used to set up a corporation. Articles of incorporation contain the most basic rules of the corporation and control other corporate rules such as the bylaws.

11. to elect directors and appoint officers, employees, and agents of the corporation, define their duties, fix their compensation, and lend them money and credit;

12. to pay pensions and establish pension plans, pension trusts, profit sharing plans, share bonus plans, share option plans, and benefit or incentive plans for any or all of its current or former directors, officers, employees, and agents;

13. to make donations for the public welfare or for charitable, scientific, or educational purposes;

14. to transact any lawful business that will aid governmental policy;

15. to make payments or donations, or do any other act, not inconsistent with law, that furthers the business and affairs of the corporation.

IN SUMMATION

- Corporations are considered artificial persons, entitled to many of the same rights as natural persons—separate from the rights of their shareholders, directors, and officers.

- Many powers are granted by state statute and may be limited or enhanced by the corporation's articles of incorporation.

§ 7.4 ADVANTAGES OF DOING BUSINESS AS A CORPORATION

The advantages of doing business as a corporation are both numerous and unique. Most of the advantages stem from the separate-entity characteristic of the corporation. This section discusses the corporation's advantages over limited liability companies, partnerships, and sole proprietorships. The advantages we focus on include the limited liability available to the officers, directors, and shareholders of the corporation; the continuity of the business of a corporation; and the increased opportunities to raise capital for corporations. We also examine the benefits of the centralized management structure of a corporation and the relative ease with which corporate ownership can be transferred.

LIMITED LIABILITY

One of the most important benefits to forming a corporation is the limited liability that the corporate structure offers to its shareholders, directors, and officers. Theoretically, the corporation is responsible for its own debts and obligations, leaving the shareholders, directors, and officers free from personal liability.

This can be a benefit to an individual or group of individuals wanting to start a business in several ways. Most obviously, the founders of the corporation put at risk only their initial investment in the corporation and protect their personal assets.

Also, the ability to raise capital to start and operate the business is increased, because potential investors may own a piece of the corporation and put at risk no more than their investment to purchase shares of stock.

The limited liability benefit of incorporating does have its boundaries, however. As discussed in § 7.6, the corporate veil may be pierced under certain circumstances, leaving the individual shareholders exposed to personal liability for the corporation's debts and obligations. Also, as a practical matter, shareholders of a new or small corporation are often required to give their personal guarantees to obtain financing on behalf of the corporation. If the corporation has few assets in its own name, banks and other lenders often refuse financing to the corporation without the personal guarantee of individual shareholders who have an adequate net worth to secure the corporation's loans.

Business Continuity

Another important advantage of doing business as a corporation is that the corporation has the ability to exist perpetually. Unlike the sole proprietorship or partnership, the corporation does not dissolve upon the death or withdrawal of any of its principals. Shares of stock may be sold, given, or bequeathed to others without affecting the continuity of the corporation or its business.

Ability to Raise Capital

Compared to sole proprietorships or partnerships, the corporation has an increased potential for raising capital. Investors may be enticed by the potential for dividends and stock appreciation, as well as the limited liability offered by corporations. The flexible nature of the corporate capital structure allows corporations to appeal to a wide variety of investors with varying needs; for example, the corporation may sell shares of stock of different classes. The financial structure of corporations is discussed in Chapter 10 of this text. Securities are discussed in Chapter 11.

Centralized Management

Although the shareholders of a corporation have the right to vote for directors of the corporation, they generally do not have an automatic right to participate directly in the management of the business, as general partners do. Shareholders participate in management of the corporation through their votes for the directors of the corporation. The directors, in turn, are given the right to elect the officers of the corporation—the individuals they feel are the best people to operate the day-to-day business of the corporation. The officers are given the authority to operate the business as they see fit, under the oversight of the board of directors. Shareholder or director approval, or both, must be given to certain extraordinary actions taken by the officers on behalf of the corporation, however.

In small corporations with just a few shareholders, those shareholders often elect themselves to be the directors and officers of the corporation. In effect, the small corporation is often run by its owners. In contrast, directors and officers of larger corporations may own little or no stock in the corporations they work for. Corporate management and the roles of the officers, shareholders, and directors are discussed in more detail in Chapter 9 of this text.

TRANSFERABILITY OF OWNERSHIP

In contrast to the sole proprietorship, limited liability company, and partnership, the ownership interest of a corporation is easily transferred. Barring a prohibitive agreement among the shareholders, or restrictions in the corporation's articles of incorporation or bylaws, shares of stock may be bought and sold freely. Because a shareholder's interest in the corporation is represented by stock certificates, the transfer of unrestricted stock may be as simple as an endorsement by the shareholder, on the back of the certificate, to the purchaser or transferee of the stock.

However, restrictions may be placed on the transfer of shares of closely held corporations, either by statute, the articles of incorporation, bylaws, or in an agreement between the shareholders. These agreements often give the corporation or existing shareholders the first option to purchase the shares of a shareholder who would like to sell stock in the corporation. An agreement of the shareholders may also provide for the purchase of shares of a deceased shareholder by the corporation or the other shareholders. Unless addressed in a written agreement, a deceased shareholder's shares of stock are passed on to his or her heirs, just like any other asset. Shareholder agreements restricting the transfer of stock are discussed in more detail in Chapter 9 of this text.

EMPLOYEE BENEFIT PLANS

The owners of a corporation may be in a position to take advantage of employee benefit plans that can be used both to compensate employees and to reduce the income tax liability of the corporation. These benefits may be in the form of stock option or bonus plans or contributions to qualified pension and profit-sharing plans, group-term life insurance, health insurance, medical reimbursement plans, and other employee benefits. Many of these benefits constitute tax-deferred or nontaxable income to the employee/shareholders of the corporation and can be used as a means to pass tax-free income through to the shareholders of the corporation, while giving the added bonus of a tax deduction to the corporation. Employee benefit plans are discussed in Chapter 15 of this text.

CHOICE OF TAX YEAR

With the exception of S Corporations, which are discussed in § 7.9, corporations may freely choose their fiscal tax year, which may be different from the calendar year. The corporation can choose the tax year that is most advantageous to its business and that best fits its natural business cycle. For example, a corporation formed to operate a marina may find that it would be advantageous to have its fiscal year end in November, one of the business's slowest months of the year.

IN SUMMATION

- Some of the advantages to doing business as a corporation as opposed to other forms of business organization include:
  - Limited liability status is available to all owners, directors, and officers of the corporation.
  - The business may exist perpetually.
  - The corporation may raise additional capital by selling shares of stock.
  - Corporate management is typically centralized with the officers, who are overseen by the directors of the corporation.
  - Unless specific restrictions are placed on shares of stock, corporation ownership may be transferred freely by selling or assigning shares of stock.
  - Compensation of corporate owners and employees can be very flexible and can include employee benefit plans, which provide tax breaks for corporations.
  - Most corporations may choose a tax year that is convenient to the business.

§ 7.5 DISADVANTAGES OF DOING BUSINESS AS A CORPORATION

The many advantages of doing business as a corporation must be weighed against the disadvantages before a determination can be made as to whether to incorporate. Exhibit 7-3 summarizes both sides of the question. In this section we explore some of the disadvantages of doing business as a corporation, including the formalities and reporting requirements that must be followed by corporations and the income taxation disadvantages.

CORPORATE FORMALITIES AND REPORTING REQUIREMENTS

The corporation is the most complex type of business entity, and there are numerous formalities and reporting requirements associated with its formation and maintenance.

First, because the corporation is a creature of statute, it does not exist until the proper documentation is filed with the designated state authority in accordance with state law. Articles of incorporation must be filed, and all other statutory requirements for incorporating must be complied with before the corporate existence begins. Unlike a partnership, a corporation may not be formed by a verbal agreement. Corporate formation is discussed in detail in Chapter 8 of this text. Also, unlike sole proprietorships and most partnerships, for a corporation to transact business in any state other than its state of domicile, it must qualify with the proper state authority in the foreign state.

Once the corporation is formed, several ongoing statutory requirements must be complied with. Annual shareholder and director meetings may be required, and annual reports often are required by the state of domicile. In addition, corporations may be subject to securities regulations that include securities registration and periodic reporting.

The corporation, as a separate entity, must file a separate corporate income tax return and pay income tax each year to the Internal Revenue Service, its state of domicile, and states in which it transacts business.

All of the foregoing requirements can be time consuming and costly. However, as mentioned previously in this chapter, it is important that a corporation comply with all corporate formalities to ensure that there is no cause for the corporate veil to be pierced.

TAXATION

Although the corporate structure can offer advantages under certain circumstances, in other instances the tax disadvantages may be enough reason to choose another form of business organization.

Double Taxation

The most serious corporate tax drawback is double taxation of the corporate income. Unlike sole proprietorships, partnerships, and limited liability companies, most corporations are taxed as entities separate from their shareholders, and must pay income tax on their earnings. Income tax will be payable by the corporation on the income reported. Most states also require that a state income tax form be filed and state income taxes paid annually. In addition, the shareholders of the corporation must pay income tax on income or dividends received from the corporation. The income of the corporation is, in effect, taxed twice. For example, suppose that four friends decide to form a corporation to own and operate a real estate investment business. The corporation is successful, and the four friends receive dividends from the corporation throughout the year. At tax time, the corporation must report all of its income on a corporate income tax return and pay the income tax owed. In addition, the four friends must pay income tax on the dividends they received from the corporation. The income is taxed once as income of the corporation and again as income of the shareholders. Corporate income must be reported to the Internal Revenue Service each year on Form 1120. Exhibit 7-2 is a sample IRS Form 1120.

Other Taxes on Corporations

In addition to income tax, corporations may be subject to special state taxes, including incorporation taxes and franchise taxes. Corporations are also subject to fees and taxes in any foreign states in which they transact business.

As mentioned, Exhibit 7-3 summarizes the advantages and disadvantages of corporations.

EXHIBIT 7-2 FORM 1120, U.S. CORPORATION INCOME TAX RETURN

Form **1120**

Department of the Treasury
Internal Revenue Service

U.S. Corporation Income Tax Return

For calendar year 2010 or tax year beginning _____ , 2010, ending _____ , 20___

▶ See separate instructions.

OMB No. 1545-0123

20**10**

A Check if:		
1a Consolidated return (attach Form 851) . . ☐	**Print or type**	Name
b Life/nonlife consoli- dated return . . . ☐		Number, street, and room or suite no. If a P.O. box, see instructions.
2 Personal holding co. (attach Sch. PH) . . ☐		City or town, state, and ZIP code
3 Personal service corp. (see instructions) . . ☐		
4 Schedule M-3 attached ☐		

B Employer identification number

C Date incorporated

D Total assets (see instructions)

$

E Check if: **(1)** ☐ Initial return **(2)** ☐ Final return **(3)** ☐ Name change **(4)** ☐ Address change

Income

1a	Gross receipts or sales _____ **b** Less returns and allowances _____ **c** Bal ▶	**1c**	
2	Cost of goods sold (Schedule A, line 8)	**2**	
3	Gross profit. Subtract line 2 from line 1c	**3**	
4	Dividends (Schedule C, line 19)	**4**	
5	Interest	**5**	
6	Gross rents	**6**	
7	Gross royalties	**7**	
8	Capital gain net income (attach Schedule D (Form 1120))	**8**	
9	Net gain or (loss) from Form 4797, Part II, line 17 (attach Form 4797)	**9**	
10	Other income (see instructions—attach schedule)	**10**	
11	**Total income.** Add lines 3 through 10 . . . . ▶	**11**	

Deductions (See instructions for limitations on deductions.)

12	Compensation of officers (Schedule E, line 4) . . . . ▶	**12**	
13	Salaries and wages (less employment credits)	**13**	
14	Repairs and maintenance	**14**	
15	Bad debts	**15**	
16	Rents	**16**	
17	Taxes and licenses	**17**	
18	Interest	**18**	
19	Charitable contributions	**19**	
20	Depreciation from Form 4562 not claimed on Schedule A or elsewhere on return (attach Form 4562) . .	**20**	
21	Depletion	**21**	
22	Advertising	**22**	
23	Pension, profit-sharing, etc., plans	**23**	
24	Employee benefit programs	**24**	
25	Domestic production activities deduction (attach Form 8903)	**25**	
26	Other deductions (attach schedule)	**26**	
27	**Total deductions.** Add lines 12 through 26 . . . . ▶	**27**	
28	Taxable income before net operating loss deduction and special deductions. Subtract line 27 from line 11.	**28**	
29	**Less: a** Net operating loss deduction (see instructions) . . . . **29a** _____		
	b Special deductions (Schedule C, line 20) . . . . . . **29b** _____	**29c**	

Tax, Refundable Credits, and Payments

30	**Taxable income.** Subtract line 29c from line 28 (see instructions)	**30**	
31	**Total tax** (Schedule J, line 10)	**31**	
32a	2009 overpayment credited to 2010 . . **32a** _____		
b	2010 estimated tax payments . . . **32b** _____		
c	2010 refund applied for on Form 4466 **32c** (_____) **d Bal** ▶ **32d** _____		
e	Tax deposited with Form 7004 . . . . **32e** _____		
f	Credits: **(1)** Form 2439 _____ **(2)** Form 4136 _____ **32f** _____		
g	Refundable credits from Form 3800, line 19c, and Form 8827, line 8c . . . **32g** _____	**32h**	
33	Estimated tax penalty (see instructions). Check if Form 2220 is attached . . . ▶ ☐	**33**	
34	**Amount owed.** If line 32h is smaller than the total of lines 31 and 33, enter amount owed . . .	**34**	
35	**Overpayment.** If line 32h is larger than the total of lines 31 and 33, enter amount overpaid . . .	**35**	
36	Enter amount from line 35 you want: **Credited to 2011 estimated tax** ▶ _____ Refunded ▶	**36**	

Sign Here

Under penalties of perjury, I declare that I have examined this return, including accompanying schedules and statements, and to the best of my knowledge and belief, it is true, correct, and complete. Declaration of preparer (other than taxpayer) is based on all information of which preparer has any knowledge.

▲ _____ _____ ▶ _____
Signature of officer   Date   Title

May the IRS discuss this return with the preparer shown below (see instructions)? ☐ Yes ☐ No

Paid Preparer Use Only

Print/Type preparer's name	Preparer's signature	Date	Check ☐ if self-employed	PTIN
Firm's name ▶			Firm's EIN ▶	
Firm's address ▶			Phone no.	

For Paperwork Reduction Act Notice, see separate instructions.   Cat. No. 11450Q   Form **1120** (2010)

Internal Revenue Service

EXHIBIT 7-3	ADVANTAGES AND DISADVANTAGES OF DOING BUSINESS AS A CORPORATION

Advantages	Disadvantages
• Limited liability for shareholders	• Corporate formalities and reporting requirements
• Business continuity	
• Ability to raise capital	• Double taxation
• Centralized management	• Legal expenses
• Transferability of ownership	

© Cengage Learning 2013

IN SUMMATION

- Some of the disadvantages to doing business as a corporation as opposed to other forms of business organization include:

  - The corporation must be formed by filing articles of incorporation or a similar document with the appointed state authority and paying a filing fee.

  - Corporations are subject to formalities such as holding annual meetings, annual reporting, and filing tax returns. Publicly held corporations are subject to many more reporting requirements and formalities.

  - Corporations are subject to double taxation.

  - Corporations may be subject to certain taxes and fees unique to that form of business.

§ 7.6 PIERCING THE CORPORATE VEIL

Although the shareholders of a corporation are generally free from personal liability for the corporation's obligations, there are certain circumstances under which the corporate entity may be disregarded and shareholders may be considered personally liable for corporate debts and obligations. This is referred to as "piercing the corporate veil." If a court finds that the circumstances warrant, corporate shareholders, directors, and officers may be held personally liable for certain obligations. In fact, whether to pierce the corporate veil is the most highly litigated issue in corporate law.

Courts are reluctant to pierce the corporate veil, but may do so when the corporation is used "as a cloak or cover for fraud or illegality, to work an injustice, to defend a crime or defeat an overriding public policy, or where necessary to achieve equity."[10] When a corporation is formed or operated to commit fraud or other illegal activity, or to defend a crime, the corporate veil may be pierced and any shareholder, director, or officer who is responsible for the wrongdoing may be held personally accountable.

The corporate veil of a small or closely held corporation may be pierced when the corporation is found to be an alter ego of an individual and if such attribution of liability is in the interest of securing a just determination of the action. Courts have found that the "corporate entity may be disregarded where there is such unity of interest and ownership that the separate personalities of the corporation and the individual no longer exist and where, if the acts are treated as those of the corporation alone, an inequitable result will follow."[11]

Keeping in mind that courts will usually seek to pierce the corporate veil only to prevent inequity, injustice, or fraud, other factors are taken into consideration. The corporation is closely scrutinized to determine if it is actually being operated as a corporation and to determine if statutory formalities for incorporating and operating the corporation have been followed. The following factors are often taken into consideration in support of piercing the corporate veil:

1. Improper or incomplete incorporation
2. Failure to issue stock
3. Commingling of corporate and shareholder funds
4. Failure to follow statutory formalities
5. Failure to hold regular shareholders' and directors' meetings
6. Nonpayment of dividends
7. Failure of shareholders to represent themselves as agents of a corporation, rather than individuals, when dealing with outside parties
8. Undercapitalization

To provide an equitable settlement of the corporation's debts and to preserve the rights of certain creditors, the corporate veil may be pierced and the corporate existence ignored by a bankruptcy court under the Federal Bankruptcy Act. The Internal Revenue Service also may seek to pierce the corporate veil when the corporate entity is used solely for the purpose of income tax evasion.

The fact that it is possible for the corporate veil to be pierced under certain circumstances makes it imperative that all corporate formalities be followed by the corporation and that those formalities be properly documented. In the case that follows in this chapter, the corporation's majority shareholder was found to be the alter ego of the corporation and the corporate veil was pierced, holding the shareholder personally liable for damages resulting from a suit brought against the corporation and shareholder.

CASE

359 S.C. 217, 597 S.E.2D 803 COURT OF APPEALS OF SOUTH CAROLINA

Carol HUNTING, as Guardian *ad Litem* for Catherine L. Hitchcock, Respondent, v. William ELDERS, Samuel Chris Gordon and Elmyer Enterprises, Inc., Defendants of whom William Elders is, Appellant

No. 3778.
Heard Oct. 8, 2003.
Decided April 19, 2004.
Rehearing Denied June 25, 2004.
Certiorari Granted August 12, 2005.

STILWELL, J.:

This action was commenced to recover damages sustained by Catherine L. Hitchcock in an accident caused by a drunk driver. Carol Hunting, as guardian *ad litem* for Hitchcock, brought suit

continues

CASE *(continued)*
359 S.C. 217, 597 S.E.2D 803 COURT OF APPEALS OF SOUTH CAROLINA

against Chris Gordon as the drunk driver, Elmyer Enterprises, Inc. as the owner and operator of the bar, and William Elders as the alter ego of the corporation. In the first portion of the bifurcated trial, damages of $1.5 million were awarded against Gordon and Elmyer Enterprises. The second phase of the trial, which is the subject of this appeal, resulted in a holding that Elders was the alter ego of Elmyer Enterprises, justifying piercing the corporate veil, thereby holding Elders personally liable for the $1.5 million verdict and the interest which had accrued from the date of the original judgment against the corporation. We affirm.

FACTS

We discern the following facts from the order of the unappealed first phase of the trial. Gordon became intoxicated while at Willie's, a bar operated by Elmyer Enterprises. Gordon was served alcohol despite being obviously intoxicated. After leaving the bar in an intoxicated state, he caused the accident in which Hitchcock was left permanently brain damaged. Hunting was awarded $1.5 million in actual damages against Gordon and Elmyer Enterprises. The jury also awarded $3,000 and $25,000 in punitive damages against Gordon and Elmyer Enterprises respectively. Subsequently, a non-jury trial was held on the issue of whether to pierce the corporate veil of Elmyer Enterprises and hold Elders liable for the judgment as its alter ego.

The facts as gleaned from the second trial reveal that Elmyer Enterprises was originally incorporated in 1981 and engaged in the business of selling tires. Elders and another shareholder operated the business until Elders bought out the other shareholder. The business then became inactive for several years.

In 1990, Elders opened two bars on property he owned. He originally held the liquor licenses in his own name. In 1993, he reinstated Elmyer Enterprises for the purpose of operating the bars. Each bar was capitalized with $1,000, which was deposited into separate bank accounts. The property and equipment used to operate the bars were leased to Elmyer Enterprises by other businesses formed and owned by Elders. . . .

In December 1993, Elders transferred several shares of stock in Elmyer Enterprises to his wife and niece. He designated his wife as a vice president and his niece as secretary and treasurer. However, his niece testified that she knew nothing about her ownership of shares of stock of Elmyer Enterprises or her selection as an officer of the company. . . .

During the trial, Hunting presented the testimony of Jan Waring-Woods, a forensic accountant, . . . she testified Elders siphoned off between $400,000 and $800,000 from the business over a three-year period. . . .

Hunting also presented testimony from John Freeman, a law professor at the University of South Carolina. He testified that in his opinion the company was operated as a facade by Elders. Freeman maintained Elmyer Enterprises was grossly undercapitalized given its purpose of operating bars and considering the inherent risks associated with a business dispensing alcohol. His conclusion was that Elmyer Enterprises had income that was unaccounted for and profit that was not adequately revealed. He further testified that, in his opinion, Elders was the alter ego of Elmyer Enterprises.

Elders testified the income was as reported. He claimed detailed records were never kept by

continues

the company. . . . He also argued the business was run as a statutory close corporation and as an S corporation. Therefore, it did not have to meet the normal business formalities and would likely mirror Elders as the majority shareholder. Elders claimed the business met its ongoing financial obligations and therefore was not undercapitalized. . . .

LAW/ANALYSIS

Elders contends the trial court erred in piercing the corporate veil of Elmyer Enterprises and therefore holding him personally liable for the judgment. We disagree.

"At the outset, it is recognized that a corporation is an entity, separate and distinct from its officers and stockholders, and that its debts are not the individual indebtedness of its stockholders." *DeWitt Truck Brokers, Inc. v. W. Ray Flemming Fruit Co.*, 540 F.2d 681, 683 (4th Cir.1976). . . .

If any general rule can be laid down, it is that a corporation will be looked upon as a legal entity until sufficient reason to the contrary appears; but when the notion of legal entity is used to protect fraud, justify wrong, or defeat public policy, the law will regard the corporation as an association of persons. . . .

In *Sturkie*, this court set forth a two-pronged test to be used to determine whether to pierce the corporate veil. "The first part of the test, an eight-factor analysis, looks to observance of the corporate formalities by the dominant shareholders. The second part requires that there be an element of injustice or fundamental unfairness if the acts of the corporation be not regarded as the acts of the individuals." *Id.* at 457–58, 313 S.E.2d at 318. The first eight factors were delineated in *Dumas*

v. InfoSafe Corp., 320 S.C. 188, 463 S.E.2d 641 (Ct.App.1995):

1. whether the corporation was grossly undercapitalized
2. failure to observe corporate formalities
3. nonpayment of dividends
4. insolvency of the debtor corporation at the time
5. siphoning of funds of the corporation by the dominant stockholder
6. nonfunctioning of other officers or other directors
7. absence of corporate records, and
8. the fact that the corporation was merely a facade for the operations of the dominant stockholder

. . . The *Sturkie* factors, which now have less importance, include the failure to observe corporate formalities, nonfunctioning of other officers or other directors, the absence of corporate records, and, as stated above, the nonpayment of dividends. The adoption of the statutory device allowing the creation of a statutory close corporation was designed to lessen the formalities necessary to maintain a corporation. . . . The failure to observe the formality "is not a ground for imposing personal liability on the shareholders for liabilities of the corporation." S.C.Code Ann. § 33-18-250 (1990). . . .

Although Elders maintained a bare minimum of corporate records, normal business records were definitely lacking in sufficiency. The corporation did not have adequate records of income from the video poker machines or from the operation of the bars. It did not have records of cash receipts, cash expenses, sales, inventory, or other profit and loss statements that normally would be expected.

continues

In the same fashion, although the corporate minutes indicated the election of officers, Elders's niece, who served as secretary-treasurer, stated she did not know she was an officer in the corporation. Elders produced minutes indicating that his wife and niece were present during meetings. However, the niece testified she never attended any corporate meetings.

Admittedly, Elmyer Enterprises was not required to follow the same corporate formalities as a regular business corporation. Although the failure to adhere to these formalities alone cannot be used to pierce the corporate veil, coupling the dearth of corporate business records and the inactivity of other corporate officers with the evidence of substantial siphoning of funds provides evidence upon which the trial court, at least in part, based its decision. . . .

The corporation was originally funded with only $2,000, which represented $1,000 for each of the two operating locations. Elders asserts that the corporation was properly capitalized at all times, even though the capitalization never appeared to increase over time.

One fact which all the authorities consider significant in the inquiry, and particularly so in the case of the one-man or closely-held corporation, is whether the corporation was grossly undercapitalized for the purposes of the corporate undertaking. See *DeWitt,* 540 F.2d at 685. . . .

The corporation's initial funding was minimal at best. However, as an ongoing concern, the corporation was not properly capitalized. . . .

Additionally, as Professor Freeman testified, a corporation established for the purpose of serving alcohol has more inherent risks and should be adequately protected from liability associated with those risks. The failure to properly protect the business and others should be considered when determining whether the corporation is properly capitalized. Accordingly, we hold Elmyer Enterprises failed to remain properly capitalized as an ongoing business.

The factors dealing with undercapitalization, siphoning of funds, and whether the corporation was a facade for its dominant shareholder are closely related. The trial court found Elders siphoned substantial funds from the corporation, and the evidence substantiates this finding. Using documents from the corporation, the forensic accountant testified there was a significant amount of income not reported, and she determined that Elders siphoned $400,000 to $800,000 from Elmyer Enterprises over a three-year period. . . .

We therefore agree with the trial court that a sufficient number of the eight *Sturkie* factors were present to justify moving to the second prong of the analysis.

The second prong of the *Sturkie* test, requiring "that there be an element of injustice or fundamental unfairness if the acts of the corporation be not regarded as the acts of the individuals," *Sturkie,* 280 S.C. at 457–458, 313 S.E.2d at 318, is perhaps more elusive. In *Sturkie,* the court stated:

> The burden of proving fundamental unfairness requires that the plaintiff establish (1) that the defendant was aware of the plaintiff's claim against the corporation, and (2) thereafter, the defendant acted in a self-serving manner with regard to the property of the corporation and in disregard of the plaintiff's claim in the property.

continues

CASE *(continued)*
359 S.C. 217, 597 S.E.2D 803 COURT OF APPEALS OF SOUTH CAROLINA

Later cases clarified the actual knowledge requirement by stating that a person is "aware" of a claim against the corporation if he has notice of facts which, if pursued with due diligence, would lead to knowledge of the claim. *Multimedia Publ'g of South Carolina, Inc. v. Mullins,* 314 S.C. 551, 554, 431 S.E.2d 569, 572 (1993). Most recently this court has held that "the essence of the fairness test is simply that an individual businessman cannot be allowed to hide from the normal consequences of carefree entrepreneuring by doing so through a corporate shell." *Dumas,* 320 S.C. at 193, 463 S.E.2d at 644.

There is evidence that indicates Elders knew of the plaintiff's claim against the corporation and that, as the trial court found, he nevertheless acted in a self-serving and unfair manner by siphoning off substantial sums of money, commingling and transferring assets which he held in his own name to different entities, transferring stock in the corporation to other individuals without a valuable consideration, and then finally dissolving the corporation.

Elders submits there is no evidence he intended to avoid the *normal* consequences of his entrepreneurial adventures. However, the "normal" consequences of operating a bar which, at least in this instance, admittedly served alcohol to an already-intoxicated individual, transcends that which would be considered normal consequences for the average entrepreneurial endeavor. . . .

AFFIRMED.

Case material reprinted from Westlaw, with permission.
Note: The *Sturkie* test used by the court in this case to find the shareholder was the alter ego of the corporation is just one test that courts may use when deciding whether to pierce the corporate veil.

IN SUMMATION

- At times, when the circumstances dictate, the corporate veil of a corporation may be pierced and any or all of the shareholders, directors, and officers of a corporation may be found personally liable for corporate debts and obligations.
- The corporate veil will typically only be pierced to right a wrong or cure an injustice.

§ 7.7 CORPORATION TYPES AND CLASSIFICATIONS

There are many types and classifications of corporations, stemming from their financial structure, ownership, and purpose. This section deals only with the more common types and classifications of corporations, to give a general understanding of their nature and purposes, including business corporations, professional corporations, nonprofit corporations, S Corporations, statutory close corporations, and parent and subsidiary corporations.

BUSINESS CORPORATIONS

Business corporations, which include large, publicly held corporations and smaller, closely held corporations, are by far the most common type of corporation in this country. As discussed previously in this chapter, business corporations may be formed for the purpose of engaging in any lawful business, unless a more limited purpose is desired.

PROFESSIONAL CORPORATIONS

Under common law, professionals were allowed to practice only as individuals or partners. Now state statutes provide for the formation of professional corporations, or professional service corporations, as they are sometimes called. These corporations are treated in much the same way as a business corporation, with a few important distinctions.

Typically, state statutes provide that the professional corporation is subject to all the provisions of that state's business corporation act, except to the extent that it is inconsistent with the professional corporation act of that state. Many professional corporation acts are based on the Model Professional Corporation Act, which provides that professional corporations may be formed "only for the purpose of rendering professional services and services ancillary thereto within a single profession."[12] A doctor, dentist, and lawyer may not form a single professional corporation. An exception to the single profession rule permits one or more professions to be combined to the extent permitted by the licensing laws of the state of domicile.

Some state statutes enumerate the types of professions that may be incorporated under the professional corporation statutes. These lists typically include many of the following professions: physicians and surgeons, chiropractors, podiatrists, engineers, electrologists, physical therapists, psychologists, certified public accountants and public accountants, dentists, veterinarians, optometrists, attorneys, and licensed acupuncturists. Often the statutes provide that professional corporations may be formed for the performance of any type of service that may be rendered only pursuant to a license issued by law.

Many types of professionals have the option as to whether to incorporate as a professional corporation or a business corporation. Given a choice, it is usually advantageous to incorporate under the business corporation laws of the state in question, as the professional corporation laws are generally more restrictive.

The enactment of professional corporation acts has allowed professionals to realize many of the benefits normally associated with corporations that were not previously available to them as partners or sole proprietors. Of special interest to professionals is the limited liability benefit associated with the corporate structure. Although licensed professionals remain personally liable for their own acts and omissions, professionals practicing in a group may incorporate to provide protection against personal liability for the acts and omissions of their associates, or for torts committed by them.

In addition to the restricted corporate purpose, several other restrictions apply to professional corporations. For instance, stock ownership of professional corporations typically has statutory restrictions placed upon it. The stock of a professional corporation may be owned only by licensed professionals, or partnerships consisting only of partners who are licensed professionals.

SIDEBAR

In some states, a group of professionals may have the option of forming a partnership, a professional limited liability partnership, a professional limited liability company, or a professional corporation.

NONPROFIT CORPORATIONS

Another common type of corporation is the nonprofit corporation, or not-for-profit corporation as it is sometimes referred to, which is formed only for certain nonprofit purposes. Many nonprofit corporations are formed for charitable, civic, educational, and religious purposes. However, nonprofit corporations may be formed for several different reasons. Nonprofit corporations are generally governed under the nonprofit corporation statutes of the state of domicile.

Incorporating as a nonprofit corporation does not ensure exemption from federal income taxation. To qualify for federal tax exemption, the nonprofit corporation must meet the requirements of the Internal Revenue Code (IRC) and obtain approval from the Internal Revenue Service. IRC § 501(c)(3) lists specifically the purposes that may qualify a nonprofit corporation for tax-exempt status. The articles of incorporation of a nonprofit corporation should specifically indicate that the corporation has, as its purpose, one of the purposes listed under IRC § 501(c)(3).

S CORPORATIONS

The Internal Revenue Service recognizes a special category of corporations, referred to as S Corporations, for federal income tax purposes. S Corporations are formed under Subchapter S of the Internal Revenue Code. Unless otherwise specified, other corporations are formed under Subchapter C and are sometimes referred to as C Corporations. S Corporations are eligible, small business corporations that file elections to be treated as such. All shareholders of the S Corporation must agree to the election.

Unlike other business corporations, the income of S Corporations is not taxed at the corporate level, but is passed through to the corporation's shareholders, much like income is passed through to the partners of a partnership or members of a limited liability company. The pass-through taxation of S Corporations has made this type of corporation one of the most popular types of business entities in the United States.

In 1997, for the first time, the number of S Corporation income tax returns surpassed the number of income tax returns filed for other corporations. This trend has continued, and the Internal Revenue Service predicts that the number of S Corporations will continue to grow while the number of other corporations will level off and even decrease.

Exhibit 7-4 provides a comparison of the number of corporate income tax returns filed between 2002 and 2007, showing all corporations and S Corporations.

Pursuant to § 1361 of the Internal Revenue Code, S Corporations must make an election to be treated as such by filing a Form 2553 (shown in Exhibit 7-5), and they must meet the following eligibility requirements:

1. The corporation must be a domestic corporation, or a domestic entity eligible to elect to be treated as a corporation that has filed a Form 2553.
2. The corporation must have no more than 100 shareholders.
3. The corporation's shareholders must all be individuals, estates, or exempt organizations or trusts that meet certain prerequisites.
4. Nonresident aliens may not be shareholders.
5. The corporation cannot issue more than one class of stock.

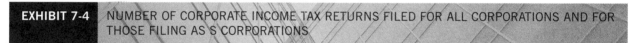

EXHIBIT 7-4 NUMBER OF CORPORATE INCOME TAX RETURNS FILED FOR ALL CORPORATIONS AND FOR THOSE FILING AS S CORPORATIONS

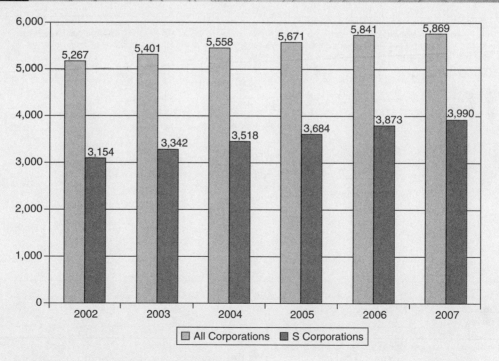

Corporations in thousands (2,000 = 2,000,000 corporations).

Statistics of Income Tax Stats — Integrated Business Data, Table 1, 1980 through 2007, Internal Revenue Service.

EXHIBIT 7-5 FORM 2553, ELECTION BY A SMALL BUSINESS CORPORATION

Form **2553**
(Rev. December 2007)
Department of the Treasury
Internal Revenue Service

Election by a Small Business Corporation
(Under section 1362 of the Internal Revenue Code)
▶ See Parts II and III on page 3 and the separate instructions.
▶ The corporation can fax this form to the IRS (see separate instructions).

OMB No. 1545-0146

Note. This election to be an S corporation can be accepted only if all the tests are met under **Who May Elect** on page 1 of the instructions; all shareholders have signed the consent statement; an officer has signed below; and the exact name and address of the corporation and other required form information are provided.

Part I	Election Information

Type or Print

Name (see instructions)	**A** Employer identification number
Number, street, and room or suite no. (If a P.O. box, see instructions.)	**B** Date incorporated
City or town, state, and ZIP code	**C** State of incorporation

D Check the applicable box(es) if the corporation, after applying for the EIN shown in **A** above, changed its ☐ name or ☐ address

E Election is to be effective for tax year beginning (month, day, year) (see instructions) ▶ / /

Caution. A corporation (entity) making the election for its first tax year in existence will usually enter the beginning date of a short tax year that begins on a date other than January 1.

F Selected tax year:

(1) ☐ Calendar year

(2) ☐ Fiscal year ending (month and day) ▶ _____

(3) ☐ 52-53-week year ending with reference to the month of December

(4) ☐ 52-53-week year ending with reference to the month of ▶ _____

If box (2) or (4) is checked, complete Part II

G If more than 100 shareholders are listed for item J (see page 2), check this box if treating members of a family as one shareholder results in no more than 100 shareholders (see test 2 under **Who May Elect** in the instructions) ▶ ☐

H Name and title of officer or legal representative who the IRS may call for more information	**I** Telephone number of officer or legal representative ( )

If this S corporation election is being filed with Form 1120S, I declare that I had reasonable cause for not filing Form 2553 timely, and if this election is made by an entity eligible to elect to be treated as a corporation, I declare that I also had reasonable cause for not filing an entity classification election timely. See below for my explanation of the reasons the election or elections were not made on time (see instructions).

Sign Here ▶

Under penalties of perjury, I declare that I have examined this election, including accompanying schedules and statements, and to the best of my knowledge and belief, it is true, correct, and complete.

Signature of officer	Title	Date

For Paperwork Reduction Act Notice, see separate instructions.   Cat. No. 18629R   Form **2553** (Rev. 12-2007)

Internal Revenue Service

6. The corporation may not be a bank or thrift institution that uses a reserve method of accounting for bad debts under Internal Revenue Code § 585.
7. The corporation may not be an insurance company taxable under Subchapter L of the Internal Revenue Code.
8. The corporation may not have elected to come under IRC § 936 concerning the Puerto Rico and possession tax credits.
9. The corporation may not be a domestic international sales corporation (DISC) or former DISC under the Internal Revenue Code.

S Corporation status may be revoked only if shareholders holding a majority of the shares of stock of the corporation consent to the revocation. If the corporation ceases to meet these requirements and all other requirements set forth in the Internal Revenue Code, the business may lose its S Corporation status.

All S Corporations have a calendar year as their tax year, unless a special election proving acceptable business purposes for a different year is filed with, and approved by, the Internal Revenue Service.

Although there were more than twice as many S Corporations than C Corporations during 2007, those C Corporations reported more than three times the amount of business receipts.

STATUTORY CLOSE CORPORATIONS

Corporations with stock that is not publicly traded, including family-owned corporations and corporations with relatively few stockholders, are often referred to as **closely held corporations** or **close corporations**. These smaller corporations are generally governed by the Business Corporation Acts of their states of domicile. However, because the needs and realities of the smaller corporations are often different from those of their larger counterparts, some states have adopted special statutes for closely held corporations.

CLOSELY HELD CORPORATION
A corporation with total ownership in a few hands.

These statutes take into consideration the true nature of the smaller corporations, which are often operated in a manner similar to partnerships. Close corporations that are formed subject to state close corporation statutory provisions are generally referred to as **statutory close corporations**. Statutory close corporations are corporations that have no more than 50 shareholders (or some other number specified by statute) that have elected to be treated as a statutory close corporation.

CLOSE CORPORATION
A corporation with total ownership in a few hands.

To be considered a statutory close corporation, the corporation's shareholders must make an election pursuant to state statute. Any corporation electing to become a statutory close corporation after its incorporation typically must have the approval of at least two-thirds of the corporation's shareholders. In addition, the stock certificates representing shares of stock of statutory close corporations must contain specific language on their face to indicate to the shareholder that the corporation is

STATUTORY CLOSE CORPORATION
A closely held corporation having no more than 50 shareholders that has elected to be treated as a statutory close corporation under the relevant statutes of its state of domicile.

a statutory close corporation and that the rights of a shareholder of a statutory close corporation may differ from those of other corporations.

Under certain circumstances, courts will decide that a corporation is a close corporation under common law and subject to the state's close corporation laws—even if the corporation has not made an election to become a statutory close corporation. In making a determination, courts will usually identify common law close corporations by three characteristics, including:

1. A small number of shareholders
2. No ready market for the stock of the corporation
3. Active shareholder participation in the business[13]

Statutory close corporations are generally allowed to operate without all of the statutory formalities imposed on other types of corporations. Recognizing that the shareholders and directors of small corporations are often the same individuals, statutory close corporations are usually permitted to operate without a board of directors, leaving the management and operation to the shareholders. The requirement to have corporate bylaws may also be waived.

State close corporation statutes are typically narrow in scope. The state's business corporation act will be applicable to all matters not specifically addressed in the close corporation statutes. See Exhibit 7-6 for a list of select state statutory provisions pertaining to close corporations.

EXHIBIT 7-6	SELECT STATUTORY PROVISIONS PERTAINING TO CLOSE CORPORATIONS
Arizona	Ariz. Rev. Stat. Ann. §§ 10-1801 *et seq.*
California	Cal. Corp. Code §§ 154, 158, 186, 202(a), 204, 300, 418, 421, 602, 1111, 1201, 1800, 1904.
Delaware	Del. Code Ann. tit. 8, §§ 341 *et seq.*
Illinois	805 ILCS 5/2A.05 *et seq.*
Kansas	Kan. Stat. Ann. §§ 17-7201 *et seq.*
Maine	Me. Rev. Stat. Ann. tit. 13-A, §§ 202, 508, 603, 604, 606, 607, 618, 623, 626, 1115.
Massachusetts	*Harrison v. NetCentric Corp.*, 433 Mass 465, 744 NE2d 622 (2001).
Maryland	Md. Corps. & Ass'ns Code Ann. §§ 4-101 *et seq.*
Michigan	MSA §§ 21.200(101) *et seq.*; MCL §§ 450.1101 *et seq.*
New Jersey	NJ Rev. Stat. § 14A:1-1.
North Carolina	NC Gen. Stat. § 55-7-31(b).
Pennsylvania	Pa. Stat. Ann. tit. 15, §§ 2301 *et seq.*
Rhode Island	RI Gen. Laws § 7-1.1-51.
Wisconsin	Wis. Stat. §§ 180.1801 *et seq.*

The statutory close corporation has much in common with the limited liability company. Both are separate entities distinct from their owners that permit flexibility with regard to management. Transfer of interests in both entities may be restricted by statute or by the entity's operating agreement.

Increasingly, smaller businesses, especially family-owned businesses, are choosing to operate as limited liability companies rather than statutory close corporations.

PARENTS AND SUBSIDIARIES

The parent and subsidiary classifications given to corporations refer to a relationship between corporations, depending on the ownership and control of the corporations. A **parent corporation** is a corporation that owns stock in a **subsidiary corporation** that is sufficient to control the subsidiary corporation.

The terms **sister corporations** and **affiliate corporations** are both used to refer to corporations that are owned or controlled by the same owners. For example, two subsidiary corporations that are owned by the same parent corporation may be referred to as sister corporations or affiliated corporations.

PARENT CORPORATION

A corporation that fully controls or owns another company.

SUBSIDIARY CORPORATION

A corporation that is owned by another corporation (the parent corporation).

SISTER CORPORATIONS

Two (or more) companies with the same or mostly the same owners.

AFFILIATE CORPORATIONS

A person or company with an inside business connection to another company. Under bankruptcy, securities, and other laws, if one company owns more than a certain amount of another company's voting stock, or if the companies are under common control, they are affiliates.

IN SUMMATION

- In most states only licensed professionals of a single profession may be shareholders of a professional corporation.
- To qualify for exemption from federal income tax, nonprofit corporations must meet the requirements of Internal Revenue Code §501(c)(3) and obtain approval from the Internal Revenue Service.
- Although S Corporations, which are not taxed at the corporate level, are subject to certain restrictions regarding ownership, they outnumber C Corporations in this country by more than two to one.
- Statutory close corporations, provided for by the statutes of many states, are smaller corporations that are generally not subject to all of the formalities typically imposed on corporations, such as the requirement to elect a board of directors.
- A parent corporation is a corporation that owns stock in a subsidiary corporation that is sufficient to control the subsidiary corporation.

§ 7.8 THE PARALEGAL'S ROLE

Short of giving legal advice to corporate clients, corporate paralegals are allowed to assist with almost all areas and aspects of corporate law. Typically the paralegal's duties will be dominated by document drafting and research.

The duties performed by paralegals who specialize in corporate law often include:

1. Drafting corporate documents
2. Reviewing and updating corporate minute books

3. Drafting corporate minutes and resolutions
4. Incorporating and dissolving corporations
5. Preparing foreign qualification documents
6. Assisting with mergers and acquisitions
7. Assisting with securities rules and regulation compliance
8. Researching state securities laws (blue sky laws)
9. Drafting all types of corporate agreements and contracts

The duties performed by paralegals who work in a corporate legal department can include all of these. In addition, the corporate legal department paralegal may be responsible for the following:

1. Subsidiary maintenance, including preparing all documents for incorporating and dissolving subsidiaries, and preparing corporate resolutions
2. Shareholder relations, including drafting correspondence to shareholders to answer questions concerning stock transfers and other matters concerning their interests in the corporation
3. Board of director communications
4. Coordinating stock transfers and notices to shareholders with the transfer agent
5. Acting as liaison between the corporation, in-house counsel, and outside counsel
6. Confirming proper service of legal process and opening files for new lawsuits brought against the corporation

OPPORTUNITIES FOR CORPORATE PARALEGALS

In the fast-growing paralegal field, the number of paralegals employed in the corporate area of law is second only to the number working in litigation. In addition to paralegals employed in the corporate law departments of law firms, approximately 18–20 percent of all paralegals work for corporations, typically in their legal departments.

Pursuant to a recent survey by the National Association of Legal Assistants, paralegals who work in the corporate specialty area reported one of the highest average salaries at $63,657, second only to paralegals specializing in securities/antitrust, a subspecialty of corporate law. See Exhibit 7-7.[14]

The paralegal working in the corporate law area often specializes in one or more areas within that field. Some of the more common paralegal specialties among those paralegals working in a corporate legal setting are:

Litigation

Contracts

Corporate governance

Mergers and acquisitions

Securities

Intellectual property

Specific duties in each of these areas are discussed in the pertinent chapters throughout this text.

EXHIBIT 7-7	AVERAGE TOTAL COMPENSATION OF PARALEGALS SPENDING MORE THAN 40 PERCENT OF THEIR TIME IN SPECIALTY AREA—TOP 10 AREAS OF SPECIALTY

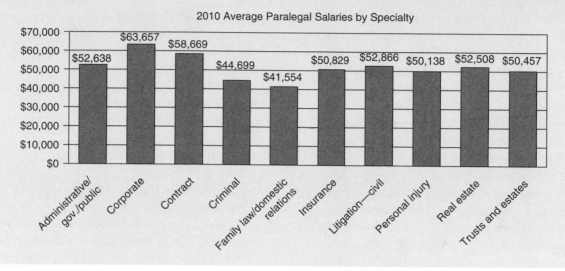

2010 Average Paralegal Salaries by Specialty

From the National Association of Legal Assistants 2010 National Utilization and Compensation Survey Report.

CORPORATE PARALEGAL PROFILE
Heather Brinkman

NAME Heather Brinkman
LOCATION Peoria, Illinois
TITLE Corporate Paralegal
SPECIALTY Commercial Transactions/Mergers and Acquisitions
EDUCATION Bachelor's Degree in Paralegal Studies, St. Mary-of-the-Woods College
EXPERIENCE 5 years—Corporate

Heather Brinkman is a paralegal with Caterpillar, Inc., a global company, based in Peoria, Illinois, that manufactures and sells construction and mining equipment, diesel and natural gas engines, and industrial turbines worldwide. Heather reports to senior corporate counsel for Caterpillar and two other attorneys in her workgroup.

Heather works in the commercial section of the legal department, where much of her job entails preparing contracts for specific divisions within the corporation and working with the mergers and acquisitions team. The contracts that she works on vary from general confidentiality agreements to highly negotiated purchase agreements that can involve millions of dollars. Under attorney supervision, Heather reviews and drafts contracts based on attorney negotiations. As drafts are negotiated between the parties to an agreement, she performs reviews and provides commentary, noting errors and potential risks. Her drafting duties and periodic reviews allow the attorneys to focus on negotiating specific points of the deal.

continues

CORPORATE PARALEGAL PROFILE
Heather Brinkman (continued)

As a member of the mergers and acquisitions team, Heather manages the due diligence process, which includes organizing a team of approximately 30 subject-matter experts, coordinating internal due diligence team meetings and external on-site visits, managing virtual data rooms, performing corporate governance and legal diligence reviews, preparing diligence reports, and working with consultants and outside counsel. She assists with the negotiation, preparation, and execution of the numerous documents necessary for each transaction. Heather also prepares antitrust filings, corporate governance documents, and at times is called upon to form and register subsidiary corporations and LLCs.

Heather enjoys the variety of her day-to-day duties, from more general commercial transactions to the potentially highly contentious mergers and acquisitions. All transactions start with a business plan and, through the legal and business teams' efforts, the plan becomes reality. While some days can be long and hectic, Heather feels that being able to play an integral role in these various corporate transactions from beginning to end is very rewarding.

Heather's advice to new paralegals?

Be open to new possibilities; be willing to experience new areas of law and take on challenges—it is one of the best ways to gain expertise and grow professionally. Keep a strong work ethic, and you will be highly regarded by your supervising attorneys, clients, and peers.

For more information on careers for corporate paralegals, log in to http://www.cengagebrain.com to access the CourseMate website that accompanies this text; then see the Corporate Careers Section.

ETHICAL CONSIDERATION

As mentioned previously, attorneys and paralegals owe a duty of loyalty to all their clients, including corporate clients. In addition to being aware of any conflicts that may arise between current and past clients you have helped to represent, you must always be aware of any personal or business interests you may have that conflict with the interests of any clients or potential clients. What if a corporation your law firm represents is suing your spouse's business?

When the interests of a client conflict with the personal interests of his or her attorney, there is a potential conflict of interest. These same rules may be applied to paralegals. If an attorney or paralegal engages in

continues

ETHICAL CONSIDERATION
(continued)

the following types of actions, there may be a conflict of interest with the client:

- Entering into certain business transactions with the client

- Drafting wills or other legal documents that provide for the transfer of a substantial gift from the client to the attorney or paralegal (unless the attorney or paralegal is related to the client)

- Using information learned during the course of a representation for the personal benefit of the attorney or paralegal

- Entering into an agreement giving the attorney or paralegal literary or media rights concerning the client's case

- Providing financial assistance to the client

- Accepting compensation for representation from someone other than the client

- Having a sexual relationship with a client, unless a consensual sexual relationship existed prior to the representation

Specific rules concerning conflicts of interest between the attorney's personal or business interests and the client's interests can be found in the code of ethics for your state. As with any type of potential conflict of interest, if you become aware that your personal or business interests may conflict with those of a potential client, you must be careful to bring it to the attention of the responsible attorney immediately so that the matter can be dealt with. In most cases a remedy can be found short of discontinuing representation of the client.

For more information on ethics for corporate paralegals, including links to the NALA and NFPA codes of ethics, log in to http://www.cengagebrain.com to access the CourseMate website that accompanies this text; then see the Ethics Section.

§ 7.9 RESOURCES

Many resources are available to assist the paralegal working in the corporate law area. In addition to the statutes that the paralegal must be familiar with, there are several sources that may provide useful information, including legal encyclopedias, form books, CLE materials, and state agencies.

STATE AND FEDERAL STATUTES

The primary source of information on business corporations is the business corporation act (or similar act) in the statutes of the corporation's state of domicile. Information regarding special types of corporations can be found in the pertinent state's close corporation act or supplement, its professional corporation act, and its nonprofit corporation act, any or all of which may be part of the state's business corporation act. Exhibit 7-8 is a list of state business corporation statutes. Links to those statutes may also be found at the CourseMate website that accompanies this text.

Although state law is the primary source of law for corporations, corporations are also subject to special federal statutes and regulations in specific areas, such as interstate commerce, income taxation, bankruptcy, intellectual property, and securities. The paralegal should be aware of the corporation's business focus and alert for possible applications of such federal statutes.

SECRETARY OF STATE OFFICES

The secretary of state offices provide a wealth of online information concerning the formation of corporations and any filing requirements for corporate documents. Most states provide downloadable forms as well. Appendix A provides a directory of secretary of state offices. Links to those secretary of state offices may be found at the CourseMate website that accompanies this text.

INFORMATION ON SPECIFIC CORPORATIONS

There are several resources available online to provide useful information about public corporations. It is more difficult to find information about private corporations. To find background information on either a private or public corporation, it is often very useful to conduct a Google search on the corporation's name to see if the corporation has its own website or if it is discussed on other sites.

Basic information, such as when a corporation was formed and where its registered office is, can often be found online at the website for the secretary of state's office of the corporation's state of domicile. The following websites are useful sources of general business and financial information on public corporations:

"Hoover's Online" provides comprehensive company, industry, and market intelligence that drives business growth. Hoover's has a database of 12 million companies. Although the more in-depth information on hoovers.com may be accessed only with a subscription, there is much information here that is available free to the public.

"Corporate Information" (CI) provides free information on public corporations, including a brief description of the corporation's business and current stock data. Several other reports are available from this site for a fee.

"Securities and Exchange Commission Edgar Filings" Corporations that have stock that is publicly traded must file initial and periodic reports with the Securities and Exchange Commission via the EDGAR system. This information may be accessed by the public at this site. More information on the Securities and Exchange Commission and public corporations may be found in Chapter 11 of this text.

EXHIBIT 7-8 STATE BUSINESS CORPORATION ACTS

State	Code
Alabama	Alabama Business Corporation Law, 10A-2-1.01 through 10A-2-17.02
Alaska	Alaska Corporations Code, Alaska Stat. §§ 10.06.005 through 10.06.995
Arizona	Arizona Revised Statutes, Ariz. Rev. Stat. Ann §§ 10.120 through 10.1635
Arkansas	Arkansas Business Corporation Act, Ark. Code Ann. §§ 4-27-101 through 4-27-1804
California	Corporations Code, Cal. Corp. Code §§ 1 through 2319
Colorado	Colorado Business Corporation Act, Colo. Rev. Stat. §§ 7-101-101 through 7-117-105
Connecticut	Connecticut Business Corporation Act, Conn. Gen. Stat. §§ 33-600 through 33-999
Delaware	Delaware General Corporation Law, Del. Code Ann. Tit. 8 §§ 101 through 391.
District of Columbia	District of Columbia Business Corporation Act, D.C. Official Code §§ 29-101.01 through 29-101.170
Florida	Florida Business Corporation Act, Fla. Stat. §§ 607.0101 through 607.1903
Georgia	Georgia Business Corporation Code, Ga. Code Ann. §§14-2-101 through 14-2-1703
Hawaii	Hawaii Business Corporation Act, Haw. Rev. Stat. Ch. 414-1 through 414-484
Idaho	Idaho Business Corporation Act, Idaho Code §§ 30-1-101 through 30-1-141
Illinois	Business Corporation Act of 1983; 805 Ill. Comp. Stat. §§ 5/1.01 through 5/17.05
Indiana	Indiana Business Corporation Law; Ind. Code §§ 23-1-17 through 23-1-55-3
Iowa	Iowa Business Corporation Act; Iowa Code §§ 490.101 50 490.1705
Kansas	Kansas General Corporation Code, Kan. Stat. Ann. §§ §§ 17-6001 through 17-7514
Kentucky	Kentucky Business Corporation Act; Ky. Rev. Stat. Ann. §§ 271B.1-010 271B.18-070
Louisiana	Louisiana Business Corporation Law; La. Stat. Ann. §§ 12:1 through 12.1607
Maine	Maine Business Corporation Act; Me. Rev. Stat. Ann. Tit. 13-C §§ 101 through 1702
Maryland	Maryland General Corporation Law, Md. Code Ann, Corps. & Ass'ns §§ 1-101 through 3-805
Massachusetts	Massachusetts Business Corporation Act, Mass. Gen. Laws ch.156D §§ 1.01 through 17.04
Michigan	Michigan Business Corporation Act; Mich. Comp. Laws Ann. §§ 450.1101 through 450.2099
Minnesota	Minnesota Business Corporation Act; Minn. Stat. §§ 302A.001 through 302A.92
Mississippi	Mississippi Business Corporation Act; Miss. Code Ann. §§ 79-4.101 through 79-4-17.04
Missouri	General and Business Corporation Law of Missouri; Mo. Rev. Stat. §§ 351.010 through 351.935
Montana	Montana Business Corporation Act; Mont. Code Ann. §§ 35-1-112 through 35-1-1315
Nebraska	Business Corporation Act; Neb. Rev. Stat. §§ 21-2001 through 20,193

continues

EXHIBIT 7-8 (*continued*)

State	Code
Nevada	Private Corporations, Business Corporation Act; Nev. Rev. Stat. §§ 78.010 through 78.795
New Hampshire	New Hampshire Business Corporation Act; N.H. Rev. Stat. Ann. §§ 293-A:1.01 through 17.04
New Jersey	New Jersey Business Corporation Act; N.J. Stat. Ann. §§ 14A:1-1 through 14A:16-4
New Mexico	Business Corporation Act; N.M. Stat Ann. §§ 53-11-1 through 53-18-12
New York	Business Corporation Law; N.Y. Bus. Corp. §§ 101 through 2001
North Carolina	North Carolina Business Corporation Act; N.C. Gen. Stat. §§ 55-1-101 through 55-17-05
North Dakota	North Dakota Business Corporation Act; N.D. Cent. Code §§ 10-19.1 through 10-19.1-152
Ohio	General Corporation Law; Ohio Rev Code Ann. §§ 1701.01 through 1701.99
Oklahoma	Oklahoma General Corporation Act; Okla. Stat tit. 18§§ 1001 through 1144
Oregon	Oregon Business Corporation Act; Or. Rev. Stat. §§ 60.001 through 60.992
Pennsylvania	Business Corporation Law of 1988; Pa. Stat. 15 Pa.C.S.A. §§ 1101 through 1998
Rhode Island	Rhode Island Business Corporation Act; R.I. Gen. Laws §§ 7-1.2-101 through 7-1.2-1804
South Carolina	South Carolina Business Corporation Act of 1988; S.C. Code Ann. §§ 33-1-101 through 33-20-105
South Dakota	South Dakota Business Corporation Act; S.D. Codified Laws Ann. §§ 47-1A-101 through 47-1A-1703.1
Tennessee	Tennessee Business Corporation Act;Tenn. Code Ann. §§ 48-11-101 through 48-27-103
Texas	Texas For-Profit Corporation Law, Tex. Stats. §§ 21.001 through 21.802
Utah	Utah Revised Business Corporation Act; Utah Code Ann. §§ 16-10a-101 through 16-10a-1705
Vermont	Vermont Business Corportion Act; Vt. Stat. Ann. Tit. 11A §§ 1.01 through 21.14
Virginia	Virginia Stock Corporation Act; Va. Code Ann. §§ 13.1-601 through 13.1-782
Washington	Washington Business Corporation Act; Wash. Rev. Code §§ 23B.01.010 through 23B.900.050
West Virginia	West Virginia Business Corporation Act; W.Va. Code §§ 31D-1-101 through 31D-17-1703
Wisconsin	Wisconsin Business Corporation Law; Wis. Stat. §§180.0101 through 180.1921
Wyoming	Wyoming Business Corporation Act; Wyo. Stat. §§17-16-101 through 1810

SUMMARY

- Corporations are considered entities separate from their owners.
- One of the greatest benefits to the corporate structure is the limited personal liability offered to the corporate owners, directors, and officers.
- Under certain circumstances, the corporate entity may be disregarded (piercing the corporate veil) when the court finds it necessary to prevent inequity, injustice, or fraud.
- Corporations are governed predominantly by state statute.
- Most state statutes are modeled on the Model Business Corporation Act (1984) as amended.
- Corporations are also subject to common law, case law, and federal law.
- As a separate entity, the corporation enjoys certain rights and powers that are typically prescribed by state statute.
- Shareholders of a corporation are usually not personally responsible for the debts and obligations of a corporation.
- There are several types of corporations, including business corporations, professional corporations, nonprofit corporations, and S Corporations.
- The S Corporation is the most common type of corporation.
- Most small business corporations can file an election with the Internal Revenue Service to become an S Corporation and receive pass-through taxation status.

REVIEW QUESTIONS

1. What are four characteristics of a corporation that distinguish it from the sole proprietorship and the partnership?

2. If a corporation defaults on its debts, may the creditors typically look to the shareholders for payment? Under what circumstances might the shareholders become personally liable for the debts of the corporation?

3. Suppose that John's Appliance, Inc. is a corporation formed by John Miller. John Miller is the only owner and employee of John's Appliance, Inc., an appliance repair service business. John Miller has formed the corporation to shelter his personal assets. He has put title to the repair truck (which he often uses for his own personal enjoyment), all of his equipment and tools, and his workshop in his own name, although he leases these items back to the corporation. What are some of the potential problems with this arrangement? What can John Miller do to decrease the risk that the corporate veil of John's Appliance could be pierced in the event of a lawsuit?

4. Dave Breen and Sue Martin would like to start a business involving themselves and D&S Equipment, Inc., a corporation that holds certain of their assets. Could they form a regular business corporation with Dave Breen, Sue Martin, and D&S Equipment, Inc. being the shareholders? Could they form an S Corporation?

5. Who elects the directors of a corporation? Who elects the officers? Could an individual be a shareholder, director, and officer all at the same time?

6. Could a group of attorneys and physicians form a single professional corporation? Why or why not?

7. Are all corporations incorporated as nonprofit corporations automatically exempt from paying income tax?

8. Explain the general differences between a regular business corporation and an S Corporation.

9. What are some of the practical differences between regular business corporations and statutory close corporations?

10. Suppose that Anna and Grace want to start a business to market a new food product they have invented. Limited liability is important to them because of the potential product liability problems associated with manufacturing and selling food products. Initially, Anna and Grace will be the only investors, and they may not see a profit in their business for a few years. What types of business organizations are available to Anna and Grace? What type of organization would you suggest? Why?

PRACTICAL PROBLEMS

1. Locate the business corporation act for your state. What is the name of the act?

2. Cite the acts, or portions of acts, in your state for forming the following types of corporations:

   a. Business corporation

   b. Statutory close corporation
   c. Nonprofit corporation
   d. Professional corporation

   There may not be provisions for all of the preceding types of corporations in your state.

EXERCISE IN CRITICAL THINKING

As briefly discussed in § 7.3 of this chapter, there is a continuing debate in the United Sates regarding the rights that should be granted to corporations and those that should be reserved for individuals. What do you see as the pros and cons to granting corporations the constitutional right to free speech as the court has done in *Citizens United v. Federal Election Commission* (2010)?

WORKPLACE SCENARIO

Assume you are a paralegal working for a corporate law firm. New clients Bradley Harris and Cynthia Lund have just finished an initial meeting with your supervising attorney. Your supervising attorney, Belinda Murphy, has briefed you on their situation. Bradley Harris and Cynthia Lund have just incorporated a business called Cutting Edge Computer Repair, Inc. After consulting with Belinda, they feel it would be in their best interests to be taxed as an S Corporation. Belinda has asked you to prepare the necessary Form 2553 to elect S Corporation status for their signatures.

Using the earlier information and the information in Appendix B-3 of this text, prepare a Form 2553 for Cutting Edge Computer Repair, Inc. This form may be downloaded from the Internal Revenue Service's website at http://www.irs.gov.

Portfolio Reminder
Save the documents prepared for the Workplace Scenario exercises in each chapter, either in hard copy or electronically, to build a portfolio of documents to be used for job interviews or as

sample documents on the job. At this point, your portfolio should include the following:

- Power of attorney
- Application for assumed name
- Application for federal employer identification number
- Application for state employer identification number

- Partnership statement of authority
- Limited partnership certificate
- Limited liability partnership statement of qualification
- Articles of organization
- Subchapter S Election by Small Business Corporation, Form 2553

ENDNOTES

1. 18 Am. Jur. 2d Corporations § 1 (March 2011).

2. Oran's Dictionary of the Law (2000).

3. 18 Am. Jur. 2d Corporations § 2 (March 2011).

4. The states of Alabama, Arizona, Arkansas, Connecticut, Florida, Georgia, Hawaii, Idaho, Indiana, Iowa, Kentucky, Maine, Massachusetts, Mississippi, Montana, Nebraska, New Hampshire, North Carolina, Oregon, Rhode Island, South Carolina, South Dakota, Tennessee, Utah, Vermont, Virginia, Washington, West Virginia, Wisconsin, and Wyoming have business corporation acts based substantially on the Model Business Corporation Act (1984).

5. Internal Revenue Service, Statistics of Income—2008, Corporation Income Tax Returns, http://www.irs.gov.

6. Internal Revenue Service, Statistics of Income, Partnership Returns, 2008, http://www.irs.gov.

7. Internal Revenue Service, Statistics of Income, Sole Proprietorship Returns, 2008, http://www.irs.gov.

8. Internal Revenue Service, Statistics of Income—2008, Corporations Income Tax Returns, Table 1, http://www.irs.gov.

9. U.S. Census Bureau. The Statistical Abstract of the United States: 2011, No. 1210.

10. 18 Am. Jur. 2d Corporations § 57. (March 2011).

11. Id. § 52.

12. Model Professional Corporation Act § 3.

13. 1A Fletcher Cyclopedia of Private Corp. § 70.10 (2004).

14. National Association of Legal Assistants, "2010 National Utilization and Compensation Survey Report," October 2010, Section 4, Table 4.14.

15. Id.

CourseMate

To access additional course materials including CourseMate, please visit www.cengagebrain.com. At the CengageBrain.com home page, search for the ISBN of your title (from the back cover of your book) using the search box at the top of the page. This will take you to the product page where the resources can be found. The CourseMate resources for this text include web links to the resources discussed above, including several resources for sole proprietors and small businesses, downloadable forms, flash cards and more. In addition to the statement of authority, prepare a cover letter filing the form with the appropriate state authority, along with any required filing fee.

CHAPTER 8

INCORPORATIONS

INTRODUCTION

The corporation is an entity that cannot exist unless it has been properly incorporated. Articles or a certificate of incorporation must be filed with the secretary of state or other appropriate state official, who will give the corporation its life and its right to transact business. For ease in discussion, here we refer to the state official responsible for accepting the articles of incorporation for filing as the secretary of state, although that responsibility is held by different state offices in some states. This chapter discusses the formation of the corporation, from preincorporation matters through the organizational meeting following incorporation. Special attention is given to preincorporation concerns, the incorporator, the articles of incorporation, organizational meeting, bylaws, and the formation of special types of corporations. This chapter concludes with a look at the role of the paralegal in corporation formations and the resources available to assist paralegals in that area.

§ 8.1 PREINCORPORATION MATTERS

The life of the corporation does not begin until the proper documentation is filed with the appropriate state authorities. Therefore, some actions involving the future corporation must be taken before the corporation actually exists. In this section, we examine the preincorporation matters that are often dealt with by the incorporators of a business corporation, including the decision to incorporate and the choice of a domicile for the corporation. We also discuss preincorporation agreements and stock subscription agreements. This section concludes with a look at the important task of gathering client information prior to incorporating a business.

DECIDING ON THE CORPORATE STRUCTURE

When an attorney meets with clients to advise them concerning the formation of a business organization or the expansion of an ongoing business, one of the first issues they must decide on is the proper format for the business. The attorney and client will consider the advantages and disadvantages of each type of available business organization, as discussed in previous chapters.

The following items must be considered and discussed with the client to determine whether to incorporate or form another type of business entity:

- Income tax implications
- Capital requirements
- Applicable statutory requirements
- Desired management structure
- The importance of limited liability
- Transferability of ownership
- Ease of forming and dissolving the business entity
- Business continuity

All of these factors must be considered to make the appropriate choice of business organization. Exhibit 8-1 is a table summarizing the basic characteristics of each type of business organization that we have looked at.

This chapter investigates the process of forming a business corporation, assuming that the corporation is being created based on an informed consideration of all possibilities.

EXHIBIT 8-1 TABLE OF BUSINESS ORGANIZATION CHARACTERISTICS

	Formation	Management	Restrictions on Ownership	Limited Personal Liability	Taxation	Duration
Sole Proprietorship	No formalities required.	Sole proprietor has sole management responsibility; may delegate to employees and agents.	Only one owner	None	Sole proprietor reports income on personal return; pays tax accordingly.	At will of sole proprietor. Business ends with sole proprietor's death or withdrawal.
Partnership	No formalities required. Written partnership agreement is recommended.	All partners have equal right to manage partnership unless otherwise agreed to in partnership agreement.	Two or more owners	None	Income allocated among partners who pay tax at personal rate. Informational return filed on behalf of partnership.	Indefinite. May dissolve on death or withdrawal of partner unless otherwise agreed to in partnership agreement.
Limited Liability Partnership	Statement of qualification must be filed at state level.	All partners have equal right to manage partnership unless otherwise agreed to in partnership agreement.	Two or more owners	Yes, for all partners	Income allocated among partners who pay tax at personal rate. Informational return filed on behalf of partnership.	Indefinite. May dissolve on death or withdrawal of partner unless otherwise agreed to in partnership agreement.
Limited Partnership	Articles of limited partnership (or similarly named document) must be filed at state level.	All general partners have equal right to manage partnership unless otherwise agreed to in partnership agreement. Limited partners may not participate in management of limited partnership in most states.	Two or more owners	Yes, for limited partners only	Income allocated among partners who pay tax at personal rate. Informational return filed on behalf of partnership.	Indefinite. May dissolve on death or withdrawal of general partner unless otherwise agreed to in partnership agreement.
Limited Liability Limited Partnership	Articles of limited partnership and statement of qualification must be filed at state level.	All general partners have equal right to manage partnership unless otherwise agreed to in partnership agreement. Limited partners may not participate in management of limited partnership in most states.	Two or more owners	Yes, for all partners	Income allocated among partners who pay tax at personal rate. Informational return filed on behalf of partnership.	Indefinite. May dissolve on death or withdrawal of general partner unless otherwise agreed to in partnership agreement.

EXHIBIT 8-1 *(continued)*

	Formation	Management	Restrictions on Ownership	Limited Personal Liability	Taxation	Duration
Limited Liability Company	Articles of organization must be filed at state level.	All members have right to participate in management of business unless otherwise agreed to in articles of organization or operating agreement. Management is often delegated to board of managers.	Minimum of two owners in a few states. No maximum number of owners.	Yes, for all owners/members	Income allocated among members/owners who pay tax at personal rate. Informational return filed on behalf of limited liability company.	Perpetual in most states
S Corporation	Articles of incorporation must be filed at state level; election to become S Corporation must be filed with Internal Revenue Service.	Shareholders elect board of directors to oversee management.	Minimum of one; maximum of 100. Shareholders must all be individuals, estates, or exempt organizations or trusts that meet certain prerequisites.	Yes, for all owners/shareholders	Income allocated among shareholders who pay tax at personal rate. Informational return filed on behalf of S Corporation.	Perpetual
Corporation	Articles of incorporation must be filed at state level.	Shareholders elect board of directors to oversee management.	No, or few, restrictions	Yes, for all owners/shareholders	Corporation responsible for tax on corporate income. Shareholders responsible for income tax on income and dividends received.	Perpetual

Choosing a Domicile

The state in which a corporation's articles or certificate of incorporation are filed is considered the corporation's home state or the state of domicile. Although it may seem obvious that incorporators should incorporate their businesses in the state in which they live and intend to operate, this is not necessarily true, and should not be taken for granted. Persons forming a corporation usually have their choice of the domicile or state in which they wish to incorporate, and their actual home state may not be the most advantageous for the business. The nature of the state's corporate law is usually the primary consideration, although there are several others. Following is a list of factors to be considered when choosing a state of domicile:

1. Does the law of the state being considered allow the corporation to be operated in the manner desired?
2. What costs are associated with incorporating in the state being considered?
3. What is the state's judicial policy toward corporations?
4. Is the proposed corporate name available in the state being considered?
5. May shareholder meetings be held out of state?
6. What is the state's statutory treatment of shareholder and director liability?
7. Must any corporate records be kept in the proposed state?
8. What are the annual reporting requirements in the proposed state (tax and informational)?

In addition to the foregoing factors, the incorporators must be aware of the foreign corporation qualification requirements in states other than the state of domicile. The corporation will be required to qualify to do business as a foreign corporation in any state, other than the state of domicile, in which it transacts business. Each state's statutes set requirements for qualifying as a foreign corporation. These requirements should be researched carefully before deciding where to incorporate. Qualification of foreign corporations is discussed in Chapter 13.

Incorporating in Delaware

Historically, many incorporators have chosen to incorporate in the state of Delaware, which is known for its liberal corporate laws and favorable judicial treatment of corporations.

The state of Delaware places a high priority on attracting corporations. Some of the laws Delaware has adopted to attract corporations include the following features:

HOSTILE TAKEOVER
A corporate takeover that is opposed by the management and board of directors.

- Maximum protection against **hostile takeovers**
- Maximum protection from personal liability for directors
- No minimum capital requirements
- No corporate state income taxation for corporations that do not conduct business in the state
- Anonymous ownership of a corporation, if desired
- Written consents and conference calls are permitted in lieu of directors' meetings

For years Delaware has attracted corporations by adopting corporate laws that are among the most liberal in the country. In addition, the Delaware Department of State, Division of Corporations, has been set up to handle an enormous number of incorporations in an easy and efficient manner. It is one of the most user-friendly systems in the country.

In recent years, many states have revised their corporate laws to conform more closely to the Delaware General Corporate Law or the Model Business Corporation Act (MBCA), which is significantly similar in many regards, and the advantages to incorporating in Delaware have somewhat diminished. One clear advantage to incorporating in Delaware remains, however, in that compared to most other states, the corporate law of Delaware has been interpreted extensively by that state's courts. Attorneys and incorporators may find more certainty in incorporating in Delaware, where there are few questions left unanswered concerning the court's interpretation of the state's corporate law.

More than 850,000 business entities are domiciled in Delaware, including more than 50 percent of all U.S. publicly traded companies and 63 percent of the Fortune 500 companies.[1]

PREINCORPORATION AGREEMENTS

Under certain circumstances, the founders of a corporation may find it beneficial to enter into a formal **preincorporation agreement** to set forth their understanding and agreement concerning the formation of a new corporation. Because the incorporation process can usually be completed within a few days at most, a formal preincorporation agreement is generally not necessary. However, under any of the following circumstances, a formal preincorporation agreement may be desirable:

1. When a considerable amount of time will lapse between the decision to incorporate and the actual incorporation
2. When considerable financial contributions are required prior to incorporation
3. When it is desirable to bind participants to make future financial contributions that may be essential to the business venture
4. When one or more participants are being induced to participate in the business by promises of employment
5. When it is necessary to protect a trade or business secret
6. When confidentiality is important
7. When the formation of the business depends on one or more agreements with outside parties

A preincorporation agreement should, in general, include the agreement of the future corporation's shareholders regarding the terms for formation of the

PREINCORPORATION AGREEMENT

Agreement entered into between parties setting forth their intentions with regard to the formation of a corporation.

corporation. The preincorporation agreement should address such matters as the content of the articles of incorporation and bylaws, the state of incorporation, the identity and initial term of the first board of directors, and the identity of the statutory agent of the corporation, if one is to be appointed. The preincorporation agreement may also include the subscription agreement of the future shareholders of the corporation who are entering into the preincorporation agreement.

STOCK SUBSCRIPTIONS

STOCK SUBSCRIPTION
Agreement to purchase a specific number of shares of a corporation.

A **stock subscription** is an agreement to purchase a stated number of shares of a corporation or a future corporation at a stated price. Often a promoter helps obtain preincorporation stock subscriptions to finance the corporation. Once the corporation is actually formed, the subscription agreements are ratified by the corporation and then executed as shares of stock are issued to the subscribers pursuant to the agreements.

The stock subscription agreement is considered a contract between the corporation and the future shareholder. If a subscriber defaults in payment or does not follow through with the purchase pursuant to the contract, the corporation may take legal action against the subscriber. Under Section 6.20 of the Model Business Corporation Act and the statutes of many states, if the subscriber defaults in payment under a subscription agreement entered into before incorporation, the corporation may collect the amount owed as any other debt. In the alternative, the corporation may rescind the agreement and sell the shares to someone else if the subscriber defaults in payment.

Stock subscription agreements may be used at any time during the life of the corporation to add new shareholders to the corporation or to document the purchase of additional shares by existing shareholders. Following is a checklist of matters to consider for inclusion when drafting a stock subscription agreement prior to incorporation:

- Name and address of each subscriber
- Name of corporation to be formed
- Number and class of shares the corporation will be authorized to issue
- Number and class of shares subscribed
- Amount of cash or description of consideration paid for subscription
- Conditions on subscription, if any
- Date on or before which stock is to be issued and paid for
- Identification of subscriber as incorporator or promoter, in appropriate case
- Date of subscription agreement

Exhibit 8-2 is an example of a stock subscription agreement form to be used by incorporators.

EXHIBIT 8-2 SUBSCRIPTION AGREEMENT FORM

Subscription

The undersigned, as incorporators of the corporation to be known as
_____ [corporate name], in accordance with the agreement to incorporate,
dated and executed by them this date, and in consideration of the mutual subscriptions now made, do agree among themselves, each with the others, and with
the corporation, to subscribe to and purchase from the corporation, at _____
[par or book] value, the class and number of shares of the corporation set forth
opposite their respective signatures below. Each of the undersigned subscribes for
the kind and number of shares set opposite his or her name, and his or her obligation under this agreement shall not be dependent upon performance by any of the
other signatories.

The respective subscription prices shall be due and paid after the formation
and organization of the corporation substantially in accordance with the agreement
to incorporate, and on issuance to and receipt by the corporation of a stock permit
from _____ [the Secretary of State or the Corporation Commission or as the
case may be] of _____ [state].

If such stock permit is not received by the corporation on or before
_____ [date], or such later date as may be agreed upon by all the subscribers
below signed, then this agreement and the obligations of the respective subscribers shall be null and void and of no further force and effect.

The subscribers have executed this subscription at _____ [place of exe-
cution] on _____ [date].

Subscribers Signatures	Class of Shares	Number of Shares
_____	_____	_____
_____	_____	_____
_____	_____	_____
_____	_____	_____

GATHERING CLIENT INFORMATION TO INCORPORATE

Once the decision has been made to incorporate, the attorney or paralegal must gather
the necessary information from the client to begin the incorporation process. This can
be done at an initial meeting between the client, attorney, and the paralegal. Collecting

this information is important for two reasons. First, the information is needed to prepare the initial incorporation documents and subsequent corporate documents. Second, the collection of this information may lead to discussions that cause the clients to consider and discuss facets of the business that have not previously been contemplated. Following is a list of information to obtain from clients to begin the incorporation process:

- Is the corporation the appropriate business organization? Has the client considered other types of business entities?
- What is the proposed corporate name?
- What are the possible alternatives if that name is unavailable?
- What is the primary business to be conducted?
- Should specific business purposes be set out in the articles of incorporation, if not required by state law?
- Where will the corporation's business be conducted?
- How much total capital is needed to begin business?
- How much of the capital will the initial investors contribute?
- Is any public financing planned?
- Are the investors' equity interests to be protected against dilution?
- Do the founders want corporate income taxed directly to stockholders (i.e., should election to be treated as an S Corporation be made if the corporation is eligible)?
- Who is to have control of the corporation?
- How many initial directors of the corporation are planned and who will they be?
- What officers will the corporation have and who will they be?
- What are the proposed salaries for each officer, including bonuses?
- What is the term of office for officers and directors?
- Where is the principal office to be located?
- Where is the annual meeting of stockholders to be held?
- What will the corporation's fiscal year be?

IN SUMMATION

- Because corporate existence does not begin until the articles of incorporation are properly filed with the secretary of state, certain actions must be taken on behalf of the corporation before its existence begins.
- The organizers of the corporation must make certain decisions, including:
  - Determining that the corporation is, in fact, the best form of business organization for their business.
  - Deciding where the corporation should be incorporated—the state of domicile.

IN SUMMATION (*continued*)

- Delaware has always been home to a disproportionately large number of business corporations due, in part, to its favorable corporate laws and legal system.

- At times, especially when a significant amount of time may lapse between initial discussions and incorporation, the founders of a corporation may enter into a preincorporation agreement to set forth their understanding.

- Individuals may enter into stock subscription agreements for the purchase of stock in a corporation once it is formed.

- It is important to gather all relevant information from the client before drafting and filing incorporation documents—a process that paralegals are often involved in.

§ 8.2 PROMOTERS

The formation of some, but not all, corporations involves one or more individuals acting in the role of a **promoter**—an individual who assists in creating and organizing the corporation. The promoter of a corporation will often bring interested parties together, obtain subscriptions for stock of the proposed corporation, and see to the actual formation of the corporation.

PROMOTER
An individual who assists in creating and organizing a corporation, often by bringing interested parties together, obtaining subscriptions for stock of the proposed corporation, and seeing to the actual formation of the corporation.

Any transactions made by the promoter on behalf of the corporation before the actual incorporation are considered to be preincorporation transactions. The corporation does not legally exist until its articles of incorporation are properly filed. Therefore, any preincorporation transactions must be approved by the corporation after it is formed if they are to be valid. Promoters may be liable for contracts entered into on behalf of the future corporation until the contracts are ratified by the corporation, unless the contracts specifically state that the promoter is acting only on behalf of the future corporation and assumes no personal liability. In *Moneywatch Companies v. Wilbers*, beginning on page 304, the appellant was held personally responsible for breach of a commercial lease entered into by him on behalf of a future corporation. The court held that promoters are released from personal liability under terms of contract only where that contract provides that performance is to be the obligation of the corporation, the corporation is ultimately formed, and corporation formally adopts the contract. Corporations are not required to have a promoter prior to their formation, and most corporations are formed without anyone assuming that role.

IN SUMMATION

- The formation of certain corporations is facilitated by a promoter who brings interested parties together, obtains subscriptions for stock, and handles the incorporation.

- All actions of a promoter taken on behalf of a corporation should be ratified by the corporation once it is formed.

POWELL, Judge.

Defendant-appellant, Jeffrey Wilbers, appeals a decision of the Butler County Court of Common Pleas in favor of plaintiff-appellee, Moneywatch Companies, in a breach of contract action.

In December 1992, appellant entered into negotiations with appellee, through its property manager, Rebecca Reed, for the lease of commercial property space in the Kitty Hawk Center located in Middletown, Ohio. During the negotiations, appellant indicated that he intended to create a corporation and needed the space for a golfing business he wanted to open. Reed testified that although appellant told her that he would be forming a corporation, she advised appellant that he would have to remain personally liable on the lease even if a corporation was subsequently created. Appellant testified that he never intended to assume personal liability on the lease and that appellee never advised him that he would have to be personally liable under the lease. At appellee's request, appellant submitted a personal financial statement and business plan.

On December 23, 1992, a lease agreement was signed naming appellee as landlord and "Jeff Wilbers, dba Golfing Adventures" as tenant. The lease agreement provided that rent would not be due until March 1, 1993. On January 11, 1993, articles of incorporation for "J & J Adventures, Inc." were signed by "Jeff Wilbers, Incorporator." On February 3, 1993, a trade name registration was signed for "Golfing Adventures" to be used by J & J Adventures, Incorporated. . . .

Appellant notified appellee of the incorporation of J & J Adventures, Inc. and asked that the name of

the tenant on the lease be changed from "Jeff Wilbers, dba Golfing Adventures" to "J & J Adventures, Inc., dba Golfing Adventures." In a letter dated March 1, 1993, from appellee to appellant, appellee informed appellant that the name of the tenant on the lease would be so changed and that "[t]his name change shall be deemed a part of the entire Lease Agreement." Reed testified that appellant did not request a release of personal liability under the lease at this time. Appellant testified that he did not seek release of personal liability because he never thought he was personally liable under the lease. . . .

At some time during 1993, the corporation defaulted and vacated the premises. Appellee brought a breach of contract action against appellant in his personal capacity. After a bench trial, the trial court entered judgment in favor of appellee and ordered appellant to pay appellee the sum of $13,922.67 plus interest and costs. . . .

In his sole **assignment of error**, appellant contends that he is not personally liable under the lease agreement because a **novation** was accomplished by the substitution of "J & J Adventures, Inc., dba Golfing Adventures," a corporate party, for "Jeff Wilbers, dba Golfing Adventures," an individual party. . . .

In this case, the substitution of tenant names on the lease does not constitute a novation because there was no discharge of appellant from his original obligations under the lease. . . .

Appellant also contends that he is not personally liable under the lease agreement because he executed the lease as a corporate promoter on behalf of a future corporation. Corporate promoters are "those who participate in bringing about the

continues

organization of an incorporated company, and in getting it in condition for transacting the business for which it is organized.". . . A promoter is not personally liable on a contract made prior to incorporation which is made "in the name and solely on the credit of the future corporation.". . .

Further, a corporation does not assume a contract made on its behalf by the mere act of incorporation. . . .

In addressing the issue of promoter liability on contracts executed on behalf of a corporation to be formed in the future, the Ohio Supreme Court recently stated:

> It is axiomatic that the promoters of a corporation are at least initially liable on any contracts they execute in furtherance of the corporate entity prior to its formation. The promoters are released from liability only where the contract provides that performance is to be the obligation of the corporation, the corporation is ultimately formed, and the corporation then formally adopts the contract. . . .

In this case, appellant can be deemed a promoter because he participated in bringing about the organization of the corporation and in getting it ready for business. However, the original lease was not made "in the name and solely on the credit of the future corporation.". . . To the contrary, the lease was executed by appellant, individually, on his own credit, as evidenced by the submission of appellant's personal financial statement during the negotiation and execution of the lease.

Promoters are released from personal liability under the terms of a contract only where the contract provides that performance is to be the obligation of the corporation, the corporation is ultimately formed and the corporation formally adopts the contract . . . In this case, the lease agreement does not provide that the corporation will be exclusively liable under its terms even though the corporation is now listed as tenant.

In fact, appellant's individual signature remains on the lease agreement. . . . In addition, there is no evidence that the corporation, once formed, formally adopted the lease agreement as executed by appellant. In the absence of the necessary steps which must be taken to ensure that appellant is not personally liable and the corporation is solely liable under the lease, appellant is liable under the lease.

. . .After thoroughly reviewing the record, we find competent, credible evidence to support the trial court's decision to hold appellant personally liable under the lease. We will not substitute our judgment for that of the trial court. . . .

Accordingly, appellant's sole assignment of error is overruled.

Judgment affirmed.

WILLIAM W. YOUNG, P.J., and

KOEHLER, J., CONCUR.

Note that the individual acting as promoter here was found to be personally liable for the contract he claimed was entered into on behalf of the corporation, in part, because the corporation did not ratify the act of the promoter once formed.

§ 8.3 INCORPORATORS

The incorporator is the individual who actually signs the articles or certificate of incorporation to form the corporation. The role played by the incorporator is usually very minor, and the involvement of the incorporator typically ceases after the articles or certificate of incorporation is filed or after the organizational meeting electing the first board of directors is held. At times, the attorney for the corporate client will serve as the incorporator so that the attorney can sign and file the articles of incorporation on behalf of the client.

Qualifications for incorporators are usually set forth in the statutes of the state of domicile. The MBCA states only that "One or more persons may act as the incorporator or incorporators of a corporation by delivering articles of incorporation to the secretary of state for filing."[2] Persons, as defined by the MBCA, means individuals and entities, including other profit or not-for-profit corporations, whether foreign or domestic, as well as business trusts, estates, partnerships, trusts, unincorporated associations, and governments. State statutes with more restrictive provisions may require that the incorporators be natural persons, meaning an adult individual.[3]

IN SUMMATION

- The incorporator is the individual who signs the articles of incorporation.
- The role of incorporator is usually very minimal and ends once the corporation is formed and the first board of directors is appointed.
- State statutes often set forth the specific requirements for the incorporator. Requirements for incorporators often provide that the incorporator must be an individual at least 18 years of age.

§ 8.4 CORPORATE NAME

One of the first items of business the incorporators or founders of the corporation will address is the selection of the corporate name. The name for the corporation must meet with state statutory requirements, and it must be available for use. It is often advisable to reserve the desired corporate name with the appropriate state authority to ensure that it is available for use when the incorporation documents are ready for filing.

As with other forms of business organizations, there are three aspects of name availability with which incorporators must comply. First, the name must include at least one of a number of specific words that may be required by statute, and must not contain any prohibited words. Second, the name of the corporation must not be the same as, or deceptively similar to, the name of another corporation or entity of record in the office of the secretary of state of the state of domicile. Third, most state statutes require that the name of the corporation not mislead as to the purpose of the corporation.

SPECIFIC WORD REQUIREMENT

Most state statutes require that corporation names contain a word or words indicating that the corporation is a corporate entity, as opposed to a partnership or other type of business entity. The names of corporations domiciled in states following the MBCA must include the word *corporation, incorporated, company*, or *limited*, or the abbreviation *corp., inc., co.,* or *ltd.*, or words or abbreviations of like import in another language.

NAME AVAILABILITY

The incorporators may not use the name of a corporation that is already in use in the state of domicile, or a name that is deceptively similar to that of another corporation incorporated in the state or qualified to do business in the state. For example, *Acme Hardware Company* would be considered deceptively similar to the name *Acme Hardware Corporation*.

There are several remedies that may be available if the first choice of a corporate name is not available. At times, the corporation already using the similar name may consent to the use of the name if the two corporate names are not identical. At other times, the incorporators may use a variation of the name to distinguish it from the similar name. For example, Chicago Acme Hardware Company may be permissible if Illinois Acme Hardware Company is already in use. The secretary of state's office will make the final determination as to whether the name is acceptable.

A preliminary check on name availability can be made in most states by consulting the secretary of state's website or by calling the secretary of state's office. See Appendix A of this text for a secretary of state directory.

NONDECEPTIVE NAME

The name of the corporation must not be misleading. A corporate name may be considered misleading if it includes language stating or implying that the corporation is organized for a purpose other than its actual purpose. For example, a corporation with the name of Main Street Bank may be considered misleading if it is a corporation that is not a bank and therefore subject to the regulations imposed on banks. Corporate names that include words such as "bank," "insurance," or "trust" may be considered misleading if those words are not indicative of the purpose of the corporation.

Exhibit 8-3 gives a brief list of requirements for corporate names.

EXHIBIT 8-3 TYPICAL REQUIREMENTS FOR CORPORATE NAMES

- The name must be available.
- The name must include the word *corporation, incorporated,* or a similar word permitted by state statute indicating that the entity is a corporation.
- The name must not be the same as, or deceptively similar to, the name of another corporation incorporated or qualified to do business in the state.
- The name of the corporation must not be misleading.

© Cengage Learning 2013

NAME RESERVATION

The statutes of most states provide that a person may reserve the exclusive use of a corporate name by filing an application for name reservation with the secretary of state, along with the required filing fee. Incorporators may reserve the name of a future corporation as long as the name is available in that state and meets with all other statutory requirements. This may be advisable when the incorporation process will take several weeks, or even several days. It is also advisable if there is any doubt that the name may not be acceptable when the articles of incorporation are filed. Typically, the secretary of state's office will not guarantee name availability until the articles of incorporation are filed, or the name is properly reserved.

In states that follow the Model Business Corporation Act in this regard, the name of a corporation may be reserved for a nonrenewable 120-day period by filing the proper documentation with the secretary of state, along with the name reservation fee.

Exhibit 8-4 is a sample name reservation form from the state of Minnesota. In Minnesota the desired corporate name can be reserved for a renewable 12-month period for $35.00. This name reservation can be completed online.

IN SUMMATION

- The name of any corporation:
  - Must meet with statutory requirements;
  - Must be available for use in the state of incorporation; and
  - Must not be deceptive.
- Before incorporation documents are filed, the secretary of state records should be checked to be sure the name is available for use.
- Most states provide for the reservation of a corporate name prior to incorporation.

EXHIBIT 8-4   REQUEST FOR RESERVATION OF NAME IN THE STATE OF MINNESOTA

MINNESOTA SECRETARY OF STATE

REQUEST FOR RESERVATION OF NAME

I hereby request the Secretary of State to reserve the name listed below. I understand that the name reservation is valid for twelve months from the date on which it is filed and may be renewed for additional twelve month periods, pursuant to Minnesota Statutes, Section 302A.117, 317A.117, 322B.125 or 321.109.

READ INSTRUCTIONS ON BACK BEFORE COMPLETING THIS FORM
All information on this form is public information.
Filing Fee: $35.00; except for the intent of forming a Foreign Limited Partnership (Chap 321) the fee is $50.00.

1. Desired Name: (Required)_____

2. Reserved For: (Required)_____
Note: If this name is reserved for an organization not yet formed, list the individual who will be signing the documents, which will be submitted at the time of the organization of the business.

3. Located at: (Required) _____
                            (Street Address)

       _____
             (City)   (State)   (Zip)

4. The applicant hereby states that the proposed name holder is:

    A person doing business in this state under that name or a deceptively similar name;
    A person intending to form an entity under Chapter 302A, 317A, 322B or 321;
    A domestic corporation, limited liability company or limited partnership intending to change its name;
    A foreign corporation, foreign limited liability company or foreign limited partnership intending to make application for a Certificate of Authority to transact business or register in this state;
    A foreign corporation, foreign limited liability or foreign limited partnership authorized to transact business in this state and intending to change its name;
    A person intending to incorporate a foreign corporation, or foreign limited liability company and intending to have the foreign corporation, or foreign limited liability company make application for a Certificate of Authority to transact business in this state; a person registering as a foreign limited partnership; or
    A foreign corporation, foreign limited liability company or foreign limited partnership doing business under that name or a name deceptively similar to that name in a state other than Minnesota and not described in clauses d, e or f.

I certify that the foregoing is true and accurate and that I have the authority to sign this document on behalf of the proposed name holder, and I further certify that I understand that by signing this reservation, I am subject to the penalties of perjury as set forth in section 609.48 as if I had signed this reservation under oath.

5. Signature: (Required) _____ Position: _____

6. Name, daytime telephone number and e-mail address of contact person:

Name: _____ Phone:_____ Ext. _____

E-Mail Address: _____

Minnesota Secretary of State's Office

§ 8.5 ARTICLES OF INCORPORATION

CHARTER

An organization's basic starting document (for example, a corporation's articles of incorporation).

The document that is actually filed with the secretary of state to form the corporation is typically called the articles of incorporation, although in some states that document may be referred to as the certificate of incorporation or **charter**. For ease in discussion, we refer to the incorporation document as the "articles of incorporation" throughout the rest of this chapter. The articles of incorporation contain essential information regarding the corporation and must comply with statutory requirements of the state of domicile.

The articles of incorporation must be filed with the secretary of state to be valid. The secretary of state's office typically supplies articles of incorporation forms. In some states, the articles of incorporation may be filed online on the secretary of state's website. Most states offer the forms online that may be downloaded and submitted by mail or e-mail. Statutes regarding the articles of incorporation vary from state to state. However, most states have provisions similar to those of the MBCA, which is discussed later in this chapter.

SIDEBAR

A growing number of states provide incorporation forms that may be completed and filed online.

This section examines the mandatory articles of incorporation provisions required by most state statutes, the articles of incorporation provisions that are usually considered optional, and the statutory provisions that apply to all corporations unless contrary provision is made in the articles of incorporation.

MANDATORY PROVISIONS

The mandatory provisions for articles of incorporation vary from state to state and depend upon the type of corporation to be formed. Under the MBCA, only the four following provisions are required:

1. A corporate name for the corporation that satisfies all statutory requirements[4]
2. The number of shares the corporation is authorized to issue[5]
3. The street address of the corporation's initial registered office and the name of its initial registered agent at that office[6]
4. The name and address of each incorporator[7]

Name

The name chosen by the corporation must comply with all requirements of the statutes of the state of domicile.

Authorized Stock

The articles of incorporation must set forth the number of shares of each class of stock that the corporation is authorized to issue in accordance with the statutes of the state of domicile. When there is only one class of stock, that class is typically referred to as **common stock**.

State statutes may require additional information regarding the corporation's authorized stock, such as the **par value** of the stock and the rights and preferences of all classes of stock. Capitalization of the corporation is discussed in further detail in Chapter 10 of this text. Following are examples of articles of incorporation paragraphs setting forth the number of shares of stock of the corporation.

EXAMPLE: Authorized Stock

The corporation is authorized to issue _____ shares (_____) of common stock of the corporation.[8]

EXAMPLE: Capitalization

The total number of shares of all classes of stock which the corporation shall have authority to issue is _____, divided into _____ [number] shares of common stock at $ ___ par value each and ___ [number] shares of preferred stock at $ _____ par value each. _____ [State designations and powers, preferences, and rights, and the qualifications, limitations, or restrictions of the classes of stock.]

This corporation will not commence business until it has received for the issuance of its shares consideration of the value of $ _____, consisting of money, labor done, or property actually received, which sum is not less than $ _____.

This Article can be amended only by the vote or written consent of the holders of _____% of the outstanding shares.[9]

Registered Office and Registered Agent

The articles of incorporation must set forth the corporation's **registered office** and its **registered agent**, or statutory agent, as it is sometimes referred to (if one is required and appointed).

Under the MBCA, each corporation must appoint and maintain both a registered office and a registered agent. The registered office of the corporation may be the same as any of the corporation's places of business within the state of domicile.

COMMON STOCK
Shares in a corporation that depend for their value on the value of the company. These shares usually have voting rights (which other types of company stock may lack). Usually, they earn a dividend (profit) only after all other types of the company's obligations have been paid.

PAR VALUE
The nominal value assigned to shares of stock, which is imprinted upon the face of the stock certificate as a dollar value. Most state statutes do not require corporations to assign a par value to their shares of stock.

REGISTERED OFFICE
Physical office location designated by corporation in articles of incorporation where service of process may be made on the corporation within the state. In addition to the registered office address in the corporation's state of domicile, the corporation must designate a registered office address in each state where it is authorized to transact business.

REGISTERED AGENT
Individual or organization designated by a corporation as agent to receive service of process for the corporation within the state where the agent is located. A corporation may appoint a registered agent in its state of domicile and an agent in each state where it is authorized to transact business.

The registered agent required by the MBCA may be an individual resident of the state of domicile, a domestic corporation, or qualified foreign corporation with a business office identical to the registered office of the corporation. This requirement is typical of most states, although there are some exceptions. For example, not all states require the appointment of a registered agent. Most states require that the registered office address be a street address (not a P.O. Box) where service of process may be made in person on the corporation.

Following is an example of an "articles of incorporation" paragraph in which the registered office and registered agent of the corporation are appointed.

EXAMPLE: Registered Agent and Registered Office

The name of the corporation's registered agent and the street address of the corporation's registered office are as follows:

Registered Office: _____

Registered Agent: _____.[10]

Name and Address of Incorporators

The name and address of each incorporator must be set forth in the articles of incorporation. The incorporators also must sign the articles of incorporation in the method prescribed by state statute. Exhibit 8-5 illustrates a form that may be used for articles of incorporation in states that follow the MBCA. Exhibit 8-6 on page 314 is a sample certificate of incorporation form to incorporate a business in Delaware.

OPTIONAL PROVISIONS

The articles of incorporation may contain any information that the incorporators choose to include regarding the management and administration of the corporate affairs. The MBCA states that the articles of incorporation may set forth the following:

1. The names and addresses of the individuals who are to serve as the initial directors[11]
2. The purpose or purposes for which the corporation is organized[12]
3. Provisions regarding the management of the business and regulation of the affairs of the corporation[13]
4. Provisions defining, limiting, and regulating the powers of the corporation, its board of directors, and shareholders[14]
5. Provisions setting a par value for authorized shares or classes of shares[15]
6. Provisions imposing personal liability on shareholders for the debts of the corporation to a specified extent and upon specified conditions[16]

EXHIBIT 8-5   SAMPLE ARTICLES OF INCORPORATION TO BE USED IN STATES FOLLOWING THE MODEL BUSINESS CORPORATION ACT

[In compliance with minimum requirements of the
Revised Model Business Corporation Act]

ARTICLES OF INCORPORATION

The undersigned, acting as Incorporator(s) of a corporation under the _____ Business Corporation Act, adopt(s) the following Articles of Incorporation for such corporation:

I. NAME

The name of this corporation is _____.

II. AUTHORIZED STOCK

The number of shares that the corporation is authorized to issue is _____ shares, all of one class.

III. INITIAL REGISTERED OFFICE AND AGENT

The name and address of the initial registered agent and office of this corporation are as follows:

_____

_____.

IV. INCORPORATOR(S)

The name(s) and address(es) of the Incorporator(s) signing these Articles of Incorporation [is] [are]:

Name   Address

_____   _____

_____   _____

_____   _____

IN WITNESS WHEREOF, the undersigned Incorporator(s) has/have executed these Articles of Incorporation this _____ day of _____, _____.

_____
Incorporator

_____
Incorporator

STATE OF _____

COUNTY OF _____

BEFORE ME, the undersigned authority, personally appeared _____ and _____ , to me known to be the persons who executed the foregoing Articles of Incorporation, and [he] [she] [they] acknowledged to and before me that [he] [she] [they] executed such instrument.

IN WITNESS WHEREOF, I have hereunto set my hand and seal this _____ day of _____, _____.

_____
Notary Public, State of _____

(Notarial Seal)

My Commission Expires:

Minnesota Secretary of State's Office

EXHIBIT 8-6 STATE OF DELAWARE CERTIFICATE OF INCORPORATION FORM

STATE *of* DELAWARE
CERTIFICATE *of* INCORPORATION
***A* STOCK CORPORATION**

- **First:** The name of this Corporation is_____
  _____.

- **Second:** Its registered office in the State of Delaware is to be located at _____
  Street, in the City of_____
  County of _____ Zip Code_____. The registered agent in
  charge thereof is _____
  _____.

- **Third:** The purpose of the corporation is to engage in any lawful act or activity for which corporations may be
  organized under the General Corporation Law of Delaware.

- **Fourth:** The amount of the total stock of this corporation is authorized to issue is _____
  shares (number of authorized shares) with a par value of _____per share.

- **Fifth:** The name and mailing address of the incorporator are as follows:
  Name _____
  Mailing Address _____
  _____ Zip Code _____

- **I, The Undersigned,** for the purpose of forming a corporation under the laws of the State of Delaware,
  do make, file and record this Certificate, and do certify that the facts herein stated are true, and I have
  accordingly hereunto set my hand this _____ day of _____, A.D. 20_____.

  BY:_____
  (Incorporator)
  NAME:_____
  (type or print)

Delaware Division of Corporations

7. Any provision that is required or permitted by statute to be set forth in the bylaws[17]
8. Provisions eliminating or limiting the liability of directors of the corporation or its shareholders for money damages for any action taken, or any failure to take any action, as a director, except under certain circumstances[18]
9. Provisions permitting or requiring indemnification of directors for liability to any person arising from their actions taken (or not taken) as directors[19]

Initial Board of Directors

In the past, most statutes have required that the initial board of directors be appointed in the articles of incorporation. The MBCA and several state statutes that are following suit now give incorporators the option of including this information. However, the directors are often appointed in the articles of incorporation to relieve the incorporators of any further responsibility.

Purpose

The purpose of the corporation is often set forth in the articles of incorporation, and the statutes of most states require it. The purpose of the corporation must be a lawful purpose in compliance with state statutes. The purpose clause in the articles serves to notify both the public and its own shareholders of the corporation's general business purposes. It is usually preferable to provide for a broad business purpose in the articles of incorporation. A corporation with a purpose too narrow in scope may have difficulty proving that it is authorized to enter into unanticipated transactions that are necessary to its main business purpose. Courts have found that "the statement of corporate purpose in the articles of incorporation serves to inform the public of the nature of the organization, thus benefiting those with whom it deals, and serves to inform its members of the scope and range of its proper activities and to assure them that they will not be involved in remote and uncontemplated activities."[20]

State statutes may require at least one specific purpose, or merely a vague statement that the purpose of the corporation is "any lawful business." Section 3.01 of the MBCA, which follows, is typical of the purpose provisions under many state statutes.

---

§ 3.01 PURPOSES

(a) Every corporation incorporated under this Act has the purpose of engaging in any lawful business unless a more limited purpose is set forth in the articles of incorporation.

(b) A corporation engaging in a business that is subject to regulation under another statute of this state may incorporate under this Act only if permitted by, and subject to all limitations of, the other statute.

SIDEBAR

The corporation's purpose as stated in its articles of incorporation should be flexible enough to change with the corporation's business plan.

Management of the Corporation

The MBCA states that the articles of incorporation may include any lawful provision regarding the management of the business and regulation of the affairs of the corporation. The incorporators may be as specific as they wish in this regard. However, because the articles of incorporation may be amended only with shareholder approval, and because an amendment requires an additional filing at the state level, specific information regarding management of the corporation is usually included in the corporation's bylaws.

Powers of the Corporation

The powers of the corporation, the directors, and the shareholders of the corporation are typically prescribed by statute, unless amended by the articles of incorporation. Any desired limitations on the statutory powers granted to the corporation, or the directors or shareholders of the corporation, must be made in the articles of incorporation within the scope of the state statutes.

Par Value of Shares of Stock and Classes of Stock

The par value of the shares of stock may be included in the articles of incorporation, if desired. Under the MBCA, this information is not mandatory. However, the statutes of many states require that the par value of each class of authorized stock be set forth in the articles. Par value is discussed further in Chapter 10.

Imposition of Personal Shareholder Liability

Shareholders are not normally responsible for any debts or obligations of the corporation. If the incorporators feel that it is desirable that the shareholders assume personal liability to a certain extent, provision must be made in the corporation's articles of incorporation.

Provisions That May Be Required or Permitted in Bylaws

There are many matters that the incorporators may choose to include in either the articles or the bylaws of the corporation. Incorporators should choose the inclusions to the articles carefully, because amendments to the articles usually involve shareholder approval and an additional filing with the secretary of state.

Limitation on Board of Director Liability

In states that have followed the MBCA in this regard, the incorporators may draft the articles of incorporation to limit the liability of directors of the corporation for actions arising based on their actions or inactions on behalf of the corporation, except in the event of wrongful financial benefit to the director, intentional infliction of harm, a violation of the director's duty of care, or an intentional violation of criminal law. Director liability is discussed further in Chapter 9.

Indemnification of Directors

The statutes of most states provide for **indemnification** of directors who are involved in lawsuits because of their actions on behalf of the corporation, so long as the director acted in good faith and believed his or her conduct was in the best interests of the corporation. Provisions for the indemnification of directors are often included in the articles, and it is often the case that statutory provisions for director indemnification may be amended only in the articles.

INDEMNIFICATION
The act of compensating or promising to compensate a person who has suffered a loss or may suffer a future loss.

STATUTORY PROVISIONS THAT MAY BE AMENDED ONLY IN THE ARTICLES OF INCORPORATION

The statutes of most states contain several provisions that govern the internal affairs of corporations, unless the corporation has provisions in its articles of incorporation to the contrary. Following is a list of some of the provisions that are most often set by statute but may be amended in the articles of incorporation:

1. A corporation has perpetual existence.[21]
2. The board of directors has the power to adopt, amend, or repeal the bylaws.
3. The affirmative vote of a majority of directors present is required for an action of the board.
4. A written action by the board, taken without a meeting, must be signed by all directors.[22]
5. The affirmative vote of the holders of a majority of the voting power of the shares present and entitled to vote at a duly held meeting is required for an action of the shareholders, except where state statutes require the affirmative vote of a majority of the voting power of all shares entitled to vote.
6. Shareholders do not have a right to cumulate their votes for directors.[23] (Cumulative voting is discussed in Chapter 9.)
7. The shareholders may remove one or more directors with or without cause.[24] (Removal of directors is discussed in Chapter 9.)
8. All shares of the corporation are of one class with identical rights.[25] (Share classes are discussed in Chapter 10.)
9. Shareholders have no preemptive rights to acquire unissued shares.[26] (Preemptive rights are discussed in Chapter 9.)

EXECUTION

The articles of incorporation must be properly executed by the incorporators, in accordance with state statutory provisions. Some state statutes require that the signature or signatures on the articles of incorporation be witnessed, acknowledged, or notarized.

FILING

The articles of incorporation must be filed with the secretary of state within the state of domicile with the appropriate filing fee. Statutes regarding filing requirements should be reviewed carefully, and the appropriate state authority should be

EXHIBIT 8-7 REASONS FREQUENTLY GIVEN BY STATE AUTHORITIES FOR REJECTING ARTICLES OF INCORPORATION FOR FILING

- Corporate name chosen is unavailable or otherwise unacceptable.
- Inclusion of a provision giving authority to the board of directors to change the authorized number of directors, where such provision is contrary to state statute.
- Improper execution and/or acknowledgment of the articles of incorporation.
- Failure to name a street address for the registered office and/or registered agent of the corporation for service of process. P.O. boxes are *not* acceptable in most jurisdictions.
- Nonpayment of fees and taxes as required by state and local law.
- Failure to state the specific number of authorized directors (where required by statute).
- Failure to state the total number of authorized shares.
- Failure to state the aggregate par value of all shares of stock having a par value (where required by statute).
- Failure to state the par value, preferences, privileges and restrictions, and number of shares of each class of authorized stock (where required by statute).

© Cengage Learning 2013

contacted, to ensure that all filing procedures are complied with. Failure to comply with filing requirements can seriously delay incorporation.

Publication

The statutes of a few states in the country have publication laws requiring that the articles of incorporation, or a notice of incorporation, be published in a legal newspaper.[27] It is important that the statutes be consulted to assure that this requirement is complied with, if necessary.

County Recording

Some state statutes require that the articles of incorporation, or a copy thereof, be filed with the county recorder or other county official of the county in which the registered office of the corporation is located.[28] Again, the state statutes must be consulted to determine if county recording is necessary.

Exhibit 8-7 provides a list of reasons frequently given by state authorities for rejecting articles of incorporation for filing.

EFFECTIVE TIME AND DATE

The effective time and date of the articles of incorporation are important because they are, in effect, the time and date for the commencement of the corporate entity.

Actions taken prior to the corporation's effective date may not be considered valid actions of the corporation. Again, this matter is addressed by state statute. Most state statutes provide that the articles of incorporation are effective when filed with the secretary of state or at a later time specified in the articles of incorporation. Most statutes that allow a later effective date and time to be specified limit that time to 90 days.

IN SUMMATION

- Articles of incorporation or a similar document must be filed with the secretary of state or other appropriate state office to form a corporation.
- Under state statute, the articles of incorporation are usually required to include:
  - An acceptable corporate name
  - The number and description of shares the corporation is authorized to issue
  - The street address of the corporation's registered office
  - The name of a registered agent who is located in the state of domicile
  - The name and address of each incorporator
- The incorporators may choose to include additional information concerning the governance of the corporation in the articles of incorporation, so long as the provisions are not contrary to law.
- State statutes generally include several default provisions that will apply to the corporation unless the articles of incorporation provide otherwise.
- In some states, there are requirements for publishing a notice of incorporation or recording the articles at the county or local level.
- The corporate existence begins when the articles of incorporation are accepted for filing with the proper state authority or at a later date stated in the articles.

§ 8.6 ORGANIZATIONAL MEETINGS

After the articles of incorporation have been filed, the organizational meeting of the corporation is usually held. The requirements for this organizational meeting and the organizational actions that must be taken vary from state to state. Depending on the statutes of the state of domicile, the incorporators or a majority of the directors named in the articles of incorporation may be required to call the organizational meeting and give notice to the directors and/or shareholders of the corporation.

This section examines the various requirements for organizational meetings, the purpose of organizational meetings, and the resolutions typically passed by incorporators, directors, and shareholders at organizational meetings. The section concludes with a discussion of the use of written consents in lieu of organizational meetings.

ORGANIZATIONAL MEETING REQUIREMENTS

The statutes of most states require that an organizational meeting of the corporation be held shortly after its incorporation to ratify preincorporation acts taken by promoters or incorporators, adopt bylaws, elect directors, and take care of other details necessary to the operation of the corporation. As a practical matter, the organizational meeting is usually attended by the incorporators, the initial board of directors, and the initial shareholders, which often total only a very few people. Under certain circumstances, a written consent in lieu of an organizational meeting may be used to approve the necessary resolutions. Written consents are discussed in § 8.6 of this chapter.

Requirements for the organizational meeting under the MBCA are set forth in § 2.05:

§ 2.05 ORGANIZATION OF CORPORATION

(a) After incorporation:

1. if initial directors are named in the articles of incorporation, the initial directors shall hold an organizational meeting, at the call of a majority of the directors, to complete the organization of the corporation by appointing officers, adopting bylaws, and carrying on any other business brought before the meeting;

2. if initial directors are not named in the articles, the incorporator or incorporators shall hold an organizational meeting at the call of a majority of the incorporators:

    (i) to elect directors and complete the organization of the corporation; or

    (ii) to elect a board of directors who shall complete the organization of the corporation.

(b) Action required or permitted by this Act to be taken by incorporators at an organizational meeting may be taken without a meeting if the action taken is evidenced by one or more written consents describing the action taken and signed by each incorporator.

(c) An organizational meeting may be held in or out of this state.

In any event, the statutes of the state of domicile should be consulted regarding the organizational meeting to determine the following:

1. Who is responsible for giving notice of the organizational meeting?
2. Who is entitled to receive notice of and attend the organizational meeting?
3. What are the notice requirements?
4. What actions must be taken by the incorporators, directors, and shareholders at the organizational meeting?
5. May a written resolution signed by all interested parties be substituted for an actual organizational meeting?

PURPOSE OF ORGANIZATIONAL MEETING

The purpose of the organizational meeting is to organize the corporation. This usually includes electing directors (when not appointed in the articles of incorporation), executing subscriptions for shares of the corporation, and any other steps necessary to give the corporation the capacity to transact business.

INCORPORATORS' RESOLUTIONS

When the first board of directors is not named in the articles of incorporation, the incorporators may hold the organizational meeting.

Election of Board of Directors

Typically, the first and only order of business at an organizational meeting held by incorporators is to elect the first board of directors. Following is an example of a resolution that might be made by the incorporators at the organizational meeting to elect the first board of directors.

EXAMPLE: Election of First Board of Directors

RESOLVED, by the incorporators, that the following individuals, having been duly nominated, are hereby elected as the first board of directors of this corporation, to serve until the first annual meeting of the shareholders, or until their successors are elected and qualified:

_____

_____

Adoption of Bylaws

In some jurisdictions, the incorporators may adopt the bylaws of the corporation at the organizational meeting. Exhibit 8-8 is an example of a form of minutes of an organizational meeting of the incorporators.

BOARD OF DIRECTORS' RESOLUTIONS

The items discussed in this section are often considered for action by the board of directors at the organizational meeting or the first meeting of the board of directors. Depending on state statute, some of these actions may also require shareholder approval. Exhibit 8-9 shows a sample of a form of minutes of the first board of directors' meeting, which includes the items discussed in the rest of this section.

EXHIBIT 8-8 MINUTES OF ORGANIZATIONAL MEETING OF INCORPORATORS

The organizational meeting of _____ [name of corporation], a corporation duly incorporated under the laws of the State of _____, was held on _____ [date], at _____ [address] pursuant to the attached waiver of notice.

The following incorporators were present: _____.

On motion duly made, seconded and carried, _____ [name] was chosen chairperson of the meeting and _____ [name] was chosen as secretary.

The chairperson reported that the articles of incorporation had been filed with the Secretary of State of the State of _____ on ___ [date]. The Secretary was directed to file a copy of the articles of incorporation and the certificate of incorporation in the corporate minute book.

On motion duly made, seconded, and carried, the following resolutions were adopted:

RESOLVED, that the number of initial directors of the corporation shall be _____.

FURTHER RESOLVED, that the following individuals shall serve as the initial directors of the corporation, to serve in accordance with the bylaws of the corporation until the first annual meeting of the shareholders and until their successors are elected and shall have qualified:

_____

_____

_____.

FURTHER RESOLVED, that the Board of Directors is hereby authorized to issue the capital stock of this corporation to the full extent authorized by the Articles of Incorporation in such amounts and for such consideration as from time to time shall be determined by the Board of Directors and as may be permitted by law, provided, however, that par value stock shall not be issued for less than par.

There being no further or other business to come before the meeting, on motion duly made, seconded, and carried, the meeting was adjourned.

_____
Chairman

_____
Secretary

Approval and Acceptance of Articles of Incorporation

Often, as a formality, the incorporators will present to the board of directors a copy of the articles of incorporation, and report on its filing. This action should be noted by a resolution in the minutes of the meeting of the board of directors. Following is an example of a resolution that may be made by the board of directors to approve the articles of incorporation.

EXAMPLE: Acceptance of Articles of Incorporation

RESOLVED, that the corporation's articles of incorporation, a copy of which is presented by the incorporator, are hereby ratified and approved. The secretary of the corporation is directed to file the articles in the corporate minute book of the corporation, along with the certificate of incorporation issued by the secretary of state, providing evidence of the filing and acceptance of the articles.

EXHIBIT 8-9 MINUTES OF FIRST MEETING OF THE BOARD OF DIRECTORS

Minutes of meeting of _____
[corporation]

Pursuant to _____ [notice or call and waiver of notice], the first board of directors of _____ [corporation] assembled and held its first meeting at _____ [address], City of _____, State of _____, at ___o'clock A.M., on ___, ___.

The following, being all of the directors of the corporation, were present at the meeting:

_____   _____

_____   _____

_____ [Name] called the meeting to order. On motion duly made and seconded, she was appointed temporary chairman, and _____ [name] was appointed temporary secretary.

The election of officers was thereupon declared to be in order. The following individuals were elected to the offices set forth opposite their names:

_____   President
_____   Vice President
_____   Secretary and Treasurer.

_____ [Name] took the chair and presided at the meeting.

The chairman then announced that the _____ [articles or certificate] of incorporation had been filed with the _____ [Secretary of State or other appropriate official] on ___, ___. The secretary was instructed to cause a copy of the _____ [articles or certificate] of incorporation to be inserted in the front of the minute book of this corporation.

The secretary presented a form of bylaws for the regulation of the affairs of the corporation, which were read, section by section.

On motion duly made, seconded, and carried, it was

Resolved, that the bylaws submitted at and read to this meeting be, and the same hereby are, adopted as and for the bylaws of this corporation, and that the secretary be, and he hereby is, instructed to certify the bylaws, and cause the same to be inserted in the minute book of this corporation, and to certify a copy of the bylaws, which shall be kept at the principal office of this corporation and open to inspection by the stockholders at all reasonable times during office hours.

continues

EXHIBIT 8-9 (continued)

On motion duly made, seconded, and carried, it was

Resolved, that the seal, an impression of which is herewith affixed, be adopted as the corporate seal of the corporation.

[Corporate Seal]

The secretary was authorized and directed to procure the proper corporate books.

On motion duly made, seconded, and carried, it was

Resolved, that the standard form of resolution of _____ Bank, with respect to checking accounts at said bank, is hereby adopted, and a copy thereof is ordered to be filed with the minutes of this meeting. The proper officers are hereby authorized and directed to file the necessary papers with said bank, including the signature authorization card, with respect to said checking account.

On motion duly made, seconded, and carried, it was

Resolved, that the principal office of the corporation for the transaction of its business be, and it hereby is, fixed at _____ [address], City of _____, State of _____.

On motion duly made, seconded, and carried, the following preambles and resolutions were unanimously adopted:

Whereas, this corporation is authorized, in its _____ [articles or certificate] of incorporation, to issue ___ [number] shares of its capital stock without nominal or par value; and

Whereas, this corporation has received stock subscriptions for a total of ___ shares of its authorized stock, and consideration for those shares of stock, in an amount deemed sufficient by the board of directors, has been received, the following number of authorized shares of stock are to be issued to the following individuals:

Shareholder	Number of Shares
_____	_____
_____	_____
_____	_____
_____	_____.

A copy of the certificate of stock proposed to be issued by the corporation was considered, and
On motion, duly made, seconded, and carried, it was
Resolved, that the above certificate be substantially in the following form: _____ [set out certificate of stock in full].

There being no further business, the meeting was adjourned.

_____
[Signature of secretary]

Ratification of Acts of Incorporator(s)

It is usually prudent, even if not required, for the directors of the corporation to approve and ratify the acts of the incorporator or incorporators taken on behalf of the corporation, even if those acts consisted only of filing the articles of incorporation.

Acceptance of Stock Subscriptions

Although the MBCA does not require any paid-in capital before the commencement of business, the statutes of some states require that a certain proportion of the stock be subscribed for, or even paid in, before the commencement of corporate business. Other states may require subscription for, or payment for, a specified amount of stock as a condition precedent to corporate existence.

In any event, it is important that the statutory requirements regarding the subscription and payment for stock of the corporation be complied with at the organizational meeting. This typically involves the acceptance of subscriptions and the issuance of stock of the corporation in accordance with the subscription agreements. The names of the shareholders, number and class of shares received by the shareholders, and the consideration received by the corporation from each shareholder should be noted. A statement regarding the paid-in capital of the corporation, in accordance with state statute, should be agreed on and noted in the minutes of the meeting. Following is an example of a resolution that could be passed by the board of directors regarding the issuance of stock of the corporation.

EXAMPLE: Issuance of Stock

RESOLVED, that the subscriptions for the shares of the corporation, dated and filed in the corporate minute book of the corporation, are hereby accepted and the amount and fair value of the consideration recited therein are hereby approved. The corporation has received the stated consideration, and the officers of the corporation are hereby authorized to issue to each such subscriber a certificate for the shares subscribed to as follows:

Subscriber	Number of Shares	Consideration Received
_____	_____	_____
_____	_____	_____
_____	_____	_____

The corporation, having received the minimum consideration for the issuance of the shares of the corporation fixed in the articles of incorporation, is duly organized and ready to commence business.

Election of Officers

The directors of the corporation will elect the officers of the corporation, which may include a chairman of the board, chief executive officer, president, vice president(s), chief financial officer or treasurer, secretary, and any other or different officers as may be desired by the board of directors and in accordance with the statutes of the corporation's state of domicile and the corporation's bylaws. Following is an example of a resolution that could be passed by the directors to elect the officers of the corporation.

EXAMPLE: Election of Officers

RESOLVED, that the following persons are hereby elected as officers of the corporation to assume the duties and responsibilities fixed by the bylaws, and to serve until their respective successors are chosen and qualify:

Chief Executive Officer: ＿＿＿＿＿＿＿

President: ＿＿＿＿＿＿＿

Vice President: ＿＿＿＿＿＿＿

Secretary: ＿＿＿＿＿＿＿

Treasurer: ＿＿＿＿＿＿＿

Assistant Secretary: ＿＿＿＿＿＿＿

Adoption of Bylaws

The bylaws of the corporation, which are typically prepared in advance of the organizational meeting and reviewed by all directors, should be approved at the organizational meeting in accordance with state statute. Often, the bylaws are adopted by the corporation's directors and ratified by its shareholders. Following is an example of a resolution that could be passed by the board of directors to adopt the bylaws of the corporation.

EXAMPLE: Adoption of Bylaws

RESOLVED, that the proposed bylaws, a copy of which is filed in the corporate minute book of the corporation, are hereby adopted by the board of directors as the bylaws of the corporation, and the secretary of the corporation is hereby authorized to sign said bylaws on behalf of the corporation.

Approval of Accounting Methods

The board of directors should agree upon the general accounting methods to be used by the corporation, including the fiscal year of the corporation, if a fiscal year other than the calendar year is an option.

Authorization of Appropriate Securities Filings

If the corporation will be subject to any securities filings, the board of directors is generally responsible for those filings. Any potential filings should be discussed during the organizational meeting, and a resolution should be passed authorizing certain officers of the corporation to prepare and file the necessary documentation.

Approval of Form of Stock Certificate

The board of directors will often approve a form of stock certificate to be used by the corporation, including any necessary restrictive legends. Following is an example of a resolution that could be passed by the board of directors to approve a form of stock certificate for use by the corporation.

EXAMPLE: Approval of Form of Stock Certificates

RESOLVED, that the form of stock certificate attached hereto as Exhibit _____ is hereby adopted and approved.

Adoption of Corporate Seal

If a corporate seal is required by state statute, or if a seal is desired, the seal should be approved at the organizational meeting. If no corporate seal is to be used by the corporation, that should be so agreed upon and noted.

Banking Resolutions

The directors of the corporation should agree on and establish a corporate bank account or bank accounts, and the terms of the bank account(s) should be determined, including the type of account(s) to be opened, where such account(s) should be opened, and who the authorized signatories on the bank account will be. Following is an example of a resolution that could be passed by the board of directors regarding the designation of a bank for corporate accounts.

Approval of S Corporation Election

The directors should discuss the advisability of electing to be treated as an S Corporation for federal income tax purposes. If it is decided that the corporation will elect to become an S Corporation, a resolution must be completed and must be approved by

EXAMPLE: Banking Resolution

RESOLVED, that _____ [bank] of the City of _____, State of _____, is hereby selected as a depository for the monies, funds, and credits of this corporation and that _____ and _____ are hereby authorized and empowered to draw checks (including checks payable to their own order or to bearer) on the above depository, against the account of this corporation with the depository, and to endorse in the name of this corporation and receive payment of all checks, drafts, and commercial papers payable to this corporation either as payee or endorsee.

Further resolved, that the authority hereby conferred shall remain in full force and effect until revoked and until a formal written notice of such revocation is given to and received by _____ [bank] of the City of _____, State of _____.

Further resolved, that the certificate of the secretary of this corporation as to the election and appointment of persons so authorized to sign such checks and as to the signatures of such persons shall be binding on this corporation.

Further resolved, that the Secretary of this Corporation is hereby authorized and directed to deliver to _____ [bank] of the City of _____, State of _____, a copy of these resolutions properly certified by him.

the directors and all shareholders. Following is an example of a resolution that could be passed by the board of directors to approve the election of S Corporation status for the corporation.

EXAMPLE: S Corporation Election

RESOLVED, that the corporation elects to be taxed as an S Corporation in accordance with Section 1372 of the Internal Revenue Code of 1954, as amended. The officers of the corporation are hereby authorized and directed to do all acts and to execute and file all papers, documents, and instruments necessary to cause the corporation to make such election.

Adoption of Employee Benefit Plans

Any employee benefit plans to be adopted by the corporation may be approved by the board of directors at the organizational meeting or the first meeting of the board of directors. These plans may include medical insurance plans, medical expense reimbursement plans, life insurance plans, qualified retirement plans, or any other employee benefit plans.

SHAREHOLDER RESOLUTIONS

The shareholders may be required by statute to be a part of the organizational meeting or to hold a different meeting referred to as the first meeting of shareholders. This meeting is often a part of, or held immediately following, the organizational meeting or the first meeting of the board of directors. The items discussed in this section may be considered for action by the shareholders of the corporation at their first meeting.

Election of Directors

The directors of the corporation must be elected pursuant to the statutes of the state of domicile. The statutes may permit this to be done by the incorporators if not done in the articles of incorporation, or the first board of directors may be elected or ratified by the shareholders of the corporation at the organizational meeting. Following is an example of a resolution that could be used by the shareholders of the corporation to elect the first board of directors.

EXAMPLE: Election of First Board of Directors

RESOLVED, that the following individuals, having been duly nominated, are hereby elected as the first board of directors of this corporation, to serve until the next annual meeting of the shareholders, or until their successors are elected and qualified:

_____

_____

_____

_____

Approval of S Corporation Election

For a corporation to become an S Corporation, the shareholders of the corporation must unanimously approve the adoption of S Corporation status by signing the proper documents for filing with the Internal Revenue Service.

Approval of Bylaws

In most states, the directors of the corporation are granted the authority to adopt the bylaws of the corporation. However, this adoption of bylaws may be ratified by the shareholders of the corporation.

UNANIMOUS WRITINGS AND WRITTEN CONSENTS VERSUS MINUTES

Traditionally, formal organizational meetings were required by state statute. However, two changes in corporate law have made the formal organizational meeting optional in certain instances.

First, the required minimum number of directors has gone from three to one. Previously, an organizational meeting of the directors was considered necessary to have a "meeting of the minds." This is obviously not necessary when there is only one director who may also be the only shareholder of the corporation.

Second, modern corporate law typically provides for the use of unanimous writings or written consents in lieu of meetings. Written consents do away with the necessity of having to give notice of and attend a formal meeting every time an action of the board of directors or shareholders is called for. Especially when the individual directors or shareholders live far apart, the use of unanimous writings can be invaluable.

In most instances, the directors or shareholders, as the case may be, may waive their statutory right to notice and attendance at a meeting and agree to set forth the agreed-upon resolutions in the form of a written consent. Under most circumstances, the written consent must be signed and dated by all individuals entitled to notice and attendance at a meeting of the directors or shareholders (unanimous written consent). If permissible under state statute, the articles of incorporation may provide that shareholders' and directors' resolutions may be made by a written consent signed by the number of shareholders or directors required to pass the resolution at a meeting. Under those circumstances, the signature of all shareholders or directors may not be required. State statutes must be consulted and followed carefully if a written consent in lieu of a meeting is used. Exhibit 8-10 is a sample form of a unanimous writing in lieu of an organizational meeting.

EXHIBIT 8-10   SAMPLE UNANIMOUS WRITING IN LIEU OF ORGANIZATIONAL MEETING

CONSENT TO ACTION TAKEN IN LIEU OF ORGANIZATIONAL MEETING of

_____

The undersigned, being all of the incorporators, shareholders, and directors of the corporation, hereby consent to and ratify the actions taken to organize the corporation as hereafter stated:

The Certificate of Incorporation filed on_____, ___, with the Secretary of State of this state is hereby approved and it shall be inserted in the record book of the corporation.

The persons whose names appear below are hereby duly appointed directors of the corporation to serve for a period of one year and until their successors are appointed or elected and shall qualify:

The persons whose names appear below are hereby duly appointed officers of the corporation to serve for a period of one year and until their successors are appointed or elected and shall qualify:

President: _____

Vice President: _____

Secretary: _____

Treasurer: _____

EXHIBIT 8-10 *(continued)*

Bylaws, regulating the conduct of the business and affairs of the corporation, as prepared by _____, counsel for the corporation, are hereby adopted and inserted in the record book.

The corporation shall have no seal.

The directors are hereby authorized to issue the unsubscribed capital stock of the corporation at such times and in such amounts as they shall determine, and to accept in payment therefore cash, labor done, personal property, real property or leases therefore, or such other property as the board may deem necessary for the business of the corporation.

The treasurer is hereby duly authorized to open a bank account with _____, located at _____, and is authorized to execute a resolution for that purpose on the printed form of said bank.

The president is hereby duly authorized to designate the principal office of the corporation in this state as the office for service of process on the corporation, and to designate such further agents for service of process within or without this state as is in the best interests of the corporation. The president is hereby further authorized to execute any and all certificates or documents to implement the above.

Dated _____

_____

_____

_____

© Cengage Learning 2013

IN SUMMATION

- An organizational meeting is usually held following the filing of the corporation's articles of incorporation. The incorporator, shareholders, and newly elected directors typically attend the meeting.
- The following actions may be taken at an organizational meeting of the initial shareholders and board of directors:
  - Elect the first board of directors
  - Adopt bylaws
  - Ratify the acts of incorporators and promoters
  - Accept stock subscriptions and issue shares of stock
  - Approve a form of stock certificate
  - Reach an agreement on accounting and banking arrangements
  - Elect the first officers of the corporation
  - Authorize securities filings
  - Approve S Corporation status (if desired)
- Written consents signed by those entitled to attend an organizational meeting may be used in place of holding a formal meeting in most states.

§ 8.7 BYLAWS

Bylaws are considered the rules and guidelines for the internal control of a corporation. The bylaws, which are typically adopted by the board of directors, prescribe the rights and duties of the shareholders, directors, and officers with regard to the management and governance of the corporation. They are considered to be a contract between the members of a corporation and between the corporation and its members.

Some state statutes specifically address the information to be contained in the bylaws. The MBCA merely states that the "bylaws of a corporation may contain any provision for managing the business and regulating the affairs of the corporation that is not inconsistent with law or the articles of incorporation."[29]

The following paragraphs discuss and show examples of some of the more common matters addressed in corporate bylaws. See Appendix F for a sample bylaws form.

OFFICE OF THE CORPORATION

The bylaws set forth the address of the principal office of the corporation and any other significant offices to be used by the corporation.

EXAMPLE: Principal Corporate Office

The principal office of the corporation shall be located at _____, City of _____, County of _____, State of _____. The board of directors may establish and maintain branch or subordinate offices at any other locations they deem appropriate within the State of _____.

SHAREHOLDER MEETINGS

Requirements for holding shareholder meetings are sometimes specifically set by state statute. However, details regarding the shareholder meetings are typically left to the corporation. The bylaws often set the time, place, and notice requirements for the annual meetings and the requirements for calling and holding special meetings of the shareholders. In addition, the bylaws should address the question of who is entitled to receive notice of shareholder meetings.

EXAMPLE: Annual Meetings of Shareholders

The annual meeting of the shareholders shall be held on the first Tuesday of April in each year, beginning with the year 2012, at 10:00 A.M., or such other date and time during the month of April as fixed by the directors, for the purpose of electing directors and for the transaction of such other business as may come before the meeting. If the election of directors is not held on the day designated herein for any annual meeting of the shareholders, or at any adjournment thereof, the board of directors shall cause the election to be held at a special meeting of the shareholders as soon thereafter as is convenient.

EXAMPLE: Special Meetings of Shareholders

Special meetings of the shareholders may be called by the president of the corporation or the board of directors. The president of the corporation shall call a special meeting for any proper purpose at the request of holders of not less than 10 percent of the outstanding shares of the corporation entitled to vote at a meeting, pursuant to section _____ of the Business Corporation Act for the State of _____.

EXAMPLE: Place of Shareholder Meetings

Annual and special meetings of the shareholders shall be held at the principal office of the corporation in the city of _____, State of _____, or at any other place within or without the State of _____, as designated by the board of directors. A waiver of notice signed by all shareholders entitled to vote at a meeting may designate any place, either within or without the State of _____, as the place for holding such meeting.

EXAMPLE: Notice of Shareholder Meetings

Notice of annual or special shareholders meetings, stating the place, day, and hour of the meeting, shall be delivered not less than _____ nor more than _____ days before the date of the meeting to all shareholders entitled to receive notice. Notices of special meetings shall also include the purpose or purposes for which the meeting is being called. Such notice shall be delivered, either personally or by mail, by or at the direction of the president, or the secretary, or the officer or persons calling the meeting, to each shareholder of record entitled to vote at such meeting. If mailed, such notice shall be deemed to be delivered when deposited in the United States mail, addressed to the shareholder at the shareholder's address as it appears on the stock transfer book of the corporation, with postage thereon prepaid.

NUMBER AND TERM OF DIRECTORS

The bylaws often include information on the directors of the corporation, including the number of directors required, the term of office, and the qualifications of the directors.

For more flexibility, the bylaws may indicate that the number of directors will be established from time to time by the shareholders. Then, if the number of directors is increased or decreased, the action may be approved at the shareholder meeting electing the new board of directors, and it will not be necessary to amend the bylaws.

EXAMPLE: Number, Tenure, and Qualifications of Directors

The number of directors of the corporation shall be established by the shareholders of the corporation from time to time. Directors shall be elected at the annual meeting of shareholders, and the term of office of each director shall be until the next annual meeting of shareholders and the election and qualification of his or her successor. Directors need not be residents of the State of _____, and need not be shareholders of the corporation.

MEETINGS OF THE BOARD OF DIRECTORS

The bylaws should contain information regarding the annual and special meetings of the directors, such as the time and place of the meetings, who may call the meetings, and notice requirements. The bylaws should also set a quorum of directors who may take action at a meeting.

If permitted by statute, the bylaws may also provide that meetings of the board of directors may be transacted electronically, via telephone, or that meetings may be waived and replaced by a unanimous written consent of the directors in lieu of meeting.

EXAMPLE: Regular Meetings of Board of Directors

Regular meetings of the board of directors shall be held without notice immediately following the annual meeting of the shareholders and at those times fixed from time to time by resolution of the board of directors. Regular meetings of the board of directors may be held at the principal office of the corporation, or at such other place, either within or without the State of _____, as designated by resolution of the board of directors.

EXAMPLE: Special Meetings of Board of Directors

Special meetings may be held at any time upon call of the Chairman of the Board, the Chief Executive Officer, the President, or any three directors, and shall be held at the principal office of the corporation.

EXAMPLE: Notice of Board of Directors' Meetings

Notice of any special meeting shall be given by the secretary of the company at least 48 hours prior to the time fixed for the meeting by written notice delivered by mail, telegram, fax, e-mail, or by personal communication by telephone or other means of personal communication. Any director may waive notice of any meeting. The attendance of a director at a meeting shall constitute a waiver of notice of such meeting, except where a director attends a meeting for the express purpose of objecting to the transaction of any business because the meeting is not lawfully called or convened.

EXAMPLE: Quorum

A majority of the number of directors fixed by these bylaws shall constitute a quorum for the transaction of business at any meeting of the board of directors, but if less than such majority is present at a meeting, a majority of the directors present may adjourn the meeting from time to time without further notice.[30]

EXAMPLE: Board Decisions

The act of the majority of the directors present at a meeting at which a quorum is present shall be the act of the board of directors _____ [except that vote of not less than _____ (fraction) of all the members of the board shall be required for the amendment of or addition to these bylaws or as the case may be].[31]

EXAMPLE: Meetings by Telephone or Video Conference

Meetings of the board of directors may be held by means of a telephone conference, video conference, or some similar communications equipment by means of which all persons participating in the meeting can hear each other and participate at the same time. Participation by a director in such a meeting by telephone or other such means shall constitute the presence of that director at the meeting.

EXAMPLE: Written Action by Directors

Actions required to be taken at a meeting of the board of directors may be taken without a meeting if all the directors of the corporation sign a written consent, setting forth specifically the action so taken and agreeing that the same shall become effective without the formality of a meeting of the board.

REMOVAL AND RESIGNATION OF DIRECTORS

The bylaws should set forth the procedures for removing directors from the board, including who may remove the directors, for what cause directors may be removed, how resignations of directors are to be tendered, and how vacancies on the board of directors are to be handled.

DIRECTOR COMPENSATION

The compensation of the directors or the means for determining the directors' compensation should be set forth in the bylaws. The bylaws should also address the directors' expense reimbursement and the indemnification of directors.

DIRECTOR LIABILITY

The liability of the directors may be limited or expanded in the bylaws of the corporation, within the limits imposed by statute.

OFFICERS

The corporation's bylaws should name the titles of the officers that the corporation will have, define the powers and duties of each officer, and set forth the compensation for each officer, or the means for determining that compensation.

EXAMPLE: Number of Officers

The officers of the corporation shall include a chief executive officer, president, one or more vice presidents, a secretary, and a chief financial officer, each of whom shall be elected by the board of directors. Such other officers and assistant officers as may be deemed necessary may be elected or appointed by the board of directors. Any two or more offices may be held by the same person, except the offices of president and secretary.

EXAMPLE: Election and Term of Office

The officers of the corporation to be elected by the board of directors shall be elected annually at the first meeting of the board of directors held after each annual meeting of the stockholders. If the election of officers is not held at such meeting, such election shall be held as soon thereafter as is convenient. Each officer shall hold office until his or her successor has been duly elected and qualifies or until his or her death or until he or she resigns or is removed in the manner provided below.[32]

EXAMPLE: Removal of Officers

Any officer elected by the board of directors may be removed by the board of directors whenever the board determines it is in the best interests of the corporation. Such removal shall be without prejudice to the contract rights, if any, of the removed officer.

STOCK CERTIFICATES

The bylaws should approve a form of stock certificate for the corporation for each class or type of stock to be used, including the required signatures on each stock certificate.

The bylaws should also provide the means for transfer of stock and replacement of lost, stolen, or destroyed certificates. If there is any restriction on the transfer of shares, this restriction should be set forth in the bylaws, as well as on each stock certificate.

EXAMPLE: Certificates for Shares

Certificates representing shares of the corporation shall be in the form attached as Exhibit A hereto [attach sample stock certificate]. Stock certificates of the corporation shall be signed by the president or a vice president and by the secretary of the corporation. The secretary of the corporation shall enter the name and address of the person to whom the shares of stock are issued, along with the number of shares, the number of the certificate, and date of issue. Transfers of stock shall be accomplished by the cancellation of the transferor's certificate of shares and the issuance of a new certificate to the transferee representing the transferred shares.

DIVIDENDS

The bylaws may provide the method for determining the dividends to be paid on the stock of the corporation, and the timing and method for payment of those dividends.

FISCAL YEAR

The fiscal year of the corporation should be set forth in the bylaws of the corporation.

CORPORATE SEAL

If the corporation plans to use a corporate seal, the seal should be described or reproduced in the bylaws. If the corporation does not plan to use a corporate seal, a statement to that effect should be included.

CORPORATE RECORDS

The bylaws should include a statement regarding the corporate records that are to be kept, their location, and the inspection rights of the officers, directors, and shareholders. Corporate records may include the stock certificate book, the stock transfer ledger, the minute book, and records of accounts.

AMENDMENT OF BYLAWS

Procedures for amending the bylaws of the corporation, congruent with state statutes, should be set forth in the bylaws.

SIGNATURES ON BYLAWS

The bylaws of the corporation are typically dated and signed by the secretary of the corporation in accordance with statute.

IN SUMMATION

- Bylaws set forth the rules and guidelines for the internal control of a corporation.
- The following topics are typically addressed in the corporation's bylaws:
  - The corporation's office address(es)
  - Procedures for giving notice and holding shareholder meetings
  - Procedures for giving notice and holding board of director meetings
  - Guidelines for the board of directors, including number of directors, duties and responsibilities, terms of office, qualifications, and removal

- Guidelines and qualifications for officers of the corporation, including their titles, duties and responsibilities, qualifications, and removal
- The corporation's fiscal year
- Guidelines for paying dividends
- Provisions approving a form of stock certificate
- Provisions for amending bylaws
- Guidelines for keeping the corporate records.

§ 8.8 FORMATION OF SPECIAL TYPES OF CORPORATIONS

Corporations other than business corporations are often subject to statutory incorporation requirements that differ from those prescribed for business corporations. In this section, we look at the special statutory provisions for incorporating statutory close corporations, professional corporations, and nonprofit corporations.

STATUTORY CLOSE CORPORATIONS

The statutes of states that provide for statutory close corporations usually have different or additional requirements for such an entity's articles of incorporation. If a corporation is to be incorporated as a statutory close corporation, it typically must so state in its articles of incorporation.

Special attention must also be paid to the stock certificates and bylaws of a statutory close corporation. Close corporations are typically required to include a statement on each stock certificate indicating that the corporation is a statutory close corporation and including any pertinent restrictions on transfer of the stock of the corporation.

Bylaws may be optional for close corporations. Many of the provisions included in the bylaws of other types of corporations are included in the articles of a close corporation or in resolutions by the shareholders or directors, if the corporation has directors.

PROFESSIONAL CORPORATIONS

The professional corporation must be incorporated in accordance with the professional corporation act or the professional corporation supplement to the business corporation act of the state of domicile. The requirements for forming a professional corporation are generally very similar to the requirements for forming a business corporation, with the exception of the restrictions on the officers, directors, and shareholders that were discussed in Chapter 7. The name of a professional corporation must indicate that it is a professional corporation rather than a business corporation. Exhibit 8-11 is a form that may be used to incorporate a professional corporation in Nevada.

EXHIBIT 8-11 ARTICLES OF INCORPORATION FOR PROFESSIONAL CORPORATION[34]

ROSS MILLER
Secretary of State
204 North Carson Street, Suite 4
Carson City, Nevada 89701-4520
(775) 684-5708
Website: www.nvsos.gov

040401

Articles of Incorporation
Professional Corporation
(PURSUANT TO NRS CHAPTER 89)

USE BLACK INK ONLY - DO NOT HIGHLIGHT   ABOVE SPACE IS FOR OFFICE USE ONLY

1. Name of Corporation: (see instructions)

2. Registered Agent for Service of Process: (check only one box)

☐ Commercial Registered Agent: _____
Name

☐ Noncommercial Registered Agent (name and address below)   **OR**   ☐ Office or Position with Entity (name and address below)

Name of Noncommercial Registered Agent **OR** Name of Title of Office or Other Position with Entity

_____ _____ Nevada _____
Street Address   City   Zip Code

_____ _____ Nevada _____
Mailing Address (if different from street address)   City   Zip Code

3. Authorized Stock: (number of shares corporation is authorized to issue)

Number of shares *with par value:* _____ Par value per share: $ _____ Number of shares *without par value:* _____

4. Names and Addresses of the Directors/Trustees and Stockholders:

IMPORTANT:
a) A certificate from the regulatory board showing that each individual is licensed at the time of filing with this office must be presented with this form.

b) Each Director/Trustee, Stockholder and Incorporator must be a licensed professional.

1) _____
Name

_____ _____ ____ _____
Street Address   City   State   Zip Code

2) _____
Name

_____ _____ ____ _____
Street Address   City   State   Zip Code

3) _____
Name

_____ _____ ____ _____
Street Address   City   State   Zip Code

5. Purpose: (see instructions)

The purpose of this corporation shall be:

6. Name, Address and Signature of Incorporator: (attach additional page if more than one incorporator)

_____   **X** _____
Name   Incorporator Signature

_____ _____ ____ _____
Address   City   State   Zip Code

7. Certificate of Acceptance of Appointment of Registered Agent:

I hereby accept appointment as Registered Agent for the above named Entity.

X _____   _____
Authorized Signature of Registered Agent or On Behalf of Registered Agent Entity   Date

This form must be accompanied by appropriate fees.

Nevada Secretary of State NRS 89 Articles
Revised: 10-16-09

NONPROFIT CORPORATIONS

Incorporation requirements for nonprofit corporations are also set by state statute, usually a state nonprofit corporation act. Requirements will vary, although they will resemble the business corporation incorporation requirements at least in part. Typically, requirements for the articles of incorporation of a nonprofit corporation differ from those for a business corporation, but the articles must be filed in much the same way.

S CORPORATIONS

There are generally no special requirements for incorporating S Corporations. S Corporations are formed in the same manner as any other business corporation, then the shareholders make an election to become an S Corporation by filing the proper form with the Internal Revenue Service.

IN SUMMATION

- There are unique requirements for qualifying certain types of corporations, including statutory close corporations, professional corporations, and nonprofit corporations.
- The secretary of state may provide forms specifically for forming certain types of corporations.
- S Corporations are incorporated with the state in the same manner as any other business corporations.
- After a corporation has been formed, it elects S Corporation status by filing the appropriate form with the Internal Revenue Service.

§ 8.9 THE PARALEGAL'S ROLE

The paralegal can handle almost all aspects of the incorporation process under the direction of an attorney. Given correct and complete information, the paralegal can prepare the articles of incorporation, bylaws, and first minutes or written consents of the board of directors and shareholders. The specific tasks that can be performed by the paralegal include the following:

1. Attend initial attorney/client meeting to collect information required to complete incorporation process.
2. Check name availability and prepare and file application for name reservation, if desired.
3. Prepare and file articles of incorporation.

4. Check for compliance with any publication or county recording requirements.
5. Draft corporate documents, including:
    a. Bylaws
    b. Notices of organizational meetings
    c. Minutes or unanimous writings in lieu of organizational meeting or first meeting of directors and shareholders
    d. Stock subscription agreements
    e. Stock certificates
    f. Banking resolutions
6. Assist client with obtaining any required licenses to operate business.
7. Order corporate minute book, seal, and stock certificates.
8. Organize corporate minute book.
9. Prepare stock certificates and stock ledger.
10. Follow up with client concerning corporate formalities and procedures to be followed.

Initial Client Meeting

The corporate paralegal will often attend the initial attorney/client meeting. The paralegal may take notes using a customized checklist to collect the information discussed in § 8.1 of this chapter. The paralegal is often introduced as the contact person to answer procedural questions the client may have during the incorporation process.

Reserve Corporate Name

If it is determined that the corporate name must be reserved, the paralegal will often assume that responsibility. Paralegals must be familiar with the state procedures for reserving corporate names. It is very important that the corporate name be reserved promptly, as the client may be taking actions (such as ordering letterhead and supplies) on the assumption that the corporate name will be available.

Prepare Articles of Incorporation and Other Incorporation Documents

The paralegal will often assume responsibility for preparing the initial draft of the articles of incorporation and other incorporation documents for the attorney's review and approval, using the information learned during the initial client meeting and form books or standard forms that are used by the office.

Filing Articles of Incorporation

The paralegal is often responsible for filing the articles of incorporation and any other required documents with the secretary of state. Each state has its own unique filing requirements, and it is imperative that paralegals are familiar with those requirements. Exhibit 8-12 provides a sample checklist of all tasks that must be completed in the incorporation process.

EXHIBIT 8-12   INCORPORATION CHECKLIST

This is just a sample list. The exact steps to be taken, and the order in which they will be taken, will depend on the jurisdiction and other circumstances.

☐ Select corporate name.

☐ Check name availability and reserve name if necessary.

☐ Prepare articles of incorporation.

☐ Prepare designation of registered agent (in jurisdictions where required).

☐ File articles of incorporation and any other accompanying documents required in jurisdiction.

☐ Record articles of incorporation (in jurisdictions where required).

☐ Provide for publication of notice of incorporation (in jurisdictions where required).

☐ Prepare bylaws.

☐ Order corporate minute book and other supplies needed, including corporate seal and stock certificates.

☐ Prepare stock subscriptions and stock certificates.

☐ Prepare minutes of organizational meeting, or unanimous written resolution in lieu of organizational meeting.

☐ Prepare S corporation election (if desired).

☐ Prepare any required employment agreements or shareholder agreements.

☐ Prepare applications for certificates of authority to transact business as a foreign corporation.

☐ Calendar any dates that will be important to the corporation.

CORPORATE PARALEGAL PROFILE
Leah Mumford

I enjoy the ever-changing environment of the large law firm and the constant learning process required to do my job effectively.

NAME Leah Mumford

LOCATION Denver, Colorado

TITLE Corporate Paralegal

SPECIALTY Corporate and Securities Law

EDUCATION Bachelor of Arts—Southwest Studies, Fort Lewis College; Paralegal Certificate, Arapahoe Community College

EXPERIENCE 5 years

Leah Mumford is a paralegal with Holme Roberts & Owen, LLP, a law firm of 265 attorneys and 50 paralegals. Leah works in the Corporate Law and Securities Group and reports to the heads of that group, as well as any specific partner or associate she may be working with on a particular project.

Leah works with several different attorneys within the firm to form business entities, research state compliance requirements, prepare and file Uniform Commercial Code (UCC) statements, and draft a variety of corporate documents. She also assists with bank financings and mergers and acquisitions by tracking the various documents required for those transactions and preparing closing books for the involved parties. Leah helps clients track their stock issuance and keep up-to-date stock ledgers and corporate minute books.

When a corporate client of the firm makes a public securities offering, Leah assists by researching blue sky laws and preparing related memos to monitor compliance with Securities and Exchange Commission (SEC) regulations. She also prepares and submits securities-related filings to the SEC.

Leah enjoys the ever-changing work environment of the large law firm and the constant

learning process required to do her job effectively. She reports that every project is different, from the working group to the structure of the deal itself. On the downside, Leah reports that creating an organized environment for the deal team to work in and ensuring that things are not overlooked can be challenging and stressful at times. Leah often gets involved in projects toward the end of the transaction, when the closing is on the horizon. She then must quickly bring herself up to speed on the project, often without much guidance. At times, Leah finds herself putting in long hours to make sure transaction closings go smoothly.

One project Leah was involved in concerned a large bank financing for a client who, without the funding, was facing imminent bankruptcy. Leah and her team worked around the clock to negotiate the terms with the lenders and complete the transaction. While working under such a tight deadline was stressful and hours were long, it was very rewarding to Leah to know that her efforts helped to keep the company and its numerous employees in business.

Leah lives in Denver, where she has done pro bono work with two clients by helping them set up nonprofit entities. One of her pro bono projects involved an organization that operated a website for cancer patients and their families to share stories, insights, and fears. The other organization she worked for was a charity that distributed donated medical supplies to impoverished countries.

Leah's advice to new paralegals?

Working in a fast-paced, busy firm often does not allow for much of a learning curve.

continues

CORPORATE PARALEGAL PROFILE
Leah Mumford (continued)

I think it is important to have the ability to problem solve on your own. I find that many of the attorneys I work for are far too busy for more questions; what they want is an answer, and if you can provide that answer and make their jobs a bit easier you will be invaluable. Also, small details that seem unimportant may actually be very important. If you are very detail oriented and catch those minor issues and errors, your employer will greatly appreciate your efforts.

For more information on careers for corporate paralegals, log in to http://cengagebrain.com to access the CourseMate website that accompanies this text; then see the Corporate Careers Section.

ETHICAL CONSIDERATION

Access to the legal system for all Americans is a goal that members of the legal community aspire to. Attorneys and paralegals work toward this goal by providing their services pro bono. The term *pro bono publico* means "for the public good." Free legal work done by lawyers and paralegals to help society is referred to as "pro bono" work.

Most pro bono work is in the form of legal services provided to the poor who may not otherwise have access to the legal system. Attorneys may represent the poor to obtain divorces, to collect child support, to defend themselves in criminal matters, or in numerous other types of legal matters. Paralegals may work with attorneys as part of the legal team to provide pro bono services to those in need. They may also act independently to provide their services pro bono, provided their services do not constitute the unauthorized practice of law.

Attorneys and paralegals who specialize in corporate law may find pro bono work an opportunity to expand their expertise. Many legal clinics and other types of agencies that serve the poor offer free training to attorneys and paralegals who are willing to offer a certain number of hours of their time.

For those who prefer to limit their work to their area of expertise, nonprofit organizations of all types are often in need of legal services.

It is not uncommon for attorneys who specialize in corporate law to offer pro bono services to nonprofit and charitable organizations. They may serve as counsel for, or serve on the board of directors of, nonprofit corporations, community groups, environmental groups, or similar organizations.

continues

ETHICAL CONSIDERATION
(continued)

Corporate paralegals may team with attorneys to provide pro bono services by assisting with incorporations and annual reporting requirements, and by preparing all types of legal documents for a favorite charitable organization or community nonprofit corporation.

Providing pro bono services may be an ethical duty. The rules of ethics of most states provide that attorneys have an ethical duty to provide pro bono services to persons of limited means and organizations that address the needs of persons of limited means. The rules of ethics of the paralegal associations have similar provisions. Many paralegals who provide pro bono services indicate that it is one of the most rewarding experiences of their careers.

The national and state bar associations and paralegal associations are excellent resources for information and advice on providing pro bono services and finding pro bono opportunities. Most state and local paralegal associations have committees that work to match paralegal volunteers with pro bono opportunities.

For more information on ethics for corporate paralegals, including links to the NALA and NFPA codes of ethics, log in to http://www.cengagebrain.com to access the CourseMate website that accompanies this text; then see the Ethics Section.

SIDEBAR

Excerpt from the National Federation of Paralegal Association's Model Code of Ethics and Professional Responsibility, EC-1.4(b): "A paralegal shall support bona fide efforts to meet the need for legal services by those unable to pay reasonable or customary fees; for example, participation in pro bono projects and volunteer work."

§ 8.10 RESOURCES

The resources that the paralegal will find useful when working on the formation of a corporation include the state statutes, information from the secretary of state, legal form books, Internet resources, and incorporation services.

STATE STATUTES

As discussed in this chapter, incorporation requirements for business corporations are found in the business corporation act of the statutes of the corporation's state of domicile. A list of state business corporation acts can be found in Chapter 7 of this text. Links to those statutes may also be found at the CourseMate website that accompanies this text.

SECRETARY OF STATE OFFICES

The articles or certificate of incorporation must be filed with the secretary of state. Some states accept articles of incorporation and other corporate documents online, via facsimile or e-mail, with payment made by credit card or by means of a preestablished account with the secretary of state. The secretary of state's office must be contacted to ascertain the appropriate forms to use, current filing fees, and specific instructions for filing articles of incorporation and other incorporation documents. Appendix A of this text includes a directory of secretary of state offices. Links to those secretary of state offices may be found at the CourseMate website that accompanies this text.

INCORPORATION SERVICES

There are several businesses that assist attorneys and laypersons with the formation of corporations. These services usually have the ability to incorporate businesses in any state in the country within a very short time period. These services may be useful to paralegals who need to form a corporation in a distant state quickly. For the names of services in your location, you can consult your telephone directory, search the Internet, or ask for referrals from attorneys and other paralegals.

SUMMARY

- Corporations do not exist until they are properly incorporated pursuant to state statute.
- The corporation's state of domicile is the state where the corporation is incorporated.
- At times, corporations may have a promoter, an individual who organizes, promotes, and forms the corporation.
- When the incorporation is complex and may take a considerable amount of time, the initial shareholders may enter into a preincorporation agreement to formalize their understanding about the formation of the corporation.
- A stock subscription is an agreement to purchase shares of stock of a corporation at an agreed-upon price.
- The incorporator is the individual who actually signs the incorporation documents. The incorporator may not have an active role in the corporation after it is formed. At times, the corporation's attorney acts as incorporator.
- The document filed at the state level to form the corporation is usually referred to as the articles of incorporation or certificate of incorporation.
- Requirements for the articles of incorporation are established by state statute, but usually require the document to include (at a minimum) the corporation's name, number of authorized shares, street address of a registered office, and name and address of each incorporator.
- An organizational meeting of the initial shareholders and directors is often held immediately following the incorporation of the company.

- The initial board of directors is either named in the articles of incorporation or elected by the shareholders at the organizational meeting.
- The bylaws are considered the rules and guidelines for the internal control of the corporation. Most corporations are required to have bylaws.
- Shareholders and directors take action by passing resolutions at meetings pursuant to the corporation's bylaws and state statute.
- Under some circumstances, the shareholders and directors may take action by means of a unanimous written consent or a consent signed by the number of shareholders or directors required to take the action.

■ REVIEW QUESTIONS _____

1. What are some of the factors that must be taken into account when determining if a corporation is the best type of business organization for a particular business?

2. Discuss some of the factors that should be considered when determining where to incorporate a business. Why are those factors important?

3. Under what circumstances are corporations bound to contracts made by their promoters prior to incorporation?

4. Can two individuals from New York form a Florida corporation?

5. If two residents of Texas file articles of incorporation in New York and transact the majority of their business in Florida, what is their state of domicile?

6. In addition to filing articles of incorporation, what incorporation formalities are imposed by some states before the incorporation process is complete?

7. Can the incorporator also be a director of a corporation?

8. What required provisions must be included in the articles of incorporation in a state following the Model Business Corporation Act?

9. Why might it be preferable to put information in the bylaws, as opposed to the articles of incorporation, when the statute provides that the information could be in either document?

10. Would the name "Johnson Brothers Furniture Store" be a valid corporate name in a state following the Model Business Corporation Act? Why or why not?

■ PRACTICAL PROBLEMS _____

1. Find the pertinent incorporation statute in your state to answer the following questions:

   a. What is the name of the document filed to form a corporation in your state?
   b. What is the minimum information required for that document?
   c. What are the requirements for incorporators in your state? Can a corporation act as incorporator in your state?

2. What is the name of the state agency in your state that accepts incorporation documents for filing?

3. What are the basic procedures for filing incorporation documents in your state? What documents must be filed? How can that filing be accomplished? What is the filing fee for incorporation documents?

◼ EXERCISE IN CRITICAL THINKING

Why is it so important for the organizers of a corporation to make sure that corporate formalities are followed with regard to preincoroporation and incorporation matters? If formalities are not followed, what are some possible consequences to the

Promoters?
Incorporators?
Shareholders?
Board of directors?

◼ WORKPLACE SCENARIO

Assume, once again, that you are a paralegal for a corporate law firm. Our fictional clients, Bradley Harris and Cynthia Lund, have just met with your supervising attorney, Belinda Murphy. Belinda has advised them to have their business, Cutting Edge Computer Repair, incorporated. Using the information in Appendix B-3, prepare articles of incorporation and any other documents required for filing with the appropriate state office in your state to form a corporation. Also prepare a cover letter with accompanying filing fee. Note that for the Workplace Scenario in Chapter 7, this incorporation had already taken place.

Portfolio Reminder
Save the documents prepared for the Workplace Scenario exercises in each chapter, either in hard copy or electronically, to build a portfolio of documents to be used for job interviews or as

sample documents on the job. At this point, your portfolio should include the following:

- Power of attorney
- Application for assumed name
- Application for federal employer identification number
- Application for state employer identification number
- Partnership statement of authority
- Limited partnership certificate
- Limited liability partnership statement of qualification
- Articles of organization
- Subchapter S election by small business corporation, Form 2553
- Articles of incorporation

◼ ENDNOTES

1. State of Delaware, Division of Corporations, http://corp.delaware.gov, accessed March 6, 2011.

2. Model Business Corporation Act as Revised through December 2007 (MBCA) § 2.01.

3. Alaska, District of Columbia, Maryland, Minnesota, Missouri, New York, North Dakota, Rhode Island, and Vermont have statutory provisions requiring that incorporators be natural persons.

4. MBCA § 2.02(a)(1).

5. Id. § 2.02(a)(2).

6. Id. § 2.02(a)(3).

7. Id. § 2.02(a)(4).

8. Minimum required information under Revised Model Business Corporation Act § 2.02(a)(2).

9. 6 Am. Jur. Legal Forms 2d Corporations 74:76 (May 2011). Reprinted with permission from American Jurisprudence Legal Forms 2d. © 2008 West Group.

10. Minimum required information under Revised Model Business Corporation Act § 2.02(a)(3)

11. MBCA § 2.02(b)(1).

12. Id. § 2.02(b)(2)(i).

13. Id. § 2.02(b)(2)(ii).

14. Id. § 2.02(b)(2)(iii).

15. Id. § 2.02(b)(2)(iv).

16. Id. § 2.02(b)(2)(v).

17. Id. § 2.02(b)(3).

18. Id. § 2.02(b)(4).

19. Id. § 2.02(b)(5).

20. 18A Am. Jur. 2d Corporations § 175 (November 2007).

21. MBCA § 2.02 Official Comment.

22. Id. § 8.21(a).

23. Id. § 7.28(b).

24. Id. § 8.08(a).

25. Id. § 6.01.

26. Id. § 6.30.

27. Arizona, Georgia, Nebraska, and Pennsylvania have publication requirements for incorporating in those states.

28. Alabama, Illinois, Kentucky, Louisiana, and Tennessee all have requirements for filing the articles of incorporation or a copy thereof at the county or local level.

29. MBCA § 2.06.

30. 6 Am. Jur. Legal Forms 2d Corporations § 74:632 (November May 2011). Reprinted with permission from American Jurisprudence Legal Forms 2d. © 2011 West Group.

31. Id. Reprinted with permission from American Jurisprudence Legal Forms 2d. © 2011 West Group.

32. Id. Reprinted with permission from American Jurisprudence Legal Forms 2d. © 2008 West Group.

33. © 2008 West Group.

34. Nevada Secretary of State's Office This form, Articles of Incorporation Professional Corporation Form – Nevada Secretary of State NRS 89 Articles, Revised: 10-16-09, is provided by the Office of the Nevada Secretary of State or the purpose of inclusion in the 6th edition of *The Law of Corporations and Other Business Organizations*, a textbook published by Cengage Learning.

Please note that this form is for general information only and is subject to change without notice. Interested individuals should contact the Secretary of State's office to retrieve the most recent version of this form or visit the Secretary of State's website: https://www.nvsos.gov.

CourseMate

To access additional course materials, including CourseMate, please visit http://www.cengagebrain .com. At the CengageBrain home page, search for the ISBN of your title (from the back cover of your book) using the search box at the top of the page. This will take you to the product page where the resources can be found. The CourseMate resources for this text include Web links to the resources discussed above, downloadable forms, flash cards, and more.

CHAPTER 9

THE CORPORATE ORGANIZATION

CHAPTER OUTLINE

INTRODUCTION

Corporations must act through their agents, the most visible agents being corporate officers and directors. The officers, directors, and shareholders may play very different roles, but each functions as an integral part of the operation of the business corporation. This chapter discusses the role of each type of member of the corporation, beginning with the authority, duties, liabilities, and compensation of the directors of the corporation. First we examine how they are elected and how they act through directors' meetings. Next we investigate the officers, who are elected by the directors of the corporation, and follow with a study of the rights and responsibilities of the shareholders of the corporation and how they participate in the corporate affairs through shareholder meetings. We then take a brief look at the restrictions that may be placed on the transfer of shares of corporate stock. This chapter concludes with a discussion of the paralegal's role in corporate organizational matters and the resources available to assist paralegals working in that area.

§ 9.1 AUTHORITY AND DUTIES OF DIRECTORS

Corporations act through their directors, who are responsible for overseeing the operation of the corporation's business. The board of directors may range from one to several directors. State statutes may provide for a minimum number of directors—for example, some states require that the board of directors must consist of at least three directors, unless there are fewer than three shareholders.[1]

Directors of smaller corporations may also be employees, officers, and shareholders of the corporation. The board of directors of larger corporations will include a percentage of outside directors—individuals who are neither employees nor shareholders of the corporation. There is a presumption that all directors act in good faith, but that presumption is heightened with independent outside directors. Publicly traded corporations may be required to have a certain percentage of outside directors on their board, serving on particular committees.

Directors are given the statutory authority to make most decisions regarding the operation of the corporation, and it may appear that they have a free rein to operate the corporation as they see fit. However, it is important to remember that although directors have full authority in most matters, they are elected by the shareholders of the corporation. The director who does not serve what the shareholders perceive to be their best interests could be voted out of office at the next election, or even removed before his or her term expires. In this section we will look at both the authority and the duties of corporate directors.

According to one recent study, on average, companies with the highest percentage of women board directors outperform those with the lowest by 66 percent in return on invested capital.[2]

DIRECTORS' AUTHORITY

It has been said that the "corporate board of directors, exercising their reasonable and good faith business judgment, possess the paramount right to corporate control and management."[3] The corporation, in effect, acts through its directors.

Directors have statutory authority to act for the corporation. Corporate control is granted to the board of directors except as may otherwise be provided in the corporation's articles of incorporation. Section 8.01(b) of the Model Business Corporation Act (MBCA) represents the common statutory grant of authority to a corporation's board of directors:

> (b) All corporate powers shall be exercised by or under the authority of the board of directors of the corporation, and the business and affairs of the corporation shall be managed by or under the direction, and subject to the over-sight, of its board of directors, subject to any limitation set forth in the articles of incorporation or in an agreement authorized under section 7.32.

In addition to granting the board of directors the authority to manage the business and affairs of the corporation, most state business corporation acts grant the board of directors the authority to delegate the management of the business and affairs of the corporation.

Delegation of Authority to Officers

Directors generally are given the authority to appoint officers and to delegate certain authority to them. Under the MBCA, the business affairs of the corporation may be managed "under the direction of" the board of directors. This recognizes the fact that the directors of the corporation, alone, are often not the appropriate individuals to run the day-to-day business of the corporation. In larger corporations, directors are frequently employed outside the corporation, or have other interests that make demands on their time. Some individuals serve on the boards of several corporations.

There is a difference between the delegation of authority and power and the delegation of responsibility. It is generally accepted that although the board of directors may delegate authority to corporate officers, the board must continue to exercise general supervision over their activities. Directors are generally responsible for the acts of the officers whom they appoint.[4] The directors of a corporation may not delegate to others those duties that lie at the "heart of the management of the corporation."

The responsibilities the board of directors must oversee will vary depending on the size and business of the corporation, and whether the stock of the corporation is publicly traded. The MBCA includes the following list of items representative of those for which directors of a publicly traded corporation have oversight responsibilities.[5] That list includes:

- Business performance and plans
- Major risks to which the corporation is, or may be, exposed
- The performance and compensation of senior officers
- Policies and practices to foster the corporation's compliance with law and ethical conduct
- Preparation of the corporation's financial statements
- The effectiveness of the corporation's internal controls

- Arrangements for providing adequate and timely information to directors
- The composition of the board and its committees, taking into account the important role of independent directors

The powers delegated to the officers of the corporation may be very broad, or they may be set forth very specifically in the articles or bylaws of the corporation, or by director resolution. The extent to which the officers are directed and limited in their authority by the board of directors will depend on the statutes of the corporation's state of domicile and the governing instruments of the corporation.

Delegation of Authority to Committees

Directors also commonly delegate authority to one or more committees that are comprised of members of the board of directors. With the complexities of managing a modern business, groups such as executive committees, nominating committees, finance committees, compensation committees, audit committees, and litigation committees are often appointed to oversee specific areas of concern.

The authority of directors to appoint committees may come from the statutes of the corporation's state of domicile, or the articles or bylaws of the corporation. Under the MBCA, the board of directors is granted the authority to create committees, unless the articles of incorporation or bylaws of the corporation provide otherwise. The creation of the committee and the appointment of its members must be approved by a majority of the board of directors, unless a larger number is required for a **quorum** under the articles of incorporation or bylaws of the corporation.

The only authority that a committee has to act on behalf of the corporation is the authority delegated to it by the board of directors, or as authorized in the articles of incorporation or bylaws of the corporation. Restrictions on the authority of the committee and the powers that may be delegated to it are often found in the state statutes. Additional restrictions may be imposed by the articles or bylaws of the corporation. The MBCA specifically states that a committee may not do any of the following:

1. Authorize dividends or distributions to the shareholders of the corporation, except according to a formula or method or within limits, prescribed by the board of directors[6]
2. Approve or propose to shareholders action that the MBCA requires to be approved by shareholders[7]
3. Fill vacancies on the board of directors or on any of its committees[8]
4. Amend the articles of incorporation and adopt, amend, or repeal bylaws[9]

Limitations on Directors' Authority

While state statutes generally grant full authority to the board of directors to manage the business and affairs of the corporation, that authority may be limited in the articles of incorporation of the corporation. Certain corporate acts, not considered to be within the ordinary business and administration of the corporation, may require approval of the shareholders of the corporation.

QUORUM

The number of persons who must be present to make the votes and other actions of a group (such as a board) valid. This number is often a majority (over half) of the whole group, but is sometimes much less or much more.

Following is a list of actions that often require shareholder approval:

1. Amendment and restatement of the articles of incorporation
2. Enactment, amendment, or repeal of bylaws
3. Issuance of stock of the corporation
4. Dissolution of the corporation
5. Calling of shareholder meetings
6. Approval of merger and consolidation plans
7. Sale of corporate assets other than in the regular course of business

DIRECTORS' DUTIES

The duties owed to the corporation by a director are several and complex. The MBCA provides that each member of the board of directors, when discharging the duties of a director, shall act (1) in good faith, and (2) in a manner the director reasonably believes to be in the best interests of the corporation.[10]

Because the directors have the ultimate responsibility for the entire management of corporate affairs, directors owe the following **fiduciary** duties to the corporation and its shareholders:

1. The duty of care
2. The duty of loyalty
3. The duty of good faith

Duty of Care

Directors must use "due care" and be diligent in the management and administration of the affairs of the corporation and in the use or preservation of its property.[11] The exact measure of the degree of care that must be exercised is difficult to define, although one test often used is the ordinarily prudent person test, which means acting with the diligence and care that would be exercised by an ordinarily prudent person in like circumstances. Under the MBCA, directors must discharge their duties "with the care that a person in a like position would reasonably believe appropriate under similar circumstances."[12] The director's duty of care can be measured, in part, by the time and attention devoted to the affairs of the corporation and the skill and judgment used in business decisions. In addition, the directors' duty of care includes the duty to give adequate attention and supervision to the corporation and its officers and employees. Directors will, of course, have the right to delegate the management of the day-to-day corporate affairs, but in so doing they must exercise due care.[13]

In one case in Alabama, the directors of a corporation were found not to be guilty of neglecting their duties by failure to supervise the president of a company who lost $640,000 through investments in speculative commodities. In that case, the directors had not violated their duty of care since they had questioned the president about the corporation's investments and had cautioned the president to avoid any speculation.[14] The following list indicates

FIDUCIARY

1. A person who manages money or property for another person and in whom that other person has a right to place great trust.
2. A relationship like that in definition no. 1.
3. Any relationship between persons in which one person acts for another in a position of trust, for example, lawyer and client or parent and child.

typical actions required by a director's duty of care to oversee the activities of the corporation:

1. Regularly attend board of director and committee meetings
2. Require the corporate management to provide adequate information upon which to make decisions
3. Carefully read, understand, and act on (when necessary) the documentation provided to the board of directors
4. Participate in board of director and committee discussions
5. Make independent inquiries, when warranted
6. Carefully monitor the activities delegated to the officers of the corporation

Duty of Loyalty

Directors must at all times remain loyal to the corporation and its shareholders, acting in a manner that serves the best interest of the corporation, as opposed to a director's other interests or the director's personal interests. Directors who are also directors of related corporations or have interests in related businesses may find themselves in a position of a potential conflict of interest from time to time. Directors should abstain from participating in corporate decisions that might give even the appearance of a conflict of interest. Statutes modeled after the MBCA with regard to director conflicts of interest require that directors disclose the existence and nature of potential conflicting interests and all known material facts with regard to the decision as to whether to proceed with the proposed transaction.

Duty of Good Faith

The director's duty of good faith demands honesty in the performance of duties, and it precludes actions designed to benefit the director personally to the detriment of the corporation. In one recent case heard in Delaware, the court held that, in addition to the duties of care and loyalty, the directors' duty of good faith encompasses "all actions required by a true faithfulness and devotion to the interests of the corporation and its shareholders."[15] It is possible that bad decision can be made in good faith. For example, if the members of the board of directors firmly believe, after making proper study and inquiry, that the purchase of a new factory is a good decision for their manufacturing company, they have made a decision in good faith, even if the decision causes a financial loss to the corporation. If, on the other hand, certain directors know there has been toxic waste secretly dumped on the property, but they promote the purchase of the factory because they have an interest in it and stand to personally gain from the sale, that same decision is made in bad faith.

Reliance upon Information from Others

Directors cannot reasonably be expected to have firsthand knowledge of all business affairs of the corporation for which they are responsible. For that reason, it is assumed that directors are entitled to rely upon information given to them and statements made to them by those who are in immediate charge of the corporation's business. Under § 8.30 of the MBCA, if directors have no knowledge that makes their reliance unwarranted, they are entitled to rely on information, opinions, reports, or statements, including financial statements and other financial data, prepared or presented by the following:

1. One or more officers or employees of the corporation whom the director reasonably believes to be reliable and competent in the functions performed or the information, opinions, reports, or statements provided
2. Legal counsel, public accountants, or other persons retained by the corporation as to matters involving skills or expertise the director reasonably believes are matters (i) within the particular person's professional or expert competence or (ii) as to which the particular person merits confidence
3. A committee of the board of directors of which the director is not a member if the director reasonably believes the committee merits confidence

IN SUMMATION

- Corporations act through their directors, who are elected by the shareholders.
- In smaller corporations, the corporate directors may also be employees and shareholders of the corporation.
- Larger, publicly held corporations may be required to have outside directors who are not employees of the corporation.
- The board of directors has the authority to manage the business and affairs of the corporation and the authority to delegate much of that management.
- The board of directors has the authority to appoint officers and delegate certain authority to them, although the board must exercise general supervision over their activities.
- Directors may delegate authority to one or more committees comprised of board members.
- Certain actions not in the ordinary course of business will be outside the scope of the authority of the board of directors and require shareholder approval.
- Directors owe the fiduciary duties of care, loyalty, and good faith to the corporation and its shareholders.
- Directors may rely on reliable information presented to them by officers, legal counsel, accountants, and other experts when making decisions on behalf of the corporation.

§ 9.2 PERSONAL LIABILITY OF DIRECTORS

The imposition of personal liability on corporate directors for poor business decisions would be an impractical, if not impossible, task. Under the **business judgment rule**, directors generally cannot be held personally liable for any damages caused to the corporation as the result of decisions made by them in good faith.

However, there are several instances in which directors may be held personally liable for debts and obligations of the corporation—specifically those arising from actions of the directors that were not taken in good faith. Under certain conditions, personal liability is imposed on the directors of a corporation by statute, unless the corporation's articles of incorporation provide otherwise. It is therefore important that the incorporators of a business be well informed regarding the potential for director liability, and that the incorporation documents be drafted accordingly.

BUSINESS JUDGMENT RULE

The courts have recognized for years that the decisions made by directors involve a certain amount of risk, and that even an informed, good-faith decision can result in an unfavorable outcome for the corporation.

Because it would be unfair for officers and directors to be held personally liable for poor outcomes of informed decisions made in good faith, the courts have looked to the business judgment rule in deciding such cases. The business judgment rule is a standard of judicial review that provides that officers and directors will not be held personally liable for honest, careful decisions within their corporate powers. The business judgment rule protects a board of directors from being questioned or second-guessed on the conduct of corporate affairs, except in instances of fraud, self-dealing, or unconscionable conduct.

The business judgment rule protects a director or officer from liability for business decisions made:

1. in good faith;
2. where the director or officer is not interested in the subject of the business judgment;
3. where the director or officer is informed with respect to the subject of the business judgment to the extent the director reasonably believes to be appropriate under the circumstances; and
4. where the director or officer rationally believes that the business judgment in question is in the best interests of the corporation.[16]

Under the business judgment rule, directors are not liable for honest errors or mistakes of judgment made without corrupt motive and in good faith.[17]

SIDEBAR

The business judgment rule applies only where a business decision is actually made—it does not protect directors for omissions where injury results from the directors passively doing nothing.

IMPOSITION OF PERSONAL LIABILITY ON DIRECTORS

As we have discussed, personal liability is generally not imposed on corporate directors for their poor business decisions. However, the amount of litigation personally involving directors in recent years is indicative of the many exceptions to that rule.

Breach of Fiduciary Duty, Duty of Due Care, or Duty of Loyalty

A director who fails in his or her fiduciary duty, duty of due care, or duty of loyalty to the corporation may be subject to the imposition of personal liability for any damages caused to the corporation or its shareholders.

Unauthorized Acts

When directors clearly act beyond the scope of their authority, personal liability may be imposed upon them for losses to the corporation caused by their unauthorized acts. Directors acting beyond the scope of their authority may be required to use their personal assets to make good any losses caused by their acts.

Negligence

Directors are personally liable for their negligent acts that involve injury or loss to the corporation or to third parties. Personal liability of the directors for negligent acts is based on the common law rule "which renders every agent liable who violates his authority or neglects his duty to the damage of his principal."[18]

Fraud or Other Illegal Acts

Directors may also be personally liable to the corporation and to third parties for any fraudulent or other **tortious** acts committed by them, or by the corporation with their knowledge. Corporate directors are not personally liable for fraud involving the corporation that they were unaware of, if they should not have reasonably been expected to be aware of it.

TORTIOUS
Wrongful. A civil (as opposed to a criminal) wrong (tort), other than a breach of contract. For an act to be a tort, there must be: a legal duty owed by one person to another, a breach (breaking) of that duty, and harm done as a direct result of the action. Examples of torts are negligence, battery, and libel.

Statutory Imposition of Personal Liability

State statutes or the articles of incorporation of a corporation, or both, may specify that the directors of a corporation are personally liable for certain actions. Under the MBCA, directors may be held personally liable for the payment of distributions in violation of state statutes or the articles of incorporation.

Exhibit 9-1 lists some of the actions for which directors may be held personally liable.

State corporate statutes not only impose personal liability on directors under certain circumstances, they provide the means for corporations to limit the personal liability of their directors and to indemnify them for certain litigation-related expenses.

EXHIBIT 9-1 PERSONAL LIABILITY OF DIRECTORS

Directors May Be Held Personally Liable For

- Breaches of the director's fiduciary duty, duty of care, or duty of loyalty

- Unauthorized acts (acts clearly beyond the scope of their authority)

- Negligent acts

- Fraud or other illegal acts

- Acts that are controlled by state statute that provide for personal liability by directors

© Cengage Learning 2013

In addition to the business judgment rule, a director's personal liability may be further limited by the corporation's articles of incorporation. In some situations, corporate management may find it necessary to provide the maximum protection available under statute in its articles of incorporation to entice qualified outside directors to join the board. To further entice individuals to join the board of directors, corporations purchase director and officer liability insurance—insurance to protect the directors from personal liability and financial loss arising out of wrongful acts committed or allegedly committed in their capacity as corporate director.

Section 2.02 of the MBCA provides that a corporation's articles of incorporation may be drafted to eliminate or limit the liability of its directors, except liability for:

1. The amount of financial benefit received by a director to which he or she is not entitled
2. An intentional infliction of harm on the corporation or the shareholders
3. A violation of Section 8.33 (concerning unlawful distributions); and
4. An intentional violation of criminal law[19]

In *Grassmueck v. Barnett*, the following case on page 361, the outside director defendants of the suit brought a motion to dismiss the suit brought against them and others for breach of their fiduciary duties to the corporation and its shareholders. In this case, the founder and principal stockholder of the corporation allegedly diverted millions of the corporation's dollars for his own use.[20] Although the articles of incorporation of the subject corporations provided for the maximum amount of liability protection for the directors, the suit against them was not dismissed. The liability shield statutes will not protect directors who act in bad faith.

SIDEBAR

Individuals who are both directors and corporate officers may be held to even higher standards where their fiduciary duty is concerned.

CASE

United States District Court, W.D. Washington. Michael Grassmueck, Plaintiff, v. Dwayne Barnett, et al., Defendants. No. C03-122P. July 7, 2003.

BACKGROUND

The Defendants were Directors of the Znetix Inc. ("Znetix") while Znetix's founder and principal stockholder, Kevin Lawrence, served as director and controlling shareholder of Znetix and Health Maintenance Centers, Inc. ("HMC"). Mr. Lawrence is accused of exerting "unchecked power and control" over Znetix, including various improper actions and false and misleading representations regarding Znetix's business, which diverted millions of dollars from the day-to-day operation of Znetix. . . . Allegedly, Mr. Lawrence used these funds for the personal benefit of himself, his family, friends, and accomplices. . . . As a result of these wrongful acts, the Securities and Exchange Commission forced Znetix into receivership and forced liquidation of all of its assets. The Complaint alleges that the damages to Znetix and its shareholders are known to exceed $10 million . . . . Plaintiff and Receiver, Michael Grassmueck, claims on behalf of creditors and investors of HMC, Znetix and/or Cascade that the Directors and Officers should be held personally liable for damages to the creditors and investors because they were negligent and exercised bad faith by failing to act to prevent or control Lawrence's wrongful acts. . . .

It is undisputed that the Directors and Officers had fiduciary duties of care to Znetix and its shareholders to (a) discharge their duties with the care an ordinary prudent person in a like position would exercise under similar circumstances; (b) discharge their duties with a critical eye to assessing information, performing actions carefully, thoroughly, thoughtfully,

and in an informed manner; (c) seek all relevant material information before making decisions on behalf of the corporation; and (d) avoid and prevent corporate waste and unnecessary expense. . . . They also had affirmative duties to protect Znetix and its shareholders' interests and to be aware of the corporation's affairs. . . . In addition, they owed fiduciary duties of loyalty to Znetix and its shareholders, which required that each discharge his or her duties in good faith. . . . Finally, they owed undivided loyalty to Znetix and its shareholders to ensure that neither they, nor any other officer or director, obtained any profit or advantage at the expense of Znetix.

The Complaint asserts that the Directors and Officers did not uphold these obligations and alleges "negligent and bad faith performance of their duties," and "breach of fiduciary duty." . . . In particular, the complaint states that the Directors had knowledge of, or recklessly failed to learn of Lawrence's wrongful acts when they recklessly and negligently continued to work for Znetix and/or allowed their names, services, and work product to be used in furtherance of the Lawrence's wrongful acts, without disclosing those acts or taking steps to prevent them. . . . Furthermore, the Directors and Officers acted in bad faith when they accepted compensation from Znetix for a job they did not intend to properly perform, acting in their own self-interest at the expense of the corporation. . . . In addition, these same actions constituted a breach of fiduciary duty. . . .

ANALYSIS

. . . In Washington and Delaware, directors are protected against general claims for breach of the

continues

duty of care when pursuant to state law a corporation adopts a director protection provision into its articles of incorporation. . . . However, if directors breach the duty of care intentionally, knowingly, or in bad faith, the director protection statutes will not shield them from personal liability . . . Furthermore, when directors breach the duty of loyalty or act in bad faith they are not shielded by the director protection statutes . . . Therefore, to successfully plead breach of fiduciary duty against the Directors in this case, Plaintiff must sufficiently plead breach of the duty of loyalty, bad faith performance of duties, or intentional or knowing breach of the duty of care. . . . Defendants concede the Plaintiff states a negligence claim for a breach of fiduciary duty of care when he claims that "a reasonably prudent director would have discovered and stopped Lawrence's actions." . . . However, Defendants repeatedly state that the Plaintiff pleads insufficient facts to elevate his duty of care claims outside of the protection of the Articles, and that he fails to plead sufficient facts to show breach of the duty of loyalty or bad faith performance of duties, claims that would not be barred by the Articles. . . .

In Washington, plaintiffs may bring a general claim of breach of fiduciary duty against directors as long as they show that the directors' acts or omissions involved . . . (1) "intentional misconduct," (2) "a knowing violation of law," (3) "conduct violating RCW 23B.08.310" (which includes discharging duties in good faith under RCW 23B.08.300) or (4) "any transaction from which the director will personally receive a benefit in money, property, or services to which the director is not legally entitled." Wash. Rev. Code § 23B.08.320. While the Defendants maintain that Plaintiff has not sufficiently pled

that the Directors acted intentionally or knowingly, paragraphs 20 and 21 of the Complaint use those very words with respect to the Defendants' actions or inactions. In addition, the Plaintiff states that the Defendants acted in bad faith in that they knew or should have known of Lawrence's acts. Furthermore, the Plaintiff asserts that the Directors acted in their own self-interest at the expense of the company and its shareholders. In light of the federal rules, these allegations are sufficient to take the Plaintiff's claims out of the realm of the director protection statutes (and the director protection provision of the Articles) as adopted under Washington law.

. . . Similarly, in Delaware, a Plaintiff may bring a general claim of breach of fiduciary duty against a Director as long as he or she claims that Director's acts or omissions involved (i) a breach of the director's duty of loyalty to the corporation or its stockholders; (ii) acts or omissions not in good faith or which involve intentional misconduct or a knowing violation of law; (iii) under § 174 of the Delaware Code (which includes willful or negligent violation of § 160 or 173 regarding voting and trading); or (iv) any transaction from which the director derived an improper personal benefit. 8 Del.C. § 102(a)(7). Defendants claim that under Delaware law, a plaintiff cannot make allegations of "bad faith" without putting forth more facts. However, while in this case, state law determines whether the Plaintiff's claims exist and what defenses are recognized, the federal rules govern the manner in which those claims and defenses are raised . . . Therefore, while Delaware law may dictate the substance of the claim and which defenses exist, the federal rules govern how those

---

CASE *(continued)*
United States District Court, W.D. Washington. Michael Grassmueck, Plaintiff, v. Dwayne Barnett, et al., Defendants.

claims are plead. See id. As discussed above, the Plaintiff has listed several factors to show that the Defendants acted in bad faith, in that they knew or should have known about Kevin Lawrence's wrongful acts. Plaintiff's allegations are sufficient to put the Defendants on notice of the claims against them. . . . In light of the foregoing, the Plaintiff has stated a claim against the directors for breach of fiduciary duty pursuant to Delaware law, and has certainly plead with sufficient particularity under FRCP 8(a).

CONCLUSION

Plaintiff has sufficiently stated claims for negligent or bad faith performance of duties and breach of fiduciary duty under Washington law and under Delaware law. Thus, this Court DENIES Defendants' Motions to Dismiss.

Case material reprinted from Westlaw, with permission.

IN SUMMATION

- The business judgment rule provides that directors cannot be held personally liable for any damages caused to the corporation as the result of informed decisions made by them in good faith.

- While directors are not held personally liable for their poor business decisions made in good faith, personal liability may be imposed on directors under the following conditions:
  - Breach of fiduciary duty by the director
  - Unauthorized act by the director
  - Director negligence
  - Director fraud or other illegal acts
  - Certain circumstances provided for by state statute or the corporation's articles of incorporation.

§ 9.3 DIRECTOR COMPENSATION AND INDEMNIFICATION

Directors are often called upon to serve the corporation in several different ways, and they may or may not be directly compensated by the corporation. This section scrutinizes the compensation of directors and their indemnification for expenses incurred on behalf of the corporation.

DIRECTOR COMPENSATION

Directors may or may not receive compensation specifically for their roles as directors in the corporation. Director compensation is usually set by the board of directors, unless the right to set director compensation is limited to the shareholders by state statute or the corporation's articles of incorporation or bylaws.

Customarily, outside directors are compensated for their time spent attending board meetings and committee meetings, and directors who are officers and employees of the corporation do not receive additional compensation for their roles as directors.

In publicly held corporations, director compensation is usually set by a compensation committee of the board of directors. Director compensation may include monetary compensation as well as stock in the corporation. With passage of the Sarbanes-Oxley Act (discussed in Chapter 11 of this text), directors have increased oversight and reporting responsibilities. Compensation for outside directors has increased accordingly. Outside directors of larger corporations will often receive annual cash retainers, annual stock awards, fees for meeting attendance, and additional compensation for serving as chairman of the board or chairing board committees. The chairman of the audit committee, which has responsibility for overseeing the preparation of the company's annual financial reports, compliance with legal and regulatory requirements, and the qualification of the independent auditor (among other things), is often granted a larger fee for that position.

SIDEBAR

According to a recent study of the 100 largest corporations traded on NASDAQ and the 100 largest corporations traded on the NYSE, the 2010 median value of annual compensation programs for outside directors was $228,540.[21]

INDEMNIFICATION

A director generally has a right to be reimbursed for advances made or expenses incurred by him or her on behalf of the corporation. A director, however, has no right to be reimbursed for expenses incurred by his or her own wrongdoing.

Indemnification refers to the act by which corporations reimburse directors for expenses incurred by them in defending a lawsuit to which they become a party because of their involvement with the corporation. This type of reimbursement is addressed separately by law and usually by the articles and bylaws of the corporation. Typically, the statutes of the state of domicile will set guidelines directing mandatory indemnification under certain circumstances (such as when the director has acted in good faith on behalf of the corporation), and prohibiting indemnification of the directors for expenses incurred due to their own wrongdoing.

Mandatory Indemnification

Statutes typically prescribe certain conditions under which a director must be indemnified, usually when a director is successful in the defense of any proceeding to which he or she was a party because of his or her directorship of the corporation. Section 8.52 of the MBCA addresses mandatory indemnification as follows:

---

§ 8.52 MANDATORY INDEMNIFICATION

A corporation shall indemnify a director who was wholly successful, on the merits or otherwise, in the defense of any proceeding to which he was a party because he was a director of the corporation against reasonable expenses incurred by him in connection with the proceeding.

Optional Indemnification

Statutes typically address several circumstances under which directors may be indemnified if the articles of incorporation or bylaws of the corporation provide for indemnification under those conditions. Provisions such as these require careful drafting of the articles and bylaws to provide the desired indemnification of corporate directors. A corporation normally indemnifies its directors when they have conducted themselves in good faith and when they reasonably believed that their actions were in the best interests of the corporation. In the event of criminal proceedings, directors will often be indemnified, pursuant to the corporation's articles of incorporation or bylaws, if the directors had no reasonable cause to believe that their conduct was unlawful. Again, the articles of incorporation or bylaws of the corporation must provide for this type of director indemnification in accordance with statute, if desired.

   Corporations that do not indemnify their directors in accordance with the corporation's bylaws may be sued for breach of contract. Such was the case in *Salaman v. National Media Corp.*[22] In that case, tried before a Delaware jury in 1994, a director was forced to defend himself in two federal actions because of his position with the corporation. The corporation amended its bylaws after the fact to provide no indemnification for the director and refused to pay the director's attorneys fees and costs, even though the director was not found to be guilty of any wrongdoing. The jury in that case returned a verdict that awarded the director compensatory damages to cover his costs and attorneys' fees, plus an additional $1,550,000 in **punitive damages**.

PUNITIVE DAMAGES
Extra money given to punish the defendant and to help keep a particular bad act from happening again.

Prohibited Indemnification

Statutory provisions such as subsection (d) of § 8.51 of the MBCA make it clear that directors are not to be indemnified for expenses incurred for defense in proceedings involving their own wrongdoing:

   (d) Unless ordered by a court under section 8.54(a)(3), a corporation
        may not indemnify a director:

1. in connection with a proceeding by or in the right of the corporation, except for reasonable expenses incurred in connection with the proceeding if it is determined that the director has met the relevant standard of conduct under subsection (a); or

2. in connection with any proceeding with respect to conduct for which the director was adjudged liable on the basis that he received a financial benefit to which he or she was not entitled, whether or not involving action in the director's official capacity.

IN SUMMATION

- Customarily, outside directors are compensated for their service to the corporation while directors who are employees of the corporation do not receive additional compensation for their service on the board.

- Compensation for directors of publicly held corporations is usually set by a compensation committee of the board of directors.

- State statutes typically provide for mandatory indemnification of directors for legal expenses incurred while defending themselves in a lawsuit where the outcome is favorable.

- State statues may prohibit the corporation from indemnifying a director for lawsuits brought against directors in connection with the corporation's business when the director does not prevail in the suit due to his or her own wrongdoing.

- State statutes may provide for optional director indemnification that may be decided by provisions in the corporation's articles of incorporation.

§ 9.4 ELECTION AND TERM OF DIRECTORS

The board of directors is chosen by vote of the shareholders of the corporation to serve a definite term. In this section we examine the election of directors and the terms they serve.

ELECTION OF DIRECTORS

The directors of a corporation are elected by the shareholders to operate and manage the affairs of the corporation. With the possible exception of statutory close corporations, corporations are required to elect a board of directors and to have a board of directors at all times.

If the first board of directors is named in the articles of incorporation, those directors serve only until the first meeting of the shareholders. At that time, the initial directors are either reelected or replaced by a vote of the shareholders, as discussed in the section "Term of Directors."

Often, especially in smaller corporations, shareholders elect themselves, or some of themselves, to serve as directors and officers of the corporation. In larger firms, outside directors may be elected. These individuals are usually elected to the board because of their unique expertise and management experience.

NUMBER AND QUALIFICATIONS OF DIRECTORS

Traditionally, corporations were required by statute to have at least three directors on their boards. Often, those individuals were required to be shareholders of the corporation or residents of the state of the corporation's domicile, or both. With the relaxation of corporate law restrictions and the advent of the one-person corporation, most state statutes now allow the board of directors to consist of one individual, who may or may not be a shareholder of the corporation or a resident of the corporation's state of domicile.

The MBCA states that the "board of directors must consist of one or more individuals, with the number specified in or fixed in accordance with the articles of incorporation or bylaws."[23] Section 8.02 of the MBCA addresses director qualifications as follows:

§ 8.02 QUALIFICATIONS OF DIRECTORS

The articles of incorporation or bylaws may prescribe qualifications for directors. A director need not be a resident of this state or a shareholder of the corporation unless the articles of incorporation or bylaws so prescribe.

Because the directors typically have the authority to amend the bylaws of the corporation, many state statutes that allow the number of directors to be prescribed by the bylaws of the corporation also place limits on the power of the members of the board of directors to increase or decrease their own number. This may be done by providing for a range in the number of directors in the articles of incorporation of the corporation (which may only be amended with shareholder approval), or by providing that the number of directors may not be increased or decreased by more than a certain amount without shareholder approval.

Directors of professional corporations are usually subject to more specific qualifications, such as being license holders of the profession being practiced by the professional corporation. Federal securities laws and the rules of the stock exchanges may require certain qualifications for the directors of public corporations.

TERM OF DIRECTORS

Under the MBCA, the term of each director expires at the next annual meeting of the shareholders following his or her election, when the director's successor is elected and qualifies. Directors may be reelected for any number of terms.

The shareholders may decide to ensure the continuity of management of the corporation by staggering the terms of the directors. The MBCA provides that corporations may stagger their terms by dividing the total number of directors into two or three groups, as nearly equal in number as possible. These groups may be elected for one-, two-, or three-year terms that will expire in different years. At each annual shareholder meeting, directors will be elected or reelected to fill the positions of the directors whose terms are expiring that particular year.

For example, if a board of directors is eventually to consist of nine directors who will each serve for a two-year term, three of the first directors may be elected for an initial three-year term, three may be elected for an initial two-year term, and three may be elected for an initial one-year term. Annual board of director elections in subsequent years will be required only for the reelection or replacement of those directors whose terms are expiring in that particular year.

Resignation

Directors are generally allowed to resign their positions at any time, in accordance with state statute. Courts have found that directors "may resign at any time and for any reason if they act in good faith and without personal gain."[24] Resignation is generally given by written notice delivered to the chairman of the board of directors or to the board itself.

Removal of Directors

The board of directors is elected to serve the best interests of the corporation and, more specifically, the shareholders. It is generally the shareholders' right to remove any director or directors with or without cause by a majority vote at a special shareholder meeting called specifically for that purpose. Corporations that allow cumulative voting may provide that the number of votes required to elect a director, if cast in favor of retaining a director, is sufficient to keep the director in office. Cumulative voting is discussed in § 9.8 of this text.

The statutes of a few states protect the directors of the corporation by providing that they may not be removed without cause unless specific provisions for removal without cause are included in the articles of incorporation or bylaws of the corporation. Requirements and procedures for removing a director of the corporation may be set by the articles of incorporation or the bylaws of the corporation, so long as those provisions fall within the boundaries of the statutes of the state of domicile.

Under certain circumstances, when it is desirable to remove a director who is a shareholder with sufficient voting power to prevent his or her own removal, or in larger, publicly held corporations where it is impractical to call a special meeting of the shareholders for the purpose of removing a director, it may be necessary or desirable to remove a director by court order. Directors may be removed by a judicial proceeding commenced by the corporation if the court finds that:

1. the director engaged in fraudulent conduct with respect to the corporation or its shareholders, grossly abused the position of director or intentionally inflicted harm on the corporation; and

2. considering the director's course of conduct and the inadequacy of other available remedies, removal would be in the best interest of the corporation.

Filling Vacancies on the Board

In some states a vacancy on the board of directors may be filled by a vote of the remaining directors. Statutes of other states provide that a special meeting of the shareholders may be called to elect a director to fill a vacancy on the board. In either event, the replacement director serves until the next annual meeting of the shareholders, or until his or her successor is duly elected and qualified.

IN SUMMATION

- Corporate directors are elected by the shareholders of the corporation.
- Most, but not all, states permit corporations to have a board of just one director.
- The articles of incorporation typically set forth the number of directors and their qualifications.
- Under the MBCA, the term of each director expires at the next annual meeting of the shareholders following their election, but different terms may be set forth in the articles of incorporation or bylaws.
- Director terms may be staggered so that not all directors are up for reelection in the same year.
- Directors may typically resign by giving notice to the chairman of the board of directors or the board itself.
- Directors may be removed by vote of the shareholders at a special shareholders' meeting.
- Directors may also be removed for cause by a court of law.
- Vacancies on the board may be filled by the vote of shareholders at a special shareholder meeting or, under certain circumstances, by a vote of the remaining directors.

---

§ 9.5 BOARD OF DIRECTORS MEETINGS AND RESOLUTIONS

Most board of directors actions are taken through resolutions passed at board meetings. This section examines the requirements for board of directors meetings, including requirements for holding annual meetings and for notifying the directors about meetings. It also discusses the requisite quorum for passing a resolution of the board of directors at a board meeting, and the minutes taken to formalize the resolutions of the board of directors. Finally, we focus on the ability of directors to act without formal, in-person meetings, through the use of written consents, telephone conferences, and Web conferencing.

BOARD OF DIRECTORS MEETINGS

Corporate directors have no individual power to act on behalf of the corporation. Rather, they act only through the collective action of the board. Under common law, a corporation could act only through its directors at regularly held meetings. Early state statutes almost uniformly required annual meetings of the board of directors and dictated the procedures for calling and holding the annual and special board meetings that were necessary for the directors to take action.

The tendency of modern corporate law, however, recognizes the impracticality of mandatory, formal directors' meetings for all board of director actions, and the following trends have been adopted by most states to make it easier for a board of directors to take action:

1. Annual board of directors' meetings are optional.
2. Action may be taken by the board of directors by a unanimous written consent, signed by each director.
3. Telephonic meetings or Web conferencing by the board of directors are generally acceptable.
4. Notice requirements for board meetings have been relaxed.

Corporations generally address the issue of directors' meetings in the bylaws of the corporation. If regular meetings are desired, the dates are typically set forth, as well as the place and time for the meetings and the notice requirements.

Depending on the degree to which directors are directly involved in the day-to-day business of a corporation, the board of directors may meet regularly for monthly or even weekly meetings. Other corporations, especially large and publicly held corporations, may limit their board of directors meetings to quarterly and annual meetings, including an annual meeting held immediately following the annual meeting of the shareholders of the corporation, as prescribed in the bylaws of the corporation.

ANNUAL MEETINGS OF THE BOARD OF DIRECTORS

Annual board of directors meetings are held for several purposes. In almost all instances, an election is held to reelect or replace the current officers and to ratify the acts of the officers for the past year. In addition, the board of directors reviews important events that have occurred during the past year and acts on those matters requiring attention for the upcoming year.

An agenda for an annual meeting of a board of directors might include several of the following items:

1. Approve the minutes from the last meeting of the board of directors
2. Approve dividends to be paid to the shareholders of the corporation

3. Approve annual reports to be filed with the appropriate state or federal authorities (if required)
4. Review the corporation's financial reports
5. Elect officers of the corporation to serve until the next annual meeting or until their successors are duly elected and qualified
6. Set the compensation of the corporate officers for the succeeding year
7. Approve bonuses for the officers and directors
8. Ratify the acts of the officers and directors for the past year
9. Address any other matters of concern regarding the operation of the business of the corporation

NOTICE OF MEETINGS

Notice of regular and special meetings of the board of directors must be given in accordance with statute and with provisions in the articles of incorporation or bylaws of the corporation. In states that follow the MBCA in this regard, regular meetings of the board of directors may be held without notice, unless the articles or bylaws of the corporation include mandatory provisions for giving notice. Under the MBCA, "Unless the articles of incorporation or bylaws provide otherwise, regular meetings of the board of directors may be held without notice of the date, time, place, or purpose of the meeting."[25] Specific notice requirements for special meetings are usually included in state statutes, as they are in the MBCA, which provides that at least two days' notice of the date, time, and place of the meeting must be given. It is common for the statutes or the corporation's articles or bylaws to require that the purpose of a special meeting of the board of directors be included in the notice of the meeting.

Notice may be given personally, in writing, or by some other method prescribed in the articles of incorporation or bylaws of the corporation, as long as it is permissible under state statute. It is usually permissible to give notice by telephone, e-mail, or by facsimile. Typically, notice requirements set forth in the bylaws of the corporation for annual and special meetings of the board of directors include a statement to the effect that the directors of the corporation may waive any required notice and that a director's attendance at any meeting constitutes a waiver of notice for that meeting. It is not considered a waiver of notice for a meeting if a director attends a meeting only to object to the holding of the meeting or the transaction of business at the meeting.

Exhibit 9-2 shows a form that could be used to give notice of an annual board of directors' meeting.

QUORUM

A quorum is the minimum number of individuals who must be present or represented at a meeting as a prerequisite to the valid transaction of business. Section 8.24 of the MBCA, which is followed by most states in this regard, sets

---

EXHIBIT 9-2 SAMPLE NOTICE OF ANNUAL MEETING OF BOARD OF DIRECTORS

NOTICE OF ANNUAL MEETING OF THE BOARD OF
DIRECTORS OF THE _____ CORPORATION

You are hereby notified that the 2013 Annual Meeting of the Board of Directors of the _____ Corporation will be held at the registered office of the corporation, at _____ [address], _____, on_____, 2013, for the purpose of transacting all such business as may properly come before the board.

Dated the _____ day of _____, 2013.

_____
Secretary

© Cengage Learning 2013

forth the following quorum and voting requirements for taking action at a meeting of the board of directors:

1. A quorum of the board of directors consists of a majority of the fixed number of directors if the corporation has a fixed board size, or a majority of the number of prescribed directors or the number of directors in office immediately before the meeting begins if the corporation has a variable-range size board.

2. The affirmative vote of a majority of the directors present is the act of the board of directors if a quorum is present when the vote is taken.

3. A director who is present at a meeting of the board of directors when corporate action is taken is deemed to have assented to the action taken unless:

   a. The director objects at the beginning of the meeting (or promptly upon arrival) to holding it or transacting business at the meeting;

   b. The director's dissent or abstention from the action taken is entered in the minutes of the meeting; or

   c. The director delivers written notice of dissent or abstention to the presiding officer of the meeting before its adjournment or to the corporation immediately after adjournment of the meeting.

The MBCA provides that the articles of incorporation or the bylaws of the corporation may provide for the following deviations from statutory requirements:

1. The articles or bylaws may require a greater number for the quorum of a meeting.

2. The articles of incorporation may require a lesser number for a quorum of a meeting of the board of directors, so long as the number is no fewer than one-third of the number prescribed by statute.

These requirements for quorum and voting are typical of the laws of many states. However, the quorum and voting requirements vary by state, and state statutes, as well as the corporation's articles of incorporation and bylaws, must always be consulted to see that quorum and voting requirements are complied with for an action of the board of directors to be valid.

Minutes

Complete and accurate minutes must be taken at every meeting of the board of directors. These minutes of the board of directors typically are taken and signed by the secretary of the corporation, who then places them in the corporate minute book, along with a copy of the notice of the meeting that was sent to all directors, any waivers of notice received from the directors, and any other documents pertaining to the meeting. Exhibit 9-3 is a form of annual minutes that could be used for an annual meeting of a board of directors.

Board Actions without Meeting

Modern corporate law recognizes the complexity of assembling a board of directors every time a board resolution is required by allowing for such resolutions to be passed by unanimous written consents and by telephonic meetings or Web conferencing.

Written Consents

As discussed in Chapter 8, the unanimous written consent of the board of directors has become a very popular means for taking a formal action of the board of directors. The unanimous writing can be very useful to corporations whose boards of directors may be spread out over a large geographical distance. Unanimous written consents are also a useful means of formalizing the agreement of directors of smaller corporations who may work side by side every day without ever going through the formality of holding a "meeting" of the board of directors.

Unanimous writings do have some drawbacks, the foremost being that it is generally required that the consent in fact be unanimous. If any one director disagrees with the proposed action, a meeting must be held and a vote must be taken.

Some state statutes provide that, if specifically provided for in the articles of a corporation, the board of directors may take action by a written resolution signed by the number of directors required to take the action if it were voted on at a meeting of the board. Under those circumstances, the signature of all directors may not be required to take action of the board.

Exhibit 9-4 demonstrates how the same resolutions that are typically passed at an annual meeting of a board of directors can be passed by the unanimous written consent of the directors.

EXHIBIT 9-3 SAMPLE MINUTES OF ANNUAL MEETING OF BOARD OF DIRECTORS

MINUTES OF THE ANNUAL MEETING
OF THE BOARD OF DIRECTORS
OF THE_____CORPORATION

The annual meeting of the Board of Directors of the _____

Corporation was held on_____, at the registered office of the corporation at

_____.

Present at the meeting were the following persons:

_____

_____

_____

_____

which constitutes all of the members of the Board of Directors.

The Chairman of the Board of the corporation, _____, presided as chairman of the meeting, and _____acted as its secretary.

The chairman called the meeting to order and stated that a quorum of directors was present for the conduct of business.

The secretary presented and read a waiver of notice to the meeting signed by all directors of the corporation, which was ordered to be made part of the minutes of this meeting.

A discussion was had on the corporation's financial statements, salary increases and bonuses for the officers and directors of the corporation, and dividends to be paid on the outstanding stock of the corporation.

After motions duly made, seconded, and carried, the following resolutions were adopted by the Board of Directors:

RESOLVED, that the financial statements, as presented to the Board of Directors at this meeting, are hereby ratified and approved.

RESOLVED, that due to the profitable nature of the business of the corporation during the past fiscal year, the following officers shall be given a bonus in the following amounts:

_____ $ _____

_____ $ _____

_____ $ _____

_____. $ _____

continues

EXHIBIT 9-3 *(continued)*

RESOLVED, that the following persons are hereby elected to the following described offices, to serve in such capacities until their successors are elected at the next annual meeting and qualify:

Chairman of the Board   _____

Chief Executive Officer   _____

President   _____

Vice President   _____

Secretary   _____

Treasurer   _____ .

Each of the above-named officers accepted the office to which he or she was elected.

RESOLVED, that in consideration of their services to the corporation, the following annual salaries of the officers of the corporation for the fiscal year beginning _____, ____, were approved:

_____ $_____

_____ $_____

_____ $_____

_____ $_____ .

RESOLVED, that a dividend is hereby declared out of the capital surplus of the corporation to be payable to the stockholders of the corporation in an amount of $_____ per share. Such dividend shall be payable on the _____ day of _____, _____, in cash, to shareholders of record on the _____ day of _____, _____. The treasurer of the corporation is hereby authorized to set aside the sum necessary to pay said dividends.

There being no further business before the meeting, it was, on motion duly made, seconded, and unanimously carried, adjourned.

_____
Secretary

© Cengage Learning 2013

Telephonic Meetings

Another modernization of corporate law, which is found in the MBCA and has been followed by most states, allows regular or special meetings of the board of directors to be conducted through "any means of communication by which all directors participating may simultaneously hear each other during the meeting."[26] Statutes in states that follow this provision of the MBCA permit meetings via telephone conference and Web conferencing.

EXHIBIT 9-4 SAMPLE UNANIMOUS WRITTEN CONSENT OF BOARD OF DIRECTORS

UNANIMOUS WRITTEN CONSENT OF THE BOARD OF DIRECTORS OF THE _____ CORPORATION

The undersigned persons, being all of the Directors of the _____

Corporation (hereinafter referred to as the "Corporation"), hereby take the following actions by written consent in lieu of an annual meeting of the Board of Directors, pursuant to _____ [cite pertinent statute].

RESOLVED, that due to the profitable nature of the business of the corporation during the past fiscal year, the following officers shall be given a bonus in the following amounts:

_____	$_____
_____	$_____
_____	$_____
_____	$_____

RESOLVED, that the following persons are hereby elected to the following described offices, to serve in such capacities until their successors are elected at the next annual meeting and qualify:

Chairman of the Board	_____
Chief Executive Officer	_____
President	_____
Vice President	_____
Secretary	_____
Treasurer	_____

RESOLVED, that in consideration of their services to the corporation, the following annual salaries of the officers of the corporation for the fiscal year beginning _____, _____, are hereby approved:

_____	$_____
_____	$_____
_____	$_____
_____	$_____

RESOLVED, that a dividend is hereby declared out of the capital surplus of the corporation to be payable to the stockholders of the corporation in an amount of $____ per share. Such dividend shall be payable on the ____ day of ____, ____, in cash, to shareholders of record on the ____ day of ____, ____. The treasurer of the corporation is hereby authorized to set aside the sum necessary to pay said dividends.

Dated: _____.

_____   _____

_____   _____

CORPORATE MINUTE BOOKS

The minutes and unanimous written consents of both directors' and shareholder meetings are kept in a corporate minute book, along with other important documents regarding the corporation See Exhibit 9-5. The contents of the corporate minute book often include the articles or certificate of incorporation, the corporate charter, the corporate bylaws, the minutes of the organizational meeting, all minutes of meetings of the board of directors or shareholders, and all unanimous written consents of the board of directors and shareholders. One purpose for keeping correct and complete minutes of the board of directors meetings is to put corporate actions in the open and make them accessible to shareholders. Corporate minute books are often kept in the office of the corporate attorney, and the task of keeping the corporate minute book in order and up to date often falls to the paralegal.

EXHIBIT 9-5	CORPORATE MINUTE BOOKS CONTAIN THE CORPORATION'S INCORPORATION DOCUMENTS, MEETING MINUTES, AND UNANIMOUS WRITINGS

Photo Provided by Corpkit Legal Supplies

IN SUMMATION

- Most board of director actions are taken through resolutions passed at board of directors' meetings and evidenced by meeting minutes.
- Annual board of directors' meetings are held to
  - Approve the minutes from the last meeting of the directors
  - Approve shareholder dividends to be paid
  - Approve annual reports

- • Review financial reports of the corporation
- • Elect corporate officers and set their compensation
- • Approve officer and director bonuses
- • Ratify the acts of the officers and directors for the past year

- • Notice of board of directors meetings must be given in accordance with state statutes and the articles of incorporation and bylaws. In most cases, notice requirements are waived by the director's attendance at the meeting.

- • A quorum is the minimum number of directors who must be present at a meeting to take action on behalf of the corporation. The number of directors required for a quorum, which is usually a majority of the directors, is prescribed by state statute and the corporation's governing documents.

- • Board of director actions may be taken through resolutions passed by unanimous written consent signed by all directors.

- • Board of directors' meetings may be held by any means of communication by which all directors participating may simultaneously hear each other during the meeting, including telephone conference or Web conference.

§ 9.6 CORPORATE OFFICERS

Officers are considered to be agents of the corporation. They are individuals elected by the board of directors to oversee the business of the corporation, under the authority of the directors. Officers are usually charged with important managerial functions such as administering and operating the company, recruiting key personnel, and signing checks.[27] An individual may be an officer and a director at the same time; in small corporations, all of the officers are commonly directors of the corporation as well.

This section examines the titles and typical duties of various corporate officers, and the officers' potential for personal liability. The section concludes with a discussion of the election and terms of office of corporate officers.

TITLES AND DUTIES OF OFFICERS

Generally, the officers of a corporation have the titles, duties, and responsibilities assigned to them under the statutes of the state of domicile, by the articles of incorporation or bylaws of the corporation, or by resolution of the board of directors. Statutes may be very specific regarding the required officers of a corporation, naming the titles and duties that must be assumed by officers of a corporation. More often, however, the corporation is given much latitude regarding the officers it chooses and the duties assigned to those officers.

The MBCA addresses the required officers of a corporation in § 8.40:

§ 8.40 REQUIRED OFFICERS

a. A corporation has the officers described in its bylaws or appointed by the board of directors in accordance with the bylaws.

b. The board of directors may elect individuals to fill one or more offices of the corporation. An officer may appoint one or more officers if authorized by the bylaws or the board of directors.

c. The bylaws or the board of directors shall assign to one of the officers responsibility for preparing the minutes of the directors' and shareholders' meetings for maintaining and authenticating the records of the corporation required to be kept under sections 16.01(a) and 16.01(e).

d. The same individual may simultaneously hold more than one office in a corporation.

The MBCA gives further latitude to corporations in assigning duties of the officers. In states following the MBCA, officers have the authority to perform the duties set forth in the bylaws, or prescribed by the board of directors, or at the direction of an officer authorized by the board of directors to prescribe the duties of other officers.

Typically, bylaws of the corporation will set forth:

1. The titles of the officers of the corporation
2. A description of the duties of the officers of the corporation
3. The method for electing the officers of the corporation
4. Any special qualifications for the officers of the corporation

The following subsections list the officers that are often elected to serve a corporation and describe the duties often assigned to those officers, in terms that might be used in corporate articles or bylaws.

Chief Executive Officer

The chief executive officer (CEO) of the corporation shall actively manage the business of the corporation and directly and actively supervise all other officers, agents, and employees. The chief executive officer shall preside over all meetings of the shareholders and the board of directors.

President

The president of the corporation shall preside at all meetings of the board of directors and shareholders in the absence of the chief executive officer. The president shall perform all duties incident to the office of the president as may from time to time be assigned by the board of directors, and shall perform the duties of the chief executive officer in the chief executive officer's absence.

Chairman of the Board

The chairman of the board, if elected, shall be a member of the board of directors and, if present, shall preside at each meeting of the board of directors. The chairman of the board shall keep in close touch with the administration of the affairs of the corporation, advise and counsel with the chief executive officer, and perform such other duties as may from time to time be assigned by the board of directors.

Vice President

Each vice president shall perform all such duties as from time to time may be assigned by the board of directors, the chief executive officer, or the president. At the request of the chief executive officer, the vice president shall perform the duties of the president, in the president's absence, and when so acting, shall have the powers of and be subject to the restrictions placed upon the president in respect of the performance of such duties.

Chief Financial Officer

The chief financial officer of the corporation shall be the custodian of the funds, securities, and property of the corporation. The chief financial officer shall receive and give receipts for moneys due and payable to the corporation from any source whatsoever, and deposit all such moneys in the name of the corporation in such banks, trust companies, or other depositories as shall be selected. The chief financial officer shall perform all of the duties incident to the office, and such other duties as may be delegated by the board of directors. If required by the board of directors, the chief financial officer shall give a bond for the faithful discharge of duties in such sum and with such surety or sureties as the board of directors shall determine.

Treasurer

The treasurer of the corporation, if one is appointed, shall have such duties as the chief financial officer and the board of directors may delegate. The treasurer shall give bonds for the faithful discharge of his or her duties in such sums and with such sureties as the board of directors shall determine.

Secretary

The secretary shall be responsible for the prompt and correct recording of all proceedings of the board of directors. The secretary shall further supervise the preparation and publication of reports, studies, and other publications of the board of directors, and shall prepare such correspondence and perform such other duties as may be required.

Assistant Secretary

The assistant secretary of the corporation, if one is appointed, shall have such duties as the secretary and the board of directors may delegate. The assistant secretary may sign, with the president or vice president, certificates for authorized shares of the corporation.

PERSONAL LIABILITY OF OFFICERS

Under the MBCA, as in most states, officers are generally held to the same standards of conduct as directors of the corporation. Officers not acting in good faith or who breach their fiduciary duty, duty of care, or duty of loyalty, may be subject to personal liability for damages caused to the corporation by them, often in the same manner as directors of the corporation. Some courts have held officers to a higher degree of care than directors, due to responsibilities for the day-to-day operation of the corporation.

ELECTION AND TERM OF OFFICE

Officers are generally elected by a majority of the board of directors at an annual meeting of the board of directors. Traditionally, officers hold their office for one year and are either reelected or replaced at the annual meeting of the board of directors. In recent years, however, key corporate officers have negotiated contracts with the board of directors that extend well beyond the traditional one-year term.

IN SUMMATION

- Corporate officers are agents of the corporation who are elected by the board of directors to oversee the business of the corporation.
- The number and titles of officers elected by the board of directors varies from corporation to corporation, but may include the following:
  - Chief executive officer
  - President
  - Chairman of the board
  - Vice president
  - Chief financial officer
  - Treasurer
  - Secretary
  - Assistant secretary
- Officers have a fiduciary duty to the corporation and its shareholders and are generally held to the same standards of conduct as directors.
- Officers may be held personally liable when not acting in good faith, much like the directors of the corporation.

§ 9.7 WHITE-COLLAR CRIME AND CORPORATE COMPLIANCE PROGRAMS

Each year, **white-collar crime** costs corporations and their shareholders millions of dollars. White-collar crime includes various nonviolent crimes such as theft, fraud, insider trading, embezzlement, bribery, racketeering, and other forms of theft that involve the violation of trust.

WHITE-COLLAR CRIME
Term signifying various types of unlawful, nonviolent conduct committed by corporations and individuals, including theft or fraud and other violations of trust committed in the course of the offender's occupation (e.g., embezzlement, commercial bribery, racketeering, anti-trust violations, price-fixing, stock manipulation, insider trading, and the like). RICO laws are used to prosecute many types of white-collar crimes.

SIDEBAR

According to one report, corporations lose an estimated 5 percent of their annual revenue to fraud.[28]

While losses due to white-collar crime are of great concern to corporate executives, so is the increasing federal prosecution of white-collar criminals and possible criminal liability for corporate executives. White-collar crime can be doubly dangerous for the corporation and its executives. Not only can corporate executives face personal prosecution for criminal violations of the corporation, but the corporation can also be liable for crimes committed by its executives.

Corporate executives who commit white-collar crimes such as insider trading or fraud may face severe penalties, including fines and imprisonment. Corporations that are implicated in white-collar crime can face prosecution and millions of dollars in fines. Because a penalty to the corporation may ultimately mean a penalty to innocent shareholders, in recent years, the tendency has been to also hold the officers and directors responsible for their criminal actions, penalizing the individual wrongdoers instead of just the corporation. In 2010, Thomas J. Petters, founder of Petters Group Worldwide LLC, was sentenced to 50 years in prison for mail and wire fraud, conspiracy, and money laundering. Petters obtained loans from hedge funds and investment groups for the stated purpose of financing sales to well-known, big box retailers, including Costco and Sam's Club. Subsequent investigation revealed that the purchase and sale of merchandise to the retailers were fabricated transactions supported by fictional documentation. The fraud scheme was valued at an estimated $3.4 billion.

In 2009, Bernard Madoff was sentenced to 150 years in prison (the maximum sentence allowed) for orchestrating an estimated $50 billion Ponzi scheme, what has been referred to as "the biggest financial swindle in history."[29] These are just a couple examples of the stiff penalties that have been handed down for white-collar crime.

Although corporate attorneys are generally not too concerned with criminal law, they are becoming increasingly aware of the criminal liability risks faced by their corporate clients. Many are assisting their corporate clients in taking a proactive stance to prevent criminal liability by helping them enact **corporate compliance programs**. Under the U.S. Federal Sentencing Guidelines, consideration is given to corporations that have implemented an effective corporate compliance program. Under the Sentencing Guidelines, to have an effective compliance and ethics program an organization must (1) exercise due diligence to prevent and detect criminal conduct and (2) otherwise promote an organizational culture that encourages ethical conduct and a commitment to compliance with the law.[30]

The seven elements of an effective corporate compliance program are:

1. Standards and procedures must be established to prevent and detect criminal conduct.
2. Board and senior management must be engaged in the design, implementation, and maintenance of compliance and ethics programs.
3. Reasonable efforts must be made not to give substantial authority to any individual the organization knew, or should have known, engaged in past illegal or unethical conduct.
4. Compliance and ethics training must be undertaken at all levels.
5. Efforts must be made to encourage and monitor compliance with, and to evaluate the effectiveness of, the compliance and ethics program.

CORPORATE COMPLIANCE PROGRAM

Programs established by corporate management to prevent and detect misconduct among officers, directors, and employees of the corporation, and to ensure that corporate activities are conducted legally and ethically.

6. Incentives and discipline must be used to promote compliance.

7. The corporation must respond appropriately if and when criminal conduct occurs.

Corporate compliance plans are designed to deter and detect activity that may be grounds for both criminal and civil liability. If the corporation is found guilty of criminal wrongdoing, the fine imposed on the corporation may be reduced if an effective compliance program is in place.

An integral part of any corporate compliance program is the adoption of a code of ethics or code of conduct that applies to the board of directors and executive management of the corporation. Not only is the adoption of such a code considered advisable, but it is also mandatory for public corporations. Rules of the stock exchanges require listed companies to adopt a code of business conduct and ethics for directors and employees. The Sarbanes-Oxley Act (which is discussed further in Chapter 11 of this text) requires the implementation of an internal control system that includes, among other things, a code of conduct or code of ethics, and a procedure for reporting unethical conduct within the corporation.

IN SUMMATION

- White-collar crime includes theft, fraud, insider trading, embezzlement, bribery, racketeering, and other forms of theft that involve the violation of trust.

- Corporate executives who commit white-collar crimes such as insider trading or fraud may face severe penalties, including fines and imprisonment.

- Corporations can be liable for crimes committed by their executives.

- Most corporations adopt corporate compliance and ethics programs to promote ethical conduct and the compliance with law within their corporations.

§ 9.8 SHAREHOLDERS' RIGHTS AND RESPONSIBILITIES

A shareholder, or stockholder, is the owner of one or more shares of the stock of a corporation. The shareholder is, in effect, at least part owner of the corporation itself. The relationship between the shareholder and the corporation is a contractual relationship separate from any other relationship the shareholder may have with the corporation.

There are generally no qualifications to be met by shareholders of business corporations. A shareholder may be an individual or an entity. There are, however, restrictions on who may be a shareholder of special types of corporations. For example, the shareholders of professional corporations may be required to be licensed professionals; shareholders of S Corporations generally must be individuals (and may not be entities).

This section examines the rights of shareholders, including the shareholder's **preemptive right** to purchase shares of the corporation and the shareholder's right to inspect the books of the corporation. We also discuss the possibility of shareholders being held personally liable for the debts and obligations of the corporation.

SHAREHOLDERS' PREEMPTIVE RIGHTS

Preemptive rights give shareholders the opportunity to protect their position in the corporation by granting them the right to purchase newly issued shares of the corporation's stock in an amount proportionate to their current stock ownership.

Shareholders who have preemptive rights are entitled to a fair and reasonable opportunity to purchase newly issued shares sufficient to preserve their proportionate interest in the corporation. This can be very important in smaller corporations with only a few shareholders. For example, suppose a corporation has four shareholders who each own 200 shares of common stock. If the board of directors decides to raise funds by selling an additional 1,000 shares of the corporation, the existing shareholders could lose their voting influence on all decisions to be made by the shareholders of the corporation. If the existing shareholders have been granted preemptive rights by statute or the corporation's articles of incorporation, they must each be given the opportunity to purchase additional shares at a price not less favorable than the price proposed for sale to those outside the corporation. They must each have the opportunity to purchase shares sufficient to maintain their ownership position in the corporation.

In corporations that have many shareholders, especially publicly held corporations, the average shareholder is not as concerned with his or her proportionate ownership of the corporation. In addition, the number of shareholders in larger corporations would make preemptive rights extremely difficult to execute. For these reasons, shareholders in larger and publicly held corporations are very rarely granted preemptive rights.

In some states, statutes provide for no preemptive rights unless specifically provided in the articles of incorporation. However, in other states the opposite is true and shareholders are granted preemptive rights unless the articles of incorporation state otherwise.[31] Under the MBCA, shareholders do not have a preemptive right unless granted in the articles of incorporation. Special consideration must be given to the statutory treatment of preemptive rights in the corporation's state of domicile, and the incorporation documents must be drafted accordingly.

SHAREHOLDERS' RIGHT TO INSPECT CORPORATE RECORDS

The shareholders are the owners of the corporation. As such, they are entitled to certain rights to inspect the corporate records of the corporation. These rights are usually set forth in the statutes of the state of domicile and may be further elaborated on in either the bylaws or the articles of incorporation of the corporation.

Section 16.02 of the MBCA provides that shareholders are entitled to inspect and copy minutes of meetings, accounting records, and shareholder records. To exercise these rights, the shareholder must give the corporation at least five business days' notice, and the inspection and copying must be done during regular business hours. In addition, the demand for inspection must be made "in good faith for a proper purpose" and the demand must describe the shareholder's purpose for the inspection. Further, the records inspected must be directly connected with the shareholder's purpose.

PERSONAL LIABILITY OF SHAREHOLDERS

One of the greatest advantages of incorporating is that the corporate entity shelters the individual shareholders from personal liability for the corporation's debts and obligations. A shareholder's liability generally consists of no more than the consideration paid for the shareholder's own stock in the corporation.

The two most common exceptions to the rule of nonliability occur when the corporate veil is pierced, or when the individual shareholder grants a personal guarantee for some obligation of the corporation. Both of these occurrences are discussed in Chapter 7.

Although, in most cases, the imposition of personal liability stems from disregard of the corporate entity, at times a shareholder can be held personally liable for the tortious acts of the corporation if it can be proved that the shareholder participated in the commission of the action. Certainly, a shareholder who participates directly in the management of the corporation is exposed to a higher degree of risk for the imposition of personal liability than that commonly associated with shareholders.

IN SUMMATION

- Shareholders are the owners of a corporation.
- Shareholders of most corporations may be either individuals or entities.
- Preemptive rights give shareholders a fair and reasonable opportunity to purchase newly issued shares sufficient to reserve their proportionate interest in the corporation.
- Some state statutes provide for no preemptive rights unless specifically provided for in the articles of incorporations.
- Some state statutes provide that shareholders are granted preemptive rights unless the articles of incorporation provide otherwise.
- Shareholders have certain rights to inspect the corporate records of the corporation.
- Shareholders are generally shielded from personal liability for the debts and obligations of the corporation.

§ 9.9 SHAREHOLDER MEETINGS

Shareholder meetings are often the forum for the most important decisions made regarding the future of the corporation (Exhibit 9-6). This section discusses the requirements for annual and special meetings, including their location and notice. It also examines the use of proxies for voting at shareholder meetings and the necessity of having a quorum to adopt a shareholder resolution. We then focus on the actual voting at shareholder meetings, concentrating on the election of directors and other acts that require shareholder approval. This section concludes with an investigation of the documents that formalize shareholder resolutions, the minutes of shareholder meetings, and the unanimous written consents of shareholders.

REQUIREMENTS FOR ANNUAL MEETINGS

Annual meetings of the shareholders are often required under state statutes, although the statutes generally allow that the time and place for holding the annual meeting may be set in the bylaws of the corporation. Statutory provisions for holding annual meetings require only that a meeting of the shareholders be held annually at

EXHIBIT 9-6 SHAREHOLDERS PARTICIPATE IN THE MANAGEMENT OF THE CORPORATION THROUGH PARTICIPATION IN ANNUAL SHAREHOLDER MEETINGS

© Cengage Learning 2013

a time stated in, or fixed by, the bylaws. Under the MBCA, shareholder meetings may be held at any place indicated in the corporate bylaws within or without the state of domicile. If no place for the meeting is set forth in the bylaws, the meeting will be held at the corporation's principal office.

If a corporation does not call an annual meeting of the shareholders in accordance with its bylaws, shareholders are generally granted the statutory right to move for a court order to compel the corporation to call and hold an annual shareholder meeting. Typically, any shareholder may apply to the appropriate court for an order to compel an annual meeting if an annual meeting was not held within 6 months after the end of the corporation's fiscal year, within 15 months after the last annual meeting of the shareholders, or within some other time prescribed by statute.

REQUIREMENTS FOR SPECIAL MEETINGS

It is sometimes necessary or desirable to hold shareholder meetings between the regularly scheduled annual meetings of a corporation. These meetings are referred to as special meetings. Special meetings are held for special and specific purposes. Some of the purposes for holding special meetings include the replacement of directors who have died or resigned before the expiration of their term, the consideration of merger proposals, and other extraordinary events that affect the corporation and require attention prior to the next annual meeting. Business outside the scope of the purpose for which a special meeting is called may not be transacted at a special meeting. Specific requirements as to who may call a special meeting are prescribed by statute and generally may be further specified in the articles of incorporation or bylaws of a corporation. The MBCA provides that a special meeting may be called by the corporation's board of directors, persons holding at least 10 percent of all the votes entitled to be cast on the proposed matter, or persons authorized by the articles of incorporation or bylaws.

LOCATION

Requirements for the location of both annual and special meetings of the shareholders of a corporation are usually outlined in the state's statutes and set forth in further detail in the corporation's bylaws. Modern corporate law tends to be very liberal regarding the location of both annual and special meetings. Requirements in the MBCA for both annual and special meetings dictate only that the meeting "may be held in or out of this state at the place stated in or fixed in accordance with the bylaws."[32] If no provision is made in the bylaws regarding the location of annual and special meetings of the shareholders, the MBCA provides that such meetings must take place at the corporation's principal office.

NOTICE

The actual notice given of an annual shareholder meeting will vary, depending on the size and circumstances of the corporation. In smaller corporations, the notice may be a telephone call to one or two individuals, followed by waivers of notice signed at the actual meeting. Giving notice to shareholders of corporations that have hundreds of shareholders is a much more complicated matter.

First, there must be a determination as to which individuals are entitled to receive notice of the meeting. A record date for determining the shareholders of the corporation is generally fixed by the bylaws of the corporation or by the board of directors. All shareholders of the corporation on the record date are entitled to notice of the annual meeting and are entitled to vote at the meeting. Because any purchasers of stock subsequent to that date, but before the annual meeting, will not be entitled to receive notice of the meeting, the record date must be chosen carefully. The date picked will depend on the number of shareholders and the complexity of sending the notice. State statutes usually place restrictions on the record date as well.

In states following the MBCA, the record date may be fixed by the directors as directed in the bylaws of the corporation. However, the record date cannot be more than 70 days before the annual meeting.

The bylaws of the corporation typically prescribe the exact method for determining the record date. Following is an example of a bylaw paragraph regarding the record date.

EXAMPLE: Fixing of Record Date

Fixing of Record Date. For the purposes of determining the shareholders entitled to notice of or to vote at any meeting of shareholders or any adjournment, or to express consent to corporate action in writing without a meeting, or to receive payment of any dividend, or other distribution or allotment of any rights, or to exercise any rights in respect of any change, conversion or exchange of shares or for the purpose of any other lawful action, the board of directors of the corporation may fix in advance a record date which shall not be more than *[60]* days and, for a meeting of shareholders, not less than *[10]* days, or in the case of a merger or consolidation not less than *[20]* days before the date of the meeting. If no record date is fixed, the record date for the determination of shareholders entitled to notice of or to vote at a meeting of shareholders, shall be the date on which notice of the meeting is mailed, and the record date for the determination of shareholders for any other purpose shall be the date on which the board of directors adopts the resolution relating to that matter. A determination of shareholders of record entitled to notice of or to vote at a meeting of shareholders shall apply to any adjournment of the meeting.[33]

Once the record date has been set, the corporation must prepare a list of shareholders entitled to notice of the meeting. This task typically falls to the individual who is responsible for overseeing all stock transfers of the corporation. In the case of a small corporation, this may be the corporate secretary who keeps the stock certificate ledger in the corporate minute book. In larger corporations, on the other hand, this may be a significant task that is delegated to an individual or another company referred to as the **transfer agent**. The transfer agent is responsible for overseeing all transfers of stock, including the surrender of old stock certificates and the issuance of new ones, and for maintaining an up-to-date record of all shareholders.

The list of shareholders entitled to receive notice of the annual meeting must be made available to all shareholders for inspection for a period prior to the annual meeting that is usually prescribed by statute. Under the MBCA, the shareholder list must be available for inspection by any shareholder beginning two business days after notice of the meeting is given and continuing through the time of the meeting.

Once a record date has been set and a list of shareholders entitled to receive notice has been compiled, the directors, the corporate secretary, or other officer or individual, who is normally designated by the corporation's bylaws, must be sure that proper notice is given to all shareholders entitled to receive notice in compliance with the statutes of the state of domicile and the articles and bylaws of the corporation.

The notice of the meeting typically includes the date, time, and place of the meeting. If the meeting is a special meeting, the purpose for the meeting is given, as required by state statute or corporate bylaws. The statutes of the state of domicile usually provide guidelines within which the notice of shareholder meetings must be given, and the bylaws of the corporation typically set forth a more precise manner for giving notice.

Section 7.05(a) of the MBCA sets forth the notice requirements for annual shareholder meetings:

> (a) A corporation shall notify shareholders of the date, time, and place of each annual and special shareholders' meeting no fewer than 10 nor more than 60 days before the meeting date. Unless this Act or the articles of incorporation require otherwise, the corporation is required to give notice only to shareholders entitled to vote at the meeting.

Exhibit 9-7 shows a sample notice of annual shareholder meeting.

TRANSFER AGENT

A person (or an institution such as a bank) who keeps track of who owns a company's stocks and bonds. Also called a registrar. A transfer agent sometimes also arranges dividend and interest payments.

EXHIBIT 9-7 SAMPLE NOTICE OF ANNUAL SHAREHOLDER MEETING

NOTICE OF ANNUAL MEETING
OF THE SHAREHOLDERS
OF THE _____ CORPORATION

PLEASE TAKE NOTICE that the ___ Annual Meeting of the Shareholders of the _____ Corporation will be held on the _____ day of _____, ____, at ____ P.M., at the office of the corporation at _____, for the purpose of electing directors of the corporation and transacting such other business as may properly come before the meeting.

Dated this ____ day of _____, ____.

_____
Secretary

EXHIBIT 9-8   SAMPLE AFFIDAVIT OF MAILING NOTICE

AFFIDAVIT OF MAILING OF NOTICE
OF ANNUAL SHAREHOLDERS' MEETING
OF THE _____ CORPORATION

STATE OF _____)

) SS

COUNTY OF _____)

_____, being first duly sworn on oath, deposes and says:

I am the Secretary of the _____ Corporation and that on the ____ day of _____, ____, I personally deposited in a post-office box in the City of _____, State of_____, each in a postage-paid envelope, one Notice of the Annual Meeting of the Shareholders of the Corporation to each person whose name appears on the annexed list, and to their respective post-office addresses as therein set forth.

                                                 _____

                                                   Secretary

Subscribed and sworn to before me this ___ day of _____, ___.

_____

Notary Public

© Cengage Learning 2013

    The secretary of the corporation, or any other individual responsible for mailing the notice of annual meeting, will often prepare an affidavit of mailing to evidence the proper mailing of the notice of the annual meeting in a timely manner. Exhibit 9-8 is an example of an affidavit of mailing of notice of annual shareholder meeting.

Waiver of Notice

Shareholders may waive notice of a meeting if they so choose. Typically, shareholders may waive notice by delivering to the corporation a signed waiver of notice, or by attending the meeting. In small corporations with only a few shareholders, the shareholders often meet without ever sending any formal notice. The shareholders' attendance at the meeting, as well as their waiver of formal notice, should be noted in the minutes of the meeting. A shareholder's attendance at any meeting is generally considered to constitute a waiver of notice, unless at the beginning of the meeting, the shareholder objects to the holding of the meeting or the transaction of business at the meeting. The waiver of notice in Exhibit 9-9 is a sample form that could be used at an annual meeting of the shareholders of a small corporation, when notice of the meeting was not mailed.

EXHIBIT 9-9   SAMPLE WAIVER OF NOTICE

WAIVER OF NOTICE OF THE ANNUAL MEETING OF THE SHAREHOLDERS OF THE _____ CORPORATION

We, the undersigned being all of the shareholders of the above corporation, hereby agree and consent to the annual meeting of the shareholders held on the __ day of _____, ____, at ____ P.M., at the office of the corporation at _____, for the purpose of electing directors of the corporation and all such other business as may lawfully come before said meeting and here by waive all notice of the meeting and any adjournment thereof. Dated This ___ day of _____, ___.

_____

_____

_____

_____

© Cengage Learning 2013

PROXIES

A **proxy** is an authorization given by a shareholder to another to exercise the shareholder's voting rights. Shareholders who are unable to attend shareholder meetings may vote through the use of a proxy. The term *proxy* is often used both to define the person who will cast the vote in the place of the shareholder and the document that transfers the voting power to the person voting in place of the shareholder.

A proxy may be a general proxy, which grants the right to vote the shareholder's shares of stock on all matters with limited restrictions, or it may be a limited proxy, which is specific to the situation and authorizes the proxy holder to vote the shares on a specific matter in a specific way.

General proxies are often used by shareholders of small corporations when one shareholder will be unavailable to attend shareholder meetings for an extended period. The shareholder of a closely held corporation may grant the power to vote his or her shares to an individual who is trusted to vote as the shareholder would if he or she were attending the meeting. Exhibit 9-10 is an example of a proxy conveying general authority to the proxy holder.

Larger, publicly held corporations use limited proxies to solicit the vote of shareholders who will not be attending the shareholder meeting. The officers or directors of the corporation send a **proxy statement** to each shareholder along with the notice of a meeting of the shareholders. The proxy statement describes the matters to be voted on at the meeting to give shareholders the information needed to make an informed decision. The proxy statement is accompanied by a proxy form for the shareholder to complete and return to the corporation. The shareholder indicates his or her voting preferences on the proxy and returns it to the corporation. The proxy

PROXY
A person who acts for another person (usually to vote in place of the other person in a meeting the other cannot attend). A document giving that right.

PROXY STATEMENT
The document sent or given to stockholders when their voting proxies are requested for a corporate decision. The Securities and Exchange Commission (SEC) has rules for when the statements must be given out and what must be in them.

EXHIBIT 9-10   PROXY

I, _____ [name of stockholder], do constitute and appoint
_____[name], attorney and agent for me, and in my name,
place, and stead, to vote as my proxy at any stockholders' meetings to be held
between the date of this proxy and_____ [date], unless sooner revoked, with
full power to cast the number of votes that all my shares of stock in _____
[corporation] should entitle me to cast as if I were then personally present, and
authorize _____ [name of proxy] to act for me and in my name
and stead as fully as I could act if I were present, giving to _____[name
of proxy], attorney and agent, full power of substitution and revocation, and I
revoke all previous proxies.

I have executed this proxy on _____[date].

_____
[Signature of stockholder]

Witness: [Signature]

_____

© Cengage Learning 2013

may appoint an officer or director of the corporation to vote as indicated on the proxy
form, unless prohibited by state statute. Often, the voting at the meetings of large
corporations is merely a formality, as the corporation will receive enough proxy votes
prior to the meeting to reach a majority voting consensus.

Rules for the solicitation of proxies and their use by publicly held corporations
are discussed in Chapter 11.

QUORUM

For an action to be taken at a meeting of the shareholders, (1) a quorum must be
present, and (2) a sufficient number of shareholders present must vote in favor of the
proposed action. Unless the articles of incorporation provide otherwise, a majority
of the votes entitled to be cast typically constitutes a quorum. State statutes usually
provide that the articles may prescribe a different quorum within certain limitations.
For action to be taken at a meeting, a majority of the votes cast must be in favor of
the action, unless some other manner for approving an action is prescribed by statute
or set forth in the corporation's articles of incorporation.

VOTING AT SHAREHOLDER MEETINGS

It is generally assumed that each share of stock is entitled to one vote, although
corporations with more than one class of stock may include a class of stock that
has no voting rights or limited voting rights. Votes are cast by ballot at most formal

shareholder meetings, and those ballots, along with the proxies received from shareholders not in attendance, are tallied to determine whether a quorum is present and whether enough votes were received to adopt the proposed resolutions. The ballot used at a shareholder meeting must be in accordance with the provisions of the statutes of the corporation's state of domicile and the corporation's articles and bylaws, and must be in a form that clearly shows the intent of the voting shareholder.

Some public corporations provide for shareholder voting via the Internet or an electronic telephone system. Detailed instructions for voting by these new methods are given on the proxy card and statement that are mailed to all shareholders of record prior to the meeting. Votes received via the Internet or phone can be counted prior to the shareholder meeting.

Voting at meetings held by small corporations may be done by a voice vote that is properly noted by the secretary, or other appointed individual, in the minutes of the meeting.

Although it is generally not required by statute, **inspectors of election** are often appointed to oversee the election of directors at the shareholder meetings of large corporations. These inspectors are impartial individuals who are sworn to oversee the election of directors. Inspectors must determine the number of outstanding shares of stock, the presence of a quorum, and the validity of all proxies used. It is the inspectors' duty to count all votes, whether by ballot or proxy, to determine the outcome of the election.

INSPECTORS OF ELECTION
Impartial individuals who are often appointed to oversee the election of directors at the shareholder meetings of large corporations.

Voting Trusts

To gain voting control of a corporation, a group of shareholders with common interests may decide to form a voting trust. A voting trust is an agreement among shareholders and a trustee whereby rights to vote the stock are transferred to the trustee, and all other rights incident to the ownership of the stock are retained by the shareholders. State statutes generally recognize voting trusts as valid, and the following three criteria are often used to identify a true voting trust:

1. A grant of voting rights for an indefinite period of time
2. Acquisition of voting control of the corporation as the common purpose of the shareholders to the trust
3. Voting rights are separated from the other attributes of stock ownership

Voting Agreements

Shareholders may also seek to gain voting control of a corporation by means of a voting agreement, which is recognized and regulated in the statutes of most states. A voting agreement is an agreement among two or more shareholders that provides for the manner in which they will vote their shares for one or more specific purposes.

ELECTION OF DIRECTORS

The involvement of the shareholder in the corporate affairs is often dominated by the annual meeting of the shareholders, when the shareholders vote for the directors of the corporation. Annual meetings are held for the purpose of electing directors of the corporation and for any other matters that may require the attention or approval of shareholders.

Straight Voting versus Cumulative Voting

CUMULATIVE VOTING

The type of voting in which each person (or each share of stock, in the case of a corporation) has as many votes as there are positions to be filled. Votes can be either concentrated on one or on a few candidates or spread around.

There are two methods of voting for the election of directors: straight voting and **cumulative voting**. Cumulative voting is designed to give minority shareholders a chance to elect at least one director to the board of directors. Incorporators of closely held corporations often opt for cumulative voting to protect minority shareholders. Cumulative voting is rarely seen in larger corporations.

When straight voting is the method used for electing the directors of the corporation, each share of stock may cast a vote for the number of directors that will be elected to the board of directors. For example, if the board of directors is to consist of three individuals, a shareholder voting under the straight method who owns 100 shares in the corporation could cast 100 votes for Candidate 1, 100 votes for Candidate 2, and 100 votes for Candidate 3. If cumulative voting were used, the shareholder would have the same total number of votes to cast (300), but could choose to vote all 300 shares for Candidate 4 if desired, thereby granting the shareholder a better chance of getting at least one director of his or her choice elected to the board of directors. Statutory provisions for cumulative voting vary among the states. The statutes of some states permit cumulative voting unless the articles of incorporation provide otherwise; the statutes of other states prohibit cumulative voting unless it is provided for in the articles of incorporation. In yet another group of states, cumulative voting is mandatory under certain circumstances. State statutes must be checked carefully when the business is incorporated to ensure that the cumulative voting provisions in the articles of incorporation are as the incorporators intend.

OTHER ACTS REQUIRING SHAREHOLDER APPROVAL

In addition to electing the directors of the corporation, shareholders typically vote to ratify acts of the directors taken during the past year, and vote on any other business that might require shareholder approval, such as amendment of the articles of incorporation, issuance of stock, acquisitions and mergers involving the corporation, sale of corporate assets outside the normal course of business, or dissolution of the corporation. See Exhibit 9-11. The state statutes or the articles of incorporation or bylaws of the corporation may set forth other or different actions that require shareholder approval.

MINUTES OF SHAREHOLDER MEETINGS

Just as it is important that minutes be taken at every meeting of the board of directors, accurate minutes of shareholder meetings are crucial. Minutes of the shareholder meetings are typically taken and signed by the secretary of the corporation, who then places them in the corporate minute book, along with a copy of the notice of the meeting that was sent to all shareholders, any waivers of notice received from the shareholders, any proxies received, and any other documents pertaining to the meeting. Exhibit 9-12 is an example of minutes of an annual shareholder meeting.

EXHIBIT 9-11	ACTS THAT TYPICALLY REQUIRE SHAREHOLDER APPROVAL

- Election of directors

- Amendment of bylaws

- Amendment of articles of incorporation

- Issuance of corporate stock

- Mergers and acquisitions

- Sale of corporate assets outside the normal course of business

- Dissolution of the corporation

© Cengage Learning 2013

EXHIBIT 9-12	SAMPLE MINUTES OF ANNUAL SHAREHOLDER MEETING

MINUTES OF ANNUAL MEETING OF
SHAREHOLDERS OF THE _____ CORPORATION

The annual meeting of the Shareholders of the _____ Corporation was held on _____, at the registered office of the corporation at _____.

_____ presided as chairman of the meeting, and acted as its secretary.

The secretary reported that the notice of meeting of the annual shareholders' meeting was mailed in accordance with state statute and with the articles and bylaws of the corporation, and that the notice of meeting and affidavit of mailing were filed in the corporate minute book of the corporation.

The following shareholders were present in person:

_____
_____
_____
_____.

The following shareholders were present by proxy:

_____
_____.

continues

EXHIBIT 9-12 (continued)

It was determined that at least __% of the shareholders were present, and the meeting was called to order.

The reports of the president, secretary, and treasurer were presented to the shareholders, received, and filed in the corporate minute book.

The chairman then called for the election of the directors of the corporation.

Upon motion duly made, seconded, and carried, the following persons were elected to the board of directors, to serve as director of the Corporation until their successors are elected at the next annual meeting and qualify:

_____

_____

_____

_____.

There being no further business before the meeting, it was, on motion duly made, seconded, and unanimously carried, adjourned.

_____
Secretary

© Cengage Learning 2013

Unanimous Consents of Shareholders

The MBCA and the statutes of most states allow shareholders to take action without a meeting through means of a written consent signed by all shareholders entitled to vote on the action. For small corporations, this written consent or "unanimous writing of the shareholders in lieu of meeting" has become an invaluable tool for approving matters that require shareholder consent, especially matters that require attention between the regularly scheduled shareholder meetings.

In recent years, revisions to the MBCA and many state statutes make it clear that the approved action may be evidenced by more than one document, making it even easier to obtain the consent of a large number of shareholders within a relatively short time period. For example, if there are 10 shareholders of a corporation, the corporate secretary can send out 10 identical consents, one to each shareholder, to be signed and returned, instead of having one document that must be circulated to all 10 shareholders for signature.

Exhibit 9-13 shows a sample unanimous written consent of the shareholders in lieu of an annual meeting.

EXHIBIT 9-13 SAMPLE UNANIMOUS WRITING IN LIEU OF ANNUAL SHAREHOLDER MEETING

UNANIMOUS WRITING IN LIEU OF ANNUAL MEETING
OF THE SHAREHOLDERS OF THE _____ CORPORATION

The undersigned, being all of the shareholders of _____ (the "Corporation"), hereby adopt the following resolutions in lieu of holding an annual meeting of the shareholders, effective the _____ day of _____, _____.

RESOLVED, that the following persons are hereby elected to the board of directors, to serve as directors of the Corporation until their successors are elected at the next annual meeting and qualify:

_____

_____

_____

_____.

FURTHER RESOLVED, that the acts of the directors on behalf of the corporation for the past fiscal year are hereby ratified, affirmed, and approved.

_____

_____

_____

© Cengage Learning 2013

IN SUMMATION

- The most important decisions made regarding the future of a corporation are often made at shareholder meetings.
- Annual shareholder meetings may be required by state statutes.
- Special shareholder meetings may be held for special and specific purposes in between annual shareholder meetings.
- Shareholder meetings are typically held at the corporation's principal office, although if permitted by the corporation's articles or bylaws, a different location may be chosen.
- Shareholders are entitled to proper notice of meetings pursuant to state statute and the articles and bylaws of the corporation.
- Notice of shareholder meetings of smaller corporations is often very informal, with shareholders waiving formal notice by their attendance at the meeting.
- Notice of shareholders meetings for larger, publicly held corporations is much more formal.

- Pursuant to the MBCA, shareholders entitled to vote at a meeting must receive notice of the date, time, and place of each annual and special shareholder meeting no fewer than 10 nor more than 60 days before the meeting date. Shareholders may waive notice of a meeting by delivering a signed waiver of notice to the corporation or by attending the meeting.
- A proxy is an authorization given by a shareholder to another to exercise the shareholder's voting rights.
- A general proxy grants the holder the right to vote the shareholder's shares of stock on all matters with limited restrictions.
- A limited proxy grants authority to the proxy holder to vote the shares on a specific matter in a specific way.
- A proxy statement may be used to solicit the vote of shareholders who will not be attending the shareholder meeting.
- For an action to be taken at a shareholder meeting, a quorum must be present and a majority of the votes entitled to be cast must be voted in favor of the proposed action.
- Unless a corporation has more than one class of votes with different voting rights, each share of stock is entitled to one vote.
- Large, publicly held corporations may allow their shareholders to vote via the Internet or an electronic telephone system.
- A group of shareholders with common interests may decide to form a voting trust or enter into a voting agreement to gain voting control of a corporation.
- Cumulative voting is designed to give minority shareholders a chance to elect at least one director to the board by allowing shareholders to cumulate their votes for one or more directors.
- Minutes of shareholder meetings are taken to evidence the actions taken at the meeting.
- In lieu of a meeting, shareholders may take action by a unanimous written consent signed by all shareholders of the corporation.
- In some states, shareholder action may be taken by a written resolution signed by the holders of the number of shares that would be required to pass the resolution at a meeting—less than unanimous.
- Certain acts of the corporation require shareholder approval, including:
  - Election of directors
  - Amendment of bylaws
  - Amendment of articles of incorporation
  - Issuance of corporate stock
  - Mergers and acquisitions
  - Sale of corporate assets outside the normal course of business
  - Dissolution of the corporation

§ 9.10 RESTRICTIONS ON TRANSFER OF SHARES OF CORPORATE STOCK

The freedom to transfer corporate stock without restrictions has always been considered a basic shareholder right. However, recognizing the value of limited restrictions on the transfer of stock under certain conditions, the courts have found that "the right to transfer shares of stock may be restricted by agreement of the shareholders so long as such restriction is not contrary to public policy as being in restraint of trade."[34]

This section focuses on the restrictions placed on stock transfers by shareholder agreements and considerations in drafting shareholder agreements. The section concludes with a look at other restrictions that may be placed on share transfers.

SHAREHOLDER AGREEMENTS RESTRICTING STOCK TRANSFERS

The shareholders of a corporation may want to place certain restrictions on the transfer of shares to protect their status in the corporation and to monitor the inclusion of new shareholders in the corporation. Shareholders of a close corporation may wish to have the option to purchase shares of a withdrawing shareholder before the shares are sold to an outsider. Also, shareholders looking toward the future may want to ensure a market for their stock when they decide to sell. For all these reasons, shareholders of a corporation may agree to place restrictions on the sale of their stock.

Restrictions on the transfer of stock may be placed in the articles of incorporation, in the bylaws of the corporation, or in a separate shareholder agreement, or **buy-sell agreement**, as it may be called. Restrictions on the transfer of stock of statutory close corporations may also be prescribed by statute.

BUY-SELL AGREEMENT
An agreement among partners or owners of a company that if one dies or withdraws from the business, his or her share will be bought by the others or disposed of according to a prearranged plan.

Agreements Granting Option to Purchase Stock

Shareholder agreements that give the corporation or shareholders the option to purchase the shares of any shareholder upon the happening of a specified event are the least restrictive type of agreement. This sort of agreement does not obligate the shareholders to purchase the shares of a selling shareholder, nor does it guarantee a market for a shareholder who desires to sell his or her shares.

Agreements Mandating the Purchase of Stock

Corporate shareholders may decide it is in their best interests to enter into mandatory stock purchase agreements. This type of agreement among the shareholders obligates the corporation or other shareholders to purchase the shares of a deceased or withdrawing shareholder upon the happening of a particular event, at a preestablished price. This type of agreement guarantees a market for the shares of a shareholder who wishes to withdraw from the corporation, upon certain conditions.

CONSIDERATIONS IN DRAFTING SHAREHOLDER AGREEMENTS

The shareholder agreement, or buy-sell agreement, need not be exclusively for the optional or mandatory purchase for shares. It may be a hybrid of these two types of agreements, giving shareholders the option to purchase shares of a withdrawing shareholder under certain circumstances and mandating purchase under other circumstances.

Events Triggering Agreement

The events that trigger a buy-sell agreement will vary, depending on the purpose and intent of the shareholders. Buy-sell agreements may be triggered by any of the following events:

1. Death of a shareholder
2. Retirement of a shareholder-employee
3. Disability of a shareholder-employee
4. Proposed sale by any shareholder to a third party

Purchase Price

The purchase price found in buy-sell agreements that mandate the purchase of stock of a shareholder upon the happening of a specific event is one of the most important elements in the agreement. The agreement rarely sets a specific price for the stock purchase, but rather specifies a formula for determining the price of the stock. Determining the price of stock of a closely held corporation can be very difficult, because there is no "market value" for stock.

Shareholders may agree on a price per share in a supplement to the buy-sell agreement. This supplement is then updated periodically, with the most recent supplement providing the price in effect in the event the agreement is activated. The corporation may use the book value of the stock or the best offer of a third party to determine the price. Other formulas may be used so long as the formula is agreed upon by all shareholders in the buy-sell agreement.

Insurance Funding

Shareholders usually recognize that the mandated buyout of a deceased shareholder could impose a severe financial hardship on the corporation, so they seek to cover that loss by purchasing life insurance on the life of major shareholders. The proceeds of the life insurance policy can then be used to purchase the deceased's shares of stock from the estate.

OTHER RESTRICTIONS ON SHARE TRANSFERS

Corporate shareholders may find it necessary or desirable to place restrictions on the transfer of corporate stock for reasons other than monitoring the ownership of the corporation and ensuring a market for the corporation's stock. For example, shareholders of S Corporations may have to place restrictions on the transfer of corporate stock to remain in compliance with the S Corporation requirements. Large corporations and publicly held corporations may find it necessary to restrict the transfer of corporate shares in order to comply with securities regulations.

In any event, any restriction on the transfer of shares of stock must be considered reasonable and generally must be approved by all shareholders of the corporation. In addition, the specific restriction must be located on the face or reverse of the stock certificate of any affected shares.

IN SUMMATION

- Generally, corporate stock may be transferred freely, without restrictions.
- Shareholders may enter into agreements to restrict the transfer of stock to protect their status in the corporation and monitor the inclusion of new shareholders.
- Certain shareholder agreements give the corporation or shareholders the option to purchase shares of any shareholder upon the happening of a specified event.
- Shareholder agreements may provide for the mandatory purchase of a shareholder's stock upon the happening of a specified event, such as the shareholder's death, retirement, disability, or withdrawal from the corporation.
- The purchase price pursuant to buy-sell agreements is often established pursuant to a formula set forth in the agreement.
- The purchase of a shareholder's stock on the death of the shareholder is often funded by proceeds of life insurance purchased by the corporation on the life of each shareholder.

§ 9.11 SHAREHOLDER ACTIONS

There are three general types of shareholder lawsuits:

1. Direct shareholder actions
2. Representative actions
3. Derivative actions

The nature of and requirements for each of these types of actions are discussed briefly in this section.

DIRECT ACTIONS

An individual shareholder who is injured by an action of the corporation may bring suit against the corporation for damages. An individual shareholder may maintain a suit against a corporation in much the same way as any other individual would.

DIRECT ACTION

A lawsuit by a stockholder to enforce his or her own rights against a corporation or its officers rather than to enforce the corporation's rights in a derivative action.

Direct actions are brought only when one or a few shareholders allege that the action committed by the corporation is a direct wrong to the individual shareholder(s) and that such wrong does not affect the other shareholders. Following are some examples of the types of actions that may be appropriately brought as a direct shareholder lawsuit:

- Action based on a contract made with one or more individual shareholders
- Action for a tort where one or more individual shareholders suffer personal damages
- Action for the refusal to recognize the valid transfer of stock of one or more shareholders
- Action for the wrongful denial of one or more shareholders' rights to subscribe to additional stock
- Action relating to one or more shareholders' rights to vote at a shareholders' meeting

REPRESENTATIVE ACTIONS

REPRESENTATIVE ACTION

A lawsuit brought by one stockholder in a corporation to claim rights or to fix wrongs done to many or all stockholders in the company.

Representative actions are actions in which the parties who have a direct claim against a corporation are too numerous to be joined in a direct action.[35] One party or a few are permitted to sue on behalf of all shareholders who are similarly situated. The representative action is typically brought by a shareholder on behalf of the shareholder and his or her entire class of shareholders against the corporation.

Any benefit derived from a representative action belongs to the shareholders. Some typical representative actions include actions against the corporation and its management for fraudulent public statements made affecting the stock price, actions to compel the payment of dividends, and actions to preserve shareholders' voting rights.

DERIVATIVE ACTIONS

DERIVATIVE ACTION

A lawsuit by a stockholder of a corporation against another person (usually an officer of the company) to enforce claims the stockholder thinks the corporation has against that person.

A shareholder's **derivative action** is an action brought by one or more shareholders to enforce a right or remedy of the corporation when the officers of the corporation who would normally bring such a suit fail or refuse to take appropriate action on behalf of the corporation.

Shareholders may prosecute derivative lawsuits on behalf of the corporation to protect their own interests in the corporation, especially if they feel that the directors of the corporation are not acting with the corporation's best interests in mind. The derivative action is distinguished from other types of shareholder lawsuits in that the cause of action belongs to the corporation, not to individual shareholders. Although most derivative actions are against corporate management for waste of corporate assets, self-dealing, or mismanagement, it is also possible for shareholders to maintain derivative actions against unrelated third parties to enforce rights of the corporation. Any benefit derived from a derivative action belongs to the corporation itself and not the shareholders.

In states that follow the MBCA, to have standing to bring a derivative suit on behalf of a corporation the individual must be (1) a shareholder of the corporation who (2) fairly and adequately represents the interests of the corporation in enforcing the corporation's rights.[36]

Many states have enacted legislation in an attempt to alleviate unnecessary litigation. Most state statutes require shareholders to make a good-faith attempt to prompt the corporation to take action on its own behalf to prevent or remedy the injustice that the shareholders are seeking to cure, before a derivative action may be commenced. Section 7.42 of the MBCA, which is typical of such statutory provisions, sets forth strict requirements for the commencement of derivative suits.

See Exhibit 9-14 for a summary of shareholder lawsuit characteristics.

EXHIBIT 9-14 SHAREHOLDER LAWSUIT CHARACTERISTICS

Type of Shareholder Lawsuit	Individual/Direct	Representative	Derivative
Lawsuit brought on behalf of	Lawsuit brought on behalf of individual shareholder.	Lawsuit brought on behalf of a class or group of shareholders.	Lawsuit brought on behalf of corporation.
Sample of the types of suits that may be brought	• Breach of contract between corporation and individual shareholder • Disputes regarding voting rights • Torts that have caused shareholder damages	• Suit to enforce voting rights of minority shareholders • Disputes regarding dividends payable to a class of shareholders • Disputes regarding distribution of assets on dissolution of corporation	• Suits against third party for trespass or conversion of corporation property • Claim of waste of corporate assets by corporate management • Claim of impairment or destruction of the corporation

© Cengage Learning 2013

§ 7.42 DEMAND

No shareholder may commence a derivative proceeding until:

1. a written demand has been made upon the corporation to take suitable action; and
2. 90 days have expired from the date the demand was made unless the shareholder has earlier been notified that the demand has been rejected by the corporation or unless irreparable injury to the corporation would result by waiting for the expiration of the 90-day period.

IN SUMMATION

- Direct shareholder actions may be brought by shareholders when one or a few shareholders allege that an action by the corporation has been a direct wrong to the individual shareholders and does not affect the other shareholders.

- Representative actions may be brought by shareholders when the parties having a direct claim against the corporation are too numerous to be joined in a direct action.

- A derivative action is brought by one or more shareholders on behalf of the corporation to enforce a right or remedy of the corporation.

§ 9.12 THE PARALEGAL'S ROLE

Whether working in a law firm or in a corporation, paralegals are often asked to assist the attorneys and the corporate clients in complying with statutory requirements for corporate formalities. This can include extensive research to ascertain the rights, duties, and potential for personal liability of the corporation's officers, directors, and shareholders. Statutory research may also be necessary to ensure that the formalities for director and shareholder meetings and elections are being complied with.

BOARD OF DIRECTOR AND SHAREHOLDER MEETINGS

Paralegals who work for corporations, especially publicly held corporations, may be very involved in preparing for meetings of the board of directors. They may also be asked to assist with the many tasks undertaken to hold the annual shareholder meeting. Specifically, the paralegal may be involved in the following:

- Researching statutes and corporate bylaws to determine requirements for annual meeting
- Preparing notices and proxy statements
- Arranging for the mailing of notices of the meeting and proxy materials
- Making physical arrangements for the meeting, including reserving a place for the meeting and making sure all needed equipment and refreshments are available
- Arranging for press coverage
- Coordinating travel arrangements for the directors

CORPORATE MINUTE BOOK REVIEW AND UPDATING

Corporate paralegals who work in law firms are often assigned the task of maintaining and updating the corporate minute books that the law firm maintains for its corporate clients.

Paralegals may be asked to draft letters to all corporate clients, reminding them of the statutory annual meeting requirements and the annual meeting requirements established by the articles of incorporation or bylaws of the corporation. Paralegals frequently follow up with each client by drafting and sending out notices of annual meetings and preparing minutes for the minute book, or by drafting written consents in lieu of meetings of the board of directors of the corporation and seeing to their execution.

Paralegals who work in-house, in corporate legal departments, are often responsible for maintaining the corporate minute books for the corporation and its subsidiaries. When conducting a thorough review of a corporate minute book, you should answer the following questions:

Incorporation Documents

- What is the exact name of the corporation?
- What was the corporation's date of incorporation?
- What is the corporation's registered office address, and who is the registered agent?
- How many shares of each type of stock is the corporation authorized to issue?
- Is the corporation in compliance with any statutory incorporation formalities concerning publication of notice of incorporation or filing notice of incorporation at the local level?
- Has the corporation received certificates of authority to transact business in any foreign state in which it transacts business?
- Does the minute book contain other pertinent incorporation documentation required by the statutes of the corporation's state of domicile?

Corporate Bylaws

- How many directors are required under the bylaws? Does the corporation currently have the requisite number of directors?
- If the fiscal year is set forth in the bylaws of the corporation, is it correct?
- Are other procedures for managing the corporation's affairs, as set forth in the bylaws, being complied with?

Corporate Minutes

- Are there any missing minutes (for example, minutes not prepared for a certain year or years)?
- Are there minutes or unanimous writings of the shareholders electing the current directors of the corporation?
- Are there minutes or unanimous writings of the directors electing the current officers of the corporation?
- Are there any missing signatures (for example, all elected directors must sign unanimous writings of the board of directors)?
- Have resolutions made by the board of directors or shareholders been carried through?

Stock Certificates

- Are the certificates, subscription agreements, and ledgers consistent with each other?
- Are all stock certificates signed and in place?
- Is there a record of the location of all stock certificates not kept in the minute book?
- If the corporation has a shareholder agreement, do the stock certificates have the appropriate legends concerning restrictions on their transfer?

CORPORATE PARALEGAL PROFILE
Marianne Stark Bradley

The opportunity to work with entrepreneurs to accomplish their goals for their technology is truly a lot of fun.

NAME Marianne Stark Bradley
LOCATION Palo Alto, California
TITLE Senior Legal Assistant
SPECIALTY Blue Sky Specialist
EDUCATION Bachelor of Arts in Political Science, UC Berkeley; Paralegal Generalist Program, University of San Diego
EXPERIENCE 29 years

Marianne Stark Bradley is a senior legal assistant with the Palo Alto office of Wilson Sonsini Goodrich & Rosati, P.C., a firm with 659 attorneys and 153 paralegals spread across seven offices in the United States, an office in Hong Kong, and an office in Shanghai, China. Marianne works directly with six partners and 10 associates. She also serves as the blue sky resource to all corporate attorneys and paralegals in the firm as needed.

Marianne's responsibilities include the incorporation of new businesses and intake of new clients. She works with both public and privately held corporations to prepare board of director and shareholder resolutions, proxy materials, and financing documents. Marianne helps to maintain the corporate minute books and make sure they are kept upto date. This requires drafting minutes for each meeting of the board or shareholders to be approved at the next meeting and ensuring that executed copies of such minutes are contained in the company's minutes books. She also reviews the articles and bylaws for each corporation to see that they reflect the current status of the corporation and drafts any amendments that may be necessary for approval by the board of directors and shareholders. In addition, Marianne acts as transfer agent for each company. She prepares the stock certificates and confirms that the capitalization of the company is current and correct.

Because of her experience in the securities area, Marianne is also frequently called on by the attorneys in the firm to assist both private and public clients in their compliance with securities laws and regulations, especially blue sky laws and Section 16 requirements.

continues

CORPORATE PARALEGAL PROFILE
Marianne Stark Bradley (continued)

Marianne enjoys the direct contact she has with clients. She is able to assist them with many issues and questions without direct attorney involvement. With her level of experience, she is given the opportunity to handle various projects that are typically assigned to attorneys. Often, she can assist clients more efficiently and cost-effectively than attorneys can. Marianne feels that every transaction is a learning experience and that the opportunity to work with entrepreneurs to accomplish their goals for their technology is truly a lot of fun.

Marianne is a member of the National Association of Legal Assistants and the Santa Clara County Paralegal Association. She is also a member of the San Francisco Bar Association and an associate member of the American Bar Association.

Marianne's advice to new paralegals?

- *Always ask questions. Become a sponge.*
- *Never leave an attorney's office without complete understanding of the project that you've been given.*
- *When called into an attorney's office, always have paper and a pencil/pen in hand.*
- *Always ask when the project is due, and if you have a conflict in your schedule due to another project, let the assigning attorney know in advance.*

For more information on careers for corporate paralegals, log in to http://www.cengagebrain.com to access the CourseMate website that accompanies this text; then see the Corporate Careers Section.

ETHICAL CONSIDERATION

Attorneys, paralegals, and everyone involved in the legal profession have a duty to maintain the integrity and public respect for the legal profession. In addition to following the rules of professional conduct prescribed for attorneys, paralegals, and judges, those involved in the legal profession must remain honest, stay within the law, and avoid the appearance of impropriety. They must avoid misconduct and report any serious misconduct they witness within their profession.

Some of the consequences to unethical attorney behavior include:

- *Reprimand* by the bar association or disciplinary board
- *Probation* allowing the attorney to continue practicing law with supervision
- *Suspension* of an attorney's license to practice law for a set amount of time
- *Disbarment* revoking the attorney's license to practice law

continues

ETHICAL CONSIDERATION
(continued)

- *Civil lawsuit* brought by any party harmed by the attorney's unethical behavior

- *Criminal prosecution* when the attorney's unethical behavior is also illegal behavior

Although paralegals may not be disbarred nor have their licenses suspended, there are also consequences to the unethical behavior of paralegals. It is important to all paralegals to maintain respect for the profession, and the unethical behavior of paralegals reflects poorly on the entire profession. Some of the consequences paralegals may face for unethical behavior include:

- *Loss of respect.* The unethical paralegal will often lose the respect of his or her coworkers and others within the legal community.

- *Loss of clients.* A paralegal's unethical behavior can cause the law firm he or she works for to lose clients.

- *Disciplinary action against a responsible attorney.* The paralegal's supervising attorney is usually considered to be responsible for the actions of the paralegals. Unethical behavior by a paralegal can lead to disciplinary action against the paralegal's supervising attorney.

- *Loss of employment.* A paralegal who acts unethically may lose his or her job.

- *Criminal prosecution.* As with an attorney, if the paralegal's unethical behavior is also illegal behavior, the paralegal may be subject to criminal charges.

- *Civil lawsuits.* If a paralegal's unethical behavior causes financial damages to a client or other party, the party who suffered the damages may bring a lawsuit against the paralegal's law firm and the paralegal.

- *Discipline by paralegal association.* Paralegals who are members of a local or state paralegal association may find that they are subject to discipline for breaching the rules of ethics of that association.

To be sure your behavior is always ethical, you must be familiar with the rules of ethics in your state and you must follow those rules.

For more information on ethics for corporate paralegals, including links to the NALA and NFPA codes of ethics, log in to http://www.cengagebrain.com to access the CourseMate website that accompanies this text; then see the Ethics Section.

§ 9.13 RESOURCES

STATE STATUTES

By far the most important resource in working with corporate organizational matters is the statutes of the state of domicile. The corporate paralegal should be so familiar with state statutes that he or she can quickly locate statutory provisions regarding the organizational formalities that must be complied with by corporations. Links to these statutes may be accessed from CourseMate.

CONTINUING LEGAL EDUCATION MATERIALS

Other important resources are the state-specific corporate procedure manuals that are available for every state, and continuing education materials published on a state-by-state basis. Much of this information is also available online.

CORPORATE RESOLUTION FORMS

Generic forms for board of director and shareholder resolutions and other documents related to the corporate organization and corporate maintenance can be found online from several different sources. Before any of these forms are used, they must be carefully reviewed and edited to be certain that they meet the statutory requirements of your state and that they meet the corporation's intended purpose. Links to several websites that provide such forms for downloading may be accessed through CourseMate.

SUMMARY

- Corporations act through officers and directors who serve as agents of the corporation.
- State statutes grant the directors the authority to act on behalf of the corporation.
- In most corporations, the shareholders elect directors at annual meetings and the directors elect the officers of the corporation.
- Directors may delegate certain authority to officers, but they are generally responsible for the acts of the officers they appoint.
- Directors may delegate authority to one or more committees that are comprised of members of the board of directors.
- Directors owe a fiduciary duty, a duty of care, and a duty of loyalty to the corporation and its shareholders.
- The business judgment rule provides that directors cannot be held personally liable for the poor outcome of their informed decisions made in good faith.
- Indemnification refers to the act by which corporations reimburse officers and directors for expenses incurred by them in defending lawsuits to which they become a party due to their involvement with the corporation.

- The number of directors a corporation has may be set by the articles of incorporation, the bylaws, or by corporate resolution (depending on state statute).

- In lieu of holding a meeting, the board of directors and the shareholders may take action by a written resolution signed by all directors or all shareholders.

- The corporate secretary generally maintains a corporate minute book that contains the corporation's articles of incorporation, bylaws, minutes of meetings of both shareholders and directors, stock certificates, and a ledger of all issued shares of stock.

- Preemptive rights give shareholders the opportunity to protect their position in the corporation by giving them priority to purchase newly issued shares of the corporation.

- A corporation's officers may include a chief executive officer, chairman of the board, president, one or more vice presidents, chief executive officer, treasurer, assistant treasurer, secretary, and assistant secretary.

- Some of the most important decisions made on behalf of the corporation are made by the vote of shareholders at annual shareholder meetings.

- Shareholder meetings are typically called by the directors of the corporation. However, if the directors fail to call the meeting within a reasonable time, state statutes and the corporation's bylaws usually provide a means for the shareholders to call an annual meeting.

- Special meetings of the shareholders may be called to transact extraordinary business that requires shareholder approval.

- Shareholders may grant proxies to others to vote in their place at shareholder meetings.

- Cumulative voting grants each shareholder as many votes for each share of stock as there are directors to be elected. Shareholders may cumulate their votes for one director or spread them among the directors to be elected. Cumulative voting rights are designed to give minority shareholders a chance to elect at least one director to the board.

- Corporate actions that typically require shareholder approval include: the election of directors, the adoption of amendments to the bylaws or articles of incorporation, the issuance of corporate stock, the approval of mergers and acquisitions, the sale of corporate assets, and the dissolution of the corporation.

- Shareholders may enter into agreements to restrict the transfer of corporate stock and to provide a market for their stock in the event of their retirement or death.

- Derivative actions are lawsuits brought by shareholders on behalf of the corporation.

- Paralegals often assist with preparing minutes of board of directors' and shareholders' meetings, with preparation for annual meetings, and with corporate minute book maintenance.

■ REVIEW QUESTIONS

1. Where does a committee get its authority? Who is ultimately responsible for the acts of the committee?

2. What are the three types of duties a director owes to the corporation?

3. If a board of directors, exercising due care, makes a poor business decision that results in a substantial financial loss to the corporation, can the shareholders of the corporation look to the directors' personal assets to recover their damages? What if one director withheld information from the other directors and personally benefited from the decision?

4. Suppose that Albert is on the board of directors of Acme Sailboard Company, Inc. As the result of a contract dispute, Acme Sailboard Company, Inc., and Albert are both named in a lawsuit brought by one of their suppliers. If Albert is found at the trial to be innocent of any wrongdoing, who is responsible for paying his attorneys' fees and legal expenses?

What if it is determined at trial that there has been an illegal conversion of funds by Albert that resulted in the lawsuit?

5. Can a corporation incorporated under a state following the MBCA consist of one individual who is an officer, director, and shareholder?

6. Must all corporations have a board of directors?

7. Who typically elects the officers of the corporation?

8. Under the MBCA, what is the minimum number of votes required to pass a resolution of the shareholders if 1,000 shares of the corporation's stock have been issued?

9. If the shareholders of a corporation feel that their stock has lost its value due to the mismanagement and/or misconduct of the corporation's officers and directors, what, if any, recourse do they have?

10. Who typically benefits when cumulative voting for the directors of a corporation is allowed?

■ PRACTICAL PROBLEMS

1. How do the statutes in your state address preemptive rights for shareholders? Locate the pertinent section in your state's statutes to answer the following questions:

   a. In what section of your state's statutes are preemptive rights addressed?
   b. If a corporation's articles of incorporation are silent on the issue, are the shareholders granted preemptive rights?

2. How do the statutes in your state address cumulative voting rights for the directors of a corporation? Locate the pertinent section in your state's statutes to answer the following questions:

   a. In what section of your state's statutes is cumulative voting for directors addressed?

   b. If a corporation's articles of incorporation are silent on the issue, are the shareholders granted cumulative voting rights?

3. How does your state's business corporation act treat written consents in lieu of meetings? Is it ever permissible for a board of directors to take action by means of a consent signed by less than all of the directors? If yes, under what circumstances? Is it ever permissible for a shareholder resolution to be passed by means of a consent signed by less than all of the shareholders? If yes, under what circumstances?

■ EXERCISE IN CRITICAL THINKING

Why is the business judgment rule so important to both directors and shareholders? What would be some possible consequences if directors could not rely on the business judgment rule?

■ WORKPLACE SCENARIO

Assume that one year has passed since you assisted with the incorporation of our fictitious corporation, Cutting Edge Computer Repair, Inc. It is time for annual meetings of the shareholders and directors of the corporation. Bradley Harris and Cynthia Lund have met again with Belinda Murphy to discuss the progress of the business over the past year and the formalities required for holding annual meetings. Belinda has decided, with her clients, that it will not be necessary to hold a formal meeting. Belinda will instead prepare unanimous writings of the directors and the shareholders of Cutting Edge Computer Repair, Inc., to approve certain transactions that have occurred during the past year and reelect officers and directors.

Using the information in Appendix B-3 of this text and the forms and examples throughout this chapter, prepare unanimous writings of the board of directors and shareholders to approve the following resolutions:

Unanimous Written Consent of the Shareholders

1. Reelect the current directors of the corporation

2. Approve and ratify the acts of the directors for the previous year

Unanimous Written Consent of the Board of Directors

1. Reelect the current officers of the corporation

2. Approve salaries of the officers of the corporation for the next year in the amount of $75,000 each

3. Approve and ratify the acts of the officers for the previous year

Portfolio Reminder

Save the documents prepared for the Workplace Scenario exercises in each chapter, either in hard copy or electronically, to build a portfolio of documents to be used for job interviews or as sample documents on the job. At this point, your portfolio should include the following:

- Power of attorney
- Application for assumed name
- Application for federal employer identification number
- Application for state employer identification number
- Partnership statement of authority
- Limited partnership certificate
- Limited liability partnership statement of qualification
- Articles of organization
- Subchapter S election by small business corporation, Form 2553
- Articles of incorporation
- Unanimous written consent of shareholders
- Unanimous written consent of the board of directors

END NOTES

1. California, Massachusetts, and Utah all require more than one director if the corporation has more than one shareholder.

2. Kirdahy, Matthew, "Women Directors Linked to Performance," *Forbes.com,* October 1, 2007, accessed November 8, 2007.

3. 18B Am. Jur. 2d Corporations § 1289 (March. 2011).

4. *Chapin v. Benwood Foundation, Inc.,* 402 A2d 1205 (1979).

5. Model Business Corporation Act revised through December 2007 (hereinafter MBCA) § 8.01(c).

6. MBCA § 8.25(e)(1).

7. Id. § 8.25(e)(2).

8. Id. § 8.25(e)(3).

9. Id. § 8.25(e)(4).

10. Id. § 8.30(a).

11. 18B Am. Jur. 2d Corporations § 1465 (March 2011).

12. MBCA § 8.30(b).

13. Brodsky, Edward. *Law of Corporate Officers and Directors: Rights, Duties and Liabilities* § 2:17 (2007).

14. Id., *Deal v. Johnson,* 362 So. 2d 214 (Ala. 1978).

15. *In re Walt Disney Co. Derivative Litigation,* 907 A2d 693 (Del. Ch 2005).

16. 18 Am. Jur. 2d Corporations § 1470 (March 2011).

17. 3A Fletcher Cyclopedia of Private Corp. § 1036.

18. 18 Am. Jur. 2d Corporations § 1468 (March 2011).

19. MBCA § 2.02(b)(4).

20. Founder and principal stockholder Kevin Lawrence is currently serving a 20-year sentence in this case for mail fraud and conspiracy to commit securities, mail, and wire fraud, and money laundering. A total of 12 individuals either pleaded guilty or were convicted in criminal charges connected with this case—several of them received prison sentences.

21. Frederic W. Cook & Co., Non-Employee Director Compensation at the 100 Largest NASDAQ and 100 largest NYSE Companies (2010), available at http://www.fwcook.com.

22. *Salaman v. National Media Corp.,* 1994 WL 465534.

23. MBCA § 8.03.

24. 18B Am. Jur. 2d Corporations § 1233 (March 2011).

25. MBCA § 8.22(a).

26. Id. § 8.20(b).

27. 2 Fletcher Cyclopedia of Private Corp. § 269 (February 2011).

28. Association of Certified Fraud Examiners, 2010 Report to the Nation on Occupational Fraud and Abuse, available at http://www.acfe.com.

29. *NY Daily News,* "Swindler Bernard Madoff faces up to 150 years in jail for a $50 billion Ponzi scheme." Tuesday, March 10, 2009. http://www.nydailynews.com (accessed April 30, 2011).

30. Shilling, Monica. Educating the Board on Compliance-Related Responsibilities. Practicing Law Institute, Corporate Law and Practice Course Handbook Series 1479 PLI/Corp 567 (March–June 2005).

31. Alabama, Alaska, Minnesota, New Mexico, North Dakota, South Carolina, South Dakota, and Washington are among the states that provide preemptive rights unless limited by the articles of incorporation.

32. MBCA § 7.01.

33. 6 Am. Jur. Legal Forms 2d Corporations § 74:634 (May 2011). Reprinted with permission from American Jurisprudence Legal Forms 2d. © 2012 West Group.

34. 18B Am. Jur. 2d Corporations § 574 (March 2011).

35. 18B Am. Jur. 2d Corporations § 1936 (March 2011).

36. MBCA § 7.41.

CourseMate

To access additional course materials, including Course-Mate, please visit http://www.cengagebrain.com At the CengageBrain home page, search for the ISBN of your title (from the back cover of your book) using the search box at the top of the page. This will take you to the product page where these resources can be found. The CourseMate resources for this text include Web links, downloadable forms, flash cards, and more.

CHAPTER 10

THE CORPORATE FINANCIAL STRUCTURE

CHAPTER OUTLINE

INTRODUCTION

Three main concerns must be addressed regarding a corporation's financial structure: (1) its ability to raise and maintain the level of capital necessary to operate the business, (2) the distribution of earnings and profits to its shareholders, and (3) the division of its assets upon dissolution. This chapter explores many of the options available to the incorporators or directors of a corporation when deciding which choices will best raise capital for the corporation and distribute profits to the corporation's shareholders in a manner that is equitable and beneficial to both the corporation and its shareholders. The distribution of assets when the corporation dissolves is discussed in Chapter 14.

Paralegals are not responsible for advising corporate clients on the financial structure of their organizations. Nevertheless, a basic understanding of the corporation's financial structure will benefit paralegals who are often responsible for drafting articles of incorporation, minutes, and other corporate documents that deal with corporate financial matters.

This chapter begins with a general discussion of the capitalization of a corporation. Next, we focus on equity financing, including par value of stock, the consideration given in exchange for corporate stock, and the issuance of stock. Our focus then shifts to the redemption of equity shares, **dividends**, and stock splits. This chapter concludes with an examination of debt financing and a look at the paralegal's role in corporate financial matters.

DIVIDEND

A share of profits or property; usually a payment per share of a corporation's stock.

SIDEBAR

Financial management includes all actions taken by a corporation to enable it to obtain capital for growth, allocate resources, maximize corporate income, and monitor the corporation's results through accounting procedures.

---

§ 10.1 CORPORATE CAPITALIZATION

Before a corporation can begin transacting business, it must have capital with which to work. The capital of a corporation is generally considered to be all of the corporation's assets, although the term is sometimes used more narrowly to define only the portion of the corporation's assets that is utilized for operation of the corporation's business.[1] The amount of capital a corporation needs depends, in part, on the type of business it transacts. Some businesses, such as those that offer services rather than material goods, may require little capital. Businesses that require significant inventory, equipment, or other tangible assets may require much more capital.

Not only is adequate capitalization of a corporation crucial to its financial success, it can also be important to protect the personal liability of the shareholders. If a corporation is organized and carries on business without substantial capital and is unlikely to have sufficient assets available to meet its debts, it is inequitable to allow the shareholders to escape personal liability.[2] Inadequate capitalization of the corporation is one factor that courts look at when deciding whether to pierce the corporate veil and hold the shareholders personally responsible for the debts of a corporation.

The board of directors, with corporate management, is responsible for determining how much capital and what type of capital the corporation requires. Most corporations rely on a combination of equity and debt financing.

IN SUMMATION

- The corporation's assets are referred to as the corporate capital.

- Adequate capitalization of a corporation is important to its financial success and to protect the shareholders from personal liability for corporate debts and obligations.

- The board of directors is generally responsible for determining the appropriate mix of equity financing and debt financing for the corporation.

---

§ 10.2 EQUITY FINANCING

Equity financing involves the issuance of shares of stock of the corporation in exchange for cash or other consideration that will become corporate capital. **Equity securities** must be authorized in the corporation's articles of incorporation and are usually designated as **common stock** or **preferred stock**. The sale of stock is noted in the corporation's books by a debit to the assets column (usually cash) and a credit to the capital account column (or shareholder equity column, as it is sometimes referred to). See Exhibit 10-1.

The usual method of equity financing is the issuance of common stock in exchange for cash. However, there are many other possibilities. The issuance of equity securities means granting certain rights to the individuals who have given consideration for those securities. Those rights generally include the shareholder's

EQUITY SECURITIES

Securities that represent an ownership interest in the corporation.

COMMON STOCK

Shares in a corporation that depend for their value on the value of the company. These shares usually have voting rights (which other types of company stock may lack). Usually, they earn a dividend (profit only after all other types of the company's obligations and stocks have been paid).

PREFERRED STOCK

A type of stock that is entitled to certain rights and privileges over other outstanding stock of the corporation.

EXHIBIT 10-1	BALANCE SHEET DEPICTING ISSUANCE OF $10,000 IN COMMON STOCK

Balance Sheet

Assets		*Liabilities*	
Cash	$10,000		
		Shareholder's Equity	
		Common Stock	$10,000

© Cengage Learning 2013

proportionate right in the corporation with respect to its earnings, assets, and management. Unlike debt security holders, the holders of equity securities are typically not guaranteed a return on their investment in the corporation, and therefore place at risk their entire investment in the equity securities.

The rest of this section focuses on defining the authorized and issued stock of a corporation and the distinctions between common stock and preferred stock.

AUTHORIZED AND ISSUED STOCK

Corporate shares, or stock, are the basic units into which the ownership interest of a business corporation are divided.[3] This division of ownership into shares is a unique feature that differentiates corporations from partnerships and other forms of business organizations. When a corporation is formed, the articles of incorporation must set forth the number and type of shares the corporation is authorized to issue and any other information required by statute. These shares are referred to as the **authorized shares**. Following is a sample provision from the articles of incorporation for a corporation that has authorized only one class of stock.

AUTHORIZED SHARES

Total number of shares, provided for in the articles or certificate of incorporation, that the corporation is authorized to issue.

EXAMPLE: Authorized Stock

The authorized stock of the corporation shall consist of 10,000 shares of Class A Common Stock, without par value.

ISSUED AND OUTSTANDING SHARES

The total shares of stock of a corporation that have been authorized by the corporation's articles or certificate of incorporation and issued to shareholders.

Once consideration has been received for shares of stock and the shares have been delivered to the shareholders, they are considered to be **issued and outstanding shares**. Shares of stock remain issued and outstanding until they are reacquired, redeemed, converted, or canceled. See Exhibit 10-2.

The board of directors may not issue equity shares in excess of the authorized shares. If the directors deem it appropriate to increase the number of authorized shares, the articles of incorporation must be amended to provide for the increased number of authorized shares. Such an amendment usually requires shareholder approval.

The articles of incorporation generally set forth the preferences, limitations, and relative rights of each class of authorized shares before any shares of that class are issued. Although shareholder approval is typically required for amendments to the articles of incorporation concerning the authorized shares of the corporation, the Model Business Corporation Act (MBCA) provides that the board of directors may be granted the right, in the articles of incorporation, to establish the rights, preferences, and limitations of any new class of stock without shareholder approval.[4] This right does not apply to any class of stock of which there are issued and outstanding shares. Not all state statutes allow this much power to be vested in the board of directors, and it is important that the proper state statutes be consulted with regard to requirements for authorizing new classes of shares of stock. In addition to the articles of incorporation, rights and preferences granted to certain classes of common stock must be set forth on the face of the stock certificates of each class, pursuant to statute.

EXHIBIT 10-2	AUTHORIZED STOCK IS ISSUED AND BECOMES ISSUED AND OUTSTANDING STOCK	
Authorized	**Issued**	**Issued & Outstanding**
The total number and type of shares of stock a corporation is authorized to issue is set forth in the articles of incorporation.	The stock is issued by the board of directors when adequate consideration is received by the corporation.	Stock that has been issued to shareholders is considered issued and outstanding until reacquired, redeemed, converted, or canceled.
Most additions to the authorized stock of the corporation must be approved by the shareholders of the corporation by an amendment of the articles of incorporation.		

© Cengage Learning 2013

Statutory Requirements for Authorized Stock

Statutory requirements for the authorized stock of a corporation vary greatly. The MBCA grants corporations the opportunity to creatively structure the authorized stock of the corporation to meet its specific needs and the needs of its shareholders. The MBCA gives corporations the freedom to authorize classes of stock with a number of differing rights and preferences, provided that the number of each class of shares is set forth in the corporation's articles of incorporation, along with a distinguishing designation for each class of stock if more than one class is authorized.

Most states follow § 6.01(b) of the MBCA in requiring that the authorized stock of a corporation include one or more classes of shares that have unlimited voting rights and one or more classes of shares that together are entitled to receive the net assets of the corporation upon dissolution.

(b) The articles of incorporation must authorize:
1. one or more classes or series of shares that together have unlimited voting rights, and
2. one or more classes or series of shares (which may be the same class or classes as those with voting rights) that together are entitled to receive the net assets of the corporation upon dissolution.

These two stock characteristics are commonly found in one class of shares, as is required in many states. These widely accepted requirements guarantee that at all times there will be shareholders who have the voting rights necessary to take any required corporate actions, and that the corporation will always have shareholders who are entitled to receive the net assets of the corporation, should the corporation dissolve. It is important to note that shares of stock including these two fundamental rights must at all times be issued, not just authorized.

When drafting the articles of incorporation to specify the initial authorized shares, the immediate and future capital requirements of the corporation must be taken into consideration, as well as the control of the corporation, state and federal securities regulations, the potential market for sale of the stock, and any state taxation or filing fees that may be based on the authorized shares of the corporation. Many states, including Delaware, base an initial incorporation fee or franchise tax on the authorized capital stock of the corporation.

The MBCA no longer uses the term "preferred stock." However, the MBCA specifically provides that many of the characteristics commonly found in preferred stock may be found in certain classes of stock, whatever they may be called. For purposes of this discussion, we distinguish between common and preferred stock and discuss the characteristics commonly associated with those types of stock, keeping in mind that those characteristics may be assigned to any class of stock, regardless of what it is labeled.

While corporations routinely have only one class of common stock with all holders having identical rights and preferences, the corporation's articles of incorporation may be drafted to provide any number of different rights and preferences for different classes of stock. Some of the rights and preferences that may be established by the articles of incorporation include:

- Limitations on voting rights for certain classes of stock
- Preference in payment of dividends
- Preference in payment of assets on liquidation
- Rights to redeem stock
- Rights to convert one type of stock to another

IN SUMMATION

- Equity financing is the issuance of shares of stock representing the ownership of the corporation in exchange for cash or other consideration that will become corporate capital.
- When a corporation is formed, the articles of incorporation will set forth the number and preferences, limitations, and relative rights of each class of the authorized stock of the corporation.
- Once consideration has been received for authorized shares and those shares have been delivered to the shareholder, those shares are considered issued and outstanding.
- Corporations often issue just one class of common stock.
- The statutes of most states provide that every corporation must at all times have issued stock that has unlimited voting rights and the right to receive the net assets of the corporation on dissolution.

§ 10.3 COMMON STOCK

The ownership of almost all corporations is represented, at least in part, by stock referred to as "common stock." In the event no designation is made in the articles of incorporation, the authorized stock is considered to be common stock if only one class is authorized. Unless otherwise provided in the articles of incorporation, the owners of the corporation's common stock are entitled to the right to participate in the control of the corporation, a pro rata share of the corporation's profits, and a pro rata share of the corporation's assets on the corporation's dissolution. As discussed in Chapter 9, the holders of the corporation's common stock are entitled to participate in the management of the corporation by voting their shares.

Classes of Common Stock

The articles of incorporation may authorize more than one class of common stock, with different rights and preferences as set forth in the articles of incorporation. Common stock may also be issued in series in some states. In any event, all shares of common stock within the same class and series are entitled to identical rights.

Common stock may be issued in classes to certain groups with common interests to assure their representation on the board of directors. For example, the articles of incorporation may provide that Class A common stock may elect three directors to the board, and Class B common stock may elect two directors.

Voting Rights

Unless otherwise indicated in the articles of incorporation, holders of common stock are entitled to one vote per share of stock owned. Other voting rights may be prescribed in the articles of incorporation, and this is commonly done when there is more than one class of common stock of the corporation.

The initial shareholders of a corporation may, at times, consent to the subsequent issue of nonvoting common stock to new shareholders. The issue of nonvoting stock can be used to raise capital for the corporation without diluting the management power of the existing shareholders. The corporation may, for example, be authorized to issue Class A common stock that is entitled to one vote per share, and Class B common stock that is not entitled to vote. A family-owned corporation may issue nonvoting stock when the parents want their children to have a financial stake in the business, but not necessarily have management responsibilities. Following is a sample provision for the articles of incorporation that authorizes two classes of stock, one with voting rights and one without voting rights.

EXAMPLE: Authorized Shares

The authorized capital stock of this corporation shall consist of one thousand shares of Class A Common Stock, without par value, and one thousand shares of Class B Common Stock, without par value.

Each shareholder of Class A Common Stock shall be entitled to one (1) vote per share.

Shareholders of Class B Nonvoting Common Stock shall have no voting rights except those prescribed by statute for both voting and nonvoting shareholders.

Liquidation Rights

Unless otherwise prescribed by the articles of incorporation, the shareholders of the corporation's common stock will be entitled to the net assets of the corporation upon dissolution. Shareholders will divide the net assets in proportion to their share ownership.

IN SUMMATION

- If stock is not designated otherwise, it is considered common stock.
- Unless otherwise designated in the articles of incorporation, common stockholders are entitled to:
  - the right to participate in the control of the corporation by voting their shares,
  - a pro rata share of the corporation's profits, and
  - a pro rata share of the corporation's assets on its dissolution.

§ 10.4 PREFERRED STOCK

Preferred stock enjoys certain limited rights and privileges (usually dividend and liquidation priorities) over other outstanding stock. Preferred stock is distinguished from common stock in that it is entitled to a priority over other stock in the distribution of profits. This preference may include the right to cumulative or noncumulative dividends (discussed in § 10.9 of this text). The terms of the preferred stock are set forth in the articles of incorporation and on the face of the preferred stock certificate, and the specified terms and provisions serve as a contract between the preferred stockholder and the corporation.

Nonvoting preferred stock may be used to entice passive investors to invest in a corporation. Consider a small corporation formed to purchase and train racehorses. The two principals of the corporation, who are the only common-stock shareholders, are both very knowledgeable about purchasing and training racehorses and they are very active in the management of the corporation. If they want to raise some equity capital to purchase a new horse, they could offer shares of nonvoting preferred stock with terms that include preferred dividends to investors. Investors may invest in the corporation based on their confidence that the two common shareholders have the ability to operate the corporation profitably. The preferred shareholders would not have any voting rights, but when the corporation starts earning a profit, they would be paid dividends on a preferential basis, as established in the terms for the stock. The common shareholders, on the other hand, would raise the capital they need without losing control of the corporation.

The terms of preferred stock can vary and may be restricted by state statute. Typically, preferred stockholders are granted a dividend preference over the common stockholders in a fixed amount per share or in a certain percentage. Preferred stockholders may also be granted voting rights, redemption rights, **conversion rights**, and priority in entitlement to the assets of the corporation on dissolution. Following is a sample provision for the articles of incorporation of a corporation that has authorized common and preferred stock.

CONVERSION RIGHTS
Rights, often granted to preferred shareholders with the issuance of preferred stock, that allow the preferred shareholders to convert their shares of preferred stock into common stock at some specific point in time, usually at the shareholder's option.

EXAMPLE: Authorized Shares

The authorized capital stock of this corporation shall consist of one million shares of Common Stock, without par value, and one million shares of Non-voting Preferred Stock, without par value.

Each shareholder of Common Stock shall be entitled to one (1) vote per share.

The holders of Preferred Stock will be entitled to receive cumulative dividends on an annual basis of twelve percent (12%) of the stated value of the Preferred Stock prior to the distribution of any dividends to the holders of Common Stock. Holders of Common Stock will be entitled to dividends of ten percent (10%) of the surplus remaining, with the balance of such surplus to be distributed to holders of both classes of stock on a participating basis equally without distinction as to class.

Voting Rights

Preferred stock may be issued with voting rights, with limited voting rights, or with no voting rights at all, at the discretion of the board of directors. So long as at least one class of issued stock is granted unlimited voting rights, preferred stock is not required to provide unlimited voting rights. The statutes of some states provide that all shareholders, including shareholders of preferred stock, must be allowed to vote on certain matters affecting shareholder rights.

Redemption Rights

Often, when a corporation issues preferred stock, that stock will be issued with provisions that allow the corporation, or the preferred shareholder, the right of redemption at a future date, upon the terms and conditions set forth on the stock certificate or in an agreement between the preferred shareholder and the corporation. Following is a sample "articles of incorporation" provision providing for the redemption of preferred stock.

EXAMPLE: Redemption of Preferred Stock

The preferred stock of the corporation may be redeemed in whole or in part on any date after _____, _____, at the option of the board of directors on not less than _____ days' notice to the preferred stockholders of record. Such stock shall be redeemed by payment in cash of _____ percent (_____%) of par value of each share to be redeemed, as well as all accrued unpaid dividends on each such share.[5]

Redemption of equity shares is discussed in more detail in § 10.8 of this chapter.

Conversion of Preferred Stock

The preferred stock rights and preferences may include conversion rights providing that the issued shares may be converted into common stock at some specific point in time, usually at the shareholder's option. Specific provisions in the articles of incorporation and on the stock certificates, or in a separate agreement between the corporation and the preferred stockholder, should include a conversion rate indicating the number of preferred shares that may be converted into common stock and the number of common shares to be issued in the exchange. In addition, the conversion provisions should include the exact method for the conversion, including the period during which the conversion option may validly be exercised, and any other pertinent information. Following is a sample "articles of incorporation" provision providing for the conversion of preferred stock.

EXAMPLE: Right of Conversion

The holder of any shares of preferred stock of the Corporation may, after the fourth anniversary date of the issuance of such stock, and until such time as may be determined by the Board of Directors, elect to convert such shares of preferred stock to shares of common stock of the Corporation. Upon giving the Corporation ninety (90) days' notice by registered mail of such intent and on surrender at the office of the Corporation of the certificates for such preferred shares, duly endorsed to the Corporation, the shareholder shall be entitled to receive one share of common stock for every share of preferred stock so surrendered.

Priority Rights to Assets upon Dissolution

Preferred stockholders may be granted a specific preference over common stockholders with regard to the assets of the corporation upon its dissolution. The issuance of preferred stock with a priority right to assets upon dissolution may be a useful planning tool for a corporation where the initial shareholder contributions are of unequal short-term value. For example, suppose that an entrepreneur with a unique set of skills and talents would like to begin a corporation to run a consulting business. The startup costs to get the business running are $100,000, but the entrepreneur has no cash. If he were to enlist an investor to provide the cash and become a 50 percent shareholder of the company, the investor could be issued preferred stock with terms that include a preferred right to the assets of the corporation on dissolution. That way, if the corporation were to dissolve in one year, the preferred shareholder who put up all the cash would not be out his entire investment. The terms of the common and preferred stock could otherwise provide that both shareholders share equally in the profits of the corporation, if that is their desire.

Priority Rights to Dividends

Preferred stockholders may be granted a priority over other shareholders to receive dividends from the corporation. The rights granted to preferred stockholders often include dividends in specific amounts, paid on certain dates. The payment of dividends is discussed in § 10.9 of this chapter.

Series of Preferred Shares

Preferred stock may be issued in classes and series to the extent that such issuance is authorized in the corporation's articles of incorporation. A series of preferred stock refers to a type of shares within a class of preferred stock. The exact rights and preferences of a series of shares may be set by the board of directors before issuance, without shareholder approval or amendment of the articles of incorporation. This allows the board of directors to act quickly to take advantage of market conditions without having to amend the articles of incorporation. All rights and preferences of shares of stock within a series must be identical.

Factors in Deciding Whether to Issue Preferred Stock

The board of directors or incorporators must take several factors into consideration when deciding whether to authorize preferred stock in the corporation's articles of incorporation. Preferred stock may be used to attract investors who are interested in a more conservative investment that offers a steady income in lieu of growth potential. Other factors to be considered by the board of directors or incorporators include the cost of issuing preferred stock, the risk of capital, and the flexibility of the payment obligation.

IN SUMMATION

- The holders of preferred stock are entitled to a priority over other stockholders in the distribution of profits.
- The terms of the preferred stock are set forth in the corporation's articles of incorporation and on the face of the preferred stock certificate.
- Preferred stockholders may receive preference with regard to dividends and/or distribution of assets on dissolution of the corporation.
- Preferred stock may or may not come with voting rights.
- Preferred stock may be issued with redemption rights—the right of the stockholder to redeem his or her stock at a future date on conditions established in the articles of incorporation or by agreement between the preferred stockholder and the corporation.
- Preferred stock may be issued with conversion rights—the right of the stockholder to convert their shares to shares of common stock at a future date on conditions established in the articles of incorporation or by agreement between the preferred stockholder and the corporation.
- Preferred stock may be issued in classes and series as provided in the corporation's articles of incorporation.
- A corporation's board of directors may issue preferred stock to attract investors who are interested in a more secure investment with a steady income.

§ 10.5 PAR VALUE

Par value is the nominal value assigned to shares of stock and imprinted upon the face of the stock certificate as a dollar value. The par value requirement was primarily intended to protect corporate creditors, senior security holders, and other shareholders by setting a benchmark to ensure fair contribution from all shareholders. It was also intended to establish the corporation's permanent capital on which creditors could rely.[6] Corporations were not allowed to make distributions out of the "stated capital account"—an account that equaled the total par value of all issued shares.

Because the actual value of all stock fluctuates and because corporations often set a nominal value for the par value of their stock, the par value provided for in articles of incorporation and on the face of stock certificates may have little actual meaning. Requiring corporations to issue stock with a par value has provided little actual benefit to shareholders or creditors. It is widely accepted that "par value and actual value of issued stock are not synonymous, and there is often a wide disparity between them."[7] There is a trend toward eliminating par value and the consideration and accounting requirements for par value stock.

TREND TOWARD ELIMINATING PAR VALUE

Most states provide that a corporation's authorized stock can be without par value or with no par value. However, if no par value is assigned to the stock of a corporation, the authorities in some states will assign a specific par value to the shares of stock for certain purposes, such as taxation and filing fees. The statutes of states following the MBCA do not require that a par value be assigned to the authorized stock of the corporation. However, if a par value is assigned, it must be set forth in the corporation's articles of incorporation.

EXAMPLE: One Class of Shares—without Par Value

The aggregate amount of the total authorized capital stock of this corporation is _____ shares of common stock without nominal or par value, and which shall be all of the same class. The stock may be issued from time to time without action by the stockholders, for such consideration as may be fixed from time to time by the board of directors, and shares issued in this manner, the full consideration for which has been paid or delivered, shall be deemed full paid stock and the holder of these shares shall not be liable for any further payment on them.[8]

CONSIDERATION FOR PAR VALUE STOCK

If a corporation authorizes par value stock, special consideration must be given to the issuance of that stock with regard to the corporation's accounting. Like stock with no par value, par value stock may be issued for any price deemed adequate by the board of directors, with one exception: the consideration received must be at least equal to the par value of the shares issued. For instance, 100 shares of $10 par value common stock could be issued at a price of $5,000 if the board deems it adequate consideration. However, in no event could the board of directors issue the shares of stock for less than $1,000.

Shares issued for less than the par value, which may be the case when consideration is in a form other than cash, are considered **watered stock**, and the shareholder receiving them may be liable to the corporation for the difference between the amount paid and the par value of the shares received. However, the imposition of liability on the shareholders of a corporation for purchase of watered shares, in the absence of fraud or misrepresentation, is becoming a rare event. The MBCA provides only that "[a] purchaser from a corporation of its own shares is not liable to the corporation or its creditors with respect to the shares except to pay for the consideration for which the shares were authorized to be issued,"[9] or specified in the subscription agreement.

WATERED STOCK
A stock issue that is sold as if fully paid for, but that is not (often because some or all of the shares were given out for less than full price).

ACCOUNTING FOR PAR VALUE STOCK

The amount of capital contributed by stockholders. The capital or equity of a corporation as it appears in the balance sheet.

CAPITAL SURPLUS

Property paid into a corporation by the shareholders in excess of capital stock liability.

Generally, when a corporation receives consideration for the issuance of par value stock, the total amount of the par value of the issued stock is considered **stated capital**. Any amount received in excess of the par value of the shares is considered **capital surplus**. Any amount received by the corporation that is considered stated capital must be maintained by the corporation. The issuance of stock without par value allows the directors of the corporation greater flexibility to manipulate the available capital surplus to provide for greater dividends and the redemption of issued stock. If the authorized stock of a corporation is without par value, directors are frequently allowed to make their own determination as to what part of the consideration received is stated capital and what part is capital surplus. (See Exhibit 10-3.)

Because the par value amount typically represents only the minimum amount that shares may be issued for, and because a high par value may tie up the funds of the corporation, most corporations in states that require par value opt to assign a very nominal amount of par value. Another reason for the frequent use of a nominal

EXHIBIT 10-3	BALANCE SHEETS CONTRASTING DIFFERENT TREATMENT OF STATED CAPITAL AND CAPITAL SURPLUS

Balance Sheet of a Corporation after Issuance of 10,000 Shares of Common Stock, $1.00 par value

Assets		Liabilities	
Cash	$10,000		
		Shareholder's Equity	
		Common Stock	
		Stated Capital:	$10,000
		Capital Surplus:	0

Balance Sheet of a Corporation after Issuance of 10,000 Shares of Common Stock, $.50 par value

Assets		Liabilities	
Cash	$10,000		
		Shareholder's Equity	
		Common Stock	
		Stated Capital:	$5,000
		Capital Surplus:	5,000

© Cengage Learning 2013

par value is that some state authorities employ the par value of stock as part of a taxation formula, with corporations being taxed on the par value of authorized or issued stock of the corporation. Par value may also be a factor in determining state filing fees.

IN SUMMATION

- Par value is the nominal value assigned to shares of stock.
- The modern trend is toward authorizing stock without par value as is permitted by the statutes of most states.
- State filing fees may be based on the par value of a corporation's stock.
- If a corporation issues stock with a par value, consideration received for that stock is considered stated capital.
- Shares issued for less consideration than par value are considered watered stock.

§ 10.6 CONSIDERATION FOR SHARES OF STOCK

Unless the right is granted to the shareholders under statute or the articles of incorporation, the board of directors is typically responsible for the issuance of stock for adequate consideration. This really involves two issues. First, the board must determine a fair value at which the stock should be issued; then it must determine the adequacy of the consideration. Obviously, if the consideration is in the form of cash, the second part of that task is simple.

The price per share of stock for the initial issue of shares is determined by the amount of capital required to begin the business, the number of initial investors, and the number of shares to be issued. For example, if it is determined that a corporation requires $50,000 to begin business, and five initial investors are all willing to invest $10,000, the number and price of the authorized and issued shares will be determined accordingly. The corporation may issue 50,000 shares of common stock at $1.00 per share, or the board may decide to issue five shares at $10,000 per share. For ease in transferring stock, it is advisable to put a lower price on the shares of stock. If a shareholder in this example wished to sell half of his or her shares, it would be easier to transfer 5,000 $1.00 shares than half of a single $10,000 share.

Placing a value on subsequent issues of stock of closely held corporations is a more difficult matter. Obviously, stock cannot be priced too high or it will not sell. On the other hand, if the stock price is too low, it will dilute the interest of the current stockholders by bringing down the per-share value. Also, shares of stock that are issued within a relatively short time period generally must be sold for the same price. If the shares of stock to be issued are par value stock, the consideration must be at least equal to the par value of the shares issued.

Historically, restrictions were placed on the type of consideration that could be accepted by the board of directors for shares of equity stock. Statutes generally restricted the use of promissory notes, the rendering of future services, and other types of contracts that called for payment or performance at some time in the future. The intent behind this restriction was to ensure that the corporation had enough immediate capital with which to operate its business. Many states still place some restrictions on the form of consideration that may be accepted for the issuance of stock.

The tendency of modern corporate law is to allow any consideration deemed adequate by the board of directors for the payment of shares of stock. Under the MBCA, consideration for shares of stock may be in the form of "any tangible or intangible property or benefit to the corporation."[10] This may include cash, promissory notes, services performed on behalf of the corporation, contracts for services to be performed on behalf of the corporation, or other securities of the corporation. It is typically left to the discretion of the board of directors to determine the adequacy of consideration. Obviously, if the board of directors decides to accept promissory notes, or other contracts for future benefit to the corporation, there must be an adequate mix of cash or other immediate rewards that gives the corporation the needed initial funds. When a corporation receives valid consideration for shares, the shares are issued and considered to be fully paid and nonassessable.

IN SUMMATION

- When issuing stock, the board of directors must consider:
  - The value of the stock
  - The value of the consideration received for the stock

§ 10.7 ISSUANCE OF STOCK

STOCK SUBSCRIPTION

Agreement to purchase a specific number of shares of a corporation.

Typically, the first shares of stock of a corporation are issued at the first meeting of the board of directors. This is often done by executing or ratifying **stock subscription** agreements that were received before or immediately after incorporation of the business, with the issuance of stock certificates in exchange for the agreed-upon consideration. The right to issue shares of stock is generally granted to the board of directors. However, the statutes of many states allow the shareholders to reserve that power in the articles of incorporation if desired. If the shareholders of the corporation have preemptive rights, the existing shareholders must be given the opportunity to exercise their rights prior to the issuance of any additional shares of stock.

Shares of issued stock are usually represented by stock certificates, as may be required by state statute, or the articles of incorporation or bylaws of the corporation. However, in many instances, stock issued under a valid agreement but without the formal stock certificate has been found to be a valid issue of stock.

STOCK CERTIFICATES

Although the MBCA prescribes the minimum form and content for stock certificates, it also allows corporations to issue stock without the formality of a stock certificate, so long as the information prescribed for stock certificates is included in a written statement sent to the shareholder within a reasonable time after the issue or transfer of the shares without a certificate.[11] Section 6.25(b) of the MBCA prescribes the requirements for stock certificates, as follows:

> (b) At a minimum each share certificate must state on its face:
>   1. the name of the issuing corporation and that it is organized under the law of this state;
>   2. the name of the person to whom issued; and
>   3. the number and class of shares and the designation of the series, if any, the certificate represents.

See Exhibit 10-4.

The statutes of most states also require that the stock certificates contain a summary of the designations, relative rights, preferences, and limitations of the represented class of shares if the corporation has more than one class or series of authorized shares. Alternatively, corporations may provide the pertinent information regarding share classes and series rights and preferences to shareholders upon request, so long as the stock certificate "conspicuously state[s] on its front or back that the corporation will furnish the shareholder this information on request in writing without charge."[12]

EXHIBIT 10-4	CORPORATE OWNERSHIP IS TYPICALLY REPRESENTED BY STOCK CERTIFICATES

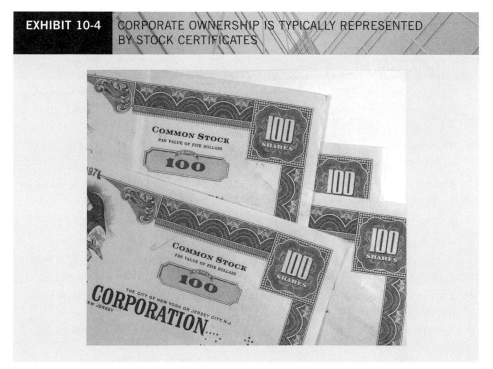

http://www.shutterstock.com/pic-1299689-corporation-common-stock-shares.html

Stock certificates must be signed by two officers of the corporation, typically the president or chief executive officer and the secretary or assistant secretary.

LOST OR DESTROYED STOCK CERTIFICATES

Lost stock certificates can usually be replaced when the shareholder submits an affidavit affirming that the certificate was lost or destroyed. The new stock certificate is typically issued with an indication that it is a "duplicate" stock certificate.

FRACTIONAL SHARES AND SCRIP

STOCK DIVIDEND

Profits of stock ownership (dividends) paid out by a corporation in more stock rather than in money. This additional stock reflects the increased worth of the company.

SCRIP

A piece of paper that is a temporary indication of a right to something valuable. Scrip includes paper money issued for temporary use, partial shares of stock after a stock split, certificates of a deferred stock dividend that can be cashed in later, and so on.

At times, because of various stock transactions involving the transfer or issuance of shares of stock, a shareholder may be entitled to own an amount of shares of stock that is represented by a fraction. For instance, the corporation may declare a **stock dividend** of one share for every 10 shares that are issued and outstanding. In that event, a shareholder holding 15 shares would be entitled to receive 1.5 more shares of stock.

A corporation may issue a fractional share, which is entitled to voting and all rights incident to stock ownership, or it may issue a **scrip**. A scrip is an instrument that represents the right to receive a fraction of a share. This instrument is freely transferable, but it does not include voting rights or other rights associated with stock ownership. Scrip is often issued with a provision that it must be combined with other fractional shares of stock and exchanged for a whole share or shares of stock within a prescribed time period. If the exchange is not completed within the time prescribed, the scrip becomes void.

IN SUMMATION

- The first stock certificates of a corporation are often issued pursuant to stock subscription agreements executed by the new shareholders and provided to the board of directors of the corporation at its first meeting.
- The exact requirements for the stock certificates issued to represent shares of a corporation may be dictated by state statute, but usually include:
  - The name of the issuing company
  - The name of the shareholder
  - The number and class of the shares and designation of the series, if any
  - Summary of the designations, relative rights, preferences, and limitation of the particular class or series of stock (if there is more than one) or a statement that that information is available to shareholders upon request.
- Lost stock certificates can usually be replaced by submitting an affidavit to the corporation.
- A scrip is a document that represents the right of the holder to receive a fraction of a share.

§ 10.8 REDEMPTION OF EQUITY SHARES

Redemption refers to the repurchase by a corporation of its own shares of stock. Often, a corporation's preferred stock will be issued with provisions that allow the corporation the right of redemption at a future date, upon the terms and conditions set forth on the stock certificate or in an agreement between the preferred stockholder and the corporation. This may be of particular interest to corporations when the market interest rate is declining, or when the corporation expects substantial profits in the near future, because redemption of preferred stock allows the corporation to terminate its obligations to pay fixed dividends on the stock. In a close corporation, rights of redemption allow shareholders to withdraw from participation in the corporation without forfeiting their investment. The corporation will buy the stock back from the shareholder.

Redemption may be at the option of the corporation, the shareholder, or a third party. Shares redeemable at the option of the corporation are often referred to as callable shares; the option of a shareholder to redeem shares is sometimes referred to as a put. The price paid to redeem shares is set in the articles of incorporation or by a formula prescribed in the articles of incorporation. A corporation may use any available funds to redeem stock, so long as the redemption would not make the corporation insolvent or impair the rights of creditors. To plan for preferred stock redemptions or the redemption of debt obligations, the corporation may establish a **sinking fund**. Contributions may be made to the sinking fund periodically in set amounts, or as a share of the corporation's income. A sinking fund may be allowed to accumulate until some future date at which the stock is redeemed, or it may be used each year to redeem a portion of the outstanding securities.

Treasury shares are shares of stock that were previously issued by the corporation but later reacquired. Reacquired shares may be subject to special accounting treatment, although the MBCA has eliminated any special treatment of treasury shares in recent years, stating merely that "corporation may acquire its own shares and shares so acquired constitute authorized but unissued shares."[13] Several states, however, require that treasury shares be accounted for under a special status as issued but not outstanding shares. Shares that are issued but not outstanding have no voting rights, and they are not counted in any necessary determinations of the number of outstanding shares of the corporation.

SINKING FUND
Money or other assets put aside for a special purpose, such as to pay off bonds and other long-term debts as they come due or to replace, repair, or improve machinery or buildings when they wear out or become outdated.

TREASURY SHARES
Shares of stock that have been rebought by the corporation that issued them.

EXAMPLE: Resolution of Directors—Authorizing Redemption

a. It is in the best interests of the corporation that it purchase out of its surplus not in excess of _____ [number] shares of the _____ [class] stock of the corporation, now offered for sale to this corporation by _____ [holder] and that immediately following the purchase of such shares, they be retired.

b. Such purchase and retirement is _____ [authorized or required] by the corporation's _____ [articles or certificate] of incorporation.

Now, therefore, it is

RESOLVED, that the executive officers of _____ [corporation] be, and they now are, empowered and directed to purchase out of the surplus of the corporation from _____ [holder] not in excess of _____ [number] shares of _____ [class] stock of the corporation at $_____ per share, plus an amount equal to accrued dividends to date of payment, and that payment for the shares so purchased be made in cash.

FURTHER RESOLVED, that immediately following such purchase, such shares be retired by the corporation pursuant to this resolution without further action by the board of directors, it being the intention of the board that this resolution shall not only authorize the purchase of the shares, but shall also effect the retirement of such shares as shall be purchased pursuant to this resolution.

FURTHER RESOLVED, that the officers of the corporation be, and they now are, authorized to take all steps required by law as a result of the retirement effected by this resolution.[14]

IN SUMMATION

- Preferred stock may be issued with the right of redemption, providing that the corporation may redeem the stock at a future date upon specified terms and conditions.
- Redemption may be at the option of the shareholder, the corporation, or a third party.
- A sinking fund may be used by a corporation to accumulate cash for a planned future acquisition.
- Treasury shares are previously issued shares of stock that have been reacquired by the corporation.

§ 10.9 DIVIDENDS

Once the business of the corporation has net earnings, the profits are usually distributed to the appropriate shareholders, in an equitable manner, in the form of dividends. A dividend is considered to be a payment to the stockholders of a corporation as a return on their investment. Generally, recurring dividends are paid on a more or less regular basis in the ordinary course of business without reducing the stockholders' equity or their position to enjoy future returns from the corporation.

These dividends are payable out of the surplus or profits of the corporation, and may be in the form of cash, stock, or other property of the corporation.

This section investigates the availability of funds for dividends and the different types of dividends. It also discusses the declaration of dividends and the shareholders' right to receive dividends after they have been declared.

AVAILABILITY OF FUNDS FOR DIVIDENDS

It is generally accepted that dividends may be paid only out of the profits of the corporation. This principle has been upheld in courts numerous times, as it has been found that "[g]enerally, the net earnings or surplus of a going corporation constitute the proper fund for the payment of dividends, whether on its common stock or preferred stock, and dividends cannot, as a rule, legally be declared and paid out of the capital of the corporation."[15] Dividends are normally payable out of the surplus or profits of a corporation, and it is usually within the discretion of the corporation's directors to decide whether to reinvest the corporation's profits in the corporation or to distribute the profits to the corporation's shareholders. Most jurisdictions have a two-pronged test to determine whether a corporation may pay a dividend. The first test is the balance sheet test, which is passed by corporations whose assets are at least equal to liabilities after the proposed dividend is paid. The second test is the solvency test that requires all corporations to be able to continue paying their debts once the proposed dividend is paid.

Newer and smaller closely held corporations may opt for the declaration of minimal dividends and keep the profits in the corporation to expand its business and increase the value of its stock. Often, the shareholders of these smaller corporations are also employees of the corporation and receive their share of the earnings of the corporation in the form of salaries.

On the other hand, larger, publicly held corporations may find it necessary to declare and pay dividends consistently at a rate attractive to potential investors who are looking for stock investments with steady income potential.

TYPES OF DIVIDENDS

Dividends may be paid in several forms. The most common types consist of cash or stock dividends.

Cash

The vast majority of corporate dividends are cash dividends. In its simplest form, the cash dividend merely divides and distributes the profits of the corporation, in cash, to the shareholders of the corporation pursuant to the terms of the shares of stock that have been issued.

Stock Dividends

At times, stock dividends may be distributed in lieu of cash. An issue of stock dividends involves the authorization and issuance of new stock to existing shareholders on a pro rata basis. Because stock dividends make no demands on the funds of a corporation, they are not regulated by statute to the extent that cash dividends are regulated.

So as not to unfairly dilute the shares of one class of stock, shareholders of one class of shares may not be issued shares of another class in a stock dividend, unless the articles of incorporation so provide, or unless, prior to declaration of the stock dividend, no shares of the class to be distributed as a dividend have been issued. Although the corporation issues additional stock, it continues with the same assets and liabilities. The declaration of a stock dividend has the effect of allowing the portion of surplus capital represented by the new stock to be transferred to the permanent capital account of the corporation.

Because the issued shares of the corporation are increased, and all shareholders receive a proportionate amount of shares in the event of a stock dividend, shareholders receiving stock dividends are, in effect, no better off than they were prior to the stock distribution. The stock dividend effectively lowers the price of the issued stock to reflect the value of the corporation.

Other Property

On occasion, dividends may be in a form other than cash or the corporation's stock. These dividends might be any property owned by the corporation, including real or personal property, bonds, scrip, or the stock of another corporation.

SIDEBAR

Stock dividends are typically declared as a percentage. For example, if a 5 percent stock dividend is declared, shareholders receive an additional one share for every 20 shares they own.

DECLARATION OF DIVIDENDS

The corporation generally has no legal obligation to pay an undeclared dividend to the shareholders. However, once a dividend is declared, it becomes a debt payable to the shareholders, and the shareholders of the corporation have the legal remedies available to creditors to collect the dividend as declared.

Dividend Preferences

Dividends that are payable, by virtue of contract, to one class of shareholders in priority over another class of shareholders are often referred to as preferred or preferential dividends. Preferred stockholders generally have a right to priority over other shareholders in the receipt of dividends. Although corporations typically pay consistent dividends to preferred stockholders at regular intervals, preferred stockholders do not have the right to dividends when there is no corporate profit or surplus earnings to justify the dividends. Courts have found in several instances that a "corporation cannot make a valid contract to pay dividends otherwise than from profits, and an agreement to pay such dividends out of capital is unlawful and void."[16]

Cumulative Dividends

Courts have held in several instances that the "omission of a dividend on either the preferred or the common stock of a corporation for any year, because net earnings which will permit the payment of a dividend are lacking, deprives such stock of all right to a share of profits for that year, unless the contract provides for the cumulation of dividends on such stock."[17] If a corporation does not earn a profit substantial enough to declare a dividend for the year, common shareholders have no right to claim an extra dividend from the following year's profits. If the preferred shareholders have a right to **cumulative dividends**, dividends omitted in one period generally must be paid in the next period before dividends are paid on the shares of common stock.

Authority to Declare Dividends

The authority to declare dividends generally rests with the board of directors, with the exception of stock dividends, which may require shareholder approval. Dividends are approved by board of director resolution and declared as a formal act of the corporation.

CUMULATIVE DIVIDEND

Type of dividend paid on preferred stock that the corporation is liable for in the next payment period if not satisfied in the current payment period. Cumulative dividends on preferred stock must be paid before any dividends may be paid on common stock.

EXAMPLE: Board of Director Resolution—Dividend Declaration

Whereas, $_____ constitutes surplus profits earned by this corporation in _____ [year];

Now, therefore, it is

RESOLVED, $_____ is now set aside from the surplus profits to be distributed to the stockholders of this corporation by a declaration of a dividend of $_____ per share for each share of common stock owned by the shareholders and by the declaration of the dividend of $_____ per share for each share of preferred stock owned by the stockholders. The dividend is payable to the stockholders of record as of the close of business on _____ [date]; and the dividend is now declared and the secretary of this corporation is instructed to distribute on _____ [date], $_____, in checks of this corporation, aggregating a dividend of $_____ per share on the common stock and a dividend of $_____ per share on the preferred stock, for every share owned by its stockholders.[18]

Board of director decisions to declare dividends are generally covered under the business judgment rule. However, pursuant to § 8.33 of the Model Business Corporation Act, and the statutes of several states, a director who votes for or assents to a distribution that does not meet the solvency test or the balance sheet test is personally liable to the corporation for the amount of the distribution that exceeds what could have been distributed under the MBCA.

Right to Receive Dividends

When a dividend is declared, the declaration includes a date on which all shareholders of record will be entitled to dividends. Once the declaration has been made, those individuals have a right to those dividends, as specified by contract and the declaration. Typically, if no date is declared to determine the shareholders of record entitled to a dividend, the record date is considered the date on which the declaration is made.

Directors are usually under no obligation to declare a dividend in the corporation and may often decide that it is in the company's best interest to reinvest the surplus and profits in the business. The corporation is not under an obligation to pay dividends unless a dividend is declared. Although the courts generally abide by the discretion of the board of directors regarding the declaration of dividends, when the rights of minority shareholders or preferred shareholders are being infringed upon, the courts may intervene. The courts have held many times that the "rights of holders of preferred stock to dividends will be enforced in equity against the corporation in accordance with the terms of the contract."[19]

In addition, if the evidence shows that the board of directors is wrongfully withholding dividends from the profits of the corporation from minority shareholders, a court of equity may order the board of directors to declare a dividend out of surplus profits.

Exhibit 10-5 illustrates the payment of corporate dividends.

IN SUMMATION

- Dividends are payments to shareholders from the profits of a corporation as a return on the shareholders' investment.
- Dividends may only be paid from the profits of the corporation.
- Dividends may only be paid when the corporation is able to continue to meet its obligations after the dividends are paid. Most dividends are paid in the form of cash, but dividends may also be in the form of stock or other property.
- Dividends are paid at the discretion of the board of directors and there is no legal obligation to pay dividends until dividends are declared.
- Preferred stockholders often have priority over common stockholders with regard to payment of dividends.
- If preferred stockholders have a right to cumulative dividends, they are entitled to payment of any missed dividends from one period before dividends are paid on shares of common stock in the next period.
- Shareholder approval may be required for the payment of stock dividends.
- Dividends are declared by the board of directors for payment to all shareholders of record on a specific date.
- Directors are typically not obligated to declare a dividend on common stock and may decide instead to reinvest profits in the corporation.

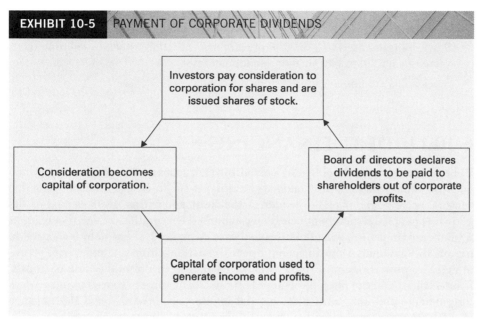

EXHIBIT 10-5   PAYMENT OF CORPORATE DIVIDENDS

Investors pay consideration to corporation for shares and are issued shares of stock.

Consideration becomes capital of corporation.

Board of directors declares dividends to be paid to shareholders out of corporate profits.

Capital of corporation used to generate income and profits.

© Cengage Learning 2013

§ 10.10 STOCK SPLITS

Although **stock splits** increase the issued number of shares, they are not considered stock dividends. Stock splits are used to lower the price of a corporation's stock. Stock splits are common among publicly held corporations with stock that has appreciated significantly, to the point where the price per share may appear prohibitive to the small investor. The effect of a stock split is to "split" the value of each share of stock into smaller denominations. For example, if a corporation's stock appreciates to the point where it is valued at the price of $100 per share, the board of directors may declare a two-for-one split and issue two $50 shares for each outstanding $100 share.

It is important to recognize the difference between a stock split and a stock dividend. Although stock splits increase the number of outstanding shares of a corporation that represent its capital, the actual amount of capital and surplus remain unchanged. A stock dividend, on the other hand, represents a transfer of earnings or profits to the capital of the corporation, together with a distribution of additional shares, which represents the addition of the earnings or profits to the corporation's capital.

STOCK SPLIT

A dividing of a company's stock into a greater number of shares without changing each stockholder's proportional ownership.

SIDE**BAR**

Although many stock splits are two-for-one splits, corporations may split their stock in any manner they deem appropriate, including three-for-one (three shares issued for each single share held), three-for-two (three shares issued for every two shares held), and so forth.

IN SUMMATION

- Stock splits are used to lower the price of a corporation's stock by splitting the value of each share into smaller denominations.
- Stock splits are not considered stock dividends.

§ 10.11 DEBT FINANCING

DEBT SECURITIES

Securities that represent loans to the corporation, or other interests that must be repaid.

Debt financing refers to obtaining capital through loans to the corporation, which must be repaid with interest upon the terms agreed to by contract between the corporation and lender or the holder of the **debt securities**. Debt is part of the permanent capital structure of nearly all established corporations. Even though debt is temporary in nature, most debt is rolled over on maturity. New debt is secured to pay off the old debt. Debt financing refers to anything from a simple loan, represented by a promissory note, to the issuance of debt securities in the form of **bonds**. Short-term capital can often be acquired by bank loans, either secured or unsecured. Intermediate and long-term **debt capital** is often acquired through the issuance of debt securities, including bonds and **debentures**. The term "bonds" generally refers to secured instruments. References to debentures are usually to unsecured instruments.

BOND

A document that states a debt owed by a company or a government. The company, government, or government agency promises to pay the owner of the bond a specific amount of interest for a set period of time and to repay the debt on a certain date. A bond, unlike a stock, gives the holder no ownership rights in the company.

Because of the significant tax (and nontax) advantages of raising capital through the issuance of bonds or other debt obligations, the board of directors often decides to maximize the use of debt financing. The interest paid to bondholders is generally deductible as a corporate expense, whereas dividends paid on shares of stock of the corporation are not deductible.

See Exhibit 10-6 for a comparison of equity financing and debt financing.

In this section, we look at the authority required to obtain debt financing on behalf of a corporation. We then focus on the two most common types of debt financing: bank loans and bonds.

DEBT CAPITAL

Capital raised with an obligation in terms of interest and principal payments. Debt capital is often raised by issuing bonds.

AUTHORITY FOR DEBT FINANCING

The board of directors usually decides what type of debt will suit the corporation's needs. Debt capital can be raised in the form of short-term, intermediate-term, or long-term financing, or any combination of the foregoing.

DEBENTURES

A corporation's obligation to pay money (usually in the form of a note or bond) often unsecured (not backed up) by any specific property. Usually refers only to long-term bonds.

The board of directors generally has the power to obtain debt financing on behalf of the corporation, although in some instances this power may be granted to the shareholders of the corporation in the articles of incorporation or state statutes. The board of directors may grant the corporation's president, or other appropriate officer, the authority to act on behalf of the corporation to obtain bank loans, within certain parameters. See Exhibit 10-7. The amount of indebtedness that a corporation can incur may be limited under the corporation's articles of incorporation.

EXHIBIT 10-6	EQUITY FINANCING vs. DEBT FINANCING

Equity	Debt
• Represents an ownership in the company.	• Represents a loan of capital to the company that must be repaid.
• Payment of dividends to shareholders is usually optional.	• Periodic payment of fixed interest to debt holders is usually mandatory.
• Dividends paid on shares of stock are not tax deductible.	• Interest paid on debt financing is tax deductible.
• Issuance of stock maintains a lower debt/equity ratio for the corporation.	• Too high a debt/equity ratio in corporation increases the likelihood of insolvency.
• Issuance of equity securities may dilute the current shareholders' control over the corporation.	• Incurring debt financing usually does not affect the current shareholders' control over the corporation.
• Shareholders are entitled to dividends only from the profits of the corporation (if any).	• Interest on debt is an expense that must be paid before profits can be calculated or dividends paid.

© Cengage Learning 2013

BANK LOANS

The terms of corporate bank loans are established in the loan agreements between the bank and the corporation. The loan can be for a specific term, or it can be in the form of a line of credit, on which the corporation can draw from time to time when additional cash is required. Depending on the corporation's credit rating, it may be able to obtain unsecured bank loans, but most corporate bank loans are secured, with the corporation pledging collateral to the bank, which will be executed or foreclosed on by the bank in the event of default.

COMMERCIAL PAPER

The term **commercial paper** refers to short-term, unsecured debt instruments that are issued by the corporation in the form of promissory notes. Commercial paper is purchased by banks, money market funds, and other large investors, typically at a discount of the face value at maturity. The difference between the purchase price and the face value, the discount, is the interest received on the investment. Commercial paper is increasingly used in place of bank borrowing as a means to quickly increase

COMMERCIAL PAPER
A negotiable instrument related to business—for example, a bill of exchange. Sometimes, the word is restricted to a company's control.

EXHIBIT 10-7	UNANIMOUS WRITTEN CONSENT OF BOARD OF DIRECTORS APPROVING BANK LOAN

UNANIMOUS WRITTEN CONSENT

OF THE BOARD OF DIRECTORS OF

_____ **CORPORATION**

The undersigned, being all of the directors of the _____ Corporation, (hereinafter referred to as the "Corporation"), hereby take the following actions by written consent in lieu of a meeting of the Board of Directors, pursuant to _____ [cite pertinent statute], effective as of this ____ day of _____, 20_____.

WHEREAS, it is agreed that it is in the best interests of the Corporation to enter into a loan agreement with the _____ Bank (hereinafter referred to as the "Bank") to provide for expansion funds for the Corporation.

IT IS HEREBY RESOLVED,

That the President of the Corporation is authorized to act on behalf of the Corporation to borrow the sum of up to Five Hundred Fifty Thousand Dollars ($550,000.00) from the Bank on the terms set out in the loan instrument attached to the minutes of this meeting,

IT IS HEREBY FURTHER RESOLVED

That the President is authorized to sign and execute the loan agreement, promissory note, and whatever other documents as necessary or required by said Bank to evidence indebtedness of Corporation to Bank; and the Secretary of the Corporation is to provide said Bank with a certified copy of these resolutions.

_____

_____

_____

_____

_____

© Cengage Learning 2013

cash flow at a relatively low interest rate. Because commercial paper is issued on a short-term basis, it is exempt from registration under federal securities law.

BONDS

Bonds can be issued to grant the bondholder a wide variety of rights. The rights of bondholders are defined by the terms of the bond contract between the corporation and the bondholder. However, the status of the bondholder differs from that of the stockholder in that the relationship of the bondholder to the corporation is more that of a creditor than an owner. Bondholders have no voting rights. Bonds are usually long-term secured debt instruments payable to the bearer, with interest, upon the terms indicated on the bond. Many bonds are coupon bonds that have detachable coupons, which may be presented to the corporation at prescribed intervals for interest payments.

Bonds that represent an unsecured loan to the corporation are referred to as debentures or simple debentures.

Bonds, or the contracts representing the agreement between the corporation and the bondholder, typically include the face value of the bond, the date when the principal repayment is due (the maturity date), and the terms for payment of interest, usually a fixed rate payable in periodic installments until the bond matures. Bonds may be issued for face value, or at a discount or premium.

Discounted Bonds

A debt obligation that bears no interest or interest at a lower-than-current-market rate is usually issued at less than its face amount—that is, at a discount. If bonds are issued at a discount, the difference between the issue price and the face value is deductible by the corporation over the life of the bonds. The discount is considered a form of interest for use of the funds received.

Premium Bonds

If the current market rate is higher than the interest rate on the debt security, the bonds may be issued at a premium. Any amount received for the bond that is over the face value on the bond is considered a premium.

Bonds are typically issued with accompanying bond contracts and indenture agreements setting forth the entire agreement between the corporation and the bondholder. The bond contract sets forth the terms for payment of interest on the bond, the maturity date of the bond, and any applicable conversion or redemption rights.

Conversion Rights

Bonds are often issued with conversion rights—the right of the bondholder to convert the bond to stock of the corporation at a set price at some time in the future. Investors who want initially to enjoy a higher income, with the potential to participate in appreciation, may find it desirable to purchase bonds with conversion rights. Basic conversion terms are typically set forth on the face of the bond, with further information in the accompanying bond contract. Bonds often have limitations within which the bondholder must exercise conversion rights, if they are to be exercised at all.

Redemption

Debt securities are often issued with a redemption right granted to the corporation. The right of redemption allows the corporation to buy back its securities on terms specified by the bond agreement. The corporation is usually required to notify the bondholder of its decision to exercise its right of redemption, and there is often a specified time after notice within which the conversion rights must be exercised.

SIDEBAR

During 2007, U.S. corporate income tax returns reported a total of more than $4.7 trillion in short-term debt and nearly $10.8 trillion in long-term debt.[20]

IN SUMMATION

- Debt financing involves obtaining capital through loans to the corporation that must be repaid upon the terms agreed to by contract between the corporation and lender.
- Short-term capital can often be acquired by bank loans.
- Long-term debt capital is often acquired through the issuance of debt securities—either bonds or debentures.
- The board of directors generally has authority to approve debt financing on behalf of the corporation.
- Commercial paper refers to short-term, unsecured debt instruments that are issued by the corporation and purchased by banks, money market funds, and other large investors.
- Bonds can be issued with a variety of rights for the bondholder that are defined by the terms of the bond contract between the corporation and the bondholder.
- A discounted bond is an obligation that is sold for a discount—less than its face value—and redeemed for its face value.
- A premium bond is a bond with a selling price that exceeds its face value.
- If a bond is issued with conversion rights, the bondholder has the right to convert the bond to stock of the corporation at a set price at some point in the future.
- Debt securities are often issued with a redemption right granted to the corporation.

§ 10.12 SECURED TRANSACTIONS AND THE UNIFORM COMMERCIAL CODE (UCC)

Corporations may obtain debt financing from several different sources, including banks, savings and loans, commercial finance companies, and the Small Business Administration.

Lenders who provide the debt financing will want assurances that they will have some recourse if the corporation should become unable to repay the loan. The lender may require the personal guarantee of shareholders, a mortgage on real estate the corporation owns, or a security interest in personal property the corporation owns. A security interest is an interest in property that secures payment or performance of an obligation. When a lender assumes a **security interest** in the borrower's **collateral**, it is a **secured transaction**.

Secured transactions are subject to Article 9 of the Uniform Commercial Code (UCC). The UCC, which was substantially revised in 2001, has been adopted by every state. It is designed to create a guide for commercial transactions under which people may predict with confidence the results of their business dealings. See Exhibit 10-8. The stated purposes of the UCC are the following:

1. To simplify, clarify, and modernize the law governing commercial transactions[21]
2. To permit the continued expansion of commercial practices through custom, usage, and agreement of the parties[22]
3. To make uniform the law among the various jurisdictions[23]

When the security interest is effective between debtor and creditor it is *attached* to the collateral. A security interest attaches to property when:

1. The debtor and creditor enter into a written security agreement that describes the collateral.
2. Value is given by the secured party to the debtor (the loan proceeds).
3. The debtor has rights in the collateral.

SECURITY INTEREST
Any right in property that is held to make sure money is paid or that something is done.

COLLATERAL
Money or property subject to a security interest.

SECURED TRANSACTION
A secured deal involving goods or fixtures that is governed by Article 9 of the Uniform Commercial Code.

EXHIBIT 10-8	ARTICLES OF THE UNIFORM COMMERCIAL CODE
Article 1.	General Provisions
Article 2.	Sales
Article 2A.	Leases
Article 3.	Negotiable Instruments
Article 4.	Bank Deposit
Article 4A.	Funds Transfers
Article 5.	Letters of Credit
Article 6.	Bulk Transfers and Bulk Sales
Article 7.	Warehouse Receipts, Bills of Lading and Other Documents of Title
Article 8.	Investment Securities
Article 9.	Secured Transactions

PERFECTION

To tie down or "make perfect." For example, to perfect title is to record it in the proper place so that your ownership is protected against all persons, not just against the person who sold it to you.

The security interest is effective against third parties when it is attached and perfected. **Perfection** gives the secured party priority over all other creditors with regard to the collateral. Under Article 9, a security interest is perfected when it is attached and the creditor is the first to file public notice of the secured interest in the collateral. The public notice gives all other creditors warning that any interest they may subsequently obtain in the collateral will be subordinate to the interest of the creditor who is first to file.

To give public notice of the secured interest, financing statements are filed at the state level. Financing statements may also be filed at the county or local level if the secured property includes fixtures. Fixtures are items that are attached to real property and considered to be a part of the real estate. Traditionally, financing statements have been in the form of a paper document, Form UCC-1. See Exhibit 10-9. More recently, most states accept electronic filing of financing statements. Regardless of the form of the filing, the financing statement is typically filed with a division of the secretary of state's office.

Financing statements filed under Article 9 include the following information:

1. The debtor's name and address
2. The secured party's name and address
3. An indication of the collateral
4. The debtor's signature (may not be required)

IN SUMMATION

- Corporations may obtain debt financing from:
  - Banks
  - Savings and loans
  - Commercial finance companies
  - Small Business Administration
- Lenders may require a security interest in the property of the corporation, either real property or personal property.
- When a lender assumes a security interest in the borrower's property, the loan is a secured transaction.
- Secured transactions are subject to Article 9 of the Uniform Commercial Code, which has been adopted by every state.
- To perfect a security interest in the borrower's collateral, the lender must be the first to file public notice of the secured interest.
- Financing statements (Form UCC-1) are filed at the state level and sometimes the county or local level to give notice of the lender's secured interest in the corporation's collateral.

EXHIBIT 10-9   UCC-1 FINANCING STATEMENT

UCC FINANCING STATEMENT
FOLLOW INSTRUCTIONS (front and back) CAREFULLY

A. NAME & PHONE OF CONTACT AT FILER [optional]

B. SEND ACKNOWLEDGMENT TO: (Name and Address)

THE ABOVE SPACE IS FOR FILING OFFICE USE ONLY

1. DEBTOR'S EXACT FULL LEGAL NAME - insert only one debtor name (1a or 1b) - do not abbreviate or combine names

1a. ORGANIZATION'S NAME			
1b. INDIVIDUAL'S LAST NAME	FIRST NAME	MIDDLE NAME	SUFFIX
1c. MAILING ADDRESS	CITY	STATE / POSTAL CODE	COUNTRY

| 1d. SEE INSTRUCTIONS | ADD'L INFO RE ORGANIZATION DEBTOR | 1e. TYPE OF ORGANIZATION | 1f. JURISDICTION OF ORGANIZATION | 1g. ORGANIZATIONAL ID #, if any | □ NONE |

2. ADDITIONAL DEBTOR'S EXACT FULL LEGAL NAME - insert only one debtor name (2a or 2b) - do not abbreviate or combine names

2a. ORGANIZATION'S NAME			
2b. INDIVIDUAL'S LAST NAME	FIRST NAME	MIDDLE NAME	SUFFIX
2c. MAILING ADDRESS	CITY	STATE / POSTAL CODE	COUNTRY

| 2d. SEE INSTRUCTIONS | ADD'L INFO RE ORGANIZATION DEBTOR | 2e. TYPE OF ORGANIZATION | 2f. JURISDICTION OF ORGANIZATION | 2g. ORGANIZATIONAL ID #, if any | □ NONE |

3. SECURED PARTY'S NAME (or NAME of TOTAL ASSIGNEE of ASSIGNOR S/P) - insert only one secured party name (3a or 3b)

3a. ORGANIZATION'S NAME			
3b. INDIVIDUAL'S LAST NAME	FIRST NAME	MIDDLE NAME	SUFFIX
3c. MAILING ADDRESS	CITY	STATE / POSTAL CODE	COUNTRY

4. This FINANCING STATEMENT covers the following collateral:

5. ALTERNATIVE DESIGNATION [if applicable]: □ LESSEE/LESSOR □ CONSIGNEE/CONSIGNOR □ BAILEE/BAILOR □ SELLER/BUYER □ AG. LIEN □ NON-UCC FILING

6. □ This FINANCING STATEMENT is to be filed [for record] (or recorded) in the REAL ESTATE RECORDS.   Attach Addendum [if applicable]   7. Check to REQUEST SEARCH REPORT(S) on Debtor(s) [ADDITIONAL FEE]   [optional]   □ All Debtors □ Debtor 1 □ Debtor 2

8. OPTIONAL FILER REFERENCE DATA

FILING OFFICE COPY — UCC FINANCING STATEMENT (FORM UCC1) (REV. 05/22/02)

Minnesota Secretary of State's Office

§ 10.13 EQUITY CAPITAL VERSUS DEBT CAPITAL

The board of directors often works with corporate management to determine the optimal capital structure—the best mix of both equity capital and debt capital. Both types of capital provide unique advantages and disadvantages to the corporation.

Some of the advantages of issuing equity securities to raise capital include the fact that the amount invested by shareholders does not have to be repaid, and dividends typically need not be paid to shareholders when the corporation is not earning a profit. As opposed to debt financing, the issuance of equity securities maintains a lower debt/equity ratio for the corporation, which increases the corporation's attractiveness to creditors and potential creditors and lowers the risk of insolvency. In addition, the corporation is not required to expend large sums of money on interest payments, as is usually the case with debt financing. One disadvantage of selling equity securities is the fact that the current shareholders' control over the corporation may be diluted.

Although debt capital must be repaid, debt financing also offers several advantages to the corporation. Most important, the control of the existing shareholders is not diluted by the issuance of debt securities. Also, the issuance of debt securities, as opposed to equity securities, offers certain tax advantages to the corporation, as the payment of interest on debt securities is generally tax deductible as an expense, whereas dividends paid to equity shareholders are not.

Some of the disadvantages of debt financing include the fact that interest must generally be paid on the securities, whether or not the corporation has any income for a particular period. If the debt-to-equity ratio in a corporation is too high, insolvency of the corporation is more likely.

It is generally the function of the corporation's board of directors to determine the best sources of capital and the best mix of equity and debt. One significant factor in that decision is the possible impact of the Federal Securities Act of 1933, the Securities Exchange Act of 1934, and the securities acts of the corporation's

IN SUMMATION

- It is generally up to the board of directors, working with the corporation's management, to determine the best mix of equity financing and debt financing to operate the corporation.
- Equity financing offers the following advantages:
  - Equity financing maintains a lower debt/equity ratio for the corporation.
  - The corporation is not required to make interest payments when it is not earning a profit.
- Debt financing offers the following advantages:
  - The control of existing shareholders is not diluted by the issuance of debt securities.
  - The payment of interest on debt securities may be tax deductible as an expense.

state of domicile. Public securities offerings are regulated by the Securities and Exchange Commission and are subject to the provisions of federal and state securities acts. Securities regulations and exemptions are discussed in Chapter 11.

§ 10.14 THE PARALEGAL'S ROLE

Paralegals are involved in corporate financial matters in several significant ways. It is important for all corporate paralegals to understand the basics of corporate financial matters and the relevant terminology.

CORPORATE PARALEGAL PROFILE
Amy Bernardino

My duties fluctuate between transactional and corporate maintenance, copyrights, drafting various agreements, and helping litigation and family law with clients who have interests in business ventures. I love that the work is so varied I can't possibly become bored.

NAME Amy Bernardino

LOCATION Encino, California

TITLE Corporate Paralegal

SPECIALTY Corporate governance and maintenance, mergers, acquisitions, and various other transactions

EDUCATION BS University of Phoenix; University of West Los Angeles School of Paralegal Studies with a Corporate Specialist Certificate

EXPERIENCE 6 years

Amy Bernardino is a paralegal with Lewitt, Hackman, Shapiro, Marshall & Harlan, a 22-attorney law firm that employs three paralegals in Encino, California. Lewitt Hackman is a full-service business, real estate, and civil litigation law firm. Amy reports to the firm's managing partner.

Amy specializes in the corporate area, with an emphasis on mergers and acquisitions. She supports tax planning, corporate, franchise and intellectual property attorneys with various matters, including property and business tax research and document preparation.

One of her primary responsibilities is to provide support for corporate mergers, acquisitions, and other transactions. She also prepares corporate minutes, forms and dissolves corporations and other business entities, and prepares franchise disclosure documents and copyright registrations. Amy provides backup support to litigation and family law attorneys and paralegals when document productions and other discovery matters are involved.

While the list of Amy's responsibilities may seem overwhelming, the variety of her position is one of the things she likes the most. According to Amy, she loves that the work is so varied she could not possibly become bored.

One of the most interesting projects Amy has been involved in was the sale of three hospitals under a local hospital district to a group of private physicians. The transaction involved compliance not only with various state rules on acquisitions, but also with various restrictions and governance issues imposed by hospital regulators (Medicare, Department of Health and Human Services, etc.). Amy was responsible for creating and maintaining due

continues

CORPORATE PARALEGAL PROFILE
Amy Bernardino (continued)

diligence and closing checklists, reviewing due diligence materials, creating and maintaining complex schedules, and drafting or otherwise preparing closing documents. One benefit of working on a project of such a large scope, and any merger, acquisition, or transactional project, is the overwhelming sense of accomplishment when the deal closes. This particular deal took 18 months to close.

In the past, Amy has served as director and secretary of the Los Angeles Paralegal Association, as well as cochair of the Association's San Fernando Valley Section. Her pro bono experience includes participation in California's Adoption Day and the filing of German ghetto work-payment applications for Holocaust survivors.

Amy's advice to new paralegals?
It can be hard for a new paralegal to get that first paralegal job. When applying, make sure your cover letter or e-mail (yes, you need one) explains how your previous career experience lends itself to being a paralegal. Also, even if you are not currently employed as a paralegal, do not let your MCLE lapse. Continuing education will set you apart from the rest.

For more information on careers for corporate paralegals, log in to http://www.cengagebrain.com to access the CourseMate website that accompanies this text; then see the Corporate Careers Section.

ETHICAL CONSIDERATION

Attorney Responsibility to Treat Clients Fairly with Regard to Financial Matters

Because attorneys owe a fiduciary duty to their clients, it is especially important that clients are treated fairly with regard to financial matters involving the attorney and client. Where attorneys' fees are concerned, attorneys have an ethical duty to bill their clients fairly and receive no excessive or unfair payment for their services.

Attorneys may charge a flat fee, an hourly fee, or a contingent fee for their services. When a client is charged a contingent fee, the attorney agrees to accept a percentage of what is collected on behalf of the client in a lawsuit or settlement (usually one-fourth to one-third of the amount collected). If the attorney collects nothing for the client, the client will not owe the attorney for any legal fees, aside from costs the attorney may have incurred on the client's behalf.

continues

ETHICAL CONSIDERATION
(continued)

Regardless of how the client is billed, the attorney's fees charged must be reasonable. Several factors may be taken into consideration when determining what a reasonable fee is. Some of those factors include:

- The time and labor the attorney spends on the representation

- The attorney's preclusion from other employment

- The customary fee charged for similar representation in the same geographical area

- The results obtained for the client

- The nature and length of the professional relationship between the attorney and client

- The experience, reputation, and ability of the attorney

- Whether the fee charged is contingent or fixed

Although paralegal time is generally billed to the client, paralegals will not have responsibility for setting their billing rates. This is typically done by the responsible attorney or law firm administrator. In most law firms, paralegals do have responsibility for keeping track of their time and providing accurate records for billing. You will probably be given a billing goal of a certain number of hours to be billed each year. If you work in a situation where you are responsible for tracking your time for billing purposes, you must be certain to keep meticulous records and always be fair and honest.

For more information on ethics for corporate paralegals, including links to the NALA and NFPA codes of ethics, log in to http://www.cengagebrain .com to access the CourseMate website that accompanies this text; then see the Ethics Section.

Corporate paralegals may be involved in researching questions concerning the requirements for debt and equity financing, and for drafting several different types of documents relating to the corporate financial structure, including:

1. Provisions in the articles of incorporation concerning the authorized stock of the corporation, including the par value and the rights and preferences associated with each class of stock issued
2. Stock subscription agreements
3. Resolutions of the board of directors approving the issuance of stock

4. Resolutions of the board of directors approving the payment of dividends on shares of issued stock
5. Resolutions of the board of directors concerning the redemption of stock
6. Resolutions of the board of directors approving stock dividends and stock splits
7. Resolutions of the board of directors approving bank loans and other types of debt financing

Paralegals are often directly involved in assisting with the closing of large bank loans and debt financing projects. Transactions involving debt financing may be very document intensive, and the corporate paralegal is often responsible for assisting with the drafting of the documents and for assembling the documents for closing. Exhibit 10-10 lists some of the documents that may be required for closing a corporate loan transaction.

When a secured transaction is involved, paralegals are often responsible for drafting the security agreement and drafting and filing the UCC forms with the secretary of state. Paralegals who work with UCC transactions must be familiar with the procedures at the secretary of state's office to conduct UCC searches (for financing statements filed previously on collateral), and they must be familiar with the procedures for filing UCC financing statements.

A typical secured transaction may include the following steps:

1. The corporation's management approaches a bank for a loan.
2. The bank and corporation come to agreement on loan terms that includes the corporation giving the bank a security interest in all equipment in its only factory.

EXHIBIT 10-10	DOCUMENTS THAT MAY BE REQUIRED FOR CLOSING A CORPORATE LOAN TRANSACTION

Loan Documents

Loan Agreement

Promissory Note

Security Documents

Security Agreement

Form UCC-1 Filings

Mortgage

Pledge Agreements

Personal Guaranties

Documents Concerning Corporate Existence and Good Standing

Certified Copy of the Corporation's Articles of Incorporation

Certificate of Good Standing from Secretary of State

Board of Directors Resolution Approving the Transaction

© Cengage Learning 2013

3. The bank conducts a UCC search at the secretary of state's office and determines that no prior financing statements have been filed on the factory equipment to be used as collateral.

4. A loan agreement and financing agreement are signed on behalf of the corporation and the bank.

5. The bank files a UCC-1 financing statement at the secretary of state's office, giving public notice of its security interest in the factory equipment.

6. Over time, the loan is paid off and a Form UCC-3 financing statement amendment is filed at the secretary of state's office, giving notice of the termination of the security interest.

§ 10.15 RESOURCES

The most important resources for paralegals who are concerned with corporate financial matters are the pertinent state statutes and forms and form books. Financial matters concerning the public offering of securities that are subject to securities laws will be discussed in Chapter 11.

STATE STATUTES

The authorized stock and par value provisions of the corporation's articles of incorporation must comply with the statutes of the corporation's state of domicile. For that reason, state statutes are a very important resource for paralegals.

FORMS AND FORM BOOKS

Paralegals who are working with corporate financial transactions will rely heavily on forms available in the office and standard forms found in form books and CLE materials. Sample resolutions and other documents relating to corporate financial matters can also be found online from several different sources. Before any of these forms are used, they must be carefully reviewed and edited to be certain that they meet the statutory requirements of your state and that they meet the corporation's intended purpose. Links to the statutes of every state and websites that provide forms may be accessed through CourseMate.

SUMMARY

- The corporation's directors and officers rely on equity and debt capital to operate the business of the corporation.
- Equity securities represent an ownership interest in the corporation.
- Common stock and preferred stock are equity securities.
- The corporation's articles or certificate of incorporation may provide for different classes of common and preferred stock, granting the holders different rights and preferences.

- If the corporation only issues one type of stock, it is common stock that grants the holders unlimited voting rights and the right to receive the assets of the corporation upon its dissolution.
- Debt securities represent a loan to the corporation that must be paid.
- Dividends are often paid to the holders of equity securities.
- Preferred stock is stock that entitles the holders of shares to a priority over the holders of shares of common stock, usually with regard to dividends and distribution of the assets of the corporation in the event of dissolution or liquidation of the corporation.
- Preferred stock is often issued with conversion rights, allowing the preferred stockholders to convert their shares to shares of common stock under prescribed conditions.
- Par value is the nominal value assigned to shares of stock, which is imprinted upon the face of the stock certificate as a dollar value. The trend in corporate law is to allow stock without par value.
- Dividends may be paid in cash, stock, or any other property deemed appropriate by the board of directors.
- Debt financing may be in the form of bank loans, loans from shareholders, or bonds or other instruments issued by the corporation.
- Interest must be paid to the holders of debt securities.
- Debt capital is an obligation that must be repaid by the corporation.
- Corporate loans are often secured by granting a security interest in collateral to the lender.
- Under Article 9 of the Uniform Commercial Code, a security interest is perfected when it is attached and the creditor is the first to file a UCC-1 financing statement with the proper state authority, giving notice of the creditor's interest in the collateral.

REVIEW QUESTIONS

1. The owners of A&S Marketing, Inc., need financing to expand their business. A&S has only three shareholders and few assets. However, it does have a marketing plan for substantial, sustained growth in revenue. What type of financing may be most beneficial to the owners of A&S Marketing, Inc.? Why?

2. Assume that G&A Corporation, an established manufacturing business, is owned by six shareholders who all actively participate in the business. G&A Corporation has an opportunity to enter into a very lucrative new contract, but the corporation needs $500,000 in capital to hire extra personnel and design and build the new equipment it will need to fulfill the contract. Why might the current shareholders want to issue preferred stock to raise the funds it will need?

3. Assume the same circumstances as in Question 2. Why might the current shareholders want to use debt capital to fund their expansion?

4. The articles of incorporation of the Jerry Corporation authorize "10,000 shares of stock, no par value." No further information is given in the articles. Are these shares of common stock or preferred stock?

5. What two widely accepted requirements must be granted to shareholders under the MBCA?

6. Are all common stockholders always granted voting rights?

7. What are redemption rights?

8. What are conversion rights?

9. What are some possible drawbacks to issuing stock with a par value?

10. What information is typically required to be included on stock certificates?

11. The authorized stock of Rob's Boatworks, Inc., is 10,000 shares of common stock, $1.00 par value. If Rob's Boatworks issues 1,000 shares to Bud Peterson for $800, what term is used to describe Mr. Peterson's shares? What are the possible consequences to Mr. Peterson?

▣ PRACTICAL PROBLEMS

What are the statutory requirements for par value in your state? Find the pertinent statutes for your state to answer the following questions:

1. Must corporations in your state issue stock with a stated par value?

2. Does the number of shares or par value of authorized stock of new corporations in your state affect the filing fee for the corporation's articles of incorporation? If yes, how?

▣ EXERCISE IN CRITICAL THINKING

What are some of the reasons new businesses may rely more heavily on equity financing in times of economic downturn? What are some potential drawbacks to relying too heavily on equity financing?

▣ WORKPLACE SCENARIO

Assume that the directors of our fictional corporation, Cutting Edge Computer Repair, Inc., have decided that it is in the best interest of the corporation to lease a retail location for their business. They will need approximately $250,000 to make the necessary improvements to the location they have decided on. Because they do not want to involve another owner in the business, Bradley Harris and Cynthia Lund have agreed on debt financing.

Using the earlier information, the information in Appendix B-3 of this text, and the information and examples in this chapter, prepare a unanimous written consent of the board of directors of Cutting Edge Computer Repair, Inc., approving a $250,000 loan from the First Bank of Center City. The First Bank of Center City will provide the loan documents. The board of directors must authorize the appropriate officers to execute the loan agreement on behalf of the corporation.

Portfolio Reminder:
Save the documents prepared for the Workplace Scenario exercises in each chapter, either in hard copy or electronically, to build a portfolio of documents to be used for job interviews or as sample documents on the job. At this point, your portfolio should include the following:

- Power of attorney
- Application for assumed name
- Application for federal employer identification number
- Application for state employer identification number
- Partnership statement of authority
- Limited partnership certificate
- Limited liability partnership statement of qualification

- Articles of organization
- Subchapter S election by small business corporation, Form 2553
- Articles of incorporation
- Unanimous written consent of shareholders

- Unanimous written consent of the board of directors
- Unanimous written consent of board of directors approving bank loan

ENDNOTES

1. 18a Am. Jur. 2d Corporations § 355 (May 2011).

2. *Radaszewski v. Telecom*, 981 F2d 305 (CA8 1982).

3. Booth, Richard A., *Financing the Corporation* § 2:1 (2005).

4. Model Business Corporation Act revised through December 2007 (hereinafter MBCA) § 6.02.

5. 6 Am. Jur. Legal Forms 2d Corporations § 74:459 (May 2011).

6. Fletcher's Cyclopedia of the Law of Private Corporations § 5080.40 (Feb. 2011).

7. 18A Am. Jur. 2d Corporations § 375 (May 2011).

8. 6 Am. Jur. Legal Forms 2d Corporations § 74:421 (May 2011). Reprinted with permission from American Jurisprudence Legal Forms 2d. © 2012 West Group.

9. MBCA § 6.22(a).

10. MBCA § 6.21(b).

11. Id. § 6.26.

12. Id. § 6.25(c).

13. Id. § 6.31(a).

14. 6A Am. Jur. Legal Forms 2d Corporations § 74:1231 (May 2011). Reprinted with permission from American Jurisprudence Legal Forms 2d. © 2012 West Group.

15. 18B Am. Jur. 2d Corporations § 1015 (May 2011).

16. Id.

17. Id. § 1093 (May 2011).

18. 6A Am. Jur. Legal Forms 2d Corporations § 74:1428 (May 2011). Reprinted with permission from American Jurisprudence Legal Forms 2d. © 2008 West Group.

19. 18B Am. Jur. 2d Corporations § 1112 (May 2011).

20. U.S. Census Bureau, *The 2011 Statistical Abstract of the United States*, Table 752 (2011).

21. U.C.C. § 1-103(a)(2).

22. U.C.C. § 1-103(a)(2).

23. U.C.C. § 1-102(2)(c).

CourseMate

To access additional course materials, including CourseMate, please visit http://www.cengagebrain.com. At the CengageBrain home page, search for the ISBN of your title (from the back cover of your book) using the search box at the top of the page. This will take you to the product page where these resources can be found. The CourseMate resources for this text include Web links, downloadable forms, flash cards, and more.

CHAPTER

11

PUBLIC CORPORATIONS AND SECURITIES REGULATIONS

CHAPTER OUTLINE

INTRODUCTION

Securities regulation of public corporations is a very complex topic that is often treated separately from the law of corporations. However, because many corporate paralegals spend a significant portion of their time working with matters related to securities, and because this topic is generally not addressed in separate paralegal texts, this chapter gives a brief overview of public corporations, also referred to as publicly held corporations, and securities regulation. This chapter looks at certain aspects of the public corporation, including the distinction between public and closely held corporations, and then examines the markets in which securities are traded, the Securities and Exchange Commission, the federal regulations imposed by the Securities Act of 1933, the Securities Exchange Act of 1934, the Sarbanes-Oxley Act, and state securities regulations or "blue sky laws." This chapter concludes with a look at the paralegal's role in working with securities matters and the resources available to those paralegals.

§ 11.1 THE PUBLIC CORPORATION

PUBLIC CORPORATION

A corporation that has shares listed on a national securities exchange or shares that are regularly traded in a market maintained by one or more members of a national securities association. Also referred to as publicly held corporation or publicly traded corporation.

A **public corporation** is a corporation that has shares listed on a national securities exchange or shares that are regularly traded in a market maintained by one or more members of a national securities association.[1] For our purposes, this term is used synonymously with the terms "publicly held corporation" and "publicly traded corporation."

Although public corporations represent only a small percentage of all corporations in the United States, their enormous economic impact in this country is immeasurable. During 2008, the value of shares traded on the New York Stock Exchange exceeded $28.27 trillion.[2]

In contrast to the closely held corporation, the public corporation has a public market for its shares, regardless of the size of the corporation. During 2007, more than half of the families in the United States had direct or indirect stock holdings.[3] Indirect ownership of stock may mean that the stock is held in an individual's pension or profit sharing plan. Also, unlike the securities of closely held corporations, securities that are offered and traded publicly are subject to federal securities regulations. Any securities offered, sold, or delivered through any means of interstate commerce (including the U.S. Postal Service) are considered to be part of a **public offering**, and must first be registered in accordance with the Securities Act of 1933 and any applicable state securities law. When the shareholders of a corporation decide to sell the corporation's securities to the public, that transaction is often referred to as going public, and the first offering of a corporation's securities to the public is often referred to as the **initial public offering (IPO)**.

PUBLIC OFFERING

Offering of securities for sale to the public by means of interstate commerce.

INITIAL PUBLIC OFFERING

The first offering of a corporation's securities to the public.

A record number of corporations went public during the late 1990s, led by a boom in high-tech and Internet company stocks. Overall, initial public offerings are much more common when stock market values and investor optimism are high. In times when market values and market confidence are lower, the number of initial public offerings tends to decline. Exhibit 11-1 shows a graph of the initial public offerings by corporations from 2004 through 2010.

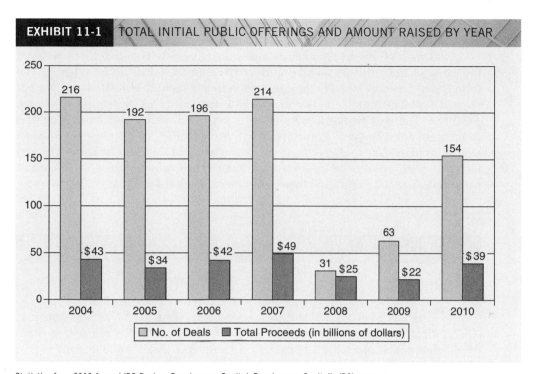

EXHIBIT 11-1   TOTAL INITIAL PUBLIC OFFERINGS AND AMOUNT RAISED BY YEAR

Statistics from 2010 Annual IPO Review, Renaissance Capital, Renaissance Capital's IPOhome.com.

The decision to go public with a corporation is typically made by its directors and principal shareholders, with the advice of their attorneys and accountants. Going public with a corporation has significant ramifications for the company's future as well as the future stake of its shareholders.

The most obvious advantage to going public is the increased availability of capital through the sale of stock, and the potential increase in the availability of future capital because of the corporation's ability to offer investors a security that is liquid and has an ascertainable market value. Public corporations also may have an advantage over closely held corporations when it comes to hiring and retaining qualified personnel. In addition, the corporation that goes public often has the advantage of gaining national exposure for itself and its products or services.

When making the decision to go public, there are considerable disadvantages that must be weighed, including the fact that the current shareholders of the corporation will experience a certain loss of control, especially in matters requiring shareholder approval. The cost of going public and complying with the federal and state securities regulations that are imposed on public corporations can be significant. Also, the federal and state reporting regulations to which public corporations are subject may require public disclosure of information that corporate management would prefer to keep private. Federal securities regulations can impose a significant burden on a corporation, both financially and on the time of the corporation's management. See Exhibit 11-2 for an overview of the advantages and disadvantages of going public.

After the decision to go public is made, an agreement is entered into between the issuer of the securities and the **underwriter** for the initial public offering. The term *issuer* generally refers to the corporation that is about to issue its stock or other securities, although the definition may include any individual who proposes to issue securities. The underwriter is any person or organization that purchases securities from an issuer, with a view to distribution of those securities, or any person who offers or sells, or participates in the offer or sale, for an issuer of any security. Large financial institutions and brokers typically serve as underwriters, who purchase the securities from the issuer and in turn sell those securities to dealers for resale.

UNDERWRITER

With regard to securities offerings, any person or organization that purchases securities from an issuer with a view to distributing them, or any person who offers or sells or participates in the offer or sale for an issuer of any security.

EXHIBIT 11-2	ADVANTAGES AND DISADVANTAGES OF GOING PUBLIC
Advantages	**Disadvantages**
• *Increased Availability of Capital.* Increased capital is available to a public corporation through the sale of the corporation's stock.	• *Current Shareholders Will Experience a Certain Loss of Control.* Current shareholders will have to submit to the vote of a majority of all shareholders on certain matters, including the election of the board of directors.
• *Potential Increase in Future Capital.* The public corporation has the ability to offer additional securities in the future.	• *The Cost of Going Public Can Be Considerable.* The fees paid to legal advisors, financial advisors, and underwriters, as well as filing fees, can be a significant burden to a corporation that goes public.
• *Ability to Hire and Retain Qualified Personnel.* Stock and other incentives that may be offered by public corporations give those corporations an advantage over smaller, privately held corporations when competing for the most sought-after directors and employees.	• *State and Federal Reporting Requirements Require Disclosure.* Once a corporation goes public, its books are open to inspection. Certain financial information concerning the corporation and its officers and directors is no longer private.
• *National Exposure.* A corporation that chooses to go public gains national exposure for itself and its products or services.	• *Compliance with Federal Securities Regulations Can Be Expensive and Time Consuming.*

© Cengage Learning 2013

The issuers and underwriters agree to the terms and details of their relationship in an underwriting agreement. The issuer may enter into underwriting agreements with more than one underwriter. The underwriters agree to sell the securities on a "firm commitment" or "best-efforts" basis. If the underwriters give a firm commitment, they commit to purchasing an agreed-upon amount of securities of the corporation at an agreed-upon price; the resale of those securities becomes the responsibility of the underwriters. Unlike the firm commitment, whereby the underwriter assumes the risk for the sale of the securities, underwriters selling on a best-efforts basis are obligated to use their best efforts to sell the securities of the issuer, but are required to take and pay for only those securities that they may sell to the public. When a best-efforts arrangement is made, the proceeds paid to the issuers will depend on the amount of securities sold by the underwriters.

IN SUMMATION

- A public corporation has its shares traded on a national securities exchange or in a market maintained by one or more members of a national securities association. Securities must be registered in accordance with the Securities Exchange Act of 1933 before they are offered to the public for sale.

- The first offering of a corporation's securities to the public is often referred to as an initial public offering (IPO).

- The decision to offer a corporation's shares to the public is usually made by the board of directors and shareholders with the advice of their attorneys and accountants.

- The primary advantage to a corporation that offers its shares to the public is the increase in available capital—both immediate and future capital—as shares of the corporation are sold.

- Disadvantages to taking a corporation public include the loss of control by current shareholders and the increased time and expense to comply with securities regulations imposed on public corporations.

§ 11.2 SECURITIES AND SECURITIES MARKETS

When a corporation goes public, it is offering shares of the corporation to the public in the form of securities. Those securities are then traded on a market.

DEFINITION OF SECURITIES

The securities offered when a corporation goes public are usually in the form of stocks, bonds, or debentures. However, securities can take on many different forms. In *SEC v. W. J. Howey Co.*, 328 U.S. 293 (1946), the Supreme Court found that the sale of individual rows of orange trees in conjunction with a service contract for maintenance of the trees and the marketing of their crop involved a "security." The test used by the Supreme Court to detect a security was whether "the person invests his money in a common enterprise and is led to expect profits solely from the efforts of the promoter or a third party." Several types of instruments are generally recognized as securities under federal regulations, including any note, stock, treasury stock, security future, bond, debenture, evidence of indebtedness, certificate of interest, or participation in any profit-sharing agreement; collateral-trust certificate, preorganization certificate or subscription, transferable share, investment contract, voting-trust certificate, or certificate of deposit for a security; fractional undivided interest in oil, gas, or other mineral rights; any put, call, straddle, option, or privilege on any security, certificate of deposit, or group or index of securities (including any interest therein or based on the value thereof); or any put, call, straddle, option, or privilege entered into on a national securities exchange relating to foreign currency; or, in general, any interest or instrument commonly known as a "security," or any certificate of interest or participation in, temporary or interim certificate for, receipt for, guarantee of, or warrant or right to subscribe to or purchase, any of the foregoing.[4]

MARKETS

SECURITIES AND EXCHANGE COMMISSION
A federal agency that administers the federal securities acts, primarily by regulating the sale and trading of stocks and other securities.

After a decision is made to take a corporation public, the decision must be made as to the best means to trade the corporation's securities. Corporations that qualify will typically trade their shares on one of the national exchanges that are regulated by the **Securities and Exchange Commission**. Corporations that do not meet the listing requirements for those exchanges may decide to sell their stock over the counter.

EXCHANGES

EXCHANGE
An organization set up to buy and sell securities such as stocks.

An **exchange** is an organization, association, or group that provides or maintains a marketplace where securities, options, futures, or commodities can be bought and sold. Traditionally, stock exchanges were actual physical locations where securities were traded by exchange members on the exchange floor. In recent years, with the advent of online trading, not all exchanges use exchange floors to trade stocks and commodities.

Registered stock exchanges in the United States currently include:

- NYSE Amex, LLC (formerly the American Stock Exchange)
- BATS Exchange, Inc.
- NASDAQ OMX BX, Inc. (formerly the Boston Stock Exchange)
- C2 Options Exchange, Inc.
- Chicago Board Options Exchange, Inc.
- Chicago Stock Exchange, Inc.
- EDGA Exchange, Inc.

- EDGX Exchange, Inc.
- International Securities Exchange, LLC
- The NASDAQ Stock Market, LLC
- National Stock Exchange, Inc.
- New York Stock Exchange, LLC
- NYSE Arca, Inc.
- NASDAQ OMX PHLX, Inc. (formerly Philadelphia Stock Exchange)

New York Stock Exchange

All stock exchanges establish minimum standards for their listing corporations. The New York Stock Exchange (NYSE), among the largest and most prestigious of the stock exchanges, has the most stringent listing standards of any of the exchanges. For example, among other requirements, U.S. corporations must meet certain minimum stock distribution requirements and certain minimum financial requirements. There are several tests corporations can choose from to meet the minimum financial requirements of the NYSE; some of these include:

- Pretax earnings of at least $10 million for the three years prior to listing
- Aggregate operating cash flow of at least $25 million for the three years prior to listing
- Revenues of $75 million for the most recent fiscal year, and $750 million in global market capitalization

In addition, the NYSE has established listing requirements that corporations must adhere to on an ongoing basis, including requirements for corporate governance.

Trading on the NYSE has always taken place on a trading floor where qualified floor brokers and specialists buy and sell stock in an auction style. In recent years, the NYSE has moved to a hybrid market that automates much of what the brokers and dealers do, although there is still trading on the floor of the NYSE.

NASDAQ

When the National Association of Securities Dealers Automated Quotation system (NASDAQ) opened in 1971, it was not considered a stock exchange, but rather an automated quotation system for **over-the-counter** stocks. With no trading floor, the NASDAQ served as a new model for the stock exchanges, and in 2006 the NASDAQ moved from a national securities association to a national securities exchange, falling under the rules of the Securities and Exchange Commission. NASDAQ, the largest U.S. electronic stock market, has approximately 3,500 listed companies, and, on average, trades more shares per day than any other U.S. market.[5]

OVER-THE-COUNTER
Describes securities, such as stocks and bonds, sold directly from broker to broker or broker to customer rather than through an exchange.

OVER-THE-COUNTER MARKETS

The stock and other securities of companies that do not meet the listing requirements of the major stock exchanges may be traded in the over-the-counter (OTC) market, by means of the OTC Bulletin Board, Pink OTC Markets, or some other electronic inter-dealer quotation system. Broker-dealers who operate in the over-the-counter market are subject to regulation of the Financial Industry Regulatory Authority (FINRA).

The OTC Bulletin Board is an electronic quotation system that provides dealers with real-time quotes, last-sale prices, and volume information on over-the-counter stocks that are not traded on a national securities exchange. Companies that want their securities quoted on this system must file current financial reports with the SEC or with their banking or insurance regulators.

Pink Quote is a similar electronic quotation system. Pink Quote is operated by Pink OTC Markets, Inc., sometimes referred to by its former name "Pink Sheets." Pink Sheets derived its name from the color of the paper used when the stock information is circulated in hard copy. There are very few requirements for companies trading on the Pink Sheets system, and most do not file financial information with the SEC.

IN SUMMATION

- In addition to shares of corporate stock, the term "securities" includes several other types of instruments, including notes, bonds, and debentures.
- Stock of public corporations is typically traded on one of the national exchanges regulated by the Securities and Exchange Commission.
- There are currently several stock exchanges operating in the United States and regulated by the SEC. The largest are the NYSE and NASDAQ.
- Both the NYSE and NASDAQ have stringent requirements for corporations listed on their exchanges, including financial requirements and corporate governance requirements.
- Corporations that do not qualify to trade their securities on one of the exchanges may trade their shares on the over-the-counter market.

§ 11.3 THE SECURITIES AND EXCHANGE COMMISSION

Prior to 1933, the only federal regulation of securities was under the jurisdiction of the Federal Trade Commission. To restore public confidence in the capital markets following the stock market crash of 1929 and the continuing Great Depression, Congress passed the **Securities Act of 1933** and the **Securities Exchange Act of 1934**. These laws were passed on the following premises:[6]

1. Companies publicly offering securities for investment dollars must tell the public the truth about their businesses, the securities they are selling, and the risks involved in investing.
2. People who sell and trade securities—brokers, dealers, and exchanges—must treat investors fairly and honestly, putting investors' interests first.

The Securities and Exchange Commission (SEC) was established in 1934 to "promote stability in the markets and, most importantly, to protect investors."[7] The SEC's primary mission is to protect investors and maintain the integrity of the securities market. The SEC is headed by five presidentially appointed commissioners, each appointed for five years. Each year, one commissioner's term expires, and one new commissioner is appointed.

The SEC has the power to enforce the Securities Act of 1933, which relates to the initial registration and issuance of securities through means of interstate commerce, and the Securities Exchange Act of 1934, which relates to ongoing public disclosures by public corporations and requires registration of all over-the-counter brokers and dealers of securities and stock exchanges. The SEC has broad rule-making powers under the statutes it administers. For example, the Securities Act of 1933 provides the SEC with authority to allow certain exemptions from registration under that act. Under that authority, the SEC has issued several rules that provide specific exemption requirements.

SECURITIES ACT OF 1933
Federal securities act requiring the registration of securities that are to be sold to the public and the disclosure of complete information to potential buyers.

SECURITIES EXCHANGE ACT OF 1934
Federal securities act regulating stock exchanges and over-the-counter stock sales.

SIDEBAR

The first chairman of the SEC was Joseph P. Kennedy, father of President John F. Kennedy. He was appointed by President Franklin Delano Roosevelt.

The SEC has civil enforcement authority—the authority to bring civil suits for the violation of securities laws. Each year the SEC brings hundreds of civil enforcement actions against individuals and corporations for violations of securities laws. The SEC also works closely with various criminal law enforcement agencies to bring criminal cases where warranted.

The SEC was the subject of much criticism for its role in the financial crisis of 2008 and its failure to detect the Bernard Madoff Ponzi scheme, despite several allegations against Madoff being brought to the attention of SEC employees. In response to that criticism, Mary Shapiro, the SEC Chairman who was appointed in

2009, has created five specialized teams of specialists to focus on particular types of fraud schemes. The five new units include:

Asset management

Market abuse

Structured and new products

Foreign corrupt practices act

Municipal securities and public pensions

SIDEBAR

In fiscal year 2010, the SEC dedicated more than $1,058 million to achieve its goals of enforcing compliance with the federal securities laws, promoting healthy capital markets, fostering informed investment decision making, and maximizing the use of agency resources.[8]

IN SUMMATION

- The Securities and Exchange Commission was created in 1934 to promote stability in the markets and protect investors following the stock market crash of 1929 and the beginning of the Great Depression.
- The SEC has the power to enforce the Securities Act of 1933, the Securities Exchange Act of 1934, and other securities laws.

§ 11.4 FEDERAL REGULATION OF SECURITIES OFFERINGS UNDER THE SECURITIES ACT OF 1933

The Securities Act of 1933 (the Securities Act) was the first significant federal legislation to be passed to protect the investor through the imposition of disclosure and antifraud requirements on corporations issuing securities through means of interstate commerce.

The SEC may prevent the distribution of securities if the disclosure requirements of the Securities Act are not complied with. Further, material misstatements in the disclosure documents or noncompliance with the antifraud provisions of the Securities Act may subject the issuer of the securities to civil liabilities or even criminal sanctions. The most significant provisions of the Securities Act for the corporation that is going public are the requirements for registering the securities to be offered to the public and for using prospectuses for the sale of all registered securities.

SECURITIES REGISTRATION

The application of the Securities Act of 1933 extends beyond stocks and bonds traded in the stock exchange and over-the-counter markets. Any "securities" as that term is defined in the Securities Act[9] must be registered under the Securities Act or offered and sold pursuant to an exemption from registration under the act. Generally, prior to the issuance of any securities through interstate commerce, the issuer must file a registration statement with the SEC. The intended purpose of the registration statement is to disclose the information necessary to allow investors to make an informed decision.

Section 5 of the Securities Act contains the major provisions regarding the registration of securities. Section 5(a) prohibits the sale and delivery of unregistered securities.

Section 5

(a) Unless a registration statement is in effect as to a security, it shall be unlawful for any person, directly or indirectly—

1. to make use of any means or instruments of transportation or communication in interstate commerce or of the mails to sell such security through the use or medium of any prospectus or otherwise; or

2. to carry or cause to be carried through the mails or in interstate commerce, by any means or instruments of transportation, any such security for the purpose of sale or for delivery after sale.

The registration statement is filed electronically via EDGAR in the form prescribed by the SEC. Form S-1 (see Exhibit 11-3) is commonly used. However, several other forms are prescribed for certain types of registrations.

The registration statement consists of two parts. Part I is the prospectus, which must be furnished to all purchasers of the corporation's securities. Part II consists of additional information required by the SEC, including very detailed information with respect to the securities being offered for sale and the corporation's operation, financial status, management, and current ownership. The information required by the registration statement is set forth in Schedule A of the Securities Act.

The registration statement is filed with the SEC and must be accompanied by a filing fee that is based on the maximum aggregate price at which the securities are to be offered. The registration statement is considered to be filed, but not effective, on the date it is received by the SEC with the proper fee.

The registration statement is effective 20 days from the date of filing with the SEC. However, the SEC often requires material amendments to the registration statement that delay the effective date beyond 20 days. Pre-effective amendments may be made in response to comments from the SEC staff, and also to reflect a change in the offering price range based on the reaction to initial marketing efforts by the underwriters.

If any amendment to the registration statement is filed prior to its effective date, the date of filing is deemed to be the date on which the amendment was filed, unless

EXHIBIT 11-3 FORM S-1 COVER PAGE

UNITED STATES
SECURITIES AND EXCHANGE COMMISSION
Washington, D.C. 20549

OMB APPROVAL
OMB Number: 3235-0065
Expires: June 30, 2014
Estimated average burden
hours per response 972.32

FORM S-1
REGISTRATION STATEMENT UNDER THE SECURITIES ACT OF 1933

_____
(Exact name of registrant as specified in its charter)

_____
(State or other jurisdiction of incorporation or organization)

_____
(Primary Standard Industrial Classification Code Number)

_____
(I.R.S. Employer Identification Number)

_____
(Address, including zip code, and telephone number,
including area code, of registrant's principal executive offices)

_____
(Name, address, including zip code, and telephone number,
including area code, of agent for service)

_____
(Approximate date of commencement of proposed sale to the public)

If any of the securities being registered on this Form are to be offered on a delayed or continuous basis pursuant to Rule 415 under the Securities Act of 1933 check the following box: ☐

If this Form is filed to register additional securities for an offering pursuant to Rule 462(b) under the Securities Act, please check the following box and list the Securities Act registration statement number of the earlier effective registration statement for the same offering. ☐

If this Form is a post-effective amendment filed pursuant to Rule 462(c) under the Securities Act, check the following box and list the Securities Act registration statement number of the earlier effective registration statement for the same offering. ☐

If this Form is a post-effective amendment filed pursuant to Rule 462(d) under the Securities Act, check the following box and list the Securities Act registration statement number of the earlier effective registration statement for the same offering. ☐

Indicate by check mark whether the registrant is a large accelerated filer, an accelerated filer, a non-accelerated filer, or a smaller reporting company. See the definitions of "large accelerated filer," "accelerated filer" and "smaller reporting company" in Rule 12b-2 of the Exchange Act.

Large accelerated filer ☐   Accelerated filer ☐

Non-accelerated filer ☐ (Do not check if a smaller reporting company)   Smaller reporting company ☐

SEC 870 (02-08)   **Persons who are to respond to the collection of information contained in this form are not required to respond unless the form displays a currently valid OMB control number.**

Securities and Exchange Commission website, http://www.sec.gov

the amendment was ordered or approved by the SEC. The SEC has the power to accelerate the effective date and generally will do so if requested by the issuer, provided that the issuer has submitted all necessary information and has acted quickly to furnish the SEC with any different or additional information requested. The SEC also has the power to delay the effective date of any registration statement that is "on its face incomplete or inaccurate in any material respect,"[10] by refusing to permit the registration statement to become effective until after it has been amended in accordance with a notice served upon the issuer not later than 10 days after the filing of the registration statement. If after the effective date of the registration statement, it appears to the SEC that the registration statement includes any untrue statements of material fact, or omits stating any material fact required to be stated therein, the SEC may issue a stop order suspending the effectiveness of the registration statement until such time as the registration statement has been amended in accordance with the stop order.

After the registration statement has been filed, a waiting period begins and lasts until the registration statement is effective. During this waiting period, securities may be offered for sale, but they may not actually be sold until the registration statement becomes effective. During the waiting period, preliminary prospectuses may be used to offer for sale securities that will be sold after the effective date of the registration statement. After the registration statement becomes effective, the securities may be sold through use of a prospectus.

PROSPECTUS REQUIREMENTS

The prospectus, which constitutes Part I of the registration statement, contains disclosures required by the SEC, including information regarding the corporation, its assets, its officers and directors, and other information material to the business of the corporation. It must be furnished to the purchaser of the securities after the securities have been registered with the SEC.

Section 5(b) of the Securities Act prohibits the use of any prospectus to sell securities, unless the prospectus meets the requirements of the Securities Act, and it prohibits the sale of securities without a prospectus:

(b) It shall be unlawful for any person, directly or indirectly—

1. to make use of any means or instruments of transportation or communication in interstate commerce or of the mails to carry or transmit any prospectus relating to any security with respect to which a registration statement has been filed under this title, unless such prospectus meets the requirements of section 10; or

2. to carry or cause to be carried through the mails or in interstate commerce any such security for the purpose of sale or for delivery after sale, unless accompanied or preceded by a prospectus that meets the requirements of subsection (a) of section 10.

The Securities Act of 1933 also permits the use of a summary prospectus to sell securities of a registered corporation. A summary prospectus includes a summary of much of the information in the registration statement, pursuant to the rules of the SEC Regulation C, 17 CFR § 230.431. Corporations may use summary prospectuses as long as the summary prospectus contains the information required by Regulation C, the summary prospectus does not include any false or misleading statements, and as long as a statement to the following effect shall be prominently set forth in conspicuous print at the beginning or at the end of every summary prospectus:

> Copies of a more complete prospectus may be obtained from (Insert name(s), address(es) and telephone number(s)). Copies of a summary prospectus filed with the Commission pursuant to paragraph (g) of this section may omit the names of persons from whom the complete prospectus may be obtained.[11]

A preliminary prospectus without the offering price and related information may be used by the issuer of securities during the waiting period to inform prospective buyers of the nature of the securities to be sold. A prospectus used before the effective date of a registration statement is often called a **red herring prospectus** because, historically, it was required to contain a legend on the cover in red ink indicating that the prospectus was preliminary and subject to completion. Although the red ink is no longer required, any preliminary prospectus must include on its cover the required "subject to completion" legend. Red ink is still often used. Exhibit 11-4 is the cover page of a preliminary prospectus for the offering of Google stock.

Also used during the waiting period to announce a securities offering, and to disseminate certain information regarding the offering, are **tombstone ads**. Tombstone advertisements are not considered to be prospectuses and are not subject to the requirements set forth for prospectuses in the rules to the Securities Act. However, they must follow certain guidelines and contain certain legends prescribed by the rules. Tombstone ads are frequently found in the business section of major newspapers and are surrounded by a thick black border, which accounts for their name. Exhibit 11-5 shows a tombstone ad.

EDGAR

Form S-1 and most disclosure documents filed with the Securities and Exchange Commission are filed via the SEC's Electronic Data Gathering, Analysis, and Retrieval system (**EDGAR**). Since May 1996, all public companies have been required to submit certain documents to the SEC in electronic form for inclusion in the EDGAR database.

Registration statements, annual reports, quarterly reports, and other disclosure documents of all public corporations may be accessed through the EDGAR database by company name, keyword, or by the EDGAR Central Index Key (CIK) lookup. The CIK is a unique identifier assigned by the SEC to all companies and people who file disclosure documents with the SEC.

RED HERRING PROSPECTUS

A preliminary prospectus, used during the "waiting period" between filing a registration statement with the SEC and approval of the statement. It has a red "for information only" statement on the front and states that the securities described may not be offered for sale until SEC approval. The red herring must be filed with the SEC before use.

TOMBSTONE AD

A stock (or other securities) or land sales notice that clearly states that it is informational only and not itself an offer to buy or sell. It has a black border that resembles one on a death notice.

EDGAR

Electronic Data Gathering, Analysis, and Retrieval system established by the Securities and Exchange Commission to collect, validate, index, and provide to the public, documents that are required to be filed with the Securities and Exchange Commission.

EXHIBIT 11-4 GOOGLE SAMPLE PRELIMINARY PROSPECTUS COVER PAGE

SAMPLE PRELIMINARY PROSPECTUS

(From the SEC EDGAR Database at www.sec.gov)

The information in this prospectus is not complete and may be changed. We may not sell these securities until the registration statement filed with the Securities and Exchange Commission is effective. This prospectus is not an offer to sell these securities and we are not soliciting any offer to buy these securities in any jurisdiction where the offer or sale is not permitted.

Prospectus (Subject to Completion)
Dated July 26, 2004

24,636,659 Shares

Class A Common Stock

Google Inc. is offering 14,142,135 shares of Class A common stock and the selling stockholders are offering 10,494,524 shares of Class A common stock. We will not receive any proceeds from the sale of shares by the selling stockholders. This is our initial public offering and no public market currently exists for our shares. We anticipate that the initial public offering price will be between $108.00 and $135.00 per share.

Following this offering, we will have two classes of authorized common stock, Class A common stock and Class B common stock. The rights of the holders of Class A common stock and Class B common stock are identical, except with respect to voting and conversion. Each share of Class A common stock is entitled to one vote per share. Each share of Class B common stock is entitled to ten votes per share and is convertible at any time into one share of Class A common stock.

Our Class A common stock has been approved for quotation on The Nasdaq National Market under the symbol "GOOG," subject to official notice of issuance.

Investing in our Class A common stock involves risks. See "Risk Factors" beginning on page 4.

	Price to Public	Price $ A Share	Proceeds to Google	Proceeds to Selling Stockholders
		Underwriting Discounts and Commissions		
Per Share	$	$	$	$
Total	$	$	$	$

EXHIBIT 11-5 TOMBSTONE ADVERTISEMENT

1,500,000 Shares

PRICE CAPITAL INVESTMENTS, INC.

Common Stock

Price $6 Per Share

This announcement is neither an offer to sell nor a solicitation of offers to buy any of these securities. The offering is made only by the Prospectus, copies of which may be obtained in any state in which this announcement is circulated from the undersigned or other dealers or brokers that may lawfully offer these securities.

Malibu Shores Securities	Montgomery & Blandon Incorporated
Bears Best Inc.	Richman Loman & Co.
Spencer Corporation	Finnegan Financial

August 16, 2009

© Cengage Learning 2013

EDGAR offers many benefits, both to filers and those seeking information about public corporations. Documents to be filed via the EDGAR system must be prepared using the SEC's online formatting. Exhibits and tables must be prepared to specification. Specific instructions for filing via the EDGAR system can be found in the SEC's Regulation S-T, and the EDGAR Filing Manual, both available at the SEC website. Regulations concerning EDGAR filings and the EDGAR Filing Manual are continually being updated as the system is improved.

IN SUMMATION

- The Securities Act of 1933 is intended to protect the investor through the imposition of disclosure and antifraud requirements on corporations.
- Section 5(a) of the Securities Act prohibits the sale or delivery of securities through the mail or by other means of transportation or communication in interstate commerce unless a registration statement has been filed for those securities.
- Section 5(b) of the Securities Act requires a prospectus prepared pursuant to the act to sell securities.

- Securities are typically registered by electronically filing a Form S-1 with the SEC.

- The prospectus that is required under Section 5(b) is Part I of the Form S-1 registration statement.

- The prospectus contains disclosures required by the SEC, including information regarding the corporation, its assets, its officers and directors, and other information material to the business of the corporation.

- A preliminary prospectus without the offering price may be used by the issuer of securities during the 20-day waiting period after the registration statement has been filed but before it becomes effective.

- Most disclosure documents filed with the SEC are filed via the SEC's Electronic Data Gathering, Analysis, and Retrieval system (EDGAR), and are available online.

§ 11.5 EXEMPTIONS FROM THE REGISTRATION REQUIREMENTS OF THE SECURITIES ACT OF 1933

Not all securities are subject to the registration requirements of the Securities Act. An issue of securities may be exempt from registration because of the type or class of the securities, or the specific transaction involving the securities. Securities that are scrutinized by other governmental agencies, such as the banking or insurance commissions, or securities that are sold to a specific group of informed investors, often fall under the category of exempted securities. Exemption from the registration requirements of the Securities Act does not provide exemption from the other provisions of the Securities Act or related securities regulations, especially the antifraud provisions. The issuer of securities that qualify under one of the exemptions may not be required to register the securities, but may be required to file other disclosure documentation with the SEC.

EXEMPTED SECURITIES

Section 3 of the Securities Act specifies certain classes of securities that are exempted from the registration provisions of the Securities Act. Some of the securities exempted by this section include:

1. Certain securities issued or guaranteed by the federal, state, or local governments
2. Certain securities issued or guaranteed by banks
3. Short-term commercial paper, including certain notes, drafts, or bills of exchange

4. Securities of nonprofit issuers
5. Securities issued by certain savings and loan associations, building and loan associations, cooperative banks, homestead associations, or similar institutions
6. Interests in railroad equipment trusts
7. Certificates issued by receivers, trustees, or debtors in possession in a case under Title 11 of the United States Code (the Bankruptcy Code), with the approval of the court
8. Insurance or endowment policies, annuity contracts, and optional annuity contracts that are subject to the supervision of the insurance commissioner, bank commissioner, or any similar agency or officer
9. Certain securities issued in exchange for one or more bona fide outstanding securities, claims, or property interests where the terms and conditions of such issuance and exchange are approved by any court, or by any official or agency of the United States, including any state or territorial banking or insurance commission
10. Certain securities exchanged by the issuer when no commission or other remuneration is paid or given for soliciting such exchange
11. Securities that are sold only to residents of a single state or territory if the issuer is both a resident of and doing business within that state or territory

In addition, Section 3(b) of the Securities Act gives the SEC authority to exempt other classes of securities from its rules and regulations, provided that the aggregate amount of the issue does not exceed $5 million. Section 3(c) gives the SEC that same authority with regard to securities issued by a small business investment company under the Small Business Investment Act of 1958.

EXEMPTED TRANSACTIONS

Section 4 of the Securities Act specifies certain transactions that are exempted from the registration provisions of the Securities Act. Some of the transactions exempted by this section include:

1. Transactions by persons other than issuers, underwriters, or dealers
2. Transactions by issuers not involving any public offering (private placement)
3. Certain transactions by dealers
4. Brokers' transactions executed upon customers' orders, but not the solicitation of such orders
5. Certain transactions involving offers or sales by an issuer solely to one or more accredited investors
6. Transactions involving offers or sales by issuers solely to one or more accredited investors if the aggregate offering price does not exceed $5 million, if there is no advertising or public solicitation by issuer, and if the issuer files notice with the SEC as it shall prescribe

EXEMPTIONS FOR LIMITED OFFERINGS AND OFFERINGS OF LIMITED DOLLAR AMOUNTS

As discussed earlier, Section 3(b) of the Securities Act of 1933 provides the SEC with the authority to exempt certain offerings from the registration requirements of the Securities Act when the securities to be offered involve a relatively small dollar amount ($5,000,000 or less). Regulations A and D under the Securities Act set forth the various conditions that must be met to qualify for the exemption authorized under Section 3(b). Regulation A (Rules 251 to 346) establishes exemptions for conditional small issues. Regulation D (Rules 501 to 508) establishes rules governing the limited offer and sale of securities without registration under the Securities Act.

Regulation A

Issuers of stock with a value of less than $5 million may find they are eligible for exemptions under the rules of Regulation A, which are available for offerings that do not exceed $5,000,000. Issuers who claim an exemption under Regulation A must comply with the provisions of Rule 251, which require the use and filing with the SEC of an offering statement and circular, among other things. The simplified registration procedure provided by Regulation A allows that the financial statements required for filing with the SEC may be in a simplified format and unaudited. In addition, issuers that have registered under Regulation A need not file periodic reports with the SEC unless the issuers have more than $5 million in assets and more than 500 shareholders.

Regulation D

Rules 501 through 508 under Regulation D provide for the limited offer and sale of securities without registration under the Securities Act of 1933. Regulation D exempts qualifying issuers of securities from the registration requirements of the Securities Act, but specifically states that "such transactions are not exempt from the antifraud, civil liability, or other provisions of the federal securities laws."[12]

Rule 504 provides exemptions for limited offerings. This rule provides exemption from registration pursuant to the following conditions:

1. The sale of securities must not exceed $1 million in a 12-month period.
2. There are no restrictions on the number of the purchasers of the securities under this exemption.
3. Securities exempted pursuant to Regulation D may not be offered through any form of general solicitation or general advertising.
4. A Form D notice must be filed with the SEC headquarters within 15 days after the first sale of securities under this rule.

Rule 505, also permitted under Section 3(b) of the Securities Act, offers exemption from registration pursuant to the following conditions:

1. The issuer may not sell securities totaling more than $5 million in any 12-month period.
2. The issuer must file financial statements as specifically required by Rule 505.
3. The offering may not be made by means of a general solicitation or general advertising.
4. There is no restriction on the number of accredited investors to which the issuer may sell its securities.
5. The issuer may sell securities to no more than 35 nonaccredited investors.
6. The issuer must make an effort to ensure that the purchase of its securities is for investment purposes only (not for resale).
7. Fifteen days after the first sale in the offering, the issuer must file a notice of sales on Form D.

An accredited investor, as defined in the Securities Act, includes:

1. Certain banks and savings and loan associations
2. Certain private business development companies
3. Certain nonprofit organizations described in § 501(c)(3) of the Internal Revenue Code
4. Directors, executive officers, or general partners of the issuer of the securities being offered or sold, or any director, executive officer, or general partner of a general partner of that issuer
5. Individuals with a net worth, or joint net worth with that person's spouse, that at the time of the purchase exceeds $1 million
6. Individuals who have an income in excess of $200,000 in each of the two most recent years, or joint income with that person's spouse in excess of $300,000 in each of those years, and has a reasonable expectation of reaching the same income level in the current year
7. Certain trusts with total assets in excess of $5 million
8. Entities in which all of the equity owners are accredited investors

PRIVATE PLACEMENT

Section 4(2) of the Securities Act, discussed earlier, provides an exemption for transactions not involving a "public offering"—in other words, a private placement. Rule 506 under Regulation D defines what is deemed not to involve a public offering. Under Rule 506, an offering is not a public offering if it meets with all the conditions of Rules 501 and 502 of Regulation D, and if there are no more than 35 purchasers of the securities. Rules 501 and 502 provide several conditions for the offering, including requirements for information that must be made available to purchasers of the securities. The purchasers must all be accredited investors, or they must have sufficient knowledge and experience in financial and business matters to allow them to evaluate the merits and risks of the investment.

To qualify for this exemption, the offering may not be made by public solicitation or general advertising, and the sale of the securities must generally be to individuals who have sufficient knowledge of the corporation to make an informed decision or are able to bear the risk. The purchasers must have access to the type of information normally provided in a prospectus and must agree not to resell or distribute the securities.

Most private placements under this rule involve the sale of large blocks of securities to institutional investors such as insurance companies or pension funds. In such private placements, the investor is in a position to insist on receiving adequate information from the issuer of securities—possibly even more than would be required by the SEC in a registration statement. The purchaser is not placed at a disadvantage because of the issuer's lack of public disclosure with the SEC. Sales to employees and those who have access to information about the corporation generally are also not considered to be public offerings. The SEC has reported that "[w]hether a transaction is one not involving any public offering is essentially a question of fact and necessitates a consideration of all surrounding circumstances, including such factors as the relationship between the offerees and the issuer, the nature, scope, size, type and manner of the offering."[13]

The issuers of a Rule 506 offering must comply with Form D filing requirements established by the SEC.

INTRASTATE OFFERING EXEMPTIONS

Section 3(a)(11) of the Securities Act offers an exemption, commonly referred to as the intrastate offering exemption, for corporations that issue securities only within the state in which they are located and doing business. To qualify for the intrastate offering exemption, the issuer must meet the following conditions:

1. The issuer must be a corporation incorporated in the state in which it is making the offering.
2. The issuer must carry out a significant amount of its business in that state.
3. The issuer must make offerings and sales only to residents of that state.

The issuer has an obligation to ensure that each investor who purchases shares of the corporation is a resident of the state of the offering. If the corporation sells shares to investors who are not residents, or if residents resell their shares to nonresidents within nine months of the date the offering is completed, the issuer may lose the right to use the exemption. For this reason, the intrastate offering exemption is usually limited to relatively small offerings to a limited number of investors.

Transactions by Persons Other Than Issuers, Underwriters, and Dealers

This exemption ordinarily permits investors to make casual sales of their securities holdings without registration. Transactions that are a part of the scheme of distribution do not qualify under this exemption, which is available only for routine trading transactions.

IN SUMMATION

- The offer and sale of securities may be exempt from the registration requirements of the Securities Act because of the type or class of the securities or the specific transaction involving the offer and sale.
- Section 4 of the Securities Act specifies certain transactions that are exempt from the registration provisions of the Securities Act.
- Transactions involving the sale of securities to a limited number of individuals with a relatively limited dollar value may be exempt from the registration provisions of the Securities Act.
- Rule 504 under Regulation D provides for an exemption for limited offerings that involve the sale of securities not exceeding $1 million in a 12-month period.
- Companies that are exempt under Regulation D do not have to register their securities; they must file a Form D with the SEC, a brief notice that includes basic information about the company's executive offers and stock promoters.
- Rule 505 under Regulation D provides an exemption for the sale of securities that do not exceed $5 million in any 12-month period to a limited number of nonaccredited investors.
- Companies that are exempt under Regulation D, Rule 505 must file financial statements with the SEC.
- Section 4(2) of the Securities Act provides an exemption for the private placement of stock—transactions not involving a "public offering."
- Section 3(a)(11) of the Securities Act provides an exemption for intrastate offerings—corporations that only issue securities within the state in which they are doing business.

§ 11.6 ANTIFRAUD PROVISIONS OF THE SECURITIES ACT OF 1933

Antifraud provisions of the Securities Act are found mainly in Sections 11, 12, and 17 of that act. These antifraud provisions are intended to protect the investors who rely on the disclosures mandated by the Securities Act of 1933. Section 11 of the Securities Act concerns the truthfulness of statements made in the registration statement of a registered corporation. Section 12 concerns the truthfulness of statements made in the prospectus and other statements made to sell the registered securities, and Section 17 covers all fraudulent conduct with regard to the offer, sale, or any other type of transaction regarding securities. The prohibited acts or practices addressed in those provisions are not limited to the common law concept of fraud, but also include acts and practices that tend to be fraudulent in nature, such as the publication of misstatements or half-truths, devices directed toward market manipulation, and improper touting of securities being offered for sale.[14] The antifraud provisions of the Securities Act are of specific concern to the issuer and all other parties signing or otherwise responsible for the information contained in the registration statement.

SECTION 11

Every person who signs or contributes information to the registration statement has a duty to provide complete and accurate information. Failure to do so may provide the purchaser of securities with a cause of action under § 11 of the Securities Act for any damages stemming from the purchase of securities for which an inaccurate or misleading registration statement was filed. A suit under § 11 places a relatively minimal burden on a plaintiff, requiring simply that the plaintiff allege that he or she purchased the security and that the registration statement contains false or misleading statements concerning a material fact. Section 11(a) of the Securities Act specifies when a purchaser may sue and who may be sued in conjunction with a registration statement containing untrue or misleading information:

Section 11

(a) In case any part of the registration statement, when such part became effective, contained an untrue statement of a material fact or omitted to state a material fact required to be stated therein or necessary to make the statements therein not misleading, any person acquiring such security (unless it is proved that at the time of such acquisition he knew of such untruth or omission) may, either at law or in equity, in any court of competent jurisdiction, sue:

1. every person who signed the registration statement;
2. every person who was a director of (or person performing similar functions) or partner in, the issuer at the time of the filing of the part of the registration statement with respect to which his liability is asserted;
3. every person who, with his consent, is named in the registration statement as being or about to become a director, person performing similar functions, or partner;
4. every accountant, engineer, or appraiser, or any person whose profession gives authority to a statement made by him, who has with his consent been named as having prepared or certified any part of the registration statement, or as having prepared or certified any report or valuation which is used in connection

with the registration statement, with respect to the statement in such registration statement, report, or valuation, which purports to have been prepared or certified by him;

5. every underwriter with respect to such security.

All the individuals named above are responsible for any misstatements and omissions throughout the registration statement, except experts. Experts are responsible for misstatements and omissions only in those parts of the registration statement that they are responsible for having prepared or certified.

The issuer of the securities is strictly liable for the information in the registration statement. For all others named above, the Securities Act provides several defenses to the liabilities in § 11. Section 11(b) provides that no persons, other than the issuer, shall be liable as provided therein if they can prove that: (1) they had resigned from the positions causing their relationships with the issuer; (2) if the registration statement became effective without their knowledge, they advised the SEC upon becoming aware of such fact, and they gave reasonable public notice that the registration statement became effective without their knowledge; or (3) they had, after reasonable investigation, reasonable ground to believe and did believe the information to be true and accurate. This is referred to as the **due diligence** defense. Corporate directors and others who participate in preparing and filing registration statements and prospectuses relating to domestic securities are required to have made a reasonable investigation of all material facts before they may avail themselves of the statutory defense of due diligence. Attorneys and paralegals often assist with gathering and verifying information to be included in the registration statement.

DUE DILIGENCE

Enough care, enough timeliness, or enough investigation to meet legal requirements, to fulfill a duty, or to evaluate the risks of a course of action. Due diligence often refers to a professional investigation of the financial risks of a merger or a securities purchase, or the legal obligation to do the investigation. Due diligence is also used as a synonym for due care.

SECTION 12

Section 12 of the Securities Act is designed to protect investors from purchasing securities based on false or misleading prospectuses or sales pitches. Section 12 provides that offers for the sale of securities, including prospectuses and oral statements, must not include any false or misleading statements of a material fact. The purchaser may not recover if he or she knew about the misstatement, but made the purchase anyway.

Section 12 also protects purchasers of securities that are unregistered in violation of Section 5 of the Securities Act.

SECTION 17

Section 17 of the Securities Act is much broader in its scope than Sections 11 and 12. It prohibits fraudulent conduct with respect to securities transactions, and pertains to the sale of, or an offer to sell, securities.

Section 17

(a) It shall be unlawful for any person in the offer or sale of any securities by the use of any means or instruments of transportation or communication in interstate commerce or by the use of the mails, directly or indirectly—

1. to employ any device, scheme, or artifice to defraud, or
2. to obtain money or property by means of any untrue statement of a material fact or any omission to state a material fact necessary in order to make the statements made, in the light of the circumstances under which they were made, not misleading, or
3. to engage in any transaction, practice, or course of business which operates or would operate as a fraud or deceit upon the purchaser.

(b) It shall be unlawful for any person, by the use of any means or instruments of transportation or communication in interstate commerce or by the use of the mails, to publish, give publicity to, or circulate any notice, circular, advertisement, newspaper, article, letter, investment service, or communication which, though not purporting to offer a security for sale, describes such security for a consideration received or to be received, directly or indirectly, from an issuer, underwriter, or dealer, without fully disclosing the receipt, whether past or prospective, of such consideration and the amount thereof.

(c) The exemptions provided in section 3 shall not apply to the provisions of this section.

In contrast to the antifraud provisions of Sections 11 and 12 of the Securities Act, Section 17 does not specifically provide a right of action to the purchasers of securities. Section 17 has been important primarily in actions brought by the SEC to seek injunctions against violations of the Securities Act, and in actions brought by the Justice Department to impose criminal liability for willful violations of the Securities Act.

IN SUMMATION

- The antifraud provisions of the Securities Act, found mainly in Sections 11, 12, and 17, are intended to protect investors who rely on the disclosures mandated by the act.

- Section 11 of the Securities Act makes it clear that every individual signing the registration statement or providing information for the registration statement is personally responsible for the truthfulness and accuracy of the information they provide.

- Section 12 of the Securities Act provides that offers for the sale of securities, including prospectuses and oral statements, must not include any false or misleading statements of a material fact.

- Section 17 of the Securities Act prohibits fraudulent conduct with respect to the sale of, or an offer to sell, securities.

§ 11.7 FEDERAL REGULATIONS IMPOSED ON PUBLIC CORPORATIONS UNDER THE SECURITIES EXCHANGE ACT OF 1934

Whereas the Securities Act of 1933 deals primarily with the registration of initial issues of securities, the Securities Exchange Act of 1934 (Exchange Act) pertains to reporting requirements and dealings in securities subsequent to their initial issue. The aim of the Exchange Act, in part, is to prevent inequitable and unfair practices and to ensure fairness in securities transactions generally, whether conducted face to face, over the counter, or on the national securities exchanges.[15]

The Exchange Act contains provisions requiring public corporations to register with the exchange on which the securities are traded. In addition, the Exchange Act contains provisions requiring periodic reporting to the exchanges and the SEC, and provisions regulating the use of proxies. The Exchange Act also contains several antifraud provisions that affect the public corporation and its officers, directors, and principal shareholders. Securities exchanges and brokers and dealers are also regulated under the Exchange Act. The Securities Exchange Act requires the registration of exchanges, securities associations, **clearing agencies**, transfer agents, and securities brokers and dealers. The Securities Exchange Act charges the SEC with the responsibility for regulation and oversight of the securities exchanges and over-the-counter trading.

Exhibit 11-6 lists the purposes of the Securities Exchange Act of 1934.

REGISTRATION UNDER THE EXCHANGE ACT

In addition to the registration requirements of the Securities Act, § 12(a) of the Exchange Act requires that every nonexempt security that is traded on a national securities exchange must be registered with that exchange. All exchanges in the United States must be registered with the SEC as a national securities exchange unless exempt from the registration requirements by the SEC because of a limited volume of trading. Section 12(a) of the Exchange Act provides:

Section 12

(a) It shall be unlawful for any member, broker, or dealer to effect any transaction in any security (other than an exempted security) on a national securities exchange unless a registration is effective as to such security for such exchange in accordance with the provisions of this title and the rules and regulations thereunder.

A security is registered by filing an application with the appropriate exchange, pursuant to the instructions of that exchange. The application contains information regarding the issuer, the corporation, and the securities to be traded. In addition, copies of corporate documents, including articles of incorporation and certain material contracts, may be required to supplement the application. The registration of the

CLEARING AGENCY

Any person who acts as an intermediary in making payments or deliveries or both in connection with transactions in securities or who provides facilities for comparison of data respecting the terms of settlement of securities transactions, to reduce the number of settlements of securities transactions, or for the allocation of securities settlement responsibilities.

EXHIBIT 11-6 PURPOSES OF THE SECURITIES EXCHANGE ACT OF 1934

- To regulate transactions by officers, directors, and principal security holders.

- To outlaw the use of insider information for the financial gain of privileged insiders to the detriment of uninformed security holders.

- To require appropriate reports.

- To make information available to persons trading in securities on the markets.

- To remove impediments to and perfect the mechanisms of a national market system for securities transactions.

- To safeguard funds and securities related to a national market system.

- To protect interstate commerce, the national credit, and the federal taxing power.

- To protect and make more effective the national banking and Federal Reserve system.

- Ensure, through regulation and self-regulation, the maintenance of fair and honest markets in transactions conducted on securities exchanges and on the over-the-counter markets.

- To prevent fraud and manipulation in the securities markets by substituting a philosophy of full disclosure for the philosophy of caveat emptor (let the buyer beware).

- To prevent those whose business is dealing in securities and who are experienced and knowledgeable in the practical process of securities and the property and potential backing of such issues from imposing upon the public by reason of such background knowledge.

From 69 § 268*American Jurisprudence2d.* © 2011 Thomson (confirm)

---

security on the exchange is generally effective 30 days after the filing of the application with the exchange and the SEC.

In addition to the issuers of securities actively traded on a national exchange, § 12(g)(1) requires registration with the SEC by every issuer that is engaged in interstate commerce, or in a business affecting interstate commerce, or whose securities are traded by use of the mails or any means or instrumentality of interstate commerce, if the corporation has total assets exceeding $10 million and a class of securities held by 500 or more persons.

PERIODIC REPORTING REQUIREMENTS

Every issuer of securities registered pursuant to § 12 of the Exchange Act is subject to the periodic reporting requirements of § 13 of the Exchange Act. Issuers who are not nominally subject to the registration requirements of the Exchange Act, but have filed a registration statement with the SEC pursuant to the Securities Act, also become subject to the reporting requirements of the Exchange Act. Corporations that do not have an active registration statement filed with the SEC, but are otherwise subject to the reporting requirements of the Exchange Act, may be required to file a special registration statement to activate those reporting requirements.

Section 13 of the Exchange Act requires issuers to make periodic disclosures electronically, on forms prescribed by the SEC, in accordance with the Exchange Act. The issuer of securities registered on a national securities exchange is required to file duplicate originals of such disclosure forms with the exchange. Issuers are further required to disclose in their annual reports where investors can obtain access to their filings. Most corporations will include references to their websites, where the corporation's annual and quarterly reports may be viewed or downloaded.

Failure to comply with the disclosure requirements of the Exchange Act can leave the public corporation liable for damages to injured parties in some instances. False reporting may subject the issuers to criminal liability.

The periodic reports required of public corporations include the 10-K, the 10-Q, and the 8-K. Section 13(d) also imposes reporting requirements on persons who own more than 5 percent of any class of equity securities that is registered under the Exchange Act.

The 10-K Report

10-K REPORT

The annual report required by the SEC of publicly held corporations that sell stock.

Annual **10-K reports** must be filed with the SEC by every issuer subject to the reporting requirements of the Exchange Act. The Form 10-K must be filed electronically via EDGAR with the SEC within 90 days after the end of the corporation's fiscal year. Certain domestic-reporting corporations considered "accelerated filers" must file within 75 days after the close of the company's fiscal year. "Large accelerated filers" must file within 60 days after the close of their fiscal year. Accelerated filers include domestic companies that have an aggregate worldwide market value of the voting and nonvoting common equity held by nonaffiliates of at least $75 million, but less than $700 million. Large accelerated filers have an aggregate worldwide market value of common equity of $700 million or more.

The information that must be included in the 10-K report is similar to that required for the initial registration statement filed by the corporation, and includes details as to the nature of the registrant's business and significant changes therein during the previous fiscal year, as well as a summary of its operation for the last 5 fiscal years, or for the life of the registrant if less than five years, and for any additional fiscal years necessary to keep the summary from being misleading. The annual 10-K report also includes identification of principal securities holders of the corporation and any transactions involving the transfer of significant percentages of the securities of the corporation. Parts I and II of the 10-K report consist of information that is typically included in the annual report to shareholders, and much of the information required by the 10-K report is often provided by reference to that information in the annual report to shareholders, which is submitted for filing with the 10-K.

The Form 10-K must be completed to the exact specifications of the SEC as set forth in the instructions to the Form 10-K, and the pertinent rules and regulations of the SEC. Exhibit 11-7 illustrates the type of information required by the Form 10-K.

EXHIBIT 11-7 PARTS OF THE FORM 10-K

Item 1.	Business.
Item 1A.	Risk Factors.
Item 1B.	Unresolved Staff Comments.
Item 2.	Properties.
Item 3.	Legal Proceedings.
Item 4.	(Removed and Reserved).
Item 5.	Market for Registrant's Common Equity, Related Stockholder Matters and Issuer Purchases of Equity Securities.
Item 6.	Selected Financial Data.
Item 7.	Management's Discussion and Analysis of Financial Condition and Results of Operations.
Item 7A.	Quantitative and Qualitative Disclosures about Market Risk.
Item 8.	Financial Statements and Supplementary Data.
Item 9.	Changes in and Disagreements with Accountants on Accounting and Financial Disclosure.
Item 9A.	Controls and Procedures.
Item 9B.	Other Information.
Item 10.	Directors, Executive Officers, and Corporate Governance.
Item 11.	Executive Compensation.
Item 12.	Security Ownership of Certain Beneficial Owners and Management and Related Stockholder Matters.
Item 13.	Certain Relationships and Related Transactions, and Director Independence.
Item 14.	Principal Accounting Fees and Services.
Item 15.	Exhibits, Financial Statement Schedules.

SIGNATURES

Securities and Exchange Commission website, http://www.sec.gov.

The Form 10-K and instructions, as well as thousands of filed Form 10-Ks, can be found on the SEC website.

The 10-Q Report

Registrants that are required to file 10-K (annual) reports must also file 10-Q quarterly reports. The **10-Q report** contains financial information regarding the registrant, the registrant's capitalization and stockholders' equity, and the registrant's sale of unregistered securities during the reporting period. Quarterly reports must

10-Q REPORT

Quarterly report that must be filed with the SEC by all corporations that are required to file 10-K reports.

be filed for the first three quarters of a corporation's fiscal year, with information concerning the fourth quarter being included in the corporation's annual report. The Form 10-Q must be filed with the SEC within 45 days of the close of the quarter. Accelerated filers and large accelerated filers have just 40 days after the close of each of the first three quarters to file their 10-Q.

Form 8-K

FORM 8-K

Form that must be filed with the SEC by the issuer of registered securities when certain pertinent information contained in the registration statement of the issuer changes.

Form 8-K must be completed and filed electronically by the issuer of registered securities when certain information contained in the registration statement of the issuer changes. Generally, within four business days after any of the events requiring reporting occur, a Form 8-K must be filed. Typical of the events that require filing of a Form 8-K are changes in control of the registrant, acquisition or disposition of a significant amount of assets (other than in the normal course of business), nonroutine legal proceedings, changes in securities of the registrant or modification of the rights of holders of securities, any material default with respect to senior securities, any increase or decrease in outstanding securities of the registrant, and any grants or extensions of options with respect to the purchase of securities of the registrant or of its subsidiaries, if such options relate to an amount of securities exceeding 5 percent of the outstanding securities of the class to which they belong. The Form 8-K, which may be found on the SEC's website, gives detailed instructions as to which items require the filing of the form. See Exhibit 11-8.

Exhibit 11-9 on page 488 is a summary of the some of the more important periodic reports required under the Securities Exchange Act of 1934.

PROXY REGULATIONS

PROXY STATEMENT

The document sent or given to stockholders when their voting proxies are requested for a corporate decision. The SEC has rules for when the statements must be given out and what must be in them.

The Exchange Act also regulates the content and use of proxies and **proxy statements** by public corporations. As discussed in Chapter 9, proxies may be used to register the vote of a shareholder not in attendance at a shareholder meeting. The proxy statement contains the information required by the SEC to be given to stockholders in conjunction with the solicitation of a proxy. The purpose of the proxy statement is to give the shareholder adequate information to make a decision regarding the use of the proxy.

Generally, any corporation that is subject to the registration requirements of the Securities Act or the Exchange Act is subject to proxy requirements of the Exchange Act. Section 14(a) of the Exchange Act specifically provides that it is unlawful to solicit proxies "in contravention of such rules and regulations as the Commission may prescribe as necessary or appropriate in the public interest or for the protection of investors." Regulation 14A contains a number of rules and a Schedule 14A, the proxy schedule, setting forth the items of information required in proxy statements. The proxy statement must disclose certain material facts concerning the matters on which shareholders are being asked to vote. Schedule 14A provides the form for the proxy statement. Following is an abbreviated list of the items required for inclusion in the proxy statement. Not every item will be included in every proxy statement. Most of these items need only be addressed if they concern an action to be taken or proposed

EXHIBIT 11-8   ACTIVITIES REQUIRING THE FILING OF FORM 8-K

- Entry into a Material Definitive Agreement.
- Termination of a Material Definitive Agreement.
- Bankruptcy or Receivership.
- Completion of Acquisition or Disposition of Assets.
- Results of Operations and Financial Condition.
- Creation of a Direct Financial Obligation or an Obligation under an Off-Balance Sheet Arrangement of a Registrant.
- Triggering Events That Accelerate or Increase a Direct Financial Obligation or an Obligation under an Off-Balance Sheet Arrangement.
- Costs Associated with Exit or Disposal Activities.
- Material Impairments.
- Notice of Delisting or Failure to Satisfy a Continued Listing Rule or Standard; Transfer of Listing.
- Unregistered Sales of Equity Securities.
- Material Modification to Rights of Security Holders.
- Changes in Registrant's Certifying Accountant.
- Non-Reliance on Previously Issued Financial Statements or a Related Audit Report or Completed Interim Review.
- Changes in Control of Registrant.
- Departure of Directors or Certain Officers; Election of Directors; Appointment of Certain Officers; Compensatory
- Amendments to Articles of Incorporation or Bylaws; Change in Fiscal Year.
- Temporary Suspension of Trading under Registrant's Employee Benefit Plans.
- Amendments to the Registrant's Code of Ethics, or Waiver of a Provision of the Code of Ethics.
- Change in Shell Company Status.
- Submission of Matters to a Vote of Security Holders.
- Asset Backed Securities (ABS) Informational and Computational Material.
- Change of Servicer or Trustee.
- Change in Credit Enhancement or Other External Support.

© Cengage Learning 2013

to be taken at the meeting for which the proxy is being solicited. Details concerning the information required for each item are set forth on Schedule 14A and in related regulations.

Item 1. Date, Time, and Place Information
Item 2. Revocability of Proxy
Item 3. Dissenters' Right of Appraisal
Item 4. Persons Making the Solicitations

EXHIBIT 11-9	SELECT PERIODIC REPORTS UNDER THE SECURITIES EXCHANGE ACT OF 1934
10-K Report	Annual report that must be filed with the SEC by every corporation subject to the reporting requirements of the Exchange Act. The Form 10-K provides information about the corporation's business operations, financial conditions, management and ownership.
10-Q Report	Quarterly report required of every corporation subject to the 10-K reporting requirements. 10-Q reports are filed with the SEC after the close of the first three quarters to provide information concerning the corporation's financial condition, legal proceedings, and sales of unregistered securities for the previous quarter. Similar information for the fourth quarter is included in the corporation's 10-K.
8-K	Form 8-K must be completed and filed by the corporation when certain information contained in the corporation's registration statement changes. The Form 8-K generally must be filed within four business days after the close of the month in which the event occurs. Events that trigger 8-K filing requirements include changes in control of the corporation, acquisition or disposition of assets other than in the normal course of business, and non-routine legal proceedings.
Form 3	Initial report filed within 10 days when a person becomes an officer, director, 10% shareholder or other reporting person of the corporation.
Form 4	Report filed to report changes in beneficial ownership after the filing of a Form 3 by officers, directors, 10% shareholders, or other reporting persons of the corporation.
Form 5	Form filed within 45 days of the end of the corporation's fiscal year to report certain transactions occurring during the year, but not previously included in a Form 3 or Form 4.

© Cengage Learning 2013

Item 5. Interest of Certain Persons in Matters to Be Acted Upon
Item 6. Voting Securities and Principal Holders Thereof
Item 7. Directors and Executive Officers
Item 8. Compensation of Directors and Executive Officers
Item 9. Independent Public Accounts
Item 10. Compensation Plans
Item 11. Authorization or Issuance of Securities Other Than for Exchange
Item 12. Modification or Exchange of Securities
Item 13. Financial and Other Information

Item 14. Mergers, Consolidations, Acquisitions, and Similar Matters

Item 15. Acquisition or Disposition of Property

Item 16. Restatement of Accounts

Item 17. Action with Respect to Reports

Item 18. Matters Not Required to Be Submitted

Item 19. Amendment of Charter, Bylaws, or Other Documents

Item 20. Other Proposed Actions

Item 21. Voting Procedures

Item 22. Information Required in Investment Company Proxy Statement

Item 23. Delivery of Documents to Security Holders Sharing an Address

Item 24. Shareholder Approval of Executive Compensation

Rules 14a-1 through 14b-1 under the Exchange Act set forth the specific requirements for soliciting proxies, including the filing of proxy statements with the SEC.

Rule 14a-6 provides for the filing of the proxy statement with the SEC. Generally, statements filed under § 14 must be filed electronically via EDGAR. The preliminary proxy statement, proxy form, and all other pertinent materials must be filed with the SEC at least 10 days prior to the mailing of the proxies. Definitive proxy statements must be filed with the SEC as of the date those proxy statements are furnished to the security holders.

Pursuant to Rule 14a-8 of the Exchange Act, eligible shareholders that follow specified procedures may notify the corporation's management of the shareholder's intent to present a proposal for action at an upcoming meeting of the shareholders, to be put to a vote. In that event, the corporation must set forth the proposal in its proxy statement. Also pursuant to Rule 14a-8, the corporate management must allow the shareholder to include in the proxy statement a statement of no more than 500 words supporting his or her proposal. By following the procedures under Rule 14a-8, disgruntled shareholders have a chance to present and support a proposal for a shareholder vote, even if the management is in opposition.

Regulations 14A and 14C require that if the proxy solicitation is made on behalf of the board of directors and relates to the election of directors, the proxy statement must be accompanied or preceded by an annual report to shareholders that meets the requirements of Rule 14a-3.

ANNUAL REPORT TO SHAREHOLDERS

The annual report to shareholders can be an important shareholder relations tool. Considerable time and expense are typically spent by the legal department, accounting, shareholder relations department, and outside counsel to prepare a report that meets statutory requirements and leaves a favorable impression on shareholders and potential shareholders. The design of these reports is often creative and related to the corporation's business—promoting a positive image.

The annual report to shareholders typically includes the following:

- Financial statements required by Rule 14a-3, meeting the requirements of Regulation S-X

- Supplementary financial information required by Item 302 of Regulation S-K
- Information concerning changes in and disagreements with accountants on accounting and financial disclosure matters
- A brief description of the business done by the registrant and its subsidiaries during the most recent fiscal year
- Information relating to the corporation's industry segments, classes of similar products or services, foreign and domestic operations, and export sales
- Information for each director and executive officer concerning his or her identity, principal occupation or employment, and the name and principal business of any organization by which such person is employed
- The market price of and dividends on registrant's common equity and related security holder matters

Although not specifically required, annual reports to shareholders usually include a letter from the president or CEO of the corporation to the shareholders, typically concerning the highlights of the corporation's business during the preceding year.

The annual report must include a statement offering to provide shareholders, without charge, with a copy of the corporation's annual report on Form 10-K. This offer usually refers to the URL of the corporation's website, and includes an offer to provide a hard copy of the report, if requested. When an annual report to shareholders is distributed to the shareholders, copies of that report must be filed with the SEC and with any exchange on which the corporation's stock is listed pursuant to the current rules of the SEC and exchange.

IN SUMMATION

- The Exchange Act deals primarily with the reporting requirements and dealings in securities subsequent to their initial issue.
- The Exchange Act requires public corporations to register with the exchanges on which they are traded.
- The Exchange Act requires the registration of exchanges with the SEC.
- The Exchange Act regulates the use of proxies and includes several antifraud provisions.
- Corporations registered under Section 13 of the Securities Act are subject to the periodic reporting requirements of the Exchange Act, including:
  - 10-K (Annual)
  - 10-Q (Quarterly)
  - 8-K (triggered by specific events)
- To protect investors, Section 14(a) of the Exchange Act and Regulation 14A specify the information that must be included in proxy statements to solicit the vote of shareholders.

- Rule 14a-8 under the Exchange Act provides procedures for eligible shareholders to follow to notify management of their intent to present a proposal for action at an upcoming meeting of the shareholders.

- The annual report to shareholders is one of the primary means for corporate management to communicate with shareholders and potential shareholders.

- The annual report must be sent to shareholders when they hold meetings to elect directors.

§ 11.8 ANTIFRAUD PROVISIONS UNDER THE SECURITIES EXCHANGE ACT OF 1934

Section 10(b) of the Exchange Act, prohibiting manipulative and deceptive devices, is the Exchange Act's principal antifraud provision. This is very broad and applies to both the sale and purchase of securities. Section 10(b) deems it unlawful for any person to use or employ any "manipulative or deceptive device or contrivance in contravention of such rules and regulations as the Commission may prescribe as necessary or appropriate in the public interest or for the protection of investors." The primary fraud-control rule adopted under § 10(b) of the Exchange Act is Securities Exchange Act Rule 10b-5:

RULE 10B-5. EMPLOYMENT OF MANIPULATIVE AND DECEPTIVE DEVICES

It shall be unlawful for any person, directly or indirectly, by the use of any means or instrumentality of interstate commerce, or the mails, or of any facility of any national securities exchange,

1. to employ any device, scheme, or artifice to defraud,

2. to make any untrue statement of a material fact or to omit to state a material fact necessary in order to make the statements made, in light of the circumstances under which they were made, not misleading, or

3. to engage in any act, practice, or course of business which operates or would operate as a fraud or deceit upon any person, in connection with the purchase or sale of any security.

The general nature of Rule 10b-5 allows its imposition on several types of securities cases, including market manipulation, insider trading, corporate misstatements, and corporate mismanagement.

INSIDER TRADING

Nowhere in Section 10(b) or Rule 10b-5 is **insider trading** mentioned. However, the SEC has held that trading in the open market by corporate insiders on the basis of material, nonpublic information is a deceptive device in violation of Section 10(b) and Rule 10b-5.[16] Public corporations must release to the public, in a timely manner,

INSIDER TRADING
The purchase or sale of securities by corporate insiders based on nonpublic information.

all information concerning their earnings, potential mergers or acquisitions, and other information that may affect the price of their stock. Disclosures of nonpublic information must be made broadly by filing the information with the SEC or by other nonexclusive means, such as a press release. This rule is intended to give all investors and potential investors the same information to base their investment decisions on. When corporate insiders become aware of nonpublic corporate information, they must disclose the information to the public or they must abstain from acting on that information. Insider trading occurs when insiders have information that has not been released to the public and they act on that information by buying or selling stock in the corporation, taking unfair advantage of the uninformed investor.

Insiders are generally considered to be individuals who have access to information intended to be available only for a corporate purpose and not for the personal benefit of anyone. When material information concerning the corporation is released, insiders must wait until the news can be widely disseminated before the insider buys or sells shares of equity securities of the corporation based on that information.

In the early 2000s, corporate fraud, including insider trading, became news. Insider trading was among the numerous charges brought against Enron and its various corporate executives. As of the spring of 2005, more than $67 million in insider-trading proceeds had been frozen.[17] In June 2003, the SEC filed charges against Martha Stewart of Martha Stewart Living and her former stockbroker, Peter Bacanovic, for illegal insider trading. The complaint alleged that Martha Stewart sold stock in a biopharmaceutical company, ImClone Systems, Inc., after learning nonpublic information communicated from Bacanovic. Bacanovic had learned that ImClone's then-CEO Samuel Waksal and his daughter had instructed Merrill Lynch to sell off their ImClone stock based on nonpublic information they received concerning a negative decision about one of their key products by the U.S. Food and Drug Administration. Martha Stewart was not convicted on the charges of insider trading; however, she was convicted on charges of obstructing justice, conspiracy, and making false statements in connection with suspicious trades. She served five months in prison for her conviction.

SIDEBAR

In 2003, Samuel Waksal, former CEO of ImClone Systems, was fined $3 million and sentenced to seven years in prison for his unlawful sale of stock in an insider trading case that involved Martha Stewart.

The SEC continues to bring numerous insider-trading cases each year. In 2010, the SEC charged billionaire Raj Rajaratnam and New York–based hedge-fund advisory firm Galleon Management with paying bribes in exchange for inside information about corporate earnings or takeovers and using that nonpublic information to illegally generate more than $52 million in illegal profits.

In *Carpenter v. United States*, the case beginning on page 493, a reporter for a financial newspaper and a stockbroker were convicted of conspiring in an insider-trading case, when the reporter passed information to his stockbroker who made trades based on that information before it appeared in the newspaper.

CASE
Supreme Court of the United States
David Carpenter, Kenneth P. Felis, and R. Foster Winans, Petitioners v. United States
No. 86-422. Argued Oct. 7, 1987. Decided Nov. 16, 1987.

Justice WHITE delivered the opinion of the Court. Petitioners Kenneth Felis and R. Foster Winans were convicted of violating § 10(b) of the Securities Exchange Act of 1934, 48 Stat. 891, 15 U.S.C. § 78j(b), and Rule 10b-5, 17 CFR § 240.10b-5 (1987) . . . They were also found guilty of violating the federal mail and wire fraud statutes, 18 U.S.C. §§ 1341, 1343, and were convicted for conspiracy under 18 U.S.C. § 371. Petitioner David Carpenter, Winans's roommate, was convicted for aiding and abetting. With a minor exception, the Court of Appeals for the Second Circuit affirmed, 791 F.2d 1024 (1986); we granted certiorari, 479 U.S. 1016, 107 S.Ct. 666, 93 L.Ed.2d 718 (1986).

In 1981, Winans became a reporter for *The Wall Street Journal* (the Journal) and in the summer of 1982 became one of the two writers of a daily column, "Heard on the Street." That column discussed selected stocks or groups of stocks, giving positive and negative information about those stocks and taking "a point of view with respect to investment in the stocks that it reviews.". . . Winans regularly interviewed corporate executives to put together interesting perspectives on the stocks that would be highlighted in upcoming columns, but, at least for the columns at issue here, none contained corporate inside information or any "hold for release" information . . . Because of the "Heard" column's perceived quality and integrity, it had the potential of affecting the price of the stocks which it examined. The District Court concluded on the basis of testimony presented at trial that the "Heard" column "does have an impact on the market, difficult though it may be to quantify in any particular case." . . .

The official policy and practice at the Journal was that prior to publication, the contents of the column were the Journal's confidential information. Despite the rule, with which Winans was familiar, he entered into a scheme in October 1983 with Peter Brant and petitioner Felis, both connected with the Kidder Peabody brokerage firm in New York City, to give them advance information as to the timing and contents of the "Heard" column. This permitted Brant and Felis and another conspirator, David Clark, a client of Brant, to buy or sell based on the probable impact of the column on the market. Profits were to be shared.

The conspirators agreed that the scheme would not affect the journalistic purity of the "Heard" column, and the District Court did not find that the contents of any of the articles were altered to further the profit potential of petitioners' stock-trading scheme . . . Over a 4-month period, the brokers made prepublication trades on the basis of information given them by Winans about the contents of some 27 "Heard" columns. The net profits from these trades were about $690,000.

In November 1983, correlations between the "Heard" articles and trading in the Clark and Felis accounts were noted at Kidder Peabody and inquiries began. Brant and Felis denied knowing anyone at the Journal and took steps to conceal the trades. Later, the Securities and Exchange Commission began an investigation. Questions were met by denials both by the brokers at Kidder Peabody and by Winans at the Journal. As the investigation progressed, the conspirators quarreled, and on March 29, 1984, Winans and Carpenter went to the SEC and revealed the entire scheme. This indictment and a bench trial followed. Brant, who had pleaded

(continues)

guilty under a plea agreement, was a witness for the Government.

The District Court found, and the Court of Appeals agreed, that Winans had knowingly breached a duty of confidentiality by misappropriating prepublication information regarding the timing and contents of the "Heard" column, information that had been gained in the course of his employment under the understanding that it would not be revealed in advance of publication and that if it were, he would report it to his employer. It was this appropriation of confidential information that underlay both the securities laws and mail and wire fraud counts. With respect to the § 10(b) charges, the courts below held that the deliberate breach of Winans's duty of confidentiality and concealment of the scheme was a fraud and deceit on the Journal. Although the victim of the fraud, the Journal, was not a buyer or seller of the stocks traded in or otherwise a market participant, the fraud was nevertheless considered to be "in connection with" a purchase or sale of securities within the meaning of the statute and the rule. The courts reasoned that the scheme's sole purpose was to buy and sell securities at a profit based on advance information of the column's contents . . .

Petitioners' arguments that they did not interfere with the Journal's use of the information or did not publicize it and deprive the Journal of the first public use of it, . . . miss the point. The confidential information was generated from the business, and the business had a right to decide how to use it prior to disclosing it to the public . . . We cannot accept petitioners' further argument that Winans's conduct in revealing prepublication information was no more than a violation of

workplace rules and did not amount to fraudulent activity that is proscribed by the mail fraud statute. Sections 1341 and 1343 reach any scheme to deprive another of money or property by means of false or fraudulent pretenses, representations, or promises . . .

We have little trouble in holding that the conspiracy here to trade on the Journal's confidential information is not outside the reach of the mail and wire fraud statutes, provided the other elements of the offenses are satisfied. The Journal's business information that it intended to be kept confidential was its property; the declaration to that effect in the employee manual merely removed any doubts on that score and made the finding of specific intent to defraud that much easier. Winans continued in the employ of the Journal, appropriating its confidential business information for his own use, all the while pretending to perform his duty of safeguarding it . . . Furthermore, the District Court's conclusion that each of the petitioners acted with the required specific intent to defraud is strongly supported by the evidence . . .

Lastly, we reject the submission that using the wires and the mail to print and send the Journal to its customers did not satisfy the requirement that those mediums be used to execute the scheme at issue. The courts below were quite right in observing that circulation of the "Heard" column was not only anticipated but an essential part of the scheme. Had the column not been made available to Journal customers, there would have been no effect on stock prices and no likelihood of profiting from the information leaked by Winans.

The judgment below is Affirmed.

LIABILITY FOR SHORT-SWING PROFITS

Because of their advantageous position and the availability of inside information to a corporation's officers, directors, and principal shareholders, the Exchange Act imposes specific reporting requirements for shareholders falling into these categories. Section 16 of the Exchange Act provides that any profits realized from the purchase and sale (or sale and purchase) of the equity securities of a corporation by its officers, directors, or 10 percent or more shareholders in any period of less than six months normally shall inure to and be recoverable by the issuer. Profits made by an insider on the purchase and sale of securities within a 6-month period are often referred to as **short-swing profits**.

Section 16(b) specifically prohibits short-swing profits as follows:

> (b) For the purpose of preventing the unfair use of information which may have been obtained by such beneficial owner, director, or officer by reason of his relationship to the issuer, any profit realized by him from any purchase and sale, or any sale and purchase, of any equity security of such issuer (other than an exempted security) within any period of less than six months, unless such security was acquired in good faith in connection with a debt previously contracted, shall inure to and be recoverable by the issuer. . . .

Section 16(a) of the Exchange Act specifically provides that a statement setting forth the beneficial ownership of the securities must be filed by "every person who is directly or indirectly the beneficial owner of more than 10 percent of any class of any equity security (other than an exempted security) which is registered pursuant to section 12 of this title, or who is a director or an officer of the issuer of such security." This initial report is made to the SEC on a Form 3 that must be filed within 10 days after a person becomes an officer, director, 10 percent shareholder, or other reporting person. A Form 4 must be filed to report most changes in beneficial ownership occurring after the filing of a Form 3. The Form 4 must be filed with the SEC before the end of the second business day following the day on which the subject transaction is executed. In addition, an annual Form 5 must be submitted within 45 calendar days after the end of the company's fiscal year to report any transactions occurring during the year, but not previously included in a Form 3 or Form 4. The Forms 3, 4, and 5 are filed electronically with the SEC and must also be posted on the issuer's website.

The rule against short-swing profits does not apply to all employees of a corporation or even all employees who hold a title generally given to an officer. The individual's access to confidential inside information, regardless of his or her title, is more determinative as to whom the short-swing profits rules apply. In *Merrill Lynch v. Livingston,* the case that follows in this chapter, the court determined that although the defendant held the title of vice president, he did not have access to "that kind of confidential information about the company's affairs that would help the particular employee to make decisions affecting his market transactions in his employer's securities."

SHORT-SWING PROFITS
Profits made by a company insider on the short-term sale of company stock.

CASE
United States Court of Appeals, Ninth Circuit. Merrill Lynch, Pierce, Fenner & Smith, Inc., Plaintiff-Appellee, v. William G. Livingston, Defendant-Appellant. No. 75-3779. Jan. 4, 1978.

HUFSTEDLER, Circuit Judge:

Merrill Lynch, Pierce, Fenner & Smith, Inc. ("Merrill Lynch") obtained judgment against its employee Livingston requiring him to pay Merrill Lynch $14,836.37 which was the profit that he made on short-swing transactions in the securities of his employer in alleged violation of Section 16(b) of the Securities Exchange Act of 1934

(15 U.S.C. § 78p (1971)). We reverse because Livingston was not an officer with access to inside information within the purview of Section 16(b) of the Securities Exchange Act of 1934. From 1951 to 1972, Livingston was employed by Merrill Lynch as a securities salesman with the title of "Account Executive." In January, 1972, Merrill Lynch began an "Account Executive Recognition Program" for its career Account Executives to reward outstanding sales records. As part of the program, Merrill Lynch awarded Livingston and 47 other Account Executives the title "Vice President." Livingston had exactly the same duties after he was awarded the title as he did before the recognition. Livingston never attended, nor was he invited or permitted to attend, meetings of the Board of Directors or the Executive Committee. He acquired no executive or policy making duties. Executive and managerial functions were performed by approximately 350 "Executive Vice Presidents."

Livingston received the same kind of information about the company as an Account Executive both before and after he acquired his honorary title. As an Account Executive, he did obtain some information that was not generally available to the investing public, such as the growth production rankings on the various Merrill Lynch retail offices. Information of this kind was regularly distributed to other salesmen for Merrill Lynch. Livingston's supervisor, a branch office manager, testified that he gave Livingston the same kind of information that he gave other salesmen about the company, none of which was useful for purposes of stock trading.

In November and December, 1972, Livingston sold a total of 1,000 shares of Merrill Lynch stock. He repurchased 1,000 shares of Merrill Lynch stock in March, 1973, realizing the profit in question.

The district court held that Livingston was an officer with access to inside information within the meaning of Section 16(b) of the Securities Exchange Act of 1934. The predicate for the district court's decision was that Section 16(b) imposes strict liability on any person who holds the title of "officer" and who has access to information about his company that is not generally available to the members of the investing public.

The district court used an incorrect legal standard in applying Section 16(b). Liability under Section 16(b) is not based simply upon a person's title within his corporation; rather, liability follows from the existence of a relationship with the corporation that makes it more probable than not that the individual has access to insider information.

Insider information, to which Section 16(b) is addressed, does not mean all information about the company that is not public knowledge. Insider information within the meaning of Section 16(b) encompasses that kind of confidential information about the company's affairs that would help the particular employee to make decisions affecting his market transactions in his employer's securities.

Strict liability to the issuer is imposed upon any "beneficial owner, director, or officer" for entering into such a short-swing transaction "(f)or the purpose of preventing the unfair use of information which may have been obtained by such . . . officer by reason of his relationship to the issuer." "The purpose of the statute was to take 'the profits out of a class of transactions in which the possibility of abuse was believed to be intolerably great' and to prevent the use by 'insiders' of confidential information, accessible because of one's corporate position or status, in speculative trading in the securities of one's corporation for personal profit.". . .

To achieve the beneficial purposes of the statute, the court must look behind the title of the purchaser or seller to ascertain that person's real duties. Thus, a person who does not have the title of an officer, may, in fact, have a relationship to the company which gives him the very access to insider information that the statute was designed to reach . . .

The title "Vice President" does no more than raise an inference that the person who holds the title has the executive duties and the opportunities for confidential information that the title

implies. The inference can be overcome by proof that the title was merely honorary and did not carry with it any of the executive responsibilities that might otherwise be assumed. The record in this case convincingly demonstrates that Livingston was simply a securities salesman who had none of the powers of an executive officer of Merrill Lynch.

Livingston did not have the job in fact which would have given him presumptive access to insider information. Information that is freely circulated among non-management employees is not insider information within the meaning of Section 16(b), even if the general public does not have the same information. Employees of corporations know all kinds of things about the companies they work for and about the personnel of their concerns that are not within the public domain. Rather, insider information to which Section 16(b) refers is the kind of information that is commonly reserved for company management and is thus the type of information that would "aid (one) if he engaged in personal market transactions.". . .

Livingston did not receive insider information within the meaning of Section 16(b). The only information that he received was that generally available to all Merrill Lynch salesmen. It was not information reserved for company management, nor was it in any way useful to give him any kind of advantage in his security transactions over any other salesmen for Merrill Lynch.

REVERSED.

IN SUMMATION

- Section 10(b) of the Exchange Act prohibits manipulative and deceptive devices in contravention of the rules and regulations of the SEC in connection with either the sale or purchase of securities.
- Insider trading is considered illegal under Section 10(b) of the Exchange Act.
- Insiders are individuals who have access to material information concerning a public corporation that has not yet been made public.
- Short-swing profits are profits made by an insider on the purchase and sale of securities within a 6-month period.
- Transactions that create short-swing profits are prohibited under Section 16(b) of the Exchange Act.

§ 11.9 THE SARBANES-OXLEY ACT OF 2002

The years 2000 and 2001 brought major corporate and accounting scandals involving several prominent companies in the United States, including Enron, WorldCom, and Tyco. These scandals dominated the headlines, shaking the public's trust in the financial markets to a degree not experienced in decades.

In addition to improper oversight by corporate directors, inadequate corporate governance, performance-based incentives, short-term focus, and greed have been blamed for the scandals, which cost shareholders and employees millions in lost equity, jobs, and pensions.

Congress's response to these scandals was to unanimously pass sweeping reform legislation—the **Sarbanes-Oxley Act**, also known as the Public Accounting Reform and Investor Protection Act of 2002. This act was signed into law effective July 30, 2002. Sarbanes-Oxley has had a major impact on the corporate governance and financial disclosures required of public corporations. It has also had a major impact on public accounting practices. The SEC promptly adopted new rules promulgated under the act. In addition to the Sarbanes-Oxley Act, the NASDAQ and NYSE quickly adopted new corporate governance requirements for companies listed on their exchanges.

The overall effect of these new laws and rules is that public companies are subject to tighter controls with regard to their accounting and auditing procedures, corporate governance, and reporting requirements. Public corporations are also subject to new rules providing for the appointment of a number of independent directors to the board and to the audit committee in particular. Following is a summary of some of the more important Sarbanes-Oxley provisions as they relate to public corporations.

CREATION OF THE PUBLIC COMPANY ACCOUNTING OVERSIGHT BOARD

Section 101 of the Sarbanes-Oxley Act establishes a new entity to oversee auditors and the audit of public companies—the Public Company Accounting Oversight Board (PCAOB).

SARBANES-OXLEY ACT OF 2002

Also referred to as the Public Accounting Reform and Investor Protection Act of 2002. Federal law signed into law effective July 30, 2002, to protect investors by improving the accuracy and reliability of corporate disclosures made pursuant to the securities laws, and for other related purposes.

OFFICER CERTIFICATIONS AND INTERNAL CONTROLS

Section 302 of the Sarbanes-Oxley Act requires that chief executive officers and chief financial officers must certify periodic reports required under the Securities Exchange Act of 1934—the 10-K and the 10-Q, and similar reports. CEOs and CFOs of reporting public corporations must certify that:

1. They have reviewed the report.
2. Based on their knowledge, the report includes no untrue statements of a material fact, and doesn't omit a necessary material fact.
3. Based on the officer's knowledge, the financial statements included in the report fairly represent the financial condition and results of operation of the corporation.
4. They have established and maintained controls as prescribed by the statute.
5. They have disclosed to their auditors and the audit committee all significant deficiencies in the internal controls and any fraud involving the management or the employees who have a significant role in the issuer's internal controls.

Section 302 of Sarbanes-Oxley makes it clear that the CEO and CFO are responsible for the financial controls of the corporation.

Closely related to Section 302 is Section 404 of Sarbanes-Oxley, which deals with the adequacy of the internal controls of the corporation to assure proper financial reporting and disclosure. Section 404 requires periodic reports under the Securities Act of 1934 to include an internal control report, stating the responsibility of management for establishing and maintaining an adequate internal control structure and procedure for financial reporting, along with an assessment of the effectiveness of the internal control structure and procedures for financial reporting. In addition, this section of Sarbanes-Oxley requires the registered public accounting firm that prepares the audit report for the corporation to attest to the management's report and assessment.

SIDEBAR

The SEC may seek orders requiring parties to pay civil penalties or **disgorge** money obtained through wrongdoing. Where appropriate, disgorged funds are returned to harmed investors. During 2010, SEC actions resulted in orders for more than $2.8 billion in disgorgement and penalties.[18]

AUDIT COMMITTEE REQUIREMENTS

Some of the more important provisions of Sarbanes-Oxley focus on the audit committee and the auditing process. Section 301, in particular, requires that all members of the corporation's audit committee be independent directors. The board's audit committee is required to actively be involved in overseeing and evaluating outside and internal audits. The audit committee is directly responsible for appointing, compensating, and overseeing the auditor.

DISGORGEMENT

To give up something (usually illegal profits) on demand or by court order.

BAN ON LOANS TO OFFICERS AND DIRECTORS

Section 402 of Sarbanes-Oxley prohibits loans or the extension of credit by a corporation to the directors and executive officers of the corporation.

WHISTLEBLOWER PROVISIONS

Section 806 of the Sarbanes-Oxley Act was adopted to encourage corporate employees to step forward and report to the authorities or a supervisor any wrongdoing they may witness. The Sarbanes-Oxley Act provides that no officer, employee, or agent of the employer-corporation may "discharge, demote, suspend, threaten, harass, or in any other manner discriminate against an employee in the terms and conditions of employment" due to the employee's lawful actions to provide information or assist in an investigation regarding any conduct that the employee reasonably believes constitutes a violation of any rule or regulation of the SEC, or any provision of federal law relating to fraud against shareholders.

Section 806 further provides procedures for whistleblowers to file complaints with the Secretary of Labor if they feel they are being retaliated against and it provides for remedy in the form of compensatory damages for any whistleblower who suffers retaliation.

ENHANCED CRIMINAL PENALTIES

Section 903 of Sarbanes-Oxley increases the maximum period of incarceration for certain mail and wire fraud violations from 5 to 20 years. Section 906 of Sarbanes-Oxley provides criminal penalties, including fines of up to $1 million and 10 years' imprisonment, for any officer who knowingly certifies a report that does not comport with the requirements of the act. Penalties of up to $5 million and imprisonment of up to 20 years may be imposed on officers who willfully certify any statement that does not comport with all the requirements of Section 302 of the Act.

Under the Securities Exchange Act of 1934, the maximum criminal penalty for individuals convicted of securities law violations was a $1 million fine and imprisonment of up to 10 years. Sarbanes-Oxley § 1106 increases the maximum penalties for such crimes to a fine of $5 million and the maximum term of imprisonment to 20 years. Organizations convicted of securities law violations can be fined up to $25 million.

EFFECT OF SARBANES-OXLEY

The full effect of Sarbanes-Oxley, which was designed to "increase the transparency, integrity, and accountability of all public companies,"[19] has yet to be felt. Most large U.S. corporations have made compliance with the Sarbanes-Oxley Act part of their regular corporate governance approach—they have integrated it with other regulatory activities.[20] However, increased accounting, auditing, and officer and director expenses have made compliance with Sarbanes-Oxley a burden for many corporations, especially the smaller corporations. While some corporate executives and analysts question whether the cost of compliance is worth the benefits, others point out the benefits to shareholders. There seems to be a general consensus that corporate governance and accountability have improved due to the Sarbanes-Oxley Act (SOX). Exhibit 11-10 is a summary of some of the major provisions of the federal securities acts discussed in this chapter.

IN SUMMATION

- The Sarbanes-Oxley Act, also known as the Public Accounting Reform and Investor Protection Act of 2002, which was signed into law in 2002, subjects public corporations to tighter controls with regard to their accounting and auditing procedures, corporate governance, and reporting requirements.

- Section 301 of the Sarbanes-Oxley Act created the Public Company Accounting Oversight Board to oversee auditors and the audit of public companies.

- Section 302 of the Sarbanes-Oxley Act requires officers to certify and take additional responsibility for periodic reports made under the Exchange Act.

- Section 402 of the Sarbanes-Oxley Act prohibits loans from public corporations to their directors and executive officers.

- Section 806 of the Sarbanes-Oxley Act provides protection for whistleblowers who report illegal actions in their workplace that constitute fraud against shareholders.

- Section 903 of the Sarbanes-Oxley Act enhances criminal penalties for certain mail and wire fraud violations and crimes involving mail and wire fraud.

- Section 906 of the Sarbanes-Oxley Act enhances criminal penalties for certification of false reports by officers.

§ 11.10 STATE SECURITIES REGULATION— BLUE SKY LAWS

Decades before the adoption of the federal Securities Act and Exchange Act, there was an attempt to regulate securities at the state level. These state statutes regulating securities were an attempt to "stop the sale of stock in fly-by-night concerns, visionary oil wells, distant gold mines, and other like, fraudulent exploitations."[21] The term **blue sky law**, which is commonly used to refer to state statutes regulating securities, was derived from an early Supreme Court case, in which the Court found that the legislative purpose of the acts were aimed at "speculative schemes which have no more basis than so many feet of blue sky."[22]

Blue sky laws act in concert with the federal securities acts and are considered to be valid so long as they do not conflict with the pertinent federal acts.

Most blue sky laws require the registration of securities and of brokers or dealers dealing in securities. They regulate the sale and purchase of securities within the state of domicile through antifraud provisions relating to securities transactions. It

BLUE SKY LAW

Any state law regulating sales of stock or other investment activities to protect the public from fly-by-night or fraudulent stock deals, or to ensure that an investor gets enough information to make a reasoned purchase of stock or other security.

EXHIBIT 11-10 SUMMARY AND HIGHLIGHTS OF SELECT PROVISIONS OF THE FEDERAL SECURITIES ACTS

Securities Act of 1933

- **Section 5(a)** makes it illegal to sell or deliver unregistered securities through the U.S. mail or by other means of transportation or communication in interstate commerce.
- **Section 5(b)** requires a prospectus prepared pursuant to the rules of Section 10 to sell securities.
- **Section 5(c)** requires registration of all nonexempt securities.
- **Section 10** establishes the rules for preparing and using a prospectus to sell securities.
- **Section 11** provides that those who sign a registration statement to register securities or who provide material information for a registration statement may be held liable for damages caused to purchasers of those securities if the registration statement contains untrue or misleading information.
- **Section 12** provides that individuals who use false or misleading prospectuses or other communications may be held liable for damages to purchasers of those securities.
- **Section 17** prohibits fraudulent conduct with respect to securities transactions pertaining to the sale of, or an offer to sell, securities.

Securities Exchange Act of 1934

- **Section 10** prohibits fraud, manipulation, and insider trading for the purchase or sale of any registered security.
- **Section 12** requires that every non-exempt security traded on a national exchange must be registered with that exchange.
- **Section 13** requires every issuer of registered securities to file with the SEC annual and quarterly reports and such other information deemed necessary by the Rules and Regulations of the SEC. These required reports include the Forms 10-K, 10-Q, and 8-K.
- **Section 14** provides that any solicitation of proxies with regard to the voting of registered securities must comply with the pertinent rules and regulation of the SEC regarding proxies.
- **Section 16** prohibits short-swing profits and provides special reporting requirements for corporate officers, directors, and the owners of more than 10% of any class of registered securities of a corporation.

Sarbanes-Oxley Act

- **Section 101** establishes the Public Company Accounting Oversight Board to oversee the audit of public companies that are subject to securities laws.
- **Section 103** gives the Public Company Oversight Board the authority to adopt auditing, quality control, and independence standards and rules.
- **Section 301** requires that all members of a registered corporation's audit committee must be independent directors.
- **Section 302** establishes requirements for the certification of the 10-K and 10-Q and similar reports by the corporation's CEO and CFO. This section makes it clear that the CEO and CFO are responsible for the financial controls of the corporation.
- **Section 402** prohibits loans by registered corporations to the directors and executive officers of the corporation.
- **Section 806** provides protection for whistleblowers who report illegal actions in their workplace that constitute fraud against shareholders.
- **Section 903** increases the penalties for certain mail and wire fraud violations.
- **Section 1106** increases the maximum criminal penalties for individuals convicted of securities law violations.

is clear that blue sky laws apply to intrastate sales of securities of a domestic corporation, but several other common circumstances raise the question of jurisdiction. Clearly, blue sky laws do not apply to transactions that occur entirely outside the state, even if residents of the state are purchasers of the securities. However, blue sky laws do apply to securities sold by foreign corporations within the state.

Blue sky laws vary from state to state, and the laws of any state where a contract for the sale of securities is entered into or executed must be consulted. Most states have adopted, at least to a significant extent, the original Uniform Securities Act (1956), the Uniform Securities Act (1985),[23] or the Uniform Securities Act (2002).[24]

IN SUMMATION

- The purchase and sale of securities is regulated at the state level by state statues referred to as blue sky laws.
- Blue sky laws are valid as long as they don't conflict with the federal securities acts.
- Most blue sky laws require the registration of securities and of brokers or dealers dealing in securities.

§ 11.11 STATE REGULATION OF STOCK OFFERINGS

Blue sky laws typically require the registration of securities of public corporations at the state level (in addition to the federal requirements). Under the Uniform Securities Act, the issuer is required to register the securities by one of three means, depending on the degree of stability of the registrant and the information already available to prospective investors by reason of a registration statement already having been filed with the SEC under the Securities Act.

REGISTRATION BY FILING

Registration by filing is a procedure available to issuers that have filed a registration statement under the Securities Act and have been actively engaged in business operations in the United States for at least three years prior to that filing. The issuer desiring to register by filing must also meet several other criteria set forth by state statute. Registration by filing is accomplished by submitting the following to the state securities authority with the appropriate filing fee:

1. A statement demonstrating eligibility for registration by filing
2. The name, address, and form of organization of the issuer
3. With respect to a person on whose behalf a part of the offering is to be made in a nonissuer distribution: name and address; the amount of securities of the issuer held by the person as of the date of the filing of the registration statement; and a statement of the reasons for making the offering

4. A description of the security being registered
5. A copy of the latest prospectus filed with the registration statement under and satisfying the requirements of § 10 of the Securities Act of 1933

REGISTRATION BY COORDINATION

The procedures for registration by coordination may be followed in most states for any securities for which a registration statement has been filed under the Securities Act. The procedures for registration by coordination are similar to those of registration by filing. Because issuers registering by coordination need not be established corporations that have been transacting business in the United States for several years, slightly more information is required to be filed with this type of registration.

REGISTRATION BY QUALIFICATION

Registration by qualification is available to the issuer of any securities. Registration by qualification is the type of registration that must be completed by corporations that are not required to file a registration statement under the Securities Act, but are required to register at the state level. This is the most complex type of registration, and it requires the most information to be filed at the state level, because there is no available copy of a prospectus filed with the SEC.

EXEMPTIONS

As with federal registration requirements, there are many exemptions from state registration requirements. The exemptions for each individual state are found in that state's statutes. Often, the securities may be exempt from registration because of either the type or class of the securities, or the specific transaction involving the securities. Exemption from the registration requirements of the state securities regulations does not guarantee exemption from the other provisions of the regulations.

IN SUMMATION

- Blue sky laws require the registration of securities of public corporations at the state level.
- Corporations that have filed a registration statement under the Securities Act may be required to register their securities by filing or by coordination.
- Registration by qualification may be completed by the issuer of securities that are not required to file a registration statement under the Securities Act, but are required to register at the state level.
- There are many exemptions from registration available under blue sky laws because of either the type or class of the securities or the specific transaction involving the securities.

§ 11.12 STATE SECURITIES REGULATION—ANTIFRAUD PROVISIONS

State statutes prohibit fraudulent activities connected with the offer, sale, and purchase of securities, as do the similar antifraud provisions found in the Securities Act and the Exchange Act. The antifraud provisions of the Uniform Securities Act are found in §§ 501 through 505. Section 505, which parallels Rule 10b-5 of the Securities Act, reads as follows:

---

§ 501 OFFER, SALE, AND PURCHASE

In connection with an offer to sell, sale, offer to purchase, or purchase, of a security, a person may not, directly or indirectly:

1. employ a device, scheme, or artifice to defraud;

2. make an untrue statement of a material fact or omit to state a material fact necessary in order to make the statements made not misleading, in light of the circumstances under which they are made; or

3. engage in an act, practice, or course of business that operates or would operate as a fraud or deceit upon a person.

The Uniform Securities Act also contains provisions prohibiting market manipulation; regulating the transactions of investment advisors; and prohibiting misleading filings and unlawful representation concerning licensing, registration, or exemption.

IN SUMMATION

- Blue sky laws prohibit fraudulent activities connected with the offer, sale, and purchase of securities.

§ 11.13 THE PARALEGAL'S ROLE

Paralegals are often involved in all aspects of the public securities offering and in complying with the ongoing reporting requirements for public corporations.

INITIAL PUBLIC OFFERINGS

Once a decision to go public has been made, a date for filing the registration statement is usually agreed upon by the corporation's directors, its attorneys, and the underwriters. All plans for the public offering depend on that target date, and it is crucial that the registration statement be filed on time. For that reason, work on securities offerings often must be completed within very tight time constraints.

The following is a sample time line for a public stock offering. This time line is by no means all-inclusive; rather, it is intended to demonstrate the ordinary sequence of the main events leading to a public stock offering.

Week 1

Organizational meeting attended by corporate management, corporate counsel, underwriters, underwriters' counsel, and corporation's accountants; schedule is decided on, as well as format for registration statement.

Preliminary agreement with underwriters.

Week 2

Circulate first draft of registration statement and underwriting agreement for comments and revisions.

Begin corporate "housekeeping" to make sure financial and corporate records are in order.

Week 3

Due diligence work; drafting and revision of registration statement and underwriting agreement.

Week 4

Continue work on drafting and revision of registration statement and underwriting agreement.

Week 5

Continue work on drafting and revision of registration statement.

Week 6

Review drafts of registration statement and underwriting agreement.

Week 7

Meeting of the board of directors to discuss and approve registration statement and other matters related to public offering.

Week 8

Finalize and file registration statement.

Submit press release regarding offering to appropriate papers. File appropriate documents with NASD.

Begin work to comply with blue sky requirements.

Weeks 8–10

Review comments from SEC.

Prepare amendments to registration statement, if necessary.

Conduct negotiations on price of stock to be offered.

Registration statement becomes effective.

Commence offering.

File prospectus with SEC, including price.

Closing with corporation and underwriters after price of stock has been set and offering has commenced.

Week 11

Continue work on blue sky requirements.

Set schedule to comply with periodic reporting requirements.

Paralegals may be assigned the task of collecting the necessary information and drafting certain sections of the registration statement and prospectus. Collecting all of the necessary information to complete the registration statement under the Securities Act of 1933 can be a monumental task. The information gathered to prepare the registration statement required under the Securities Act will also be used to complete the necessary documentation under the Exchange Act and the pertinent blue sky laws.

PERIODIC REPORTING REQUIREMENTS

Paralegals often assist with drafting and filing the periodic reports required by the Exchange Act. It is important for the paralegal or other assigned individual to keep track of the required filing dates for periodic reporting requirements, to assure that all 10-K, 10-Q, and 8-K reports are filed in a timely manner. Paralegals often work closely with the corporation's officers, directors, and major shareholders to coordinate the completion and filing of Forms 3, 4, and 5.

Another area in which the paralegal often participates is in researching the blue sky laws of the pertinent states, to determine the procedures that must be followed in each of the applicable states. Complying with blue sky laws often involves thorough research into the statutes of several states.

CORPORATE PARALEGAL PROFILE:
Brian Haberly

NAME Brian Haberly, RP®

LOCATION Seattle, Washington

TITLE Senior Paralegal

SPECIALTY Corporate and Securities

EDUCATION Bachelor of Arts, California State University, Northridge; Paralegal Certificate (Corporate Specialization), magna cum laude, University of West Los Angeles

EXPERIENCE 20 years

Brian Haberly is a Senior Corporate and Securities Paralegal in the Legal Department of Clearwire Corporation in Kirkland, Washington. He has held positions of increasing responsibility with several leading public companies, includ ing Starbucks Coffee Company, Expedia.com, and InfoSpace, as well as with two of the largest prominent Seattle law firms, Lane Powell and Williams Kastner. Clearwire's legal department consists of 12 attorneys, 4 paralegals, and 4 legal administrative assistants and staff, which provide support to more than 3,000 employees and over 8 million customers utilizing the nation's first 4G mobile broadband Internet network by working with its partners Sprint, Comcast, Time Warner Cable, Bright House Networks, Google, and Intel. It is a big task and requires a lot of cooperation and coordination by a dedicated team of professionals to make it work so well.

Brian's supervising attorney at Clearwire is the assistant general counsel and assistant corporate secretary for this publicly traded company. Brian's responsibilities include corporate securities reporting and Sarbanes-Oxley compliance. Brian assists with the preparation and filing of Clearwire's periodic and special reports that are filed with the Securities and Exchange Commission, including Forms 10-K, 10-Q, 8-K, and all Section 16 reports (Forms 3, 4, and 5). He also works on the proxy statement and annual report to shareholders. Brian works closely with the company's attorneys, internal auditors, and members of Finance, Investor Relations, and the Executive departments to ensure that the corporation is in full compliance with the Sarbanes-Oxley Act and the company's Corporate Governance Principles and Practices.

Brian also feels it is imperative to stay aware of the rapid changes in this area of the law. Significant revisions in financial accounting standards such as the handling of deferred compensation and the expensing of stock options, the requirement for quarterly CEO and CFO certifications in financial statements, increasingly shorter reporting cycles, and an increased emphasis on clear and complete reporting of executive compensation have resulted in making strong corporate compliance and good corporate governance key roles for the legal department to play, especially for attorneys and paralegals in the corporate and securities area.

Brian likes the high degree of responsibility and independence he has in his position. He enjoys being given the freedom to work on several projects for which he has primary responsibility— checking with the responsible attorney if he has

CORPORATE PARALEGAL PROFILE
Brian Haberly (continued)

questions or concerns. Brian appreciates that the paralegals at Clearwire are given a lot of responsibility and the ability to make a real difference in the success of the company.

Brian also provides support to the board of directors—he helps to organize the board of directors' briefing books delivered via a secure website, prepares minutes and resolutions, and maintains the minute books for the corporation and its subsidiaries.

Brian is a strong proponent of professional development. He has been very active in the Washington State Paralegal Association for over 17 years and completed three successive terms as state president and is currently serving as the vice president for professional development. He serves as a community member of the Paralegal Advisory Boards for the Paralegal Programs at Edmonds Community College, north of Seattle, and also the University of Washington. Brian is a frequent speaker on paralegal topics. He served on the Advisory Board for the Association of Corporate Counsel's (ACC) first-ever paralegal track at ACC's "Corporate Counsel University" (CCU) in 2007, and spoke on CCU paralegal panels in both 2007 and 2008. In 2009, he became a PACE Registered Paralegal ("RP") by passing the NFPA Paralegal

Advanced Competency Exam. At Starbucks, he founded a chapter of Toastmasters International, which is an 80-year-old international organization that helps people improve their communication and leadership skills. When not busy with work, he is usually found on the sidelines of a soccer game for one of his three children, all of whom have played select soccer for several years, or at a Seattle Sounders (Major League Soccer) match.

Brian's advice to new paralegals?

Recognize that your first paralegal position probably won't be your "dream" position, but know that if you are receptive and enthusiastic in taking on new tasks—even ones that don't initially excite you—you can learn valuable lessons that will translate into better and better positions and more financially rewarding job opportunities later on. Don't settle for being a "good" or even a "great" paralegal. Strive for "excellence," which is where all the top rewards await you. Underpromise and overdeliver, and you'll be seen as a key member of your firm or legal department. "Surprise and delight" your attorney or manager to make him or her a "raving fan customer" of you!

For more information on careers for corporate paralegals, log in to http://cengagebrain.com to access the CourseMate website that accompanies this text; then see the Corporate Careers Section.

ETHICAL CONSIDERATION

The Paralegal as an "Insider"

Suppose that one of your first duties in your new paralegal position is to organize the file of the XYZ Corporation, a public corporation, and to assemble information to be discussed at an upcoming board of directors' meeting. On review of the XYZ Corporation's preliminary financial statements, you notice that the XYZ Corporation has had a surprisingly good year. The financial forecast for the upcoming year also looks very good. With this in mind, you decide that it might be fun to buy some stock in the XYZ Corporation, just 100 shares or so.

Is this a smart move? Should you be congratulated, or sent to prison? According to the SEC, you may be guilty of insider trading, a criminal offense punishable by fine or imprisonment. Individuals who are in a position to obtain information on a corporation that is not generally available to the public and who use that information to their unfair advantage are considered to be guilty of insider trading.

In recent years, the SEC has spent considerable time and effort on detecting and prosecuting violators of the insider trading rules. Although most of this time and attention has been focused on the "big guys" on Wall Street, the SEC has also expanded its efforts to include lawyers and law firm personnel. Lawyers found to be in violation of the rules under the Securities Exchange Act are subject to sanctions under state bar association disciplinary rules, in addition to possible criminal prosecution and civil lawsuits brought by shareholders. The Model Code of Professional Responsibility Disciplinary Rule 4-101, which has been adopted by many states, requires that an attorney shall not knowingly reveal a client's confidences or secrets or use such information to his or her advantage. Further, Disciplinary Rule 4-101 provides that an attorney must use such care as is necessary to prevent his or her employees from disclosing confidential information concerning a client, or from acting on that confidential information to their advantage.

Because the penalties for insider trading can be imposed on members of a law firm's staff, most law firms that represent public corporations have written policies that must be adhered to by all office personnel. Effective law firm policies regarding trading in the securities of corporations represented by the firm serve to educate the firm's personnel about the potential risks involved in such trading. Such policies often place restrictions on trading in the securities of a corporation that the law firm represents by all individuals who may even appear to have access to inside information.

ETHICAL CONSIDERATION
(continued)

The best policy for you, as a paralegal who may be in doubt as to whether you are at risk of violating insider trading rules, is to cease any trading in the securities of corporations represented by the law firm, at least until you have had a chance to talk with a securities attorney within the firm who can advise you of your potential risks.

For more information on ethics for corporate paralegals, including links to the NALA and NFPA codes of ethics, log in to http://www.cengagebrain. com to access the CourseMate website that accompanies this text; then see the Ethics Section.

§ 11.14 RESOURCES

As discussed in this chapter, the primary sources of law regarding securities regulations are the Securities Act of 1933, 15 U.S.C. § 77a et seq., the Securities Exchange Act of 1934, 15 U.S.C. § 78a et seq., the Sarbanes-Oxley Act of 2002, 15 U.S.C. § 7201, et seq., and the rules and regulations that accompany these acts. State statutes must also be consulted for the pertinent blue sky laws.

FEDERAL AND STATE LAW

The federal securities acts are a part of the United States Code and may be found anywhere federal statutes are found. The Securities Act of 1933 is located at 15 U.S.C. § 77a et seq., the Securities Exchange Act of 1934 is located at 15 U.S.C. § 78a et seq., and the Sarbanes-Oxley Act of 2002 is located at 15 U.S.C.A. § 7201.

At times, it is necessary to research both the federal securities laws and state blue sky laws. Blue sky laws are found within the state securities acts of the state statutes of each state. Links to the statutes of each state may be accessed from the CourseMate website.

OTHER SECURITIES RESOURCES

The CCH Federal Securities Law Reporter is a comprehensive resource that may be found online or in loose-leaf volumes. Many lawyers who practice securities law subscribe to this service, which contains the federal laws, rules, and regulations. In addition, the service provides up-to-date court decisions concerning securities laws and SEC releases.

The Securities and Exchange Commission website provides the full text of securities laws and regulations, as well as the forms discussed in this chapter. In addition, the EDGAR database can be searched from the SEC website.

The Securities Lawyer's Deskbook website, published by the University of Cincinnati College of Law, provides the full text of all the securities acts and regulations discussed in this chapter. In addition, this site provides useful links to sites important to securities lawyers.

SUMMARY

- Public corporations are corporations that have shares listed on a national securities exchange or that are regularly traded on a market maintained by a member of a national securities association.

- Most securities offered, sold, or delivered through interstate commerce, including the U.S. Postal Service, are considered to be part of a public offering and must first be registered in accordance with the Securities Act of 1933.

- When a corporation first offers its securities for sale to the public, it is considered an initial public offering.

- Securities of public corporations are traded on a stock exchange, such as the New York Stock Exchange, or they are sold over the counter.

- The Securities and Exchange Commission was created by the Securities Exchange Act of 1934. It is headed by five presidential appointees and its mission is to protect investors and maintain the integrity of the securities markets.

- Section 5 of the Securities Act of 1933 makes it illegal to sell securities through interstate commerce or the mail unless a registration statement has been filed with the SEC for those securities.

- Regulations A and D provide for several exemptions to the registration requirements of the Securities Act of 1933 for smaller offerings and offerings that are made to a limited group of individuals.

- Section 11 of the Securities Act provides that everyone who signs or contributes material information to the registration statement has a duty to provide complete and accurate information.

- Section 17 of the Securities Act prohibits fraudulent conduct with respect to the sale of or offer to sell securities.

- The Securities Exchange Act of 1934 protects securities investors and the general public by regulating securities exchanges and markets, by requiring periodic reporting of information by the issuers of securities, and by prohibiting fraud and manipulation in the trading of securities.

- All securities traded on a securities exchange must be registered with that exchange.

- Every issuer subject to the reporting requirements of the Exchange Act must file Form 10-K annual reports and Form 10-Q quarterly reports in the form provided by the Securities and Exchange Commission.

- A Form 8-K must be filed with the Securities and Exchange Commission when certain information contained in the registration statement of the issuer changes.

- Profits made by an insider on the purchase and sale of securities within a 6-month period are referred to as short-swing profits and are prohibited under § 16 of the Securities and Exchange Commission Act of 1934.

- The Securities Exchange Act of 1934 provides certain requirements for the use of proxies and proxy statements.

- Section 10(b) of the Securities Exchange Act of 1934 prohibits the use of any misleading or fraudulent means in connection with the purchase or sale of any security.

- Section 10(b) of the Securities Exchange Act, which prohibits insider trading, makes it unlawful for insiders who have information that has not been released to the public to act on that information by buying or selling stock in the corporation, taking unfair advantage of the uninformed investor.

- The Sarbanes-Oxley Act of 2002, also known as the Public Accounting Reform and Investor Protection Act of 2002, was passed unanimously by Congress in 2002 to require tighter controls of corporate accounting and auditing procedures, corporate governance, and reporting requirements.

- Documents are filed electronically with the Securities and Exchange Commission via EDGAR, the Electronic Data Gathering, Analysis, and Retrieval system. Most documents filed via EDGAR are available to the public via the Internet.

- Blue sky laws are state laws regulating the sale of securities.

- In addition to filing at the federal level, blue sky laws may require the issuers of securities to file at the state level.

REVIEW QUESTIONS

1. What are some of the advantages and disadvantages of taking a privately held corporation public?

2. What are the two general requirements of § 5 of the Securities Act of 1933 with regard to securities that are offered or sold through any means of interstate commerce?

3. What is the due diligence defense? To whom is the due diligence defense available?

4. What is the purpose of Form 8-K?

5. What are short-swing profits?

6. What is the definition and the origin of the term "blue sky laws"?

7. As a 20 percent shareholder in a publicly owned corporation, Jane has decided to sell her shares. What special requirements must she comply with because she owns such a large stake in the company?

8. What is the purpose of the Sarbanes-Oxley Act, and what prompted its passage?

9. What are the purposes of the proxy and the proxy statement?

10. When is the Form 10-K filed?

▪ PRACTICAL PROBLEMS

Locate the securities act within the statutes of your state to answer the following questions:

1. What is the cite of your state's securities act?

2. What statute section requires the registration of securities in your state?

3. Where are securities registration documents filed in your state?

4. How can securities be registered in your state? List the cites of any statutes in your state permitting the following:

   a. Registration by filing
   b. Registration by coordination
   c. Registration by qualification

▪ EXERCISE IN CRITICAL THINKING

When preparing a registration statement, what steps can attorneys and paralegals follow to ensure that due diligence is used to provide factual information about the corporation? Why is it so important to use due diligence when preparing a registration statement for securities?

▪ WORKPLACE SCENARIO

Assume that our fictional clients, Bradley Harris and Cynthia Lund, have just finished meeting with your supervising attorney, Belinda Benson. Ms. Benson has informed you that Mr. Harris and Ms. Lund have been approached by a large electronics retailer in your hometown. The electronics retailer would like to purchase Cutting Edge Computer Repair, Inc., and hire Mr. Harris and Ms. Lund. They are considering the offer, but would like more information about the retailer.

Pick a public electronics company that you are somewhat familiar with. Using the above facts and the resources discussed in this chapter, locate the most current Form 10-K for the retailer to answer the following questions:

1. When was the Form 10-K report filed?

2. What is the central index key?

3. What is the company's standard industrial classification?

4. What is the company's IRS number?

5. What is the company's state of incorporation?

6. What is the company's fiscal year end?

END NOTES

1. Model Business Corporation Act, revised through December 2007 (MBCA) § 1.40(18A).

2. U.S. Census Bureau, *The Statistic Abstract of the United States (2011)* § 1209.

3. Id. § 1210.

4. Securities Act of 1933 § 2(a)(1), 15 U.S.C. § 77b(a)(1) (2000).

5. NASDAQ website, http:// www.nasdaq.com (accessed July 9, 2011).

6. Securities and Exchange Commission website, http://www.sec.gov (accessed July 9, 2011).

8. U.S. Securities and Exchange Commission FY 2010 Performance and Accountability Report, Securities and Exchange Commission website, http://www.sec.gov.

9. Section 2(a) of the Securities Act of 1933 defines the term "security" as "any note, stock, treasury stock, security future, bond, debenture, evidence of indebtedness, certificate of interest or participation in any profit-sharing agreement, collateral-trust certificate, preorganization certificate or subscription, transferable share, investment contract, voting-trust certificate, certificate of deposit for a security, fractional undivided interest in oil, gas, or other mineral rights, any put, call, straddle, option, or privilege on any security, certificate of deposit, or group or index of securities (including any interest therein or based on the value thereof), or any put, call, straddle, option, or privilege entered into on a national securities exchange relating to foreign currency, or, in general, any interest or instrument commonly known as a 'security,' or any certificate of interest or participation in, temporary or interim certificate for, receipt for, guarantee of, or warrant or right to subscribe to or purchase, any of the foregoing."

10. Securities Act of 1933 § 8(b), 15 U.S.C. § 77.

11. Reg. 17 cf. § 230.431(e).

12. Preliminary Notes, Regulation D, Securities Act of 1933.

13. United States Securities and Exchange Commission release no. 4552 (Nov. 6, 1962).

14. 69a Am.Jur.2d, Securities Regulation—Federal § 1386 (May 2011.)

15. Fletcher Cyclopedia of Private Corp. § 6826 (February 2011).

16. Cady, Roberts & Co., 40 S.E.C. 907 (1961).

17. Buchanan, Mary Beth. First Year Report to the President by the Corporate Fraud Task Force, PLI Corporate Compliance Institute 2005 (March–June 2005).

18. U.S. Securities and Exchange Commission FY 2010 Performance and Accountability Report, Securities and Exchange Commission website, http://www.sec.gov.

19. Preamble, Sarbanes-Oxley Act (2002).

20. Price Waterhouse Coopers. "Most Large Companies See Sarbanes-Oxley Compliance as Part of Broader Corporate Governance Initiative," *Management Barometer* (July 14, 2004).

21. *Hall v. Geiger-Jones Co.*, 242 U.S. 539 (1917).

22. Id.

23. Colorado, District of Columbia, Montana, Nevada, and Rhode Island have all adopted the Uniform Securities Act (1985) or substantial portions thereof.

24. Georgia, Hawaii, Idaho, Indiana, Iowa, Kansas, Maine, Michigan, Minnesota, Mississippi, Missouri, Oklahoma, South Carolina, South Dakota, Vermont, the Virgin Islands, and Wisconsin have all adopted the Uniform Securities Act (2002) or substantial portions thereof.

25. National Association of Legal Assistants 2010 National Utilization and Compensation Survey Report, 2010, http://www.nala.org (accessed July 12, 2011).

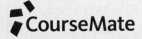
CourseMate

To access additional course materials, including CourseMate, please visit http://www.cengagebrain .com. At the CengageBrain home page, search for the ISBN of your title (from the back cover of your book) using the search box at the top of the page. This will take you to the product page where these resources can be found. The CourseMate resources for this text include links to the online resources listed earlier, downloadable forms, flash cards, and more.

12

MERGERS, ACQUISITIONS, AND OTHER CHANGES TO THE CORPORATE STRUCTURE

▪ CHAPTER OUTLINE

INTRODUCTION

While it is the big multimillion- or multibillion-dollar megamergers that make the headlines of the business section, corporations of any size can be involved in mergers and acquisitions. In addition, any corporation can find it necessary to change its corporate structure at some point. In this chapter, we will look at some of the more common changes to the corporate structure, including mergers and acquisitions, amendments to the corporation's articles of incorporation, and entity conversions.

§ 12.1 MERGERS AND ACQUISITIONS IN THE UNITED STATES

The number and value of mergers and acquisitions that take place each year rises and falls with the economy. From 2004 through the first half of 2007, mergers and acquisitions seemed to take place at an increasing and sometimes frenzied pace in the United States. During 2007, there were more than 10,500 U.S. and U.S. cross-border merger and acquisition transactions, with a total value of $1,345 trillion.[1]

During the later part of 2007, however, the financial crisis and credit crunch in the United States had a dramatic effect on mergers and acquisitions. The number of mergers fell off dramatically in the second half of 2007 and continued its downward spiral throughout 2008. The year 2008 saw the lowest number of mergers and acquisitions reported since 2003. With the slow economic recovery beginning in 2009, the pace of merger and acquisition activity also began to slowly pick up and has continued to do so through 2010. Most experts agree that merger and acquisition activity in the United States will continue to grow as the economy does. See Exhibits 12-1 and 12-2.

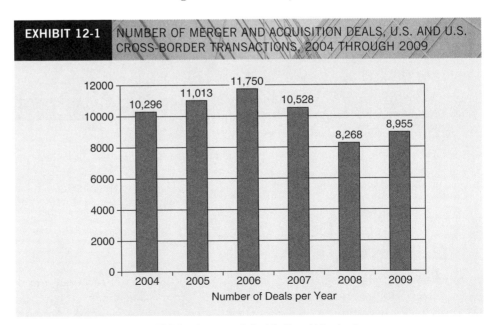

EXHIBIT 12-1 NUMBER OF MERGER AND ACQUISITION DEALS, U.S. AND U.S. CROSS-BORDER TRANSACTIONS, 2004 THROUGH 2009

Statistics MergerStat, as reported on High Rock Partners website, http://www.highrockpartners.com.

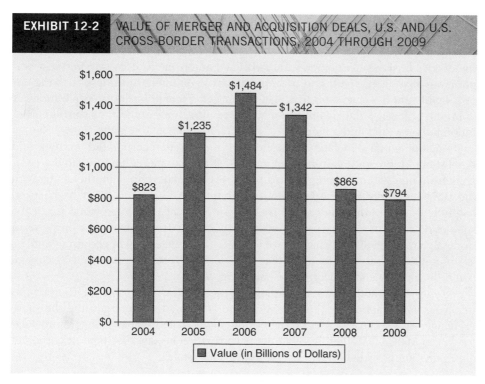

EXHIBIT 12-2 VALUE OF MERGER AND ACQUISITION DEALS, U.S. AND U.S. CROSS-BORDER TRANSACTIONS, 2004 THROUGH 2009

Statistics MergerStat, as reported on High Rock Partners website, http://www.highrockpartners.com.

While much of the volume accounting for these numbers stems from megamergers (mergers in excess of $1 billion), mergers and acquisitions also take place daily between smaller corporations—including those that are closely held.

IN SUMMATION

- The amount of merger and acquisition activity in the United States is generally dependent on the economy.
- Mergers and acquisitions may take place between large, multimillion-dollar public corporations, and also between smaller, closely held corporations.

§ 12.2 STATUTORY MERGERS AND SHARE EXCHANGES

State statutes generally set forth requirements for certain types of corporate **amalgamations**, including **mergers**, share exchanges, and consolidations. Unions that are provided for by statute are typically referred to as **statutory mergers**. Statutory mergers and **share exchanges** may be between domestic corporations or domestic

AMALGAMATION
A complete joining or blending together of two or more things into one; for example, a consolidation or merger of two or more corporations to create a single company.

MERGER
The union of two or more corporations, with one corporation ceasing to exist and becoming a part of the other.

STATUTORY MERGER
A type of merger that is specifically provided for by state statute.

SHARE EXCHANGE
Transaction whereby one corporation acquires all of the outstanding shares of one or more classes or series of another corporation by an exchange that is compulsory on the shareholders of the target corporation.

and foreign corporations, provided that the transaction is permitted by the statutes of the state of domicile of each corporation. The statutes of an increasing number of states also provide for mergers between corporate and noncorporate entities. Under the Model Business Corporation Act (MBCA), one or more domestic business corporations may merge with one or more domestic or foreign business corporations or "eligible entities" pursuant to a plan of merger. Foreign business corporations or domestic or foreign eligible entities may merge into a new domestic business corporation to be created in the merger.[2]

Eligible entities include domestic and foreign unincorporated entities and domestic and foreign nonprofit corporations.[3] For example, a limited liability company from one state may merge into a business corporation from another state, with the surviving entity being a business corporation. State statutes must be checked carefully to ensure that the type of transaction contemplated is provided for in the state of domicile of each corporate or noncorporate entity involved. For purposes of discussion throughout this chapter, we will refer to the merging or acquiring entities as corporations, but keep in mind that if permitted by state statute, our discussion could be applicable to noncorporate entities as well.

Under the statutes of states following the MBCA, two types of transactions involving the combination of corporations are addressed: the merger and the share exchange. This section focuses on the flexible mergers and share exchanges provided for in the MBCA. We then briefly discuss consolidations, another type of corporate amalgamation provided for by the statutes of some states.

MERGERS

A merger is a combination of two or more corporations whereby one of the corporations survives (the surviving corporation) and absorbs one or more other corporations (the merging corporations), which cease to exist. Mergers have the effect of transferring all assets, liabilities, and obligations of the merging corporation to the surviving corporation alone. See Exhibit 12-3.

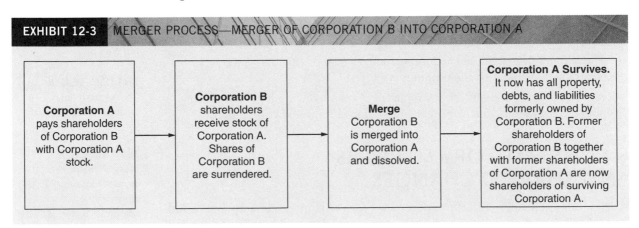

EXHIBIT 12-3 MERGER PROCESS—MERGER OF CORPORATION B INTO CORPORATION A

Corporation A pays shareholders of Corporation B with Corporation A stock. → **Corporation B** shareholders receive stock of Corporation A. Shares of Corporation B are surrendered. → **Merge** Corporation B is merged into Corporation A and dissolved. → **Corporation A Survives.** It now has all property, debts, and liabilities formerly owned by Corporation B. Former shareholders of Corporation B together with former shareholders of Corporation A are now shareholders of surviving Corporation A.

© Cengage Learning 2013

Section 11.07(a) of the MBCA sets forth the effect of a merger:

(a) When a merger becomes effective:
   (1) the corporation or eligible entity that is designated in the plan of merger as the survivor continues or comes into existence, as the case may be;
   (2) the separate existence of every corporation or eligible entity that is merged into the survivor ceases;
   (3) all property owned by, and every contract right possessed by, each corporation or eligible entity that merges into the survivor is vested in the survivor without reversion or impairment;
   (4) all liabilities of each corporation or eligible entity that is merged into the survivor are vested in the survivor;
   (5) the name of the survivor may, but need not be, substituted in any pending proceeding of the name of any party to the merger whose separate existence ceased in the merger;
   (6) the articles of incorporation or organic documents of the survivor are amended to the extent provided in the plan of merger;
   (7) the articles of incorporation or organic documents of a survivor that is created by the merger become effective; and
   (8) the shares of each corporation that is a party to the merger, and the interests in an eligible entity that is a party to a merger, that are to be converted under the plan of merger into shares, eligible interests, obligations, rights to acquire securities, other securities, or eligible interests, cash, other property, or any combination of the foregoing, are converted, and the former holders of such shares or eligible interests are entitled only to the rights provided to them in the plan of merger or to any rights they may have under chapter 13 or the organic law of the eligible entity.

Chapter 13 of the MBCA concerns dissenters' rights, which are discussed in more detail in § 12.6 of this chapter.

There are numerous reasons for merging two or more corporations. A merger is one means often employed to achieve the acquisition of one corporation by another.

When management decides that it is in the best interests of the corporation to expand into a new geographical area, or to acquire new competencies or products, this change is often accomplished by acquiring a corporation that already exists in that market, or that already has the desired expertise.

Corporate management may have a strategy that includes continued growth and expansion through acquisition and merger. Some large corporations routinely acquire and merge several corporations into the parent corporation each year. Corporations with common shareholders, and parent and subsidiary corporations, are also often merged to decrease the paperwork, taxes, and other expenses associated with maintaining two separate corporate entities.

Although megamergers involving the merger of huge conglomerates will naturally be much more complex than the merger of a closely held parent corporation with its subsidiary, the same state statutes and basic procedures apply. In addition, larger merger transactions must comply with federal antitrust statutes and require the approval of the Federal Trade Commission and the Department of Justice. Federal antitrust laws are discussed briefly in § 12.3 of this chapter.

The shareholders of the merging corporation generally receive shares of the surviving corporation in exchange for their shares and become shareholders of the surviving corporation. See Exhibit 12-3. However, the surviving corporation may pay cash as all or part of the consideration given to the merging corporation, so long as the terms are agreed to in the plan of merger.

In some instances, the majority shareholders of a corporation may seek to eliminate the interests of the minority shareholders by entering into a merger in which the minority shareholders are forced either to take cash in consideration for their shares, or to dissent and seek appraisal. This type of transaction is sometimes called a "freeze-out" or "take-out," and may be found invalid in certain jurisdictions, especially if the merger has no clear business purpose other than elimination of the minority shareholders. The management and majority shareholders owe a duty to the corporation and to the minority shareholders to enter into transactions only to promote the best interests of the corporation and all its shareholders, including the minority shareholders.

There are many variations from the simple statutory merger whereby one unrelated corporation merges into another. Some of the more common deviations from that design are upstream mergers, downstream mergers, triangle mergers, and reverse triangle mergers.

Mergers between Subsidiaries and Parents

UPSTREAM MERGER
Merger whereby a subsidiary corporation merges into its parent.

Mergers may take place between a parent and a subsidiary corporation. When the subsidiary corporation merges into its parent corporation, it is referred to as an **upstream merger**. Upstream mergers may be eligible for a short-form merger under statute, whereby the statutory merger requirements are simplified because of the relationship between the two corporations. Shareholder approval of the subsidiary corporation is not required when the parent corporation owns at least 90 percent of the outstanding stock of the subsidiary, as the minority shareholders do not have sufficient voting power to block the merger.

DOWNSTREAM MERGER
Merger whereby a parent corporation is merged into a subsidiary.

When the parent corporation is merged into a subsidiary it is referred to as a **downstream merger**. See Exhibits 12-4 and 12-5.

Triangle Mergers

TRIANGLE MERGER
Merger involving three corporations, whereby a corporation forms a subsidiary corporation and funds it with sufficient cash or shares of stock to perform a merger with the target corporation, which is merged into the subsidiary. The parent and subsidiary corporations survive.

The **triangle merger** involves three corporations: a parent corporation, a subsidiary of the parent corporation, and a target corporation. In a triangle merger, the parent corporation forms a subsidiary and funds it with sufficient cash or shares of stock to perform a merger with the target corporation, which is merged into the subsidiary

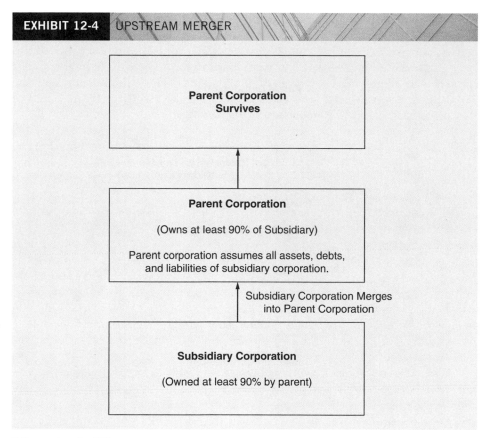

EXHIBIT 12-4 UPSTREAM MERGER

**Parent Corporation
Survives**

Parent Corporation

(Owns at least 90% of Subsidiary)

Parent corporation assumes all assets, debts,
and liabilities of subsidiary corporation.

Subsidiary Corporation Merges
into Parent Corporation

Subsidiary Corporation

(Owned at least 90% by parent)

© Cengage Learning 2013

corporation. Both the parent and the subsidiary are surviving corporations in a triangle merger. See Exhibit 12-6 on page 525.

Reverse Triangle Mergers

A **reverse triangle merger** is also a three-way merger. Its distinction from the triangle merger is that in the reverse triangle merger the subsidiary is merged into the target corporation. The end result is the survival of the parent corporation and the target corporation, which will become a new subsidiary. See Exhibit 12-7 on page 526. The survival of the target corporation may be important when it is a special type of corporation that is difficult to form, or when the target corporation being acquired is a party to nonassignable contracts.

The same result achieved by a reverse triangle merger may be achieved by a share exchange of the type permitted by § 11.3 of the MBCA. Unlike the merger, the end result of a share exchange is the survival of both corporations, one that becomes a parent and the other a subsidiary.

**REVERSE TRIANGLE
MERGER**

Three-way merger whereby a
subsidiary corporation is merged
into the target corporation. The
end result is the survival of the
parent corporation and the target
corporation, which becomes a
new subsidiary.

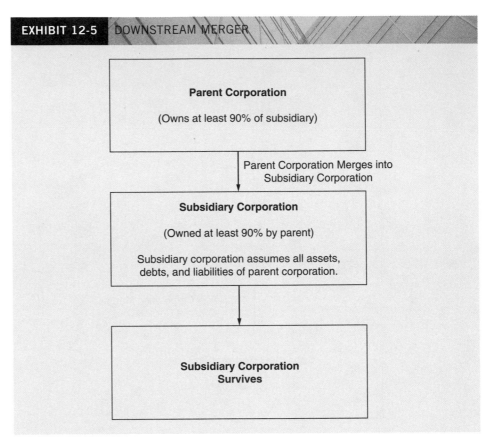

EXHIBIT 12-5 DOWNSTREAM MERGER

Parent Corporation

(Owns at least 90% of subsidiary)

Parent Corporation Merges into
Subsidiary Corporation

Subsidiary Corporation

(Owned at least 90% by parent)

Subsidiary corporation assumes all assets,
debts, and liabilities of parent corporation.

**Subsidiary Corporation
Survives**

© Cengage Learning 2013

SHARE EXCHANGES

A share exchange is a transaction whereby one corporation (the acquiring corporation) acquires all of the outstanding shares of one or more classes or series of another corporation (the target corporation) by an exchange that is compulsory on the shareholders of the target corporation. The shareholders of the target corporation may receive shares of stock in the acquiring corporation, shares of stock in a third corporation, or cash in consideration for their shares. In this type of transaction, both the acquiring and the target corporation survive, with the target corporation becoming a subsidiary of the acquiring corporation. Section 11.07(b) of the MBCA sets forth the effect of a share exchange:

> (b) When a share exchange takes effect, the shares of each acquired corporation are exchanged as provided in the plan, and the former holders of the shares are entitled only to the exchange rights provided in the articles of share exchange or to their rights under Chapter 13.

EXHIBIT 12-6 TRIANGLE MERGER

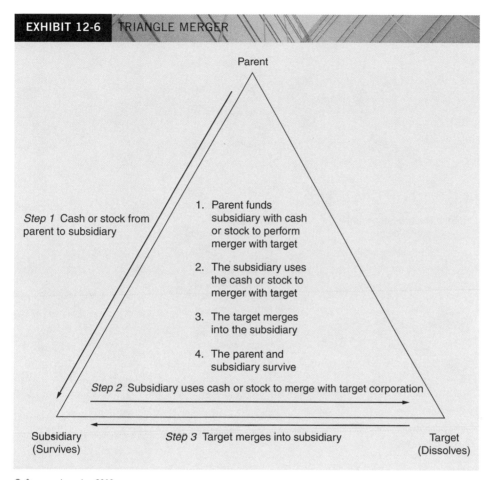

Parent

Step 1 Cash or stock from parent to subsidiary

1. Parent funds subsidiary with cash or stock to perform merger with target

2. The subsidiary uses the cash or stock to merger with target

3. The target merges into the subsidiary

4. The parent and subsidiary survive

Step 2 Subsidiary uses cash or stock to merge with target corporation

Subsidiary (Survives)   *Step 3* Target merges into subsidiary   Target (Dissolves)

© Cengage Learning 2013

CONSOLIDATIONS

A **consolidation** involves the merger of two or more corporations into a newly formed corporation and the subsequent disappearance of the merging corporations. Although the statutes of many states still allow such consolidations, the MBCA no longer provides for a statutory consolidation because it is almost always advantageous for one of the merging corporations to survive. The same result obtained in a consolidation may be obtained by a statutory merger involving the merger of two corporations into a corporation formed for the purpose of acting as the surviving corporation of the transaction.

Celotex Corporation v. Pickett, the case following on page 526, demonstrates the importance of the type of transaction used to combine businesses. It is pointed out that in a merger transaction, all debts, liabilities, and duties of the merging corporation are transferred to the surviving corporation.

CONSOLIDATION
Two corporations joining together to form a third, new one.

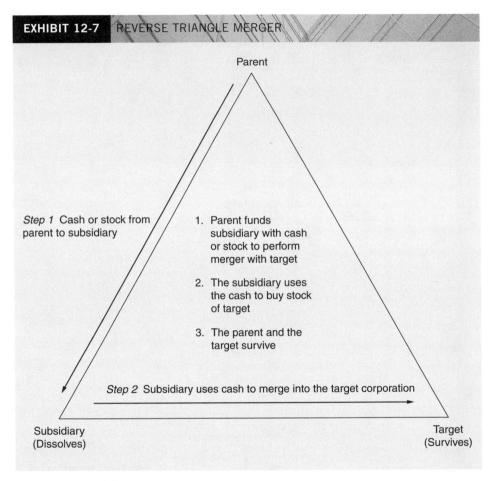

EXHIBIT 12-7 REVERSE TRIANGLE MERGER

Parent

Step 1 Cash or stock from parent to subsidiary

1. Parent funds subsidiary with cash or stock to perform merger with target

2. The subsidiary uses the cash to buy stock of target

3. The parent and the target survive

Step 2 Subsidiary uses cash to merge into the target corporation

Subsidiary (Dissolves)

Target (Survives)

© Cengage Learning 2013

CASE

Celotex Corporation, v. Pickett, Supreme Court of Florida, 490 So. 2d 35 (Fla. 1986), May 8, 1986

EHRLICH, Justice.

We have for our review a decision of the First District Court of Appeal reported as Celotex Corp. v. Pickett, 459 So. 2d 375. . . .

The facts relevant for our review here are that the respondent husband (Pickett) was employed in a Jacksonville shipyard from 1965 through June 1968, where as part of his employment as an insulator of ships, he extensively used Philip Carey asbestos cement. Pickett developed severe lung problems, due to the devastating effects on the human body which result from exposure to asbestos. The Picketts sued, on the grounds of negligence and strict liability, several defendants

continues

CASE *(continued)*
Celotex Corporation, v. Pickett, Supreme Court of Florida, 490 So. 2d 35 (Fla. 1986)

including the petitioner (Celotex) in its capacity as the corporate successor to Philip Carey. Finding that Philip Carey was negligent in placing "defective" asbestos-containing insulating products on the market which caused Pickett's injuries, the jury awarded compensatory damages of $500,000 to Pickett and $15,000 to his wife. The jury also determined that Philip Carey had acted so as to warrant punitive damages in the amount of $100,000 against Celotex. Celotex's appeal of the imposition of punitive damages formed the basis for the First District's opinion below which affirmed the award.

The threshold question involved here is the legal status of Celotex as the successor to Philip Carey. The district court opinion set forth the following background:

The Philip Carey Corporation was begun in 1888 and subsequently merged with Glen Alden Corporation in 1967. Thereafter, Philip Carey merged with another Glen Alden subsidiary, Briggs Manufacturing Company, and became known as Panacon Corporation. Celotex purchased Glen Alden's controlling interest in 1972 and later purchased the remaining shares of Panacon and merged it into Celotex.

The effect of this merger, as correctly recognized by the First District, is controlled by [Fla. Stat. §] 607.231(3) . . . (1983), which reads: "(c) Such surviving or new corporation shall have all the rights, privileges, immunities and powers, and shall be subject to all of the duties and liabilities, of a corporation organized under this chapter."

Celotex has admitted that it is liable, because of the merger, for the compensatory damages awarded to the Picketts. The sole and narrow issue before us here is whether punitive damages were properly assessed against petitioner, the surviving corporation in a statutory merger.

Celotex, however, maintains that the trial court and the district court below misapplied our prior decisions by holding Celotex liable for punitive damages, when Philip Carey, not Celotex, was the "real wrongdoer." Celotex also claims that imposition of punitive damages against Celotex, simply because it is the statutory successor of Philip Carey, contravenes the purpose of such damages in Florida. We disagree with both contentions. . . .

Celotex seeks here to characterize its liability as "vicarious,". . . since, according to it, Philip Carey/Panacon is the "real wrongdoer" and there is no evidence of fault by Celotex. We disagree with this characterization. Because of its merger agreement with Panacon, whereby "all debts, liabilities and duties" of Panacon are enforceable against Celotex, and because of the effect of Section 607.231(3), the liability imposed upon Celotex is direct, not vicarious. Liability for the reckless misconduct of Philip Carey/Panacon legally continues to exist within, and under the name of, Celotex. . . .

Further, corporations are in a very real sense, "molders of their own destinies" in acquisition transactions, with the full panoply of corporation transformations at their disposal. When a corporation, such as Celotex here, voluntarily chooses a formal merger, it will take the "bad will" along with the "good will.". . . We will not allow such an acquiring corporation to "jettison inchoate liabilities into a never-never land of transcorporate limbo." *Wall v. Owens-Corning Fiberglass Corp.*, 602 F. Supp. 252, 255 (N.D. Tex. 1985). . . .

We approve the decision of the First District Court of Appeal.

It is so ordered.

Case material reprinted from Westlaw, with permission.

IN SUMMATION

- A merger is a combination of two or more corporations whereby one merging corporation merges into a surviving corporation, with the result being one surviving corporation.
- Shareholders of the merging corporation generally receive shares of the surviving corporation in exchange for their shares and they become shareholders of the surviving corporation.
- With a merger, all liabilities of both the merging corporation and the surviving corporation become the responsibility of the surviving corporation.
- Statutory mergers and share exchanges may be between corporations or corporations and noncorporate entities, provided such a combination is permissible under the statutes of the relevant states of domicile.
- When a subsidiary corporation merges into its parent corporation, it is referred to as an upstream merger.
- When a parent corporation merges into a subsidiary corporation, it is referred to as a downstream merger.
- Triangle mergers involve three corporations: a parent corporation, a subsidiary corporation, and a target corporation that is merged into the subsidiary. With a triangle merger, both the parent and subsidiary are surviving corporations.
- A reverse triangle merger involves three corporations: a parent corporation, a target corporation, and a subsidiary corporation that is merged into the target. With a reverse triangle merger, both the parent and the target are surviving corporations.
- In a share exchange, the acquiring corporation acquires all of the outstanding shares of the target corporation by an exchange that is compulsory on the shareholders of the target corporation.
- With a share exchange, both the acquiring corporation and the target corporation survive, with the target corporation becoming the subsidiary of the acquiring corporation.
- A consolidation, which is still provided for in the statutes of some states, involves the merger of two or more corporations into a newly formed corporation with neither of the merging corporations surviving.

§ 12.3 LAWS GOVERNING MERGERS AND SHARE EXCHANGES

Statutory mergers and share exchanges may be subject to both state law and federal law. Research must be conducted throughout the merger or share exchange transaction to ensure that all state and federal laws are being complied with.

STATE LAWS AFFECTING MERGERS AND SHARE EXCHANGES

All parties to a merger or share exchange are typically subject to the statutes of their state of domicile. State statutes typically prescribe the following:

1. Requirements for the plan of merger or plan of exchange
2. The method for adopting a plan of merger or plan of exchange
3. Requirements for articles of merger or articles of share exchange
4. Requirements for filing the articles of merger or articles of share exchange at the state level
5. Provisions regarding the effect of the merger or share exchange
6. Provisions for short-form mergers
7. Provisions for dissenting shareholder rights

A foreign corporation that is being merged into a domestic corporation may also be subject to the laws of the state of domicile of the surviving corporation.

FEDERAL LAWS AFFECTING MERGERS AND SHARE EXCHANGES

In addition to the applicable state statutes regarding mergers and share exchanges, such transactions must comply with any federal securities regulations and blue sky laws applicable to mergers and share exchanges, as well as the Internal Revenue Code and pertinent provisions of the federal and state **antitrust laws**. Both the **Federal Trade Commission** and the Department of Justice have responsibility for overseeing the enforcement of federal antitrust statutes.

The Federal Trade Commission (FTC) was created by the **Federal Trade Commission Act** in 1914 to guard the marketplace from unfair methods of competition and to prevent unfair or deceptive acts or practices that harm consumers. The FTC is responsible for overseeing certain mergers to ensure that they comply with federal antitrust laws.

The FTC identifies and challenges anticompetitive mergers—those that may lessen competition and lead to higher prices, reduced availability of goods and services, lower quality of products, and less innovation.[4] Parties contemplating corporate mergers or acquisitions must be certain to comply with the antimonopoly provisions of the Sherman Act and the Clayton Act.

The **Sherman Act** was passed by Congress in 1890 to prevent or suppress devices or practices that create monopolies or restrain trade or commerce by suppressing or restricting competition and obstructing the course of trade.[5] The Sherman Act prohibits unreasonable restraint of trade, making it a felony, and grants the FTC the power to prevent unfair methods of competition. This law is violated if a company tries to maintain or acquire a **monopoly** position through unreasonable methods. The courts are left to determine what is unreasonable under the Sherman Act.

ANTITRUST LAWS

Federal and state laws to protect trade from monopoly control and from price fixing and other restraints of trade. The main federal antitrust laws are the Sherman, Clayton, Federal Trade Commission, and Robinson-Patman Acts.

FEDERAL TRADE COMMISSION

Federal agency created in 1914 to promote free and fair competition and to enforce the provisions of the Federal Trade Commission Act, which prohibits "unfair or deceptive acts or practices in commerce."

FEDERAL TRADE COMMISSION ACT

Federal Act passed in 1914, establishing the Federal Trade Commission to curb unfair trade practices.

SHERMAN ACT

(15 U.S.C. 1) The first antitrust (antimonopoly) law, passed by the federal government in 1890 to break up combinations in restraint of trade.

MONOPOLY

Control by one or a few companies of the manufacture, sale, distribution, or price of something. A monopoly may be prohibited if, for example, a company deliberately drives out competition.

CLAYTON ACT

(15 U.S.C. 12) A 1914 federal law that extended the Sherman Act's prohibition against monopolies and price discrimination.

HART-SCOTT-RODINO ACT

(15 U.S.C. § 18a) A federal law passed in 1976 that strengthens the enforcement powers of the Justice Department. The act requires entities to give notice to the Federal Trade Commission and the Justice Department prior to mergers and acquisitions when the size of the transaction is valued at $50 million or more.

In 1914 the **Clayton Act** was passed to supplement the Sherman Act and other antitrust legislation. Section 7 of the Clayton Act is an antimonopoly act. It prohibits certain acquisitions that may lessen competition or create a monopoly if it can be shown that the merger or acquisition will substantially lessen competition or tend to create a monopoly within the relevant markets.

Section 7A of the Clayton Act, called the **Hart-Scott-Rodino Antitrust Improvements Act of 1976** (Hart-Scott-Rodino Act), provides that notice of certain contemplated mergers and acquisitions must be filed with the FTC before they are completed. The parties to certain proposed mergers and acquisitions must file notification with the FTC and Department of Justice antitrust enforcement agencies, then wait for a specified period of time before completing the proposed transaction. The waiting period gives the antitrust enforcement agencies time to review the proposed transaction to see that it complies with antitrust statutes.

Currently, the premerger notification requirement applies only to certain mergers and acquisitions valued at more than $66 million. That figure may be adjusted periodically for inflation.

SIDEBAR

During 2010, 1,166 Hart-Scott-Rodino Act filings were submitted to the FTC for review.

IN SUMMATION

- Mergers and share exchanges may be subject to both state and federal law.
- All parties to a merger or share exchange are subject to the laws of their state of domicile.
- The parties to a merger or share exchange may also be subject to federal securities laws and antitrust laws.
- The Federal Trade Commission (FTC) is responsible for overseeing certain mergers and acquisitions to ensure they comply with antitrust laws.
- The primary antitrust laws are the Sherman Act, passed in 1890; the Clayton Act, passed in 1914; and the Hart-Scott Rodino Antitrust Improvements Act of 1976.
- The Hart-Scott-Rodino Act provides that premerger notification of certain mergers and acquisitions (currently those with a value in excess of $66 million) must be given to the FTC.

§ 12.4 PLANNING THE STATUTORY MERGER OR SHARE EXCHANGE

The procedures followed for planning and completing mergers and share exchanges will depend on the type of transaction and the parties involved. Obviously, mergers between related parties will involve less negotiation and due diligence than those between unrelated parties. Likewise, mergers or share exchanges involving public corporations can be much more complex than those involving smaller, closely held corporations.

This section begins with an investigation of some of the procedures common to all types of mergers and share exchanges, including negotiations and the letter of intent.

NEGOTIATIONS AND LETTER OF INTENT

The first step in the merger or share exchange process of two unrelated parties generally involves meetings and preliminary negotiations between the parties. The parties involved must agree on the general terms and conditions of the transaction and all significant issues involving the proposed merger or share exchange.

If successful, negotiations often lead to a letter of intent. The **letter of intent** is a short document, often just a few pages in length, entered into between the proposed parties to a transaction to set forth their preliminary understanding and intent with regard to the transaction. The letter of intent may contain several contingencies, including a specific date by which a formal agreement must be entered into. It may contain the parties' agreement concerning the due diligence process that will take place by both parties prior to closing and a statement concerning the confidentiality of the information exchanged during negotiations and the due diligence process. The letter of intent demonstrates the seriousness of the parties to go to the next step in the process, which involves entering into a plan of merger or plan of exchange.

LETTER OF INTENT
A preliminary written agreement setting forth the intention of the parties to enter into a contract.

IN SUMMATION

- The first step in the merger or share exchange process usually involves negotiations between the involved parties.

- Successful negotiations often lead to a letter of intent that sets forth the preliminary understanding of all parties regarding the basics of the proposed transaction, a deadline for entering a formal agreement, procedures concerning the due diligence process, and a statement concerning confidentiality of the parties involved.

§ 12.5 THE PLAN OF MERGER AND PLAN OF SHARE EXCHANGE

The **plan of merger** and **plan of share exchange**, which are generally required by state statute, set forth the agreement between the parties in detail. Specific requirements for these documents are contained in the statutes of most states.

The terms and conditions of a merger or share exchange transaction between unrelated parties may be complex and detailed, and may concern many issues in addition to those required by state statutes. In states where the plan of merger or plan of exchange is filed for public record with the secretary of state or other state

PLAN OF MERGER
Document required by state statute that sets forth the terms of the agreement between the two merging parties in detail.

PLAN OF SHARE EXCHANGE
Document required by statute that sets forth the terms of the agreement between the parties to a statutory share exchange. Also referred to as plan of exchange.

authority, those documents may include only the provisions required by statute, with additional provisions concerning the agreement between the parties set forth in a separate agreement that is not made public.

PLAN OF MERGER

Following is a list of items often included in the plan of merger or a separate agreement between the parties to a merger.

- Date of agreement
- Description of the authorized stock of each original corporation
- Name, purpose, location of the principal office, number of directors, and capital stock of the surviving corporation
- Method and rate of exchange for converting shares of the merging corporation into shares of the surviving corporation
- Provisions acknowledging the transfer of the rights, property, and liabilities of the merging corporation to the surviving corporation
- Recital that each board of directors believes it to be in the best interest of its respective corporation that the merger take place
- Provisions for submitting the plan of merger to the shareholders of each corporation for approval, as necessary
- Amendments to the articles of incorporation of the surviving corporation
- Provisions for amending the bylaws of the surviving corporation
- Provisions for dissolving the merging corporation
- Names and addresses of the directors of the surviving corporation
- Treatment of outstanding stock options, if any
- Restrictions on transactions outside the normal course of business by either corporation prior to the effective date of the merger
- Provisions for corporate distributions during the period prior to the effective date of the merger
- Provisions for possible abandonment of the merger prior to the completion thereof by the directors of either corporation
- Provisions for filing the articles of merger or share exchange with the appropriate state office, as required by statute
- Closing and effective date of the merger

In addition, the agreement between the merging corporations includes specific information (usually in the form of schedules or exhibits) regarding the business status of each corporation involved, including the corporation's financial status, assets, significant contracts, pending litigation, employees, and all matters that might affect the business or earning potential of the corporation.

Exhibit 12-8 is a sample agreement and plan of merger for a downstream merger.

EXHIBIT 12-8 SAMPLE AGREEMENT AND PLAN OF MERGER FOR DOWNSTREAM MERGER

AGREEMENT AND PLAN OF MERGER

This Agreement is made February 12, 2010, between Quality Home Repair, Inc., a corporation organized and existing under the laws of State of Minnesota, having its principal office at 3492 Oak Street, St. Paul, Ramsey County, Minnesota, and Dependable Restorations Corp., a corporation organized and existing under the laws of Minnesota, having its principal office and place of business at 2834 Main Street, Stillwater, Washington County, Minnesota.

I. SURVIVING CORPORATION

1. Dependable Restorations Corp. shall be the subsidiary corporation, and all references in this plan of merger to "subsidiary corporation" shall be to Dependable Restorations Corp.

2. Quality Home Repair, Inc., shall be the surviving corporation which owns all of the issued and outstanding stock of the above-named subsidiary corporation, and all references in this plan of merger to "surviving corporation" shall be to Quality Home Repair, Inc.

II. MANAGEMENT

1. The articles of incorporation of Quality Home Repair, Inc., shall continue to be its articles of incorporation following the effective date of the merger, until the same shall be altered or amended.

2. The bylaws of Quality Home Repair, Inc., shall be and remain the bylaws of the surviving corporation until altered, amended, or repealed.

3. The officers and directors of Quality Home Repair, Inc., in office on the effective date of the merger shall continue in office and shall constitute the directors and officers of Quality Home Repair, Inc., for the term elected until their respective successors shall be elected or appointed and qualified.

III. RIGHTS AND PRIVILEGES

On the effective date of the merger, Quality Home Repair, Inc., shall possess all the rights, privileges, immunities, powers, and franchises of a public and private nature, and shall be subject to all of the restrictions, disabilities, and duties of the subsidiary corporation. All of the property, real, personal, and mixed, and all debts due on whatever account, and all other choices in action, and all and every other interest of or belonging to or due to the subsidiary corporation shall be deemed to be transferred to and vested in Quality Home Repair, Inc., without further act or deed, and the title to any property or any interest therein, vested in the subsidiary corporation shall not revert or be in any way impaired by reason of the merger.

IV. LIABILITIES, DEBTS, AND OBLIGATIONS

On the effective date of the merger, Quality Home Repair, Inc., shall be deemed responsible and liable for all the liabilities and obligations of the subsidiary corporation; and any claims existing by or against the subsidiary corporation may be prosecuted to judgment as if the merger had not taken place, or Quality Home Repair, Inc., may be substituted in place of the subsidiary corporation. The rights of the creditors shall not be impaired by this merger. Quality Home Repair, Inc., shall execute and deliver any and all documents which may be required for it to assume or otherwise comply with the outstanding obligations of the subsidiary corporation.

continues

EXHIBIT 12-8 *(continued)*

V. SURRENDER OF SHARES

Quality Home Repair, Inc., at present owns all of the outstanding shares of stock of the subsidiary corporation. On the effective date of the merger, all the outstanding shares of stock of the subsidiary corporation shall be surrendered and canceled. The shares of common stock of Quality Home Repair, Inc., whether authorized or issued on the effective date of the merger, shall not be converted, exchanged, or otherwise affected as a result of the merger, and no new shares of stock shall be issued by reason of this merger.

VI. SUBSEQUENT ACTS

If at any time Quality Home Repair, Inc., shall consider or be advised that any further assignment or assurances in law are necessary or desirable to vest or to perfect or confirm of record in Quality Home Repair, Inc., the title to any property or rights of the subsidiary corporation or to otherwise carry out the provisions hereof, the proper officers and directors of the subsidiary corporation as of the effective date of the merger shall execute and deliver any and all proper assignments and assurances in law, and do all things necessary or proper to vest, perfect, or confirm title to such property or rights in Quality Home Repair, Inc., and to otherwise carry out the provisions hereof.

IN WITNESS WHEREOF, the directors, or a majority thereof, of Quality Home Repair, Inc., the surviving corporation, and the directors, or a majority thereof, of Dependable Restorations Corp., the nonsurviving corporation, have executed this plan of merger under their respective corporate seals on the day and year first above written.

_____

_____

© Cengage Learning 2013

SIDEBAR

Directors have a duty to act in an informed and deliberative manner with due care in determining whether to approve a merger agreement before submitting the proposal to the stockholders.

Plan of Share Exchange

Several states have requirements for the **plan of share exchange** similar to those set forth in Section 11.03(c) of the MBCA, which follows:

   (c) The plan of share exchange must include:

   (1) the name of each corporation or other entity whose shares or interests will be acquired and the name of the corporation or other entity that will acquire those shares or interests;

   (2) the terms and conditions of the share exchange;

   (3) the manner and basis of exchanging shares of a corporation or interests in an other entity whose shares or interests will be acquired

under the share exchange into shares or other securities, interests, obligations, rights to acquire shares, other securities, or interests, cash, other property, or any combination of the foregoing; and

(4) any other provisions required by the laws under which any party to the share exchange is organized or by the articles of incorporation or organic document of any such party.

As with a plan of merger, the plan of share exchange may also contain any other provisions relating to the transaction.

Following is a list of items often included in a plan of exchange:

- Date of agreement
- Name and authorized stock of each original corporation
- Recital that each board of directors believes it to be in the best interest of its respective corporation that the share exchange take place
- Provisions for the method of exchanging the shares of the target corporation for shares of the acquiring corporation and for continuing the target corporation as a subsidiary of the acquiring corporation
- Name, purposes, location of the principal offices, number of directors, and capital stock of the acquiring corporation and the subsidiary corporation after the exchange
- Amendments to the articles of incorporation of each corporation, reflecting the share exchange
- Provisions for amending the bylaws of each corporation, as necessary
- Treatment of outstanding stock options, if any
- Restrictions on transactions outside the normal course of business by either corporation prior to the effective date of the share exchange
- Provisions for corporate distributions during the period prior to the effective date of the share exchange, if desired
- Provisions for submitting the plan of exchange to the shareholders of each corporation for approval, as necessary
- Agreement regarding the inspection of books, records, and other property of each corporation
- Provisions for possible abandonment of the plan of exchange prior to the completion thereof by the directors of either corporation
- Provisions for filing the articles of share exchange with the appropriate state office, as required by statute
- Closing and effective date of the share exchange

In addition, the plan of exchange may include schedules and exhibits setting forth the specific assets and liabilities of each corporation, and any other information relevant to the business of each corporation, including pending or threatened litigation.

IN SUMMATION

- The plan of merger or plan of share exchange is typically required by state statutes to conduct merger or share exchange transactions.
- The plan of merger typically sets forth in detail the agreement between the proposed merging and surviving corporations.
- The plan of share exchange typically sets forth in detail the agreement for the share exchange between the proposed subsidiary and parent corporations.

§ 12.6 BOARD OF DIRECTOR AND SHAREHOLDER APPROVAL OF THE MERGER OR SHARE EXCHANGE

With the possible exception of upstream mergers, the plan of merger must be approved by the board of directors and shareholders of each corporation that will be a party to the merger, pursuant to state statutes. Class voting and special voting requirements unique to the plan of merger are often required. Under the MBCA, when shareholder approval is required for a plan of merger, the following procedures must be used:

1. The board of directors must recommend the plan to the shareholders, unless the board determines that it should make no recommendation and communicates the basis for its determination to the shareholders with the plan. Reasons for not rendering a recommendation may include a conflict of interest or other special circumstances.[6] The board may condition its submission of the proposed plan on any basis.[7]

2. Each shareholder, whether or not entitled to vote, must be notified of the shareholder meeting pursuant to statute. The notice must state that the purpose of the meeting is to consider the plan of merger, and it must contain or be accompanied by a summary of the plan. If the corporation is to be merged into another corporation, the notice must also include a copy or summary of the articles of incorporation of the surviving entity.[8]

3. Unless otherwise provided by state statutes, the articles of incorporation, or the board of directors, the plan must be approved by each **voting group** entitled to vote separately on the plan. Approval of each voting group is given by the majority vote of all votes within each voting group.[9] A voting group, as defined by § 1.40 of the MBCA, is:

   all shares of one or more classes or series that under the articles of incorporation or this Act are entitled to vote and be counted together collectively on a matter at a meeting of shareholders. All shares entitled by the articles of incorporation or this Act to vote generally on the matter are for that purpose a single voting group.

VOTING GROUP

All shares of one or more classes that are entitled to vote and be counted together collectively on a certain matter under the corporation's articles of incorporation or the pertinent state statute.

4. Separate voting by voting groups is required by each class or series of shares that are to be converted under the plan of merger. In addition, separate voting by voting groups is required if the plan contains a provision that, if contained in a proposed amendment to the articles of incorporation, would require action by one or more separate voting groups on the proposed amendment pursuant to statute.[10]

The following paragraphs are examples of board of director and shareholder resolutions approving plans of merger.

EXAMPLE: Resolution of Directors Authorizing Merger into Another Corporation

RESOLVED, that the plan of merger this day proposed to the board, pursuant to which this corporation will transfer to ___ [other corporation], a corporation organized and existing under the laws of the State of ___, all of the assets, tangible and intangible, of this corporation as they exist on ___, 20___, subject to the liabilities of this corporation, in the manner and to the extent set forth in the draft agreement heretofore presented and read to this meeting, be and the same hereby is declared to be in the best interests of this corporation and is hereby ratified, approved, and adopted.[11]

EXAMPLE: Stockholders' Resolution Adopting Merger Agreement

Whereas, the board of directors of this corporation has approved an agreement of merger at a meeting of the directors duly held at the corporation's [principal executive office] at ___ [address], ___ [city], ___ County, ___ [state], on ___ [date], and ordered that the agreement be submitted to the shareholders for approval at this meeting as provided by law;

RESOLVED, that the shareholders of this corporation hereby ratify, adopt, and approve the agreement of merger dated ___, between the corporation and ___ [name of other corporation(s)], and direct the secretary of the corporation to insert a copy of such agreement in the minute book of the corporation immediately following the minutes of this meeting.

FURTHER RESOLVED, that the officers of this corporation are hereby authorized and directed to execute all documents and to take such further action as may be deemed necessary or advisable to implement this resolution.[12]

Under the MBCA, as in most states, approval of the shareholders of the surviving corporation is not required under certain circumstances when the position and rights of the shareholders of the surviving corporation are not significantly affected by the merger. This allows the board of directors acting on behalf of large, publicly held corporations to acquire other businesses without the formality of a shareholder meeting to approve each merger.

The statutory requirements for approving a plan of share exchange are substantially the same as those for approving a plan of merger. State statutes generally require that the plan be recommended by the board of directors and approved by the shareholders of the corporation.

Dissenting Shareholders

Shareholders entitled to vote on a plan of merger or share exchange may be granted the right to dissent under the statutes of the corporation's state of domicile. A shareholder's right to dissent refers to the right to object to certain extraordinary actions being taken by the corporation and to obtain payment of the fair value of the shares held by the dissenting shareholder from the corporation. Under the MBCA, any shareholder who is entitled to vote on a plan of merger, or shareholders of subsidiaries that are merged with the parent in an upstream merger, have the right to dissent. Other events, including consummation of a plan of exchange and amendment of the articles of incorporation, that materially and adversely affect the rights of shareholders will also entitle shareholders to the right to dissent. Certain statutory formalities, including the submission of a written notice of intent to demand payment, must be followed by the dissenting shareholders in order to exercise their right to payment.

When the dissenting shareholder challenges the fair value placed on his or her shares by the corporation, an appraisal proceeding may be commenced. An appraisal proceeding involves judicial appraisal of the fair value of the stock of the dissenting shareholders. Exhibit 12-9 is an example of a notice that may be given to the corporation by a dissenting shareholder to demand the fair market value of his or her shares upon merger.

State statutes concerning shareholder dissent usually include very specific requirements that must be met by dissenting shareholders, including deadlines for presenting demand for the fair market value of the shareholder's shares. The dissenting shareholder must comply exactly with the provisions of state statutes to exercise his or her rights under these statutes.

EXHIBIT 12-9	DEMAND BY DISSENTING STOCKHOLDER FOR FAIR MARKET VALUE OF SHARES ON MERGER OF CORPORATION[13]

To: _____ [corporation]

_____ [address]

The shareholders of this corporation, at a [special] meeting held on [date], at its principal executive office at [address], [city], County, [state], purported to approve an agreement providing for the merger of the corporation with [constituent corporation], a [state] corporation.

EXHIBIT 12-9 (continued)

Notice of the purported approval by the shareholders was mailed to the undersigned on [date], and [30] days have not yet expired since the date of mailing of the notice, and the undersigned has not approved such proposed merger.

The undersigned is the holder of record of [number] shares of [common] stock of [name of corporation], evidenced by Certificate No.___. These shares were voted against the merger.

The undersigned now makes written demand for the payment to the undersigned of the fair market value of such shares as of [date], being the date prior to the first announcement of the terms of the proposed merger.

The undersigned states that $___ per share is the fair market value of such shares as of the date prior to the first announcement of the terms of the proposed merger.

The undersigned submits to the corporation at its principal executive office the certificate for such shares with respect to which the undersigned makes this demand, in order that the certificate may be stamped or endorsed with the statement that such shares are dissenting shares and then returned to the undersigned at the address stated below.

Dated: _____

_____
Signature

Reprinted with permission from *American Jurisprudence Legal Forms 2d.* © 2012 West Group.

IN SUMMATION

- Mergers and share exchanges typically require the approval of the board of directors and the shareholders.

- In some states the board of directors must recommend the plan of merger or share exchange to the shareholders, unless it communicates its reason for not recommending the plan.

- After board recommendation, the shareholders are entitled to vote on the plan of merger or plan of share exchange.

- Mergers and share exchanges may be subject to class voting and special voting requirements under state statutes.

- Shareholder approval of the surviving corporation is not always required.

- Shareholder approval is not always required for upstream mergers.

- Shareholders entitled to vote on a merger or plan of exchange may have the right to dissent and obtain payment of the fair value of their shares from the corporation.

- State statutes usually include very specific requirements that must be met by dissenting shareholders.

§ 12.7 ARTICLES OF MERGER OR SHARE EXCHANGE

ARTICLES OF MERGER

Document filed with the secretary of state or other appropriate authority to effect a merger.

After the plan of merger has been adopted pursuant to statute, **articles of merger** must be filed with the secretary of state or other appropriate state authority. Under § 11.06 of the MBCA, the articles of merger must set forth:

1. The names of the parties to the merger
2. Amendments to the articles of incorporation or new articles of incorporation of the surviving corporation
3. A statement that shareholder approval of the plan was not required, if that is the case
4. A statement regarding the approval of the plan of merger by the shareholders, including the number of votes voted for and against the merger in each voting group, if shareholder approval was necessary
5. A statement indicating that any foreign corporation or eligible entity involved in the merger has duly authorized the merger pursuant to the laws of the state of its domicile

ARTICLES OF SHARE EXCHANGE

Document filed with the secretary of state or other appropriate state authority to effect a share exchange.

The **articles of share exchange** must be filed with the secretary of state or other appropriate state authority to effect the share exchange. Under the Section 11.03(c) of the MBCA, the articles of share exchange must set forth:

1. The names of the parties to the share exchange
2. The terms and conditions of the share exchange
3. The manner and basis of the share exchange
4. A statement that the share exchange was approved by the shareholders of both corporations as required by state law; or a statement that shareholder approval was not required
5. Any other provisions required by statute, including amendments to the articles of incorporation of the surviving parent and subsidiary corporations (if relevant)

In some states, a copy of the plan of merger or plan of share exchange setting forth the full agreement of the parties may be required for filing, along with the articles.

Exhibit 12-10 on page 542 shows an example of an Indiana form of articles of merger or share exchange between two corporations. In Indiana, a copy of the plan of merger or share exchange is attached to the articles for filing as an exhibit.

IN SUMMATION

- State statutes typically require the filing of articles of merger or articles of share exchange with the secretary of state or other state official.
- The articles of merger must include the information required by state statute, including:
  - The names of all parties to the merger
  - Any amendments to the articles of incorporation or new articles of incorporation of the surviving corporation

- A statement concerning the shareholder approval of the merger
- A statement indicating that any foreign corporation involved in the merger has approved the merger pursuant to the laws of its state of domicile
- The articles of share exchange must set forth the information required by state statutes, which typically includes:
  - The names of the parties to the share exchange
  - The terms and conditions of the share exchange
  - The manner and basis of the share exchange
  - A statement concerning the shareholder approval of the plan of exchange
  - A copy of any amendments to articles of incorporation that may be required under the plan of exchange

§ 12.8 DUE DILIGENCE AND PRECLOSING MATTERS

Although the plan of merger or plan of exchange sets forth specific information regarding the business and financial condition of each corporation, the parties to a merger or share exchange and their professional representatives must use due diligence to ascertain the validity of the statements in the plan. Due diligence refers to the standard of care that must be exercised by each responsible party, and to the investigation done prior to closing to ascertain the validity of statements made in an agreement.

In a statutory merger or share exchange transaction, due diligence work often involves a thorough review of documents supporting the plan of merger or plan of exchange, as well as possible on-site investigations to see and inspect the real estate, buildings, assets, and inventory involved in the transaction, and also to inspect corporate books and records that are too cumbersome to photocopy or remove from the corporate offices. Due diligence work can be very time consuming, and it often involves the paralegals working on the transaction, who work on producing the documents requested by the other party or parties to the transaction and on collecting and reviewing the documents requested on behalf of the corporate client. When the supporting documents to a transaction are numerous, an electronic database may be used to track the documents, giving everyone on the legal team quick access.

Usually, the plan of merger or share exchange is used to produce a checklist of documents that must be produced by each party prior to closing. In addition to the corporate clients involved in a merger, accountants and other parties may also be responsible for producing documents. Exhibit 12-11 on page 544 is an excerpt from a sample checklist used to ensure that all documents are prepared, exchanged, reviewed, and approved before the closing of the merger or share exchange.

EXHIBIT 12-10 ARTICLES OF MERGER SHARE EXCHANGE

ARTICLES OF MERGER
State Form 39036 (R5 / 2-97)
Approved by State Board of Accounts, 1995

TODD ROKITA
SECRETARY OF STATE
CORPORATIONS DIVISION
302 W. Washington Street, Rm. E018
Indianapolis, IN 46204
Telephone: (317) 232-6576

Indiana Code 23-1-40-1 *et. seq.*

FILING FEE: $90.00

INSTRUCTIONS: *Use 8 1/2" x 11" white paper for inserts.*
Present original and two (2) copies to address in upper right corner of this form.
Please TYPE or PRINT.
Upon completion of filing the Secretary of State will issue a receipt.

ARTICLES OF MERGER / SHARE EXCHANGE
OF

_____

*(hereinafter "the **nonsurviving** corporation(s)")*

INTO

_____

*(hereinafter "the **surviving** corporation")*

ARTICLE I - SURVIVING CORPORATION

SECTION 1:

The name of the corporation surviving the merger is : _____

and such name ☐ has ☐ has not *(designate which)* been changed as a result of the merger.

SECTION 2:

a. The surviving corporation is a domestic corporation existing pursuant to the provisions of the Indiana Business Corporation Law incorporated on

_____ .

b. The surviving corporation is a foreign corporation incorporated under the laws of the State of _____ and
☐ qualified ☐ not qualified *(designate which)* to do business in Indiana.
If the surviving corporation is qualified to do business in Indiana, state the date of qualification: _____ .
(If Application for Certificate of Authority is filed concurrently herewith state "Upon approval of Application for Certificate of Authority".)

ARTICLE II - NONSURVIVING CORPORATION (S)

The name, state of incorporation, and date of incorporation or qualification *(if applicable)* respectively, of each Indiana domestic corporation and Indiana qualified foreign corporation, other than the survivor, which is party to the merger are as follows:

Name of Corporation	
State of Domicile	Date of Incorporation or qualification in Indiana *(if applicable)*
Name of Corporation	
State of Domicile	Date of Incorporation or qualification in Indiana *(if applicable)*
Name of Corporation	
State of Domicile	Date of Incorporation or qualification in Indiana *(if applicable)*

ARTICLE III - PLAN OF MERGER OR SHARE EXCHANGE

The Plan of Merger or Share Exchange, containing such information as required by Indiana Code 23-1-40-1(b), is set forth in "Exhibit A", attached hereto and made a part hereof.

continues

EXHIBIT 12-10 *(continued)*

ARTICLE IV - MANNER OF ADOPTION AND VOTE OF SURVIVING CORPORATION *(Must complete Section 1 or 2)*

SECTION 1: ☐ Shareholder vote not required.

The merger / share exchange was adopted by the incorporators or board of directors without shareholder action and shareholder action was not required.

SECTION 2: ☐ Vote of shareholders *(Select either A or B)*

The designation (*i.e., common, preferred or any classification where different classes of stock exist*), number of outstanding shares, number of votes entitled to be cast by each voting group entitled to vote separately on the merger / share exchange and the number of votes of each voting group represented at the meeting is set forth below:

A. Unanimous written consent executed on _____ 19____ and signed by all shareholders entitled to vote.
B. Vote of shareholders during a meeting called by the Board of Directors.

	TOTAL	A	B	C
DESIGNATION OF EACH VOTING GROUP *(i.e. preferred and common)*				
NUMBER OF OUTSTANDING SHARES				
NUMBER OF VOTES ENTITLED TO BE CAST				
NUMBER OF VOTES REPRESENTED AT MEETING				
SHARES VOTED IN FAVOR				
SHARES VOTED AGAINST				

ARTICLE V - MANNER OF ADOPTION AND VOTE OF NONSURVIVING CORPORATION *(Must complete Section 1 or 2)*

SECTION 1: ☐ Shareholder vote not required.

The merger / share exchange was adopted by the incorporators or board of directors without shareholder action and shareholder action was not required.

SECTION 2: ☐ Vote of shareholders *(Select either A or B)*

The designation (*i.e., common, preferred or any classification where different classes of stock exist*), number of outstanding shares, number of votes entitled to be cast by each voting group entitled to vote separately on the merger / share exchange and the number of votes of each voting group represented at the meeting is set forth below:

A. Unanimous written consent executed on _____ 19____ and signed by all shareholders entitled to vote.
B. Vote of shareholders during a meeting called by the Board of Directors.

	TOTAL	A	B	C
DESIGNATION OF EACH VOTING GROUP *(i.e. preferred and common)*				
NUMBER OF OUTSTANDING SHARES				
NUMBER OF VOTES ENTITLED TO BE CAST				
NUMBER OF VOTES REPRESENTED AT MEETING				
SHARES VOTED IN FAVOR				
SHARES VOTED AGAINST				

In Witness Whereof, the undersigned being the _____ of the surviving
Officer or Chairman of Board
corporation executes these Articles of Merger / Share Exchange and verifies, subject to penalities of perjury that the statements contained

herein are true, this _____ day of _____, 19 _____ .

Signature	Printed name

Indiana Secretary of State Author

EXHIBIT 12-11 EXCERPT FROM SAMPLE CLOSING CHECKLIST

AGREEMENT OF MERGER BETWEEN
CORPORATION A AND CORPORATION B
PROPOSED CLOSING DATE JUNE 20, 2012

Document/Page Reference	Resp. Party	Received or Prepared	Approved or Submitted
Corporation A Articles of Incorporation/ Page 3, Para. 2	Corp. A		
Corporation A Corporate Bylaws (Certified) Page 3, Para. 3	Corp. A		
Corporation A Corporate Minutes 2005 through Present Date/Page 3, Para. 4	Corp. A		
Corporation B Articles of Incorporation/ Page 3, Para. 2	Corp. B		
Corporation B Corporate Bylaws (Certified) Page 3, Para. 3	Corp. B		
Corporation B Corporate Minutes 2005 through Present Date/Page 3, Para. 4	Corp. B		
Lease to 2348 Elm Street Exhibit A	Corp. B		
Lease to 3484 Maple Street Exhibit A	Corp. B		
Title to 390 Main Street Exhibit A	Corp. A		
Agreement with ABC Mfg. Exhibit B	Corp. A		
Agreement with Acme Plastics/Exhibit B	Corp. A		

© Cengage Learning 2013

The list of documents that must be exchanged and reviewed prior to closing can be very extensive, and may include the following:

- Proof of corporate existence and good standing of each corporation
- Copies of all documents typically included in corporate minute books, including articles of incorporation and any amendments thereto, bylaws, and minutes of the board of directors and shareholder meetings
- Copies of stock ledgers and stock certificates
- Financial statements for each corporation
- Tax returns for each corporation and results of any tax audits
- Leases and/or titles to all real property that is owned and/or leased by each corporation
- Lists of all equipment and personal property at each location occupied by each corporation
- All paperwork concerning any patents, trademarks, and copyrights pending or owned by each corporation
- Copies of all employment and noncompetition agreements to which each corporation is a party
- Descriptions of all employee benefits, including the names of all employees entitled thereto
- Certified Uniform Commercial Code searches for each corporation
- Copies of any loan agreements to which each corporation is a party
- Lists of accounts payable for each corporation
- Lists of accounts receivable for each corporation
- Copies of all material contracts to which each corporation is a party
- Customer lists
- Vendor lists
- Copies of pleadings in any pending litigation

The documents that must be produced and reviewed will vary depending on the type of transaction and the relationship of the parties. If the transaction being contemplated is a merger between parent and subsidiary corporations, much of the information required for the transaction will be available to the parties in the normal course of business, and many of the documents in the preceding list will be irrelevant.

Due diligence work also involves ascertaining whether any outside parties may be required to give consent to any part of the transaction. All agreements to which the merging or target corporation is a party must be reviewed to determine whether consent of the other party to the agreement must be obtained before assigning the contract to the surviving or acquiring corporation. For example, if a merging corporation is a tenant under a lease, the landlord's consent will probably be required to transfer the lease to the acquiring corporation. If consent must be obtained, it should be requested promptly to ensure that it is received before closing.

IN SUMMATION

- Due diligence refers to the standard of care and the tasks that must be completed by each responsible party to a merger or share exchange transaction to ascertain the validity of the statements in the plan of merger or plan of share exchange.
- Due diligence reviews are typically completed with the aid of a checklist that is prepared based on the plan of merger or share exchange.
- Due diligence work involves a thorough review of the plan of merger or share exchange, all supporting documents, and, at times, on-site inspections.

§ 12.9 CLOSING THE MERGER OR SHARE EXCHANGE TRANSACTION

The plan of merger or share exchange typically sets forth a date and time for closing the transaction. At the closing, the shares of stock will change hands, assignments and transfers of contracts and real and personal property will be made, and any cash, or contractual obligations to pay out cash at a future date, will be paid out. The key officers from each corporation, the legal team for each corporation, and any other individuals who may be required to sign closing documents usually attend the closing.

The closing is typically conducted by executing and exchanging all documents referred to in the agreement and plan of merger or share exchange, as well as any supplemental documents necessary to effect the transfers referred to therein. A closing agenda is typically prepared from the plan of merger or plan of exchange and the checklist used in accumulating and reviewing the documents. Each party is responsible for preparing or producing certain documents required for the closing, as specified in the agenda. Paralegals who have been instrumental in getting the transaction to the closing table are often involved in the actual closing, and are usually responsible for seeing that each document is properly executed and that the proper parties are given copies. This may be no small task in complex transactions that could involve several boxes of documents.

MERGER CLOSINGS

Following is a list of some of the types of documents typically required for closing a merger transaction:

ARTICLES OF AMENDMENT
Document filed with the secretary of state or other appropriate state authority to amend a corporation's articles of incorporation.

1. Articles of merger, including any necessary **articles of amendment** to the articles of incorporation
2. Instruments assigning and transferring the appropriate shares of stock of each corporation
3. New stock certificates representing stock ownership pursuant to the plan of merger
4. Deeds or other instruments assigning or transferring any real property

5. Bills of sale or other instruments assigning or transferring any equipment, motor vehicles, or other personal property
6. Assignments of any patents, trademarks, or copyrights
7. Instruments assigning or transferring bank accounts
8. Legal opinions of transfer agents
9. Legal opinions of attorneys for each party
10. Notices or filings required by the Securities and Exchange Commission (SEC)
11. Officers' certificates
12. Certified copies of board of director and shareholder resolutions approving the transaction
13. Announcements to shareholders and/or employees, if necessary

SHARE EXCHANGE CLOSINGS

Closings of share exchange transactions are very similar to merger closings, with more emphasis placed on documents transferring the ownership of the target corporation. Following is a list of some of the items that may be required for closing a share exchange transaction:

1. Articles of share exchange, including amendments to the articles of the target corporation and the acquiring corporation, as needed
2. Instruments transferring the appropriate shares of stock of each corporation
3. New stock certificates representing the ownership of the acquiring corporation and the target corporation, which will become a subsidiary
4. Any necessary assignments
5. Legal opinions of attorneys for each party
6. Any notices required by the SEC or blue sky laws
7. Officers' certificates
8. Certified copies of board of director and shareholder resolutions approving the transaction

POSTCLOSING MATTERS

After the closing, there are typically several tasks that need to be completed to finalize the transaction. Most of these tasks involve notification of interested parties of the merger or share exchange and filings at the county or state level, or with the SEC. Some of the steps that may be required after the closing of a statutory merger or statutory share exchange include the following:

1. Filing the articles of merger or share exchange (if not done prior to closing) and any amendments to the articles of incorporation required by the transaction
2. Organizing new corporate minute books and stock ledgers
3. Filing any deeds transferring real estate
4. Changing title on motor vehicles, as necessary
5. Sending copies of any lease assignments to the proper landlords or tenants

6. Filing any Uniform Commercial Code documents
7. Completing any filings required by the SEC or blue sky laws

---

IN SUMMATION

- At a merger or share exchange closing, shares of stock change hands, and assignments, transfers, and cash payments take place to execute the transaction.
- Key officers from each corporation, as well as the legal teams and others required to sign documents, will typically attend the closing
- The closing is usually conducted using a checklist that has been reviewed by all parties prior to the closing.
- There are typically several postclosing matters to attend to, including documents to be filed at the state and possibly federal level after a merger or share exchange transaction has been closed.

---

§ 12.10 ASSET AND STOCK ACQUISITIONS

In addition to statutory mergers and share exchanges, there are several other means of combining or acquiring corporations and other business organizations. The discussion in this section concerns corporate acquisitions that are completed through the purchase of all or substantially all of the assets or outstanding shares of stock of a corporation. Although asset acquisitions and stock acquisitions have an economic effect that is very similar to that of statutory mergers and acquisitions, there are significant differences. When one corporation purchases the assets of another corporation, it generally assumes only those assets it contracts to assume. Debts and liabilities not specifically transferred will remain with the transferring corporation. If, however, one corporation purchases all the stock of another corporation, it would then own the corporation and be responsible for all of its debts and liabilities incurred prior to the purchase. Only under certain circumstances can the purchasers of a corporation's assets be found to be liable for the selling corporation's debts and liabilities. Courts have found:

> Where one company sells or otherwise transfers all its assets to another company the latter is not liable for the debts and liabilities of the transferor, except where: (1) the purchaser expressly or impliedly agrees to assume such debts; (2) the transaction amounts to a consolidation or merger of the seller and purchaser; (3) the purchasing corporation is merely a continuation of the selling corporation; or (4) the transaction is entered into fraudulently in order to escape liability for such debts.[14]

This section focuses on asset acquisition and stock acquisition of closely held corporations and the advantages and disadvantages of each type of transaction. It also examines the state and federal laws affecting asset and stock acquisitions.

Asset and stock acquisitions often go hand in hand with mergers, share exchanges, and corporate dissolutions. The end result of an asset purchase is often the dissolution of the corporation that has sold its assets. Stock acquisitions often result in mergers.

ASSET ACQUISITIONS

One means of acquiring the business of a corporation is to purchase all, or substantially all, of its assets. In asset acquisitions, the acquiring corporation purchases all of the assets of the target corporation, leaving the target corporation a mere corporate shell to be dissolved. This type of transaction has the advantage of permitting the buyers to know exactly what they are getting. The fact that the acquiring corporation will generally not be held liable for any future liabilities and obligations of the target corporation may also be a very important advantage. However, the necessity of identifying and transferring each specific asset being acquired can make an asset acquisition much more cumbersome than a stock acquisition.

SIDEBAR

Asset acquisitions accomplished primarily through loans are often referred to as leveraged buyouts, or LBOs.

STOCK ACQUISITIONS

A stock acquisition transaction involves the purchase of all or substantially all of the outstanding stock of a corporation, either by an individual, a group of individuals, or, more commonly, another corporation. The target corporation generally becomes a subsidiary of the acquiring corporation, or it is merged into the acquiring corporation.

One advantage of this type of purchase is the simplification in transferring the corporation from one individual or group of individuals to another. Instead of transferring each asset owned by the corporation, the ownership of the corporation itself is transferred to the new owner or owners. Disadvantages include the fact that the acquiring corporation will be responsible for all debts and liabilities of the corporation being acquired, even those that have an unknown or undisclosed value at the time of closing.

Barring any share transfer restrictions on shares of stock, shareholders of closely held or publicly held corporations may sell their shares of stock at will. However, most stock acquisitions involving the purchase of substantially all of the stock of a corporation must have a consensus of the shareholders. Obviously, the shares of a corporation may not be purchased unless the holders of those shares all agree to sell their stock.

HOSTILE TAKEOVERS

When one corporation attempts to purchase or take over another corporation against the wishes of the management and board of directors of the target corporation, the transaction is referred to as a hostile takeover.

Most hostile takeovers are completed by tender offers. This means that the acquirer makes a public offer to purchase, usually at a premium, enough shares of the target corporation to control it. In most instances, if the acquirer purchases a simple majority of the shares of the target corporation, the acquirer will have the power to replace the board of directors of the target corporation, and, effectively, to control the corporation. Tender offers and hostile takeovers are legal as long as they comply with state statutes and federal securities laws.

Hostile takeovers became popular during the 1980s and frequently made the headlines. Legislators in many states countered by drafting anti-takeover legislation—laws that allow corporations to take measures to defeat hostile takeovers.

Defensive measures adopted by a corporation to deflect hostile takeovers may be referred to as shark repellants. Some of these defensive measures include amending the corporation's articles to establish staggered terms for directors and to require the approval of a supermajority of its shareholders to approve a merger.

Corporations may also employ tactics to make themselves less attractive as takeover targets, such as authorizing additional classes of stock to give superiority to existing shareholders in the event of a takeover. Tactics that make the corporation less attractive as a takeover target are often referred to as poison pills.

The board of directors has a responsibility to the corporation and the corporation's shareholders. If the directors determine that the takeover is not in the best interests of the shareholders, the board of directors can take steps to try to prevent it. If, however, the board determines that the takeover is in the best interests of the corporation and its shareholders, they must help to facilitate the purchase.

DE FACTO MERGERS

Under some circumstances, the courts may consider a transaction between two or more corporations to be a merger, even if the parties have intended the transaction to be merely an asset purchase.

The de facto merger doctrine allows courts to view a transaction as a merger if it has the characteristics of a merger, even when it is called something else by the parties. The de facto merger is used to avoid injustices to third parties when one corporation transfers all of its assets to another corporation and disappears, making it impossible for creditors of the first corporation to collect debts owed to them.

For example, assume Corporation A sells all of its assets to Corporation B. Corporation B assumes all of the previous business of Corporation A, which then discontinues doing business. Any unpaid creditors of Corporation A are then unable to collect because Corporation A no longer has any assets. The Courts may determine that a de facto merger exists and that Corporation B is liable to Corporation A's creditors, even if the transaction between the two corporations was an asset purchase.

The following factors may be considered to determine if a de facto merger has taken place:

1. Continuation of previous business activity and corporate personnel
2. Continuity of shareholders resulting from the sale of assets in exchange for stock

3. Immediate or rapid dissolution of predecessor corporation

4. Assumption by purchasing corporation of all liabilities and obligations ordinarily necessary to continue predecessor's business operations

STATE AND FEDERAL LAWS AFFECTING ASSET AND STOCK ACQUISITIONS

Although the procedures for asset and stock purchases are not set forth in state statutes, certain aspects of these transactions, such as shareholder approval of the sale of a corporation's assets, are subject to state law. The statutes of the state of domicile of each party to the transaction must be consulted to be sure that all statutory requirements are complied with. In addition, certain asset or stock acquisition transactions may trigger SEC or blue sky law reporting requirements and the antitrust provisions found in the Hart-Scott-Rodino Act.

IN SUMMATION

- In an asset acquisition where one corporation or entity purchases the assets of another corporation or entity, the purchasing corporation acquires only the selling corporation's assets and generally assumes none of its liabilities unless specifically contracted for.

- In a stock acquisition where one corporation or entity purchases the stock of another corporation or entity, the purchasing corporation generally acquires all of the business of the selling corporation, including all of its assets and liabilities.

- With an asset acquisition, each asset must be transferred to the purchaser.

- With a stock acquisition, the stock of the selling corporation is transferred to the purchaser.

- Hostile takeovers occur when one corporation attempts to purchase or take over a target corporation against the wishes of the board of directors and management of the target corporation.

- A de facto merger occurs when the courts consider a transaction between two or more corporations to be a merger, even if the parties have intended the transaction to be merely an asset purchase.

- Corporate asset acquisitions and stock acquisitions are subject to the same federal laws that affect corporate mergers and share exchanges, including securities laws and antitrust laws.

§ 12.11 ASSET AND STOCK ACQUISITION PROCEDURES

The procedures to be followed for asset and stock acquisitions will depend on the type of transaction and the parties involved. Procedures for acquiring the assets of a corporation focus much more on the identification and transfer of the assets; stock acquisitions focus more on the entire corporate entity represented by the shares of stock.

This section looks at the procedures for completing transactions involving asset and stock acquisitions of closely held corporations. First it considers the negotiations involved in those types of transactions. Next it examines the asset purchase agreement and its approval by the shareholders of the target corporation. It then focuses on requirements for an agreement for the purchase and sale of all, or substantially all, of the outstanding stock of a corporation. This section concludes with a discussion of the due diligence and preclosing work involved in asset and stock acquisitions and the closing and postclosing matters concerning acquisitions.

NEGOTIATIONS AND LETTER OF INTENT

The first step in the asset purchase or stock purchase procedures is similar to that involved with mergers or share exchanges. Preliminary negotiations, which involve meetings between the two parties and their legal counsel, generally commence with the aim of entering into a preliminary agreement and signing a letter of intent. Price, terms, and the format of the acquisition of the corporation all must be agreed upon before an agreement can be entered into.

ASSET PURCHASE AGREEMENT

An asset purchase agreement specifically sets forth the agreement between the parties with regard to the purchase of all or substantially all of the assets of one corporation by another, based on the letter of intent or preliminary agreement entered into between the parties. The asset purchase agreement must set forth very specifically all the assets that are to be purchased by the acquiring corporation, as well as the terms for the disposition of any debts or liens related to those assets. Following is a list of items often included in an asset purchase agreement:

- Names and other identification of the parties
- Description of the property and assets subject to the agreement
- The nature and amount of the consideration to be paid for the assets
- Terms for assuming any debts and liabilities
- Acts required of the seller, including the delivery of the instruments of transfer
- Agreement regarding the inspection of books, records, and property of the selling corporation
- Warranties of the seller, including the authority to enter into the agreement, the accuracy and completeness of the books and records, title to the property and assets being acquired, and the care and preservation of the property and assets
- Indemnification of the buyer
- Buyer's right to use seller's name
- Remedies in the event of a default by either party
- Governing law

- Date of the agreement
- Signature of all parties involved
- The date, time, and place of closing

The sale of all, or substantially all, of the assets of a corporation requires shareholder approval of the selling corporation. The MBCA and most state statutes provide that shareholders must approve the sale, lease, exchange, or other disposition of corporate assets not in the usual or regular course of business. This refers especially to the sale of assets that would leave the corporation without a significant continuing business activity. Under the MBCA, if the sale of assets would leave a corporation with less than 25 percent of its total assets and continuing income from the previous year, the business is considered not to have a continuing business activity.[15] Such a sale of assets must be approved by the corporation's shareholders.

The statutory procedures for obtaining shareholder approval for the sale of all, or substantially all, of the assets of a corporation are usually very similar to those prescribed for the approval of statutory mergers and share exchanges because, in effect, the business of the corporation as it has existed will terminate upon the sale of its assets. The statutes of the selling corporation's state of domicile should always be consulted to be sure that the exact procedures for obtaining shareholder approval are followed. Shareholders of the selling corporation almost always have the right to dissent. Exhibit 12-12 is an example of a stockholders' written consent approving the sale of all, or substantially all, assets of the corporation.

STOCK PURCHASE AGREEMENT

In a stock purchase agreement, the purchaser accepts all of the rights and obligations incident to ownership of the stock of the target corporation. It is not necessary to specify the exact assets and liabilities of the selling corporation. Each selling shareholder must be in agreement with the terms of the stock purchase and enter into the stock purchase agreement. Special warranties regarding the corporation and its financial and legal status are typically given by the officers of the corporation. Common provisions in a stock purchase agreement include the following:

- Names and other identification of the parties
- Price for purchase of stock
- Method of payment
- Seller's representations regarding the authority to sell the stock being purchased
- Seller's warranty that all securities laws have been and will be complied with to the date of the contemplated transaction
- Disclosure of any pending litigation against the selling corporation
- Seller's warranties as to the good standing of the corporation; its authorized, issued, and outstanding stock; and its financial condition
- Buyer's representations with regard to its ability to finance the purchase of the stock

EXHIBIT 12-12	STOCKHOLDERS' WRITTEN CONSENT APPROVING SALE OF ALL, OR SUBSTANTIALLY ALL, ASSETS[16]

Whereas, at a _____ [regular or special] meeting of the board of directors of _____ [corporation] held on _____ [date], the board duly passed the following resolution authorizing the sale, conveyance, exchange, and transfer of all or substantially all of the property and assets of the corporation to _____ [name of purchasing corporation]: _____ [set forth board's resolution].

[If principal terms of transaction and nature and amount of consideration are not specified in board's resolution, add the following: Whereas, the principal terms of the transaction and the nature and amount of the consideration of the sale, conveyance, exchange, and transfer authorized by the board at such meeting are as follows: _____];

RESOLVED, that the undersigned shareholders, and each of them, hereby approve and consent to the principal terms of the transaction and the nature and amount of the consideration, and the resolutions of the board as set forth above.

Each of the undersigned has signed his or her name and the date of signing and the number of shares of the corporation entitled to vote held by him or her _____ [of record] on such date.

Name	Signature	Date of Execution	Number of Shares
_____	_____	_____	_____
_____	_____	_____	_____
_____	_____	_____	_____

Reprinted with permission from *American Jurisprudence Legal Forms 2d.* © 2012 West Group

- The agreement between the acquiring and selling corporations with regard to the payment of any tax liability of the selling corporation or any tax liability to be incurred as a result of the sale of the stock
- Covenants not to compete of certain officers and key employees of the corporation
- A general release of the seller from any future liability incurred by the selling corporation
- The date, location, and method of closing
- Execution by all parties

DUE DILIGENCE AND PRECLOSING MATTERS

The due diligence and preclosing procedures for asset and stock purchases are very similar to those for statutory mergers and share exchanges. The asset purchase transaction focuses more on the specific assets being purchased, whereas the stock purchase transaction involves all aspects of the corporation whose shares are being purchased, with specific attention to any potential future liability of the target corporation. The majority of the due diligence work in an asset or share acquisition transaction is done by the acquiring corporation's representatives and legal counsel. The purchase agreement is used to produce a checklist of documents to be prepared, accumulated, and reviewed in much the same way as the checklist for mergers and share exchange documents is prepared.

CLOSING THE ASSET OR STOCK ACQUISITION TRANSACTION

The procedures for closing an acquisition transaction are usually very similar to those discussed for mergers and share exchanges. The parties in attendance and the documents executed and exchanged will vary depending on the type of transaction.

In an asset purchase transaction, the purchasers and representatives of the selling corporation with authority to sign on behalf of the corporation must be present. In a share purchase, any shareholders selling their stock, who have not presigned the necessary documents, must be in attendance.

Asset Acquisition Closing

Following is a list of some of the documents that might be included in a closing agenda for an asset acquisition:

1. Certified checks, wire transfer documentation, and/or promissory notes representing the consideration being given for the assets
2. Certified copies of the resolutions of the board of directors and shareholders of the selling corporation approving the transaction
3. Deeds or other instruments assigning or transferring any real property
4. Bills of sale or other instruments assigning or transferring any equipment, motor vehicles, or other personal property, including inventory
5. Assignments or other instruments transferring any patents, trademarks, or copyrights
6. Assignments or other instruments assigning any loans on the real or personal property being purchased
7. Documents assigning the name of the corporation, if applicable
8. Legal opinions of attorneys for each party
9. Notices or filings required by the SEC
10. Officers' certificates
11. Assignments of accounts receivable and payable

Stock Acquisition Closing

Following is a list of some of the types of documents that may be included in the closing agenda for a stock acquisition transaction:

1. Instruments assigning and transferring the appropriate shares of stock of each corporation
2. New stock certificates representing stock ownership pursuant to the agreement for purchase of shares

3. Legal opinions of transfer agents
4. Legal opinions of attorneys for each party
5. Any required consents or approvals
6. Notices or filings required by the SEC
7. Officers' certificates

The transfer of real and personal property, as well as loans, contracts, and other agreements entered into by the corporation, will depend on the circumstances. In the event of a stock purchase transaction when the corporation whose shares are being sold will retain its name, it may not be necessary to prepare and execute assignments for all real and personal property, because the corporation is the owner and will remain the owner after the sale; only the shareholders have changed. However, the sale of all or substantially all of the stock of a corporation will probably require an assignment of certain assets and liabilities. Bank loans, for instance, will require an assignment, and usually permission, because the ownership of the corporation that has entered into the loan agreement is changing. In any event, the terms of all agreements to which the selling corporation is a party should be reviewed to be sure that all such transfers and assignments are ready for execution prior to closing.

POSTCLOSING MATTERS

As with the statutory merger or share exchange, there are usually several items requiring attention after the closing of an asset or stock acquisition transaction. Following is a list of some of the tasks that may need to be completed after the asset acquisition closing:

1. Deeds or other instruments assigning or transferring any real property must be filed at the proper county office.
2. Copies of any loan assignments must be sent to any interested third party.
3. If the name of any corporation involved in the transaction must be changed, the proper articles of amendment must be filed.
4. Copies of instruments assigning or transferring bank accounts must be sent to interested third parties.
5. Any reporting requirements of the SEC or state securities authorities must be complied with.

Following is a list of some of the types of documents and tasks that may require attention after the closing of a stock acquisition transaction:

1. New stock certificates must be prepared (if not done at closing).
2. Any reporting requirements of the SEC or state securities authorities must be complied with.
3. Notification to insurance companies of any insurance policies that have been assigned must be completed.

IN SUMMATION

- Successful preliminary negotiations in an asset or stock acquisition generally result in a letter of intent setting forth the price, terms, and format of the acquisition.
- A detailed asset purchase agreement must set forth very specifically all of the assets to be acquired.
- A detailed stock purchase agreement will set forth the terms for the purchase of the corporation's stock. In addition, it will set forth in detail the corporation's assets and liabilities.
- Agreements for the sale of substantially all of the corporation's assets must be approved by the shareholders of the selling corporation.

§ 12.12 ENTITY CONVERSIONS

With the growing number of noncorporate entities available for the transaction of business, corporations often convert to limited liability companies, limited liability partnerships, or similar business organizations. Likewise, the owners of noncorporate entities may decide at some point that it would be advantageous to convert to a corporation. State corporate statutes often include provisions for **entity conversions**. The secretary of state or other government office that controls the formation of corporations for each state will have established procedures to be followed and documents to be filed to convert an entity from one form to another.

    The MBCA provides for domestication, which refers to the procedure to change a corporation's state of domicile, and for conversion, which allows a corporation to become a different type of entity or a different type of entity to become a domestic business corporation.

ENTITY CONVERSION
Process whereby a domestic corporation becomes an unincorporated entity or an unincorporated entity becomes a corporation.

DOMESTICATION

Domestication of a foreign corporation may be permitted if allowed under the statutes of both the current state of domicile and the desired state of domicile. Procedures for domestication will vary. Generally, the steps to effect the domestication of a corporation include:

1. A plan of domestication must be adopted by the board of directors.
2. The corporation's shareholders must approve the plan pursuant to the statutes of its current state of domicile.
3. Articles of domestication must be executed and filed pursuant to the statutes of the new state of domicile.
4. The corporate charter must be surrendered in the old state of domicile.

    Exhibit 12-13 is a certificate of domestication form for domestication in the state of Kansas. This form must be filed with the Kansas secretary of state, along with the articles of incorporation or similar documents for other types of entities.

EXHIBIT 12-13 KANSAS CERTIFICATE OF DOMESTICATION

DMI
53-46

KANSAS SECRETARY OF STATE

Certificate of Domestication to Kansas

Foreign Entity Domesticating into Kansas

CONTACT: Kansas Secretary of State, Chris Biggs

Memorial Hall, 1st Floor
120 S.W. 10th Avenue
Topeka, KS 66612-1594

(785) 296-4564
kssos@kssos.org
www.kssos.org

Above space is for office use only.

INSTRUCTIONS: *All information must be completed or this document will not be accepted for filing.*
Please read instructions before completing.

Domesticating Entity (This is the entity as it was known before becoming a Kansas entity)

1. Business entity ID number:
If the foreign entity is on file with the Secretary of State. This is not the Federal Employer ID Number (FEIN).

_____

2. Entity name: _____

3. Type of entity:

___ For-Profit Corporation   ___ General Partnership   ___ Limited Liability Partnership
___ Not-for-Profit Corporation ___ Limited Liability Company ___ Limited Partnership

4. State or country of organization: _____

Domesticated Entity (This is the entity that will be known as the new Kansas entity)

5. Entity name: _____

6. Effective date:

☐ Upon filing

☐ Future effective date (cannot exceed 90 days from the file date) _____
                                                                    Month   Day   Year

---

This domestication was approved in accordance with the laws of the domesticating entity's state or country of origin. The formation document and fee for the domesticated entity are attached.

I declare under penalty of perjury under the laws of the state of Kansas that the foregoing is true and correct and that I have remitted the required fee.

_____   _____
Signature of authorized person of domesticatng entity   *Date*

_____   _____
Name of signer, printed or typed   *Title*

ℹ **Instructions:**

☐ 1. Submit this form with the **$75** filing fee. Include the formation document and fee for the domesticated entity.

☐ 2. Fees may be combined in one check. Make checks payable to the Kansas Secretary of State.

NOTICE: *There is a $25 service fee for all checks returned by your financial institution.*

Rev. 7/01/10 nr   *Page 1 of 1*   K.S.A. 17-78-505, 17-78-506

Kansas Secretary of State

CONVERSION

Conversion of an entity to another form of entity is done pursuant to the statutes of the state of domicile. An entity conversion may be done in conjunction with a merger or acquisition. An entity conversion may also be done at the same time as a domestication, changing the entity from one form in one state to another form in another state. Conversions generally must be approved by the directors and shareholders of a corporation, by the partners of a partnership, or by the members of a limited liability company. Conversions may be completed by filing the proper documentation with the secretary of state or other state authority, pursuant to statute. Typically, articles of conversion are filed with the proper document to form the new entity. For example, converting a corporation to a limited liability company may require the filing of articles of conversion along with articles of organization for the new limited liability company. Exhibit 12-14 is a sample articles and plan of conversion to convert a Minnesota LLC to a corporation or a Minnesota corporation to an LLC.

IN SUMMATION

- At times, it may be advisable for noncorporate entities, such as limited liability companies, to convert to a corporation and for corporations to convert to noncorporate entities as provided for in state entity conversion statutes.

- Domestication of a foreign corporation may be permitted if provided for under the statutes of both the foreign corporation and the desired state of domicile and if the appropriate plan of domestication is adopted by the board of directors and shareholders.

- Articles of domestication must be filed in the new state of domicile.

- Conversions must be performed as provided for in state statutes and may be done at the same time as a domestication.

§ 12.13 AMENDMENTS TO ARTICLES OF INCORPORATION

Many of the transactions discussed previously in this chapter require amendments to the articles of incorporation of one or more corporations. Under the MBCA, "A corporation may amend its articles of incorporation at any time to add or change a provision that is required or permitted in the articles of incorporation as of the effective date of the amendment or to delete a provision that is not required to be contained in the articles of incorporation."[17] Generally, whenever any significant information contained in a corporation's articles of incorporation changes, the articles must be amended in accordance with the statutes of the corporation's state of domicile.[1]

EXHIBIT 12-14 MINNESOTA ARTICLES AND PLAN OF CONVERSION

STATE OF MINNESOTA
SECRETARY OF STATE
ARTICLES AND PLAN OF CONVERSION
Minnesota Corporations & Limited Liability Companies
Minnesota Statutes, Chapter's 302A & 322B
Fee $35.00

Read the instructions before completing this form.

1. Name of the Organization before the Conversion is: (Required)

_____

2. Name of the Organization after the Conversion shall be: (Required)

_____

3. After the Conversion, the Organization shall be a: (Required) *(Check one of the following filing types.)*

☐ Corporation ☐ Limited Liability Company

4. The Terms and Conditions of the Proposed Conversion are: (Required)

_____

5. The manner and basis of converting each ownership interest in the organization immediately before the conversion into ownership interests of the organization immediately after the conversion, in whole or in part, into money or other property is: (Required)

_____

6. Include a Copy of the Proposed Articles of Incorporation or Articles of Organization of the Organization after the Conversion, with the Articles and Plan of Conversion. (Required)

7. I, the undersigned, certify that I am signing this document as the person whose signature is required, or as agent of the person(s) whose signature would be required who has authorized me to sign this document on his/her behalf, or in both capacities. I further certify that I have completed all required fields, and that the information in this document is true and correct and in compliance with the applicable chapter of Minnesota Statutes. I understand that by signing this document I am subject to the penalties of perjury as set forth in Section 609.48 as if I had signed this document under oath.

_____
Authorized Signature of Individual on Behalf of the Converting Company or Authorized Agent (Required)

8. Name, daytime telephone number and e-mail address of contact person:

Name

Phone Number

E-Mail Address

APPROVAL OF THE ARTICLES OF AMENDMENT

The statutes of the corporation's state of domicile provide the necessary procedures for approving and filing amendments to the articles of incorporation. In general, any amendments that affect the rights or position of the shareholders in any way must be approved by the shareholders.

Amendments Not Requiring Shareholder Approval

Although shareholder approval is generally required to amend a corporation's articles of incorporation, the incorporators or board of directors have the authority to amend the articles under certain circumstances. The incorporators or the board of directors of the corporation are usually authorized to amend the articles of incorporation prior to the issuance of shares of stock of the corporation.

The statutes of the state of a corporation's domicile may also expressly provide that the board of directors may amend the articles of incorporation after issuance of the corporation's shares if the amendment is routine and does not affect the rights of the shareholders. For example, the board of directors may have the statutory authority to amend the articles of incorporation to change the corporation's registered office address without shareholder approval.

Amendments Requiring Shareholder Approval

For amendments that require shareholder approval, the method of obtaining approval is similar to that required for approving a statutory merger or plan of exchange. Under § 10.03 of the MBCA, when shareholder approval is required for an amendment to the articles of incorporation, these procedures must be followed:

1. The board of directors adopts the proposed amendment.
2. The board of directors must recommend the amendment to the shareholders, unless the board determines that it should make no recommendation and communicates the basis for its determination to the shareholders with the amendment. Reasons for not rendering a recommendation may include a conflict of interest or other special circumstances. The board may condition its submission of the proposed amendment on any basis.
3. Each shareholder, whether or not entitled to vote, must be notified of the shareholder meeting pursuant to statute. The notice must state that the purpose of the meeting is to consider the proposed amendment, and it must contain or be accompanied by a copy or summary of the amendment.
4. Unless the articles of incorporation or the board of directors require a greater vote or a vote by voting groups, the amendment to be adopted must be approved by a majority of the votes entitled to be cast on the amendment by any voting group with respect to which the amendment would create dissenters' rights, and the votes generally required by statute with regard to every other voting group entitled to vote on the amendment.

Generally, the holders of the outstanding shares of a class are entitled to vote as a separate voting group on a proposed amendment if the rights of that class of shareholder would be affected by the proposed amendment.

Right to Dissent

A shareholder is generally entitled to dissent and be paid the fair value of his or her shares if the amendment of the articles of incorporation adversely affects the shareholder's position in the corporation.

ARTICLES OF AMENDMENT

The document amending the articles of incorporation is typically called the articles of amendment or the certificate of amendment. The requirements for the articles of amendment are set by state statute. In general, the amendment must include the information required by statute, and it must be filed in the office where the original articles of incorporation are filed. Any state requirements for county filing and publishing articles of incorporation generally apply to amendments of the articles of incorporation as well. State statutes typically require the inclusion of the following information in articles of amendment:

1. The name of the corporation
2. The text of each amendment adopted
3. Provisions for implementing any exchange, reclassification, or cancellation of issued shares that prompted the amendment of the articles (if not contained in the amendment itself)
4. The date of each amendment's adoption
5. If an amendment was adopted by the incorporators or board of directors without shareholder approval, a statement that the amendment was duly approved by the incorporators or by the board of directors, as the case may be, and that shareholder approval was not required
6. If the amendment required approval by the shareholders, a statement that the amendment was duly approved by the shareholders in the manner required by statute by the articles of incorporation

The secretary of state's office or other appropriate state office should always be contacted to be sure that the proper rules are followed for amending the articles of incorporation. Forms for amending the articles of incorporation are available from the secretary of state's office in most states. Exhibit 12-15 is an example of a form that may be filed to amend the articles of incorporation in the state of Alabama.

RESTATED ARTICLES OF INCORPORATION

Most state statutes grant corporations the right to restate their articles of incorporation at any time. If the restated articles contain no amendments that require shareholder approval, shareholder approval is generally not required merely to restate

EXHIBIT 12-15 ARTICLES OF AMENDMENT TO ARTICLES OF INCORPORATION

STATE OF ALABAMA

DOMESTIC FOR-PROFIT CORPORATION
ARTICLES OF AMENDMENT TO ARTICLES OF INCORPORATION GUIDELINES

INSTRUCTIONS

STEP 1: IF CHANGING THE CORPORATION'S NAME, CONTACT THE OFFICE OF THE SECRETARY OF STATE AT (334) 242-5324 TO RESERVE A CORPORATE NAME.

STEP 2: FILE THE ORIGINAL AND TWO COPIES IN THE JUDGE OF PROBATE'S OFFICE WHERE THE ORIGINAL ARTICLES OF INCORPORATION ARE FILED. (IF THE AMENDMENT CHANGES THE NAME, THE CERTIFICATE OF NAME RESERVATION MUST BE ATTACHED.) IF CHANGING THE NAME, THE SECRETARY OF STATE'S FILING FEE IS $10. TO VERIFY JUDGE OF PROBATE FILING, PLEASE CONTACT THE JUDGE OF PROBATE'S OFFICE.

PURSUANT TO THE PROVISIONS OF THE ALABAMA BUSINESS CORPORATION ACT, THE UNDERSIGNED HEREBY ADOPTS THE FOLLOWING ARTICLES OF AMENDMENT.

Article I   The name of the corporation:

_____

Article II   The following amendment was adopted in the manner provided for by the Alabama Business Corporation Act:

_____

_____

_____

Article III The amendment was adopted by the shareholders or directors in the manner prescribed by law on _____, 20___.

Article IV   The number of shares outstanding at the time of the adoption was _____; the number of shares entitled to vote thereon was _____. If the shares of any class are entitled to vote thereon as a class, list the designation and number of outstanding shares entitled to vote thereon of each such class:

_____

Article V   The number of shares voted for the amendment was _____ and the number of shares voted against such amendment was _____. (If no shares have been issued attach a written statement to that effect.)

Date: _____   _____

Printed Name and Business Address   Type or Print Corporate Officer's Name and Title
of Person Preparing this Document:

                                                   _____

                                                   Signature of Officer

REV. 7/03

Alabama Secretary of State

the articles. If any amendments in the restated articles of incorporation do require shareholder approval, the restated articles must be approved by the shareholders in the manner prescribed by law. Restated articles are generally filed in the same manner as articles of amendment.

The corporate secretary may decide it is in the corporation's best interest to restate the articles of incorporation if the articles have been amended numerous times. For example, if a corporation has amended its articles of incorporation 12 times, a review of the corporation's articles would mean review of the original and all 12 amendments. To simplify things, the secretary may choose to restate the articles of incorporation to incorporate the articles and all past amendments into one document.

IN SUMMATION

- Whenever information contained in the articles of incorporation changes, the articles should be amended as provided for in the statutes of the corporation's state of domicile.

- Most amendments to the articles of incorporation require the approval of the board of directors and shareholders.

- Shareholders generally have the right to dissent and be paid the fair value of their shares by the corporation if the articles of incorporation are amended in a manner that adversely affects them.

- Articles of amendment must be prepared pursuant to state statute and filed with the secretary of state in the same manner in which the articles of incorporation were filed.

- A corporation may restate its articles of incorporation to incorporate several amendments.

§ 12.14 THE PARALEGAL'S ROLE

Paralegals are essential members of most merger and acquisition teams. While the attorneys may be negotiating the details of the merger or acquisition agreement—often until the final documents are signed at the closing table—the paralegals may be responsible for preparing the necessary supplementary documents on behalf of the client, collecting and reviewing the necessary documents from other parties, and preparing for the closing. The paralegal is often instrumental in organizing and conducting the closing of the transaction and in completing the follow-up work after closing. If the paralegal is working on the legal team that represents the seller of assets or shares of stock in a transaction, he or she may directly assist the corporate client at their offices to assemble information required by the buyers.

Paralegals who perform tasks associated with mergers and acquisitions may be asked to:

- Assist in preparation of the letter of intent
- Assist in preparation of the agreement for merger, share exchange, stock purchase, or asset purchase

- Assist in complying with federal antitrust laws
- Review the agreement and prepare the closing checklist
- Assist with the preparation of supplementary documents
- Collect documents from the client for review by opposing counsel
- Review documents supplied by the other party
- Prepare the plan of merger and articles of merger or plan of exchange and articles of exchange
- Prepare necessary corporate resolutions
- Prepare articles of amendment to articles of incorporation
- Prepare consents to assignment of leases and other contracts
- Prepare new stock certificates
- Prepare documents transferring assets
- Assemble all documents for closing
- Attend the closing
- Assist with postclosing filings

LETTER OF INTENT

Paralegals may be asked to assist with drafting the letter of intent establishing the parameters of the agreement between the parties, using samples from form books and transactions previously done in the office.

AGREEMENT

Paralegals may assist with preparing the main agreement between the parties. This often involves several drafts of the agreement that may be passed back and forth between the attorneys and amended several times before signing.

Paralegals are often responsible for reviewing the agreement once it has been signed by the parties, or even reviewing the drafts as they are prepared, to determine what further documents will be required to close the transaction. A thorough review of the agreement should be made and every action that must be taken and every document that must be prepared or produced should be included in a closing checklist. The closing checklist should include all of the documents that will be drafted or reviewed prior to or at the closing, along with a reference as to who is responsible for preparing or producing the document. It should also include any actions that must be taken by any party to the agreement prior to closing. Once this checklist has been prepared, copies should be circulated to all parties involved in the transaction or to all parties who are in any way responsible for producing documents or materials prior to or at closing. Paralegals often use electronic databases to track the documents required for the due diligence process prior to closing a merger or acquisition closing. The documents may be scanned and stored electronically as they are received, allowing for prompt retrieval when required.

FEDERAL ANTITRUST LAW COMPLIANCE

Experienced paralegals are often responsible for seeing that the transaction complies with federal antitrust laws. Often, this includes researching the appropriate requirements and filing Hart-Scott-Rodino notification with the Federal Trade Commission.

SUPPLEMENTARY DOCUMENTS

It is not unusual for a merger or acquisition agreement to require several certifications and warranties by all parties involved. These supplementary documents, which are often drafted by paralegals for attorney approval, may include certifications by the secretaries or other officers of the corporations, and the attorneys for all parties involved. These documents may certify certain facts concerning the corporate existence of the parties, and other warranties and representations. The agreement between the parties may establish exactly what must be included in each supplementary document.

REVIEW AND PRODUCTION OF DOCUMENTS

Between the time of the initial agreement between the parties and the closing of the transaction, numerous documents typically trade hands for review by the other party. Using the closing checklist, paralegals may be responsible for assisting the client to produce the required documents and for obtaining the documents required of the other party. The paralegal is often responsible for ensuring that the documents arrive in time to be reviewed prior to closing, and possibly for summarizing longer documents to save the time of the attorney and client, who will undoubtedly be busy with other aspects of the transaction. Each document that leaves the office should be copied, tracked on the appropriate checklist, and approved by the responsible attorney. Each document that is received in the office should be reviewed, noted on the appropriate checklist, and filed for quick retrieval. Documentation for larger merger and acquisition transaction is often tracked with the aid of electronic databases.

PLAN AND ARTICLES OF MERGER OR SHARE EXCHANGE

When the transaction involves a statutory merger or share exchange, the appropriate documents must be drafted for filing with the secretary of state or other appropriate state authority. If the plan of merger or share exchange includes an amendment to the articles of incorporation, that document must be prepared for filing as well. Often, the secretary of state's office supplies forms that may be completed and filed. The paralegal should check with the appropriate state authority to determine the availability of forms, the appropriate filing fee, and filing procedures.

CORPORATE RESOLUTIONS

Paralegals often assist with preparing the corporate resolutions approving the transaction. If a meeting of the shareholders is required, the paralegal may assist with all formalities associated with calling a meeting of the shareholders pursuant to state statute.

STOCK AND ASSET TRANSFER DOCUMENTS

If the transaction is to be an asset transfer, separate documents must be prepared transferring all affected assets. Paralegals may assist by preparing bills of sale for all personal property and deeds for all real estate included in the agreement between the parties. Extra documentation may be required to transfer motor vehicles and intangible property.

New stock certificates must be prepared for stock purchase transactions and share exchanges.

ASSIGNMENTS OF CONTRACTS

Depending on how the transaction is structured, assignments may be required for all contracts that the acquiring party is assuming. The paralegal may be responsible for drafting such assignments pursuant to the acquisition agreement and the provisions of each contract. The individual contracts must be reviewed to determine if it is necessary to obtain permission or consent for the assignment from other parties to the contract.

CLOSING

By the closing date, the responsible paralegal should have a closing checklist indicating that all tasks have been completed. All documents should be assembled so that they are readily available. With the multitude of documents often required to close mergers and acquisitions, organization is crucial. Often, documents are arranged by responsible party, or in groups, such as real estate assets, equipment and machinery, and so on. Other times, they may be assembled in the order of their reference in the agreement between the parties, so that the agreement can be reviewed and each document executed in order at the closing table. Whatever order is chosen, sufficient copies should be made for each party involved, usually with one or two extra sets. These documents are usually placed in labeled file folders, numbered, and indexed as they are drafted or received at the office. This system also allows for good organization at the closing, when the paralegal may be responsible for seeing that each document is signed by the proper individual or individuals and witnessed and notarized (if necessary), and that each copy is delivered to the appropriate person. The paralegal may also be responsible for arranging for the physical location of the closing and wire transfers of funds.

POSTCLOSING

After the closing, the paralegal may be responsible for any loose ends. Typically, documents will need to be filed at state and local levels. The paralegal may also assist with the compilation of copies of all merger and acquisition documents in a bound closing book.

Many corporate paralegals work in the mergers and acquisitions area and find it very exciting work. It is also very demanding work that requires exceptional organizational skills, attention to detail, and the ability to work under a certain amount of pressure.

CORPORATE PARALEGAL PROFILE
Michael L. Whitchurch

As you become more experienced and get more involved, people trust your work and assume it's going to get done.

NAME Michael L. Whitchurch

LOCATION Chicago, Illinois

TITLE Senior Paralegal/Corporate Department Paralegal Coordinator

SPECIALTY Mergers and Acquisitions/ Transactional

EDUCATION Bachelor of Arts Degree, Arizona State University

EXPERIENCE 16 years

Michael Whitchurch is a senior paralegal with Jenner & Block LLP, a Chicago law firm with approximately 470 attorneys and 50 paralegals. Michael specializes in mergers and acquisitions and transactional work. He holds the position of senior paralegal, as well as the Corporate Department's paralegal coordinator, and is responsible for the management of the department.

Michael is involved in merger and acquisition transactions throughout the entire process. His responsibilities in a particular acquisition might start with putting together a data room to facilitate due diligence during the early stages of a transaction, before an agreement has been reached. After an agreement is entered into, Michael will create a closing checklist from the acquisition document and prepare and collect the documents required for closing. He also attends closings to see that the proper documentation is signed and exchanged between the parties. Michael works on transactions of all sizes, including some that have been valued in the hundreds of millions of dollars.

Michael reports to all 50 attorneys in the Corporate Department of Jenner & Block, as well as the attorneys in the firm's tax department. They understand his specialty and come to him when they need his help with a particular project or transaction. His management responsibilities mean that he is able to keep up to date with the projects that other paralegals in the department are working on, and see that the work is evenly distributed.

Michael enjoys the freedom associated with his position. The attorneys he works with have learned to trust his abilities and assign projects with confidence that they will get done. He also enjoys the nature of the transactional work.

He has been very involved in a groundbreaking project involving 1031 exchanges. These

continues

CORPORATE PARALEGAL PROFILE (*continued*)
Michael L. Whitchurch

exchanges involve tax-free, like-kind exchanges of property. The partner overseeing these transactions was able to obtain a favorable IRS ruling permitting the use of Delaware Statutory Trusts as a vehicle for use in these types of transactions, greatly simplifying the transactions for Jenner & Block's clients. Branching out somewhat from corporate law, this transactional work also involves tax, real estate, and estate planning elements.

According to Michael, the one drawback to working for a law firm? Billing.

Michael's advice to new paralegals?

Find someone at your new job—either an attorney or experienced paralegal—who is always willing to take the time to explain things to you. When you have the experience, don't forget to take the time to help out someone else who's new. Also, it's not the end of the world if you make a mistake, but you must "'fess up" and take responsibility. Admit your error and present a solution to the problem as soon as possible.

For more information on careers for corporate paralegals, log in to http://www.cengagebrain.com to access the CourseMate website that accompanies this text; then see the Corporate Careers Section.

ETHICAL CONSIDERATION

Keeping a client's confidentiality is very important in every aspect of a paralegal's work, but it is absolutely crucial when dealing with mergers and acquisitions, especially if one or more public corporations are involved. Leaks from a law firm that might appear to be harmless can actually lead to serious consequences, including fluctuation in the price of a corporation's stock. In some cases, it may not only be unethical for a paralegal to divulge information about a corporate client to the press or other outsiders, but it may be in violation of federal statutes.

Law firms have strict policies with regard to divulging information regarding any clients to the press or any outsider. Typically, all requests for information regarding a client should be directed to an attorney who is responsible for the client's affairs. No one else will be permitted to pass on any information regarding a client without permission, even information that may seem quite inconsequential.

For more information on ethics for corporate paralegals, including links to the NALA and NFPA codes of ethics, log in to http://www.cengagebrain.com to access the CourseMate website that accompanies this text; then see the Ethics Section.

§ 12.15 RESOURCES

Resources that paralegals may find particularly useful in the mergers and acquisitions area include state statutes, federal statutes, and the office of the secretary of state or other pertinent state office.

STATE AND FEDERAL STATUTES

Statutes concerning mergers and acquisitions are typically found within the business corporation act of each state. State statutes of most states include requirements for the plan of merger or plan of share exchange, the articles of merger or articles of share exchange, and obtaining shareholder approval for the transactions. State statutes may also have special provisions for mergers between related corporations, such as the merger of a subsidiary into a parent corporation. At times you may find it necessary to research both state and federal law. Links to the federal statutes and statutes of each state may be accessed from the CourseMate website.

FEDERAL ANTITRUST LAW AND INFORMATION

Larger transactions will require research of the pertinent federal antitrust laws, especially the provisions of the Hart-Scott-Rodino Act. Following is a list of the primary federal statutes affecting mergers and acquisitions:

> The Clayton Act, 15 U.S.C. § 18.
>
> The Sherman Act, 15 U.S.C. § 1.
>
> The Federal Trade Commission Act, 15 U.S.C. § 45.
>
> The Hart-Scott-Rodino Act, 15 U.S.C. § 18a.

The Federal Trade Commission website provides a variety of information for businesses and consumers, as well as a section of legal resources, including information on federal antitrust law and required filings under the Hart-Scott-Rodino Act. Links to these federal statutes, as well as the Federal Trade Commissioní's website, may be accessed from CourseMate.

SECRETARY OF STATE OFFICES

Most merger and acquisition transactions involve filings at the secretary of state's office or the office of another appropriate state official. The appropriate office should be contacted to ensure that all rules for filing are complied with, and to obtain any forms that are needed. Appendix A of this text is a directory of secretary of state offices. Links to these office websites may be found on CourseMate.

SUMMARY

- The state business corporation act of most states includes provisions for statutory mergers and share exchanges between corporations.

- A merger is a combination of two or more corporations whereby one of the corporations survives (the surviving corporation), and the other merges into it and ceases to exist (the merging corporation).

- A triangle merger is a type of merger that uses a subsidiary corporation to acquire a target corporation. The parent corporation funds a subsidiary corporation with cash or shares of stock. The target corporation is then merged into the subsidiary corporation. The parent and subsidiary corporation are both surviving corporations.

- In a reverse triangle merger, the subsidiary is merged into the target corporation (which then becomes a subsidiary of the parent corporation). Both the target corporation and parent corporation survive.

- In a statutory share exchange, all of the stock of the target corporation is acquired by another corporation, which becomes its parent corporation. The shareholders of the target corporation may receive cash or shares of stock in exchange for their shares.

- Larger mergers and acquisitions may be subject to federal antitrust laws, including reporting requirements under the Hart-Scott-Rodino Act.

- A plan of merger and articles of merger are executed and filed with the secretary of state or other appropriate state authority to effect a statutory merger.

- A plan of share exchange and articles of share exchange are executed and filed with the secretary of state or other appropriate state authority to effect a statutory share exchange.

- Statutory mergers and statutory share exchanges, as well as the sale of assets or all of the stock of a corporation, require the approval of at least the majority of the shareholders of the corporation.

- Shareholders who object to a corporate merger or acquisition may be eligible to dissent and obtain payment of the fair value of their shares.

- The investigation and examination of documents prior to the closing of a merger or acquisition transaction is referred to as the due diligence process.

- If a corporation is acquired by the purchase of all its outstanding stock, the acquiring corporation typically assumes the obligations and liabilities of the target corporation.

- If a corporation is acquired by the purchase of all of its assets, the acquiring corporation typically does not assume the obligations and liabilities of the target corporation.
- The statutes of most states provide for the domestication of foreign corporations and noncorporate entities.
- The statutes of most states provide for the conversion of corporations into noncorporate entities and for the conversion of noncorporate entities into corporations.
- The de facto merger doctrine allows courts to consider a certain transaction with characteristics of a merger to be a merger, regardless of what it is called, to prevent an injustice to third parties.
- When the information that must be included in the corporation's articles of incorporation changes, articles of amendment must usually be filed with the secretary of state or other appropriate state official.
- Under most circumstances, amendments to the articles of incorporation require the consent of shareholders.

REVIEW QUESTIONS

1. What is the difference between a consolidation and a merger?

2. What is the final relationship between two corporations that were parties to a share exchange?

3. What is a "surviving" corporation in a merger transaction?

4. What general rights does a dissenting shareholder have?

5. What are the main purposes of the federal antitrust laws?

6. Do all mergers and acquisitions require shareholder approval? Give examples.

7. If the sole shareholder of Diane's Auto Parts, Inc., which holds the stock of 95 percent of the D.G. Auto Parts Corporation, decides to merge the two corporations together, with Diane's Auto Parts, Inc., being the surviving corporation, what type of merger would it be?

Why are the requirements for shareholder approval different for this type of merger? Why are approval requirements different for upstream mergers?

8. What is a letter of intent?

9. What constitutes due diligence work?

10. Suppose that the shareholders of Kate's Household Products, Inc., are interested in acquiring one of their biggest suppliers, Nixon Chemical Corporation, but they are concerned about past problems that Nixon Chemical has had with toxic waste disposal. What type of acquisition might be the most beneficial to Kate's Household Products, Inc.?

11. What are some possible disadvantages of acquiring an auto dealer, or a corporation that owns several pieces of real estate, through an asset acquisition rather than a stock acquisition transaction?

■ PRACTICAL PROBLEMS

1. Locate the statute sections in your state that deal with mergers and share exchanges to answer the following questions:
   a. What is the cite for the statute section dealing with corporate mergers in your state?
   b. Do the statutes of your state provide for both statutory mergers and share exchanges? If yes, what is the cite for the statute section dealing with share exchanges in your state?
   c. What information is required for articles of merger (or similarly named document) in your state?

2. Do the statutes of your state provide a process for converting a limited liability company into a corporation? Do they provide for the conversion of a corporation into a limited liability company? If yes, pick one type of conversion and outline the steps that must be completed.

■ EXERCISE IN CRITICAL THINKING

Why is it important to enter into a letter of intent early in the negotiation process of a proposed merger or acquisition, even when the parties are just exploring the possibility of a transaction and there is a good possibility that the proposed deal will never close?

■ WORKPLACE SCENARIO

Assume that our fictional clients, Bradley Harris and Cynthia Lund, have decided to merge their business with a competing computer repair business by the name of Kohler's Computer Repair, Inc. Your supervising attorney has asked you to prepare drafts of the merger documents, including a plan of merger and articles of merger. Sandra and Scott Kohler, the shareholders of Kohler's Computer Repair, Inc., will surrender all the shares they hold in Kohler's Computer Repair, Inc., and they will be issued an identical number of shares of Cutting Edge Computer Repair, Inc. Cutting Edge Computer Repair, Inc., will be the surviving corporation. Kohler's Computer Repair, Inc., will be dissolved. Bradley Harris and Cynthia Lund will retain their current offices in Cutting Edge Computer Repair, Inc. Sandra and Scott Kohler will both become vice presidents and directors of the surviving corporation. Using the above information and the information found in Appendices B-3 and B-4 of this text, prepare a plan of merger and articles of merger for filing in your home state. Also prepare a cover letter filing the required documents with the appropriate state authority, and enclosing the required filing fee.

Portfolio Reminder:
Save the documents prepared for the Workplace Scenario exercises in each chapter, either in hard copy or electronically, to build a portfolio of documents to be used for job interviews or as sample documents on the job. At this point, your portfolio should include the following:

- Power of attorney
- Application for assumed name
- Application for federal employer identification number
- Application for state employer identification number
- Partnership statement of authority
- Limited partnership certificate
- Limited liability partnership statement of qualification
- Articles of organization
- Subchapter S election by small business corporation, Form 2553

- Articles of incorporation
- Unanimous written consent of shareholders
- Unanimous written consent of the board of directors

- Unanimous written consent of board of directors approving bank loan
- Plan of merger
- Articles of merger

END NOTES

1. FactSet Mergerstat's M&A Activity U.S. and U.S. Cross-Border Transactions, as reported on High Rock Partners website, http://www.highrockpartners.com.

2. Model Business Corporation Act revised through December 2007 (hereinafter MBCA) § 11.02(a).

3. Id. § 1.40 (7B).

4. Federal Trade Commission website, http://www.ftc.gov (accessed July 16, 2011).

5. 54 Am. Jur. 2d Monopolies and Restraints of Trade § 1 (May 2011).

6. MBCA § 11.04(b).

7. Id. § 11.04(c).

8. Id. § 11.04(d).

9. Id. § 11.04(e).

10. Id. § 11.04(f).

11. 6B Am. Jur. Legal forms 2d (May 2011) § 74:1545. Reprinted with permission from American Jurisprudence Legal Forms 2d © 2011Thomson/West.

12. Id. § 74:1552. Reprinted with permission from American Jurisprudence Legal Forms 2d © 2011 Thomson/West.

13. Id. § 74:1557. Reprinted with permission from American Jurisprudence Legal Forms 2d © 2011 Thomson/West.

14. *Ladjevardian v. Laidlaw-Coggeshall, Inc.*, 431 F Supp 834 (SD NY).

15. MBCA § 12.02.

16. MBCA § 10.01(a).

17. 6B Am. Jur. Legal Forms 2d (May 2011) § 74:1583. Reprinted with permission from American Jurisprudence Legal Forms 2d © 2011 Thomson/West.

CourseMate

To access additional course materials, including CourseMate, please visit http://www.cengagebrain.com. At the CengageBrain home page, search for the ISBN of your title (from the back cover of your book) using the search box at the top of the page. This will take you to the product page where these resources can be found. The CourseMate resources for this text include Web links, downloadable forms, flash cards, and more.

13

FOREIGN CORPORATION QUALIFICATION

◼ CHAPTER OUTLINE

INTRODUCTION

Few corporations of size transact business solely within their state of domicile. The state where the corporation is incorporated is considered to be the corporation's state of domicile, regardless of where the company is physically located or transacts the majority of its business. A corporation is considered to be a **foreign corporation** in every state or jurisdiction other than its state of domicile. Foreign corporations must be qualified to transact business by obtaining permission from the appropriate authority of each state in which they are considered to be doing business.

Although the focus of this chapter is on the qualification of foreign business corporations, limited liability companies, limited partnerships, limited liability partnerships, and other entities that are formed by filing documents at the state level may be required to follow the same or similar procedures for qualifying to do business in any state other than their states of domicile.

This chapter examines the factors to be considered when deciding whether foreign corporation qualification is necessary. Next, it examines the qualification requirements typically imposed by state statutes, followed by a discussion of what is required to maintain the good standing of a foreign corporation and to withdraw it from doing business in a foreign state. After a brief discussion regarding foreign corporation name registration, this chapter concludes with a look at the paralegal's role in qualifying foreign corporations and the resources available to assist in that area.

§ 13.1 DETERMINING WHEN FOREIGN CORPORATION QUALIFICATION IS NECESSARY

A corporation does not legally exist beyond the boundaries of its state of domicile and must therefore be granted permission, or qualify, to do business with the proper authorities of any state, other than its state of domicile, in which it transacts business. When a corporation is formed or when an existing corporation expands, a decision must be made as to where the corporation must qualify to do business as a foreign corporation. An examination of the corporation's business must be made and research must be done on any state in which there is potential for business to be transacted. The following factors must be considered when deciding whether it is necessary to qualify a corporation to do business in a particular foreign state:

1. The extent, duration, and nature of the corporation's involvement in the foreign state
2. The foreign state's statutory interpretation of what does, or does not, constitute transacting business in that state
3. The cost of qualification and the penalties for transacting business in the foreign state without authority

STATE LONG-ARM STATUTES AND JURISDICTION OVER FOREIGN CORPORATIONS

Whenever a corporation transacts business in a state other than its state of domicile, it subjects itself to the jurisdiction of the courts of that other state for any causes of action arising from the corporation's activities in that state. State **long-arm statutes** give the courts of each state personal jurisdiction over corporations that voluntarily go into that state for the purpose of transacting business. The defendant corporation need not be physically present in a foreign state for the courts of that state to render a binding judgment against it, but it must have minimum contacts within the state. In many instances courts have found that a defendant who is not present in the jurisdiction may be subject to a judgment in personam if the defendant has certain minmum contacts that do not offend the "traditional notions of fair play and substantial justice."[1] Because corporations are subject to the jurisdiction of the courts in any state in which they transact business, in addition to qualifying or registering to do business as a foreign corporation, they must provide an agent to receive service of process in the foreign state in accordance with the laws of that state.

STATUTORY REQUIREMENTS FOR QUALIFICATION OF FOREIGN CORPORATIONS

Exactly what does, or does not, constitute transacting business in each state is defined by the state's code or statutes. Typically, the state statutes list a number of activities that do not constitute transacting business, but remain silent on exactly what does constitute transacting business. Most states have adopted a modified version of 15.01 of the Model Business Corporation Act (MBCA), which reads:

(a) A foreign corporation may not transact business in this state until it obtains a certificate of authority from the secretary of state.

(b) The following activities, among others, do not constitute transacting business within the meaning of subsection (a):
   (1) maintaining, defending, or settling any proceeding;
   (2) holding meetings of the board of directors or shareholders or carrying on other activities concerning internal corporate affairs;
   (3) maintaining bank accounts;
   (4) maintaining offices or agencies for the transfer, exchange, and registration of the corporation's own securities or maintaining trustees or depositories with respect to those securities;
   (5) selling through independent contractors;
   (6) soliciting or obtaining orders, whether by mail or through employees or agents or otherwise, if the orders require acceptance outside this state before they become contracts;
   (7) creating or acquiring indebtedness, mortgages, and security interests in real or personal property;
   (8) securing or collecting debts or enforcing mortgages and security interests in property securing the debts;
   (9) owning, without more, real or personal property;
   (10) conducting an isolated transaction that is completed within 30 days and that is not one in the course of repeated transactions of a like nature;
   (11) transacting business in interstate commerce.

(c) The list of activities in subsection (b) is not exhaustive.

Although the list set forth in this statute section is helpful, determining whether qualification as a foreign corporation is necessary is usually a judgment call. One test that may be applied when making the determination is whether the corporation is engaging in regular and continuous business in the foreign state in question.

CONSEQUENCES OF NOT QUALIFYING AS A FOREIGN CORPORATION

When making a determination as to whether to qualify to do business in a particular state, the consequences of not qualifying must be considered. Penalties for transacting business in a foreign state without first qualifying vary from state to state. One of the most severe consequences is that the corporation usually is prohibited from commencing legal action to enforce contracts in the foreign state. This penalty is enforced under state **door-closing statutes**, which provide that a corporation doing business in the state without the necessary authority is precluded from maintaining an action in that state.

DOOR-CLOSING STATUTE
State statute providing that a corporation doing business in the state without the necessary authority is precluded from maintaining an action in that state.

In the two cases that follow in this chapter, the defendants claimed that the plaintiffs did not have the right to bring suits against them in the state where the suits were heard because they were not qualified to do business in the state where the dispute arose.

In *Harold Lang Jewelers, Inc. v. Johnson*, the court found that the plaintiff was transacting business in North Carolina and was not qualified to do business in that state. The trial court's dismissal of the suit before trial was affirmed. In *Bayonne Block Co., Inc. v. Porco*, the civil court of New York City, Bronx County, found that the plaintiff's contact within the state of New York was limited to taking orders from and delivering goods to buyers in New York State. The Court determined that the plaintiff was not doing business in the state of New York for purposes of the pertinent state statute and was not barred from bringing suit in that state for that reason.

CASE

Court of Appeals of North Carolina. Harold Lang Jewelers, Inc., Plaintiff, v. Jerger Johnson d/b/a Johnson Jewelers, and Terrell Kent Johnson d/b/a Jerger Johnson Jewelers, defendants.

No. COA02-429. Feb. 18, 2003.

Appellant Harold Lang Jewelers, Inc. (Lang), a Florida corporation, filed suit against the appellees (Johnson). As one of its affirmative defenses, Johnson argued that Lang could not sue in a North Carolina court because Lang was transacting business in the state without a certificate of authority

to do so. The trial court agreed and dismissed the suit prior to trial. Lang appealed. For the reasons set forth below, we affirm the decision of the trial court.

Lang filed suit in April 1999, alleging that Johnson owed it $160,322.90 plus interest for jewelry sold or consigned. Johnson answered in

May 1999, asserting as one of its eight affirmative defenses that Lang could not sue in a North Carolina court because Lang had failed to obtain a certificate of authority to transact business in the state. On January 7, 2002, the case was called for trial. At that time, Johnson orally raised the defense of Lang's failure to obtain a certificate of authority and requested a hearing on that issue. After hearing evidence and argument, the district court granted the motion and dismissed Lang's action. Lang now appeals.

. . . Pursuant to N.C. Gen.Stat. 55-15-02, a foreign corporation that transacts business in North Carolina is barred from maintaining an action in any state court unless it has obtained a certificate of authority to transact business prior to trial.

. . . Lang argues that the trial court did not find sufficient facts to support its conclusion that Lang was, in fact, transacting business in the state of North Carolina. Again, we disagree.

. . . Our courts have interpreted transacting business in the state to "require the engaging in, carrying on or exercising, in North Carolina, some of the functions for which the corporation was created." The business done by the corporation must be of such nature and character "as to warrant the inference that the corporation has subjected itself to the local jurisdiction and is, by its duly authorized officers and agents, present within the State." . . . In other words, the activities carried on by the corporation in North Carolina must be substantial, continuous, systematic, and regular.

Here, the trial court concluded that Lang's business activity in North Carolina was regular,

continuous, and substantial such that it was transacting business in the state. We uphold this conclusion only if it is supported by the findings of fact, and, contrary to Lang's assertion, we hold that it is.

Specifically, the court found that Lang, through its single employee, had sold and consigned merchandise to jewelry stores in Franklin, Asheville, and Highlands, North Carolina, since 1970. The court also found that Lang's employee came to North Carolina at least twice every six weeks during the year and at least twice every four weeks during the summer months for the purpose of transacting business. Sometimes he came to North Carolina to transact business as often as three times a month. The court found that when the employee came to North Carolina, he always brought jewelry with him for delivery. When he visited jewelry stores in the state, he would either (1) make a direct sale on the spot without any confirmation from any other person or entity in any other place or (2) consign the jewelry, also without any further confirmation or approval from any other person or entity anywhere. When the employee took orders, he either shipped the ordered items to the business in North Carolina or personally delivered the merchandise. He also took returns of merchandise from customers in the state. The court further found that the business that Lang conducted in North Carolina did not require it to communicate with any other person or seek any authority from any other person.

In sum, we conclude that the trial court's conclusions of law are adequately supported by the

continues

CASE *(continued)*
Court of Appeals of North Carolina. Harold Lang Jewelers, Inc., Plaintiff, v. Jerger Johnson

---

facts found in this case. There is ample evidence that Lang's business in this state has been regular, systematic, and extensive. Lang has been coming to North Carolina since about 1970 to sell and consign merchandise to several jewelry stores. In fact, Lang routinely came to North Carolina as frequently as twice every four weeks during some parts of the year, and each time he brought with him merchandise to deliver. Moreover, the orders did not require "acceptance without this State before becoming binding contracts"; instead, Lang's employee finalized the sales in North Carolina. Accordingly, Lang's assignments of error on this ground are overruled.

Finally, Lang contends that the trial court erred when it dismissed the action, arguing that the court should have continued the case to permit Lang to obtain the requisite certificate of authority. The applicable statute, N.C. Gen.Stat. 55-15-02,

does not specify the procedure in the event of failure to obtain a certificate of authority. The statute simply indicates that an action cannot be maintained unless the certificate is obtained prior to trial. N.C. Gen.Stat. 55-15-02(a). Lang has not cited, nor have we found, a case where a continuance has been granted by a court in these circumstances. Moreover, Lang was aware that Johnson's motion was pending and could have obtained the certificate in the year and a half that passed between the filing of the motion and the court's dismissal of the case. In the absence of statutory or other authority dictating a continuance, we hold that the trial court acted within its discretion in dismissing the action.

For the reasons set forth above, we affirm the decision of the trial court.

Affirmed.

Case material reprinted from Westlaw, with permission.

CASE
Civil Court, City of New York, Bronx County. Bayonne Block Co., Inc.,
Plaintiff, v. Frank T. Porco, Defendant. Nov. 26, 1996. DORIS LING-COHAN, Justice.

Defendant moves for an order pursuant to CPLR 3015(e), 3211(a)(7) and Business Corporation Law 1312 striking the complaint or, in the alternative, vacating the Notice of Trial for lack of discovery, and imposing sanctions against plaintiff.

Plaintiff commenced this action to receive monies it is allegedly owed for providing construction materials to Mulford Construction Corp.

("Mulford"). Defendant Frank T. Porco ("Porco") is named as a defendant pursuant to a guaranty of payment he executed.

. . . BCL 1312

. . . BCL 1312 bars a foreign corporation "doing business" within this State from using the courts unless the corporation is authorized to do business in New York State.

CASE *(continued)*

Civil Court, City of New York, Bronx County. Bayonne Block Co., Inc., Plaintiff, v. Frank T. Porco, Defendant.

The issue presented to the Court is whether plaintiff corporation's contacts with New York constitute "doing business" for purposes of BCL 1312. There is no precise measure of the nature or extent of the activities which may be determinative of whether a foreign corporation is doing business in New York for purposes of BCL 1312, and each case must be decided on its own facts. . . . However, it is clear that not all business activity engaged in by a foreign corporation constitutes doing business in New York. . . . In fact, business activity which may subject a foreign corporation to the jurisdiction of New York would not necessarily constitute doing business under BCL 1312. The Court of Appeals has articulated the standard in its discussion of the predecessor of BCL 1312 in *International Fuel & Iron Corp. v. Donner Steel Co.*, 242 N.Y. 224, 230, 151 N.E. 214, 215 (1926):

"To come within this section, the foreign corporation must do more than make a single contract, engage in an isolated piece of business, or an occasional undertaking; it must maintain and carry on business with some continuity of act and purpose."

Here, it is undisputed that plaintiff foreign corporation's connection to and its "doing business" in this State is limited to taking orders from and delivering goods to buyers in New York State. There is no claim that plaintiff has an office, advertises, regularly induces the purchase of its products by New York users from its New York distributors, or otherwise transacts business in New York State. "If the foreign corporation's contacts here, no matter how extensive, are merely for the purpose of soliciting business and activities incidental to the sale and delivery of merchandise into the State, then the foreign corporation is engaged in interstate commerce and is constitutionally beyond the reach of section 1312 of the Business Corporation Law." *Paper Mfrs. Co. v. Ris Paper Co. Inc.*, 86 Misc.2d at 98, 381 N.Y.S.2d 959. On these facts, this Court holds that plaintiff does not do business for purposes of BCL 1312 and thus need not be licensed or registered by the Secretary of State in order to utilize this State's courts. To hold otherwise would violate the Commerce Clause, as the business activity described in the instant case is, in essence, interstate commerce and not subject to BCL 1312(a). . . .

Case material reprinted from Westlaw, with permission.

Following is Minnesota Statutes Ann. 303.20, which provides the consequences of transacting business in the state of Minnesota without a **certificate of authority**. Many states have similar statutes.

§ 303.20 Foreign Corporation May Not Maintain Action Unless Licensed

No foreign corporation transacting business in this state without a certificate of authority shall be permitted to maintain an action in any court in this state until such corporation shall have obtained a certificate of authority; nor shall an action be maintained in any court by any successor or assignee of such

CERTIFICATE OF AUTHORITY
Certificate issued by a secretary of state or similar state authority granting a foreign corporation the right to transact business in that state.

corporation on any right, claim, or demand arising out of the transaction of business by such corporation in this state until a certificate of authority to transact business in this state shall have been obtained by such corporation or by a corporation which has acquired all, or substantially all, of its assets. If such assignee shall be a purchaser without actual notice of such violation by the corporation, recovery may be had to an amount not greater than the purchase price. This section shall not be construed to alter the rules applicable to a holder in due course of a negotiable instrument.

The failure of a foreign corporation to obtain a certificate of authority to transact business in this state does not impair the validity of any contract or act of such corporation, and shall not prevent such corporation from defending any action in any court of this state.

Any foreign corporation which transacts business in this state without a certificate of authority shall forfeit and pay to this state a penalty, not exceeding $1,000, and an additional penalty, not exceeding $100, for each month or fraction thereof during which it shall continue to transact business in this state without a certificate of authority therefor. Such penalties may be recovered in the district court of any county in which such foreign corporation has done business or has property or has a place of business, by an action, in the name of the state, brought by the attorney general.

SIDEBAR

As a condition of doing business in a state, foreign corporations are required to consent to the jurisdiction of the state's courts.

IN SUMMATION

- A corporation is considered to be a foreign corporation in every state or jurisdiction other than its state of domicile.
- Corporations that transact business in a foreign state must be qualified to transact business by receiving a certificate of authority or some similar document from the foreign state.
- State long-arm statutes give the courts of each state personal jurisdiction over foreign corporations that voluntarily transact business in their state, even if there is no corporate headquarters physically present in that state.
- When a corporation has any type of presence in a foreign state, it is important to determine if that corporation is considered to be "doing business" in that state and therefore required to qualify as a foreign corporation.
- Under state door-closing statutes, foreign corporations that transact business in a state where they are not qualified may be barred from commencing legal action in that state to enforce contracts in the foreign state.

§ 13.2 FOREIGN CORPORATION RIGHTS, PRIVILEGES, AND RESPONSIBILITIES

Except where otherwise specified by state statute, qualified foreign corporations have the same, but no greater, rights and privileges as domestic corporations. As a general rule, a qualified foreign corporation may transact all of the business conferred by its own charter and the laws of its state of domicile, unless those laws are in conflict with the laws of the foreign state. The foreign corporation also is subject to many of the same duties and restrictions applicable to domestic corporations in the foreign state. However, most state statutes provide that the laws of the state of domicile shall govern over all matters concerning the internal affairs of the corporation.

IN SUMMATION

- Qualified foreign corporations have the same, but no greater, rights and privileges as domestic corporations
- Internal matters of a qualified foreign corporation continue to be governed under the foreign corporation's state of domicile.

§ 13.3 QUALIFICATION REQUIREMENTS

Although the requirements for qualifying to do business vary from state to state, in general, the corporation must obtain a certificate of authority or similar document from the proper state authority before it begins transacting business in that state. For ease of explanation, we refer to the document granting authority to the foreign corporation as the "certificate of authority" throughout the rest of this chapter, although that document may have a different name in some states. Usually the secretary of state's corporate division has jurisdiction over all foreign corporations doing business in the state. However, in some states the agency with jurisdiction is the Corporation Commission or a similar agency. For ease of explanation, we refer to the state agency with jurisdiction over foreign corporations as the "secretary of state" throughout the rest of this chapter.

Qualification requirements are usually the same or similar for all types of corporations and other business organizations that must qualify. However, some of the fees and forms required by the secretary of state may vary for these different types of entities. The foreign state's statutes and the appropriate secretary of state must be consulted to make sure that all requirements are met for limited partnerships and other types of business organizations.

SIDEBAR

California qualified more than 8,000 foreign corporations to do business in that state during 2010.[2]

APPLICATION FOR CERTIFICATE OF AUTHORITY

The certificate of authority is obtained by filing an application, along with any other required documents, with the secretary of state in the foreign state. Many states require that the application be made on a form prescribed by their offices. It is important to consult the secretary of state of the foreign state and the foreign state's statutes or code to be sure that all application requirements have been complied with. Most states have adopted a version of 15.03 of the MBCA, which sets forth the requirements for the application for certificate of authority:

§ 15.03. Application for Certificate of Authority

(a) A foreign corporation may apply for a certificate of authority to transact business in this state by delivering an application to the secretary of state for filing. The application must set forth:

(1) the name of the foreign corporation or, if its name is unavailable for use in this state, a corporate name that satisfies the requirements of section 15.06;

(2) the name of the state or country under whose law it is incorporated;

(3) its date of incorporation and period of duration;

(4) the street address of its principal office;

(5) the address of its registered office in this state and the name of its registered agent at that office; and

(6) the name and usual business addresses of its current directors and officers.

(b) The foreign corporation shall deliver with the completed application a certificate of existence (or a document of similar import) duly authenticated by the secretary of state or other official having custody of corporate records in the state or country under whose law it is incorporated.

Exhibit 13-1 is a sample of an application for certificate of authority form that may be used in states following the MBCA.

In many states, the application must be accompanied by a certificate of existence or **certificate of good standing** from the corporation's state of domicile and a filing fee. Some states require that the application be recorded at the county level in the foreign state, and some states require publication of the application or a notice of the application in a legal newspaper in the county where the registered office is located within the foreign state.

A thorough review of the pertinent state statutes, as well as any information available from the secretary of state, must be made to ensure that all application procedures are properly followed.

CERTIFICATE OF GOOD STANDING
Sometimes referred to as a "certificate of existence." Certificate issued by the secretary of state or other appropriate state authority proving the incorporation and good standing of the corporation in that state.

FOREIGN NAME REQUIREMENTS

Each state has its own requirements that must be met with respect to the names of foreign corporations. These name requirements can be found in the state statutes, or they may be obtained by contacting the secretary of state of the foreign state. In general, most states require that the corporate name be available and that the corporate name meet the same requirements set for the names of domestic corporations in that state.

EXHIBIT 13-1 SAMPLE APPLICATION FOR CERTIFICATE OF AUTHORITY

APPLICATION FOR CERTIFICATE OF AUTHORITY OF

_____

The undersigned corporation hereby makes application for a Certificate of Authority to Transact Business in the State of _____, pursuant to the provisions of § ___ of the _____ Business Corporation Act.

1. The name of the corporation is _____.

2. The name that the corporation desires to use in your state, if its name is unavailable for use in this state, is _____.

3. This corporation is incorporated under the laws of the state of _____, and is currently in good standing, as evidenced by the attached Certificate of Good Standing.

4. The corporation was incorporated on ___, ___, and its period of duration is _____.

5. The street address of the corporation's principal office is _____.

6. The address of the corporation's registered office in this state and the name of its registered agent at that office are _____.

7. The names and usual business addresses of the corporation's current directors and officers are as follows:

Name	Title	Address
_____	_____	_____
_____	_____	_____
_____	_____	_____
_____	_____	_____

Dated this _____ day of _____, _____.

By _____

Its _____

© Cengage Learning 2013

Mandatory Inclusions

Corporate names must clearly indicate that the corporation is a corporate entity, not an individual or partnership. State statutes typically require that the names of foreign corporations include one of the following words or abbreviations:

Corporation	Corp.
Limited	Ltd.
Incorporated	Inc.
Company	Co.

If the name of the corporation does not include a word or abbreviation that is required by the foreign state's statutes, the secretary of state will usually allow the corporation to add one of the required words or abbreviations to its name for use in the foreign state to comply with this requirement.

Name Availability

Each state requires that the name of the foreign corporation be available for use in the foreign state. For example, if AB Johnson Corporation, a Minnesota corporation, decides to do business in Wisconsin, it must first make sure that its name is not already in use in Wisconsin and that no deceptively similar name is in use. If there is already a Wisconsin corporation by the name of AB Johnson Corporation, or even AB Johnson Company, there is a conflict.

Several different means are prescribed by law to get around this problem. Many states allow the addition of a distinguishing word or words to the name of the foreign corporation for use in the foreign state. Following the preceding example, AB Johnson Corporation, the Minnesota corporation, might be able to qualify to do business in Wisconsin under the name of "AB Johnson of Minnesota, Inc." or a similar name. In such an event, the foreign corporation must use this full name designation for all of its transactions within the foreign state.

Another common solution to the problem of an unavailable name is to obtain permission to use the name from the corporation or entity with a similar name. Most states that allow this option also require that the established corporation or entity change its name to a distinguishable name. This is sometimes possible if the existing corporation with the conflicting name is dormant, or if the holders of the name do not advertise their name to the public.

Finally, many states allow foreign corporations to adopt an available fictitious name for use in their state if the company's name is unavailable. A fictitious name is simply a different name that the foreign corporation uses for all its business transactions within the foreign state. Often, it is a name similar to its own name, but distinguishable from the conflicting name of the established corporation or entity.

The state's statutes or code should be consulted for further details of the options available in each foreign state. Most states provide a service that allows you to check name availability over the telephone or via the Internet. This is a preliminary check and does not guarantee that the name will be available when the application for certificate of authority is filed. (See Appendix A for a secretary of state directory.)

Corporate Name Reservation

Often, the best way to assure that a name will be available before submitting an application for certificate of authority is to reserve the name with the secretary of state of the foreign state. Most state statutes provide that an available name may be reserved for a period of up to 120 days, at a minimal cost. This is usually done by submitting the appropriate name reservation form to the secretary of state with the correct filing fee. Some states will accept a letter requesting the reservation, and a few will reserve an available name over the telephone or via the Internet.

REGISTERED AGENT AND REGISTERED OFFICE

Foreign corporations must appoint and maintain a registered agent and registered office in each state in which they are qualified to do business. The registered office must be an actual physical location in the foreign state where service of process may be made personally on an individual who is authorized to accept service on behalf of the corporation. In most states, the registered agent must be a resident of the foreign state, a domestic corporation, or qualified foreign corporation. The registered agent must be appointed by the foreign corporation to receive service of process on behalf of the corporation. In many states, the statutes provide that if no registered agent is appointed and serving, the secretary of state of the foreign state is authorized to accept service on behalf of the foreign corporation.

Thus, a foreign corporation often has an officer or employee in each foreign state who acts as the registered agent for that state. Other times, a professional registered agent is appointed. There are corporation service companies that will act as a registered agent for foreign corporations in each state. These services can be appointed, for a fee, to provide a registered office address and an agent to accept service for corporations in each state.

IN SUMMATION

- In most states, foreign corporations must file an application for certificate of authority with the secretary of state and obtain a certificate before transacting business in that state.

- In states that follow the Model Business Corporation Act, the following information must be included in the application for certificate of authority:
  - Name of the foreign corporation
  - State or country of domicile
  - Street address of principal office
  - Street address of registered agent within the state
  - Name and business address of current directors and officers

- In several states, the application for certificate of authority must be filed with a certificate of existence or certificate of good standing from the foreign corporation's state of domicile.

- If the name of the corporation is not available or permissible in the foreign state, the corporation may be required to adopt a fictitious name for use in the foreign state.

§ 13.4 AMENDING THE CERTIFICATE OF AUTHORITY

When any significant information in the certificate of authority changes, an application for an amended certificate of authority must be completed and filed. The same filing requirements that cover the application for certificate of authority in each state are generally applied to any amendments. The MBCA provides that whenever the authorized foreign corporation changes its corporate name, the period of its duration, or the state or country of its incorporation, an application for amended certificate of authority must be filed.[3]

Whenever any change in information concerning service of the foreign corporation in the foreign state occurs, such as a change in the registered agent or office in the state, the secretary of state must be notified immediately, either by an amended application for certificate of authority or by other means prescribed by the foreign state's statutes. Again, a thorough review of the state statutes or code of the foreign state must be made to be sure that all requirements are met.

Exhibit 13-2 is a sample form that may be used to amend the certificate of authority for a foreign corporation in the state of New York.

IN SUMMATION

- When significant information contained in the certificate of authority changes, the corporation must file an application to amend the certificate of authority in any foreign state in which it is qualified.

---

§ 13.5 MAINTAINING THE GOOD STANDING OF THE FOREIGN CORPORATION

A corporation may continue to transact business as a foreign corporation as long as it continues to meet the requirements of the foreign state, including timely filing of any required reports and the payment of all required fees and taxes. Most states require annual reports from every domestic and qualified foreign corporation. This is usually done on forms generated by the office of the secretary of state and sent to the principal office or registered office of the corporation, to be completed and returned within a prescribed time period. Many states require that the reports be filed with an annual fee, either a flat fee or a fee based upon the amount of business transacted within the foreign state.

Although these forms may be generated by the secretary of state, it is the responsibility of the corporation to be aware of the annual reporting requirements in each state in which it transacts business and to see that the reports are filed in a timely manner. The secretary of state must be contacted immediately if the corporation does not receive an annual report form to be completed when prescribed by law. Failure to file an annual report may have severe consequences, such as an additional fee or a fine, and even loss of good standing in the state.

Often, any state taxes that are payable by the qualified foreign corporation are included in the fee paid to the secretary of state. In some instances, however, a separate tax report may be required by a separate tax authority within the foreign state. Again, it is the responsibility of the corporation to see that all necessary tax reporting is completed in a timely manner.

New York State Department of State
Division of Corporations, State Records and Uniform Commercial Code
One Commerce Plaza, 99 Washington Avenue
Albany, NY 12231
www.dos.state.ny.us

CERTIFICATE OF AMENDMENT
OF

_____

(Insert Name of Foreign Corporation)

Under Section 1309 of the Business Corporation Law

FIRST: The name of the corporation as it appears on the index of names in the Department of State is: _____.

(Complete this paragraph only if the corporation has agreed to use a fictitious name in New York State.) The fictitious name the corporation has agreed to use in New York State is:

_____.

SECOND: The jurisdiction of incorporation of the corporation is:

_____.

THIRD: The date on which the corporation was authorized to do business in New York State is:

_____.

FOURTH: The Application for Authority is amended as follows:

(If the true name of the foreign corporation has been changed, set forth a statement that the change of name has been effected under the laws of the jurisdiction of incorporation and the date the change was so effected.)

Paragraph _____ of the Application for Authority is amended to read in its entirety as follows:

continues

EXHIBIT 13-2 *(continued)*

Paragraph _____ of the Application for Authority is amended to read in its entirety as follows:

_____

_____   _____
(Signature)   *(Name of Signer)*

                                          _____
                                                 (Title of Signer)

CERTIFICATE OF AMENDMENT
OF

_____
(Insert Name of Foreign Corporation)

Under Section 1309 of the Business Corporation Law

Filer's Name: _____

Address: _____

City, State and Zip Code: _____

NOTE: This form was prepared by the New York State Department of State. It does not contain all optional provisions under the law. You are not required to use this form. You may draft your own form or use forms available at legal stationery stores. The Department of State recommends that all documents be prepared under the guidance of an attorney. The certificate must be submitted with a $60 filing fee.

For Office Use Only

New York Secretary of State

Failure to comply with the annual reporting and fee requirements may constitute grounds for revocation of the corporation's certificate of authority. Pursuant to 15.30 of the MBCA:

§ 15.30. Grounds for Revocation

The secretary of state may commence a proceeding under 15.31 to revoke the certificate of authority of a foreign corporation authorized to transact business in this state if:

(1) the foreign corporation does not deliver its annual report to the secretary of state within 60 days after it is due;

(2) the foreign corporation does not pay within 60 days after they are due any franchise taxes or penalties imposed by this Act or other law;

(3) the foreign corporation is without a registered agent or registered office in this state for 60 days or more;

(4) the foreign corporation does not inform the secretary of state under 15.08 or 15.09 that its registered agent or registered office has changed, that its registered agent has resigned, or that its registered office has been discontinued within 60 days of the change, resignation, or discontinuance;

(5) an incorporator, director, officer, or agent of the foreign corporation signed a document he knew was false in any material respect with intent that the document be delivered to the secretary of state for filing; or

(6) the secretary of state receives a duly authenticated certificate from the secretary of state or other official having custody of corporate records in the state or country under whose law the foreign corporation is incorporated stating that it has been dissolved or disappeared as the result of a merger.

IN SUMMATION

- Most states require annual reports from qualified foreign corporations.
- To maintain good standing in every state where the corporation is qualified as a foreign corporation, all annual reports must be filed in a timely manner with the appropriate filing fees.

§ 13.6 WITHDRAWING FROM DOING BUSINESS AS A FOREIGN CORPORATION

When a corporation dissolves or ceases to do business in any state in which it is qualified, and there are no plans to recommence business in that state in the near future, it is beneficial for the corporation to withdraw from doing business so that the corporation no longer will be subject to annual reporting, registered office, registered agent, and taxation requirements in the foreign state. The procedures for withdrawing from doing business as a foreign corporation are set by state statute and generally involve obtaining a certificate of withdrawal from the secretary of state of the foreign state. Under the MBCA, the qualified foreign corporation may not withdraw from the foreign state until it obtains a certificate of withdrawal from that secretary of state.

The certificate of withdrawal is obtained by filing an application for withdrawal with the secretary of state. MBCA 15.20(b) sets forth the requirements for the application for withdrawal:

> (b) A foreign corporation authorized to transact business in this state may apply for a certificate of withdrawal by delivering an application to the secretary of state for filing. The application must set forth:
>
> (1) the name of the foreign corporation and the name of the state or country under whose law it is incorporated;
>
> (2) that it is not transacting business in this state and that it surrenders its authority to transact business in this state;
>
> (3) that it revokes the authority of its registered agent to accept service on its behalf and appoints the secretary of state as its agent for service of process in any proceeding based on a cause of action arising during the time it was authorized to transact business in this state;
>
> (4) a mailing address to which the secretary of state may mail a copy of any process served on him under subdivision (3); and
>
> (5) a commitment to notify the secretary of state in the future of any change in its mailing address.

Most states provide a form to be completed and filed with the secretary of state. Others prescribe instructions in the state statutes that must be followed. It is important to familiarize yourself with the state statutes on withdrawing from doing business in the state you are concerned with and to be certain all possible requirements, such as county recording and publication, are complied with.

Exhibit 13-3 is a sample of a form that may be used in the state of Indiana to apply for a certificate of withdrawal.

IN SUMMATION

- When a corporation is no longer doing business in a foreign state, it must withdraw from that foreign state by filing an application for certificate of withdrawal.
- The foreign corporation will continue to be subject to the requirements for filing annual reports and paying annual fees in the foreign state until it is properly withdrawn from the foreign state.

EXHIBIT 13-3	APPLICATION FOR CERTIFICATE OF WITHDRAWAL OF A FOREIGN CORPORATION

**APPLICATION FOR CERTIFICATE OF
WITHDRAWAL OF A FOREIGN CORPORATION**
State Form 39077 (R9 / 2-11)
Approved by State Board of Accounts, 1995

**CHARLES P. WHITE
SECRETARY OF STATE
CORPORATIONS DIVISION**
302 W. Washington St., Rm. E018
Indianapolis, IN 46204
Telephone: (317) 232-6576

Indiana Code 23-1-50-2; 23-17-26-11

FILING FEE IS $30.00

INSTRUCTIONS: *Use 8 1/2" x 11" white paper for attachments.*
Present original and one (1) copy to address in upper right corner of this form.
Please TYPE or PRINT.
Please visit our office on the web at www.sos.in.gov.

APPLICATION FOR CERTIFICATE OF WITHDRAWAL OF

Name of corporation

A FOREIGN CORPORATION ADMITTED TO TRANSACT BUSINESS IN THE STATE OF INDIANA

The undersigned officer of _____

(hereinafter referred to as the "Corporation"), which exists pursuant to the provisions of _____
(state or country)

as amended, desiring to effectuate the withdrawal of the Corporation from the State of Indiana, certifies the following facts:

ARTICLE I - NAME

Name of Corporation

State or country in which it is incorporated

ARTICLE II - REPRESENTATION BY THE WITHDRAWING CORPORATION

The Corporation received its Certificate of Authority from the State of Indiana on *(month, day, year)* _____

and is no longer transacting business in Indiana. The Corporation surrenders its authority to transact business in Indiana.

ARTICLE III - SERVICE OF PROCESS

The Corporation revokes the authority of _____,
its Registered Agent to accept service of process on its behalf and appoints the Secretary of State as its agent for service of process in any proceeding based on a cause of action arising during the time it was authorized to transact business in Indiana. A copy of any such process served on the Secretary of State should be mailed to the following address of the corporation:

Address of Corporation *(number and street, city, state, and ZIP code)*

The Corporation shall notify the Secretary of State in the future of any change in its mailing address.

In witness whereof, the undersigned being the _____ of
Title

said Corporation executes this Application for Certificate of Withdrawal and verifies, subject to penalties of perjury, that the

statements contained herein are true this _____ day of _____ , 20_____ .

Signature

Printed name

Indiana Secretary of State's office

EXHIBIT 13-4   REGISTRATION OF CORPORATE NAME BY FOREIGN CORPORATION

REGISTRATION OF FOREIGN CORPORATION NAME
State Form 26234 (R8 / 2-11)
Approved by State Board of Accounts, 2001

CHARLES P. WHITE
SECRETARY OF STATE
CORPORATIONS DIVISION
302 W. Washington Street, Rm. E018
Indianapolis, IN 46204
Telephone: (317) 232-6576

Indiana Code 23-1-18-3 and 23-1-23-3

FILING FEE: $30.00

INSTRUCTIONS:
1. *Use 8 1/2" x 11" white paper for attachments.*
2. *Present original and one (1) copy to the address in the upper right corner of this form.*
3. *Attach Certificate of Existence or document of similar import from state or country of domicile and send to the address in the upper right corner of this form.*
4. *Please TYPE or PRINT.*
5. *Please visit our office on the web at www.sos.in.gov.*

A. Name of Corporation to be registered (*Name of Corporation as it appears on the Articles of Incorporation, or the Amended Articles of Incorporation including additions required by IC 23-1-49-6: Incorporated, Corporation, Company, Limited, Corp., Co., Ltd. and IC 23-1.5 -2-8 if it is a Professional Corporation, the words Professional Corporation or P.C.*)

B. State or Country of Incorporation:

C. Address to which correspondence can be mailed (*number and street, city, state, and ZIP code*):

D. Date of Incorporation (*month, day, year*):

E. A brief description of the nature of the business in which the corporation is engaged:

NOTE: *Registration is for one calendar year, January 1 through December 31. Registration must be renewed each year by filing a renewal application between October 1 and December 31 for the following year.*

In witness whereof, the undersigned being the _____
(Title: Officer or Director)

of said Corporation executes this Registration of Foreign Corporation Name and verifies, subject to the penalties of perjury,

that the statements contained herein are true this _____

day of _____, 20 _____ .

Signature	Printed name

Indiana Secretary of State's Office

§ 13.7 REGISTRATION OF A CORPORATE NAME

Several states provide that a foreign corporation that is not doing business in the state may register its name with the state, in lieu of qualifying to do business. This is very useful to corporations that may commence doing business in a particular state at some time in the future, and would like to reserve their names for an extended period of time. It is also useful to corporations that want to use their names in a state but are not considered to be transacting business in that state under the statutes of that state.

The name to be registered must be available for use in that foreign state and, in most instances, must comply with the requirements for names of foreign corporations that are applying for a certificate of authority. The name of the foreign corporation typically is registered for renewable one-year period.

Exhibit 13-4 is a form to register the name of a foreign corporation in the state of Indiana.

IN SUMMATION

- In most states, foreign corporations may register their names for current or future use in that state.

§ 13.8 THE PARALEGAL'S ROLE

The role of the paralegal in working with foreign corporations must be defined by the paralegal, the responsible attorney, and the client. In general, with the exception of providing the client with legal advice, the paralegal can perform almost all of the services required to qualify a foreign corporation, see that it remains in good standing, or withdraw the foreign corporation from doing business in the foreign state. In some instances, the paralegal will work closely with the corporate secretary to assist in complying with the necessary requirements imposed on foreign corporations. In other instances, the corporate secretary may not be so closely involved, and the paralegal and responsible attorney will see to these matters, while keeping the corporate client informed.

More specifically, in the qualification process, the paralegal can locate the pertinent state statutes and any other available information to help the attorney and client make a decision on the necessity of qualifying as a foreign corporation. From there, the paralegal can obtain the necessary paperwork from the secretary of state and assist the client with the completing and filing of these documents. The paralegal should also check to see that any county recording, publishing, and other detail requirements are complied with. Following is a checklist to assist paralegals with the foreign corporation qualification process.

Foreign Corporation Qualification Checklist

☐ Locate and review copy of pertinent state statutes relating to the necessity of qualifying as a foreign corporation to determine if qualification is required.

☐ Review statutes relevant to qualification requirements in foreign state, including any publication requirements, county recording requirements, or other requirements unique to that foreign state.

☐ Contact secretary of state of foreign state to check name availability in foreign state and request all forms necessary for qualifying as a foreign corporation, including application for corporate name reservation, when appropriate, and application for certificate of authority. Also request up-to-date fee schedule and any printed information and instructions for qualifying as a foreign corporation in that state.

☐ Contact tax authority of foreign state, if separate from secretary of state, to request information on taxation of foreign corporations.

☐ Resolve any name conflicts, if applicable.

☐ Decide on registered agent and registered office and contact corporation service company, if necessary.

☐ When information and forms are received from secretary of state of foreign state, complete necessary forms and send to client for review and signature.

☐ Obtain certificate of good standing or certificate of existence and certified copy of articles or certificate of incorporation, when necessary, from secretary of state of state of domicile.

☐ Submit application for certificate of authority to proper state authority, along with any of the following that may be required:

    ☐ Any additional copies of the certificate of authority that may be required

    ☐ A current certificate of existence or certificate of good standing from the state of domicile

    ☐ A certified copy of the corporation's articles or certificate of incorporation

    ☐ The appropriate filing fee

    ☐ Separate documents appointing registered agent

    ☐ Any other documents required by the state statutes or secretary of state of the foreign state

☐ Make sure any publication requirements are complied with.

☐   Make sure any county recording requirements are complied with.

☐   Recheck statutes of foreign state to make sure that all qualification requirements have been met and to see when first annual report will be due, if applicable.

The paralegal will often perform similar tasks involved in amending the certificate of authority and in withdrawing the foreign corporation from each state when necessary. When corporations are qualified to do business in several different states, paralegals are often involved in researching the requirements for each state and filing the correct documentation to ensure that the corporation's records are up-to-date in each state where it is qualified to do business.

Another important task that the paralegal can perform is to keep track of all necessary annual reporting requirements and see that the annual report of each foreign corporation is completed and filed in a timely manner.

CORPORATE PARALEGAL PROFILE
Rhea Jared

I enjoy the diversity of my position—no two days are ever the same. Sometimes, however, the diversity can also be a real challenge.

NAME Rhea Jared
LOCATION Houston, Texas
TITLE Corporate Paralegal
SPECIALTY General Corporate
EDUCATION Graduate of the Center for Advanced Legal Studies, Houston
EXPERIENCE 9 years

Rhea Jared is a corporate paralegal in the legal department of Weatherford International in Houston, Texas. Weatherford is a Swiss-based, multi-national oilfield service company. It is one of the largest global providers of innovative mechanical solutions, technology, and services for the drilling and production sectors of the oil and gas industry. Weatherford operates in more than 100 countries and employs more than 55,000 people worldwide.

There are 16 in-house attorneys and 6 paralegals in the Houston office where Rhea works and several regional legal teams. She reports to one attorney in her office, but works closely with local counsel and paralegals in several foreign countries.

Rhea's work is with foreign entities and consists of maintaining duplicate minute books and drafting minutes and written consents and documents related to transactions for some of Weatherford's entities. Her past work with domestic corporations included forming, qualifying, withdrawing, merging, and setting up or assumed names in various states throughout the United States. Her work with Weatherford's foreign corporations sometimes includes registering branches in various countries throughout the world and working closely with local counsel.

continues

CORPORATE PARALEGAL PROFILE (continued)
Rhea Jared

Rhea is also a system administrator of a business-entity database holding corporate data for Weatherford's hundreds of subsidiary companies. She is responsible for training users and the subsequent rollout of the database to the regional legal teams. In addition, Rhea is part of a project team implementing an e-billing and matter-management application.

Rhea loves the diversity of her position—no two days are ever alike. However, at times she has found that having so many diverse responsibilities can also present challenges and conflicts.

Rhea's advice to new paralegals?

Be flexible in your career. Be willing to take on responsibilities that may go beyond the typical responsibilities of a paralegal. You may find an additional interest and develop skills that will make you invaluable to a current or future employer.

For more information on careers for corporate paralegals, log in to http://www.cengagebrain.com to access the Course Mate website that accompanies this text; then see the Corporate Careers Section.

ETHICAL CONSIDERATION

The legal profession is, in many respects, self-governing. Attorneys are responsible for establishing and enforcing the ethical guidelines for the members of their profession to follow. For that reason, every attorney has an ethical duty to report serious misconduct that he or she has knowledge of.

Attorneys have an obligation to report misconduct when:

1. The attorney has knowledge of the misconduct;

2. The misconduct calls into question the other attorney's honesty, trustworthiness, or fitness as an attorney; and

3. The attorney's knowledge is not protected as a confidence or secret.

Attorneys must report misconduct to the state bar disciplinary agency or the proper authority as designated in the state code of ethics. If an attorney fails to report misconduct as required, he or she will be in violation of the applicable rules of professional conduct.

Paralegals also have an ethical duty to report the misconduct of attorneys and other paralegals. According to the National Federation of Paralegal

continues

ETHICAL CONSIDERATION
(continued)

Association's Model Code of Ethics and Professional Responsibility, paralegals are required to report the following types of misconduct:

(a) Any action of another legal professional that clearly demonstrates fraud, deceit, dishonesty, or misrepresentation

(b) Dishonest or fraudulent acts by any person pertaining to the handling of the funds, securities, or other assets of a client

If you witness misconduct, especially ongoing misconduct that is detrimental to clients or others, you must determine if you have an obligation to report that misconduct and you must determine whom to report that misconduct to. Here are some first steps you may take:

• Consult your supervising attorney or manager.

• Consult your office policy—there may be a procedure in place for reporting misconduct within the office.

• Report the misconduct to your office ethics committee.

• Seek the advice of your paralegal association ethics committee.

• Report serious misconduct by an attorney to the state bar association disciplinary agency.

• Report serious criminal misconduct to the appropriate law enforcement authority.

    A paralegal who reports misconduct by his or her employer may be protected from employer retaliation under state or federal whistle blower acts. If you are in doubt, seek the advice of an outside attorney who is not connected with the matter in any way.

For more information on ethics for corporate paralegals, including links to the NALA and NFPA codes of ethics, log in to http://www.cengagebrain.com to access the Course Mate website that accompanies this text; then see the Ethics Section.

§ 13.9 RESOURCES

As discussed previously, the requirements for qualifying to do business as a foreign corporation vary among the states. Paralegals will often need to become familiar with the requirements in several different states. The most important resources for paralegals working with foreign corporations are the state statutes and secretaries of state of the foreign states. In certain circumstances, corporation service companies can be very helpful and efficient.

STATE STATUTES

It is important when you are qualifying a corporation in various states to carefully review the business corporation act or similar act for every state in which the corporate client may be considered a foreign corporation. Links to the statutes of each state may be accessed from the Course Mate website.

SECRETARY OF STATE OFFICES

One of the most important online resources for qualifying foreign corporations will be the website of the secretary of state. The secretary of state's website for most states includes detailed instructions on how to qualify to do business in that state, as well as downloadable forms. Appendix A of this text is a directory of secretary of state offices. Links to these office websites may be found on Course Mate.

CORPORATION SERVICE COMPANIES

Corporation service companies can be found throughout the United States. These services can help you complete and file all the necessary paperwork to qualify a foreign corporation. In addition, the services can act as a registered agent for a foreign corporation in any foreign state in the country. Using these services involves paying a third party to perform work on behalf of the corporate client. However, they are usually quick and convenient. Information concerning specific corporation service companies can be found online or by contacting the secretary of state's office to request a list.

Some of the services typically offered by corporate service companies include:

- Preparing and filing incorporation documents
- Preparing and filing organization documents for non-corporate entities
- Preparing and filing foreign corporation qualification documents
- Preparing and filing foreign qualification documents for non-corporate entities
- Filing miscellaneous corporate documents at state and county levels

- Performing Uniform Commercial Code (UCC) filings and searches
- Searching court records
- Performing motor vehicle searches
- Performing various real estate searches and filings

SUMMARY

- The state of the corporation's charter or incorporation is the corporation's state of domicile, regardless of where the corporation transacts its business.
- A corporation is considered a foreign corporation in every state or jurisdiction other than its state of domicile.
- If a corporation is to transact business as a foreign corporation, it must first obtain a certificate of authority from the proper state official of the foreign state.
- Non-corporate entities, such as limited liability companies and limited liability partnerships, are often subject to the same or similar requirements for qualifying to transact business in foreign states.
- State long-arm statutes give the courts of each state personal jurisdiction over corporations that voluntarily go into that state for the purpose of transacting business.
- Although guidance can be found in the statutes of the foreign state, determining exactly when a corporation is considered to be transacting business in a particular state, and is subject to foreign corporation qualification requirements, is usually a judgment call.
- State door-closing statutes provide that corporations that do business in a state without the necessary authority are precluded from maintaining an action in that state.
- Qualified foreign corporations are subject to the statutes of the foreign states in which they are qualified. However, the internal affairs of the corporation are usually governed by the laws of the corporation's state of domicile.
- An application for a certificate of authority is usually filed with the appropriate state authority, along with any other required documents, to qualify a corporation to do business in a foreign state.
- Corporations may register their names in most states, giving them the exclusive right to use that name in the state of registration.
- A corporation that does not comply with state requirements imposed on foreign corporations, such as annual filing and fee payment, may be subject to a proceeding for the revocation of its certificate of authority.

■ REVIEW QUESTIONS

1. Assume that Quality Liquor Company has its main office in your home state, where it transacts the majority of its wholesale liquor business. Recently, Quality Liquor has been taking orders from a neighboring state. It has begun sending its salespeople into the state in an attempt to increase its business. Assuming that the neighboring state follows the Model Business Corporation Act, does Quality Liquor need to qualify as a foreign corporation in that state? What if Quality Liquor were to set up a branch office in the neighboring state?

2. What are "door-closing" statutes as they relate to foreign corporations?

3. Explain why a corporation that is qualified in a foreign state may not be able to transact all of the same business in the foreign state that it is authorized to transact in its state of domicile.

4. Assume that it is your responsibility to qualify your corporate client, Alex Enterprises, in a foreign state that has adopted the Model

Business Corporation Act. Will there be a problem getting a certificate of authority issued under the name "Alex Enterprises"? What are the possible solutions to this problem?

5. What is a fictitious name, and why is it used?

6. What is the purpose of a registered agent in a foreign state?

7. What are the possible consequences of neglecting to file an annual registration statement for a foreign corporation?

8. Why do many states require that the registered office address used in their state not be a post office box?

9. In states that follow the Model Business Corporation Act, what steps must be taken when the corporation amends its articles of incorporation to change its authorized shares of stock?

10. Under what circumstances might it be beneficial for a corporation to register its name in a foreign state?

■ PRACTICAL PROBLEMS

1. Locate the pertinent provisions for foreign corporations in your state's business corporation code and contact the secretary of state's office, if necessary, to answer the following questions:

   a. What is the cite for the statute that requires foreign corporations to qualify to do business in your state?

   b. What guidance is given by your state's statutes to foreign corporations trying to determine whether or not they are "doing business" in your state and need to qualify?

   c. What are the procedures for qualifying to do business as a foreign corporation in your state?

■ EXERCISE IN CRITICAL THINKING

With an increasing amount of business taking place electronically or over the Internet, what special considerations do you see when businesses are contemplating whether or not they should qualify their corporations to transact business in a foreign state?

■ WORKPLACE SCENARIO

Assume that our fictional corporation, Cutting Edge Computer Repair, Inc., has decided to hire an employee to set up a shop in a neighboring state. Bradley Harris and Cynthia Lund have discussed the details with your supervising attorney, Belinda Murphy. Ms. Murphy has advised the clients to qualify Cutting

Edge Computer Repair, Inc., as a foreign corporation in the neighboring state, and she has asked you to prepare the necessary paperwork.

Using the previous information and the information in Appendix B-3, prepare the necessary paperwork to qualify Cutting Edge Computer Repair, Inc., to do business as a foreign corporation in a neighboring state of your choice. Is the name available in the state you have chosen? For purposes of this assignment, you may disregard the merger performed between Cutting Edge Computer Repair, Inc., and Kohler's Computers, Inc., in Chapter 12.

Portfolio Reminder

Save the documents prepared for the Workplace Scenario exercises in each chapter, either in hard copy or electronically, to build a portfolio of documents to be used for job interviews or as sample documents on the job. At this point, your portfolio should include the following:

- Power of attorney
- Application for assumed name
- Application for federal employer identification number

- Application for state employer identification number
- Partnership statement of authority
- Limited partnership certificate
- Limited liability partnership statement of qualification
- Articles of organization
- Subchapter S election by small business corporation, Form 2553
- Articles of incorporation
- Unanimous written consent of shareholders
- Unanimous written consent of the board of directors
- Unanimous written consent of board of directors approving bank loan
- Plan of merger
- Articles of merger
- Application for certificate of authority by a foreign corporation

END NOTES

1. *International Shoe Co. v. Washington*, 326 U.S. 310, 66 S. Ct. 154, 90 L Ed 95 (1945).

2. International Association of Commercial Administrators, 2010 Annual Report of California, http://www.IACA.org.

3. 1984 Revised Model Business Corporation Act as revised through December 2007 § 15.04.

CourseMate

To access additional course materials, including Course Mate, please visit http://www.cengagebrain .com. At the CengageBrain home page, search for the ISBN of your title (from the back cover of your book) using the search box at the top of the page. This will take you to the product page where these resources can be found. The Course Mate resources for this text include Web links, downloadable forms, flash cards, and more.

14

CORPORATE DISSOLUTION

CHAPTER OUTLINE

INTRODUCTION

Corporations are given life by the statutes of their state of domicile, and when the corporation no longer serves a purpose, that life must be terminated in accordance with those statutes. Although articles of incorporation can generally provide for a date or an event that will dissolve the corporation, most corporations exist perpetually and must be dissolved when there is no further reason for their existence. The dissolution of a corporation generally refers to the termination of the legal existence of the corporation. However, as discussed in § 14.3, the corporate existence continues after dissolution for certain purposes.

Corporations are dissolved for many reasons, including bankruptcy or insolvency, the cessation of the business of the corporation, the sale of all or substantially all of the assets of the corporation, or the death of key shareholders, directors, or officers. Extensive planning involving the corporation's management, board of directors, attorneys, and accountants is usually necessary to execute the dissolution, winding up, and liquidation of the corporation in the manner most beneficial to the shareholders of the corporation.

In addition to dissolving in accordance with the statutes of its state of domicile, the corporation is required to surrender its certificate of authority to transact business in any state in which it is qualified to transact business, and to file the appropriate forms and returns with the Internal Revenue Service. Corporate dissolution statutes vary considerably from state to state. Every state requires, at a minimum, that one document be filed with the secretary of state, or other appropriate state authority, notifying the state of the dissolution. Other common statutory provisions include requirements for obtaining and filing good-standing certificates from all state tax authorities, publishing notice in a legal newspaper of the corporation's intent to dissolve, and a second and final filing with the state after all corporate debts have been paid and all assets distributed. There are also significant differences in state statutes for obtaining director and shareholder approval of the corporate dissolution.

This chapter examines the procedures under the Model Business Corporation Act (MBCA) to effect the most common type of dissolution, the **voluntary dissolution**. We look at approval of the voluntary dissolution, the articles and notice of intent to dissolve, winding up and liquidation, and postdissolution claims. Next we investigate administrative dissolution and involuntary dissolution by the state of domicile, the shareholders of the corporation, and the creditors of the corporation. The chapter concludes with a brief discussion of corporate bankruptcy and the role of the paralegal in dissolving a corporation.

VOLUNTARY DISSOLUTION
Dissolution that is approved by the directors and shareholders of the corporation.

According to estimates of the Small Business Administration, 627,200 new employer businesses were started and 595,600 businesses were closed during 2010.

§ 14.1 VOLUNTARY DISSOLUTION

The most common type of corporate dissolution is the voluntary dissolution, which is approved by the directors and shareholders of the corporation. The procedures followed for voluntarily dissolving a corporation depend on the statutes of the state of domicile, but generally involve obtaining the appropriate approval from the directors and shareholders, filing **articles of dissolution** with the proper state authority, and winding up the affairs of the corporation by liquidating its assets, paying the creditors' claims, and distributing the balance to the shareholders.

ARTICLES OF DISSOLUTION
Document filed with the secretary of state or other appropriate state authority to dissolve the corporation.

BOARD OF DIRECTOR AND SHAREHOLDER APPROVAL OF DISSOLUTION

The voluntary dissolution of a corporation must be approved by at least a majority of the corporation's shareholders in most instances. Under certain circumstances, the incorporators or initial board of directors of the corporation may act to dissolve a corporation.

Dissolution Prior to Commencement of Business

If a decision is made to dissolve a corporation before it commences doing business or before it issues stock, a streamlined method for dissolution is generally provided by statute. The dissolution of a corporation that has not issued stock may be approved by the incorporators or the initial board of directors, if one was named in the articles of incorporation. The MBCA provides the method for dissolving a corporation by the incorporators or board of directors in § 14.01:

§ 14.01. Dissolution by Incorporators or Initial Directors

A majority of the incorporators or initial directors of a corporation that has not issued shares or has not commenced business may dissolve the corporation by delivering to the secretary of state for filing articles of dissolution that set forth:

(1) the name of the corporation;

(2) the date of its incorporation;

(3) either (i) that none of the corporation's shares has been issued or (ii) that the corporation has not commenced business;

(4) that no debt of the corporation remains unpaid;

(5) that the net assets of the corporation remaining after winding up have been distributed to the shareholders, if shares were issued; and

(6) that a majority of the incorporators or initial directors authorized the dissolution.

When a corporation has not commenced business, it will typically have no debts to satisfy and no assets to distribute. Unless there are other statutory requirements in the state of domicile, the dissolution process can be satisfied merely by filing the articles of dissolution as prescribed by statute. Articles of dissolution are discussed later in this section.

Dissolution Subsequent to Commencement of Business

After the corporation has commenced business or after shares of the corporation's stock have been issued, its dissolution must be approved by the shareholders of the corporation pursuant to statute. The statutes of the state of domicile may set forth special requirements for obtaining shareholder approval. Those requirements are often similar to the requirements for approving a merger or share exchange (discussed in Chapter 12). Shareholders are generally not granted the right to dissent in the event of a dissolution. However, courts may prohibit dissolutions that are aimed at freezing out the minority shareholders of the corporation if the board of directors and majority shareholders are not acting in good faith. Courts have held that "majority stockholders cannot vote to discontinue the business of the corporation for the purpose of turning it over to another corporation and excluding minority stockholders from participating therein."[1] The MBCA sets forth the requirements for approving a voluntary corporate dissolution in § 14.02:

§ 14.02. Dissolution by Board of Directors and Shareholders

(a) A corporation's board of directors may propose dissolution for submission to the shareholders.

(b) For a proposal to dissolve to be adopted:

    (1) the board of directors must recommend dissolution to the shareholders unless the board of directors determines that because of conflict of interest or other special circumstances it should make no recommendation and communicates the basis for its determination to the shareholders; and

    (2) the shareholders entitled to vote must approve the proposal to dissolve as provided in subsection (e).

(c) The board of directors may condition its submission of the proposal for dissolution on any basis.

(d) The corporation shall notify each shareholder, whether or not entitled to vote, of the proposed shareholders' meeting. The notice must also state that the purpose, or one of the purposes, of the meeting is to consider dissolving the corporation.

(e) Unless the articles of incorporation or the board of directors acting pursuant to subsection (c) require a greater vote, a greater number of shares to be present, or a vote by voting groups, adoption of the proposal to dissolve shall require the approval of the shareholders at a meeting at which a quorum consisting of at least a majority of the votes entitled to be cast exists.

Following are sample resolutions that might be passed by the board of directors and by the shareholders of a corporation, respectively, to approve the dissolution of the corporation.

EXAMPLE: Directors' Resolution to Dissolve Corporation—Submission of Proposition to Stockholders[2]

Whereas, this corporation has entirely ceased to do the business for which it was formed and organized; and

Whereas, all indebtedness has been paid, and it appears to be to the best interests of the stockholders that it should be dissolved, its business terminated, and its remaining assets distributed among the stockholders, or otherwise disposed of according to law;

Now, therefore, it is

RESOLVED, that in the opinion of this board of directors it is advisable to dissolve this corporation as soon as possible, and that a meeting of the stockholders be held on _____ [date], at _____ [time], at the corporation's office at _____ [address], _____ [city], _____ [county],

continues

_____ [state], for the purpose of voting upon the proposition that the corporation be immediately dissolved.

FURTHER RESOLVED, that unless notice of such meeting be waived by all the stockholders, the secretary shall cause notice of such meeting to be both published and served as prescribed by law.

FURTHER RESOLVED, that the president or vice-president and secretary execute a certificate showing the adoption of these resolutions and setting forth the proceedings of the meeting of stockholders, and that they also attest the written consent of the stockholders that the corporation be dissolved, and execute and verify all statements required by law to dissolve the corporation.

FURTHER RESOLVED, that the president or vice president and the secretary cause such certificate and consent to be filed in the office of the [Secretary of State] of _____ [state], together with a duly verified statement of the names and residences of the members of the existing board of directors and of the names and residences of the officers of the corporation, and all certificates and waivers of all notices required by law, and that the officers and board of directors of the corporation take such further action as may be required to effectuate the dissolution of the corporation and wind up its business affairs.

EXAMPLE: Stockholders' Resolution—Election to Dissolve Corporation—Approval and Adoption of Directors' Resolution[3]

Whereas, a special meeting of the stockholders of _____ [name of corporation] was held on _____ [date], at the principal office of the corporation at _____ [address], _____ [city], _____ [county], _____ [state];

Whereas, the secretary of the corporation reported that _____ shares of the outstanding capital stock of the corporation were represented in person or by proxy, being _____% of the total stock outstanding; and

Whereas, the secretary presented the resolution that had been adopted at a meeting of the board of directors held on _____ [date], which resolution provided that the corporation go into liquidation, dispose of its assets, wind up its affairs, be dissolved, and the charter of the corporation be surrendered and cancelled;

Now, therefore, after full consideration of the directors' resolution and on motion duly made and seconded, the stockholders have:

RESOLVED, that _____ [name of corporation], a corporation chartered by _____ [state], be completely liquidated at the earliest practicable date, that all debts of the corporation be paid and the remaining cash together with securities owned, or the cash realized from the sale of the same, be distributed pro rata to its stockholders prior to _____ [date], and that all other assets of the corporation be disposed of as soon as practicable and the proceeds from such disposition, after payment of any remaining liabilities, be distributed pro rata to the stockholders on surrender by the stockholders to the corporation of all the outstanding stock of the corporation.

FURTHER RESOLVED, that the officers of the corporation be authorized and directed to take immediate steps to complete the liquidation of the corporation so that its assets or their proceeds can be distributed to its stockholders prior to _____ [date], and that promptly afterward steps be taken to surrender the charter and franchise of the corporation to _____ [state] and to dissolve the corporation.

FURTHER RESOLVED, that the corporation cease the transaction of all business as of this date, except such as may be necessary or incidental to the complete liquidation of the corporation and the winding up of its affairs, including the payment of any obligations of the corporation now outstanding and any expenses incident to the liquidation.

IN SUMMATION

- Most corporate dissolutions are voluntary dissolutions approved by the board of directors and shareholders of the corporation.

- State statutes include simplified procedures for the incorporators or initial board of directors to dissolve a corporation before it issues any shares or commences business.

§ 14.2 ARTICLES OF DISSOLUTION AND NOTICE OF INTENT TO DISSOLVE

In states following the MBCA, the first and only filing required with the secretary of state, or other appropriate state authority, is the articles of dissolution. (See Exhibit 14-1 for individual state requirements.) After the articles of dissolution are filed, the corporate existence continues, but the corporation is considered to be a "dissolved

EXHIBIT 14-1 STATE CORPORATE DISSOLUTION STATUTES

State	Corporate Dissolution Statute	Document(s) Filed at State Level to Dissolve Corporation
Alabama	Ala. Code § 10A-2-14.01 *et seq.*	Articles of Dissolution[4]
Alaska	Alaska Stat. § 10.06.605 *et seq.*	Certificate of Election to Dissolve and Articles of Dissolution
Arizona	Ariz. Rev. Stat. Ann. § 10-1401 *et seq.*	Articles of Dissolution
Arkansas	Ark. Stat. Ann. § 4-27-1401	Articles of Dissolution
California	Cal. Corp. Code § 1900 *et seq.*	Certificate of Election to Wind Up and Dissolve and Certificate of Dissolution
Colorado	Colo. Bus. Corp. Act § 7-114-101	Articles of Dissolution
Connecticut	Conn. Gen. Stat. § 33-880 *et seq.*	Certificate of Dissolution
Delaware	Del. Code Ann. tit. 8 § 275	Certificate of Dissolution
District of Columbia	D.C. Code Ann. § 29-101.76 *et seq.*	Statement of Intent to Dissolve and Articles of Dissolution[5]
Florida	Fla. Stat. § 607.1401	Articles of Dissolution
Georgia	Ga. Code Ann. § 14-2-1401 *et seq.*	Notice of Intent to Dissolve and Articles of Dissolution[6]
Hawaii	Haw. Rev. Stat. § 414-381 *et seq.*	Articles of Dissolution
Idaho	Idaho Code § 30-1-1401 *et seq.*	Articles of Dissolution
Illinois	805 ILCS § 5/12.05 *et seq.*	Articles of Dissolution
Indiana	Ind. Code § 23-1-45-1 *et seq.*	Articles of Dissolution
Iowa	Iowa Code § 490.1401 *et seq.*	Articles of Dissolution
Kansas	Kan. Stat. Ann. § 17-6803 *et seq.*	Certificate of Dissolution
Kentucky	Ky. Rev. Stat. Ann. § 271B.14-010 *et seq.*	Articles of Dissolution
Louisiana	La. Rev. Stat. Ann. § 12:141	Certificate of Dissolution
Maine	Me. Rev. Stat. Ann. tit. 13-C § 1401 *et seq.*	Articles of Dissolution
Maryland	Md. Corps. & Ass'ns Code Ann. § 3-401 *et seq.*	Articles of Dissolution
Massachusetts	Mass. Gen. Laws Ann. ch. 156D, § 14.01 *et seq.*	Articles of Dissolution
Michigan	Mich. Comp. Laws § 450.1801 *et seq.*	Certificate of Dissolution
Minnesota	Minn. Stat. 302A.701 *et seq.*	Notice of Intent to Dissolve and Articles of Dissolution

continues

EXHIBIT 14-1 *(continued)*

State	Corporate Dissolution Statute	Document(s) Filed at State Level to Dissolve Corporation
Mississippi	Miss. Code Ann. § 79-4-14.01 *et seq.*	Articles of Dissolution
Missouri	Mo. Rev. Stat. § 351.462 *et seq.*	Articles of Dissolution
Montana	Mont. Code Ann. § 35-1-931 *et seq.*	Articles of Dissolution
Nebraska	Neb. Rev. Stat. § 21-20,151 *et seq.*	Articles of Dissolution
Nevada	Nev. Rev. Stat. § 78.580 *et seq.*	Certificate of Dissolution
New Hampshire	N.H. Rev. Stat. Ann. § 293-A:14.01 *et seq.*	Articles of Dissolution
New Jersey	N.J. Rev. Stat. § 14A:12-1 *et seq.*	Certificate of Dissolution
New Mexico	N.M. Stat. Ann. § 53-16-1 *et seq.*	Statement of Intent to Dissolve and Articles of Dissolution
New York	N.Y. Bus. Corp. Law § 1001 *et seq.*	Certificate of Dissolution
North Carolina	N.C. Gen. Stat. § 55-14-01 *et seq.*	Articles of Dissolution
North Dakota	N.D. Cent. Code § 10-19.1-105 *et seq.*	Notice of Intent to Dissolve and Articles of Dissolution
Ohio	Ohio Rev. Code Ann. § 1701.86 *et seq.*	Certificate of Dissolution
Oklahoma	Okla. Stat. tit. 18 § 1096 *et seq.*	Certificate of Dissolution
Oregon	Or. Rev. Stat. § 60.621 *et seq.*	Articles of Dissolution
Pennsylvania	Pa. Cons. Stat. tit. 15 § 1971 *et seq.*	Articles of Dissolution
Rhode Island	R.I. Gen. Laws § 7-1.2-1301 *et seq.*	Articles of Dissolution
South Carolina	S.C. Code Ann. § 33-14-101 *et seq.*	Articles of Dissolution
South Dakota	S.D. Codified Laws Ann. § 47-1A-1401 *et seq.*	Articles of Dissolution
Tennessee	Tenn. Code Ann. § 48-24-101 *et seq.*	Articles of Dissolution
Texas	Tex. Bus. Corp. Act arts. 6.01 *et seq.*	Articles of Dissolution
Utah	Utah Code Ann. § 16-10a-1401 *et seq.*	Articles of Dissolution
Vermont	Vt. Stat. Ann. tit. 11A § 14-01 *et seq.*	Articles of Dissolution
Virginia	Va. Code § 13.1-742 *et seq.*	Articles of Dissolution
Washington	Wash. Rev. Code Ann. § 23B.14.010 *et seq.*	Articles of Dissolution
West Virginia	W. Va. Code § 31D-14-1401 *et seq.*	Articles of Dissolution
Wisconsin	Wis. Stat. § 180.1401 *et seq.*	Articles of Dissolution
Wyoming	Wyo. Stat. § 17-16-1401 *et seq.*	Articles of Dissolution

corporation" and may continue its business only for the purpose of winding up its affairs. The MBCA sets forth the requirements for articles of dissolution in § 14.03:

§ 14.03. Articles of Dissolution

(a) At any time after dissolution is authorized, the corporation may dissolve by delivering to the secretary of state for filing articles of dissolution setting forth:

    (1) the name of the corporation;

    (2) the date dissolution was authorized;

    (3) if dissolution was approved by the shareholders, a statement that the proposal to dissolve was duly approved by the shareholders in the manner required by this Act and by the articles of incorporation.

(b) A corporation is dissolved upon the effective date of its articles of dissolution.

(c) For purposes of this subchapter, "dissolved corporation" means a corporation whose articles of dissolution have become effective and includes a successor entity to which the remaining assets of the corporation are transferred subject to its liabilities for purposes of liquidation.

The articles of dissolution must be submitted with the appropriate filing fee in accordance with state statute. Exhibit 14-2 shows sample articles of dissolution that may be appropriate in states following the MBCA. Exhibit 14-3 is a sample certificate of dissolution form for dissolving New York corporations.

In several jurisdictions that deviate from the MBCA in this regard, a notice of intent to dissolve must be filed with the secretary of state or other appropriate state authority prior to the winding-up process. This document may also be referred to as a statement of intent to dissolve. The articles of dissolution are generally filed in these jurisdictions only after all of the corporation's debts have been paid, including any tax liabilities, and all the corporation's assets have been distributed. Exhibit 14-4 is a sample notice of intent to dissolve. Exhibit 14-5 is a sample statement of intent to dissolve from the state of New Mexico. Note that the form from New Mexico is just one page of a seven-page packet provide by the New Mexico Corporations Bureau to assist with corporate dissolutions. In addition to detailed instructions, that packet also includes an application for tax clearance, a form for obtaining the written consent of the corporation's shareholders, and a form for articles of dissolution.

In addition to requiring that the notice of intent to dissolve be filed with the secretary of state, state statutes often require that the notice be published in a legal newspaper in the county in which the registered office of the corporation is located.

IN SUMMATION

- In most states the only document required for filing with the secretary of state to dissolve a corporation is the articles or certificate of dissolution.

- In some states a notice of intent to dissolve must be filed prior to the articles or certificate of dissolution.
- At a minimum, the articles or certificate of dissolution generally include:
  - The name of the corporation
  - The date the dissolution was authorized
  - A statement concerning the approval of the dissolution by the shareholders
- The articles or certificate of incorporation must be filed with the appropriate filing fee and any other documentation requested by the secretary of state's office.

EXHIBIT 14-2 SAMPLE ARTICLES OF DISSOLUTION

ARTICLES OF DISSOLUTION

OF

_____

Pursuant to _____ [statute], as amended, the undersigned, does hereby state the following as the Articles of Dissolution of said Corporation.

I.

The name of the corporation is _____.

II.

The authorized stock of the corporation consists of 10,000 shares of Class A Common Stock, without par value, 5,000 of which are issued and outstanding. At a meeting of the shareholders held on_____,____, at the registered office of the corporation, a resolution to dissolve the corporation effective _____, ____, was passed by unanimous vote of all 5,000 issued and outstanding shares of the corporation.

Dated: _____, _____.

_____

By _____

_____

Subscribed and Sworn to before me
this_____day of _____, _____.

_____
Notary Public

EXHIBIT 14-3 CERTIFICATE OF DISSOLUTION FORM

New York State Department of State
Division of Corporations, State Records and Uniform Commercial Code
One Commerce Plaza, 99 Washington Avenue Albany, NY 12231
www.dos.state.ny.us

CERTIFICATE OF DISSOLUTION

OF

_____

(Insert Name of Corporation)

Under Section 1003 of the Business Corporation Law

FIRST: The name of the corporation is:

_____

If the name of the corporation has been changed, the name under which it was formed is:

_____

SECOND: The certificate of incorporation was filed with the Department of State on:

_____

THIRD: The name and address of each officer and director of the corporation is:

_____

FOURTH: *(Check the statement that applies)*

☐ The dissolution was authorized at a meeting of shareholders by two-thirds of the votes of all outstanding shares entitled to vote.

☐ The dissolution was authorized at a meeting of shareholders by a majority of the votes of all outstanding shares entitled to vote.

☐ The dissolution was authorized by the unanimous written consent of the holders of all outstanding shares entitled to vote without a meeting.

continues

EXHIBIT 14-3 *(continued)*

FIFTH: The corporation elects to dissolve.

X _____
(Signature)

_____
(Print or Type Name of Signer)

_____
(Print or Type Title of Signer)

CERTIFICATE OF DISSOLUTION
OF

_____
(Insert Name of Corporation)

Under Section 1003 of the Business Corporation Law

Filer's Name: _____

Address: _____

City, State and Zip Code: _____

NOTES:
1. The name of the corporation and its date of incorporation must be exactly as they appear on the records of the Department of State. This information should be verified on the Department of State's web site at www.dos.state.ny.us.
2. This certificate must be signed by an officer, director or duly authorized person.
3. Attach the consent of the NYS Department of Taxation and Finance.
4. Attach the consent of the New York City Department of Finance, if required.
5. The fee for filing this certificate is **$60**, made payable to the Department of State.

For DOS Use Only

New York State, Division of Corporations

§ 14.3 WINDING UP AND LIQUIDATION

After the dissolved corporation has filed its articles or notice of dissolution, it will begin the process of winding up its affairs and **liquidation**. The statutes of virtually every state provide for the complete and orderly winding up of the affairs of dissolved

LIQUIDATION
Winding up the affairs of a business by identifying assets, converting them into cash, and paying off liabilities (liquidate the company).

EXHIBIT 14-4 SAMPLE NOTICE OF INTENT TO DISSOLVE

NOTICE OF INTENT TO DISSOLVE

_____

Pursuant to _____ [statute], the undersigned hereby provides the following notice of intent to dissolve _____ to the Secretary of State.

I.

The name of the corporation is _____.

II.

On _____, ___, a meeting of the shareholders of the corporation was held at the principal office of the corporation. At that meeting a resolution was unanimously adopted by all of the shareholders to begin a voluntary dissolution of the Corporation, effective _____, ____.

III.

The board of directors of the corporation is hereby authorized to take any and all actions necessary to wind up the business of the corporation, and distribute the corporation's assets in accordance with statute.

Dated: _____.

By _____

Its _____

Subscribed and Sworn to before me
this_____day of _____, ____.

_____
Notary Public

© Cengage Learning 2013

corporations and for the protection of the creditors and shareholders of liquidating corporations. In § 14.05, the MBCA lists the following activities that may be appropriate to wind up the affairs of a corporation and liquidate its business:

1. Collection of assets
2. Disposition of properties that will not be distributed in kind to shareholders
3. Discharge, or making provision for discharge, of liabilities of the corporation
4. Distribution of remaining property among shareholders according to their interests
5. Every other act necessary to wind up and liquidate the business and affairs of the corporation

EXHIBIT 14-5 STATEMENT OF INTENT TO DISSOLVE

SUBMIT ORIGINAL AND A COPY
TYPE OR PRINT LEGIBLY

STATEMENT OF INTENT TO DISSOLVE
BY ACT OF THE CORPORATION

Pursuant to Section 53-16-3 of the New Mexico Business Corporation Act, the undersigned corporation submits the following statement of intent to dissolve the corporation by act of the corporation:

ARTICLE ONE: The name of the corporation is (include NMPRC#): _____

_____

ARTICLE TWO: The names and respective addresses of its **officers** are: *(at least one officer must be listed)*

NAME   ADDRESS

PRES: [   ]

V-PRES: [   ]

SEC: [   ]

TREAS: [   ]

ARTICLE THREE: The names and respective addresses of its **directors** are: *(at least one director must be listed)*

NAME   ADDRESS

[   ]

[   ]

[   ]

ARTICLE FOUR: **Attached** is a **copy of the resolution** adopted by the shareholders authorizing the dissolution of the corporation.

ARTICLE FIVE:
The number of shares **issued** at the time of the adoption of the resolution was_____
The number of shares that voted **for** the resolution was _____
The number of shares that voted **against** the resolution was _____

Dated: _____

_____
Name of Corporation

By_____
Signature of Authorized Officer

Form DPR-SDACT
(revised 07/03)

New Mexico Bureau of Corporations

The liquidation of a corporation refers to the winding up of the affairs of the corporation by paying its debts, reducing its assets, and apportioning the profit or loss. Depending on the provisions of the pertinent state statutes, corporations may be liquidated either before or after they are dissolved. Exhibit 14-6 is a sample plan of liquidation that might be adopted by the board of directors and shareholders of a dissolving corporation.

Voluntary dissolutions in jurisdictions that follow the MBCA are typically nonjudicial dissolutions. This means that it is not necessary for the courts to supervise or approve either the liquidation or the dissolution process. Under certain circumstances, the court may supervise the liquidation of a corporation that is voluntarily dissolving, if requested to do so by a shareholder or creditor. The statutes of some jurisdictions may require judicial liquidation or offer incentives to corporations to choose judicial liquidations.

NOTICE TO CREDITORS

As a part of the winding up and liquidation process, state statutes may require that the creditors of the corporation be given notice and that they must be allowed to submit claims to the corporation for payment of any debt owed by the corporation.

EXHIBIT 14-6 SAMPLE PLAN OF LIQUIDATION

PLAN OF LIQUIDATION

WHEREAS, the Board of Directors and Shareholders have approved the dissolution, winding up, and liquidation of the corporation pursuant to _____ [statute]; and

WHEREAS, it is the desire of the directors and shareholders to adopt a plan of liquidation to provide for the liquidation and winding up of the corporation.

NOW, THEREFORE, the following plan is hereby adopted:

1. The officers of the corporation are hereby authorized and directed to wind up the affairs of the corporation, collect its assets, and pay or provide for the payment of the corporation's debts and liabilities.
2. As soon as may be reasonably practicable, the officers of the corporation shall transfer all its remaining property (subject to all its remaining liabilities) to the corporation stockholders, in proportion to their stock ownership, in cancellation of their shares.
3. As soon as may be reasonably practicable, the officers of the corporation shall cause it to be dissolved.

Dated this _____ day of _____, ___.

_____
By: _____
Its: _____

© Cengage Learning 2013

Often notification must be sent to each individual creditor, and notice must be given to the public.

NOTICE TO KNOWN CLAIMANTS

Corporations domiciled in states following the MBCA are given guidelines to follow for notifying creditors of known claims, and for notifying the public in the event there are any unknown claims against the corporation. Section 14.06 of the MBCA provides procedures for disposing of known claims against a dissolved corporation. Corporations following the procedures of this section must notify known creditors in writing of the dissolution at any time after the effective date of the dissolution and allow creditors sufficient time to make claim on the corporation's assets. The notice must include the following:

1. A description of the information that must be included in a claim
2. A mailing address to which the claim may be sent
3. The deadline, which may not be fewer than 120 days from the effective date of the written notice, by which the dissolved corporation must receive the claim
4. A statement that the claim will be barred if not received by the deadline

Exhibit 14-7 shows a sample notice to creditors that might be used in compliance with state statutes modeled after the MBCA.

EXHIBIT 14-7 SAMPLE NOTICE TO CREDITORS

NOTICE TO THE CREDITORS OF

_____

The directors and shareholders of the above corporation have adopted a resolution to voluntarily dissolve the corporation pursuant to _____ [statute].

1. Any claims against the assets of the corporation must be made in writing and include the amount of the claim, the basis of the claim, and the date on which the claim originated.
2. The claim must be sent, by U.S. Mail, to the registered office address of the corporation at_____.
3. The deadline for submitting claims to this corporation is ____, _____ [no sooner than 120 days from the effective date of this notice].
4. Any claims not received by the corporation on or prior to the above deadline will be barred.

Dated this _____day of _____, _____.

_____
Secretary

Claims against corporations that follow this procedure are barred if the claimant received proper notice and did not deliver a claim to the corporation by the stated deadline. Claims are also barred if they are rejected by the corporation and the claimant does not commence a proceeding to enforce the claim within 90 days of the rejection.

Notice to Unknown Claimants

The MBCA and the statutes of several states also provide procedures for disposing of unknown claims—claims against the corporation of which the corporation's principals are unaware at the time of dissolution. Corporations following this procedure publish notice of their dissolution and request that any persons with claims against the corporation present them in accordance with the notice.

When corporations follow this procedure, all claims against the corporation will be barred unless a proceeding to enforce a claim is commenced within five years after the date of publication.

Requirements for notifying claimants of a corporation's dissolution vary among the states. It is very important that the appropriate procedures set forth in state statutes are reviewed and followed carefully.

Distributions to Shareholders

As a part of the winding-up and liquidation process, the assets remaining after the debts of the corporation have been paid must be distributed to the shareholders of the dissolved corporation. The assets may be reduced to cash prior to distribution, or they may be distributed in kind. The shareholders will receive a pro rata portion of the assets of the corporation, based on the number of shares owned by them and the rights of each particular class of shares. Preferred shareholders may have a priority right to the distribution of assets upon the dissolution of a corporation.

Postdissolution Claims

The dissolution of a corporation does not invalidate claims against the corporation that have not been paid or provided for in the liquidation proceedings. Dissolution does not relieve a corporation of liability to creditors, including tort claimants. State statutes vary in their treatment of postdissolution claims. Several states set a specific number of years after a corporation is dissolved in which a claimant must commence an action. As discussed in the previous section, even if a dissolving corporation publishes notice of its dissolution as provided under the MBCA, certain claimants have up to five years to commence an action against the dissolved corporation. In the *Hunter v. Fort Worth Capital Corporation* case that follows, the court found that the defendant corporation was not liable to the petitioner for injuries sustained as the result of a defective product that was manufactured by the defendant, a corporation that had dissolved 11 years prior to the injury.

CASE
Hunter v. Fort Worth Capital Corporation Supreme Court of Texas 620 S.W.2D 547, 20 A.L.R.4TH 399 (TEX. 1981) JULY 15, 1981

The question is whether Theodore Moeller can recover damages against the former shareholders of Hunter-Hayes Elevator Company (Hunter-Hayes) for postdissolution injuries resulting from the negligence of the company. The trial court rendered summary judgment for the shareholders. The court of civil appeals reversed the judgment and remanded the cause for trial. 608 S.W.2d 352. We reverse the judgment of the court of civil appeals and affirm the judgment of the trial court.

In 1960, Hunter-Hayes installed an elevator in a building under construction in Fort Worth, Texas. The company inspected and serviced the elevator until February 1, 1964, when it transferred its assets to Dover Corporation for 25,000 shares of Dover preferred stock. Hunter-Hayes then changed its name to H. H. Hunter Corporation and distributed the shares of Dover stock among its shareholders. On March 11, 1964, H. H. Hunter Corporation (formerly Hunter-Hayes) was issued a certificate of dissolution by the Secretary of State.

Approximately eleven years later, on May 13, 1975, Theodore Moeller was permanently injured when the elevator fell on him. At the time of the accident, Moeller was working in the elevator pit, which is located in the bottom of the elevator shaft, at the direction of his employer, Dover Elevator Company. The elevator fell when a valve in the elevator pit allegedly came apart, allowing its hydraulic system to lose fluid.

Theodore Moeller sued the former shareholders of Hunter-Hayes and others to recover damages for his personal injuries. He alleged causes of action based on negligence and strict liability. The other defendants filed cross-actions against

the shareholders, seeking contribution and indemnity. In his suit against the shareholders, Moeller alleged his injuries were proximately caused by the negligent installation, inspection, and maintenance of the elevator by Hunter-Hayes. He also alleged the shareholders were personally liable to him, to the extent of the assets they received on dissolution, under the "trust fund theory."

In response, the shareholders moved for a summary judgment. They alleged Moeller's action and the cross-actions against them were barred because they were not brought within three years after the company dissolved as required by Article 7.12 of the Texas Business Corporation Act. The trial court granted the motion and severed all causes of action against the shareholders so that it could render a final and appealable judgment. . . . The court of civil appeals reversed the judgment and remanded the cause for trial. The court of civil appeals held that Article 7.12 was vitiated in this cause by the "trust fund theory."

Article 7.12, which is derived from Section 105 of the Model Business Corporation Act, provides:

SURVIVAL OF REMEDY

After Dissolution

A. The dissolution of a corporation . . . shall not take away or impair any remedy available to or against such corporation, its officers, directors, or shareholders, for any right or claim existing, or any liability incurred, prior to such dissolution. . . .

Article 7.12 provides statutory remedies for pre-dissolution claims only and thus is in the nature of a survival statute. Moeller's cause of action did not accrue until he was injured more than

continues

CASE *(continued)*
Hunter v. Fort Worth Capital Corporation Supreme Court of Texas 620 S.W.2D 547, 20 A.L.R.4TH 399 (TEX. 1981) JULY 15, 1981

---

eleven years after the company dissolved. . . . Consequently, Moeller cannot recover against the shareholders for his post-dissolution claim against the corporation, unless his suit is authorized by some other statute or legal theory. . . .

At common law, dissolution terminated the legal existence of a corporation. Once dissolved, the corporation could neither sue nor be sued, and all legal proceedings in which it was a party abated. . . .

To alleviate the harsh effects of the common law on creditors, an equitable doctrine evolved. This doctrine provided that when the assets of a dissolved corporation are distributed among its shareholders, a creditor of the dissolved corporation may pursue the assets on the theory that in equity they are burdened with a lien in his favor . . . . This doctrine is often referred to as the "trust fund theory." Actually, the equitable doctrine has a much broader application. The trust fund theory applies whenever the assets of a dissolved corporation are held by any third party, including corporate officers and directors, so long as the assets are traceable and have not been acquired by a bona fide purchaser. . . .

We agree with defendant that extension of the trust fund theory to cover plaintiff's claim would mean that the corporation could never completely dissolve but would live on indefinitely through its shareholders. We do not believe that this result would be in accordance with the spirit of the laws governing the dissolution of corporations. . . .

We reverse the judgment of the court of civil appeals and affirm the judgment of the trial court.

Case material reprinted from Westlaw, with permission.

Valid claims may be enforced against the undistributed assets of a dissolved corporation, or against a shareholder of the dissolved corporation to the extent of the shareholder's share of the distribution upon the corporation's liquidation. Shareholders may not be held liable in excess of their distribution received upon dissolution of the corporation.

TAX CONSIDERATIONS

The dissolving corporation's attorneys often work closely with its accountants to dissolve the corporation in the manner that is the most tax advantageous to its shareholders. The dissolving corporation must notify the Internal Revenue Service by filing a Corporate Dissolution or Liquidation Form 966 (see Exhibit 14-8), together with a certified copy of the resolution or plan of liquidation, within 30 days of adoption of the liquidation plan. In addition, the distributions of the liquidating corporation must be reported on Forms 1096 and 1099.

EXHIBIT 14-8 FORM 966—CORPORATE DISSOLUTION OR LIQUIDATION

Form 966
(Rev. December 2010)
Department of the Treasury
Internal Revenue Service

Corporate Dissolution or Liquidation
(Required under section 6043(a) of the Internal Revenue Code)

OMB No. 1545-0041

Please type or print

Name of corporation	Employer identification number
Number, street, and room or suite no. (If a P.O. box number, see instructions.)	Check type of return ☐ 1120 ☐ 1120-L ☐ 1120-IC-DISC ☐ 1120S ☐ Other ▶
City or town, state, and ZIP code	

1 Date incorporated	2 Place incorporated	3 Type of liquidation ☐ Complete ☐ Partial	4 Date resolution or plan of complete or partial liquidation was adopted
5 Service Center where corporation filed its immediately preceding tax return	6 Last month, day, and year of immediately preceding tax year	7a Last month, day, and year of final tax year	7b Was corporation's final tax return filed as part of a consolidated income tax return? If "Yes," complete 7c, 7d, and 7e. ☐ Yes ☐ No
7c Name of common parent		7d Employer identification number of common parent	7e Service Center where consolidated return was filed

	Common	Preferred
8 Total number of shares outstanding at time of adoption of plan of liquidation		
9 Date(s) of any amendments to plan of dissolution		
10 Section of the Code under which the corporation is to be dissolved or liquidated		
11 If this form concerns an amendment or supplement to a resolution or plan, enter the date the previous Form 966 was filed		

Attach a certified copy of the resolution or plan and all amendments or supplements not previously filed.

Under penalties of perjury, I declare that I have examined this form, including accompanying schedules and statements, and to the best of my knowledge and belief, it is true, correct, and complete.

▶

Signature of officer	Title	Date

Instructions

Section references are to the Internal Revenue Code unless otherwise noted.

Who Must File

A corporation (or a farmer's cooperative) must file Form 966 if it adopts a resolution or plan to dissolve the corporation or liquidate any of its stock.

Exempt organizations and qualified subchapter S subsidiaries should not file Form 966. Exempt organizations should see the instructions for Form 990, Return of Organization Exempt From Income Tax, or Form 990-PF, Return of Private Foundation or Section 4947(a)(1) Nonexempt Charitable Trust Treated as a Private Foundation. Subchapter S subsidiaries should see Form 8869, Qualified Subchapter S Subsidiary Election.

 Do not file Form 966 for a deemed liquidation (such as a section 338 election or an election to be treated as a disregarded entity under Regulations section 301.7701-3).

When To File

File Form 966 within 30 days after the resolution or plan is adopted to dissolve the corporation or liquidate any of its stock. If the resolution or plan is amended or supplemented after Form 966 is filed, file another Form 966 within 30 days after the amendment or supplement is adopted. The additional form will be sufficient if the date the earlier form was filed is entered on line 11 and a certified copy of the amendment or supplement is attached. Include all information required by Form 966 that was not given in the earlier form.

Where To File

File Form 966 with the Internal Revenue Service Center at the address where the corporation (or cooperative) files its income tax return.

Distribution of Property

A corporation must recognize gain or loss on the distribution of its assets in the complete liquidation of its stock. For purposes of determining gain or loss, the

For Paperwork Reduction Act Notice, see page 2.   Cat. No. 17053B   Form **966** (Rev. 12-2010)

IN SUMMATION

- After the articles of dissolution are filed, or the notice of intent to dissolve in some jurisdictions, the corporation will commence winding up its affairs and liquidating its assets.
- The winding-up process may include the following activities:
  - Collection of assets
  - Disposition of properties to shareholders
  - Discharging the liabilities of the corporation
  - Distribution of the remaining property among the shareholders according to their interest.
- In most instances, corporate dissolutions are nonjudicial and don't require the supervision or approval of a court.
- As part of the winding-up process, creditors of the corporation must be given notice pursuant to state statute.
- Under some circumstances, it may be necessary for the corporation to publish notice of its dissolution to notify unknown creditors.
- After the creditors of the dissolving corporation have been paid, the remaining assets will be distributed to the shareholders on a pro rata basis based on the number of shares owned by them.
- Under some circumstances, dissolution does not relieve a corporation of liability to creditors. Some states set a specific number of years during which claimants, including tort claimants, can come forward to make claims against a dissolved corporation.
- The dissolving corporation must notify the Internal Revenue Service by filing a Form 966 together with a copy of its plan of liquidation within 30 days of adoption of the liquidation plan.
- Distributions of the liquidating corporation must be reported on IRS Forms 1096 and 1099.

§ 14.4 REVOCATION OF DISSOLUTION

Because the dissolution of a corporation is such a final step, the statutes of most states provide for the revocation of dissolution proceedings. The revocation of dissolution typically must be approved by the directors and shareholders of a corporation in the same manner in which the dissolution was approved. The MBCA provides that a corporation may revoke its dissolution within 120 days after its effective date.[7]

Articles of revocation of dissolution, or some other similar document, typically must be filed with the secretary of state to revoke the dissolution of a corporation.

Section 14.04(c) of the MBCA sets forth the requirements for the articles of revocation of dissolution:

> (c) After the revocation of dissolution is authorized, the corporation may revoke the dissolution by delivering to the secretary of state for filing articles of revocation of dissolution, together with a copy of its articles of dissolution, that set forth:
> (1) the name of the corporation;
> (2) the effective date of the dissolution that was revoked;
> (3) the date that the revocation of dissolution was authorized;
> (4) if the corporation's board of directors (or incorporators) revoked the dissolution, a statement to that effect;
> (5) if the corporation's board of directors revoked a dissolution authorized by the shareholders, a statement that revocation was permitted by action by the board of directors alone pursuant to that authorization; and
> (6) if shareholder action was required to revoke the dissolution, the information required by section 14.03(a)(3).

The MBCA further provides that the revocation of dissolution is effective upon the effective date of the articles of revocation of dissolution, and that it relates back to the effective date of the dissolution as if the dissolution had never occurred.

SIDEBAR

According to the Small Business Administration, after four years, 17 percent of new employers are closed and successful, 33 percent of new employers are closed and unsuccessful, and 50 percent are surviving.

IN SUMMATION

- The statutes of most states provide for the revocation of a dissolution after it is authorized and before its completion.
- Articles of revocation or some similar document is filed with the secretary of state to revoke the dissolution.

§ 14.5 INVOLUNTARY DISSOLUTION

Whereas most corporate dissolutions are voluntary, under certain circumstances a corporation may be forced into dissolving by the state in which it is domiciled, by shareholders of the corporation, or by unsatisfied creditors of the corporation. State statutes generally require that **involuntary dissolutions** be accomplished through judicial proceedings. However, the statutes of several states that have adopted the provisions of the MBCA in this regard provide for an **administrative dissolution** by the secretary of state or other appropriate state official, without the necessity of a judicial proceeding.

INVOLUNTARY DISSOLUTION
Dissolution that is not approved by the board of directors or shareholders of a corporation, often initiated by creditors of an insolvent corporation.

ADMINISTRATIVE DISSOLUTION
Dissolution of a corporation by the state of the corporation's domicile, usually for failing to pay income taxes or file annual reports.

ADMINISTRATIVE DISSOLUTION

A corporation's life is granted to it by the state, and that life may be taken away by the state. Courts have held that "[c]orporate privileges may be withdrawn by a state if they are abused or misemployed."[8] In an administrative dissolution, the state of the corporation's domicile dissolves the corporation. The corporation forfeits its right to exist, usually by failing to pay income taxes, failing to file annual reports, or failing to provide a registered agent or office in compliance with state statutes.

Although state statutes provide several different grounds for dissolution of a corporation by its state of domicile, the corporation is generally given several opportunities to rectify the situation that creates the grounds for involuntary dissolution. Section 14.20 of the MBCA sets forth the grounds for administrative dissolution in states patterned on the model act:

§ 14.20. Grounds for Administrative Dissolution

The secretary of state may commence a proceeding under section 14.21 to administratively dissolve a corporation if:

    (1) the corporation does not pay within 60 days after they are due any franchise taxes or penalties imposed by this Act or other law;

    (2) the corporation does not deliver its annual report to the secretary of state within 60 days after it is due;

    (3) the corporation is without a registered agent or registered office in this state for 60 days or more;

    (4) the corporation does not notify the secretary of state within 60 days that its registered agent or registered office has been changed, that its registered agent has resigned, or that its registered office has been discontinued; or

    (5) the corporation's period of duration stated in its articles of incorporation expires.

The fact that one or more of the grounds for involuntary dissolution exist does not automatically dissolve the corporation. Specific statutory procedures must be followed for involuntary dissolution of a corporation. Typically, notice must be given to the corporation, and the corporation will have a prescribed time period within which to rectify the offending situation. Under the MBCA, the secretary of state must serve the corporation with written notice and the corporation must be given 60 days after service of the notice to correct the grounds for dissolution to the reasonable satisfaction of the secretary of state. If the grounds for dissolution are not corrected within that 60-day period, the secretary of state may administratively dissolve the corporation by signing and filing a certificate of dissolution. Any corporation that has been administratively dissolved may continue its existence only for the purpose of winding up and liquidating its business and affairs.

Even after the corporation has been administratively dissolved, statutes typically provide a time period within which the corporation may be reinstated. However, once a corporation is dissolved, it may lose the right to use its name in the state, and that name may be taken by another corporation. In order for a corporation to be reinstated, its corporate name must be available, or it must use a different name. Section 14.22(a) of the MBCA provides for the reinstatement of a corporation following an administrative dissolution:

> (a) A corporation administratively dissolved under section 14.21 may apply to the secretary of state for reinstatement within two years after the effective date of dissolution. The application must:
>   (1) recite the name of the corporation and the effective date of the administrative dissolution;
>   (2) state that the ground or grounds for dissolution either did not exist or have been eliminated;
>   (3) state that the corporation's name satisfies the requirements of section 4.01; and
>   (4) contain a certificate from the [taxing authority] reciting that all taxes owed by the corporation have been paid.

If the reinstatement is determined by the secretary of state to be effective, it relates back to the effective date of the administrative dissolution, and the corporation resumes its business as if the administrative dissolution had never occurred.

JUDICIAL DISSOLUTIONS

Judicial dissolutions are supervised by the proper court. Although in some instances the shareholders and directors of a dissolving corporation will request judicial supervision over a voluntary dissolution, judicial dissolutions are usually involuntary. Judicial proceedings for dissolutions are usually initiated by a petition of the state attorney general, by minority shareholders, or by an unsatisfied creditor. After it is determined that grounds for a judicial dissolution exist, the court may enter a decree dissolving the corporation and directing the commencement of the winding up of the corporation's affairs and the liquidation of its assets.

The court in which the judicial proceedings are brought often appoints a receiver to manage the business and affairs of the corporation during the winding-up process. This court-appointed receiver typically has all the rights and powers assigned by the court to sell and dispose of the assets of the corporation and to distribute the remaining assets of the corporation to the shareholders as directed by the court.

Judicial Proceedings by State Authority

State statutes usually provide for involuntary dissolution of corporations by judicial proceedings at the behest of the attorney general or other appropriate state authority. Under the MBCA, the court may dissolve a corporation in a proceeding by the attorney general if it is found that the corporation obtained its articles of incorporation through fraud or the corporation has continued to exceed or abuse the authority conferred upon it by law.[9]

Judicial Proceedings by Shareholders

Although the consensus of a majority of the shareholders is usually required to dissolve a corporation, a corporation may be dissolved by judicial proceedings brought by minority shareholders under certain circumstances. Some of the grounds set forth in state statutes for the judicial dissolution of a corporation by minority shareholders include insolvency of the corporation, corporate mismanagement or deadlock, and oppressive conduct by the controlling shareholders. It has been held that "even if there is no explicit statutory authority for dissolution of a corporation upon the petition of a minority stockholder, such relief is available as a matter of judicial sponsorship."[10] Section 14.30(2) of the MBCA sets forth the grounds for shareholder-initiated judicial dissolution in states following the model act:

The [name or describe court or courts] may dissolve a corporation: . . .

(2) in a proceeding by a shareholder if it is established that:
(i) the directors are deadlocked in the management of the corporate affairs, the shareholders are unable to break the deadlock, and irreparable injury to the corporation is threatened or being suffered, or the business and affairs of the corporation can no longer be conducted to the advantage of the shareholders generally, because of the deadlock;
(ii) the directors or those in control of the corporation have acted, are acting, or will act in a manner that is illegal, oppressive, or fraudulent;
(iii) the shareholders are deadlocked in voting power and have failed, for a period that includes at least two consecutive annual meeting dates, to elect successors to directors whose terms have expired; or
(iv) the corporate assets are being misapplied or wasted.

Judicial Proceedings by Creditor

At times, corporations that are in severe financial trouble may continue to transact business despite having several judgments filed against them. Creditors may be unable to collect on their judgments if the corporation has insufficient liquid assets. For this reason, the statutes of most states provide for the involuntary dissolution of a corporation in a proceeding initiated by the corporation's creditors. The MBCA provides that the court may dissolve a corporation in a proceeding initiated by a creditor if the creditor's claim has been reduced to judgment, the execution on the judgment is returned unsatisfied, and the corporation is insolvent; or if the corporation has admitted in writing that the creditor's claim is due and owing and the corporation is insolvent.[11]

Buyouts and Other Alternatives to Involuntary Dissolutions

The MBCA further provides that, under certain circumstances, when a shareholder has brought a petition for judicial dissolution, for any of the reasons given under § 14.30(2), the corporation or one or more of the other shareholders may elect to purchase all of the shares of the petitioning shareholder for their fair value. Election to purchase the shares of the petitioning shareholders in lieu of corporate dissolution under the MBCA is subject to many restrictions and conditions designed to protect the interests of the petitioning shareholders. The statutes of several states contain provisions similar to those of the MBCA, which recognize the fact that restructuring a corporation or buying out disgruntled shareholders is often a better alternative than the dissolution of a deadlocked corporation or a corporation that is otherwise unable to operate as presently structured.

IN SUMMATION

- Under certain circumstances, a corporation may be forced into an involuntary dissolution by the state in which it is domiciled, by its shareholders, or by unsatisfied creditors.

- An administrative dissolution occurs when the state of a corporation's domicile dissolves the corporation—usually for failure to pay taxes, maintain a registered agent in the state, or file required documentation.

- A corporation may be dissolved by a judicial proceeding, typically in an involuntary dissolution.

- Judicial dissolutions may be initiated by petition of:
  - The state attorney general
  - Minority shareholders
  - Unsatisfied creditors

§ 14.6 CORPORATE DISSOLUTION AND BANKRUPTCIES

Corporations dissolve for numerous reasons. Corporate dissolutions are not necessarily due to failure or bankruptcy of the corporation. Likewise, corporate bankruptcies do not necessarily result in dissolution of the corporation. However, the two often go hand in hand. In 2010, 56,282 businesses filed bankruptcy petitions in the United States.[13] See Exhibit 14-9.

Paralegals who assist with corporate dissolutions may find themselves working with corporations that are involved in the bankruptcy process. For that reason, it is important to have a basic knowledge of corporate bankruptcy procedures in the United States.

Bankruptcy is a procedure provided for under the Federal Bankruptcy Act (11 U.S.C. 101). Federal bankruptcy courts have jurisdiction over all bankruptcy proceedings. Filing a bankruptcy petition suspends the normal relationship between the debtor and the creditor. Bankruptcy allows debtors to eliminate their debts or repay them under the protection of the bankruptcy court. A corporation filing for bankruptcy protection may petition for a liquidation bankruptcy, or it may seek a reorganization.

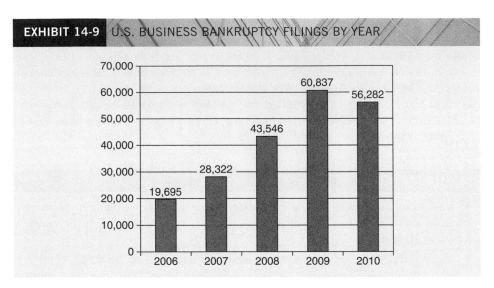

EXHIBIT 14-9   U.S. BUSINESS BANKRUPTCY FILINGS BY YEAR

American Bankruptcy Institute, http://www.abiworld.org

If the directors of a corporation feel that their business is so far in debt that there is no hope of becoming profitable again, they may seek a liquidation bankruptcy under Chapter 7 of the Bankruptcy Code. Under Chapter 7, the corporation ceases all operation and goes completely out of business. A trustee is appointed to liquidate the corporation's assets and use the money to pay off as much of the debt as possible to the corporation's creditors and investors as provided by bankruptcy law.

Chapter 11 of the Bankruptcy Code allows companies that are in serious financial trouble to reorganize their business without liquidating. Chapter 11 provides a rehabilitative procedure for corporations to retain their assets, restructure their debt, and repay obligations over an extended period of time. Under Chapter 11, the debtor company works with committees appointed to represent the interests of creditors and stockholders to create a proposed plan of reorganization to help the company get out of debt. The reorganization plan usually includes provisions for paying off at least a portion of the debt owed by the corporation. The plan must be accepted by creditors and stockholders, and it must be confirmed by the Bankruptcy Court. Corporations may complete their plan of reorganization and emerge from a Chapter 11 bankruptcy to continue their business—sometimes more successfully than ever.

IN SUMMATION

- If a corporation files for bankruptcy under Chapter 7 of the Bankruptcy Code, the corporation ceases all operation and goes out of business, leaving a trustee to liquidate the corporation's assets and pay creditors as much as possible.
- Chapter 11 under the Bankruptcy Code provides financially troubled corporations the opportunity to reorganize their business without liquidating.

§ 14.7 THE PARALEGAL'S ROLE

Corporate dissolutions and liquidations often involve the corporation's attorney, an assisting paralegal, corporate management, and the corporation's accountants. The attorney and paralegal work with the client to see that all statutory formalities are complied with, while the accountant advises the client regarding the income tax aspects of dissolving and liquidating a corporation and the necessary tax filings.

Paralegals assist with all aspects of the dissolution process, including drafting the plans of dissolution and liquidation and the resolutions of the board of directors and shareholders approving the plan. Paralegals may also be responsible for drafting the articles of dissolution or other documents required for filing in the state of domicile, as well as drafting and publishing notices to the creditors of the dissolving corporation. Corporate paralegals often work directly with clients to obtain necessary information regarding the corporation's assets, liabilities, and creditors. The paralegal also may assist the corporate client with the distribution of assets by drafting deeds, assignments, and other instruments of transfer.

CORPORATE PARALEGAL PROFILE
Donna Sorensen

I enjoy being a part of a legal team that relies on my expertise and experience and respects the time and dedication that I have put into my career.

NAME Donna Sorensen
LOCATION Grand Prairie, Texas
TITLE Paralegal
SPECIALTY Corporate and Export Control
EDUCATION University of North Texas, Paralegal Certificate
EXPERIENCE 20+ years

Donna Sorensen is a paralegal with Safran USA, Inc., a wholly owned subsidiary of Safran Group, a leading international high-technology aerospace, defense, and security group. Safran Group has more than 54,000 employees worldwide.

Donna reports to Safran USA's general counsel in Grand Prairie, a city of more than 175,000 located between Dallas and Fort Worth, Texas. She is the only paralegal in the legal department.

Donna is an experienced paralegal and her position carries a lot of responsibility. The Safran Group is a global company with numerous subsidiaries and affiliates throughout the United States. Donna performs corporate governance filings, incorporates and dissolves U.S. entities, and she uses the company's entity-management software to maintain corporate records for more than 50 entities.

Donna manages records throughout the entire life of the corporations. Even though entities are merged out of existence and in essence dissolved, maintaining corporate records for inactive entities is very important. Unwinding a company can be a very time-consuming process, and maintaining corporate records makes this process seamless.

In addition to her subsidiary maintenance responsibilities, Donna works in the very specialized area of export control. She assists Global Trade &

continues

CORPORATE PARALEGAL PROFILE (continued)
Donna Sorensen

Compliance counsel in import and export control and compliance for numerous entities relating to issues that arise under the parent company's Directorate of Defense Trade Controls (DDTC) Registration and the Export Administration Regulations.

Her responsibilities also include drafting and reviewing contracts, preparing board and shareholder consents, preparing state compliance filings, and assisting in governmental filings.

Donna reports that as the only paralegal in the legal department, her typical day starts out by checking e-mails and putting out the largest fires first. She answers phone calls and visitor requests throughout the day relating to corporate-governance and export-control issues. In her "spare time" she organizes and manages legal files and the entity-management software. Donna's job responsibilities also include fielding questions and requests relating to insurance, limited human resource issues, and various other legal issues.

Throughout her career, Donna has worked on some very interesting projects. One of her most memorable involved a case she worked on for a previous law firm employer. It involved one of her firm's corporate finance clients that had entered into loan agreements, issuing many promissory notes that were backed by U.S. government guarantees. The debtors in that case defaulted for a

combined debt of over $100 million. The attorneys in the firm called on Donna's communication skills and appointed her as the liaison between the client and the government. In a long and arduous process, Donna helped to recover $81 million from the government for the firm's client.

Donna has been a member of the North Texas Paralegal Association (NTPA) since 2003, serving in numerous positions, including two terms as president. She is also a member of the National Association of Legal Assistants (NALA), one of the nation's leading professional associations for paralegals.

Donna's advice to new paralegals?

The best advice I can give paralegal students is to network, network, network! Join as many paralegal associations as you can manage and afford and get involved. I have rarely been offered a job when I didn't have an inside associate or friend that put in a good word or offered to present my resume. After over 20 years in the legal field, I still maintain my connections, because you never know when you will have a question or need a service that is out of your area of expertise. Having a network ensures that you always have an answer for any situation.

For more information on careers for corporate paralegals, log in to http://www.cengagebrain.com to access the CourseMate website that accompanies this text; then see the Corporate Careers Section.

ETHICAL CONSIDERATION

Attorneys are licensed to practice law by the highest court in the state or, if the court delegates that authority, by the state bar association. The state
continues

ETHICAL CONSIDERATION
(continued)

courts or bar associations are responsible for overseeing the ethical conduct of attorneys and for disciplining attorneys for misconduct. But who is responsible for licensing and disciplining paralegals?

At this time, the answer may be no one. There is currently no state law requiring the licensing of all paralegals. However, there are other means by which paralegals may be regulated.

In several states, a definition of the term "paralegal" has been adopted by the state legislature. Anyone who works within that state and refers to himself or herself as a paralegal must meet with the requirements of that definition. The state definitions of paralegal are not uniform, but there are some similarities. Several definitions are similar to the American Bar Association's definition, which follows:

A legal assistant or paralegal is a person qualified by education, training or work experience who is employed or retained by a lawyer, law office, corporation, governmental agency or other entity who performs specifically delegated substantive legal work for which a lawyer is responsible.

Some states regulate certain types of paralegals who offer their services directly to the public, without attorney supervision. California, for example, regulates paralegals who work as legal document assistants, providing self-help services to the public, without direct supervision of attorneys. Legal document assistants are subject to registration requirements under state statutes.

Over the years, there have been several proposals for paralegal regulation by various groups. The NFPA endorses a two-tiered regulatory scheme with licensing and specialty licensing at the state level. The NFPA would like to see its Paralegal Advanced Competency Exam (PACE) used as one means for states to measure competency as part of a regulatory scheme. The NALA would prefer to see its Certified Legal Assistant (CLA) exam used for voluntary certification. The NALA is against mandatory licensing or regulation of paralegals.

As a paralegal, it will be important for you to be aware of any regulation that may apply to you in the state in which you work, and to be aware of any new laws that may be passed that will result in some form of paralegal regulation in your state.

For more information on ethics for corporate paralegals, including links to the NALA and NFPA codes of ethics, log in to http://www.cengagebrain.com to access the CourseMate website that accompanies this text; then see the Ethics Section.

Following is a checklist of tasks that are typically undertaken in connection with a corporate dissolution:

- A plan of dissolution is agreed upon. This will usually take some planning involving the attorney, the corporate client, and the corporation's accountants.
- A board of director resolution is prepared approving the dissolution and recommending the dissolution to the shareholders. This may be in the form of a unanimous writing, or the directors may hold an actual meeting.
- Notice of shareholders' meeting to approve the dissolution is prepared.
- A shareholder resolution approving the dissolution is prepared and adopted. Again, this may be in the form of a unanimous writing, or the resolution may be passed at a meeting of the shareholders.
- A statement of intent to dissolve is filed in states requiring the filing of such a document.
- Proper notice is given to all known creditors.
- In some cases, notice of the dissolution is published.
- Form 966 is prepared and filed with the IRS.
- The corporation's assets are liquidated and distributed.
- Final tax payments are made on behalf of the corporation.
- Articles of dissolution are filed.

§ 14.8 RESOURCES

The most valuable resources for information regarding corporate dissolutions, and assistance in filing corporate dissolution documents, are the state statutes, forms and form books, the appropriate secretary of state office, and corporation service companies.

STATE STATUTES

When working to dissolve a corporation, the statutes of the corporation's state of domicile must be consulted for specific dissolution and liquidation requirements, and the statutes of each state where the corporation is qualified to do business must be consulted to ensure that the corporation complies with any requirements for withdrawing from that state.

Provisions for corporate dissolutions are typically found in the business corporation act or similar act adopted by the state of domicile. See Exhibit 14-1 of this chapter for a list of state corporation dissolution statutes. Links to the statutes of each state may be accessed from the CourseMate website.

LEGAL FORMS AND FORM BOOKS

Corporate dissolution can be a very document-intensive procedure. Legal form books, such as Am. Jur. Legal Forms 2d, Nichols Cyclopedia of Legal Forms Annotated, Rabkin & Johnson Current Legal Forms, and West's Legal Forms (second edition), can be good sources for forms for the corporate resolutions approving the dissolution, notices of dissolution, statements of intent to dissolve, and articles of dissolution. Some secretary of state offices provide forms and a few even require the use of their forms for certain dissolution purposes. Any forms used for the corporate dissolution process must be tailored to meet the specific circumstances of the dissolving corporation and the specific requirements of the state of dissolution.

SECRETARY OF STATE OFFICES

The websites of most secretary of state's offices include procedures and instructions for dissolving corporations in their states, as well as downloadable forms for articles of dissolution and related documents. Most secretary of state websites also include information and forms for withdrawing foreign corporations. Appendix A of this text is a directory of the secretary of state's offices. Links to the websites of those offices may be found on CourseMate.

CORPORATION SERVICE COMPANIES

When a corporation dissolves, it must withdraw from every state where it is qualified to do business as a foreign corporation. Some states require the filing of a certificate of termination from the corporation's state of domicile. For corporations that are qualified in several states, this can be quite an undertaking. Corporation service companies can assist you with this process. They can provide the necessary forms for each state and take care of filing them for you. For the names of services in your location, you can search online or ask for referrals from attorneys and other paralegals.

LOCAL AND FEDERAL TAX OFFICES

The Internal Revenue Service provides information concerning filing of the required forms by dissolving corporations on its website.

SUMMARY

- Corporations are given their life by state statutes and they must be dissolved according to state statute.
- A dissolving corporation must surrender its certificate of authority in every state in which it is qualified to do business as a foreign corporation.
- A dissolving corporation must file a Form 966, Corporate Dissolution or Liquidation, with the IRS, and it must file a final income tax return.
- Voluntary dissolutions are approved by the directors and shareholders of the corporation.

- In some states the corporation is dissolved by filing articles of dissolution or a certificate of dissolution with the secretary of state.
- In some states the corporation first files a notice (or statement) of intent to dissolve with the secretary of state, and then files articles of dissolution at a later date.
- All state statutes provide procedures for notifying a corporation's creditors of its dissolution.
- After a dissolving corporation has filed either its notice of dissolution (in states that require such a document) or its articles of dissolution with the secretary of state, it begins the process of winding up its affairs and liquidating its assets.
- Shareholders may be liable for valid claims made after the dissolution of a corporation, but only to the extent of the distribution they received when the corporation dissolved.
- Corporations may be dissolved involuntarily by a court action brought by creditors.
- In an administrative dissolution, the corporation is dissolved by its state of domicile, usually for failure to pay taxes or file annual reports.

REVIEW QUESTIONS

1. Suppose that Ann, Bob, and Christie are all incorporators of the ABC Corporation. Don and Elaine are elected directors, and all five are to become shareholders of the new corporation. Before shares of stock are actually issued, the five investors decide to form a limited liability company instead. Bob has taken on responsibility for dissolving the corporation. Who must approve the dissolution? What if shares of stock had been issued?

2. What are the duties of the individual or individuals who are responsible for winding up the affairs of a dissolving corporation?

3. In states following the MBCA, what documentation must be filed with the secretary of state to dissolve the corporation?

4. Does the corporate existence dissolve upon the filing of the articles of dissolution in states following the MBCA? If not, for what purpose(s) is the corporate existence extended?

5. Under the MBCA, what notice of liquidation must be given to the creditors of a corporation?

6. What possible recourse does a minority shareholder have when the corporate management is deadlocked?

7. To what extent may the shareholders of a dissolved corporation be held liable for the debts of the corporation incurred prior to dissolution?

8. Suppose that the ABC Corporation is administratively dissolved on January 1, 2012, for

failure to file annual reports in compliance with the statutes of its state of domicile. On June 30, 2012, the ABC Corporation eliminates the grounds for its dissolution to the satisfaction of the secretary of state and becomes reinstated. Could the shareholders of the ABC Corporation be held personally liable for obligations incurred on behalf of the corporation on March 15, 2012, on the grounds that the corporation did not legally exist?

9. In a state following the MBCA, can a creditor of a dissolved corporation who has received proper notice collect on that claim six months after the notice was received?

10. Name three grounds for administrative dissolution in states following the MBCA.

■ PRACTICAL PROBLEMS

1. Find the pertinent corporate dissolution statute in your state to answer the following questions:

   a. What document(s) must be filed in your state to dissolve a corporation?

   b. What information is required in the document(s) that needs to be filed to dissolve a corporation?

2. What provisions are made in your state for notifying the creditors of a dissolving corporation?

   a. Briefly describe the notice that must be given to known creditors of a dissolving corporation.

   b. If your state provides for publishing a notice of dissolution, how long do claimants have to commence proceedings to collect a claim after notice of a corporation's dissolution has been published?

■ EXERCISE IN CRITICAL THINKING

Postdissolution claims may be allowed against the shareholders of a corporation—sometimes several years after they receive their final distribution from the corporation. Why do you think the courts allow this? What might shareholders of a dissolving corporation do to protect themselves from postdissolution claims?

■ WORKPLACE SCENARIO

Assume that our fictional clients, Bradley Harris and Cynthia Lund, have decided to go their separate ways, and they want to dissolve their corporation. Your supervising attorney has asked you to draft the necessary paperwork for her review.

Using the information in Appendix B-3, prepare the documents required for filing with the appropriate state authority in your state to dissolve Cutting Edge Computer Repair, Inc. Also prepare a cover letter with accompanying filing fee. Again, disregard the merger performed in Chapter 12.

> **Portfolio Reminder:**
> Save the documents prepared for the Workplace Scenario exercises in each chapter, either in hard copy or electronically, to build a portfolio of documents to be used for job interviews or as

XRS JJ1B.14-020

sample documents on the job. At this point, your portfolio should include the following:

- Power of attorney
- Application for assumed name
- Application for federal employer identification number
- Application for state employer identification number
- Partnership statement of authority
- Limited partnership certificate
- Limited liability partnership statement of qualification
- Articles of organization
- Subchapter S election by small business corporation, Form 2553
- Articles of incorporation
- Unanimous written consent of shareholders
- Unanimous written consent of the board of directors
- Unanimous written consent of board of directors approving bank loan
- Plan of merger
- Articles of merger
- Application for certificate of authority by a foreign corporation
- Articles of dissolution

■ END NOTES

1. 19 Am. Jur. 2d Corporations § 2362 (May 2011).

2. 6B Am. Jur. 2d Legal Forms 2d § 74:1623 (May 2011). Reprinted with permission from American Jurisprudence Legal Forms 2d. © 2011.

3. Id. § 74:1640 (May 2011). Reprinted with permission from American Jurisprudence Legal Forms 2d. © 2011 West Group.

4. Articles of dissolution are filed with probate judge.

5. Articles of dissolution are filed with mayor.

6. Notice of intent to dissolve must be published.

7. Model Business Corporation Act Revised through December 2007 (hereinafter MBCA) § 14.04.

8. 19 Am. Jur. 2d Corporations § 2391 (May 2011).

9. MBCA § 14.20(1).

10. 19 Am Jur. 2d Corporations § 2364 (May 2011).

11. MBCA § 14.30(3).

12. Annual Business and Non-Business Filings Per Year, American Bankruptcy Institute, http://www.abiworld.org (accessed July 17, 2011.)

◢ CourseMate

To access additional course materials, including CourseMate, please visit http://www.cengagebrain.com. At the CengageBrain home page, search for the ISBN of your title (from the back cover of your book) using the search box at the top of the page. This will take you to the product page where these resources can be found. The CourseMate resources for this text include Web links, downloadable forms, flash cards, and more.

CHAPTER 15

EMPLOYEE BENEFIT PLANS AND EMPLOYMENT AGREEMENTS

▣ CHAPTER OUTLINE

INTRODUCTION

The owners of a corporation or any type of business organization that hires employees must be concerned with the fair compensation of those employees. In this chapter we will take a look at executive compensation and employee benefits. Our focus then turns to employment agreements, which are often entered into between corporations and their key employees.

§ 15.1 EXECUTIVE COMPENSATION

Executive compensation can be a controversial subject. On the one hand is the argument that executive compensation packages have skyrocketed in recent years to inappropriate levels. On the other hand is the argument that executive compensation is dictated by the market, and shareholders benefit when the best talent is hired. In any regard, executive compensation, which includes both cash and equity-based compensation, is of concern to all corporate stockholders and it may be subject to scrutiny by the Internal Revenue Service (IRS) and the U.S. Securities and Exchange Commission (SEC).

Cash compensation paid to executives includes salaries and bonuses. Bonuses are a form of incentive compensation, usually paid to reward accomplishments and corporate performance. Many corporations have formal bonus plans in place that prescribe formulas for awarding cash bonuses to their executives. In 1993, in an attempt to combat the public perception that many corporate executives in this country were being excessively compensated, Congress passed a bill adding Section 162(m) to the Internal Revenue Code. Section 162(m) of the Internal Revenue Code disallows the deductibility of certain executive compensation that exceeds $1 million per year, unless the compensation in excess of $1 million is part of a performance-based plan that meets certain criteria. Enactment of 162(m) prompted the increased use of **equity compensation** plans to compensate executives. Large, public corporations often have plans in place that allow them to pay their executives approximately $1 million cash per year, plus additional performance-based compensation. Other corporations have opted to pay the penalties for compensating their executives with salaries in excess of $1 million per year—raising the total executive compensation cost to those corporations.

Federal securities laws require public corporations to disclose to shareholders the nature and amount of compensation paid to their top five executives in their proxies and information statements filed with the SEC.

EQUITY COMPENSATION

Stock awards, stock options, and other compensation paid to employees and executives in the form of equity of the corporation.

SIDEBAR

During 2010, the CEOs of the largest companies in the United States received, on average, $11.4 million in total compensation, according to the AFL-CIO analysis of 299 companies in the S&P 500 Index.[1]

STOCK OPTIONS

The right to buy a designated stock, at the holder's option, at a specified time for a specified price. Stock options are often granted to executives and key employees as a form of incentive compensation.

Executive compensation often includes equity compensation in the form of **stock options**. Stock options are a form of incentive compensation that gives the option holder the right to buy shares of stock at a specific price within a specified period of time. As the corporation's stock increases, the executive's options become more valuable. For example, if on January 1, 2012, an executive is awarded an option to purchase 10,000 shares of the corporation's stock for $20 per share between January 1, 2017, and December 31, 2017, the options will be very valuable if the corporation's stock becomes worth $60 per share by 2017.

Also typical of executive compensation packages are **golden parachutes**. The golden parachute refers to an agreement to protect the executive with a severance bonus that may rank into the millions of dollars, payable upon the executive's termination from the corporation under certain circumstances. Criticism that executives are often paid excessive severance bonuses as part of their golden parachutes prompted Congress to pass legislation that disallows deduction for any golden parachute in excess of three times the executive's annual compensation during the last five years of his or her employment.[2] In addition, the executive can be subject to a nondeductible 20 percent excise tax on any excess golden parachute payment.[3] Public corporations may also be subject to executive compensation guidelines established by the NASDAQ or other stock exchanges on which they are listed.

GOLDEN PARACHUTE

An employment contract or termination agreement that gives a top executive a big bonus or other major benefits if the executive loses his or her job (usually due to a change in corporate control).

SIDEBAR

Kerry Killinger, who was fired from Washington Mutual in 2008 shortly before it hosted the largest bank failure in U.S. history, left with a severance payment totaling more than $16 million.[4] Killinger and Washington Mutual later became targets of several lawsuits by shareholders and the Federal Deposit Insurance Corporation (FDIC).

IN SUMMATION

- IRC § 162(m) sets a limit of $1 million of non-performance-based compensation paid to CEOs and certain other executives that public corporations may claim as a deduction on their tax returns.

- Many public corporations make performance-based compensation a significant part of their executive compensation packages—there is no limit set on the deductibility of performance-based income.

- Federal securities laws require public corporations to disclose to shareholders the nature and amount of compensation paid to their top five executives.

- Executive compensation often includes stock options—the option to purchase stock of the corporation at a set price at some future date.

- Executive compensation packages often include golden parachutes—an agreement to provide severance bonuses to executives upon termination or retirement from the corporation under certain circumstances.

§ 15.2 EMPLOYEE BENEFITS AND QUALIFIED PLANS

The salary and bonuses paid to executives and all employees by a corporation accounts for only a portion of their total compensation.

Employers also compensate their employees with a mixture of other benefits, some of which are mandated by law, such as Social Security and workers' compensation, and some of which the employer may elect to offer to compensate its current employees and entice new employees. There is a wide variety of employee benefit plans that employers may elect to adopt, including pension plans and welfare

QUALIFIED PLAN

Pension plan that meets IRS requirements for the payments to be deducted by the employer and initially tax-free to the employee.

EMPLOYEE RETIREMENT INCOME SECURITY ACT OF 1974 (ERISA)

(29 U.S.C. 1000) A federal law that established a program to protect employees' pension plans. The law set up a fund to pay pensions when plans go broke and regulates pension plans as to vesting (when a person's pension rights become permanent), nondiversion of benefits to anyone other than those entitled, nondiscrimination against lower-paid employees, and so on.

SPONSOR

In ERISA terms, an employer who adopts a qualified plan for the exclusive benefit of the sponsor's employees and/or their beneficiaries.

SUMMARY PLAN DESCRIPTION

Document required by ERISA to communicate the contents of a qualified plan to plan participants.

PLAN ADMINISTRATOR

Individual or entity responsible for calculating and processing all contributions to and distributions from a qualified plan, and for all other aspects of plan administration.

PLAN PARTICIPANT

Employees who meet with certain minimum requirements to participate in a qualified plan.

benefit plans. Plans that meet with certain requirements of the Internal Revenue Code (IRC) and qualify for special tax treatment are referred to as qualified plans.

QUALIFIED PLANS

Qualified plans offer tax incentives to employers by allowing a tax deduction for the employers' contributions to the plans. In addition, investment income earned on contributions may be tax-free until it is distributed to plan participants.

Tax benefits to the qualified pension plan participant include deferred income tax payments: No income tax is payable on the contribution to the plan, only on the benefit received from it in the future.

Qualified welfare benefit plans allow the employer a tax deduction for certain health and welfare benefits they offer to their employees. In addition, employees may be allowed to pay for their portion of welfare benefits with pre-tax dollars.

Qualified plans are subject to the restrictions and requirements set forth in the IRC 401–418E, the **Employee Retirement Income Security Act of 1974 (ERISA)**, which is the primary act regulating qualified plans. Several acts passed subsequent to ERISA have amended and updated the rules for pension plans, including the Pension Protection Act of 2006.

Qualified plans are adopted by an employer—typically a corporation—that acts as **sponsor** of the plan. The plan must be a written document that includes certain provisions required by law. Certain important provisions must be summarized and communicated to plan participants through use of a document referred to as a **summary plan description**. Qualified plans are administered and managed by one or more individuals acting as **plan administrators**, who are considered to be fiduciaries of the plan. The plan administrator is responsible for calculating and processing all contributions to and distributions from the plan.

The terms of the qualified plan document determine who may participate in the plan. **Plan participants** are generally all employees of the sponsor who meet certain minimum requirements set forth in the plan in compliance with ERISA. Qualified plans must meet certain minimum participation and minimum coverage standards set forth in the IRC and ERISA, or the plan will lose its qualified status. Minimum participation and minimum coverage rules are established to ensure that the qualified plans do not discriminate in favor of the corporation's owners or its most highly compensated employees. To reap the tax benefits available to employers, qualified plans must be designed to benefit the workers of the corporation—not just the owners and executives.

When employers adopt qualified plans, they want to be assured that the plans will be considered "qualified" and that the tax benefits associated with qualified plans will be available. The employer can attain that assurance by submitting the plan to the IRS to request a favorable **determination letter**, which states that the plan has been reviewed by the IRS and that it complies with the requirements for a qualified plan. The request for favorable determination letter is made by filing a Form 5300 with the IRS, along with a copy of the plan and any other required information as indicated on the form. Exhibit 15-1 is a sample first page of Form 5300.

EXHIBIT 15-1 FORM 5300 APPLICATION FOR DETERMINATION FOR EMPLOYEE BENEFIT PLAN

Form **5300**
(Rev. September 2001)
Department of the Treasury
Internal Revenue Service

**Application for
Determination for Employee Benefit Plan**
(including collectively bargained plans formerly filed on Form 5303)
(Under sections 401(a) and 501(a) of the Internal Revenue Code)

OMB No. 1545-0197

For IRS Use Only

Review the **Procedural Requirements Checklist** on page 5 before submitting this application.

1a Name of plan sponsor (employer if single-employer plan)

1b Employer identification number

Number, street, and room or suite no. (If a P.O. box, see instructions.)

1c Employer's tax year ends—Enter (MM)

City   State   ZIP code

1d Telephone number

2a Person to contact if more information is needed. (See instructions.) (If **Form 2848**, Power of Attorney and Declaration of Representative, or other written designation is attached, check box and do not complete the rest of this line.) ▶ ☐
Name

1e Fax number ( )

Number, street, and room or suite no. (If a P.O. box, see instructions.)

2b Telephone number ( )

City   State   ZIP code

2c Fax number ( )

3a Determination requested for (enter applicable number(s) in the box and fill in required information). (See instructions.)

☐ Enter 1 for Initial Qualification—Date plan signed ▶ ___/___/___

☐ Enter 2 for a request after initial qualification—Is complete plan attached? (See instructions.) ▶ Yes ☐ No ☐
Date amendment signed ▶ ___/___/___ Date amendment effective ▶ ___/___/___

☐ Enter 3 for Affiliated Service Group status (section 414(m))—Date effective ▶ ___/___/___

☐ Enter 4 for Leased Employee status

☐ Enter 5 for Partial termination—Date effective ▶ ___/___/___

☐ Enter 6 for Termination of collectively bargained multiemployer or multiple-employer plan covered by PBGC insurance—Date of Termination ▶ ___/___/___

b Has the plan received a determination letter? Yes ☐ No ☐
Date of letter ▶ ___/___/___
If "Yes" submit a copy of the latest letter and subsequent amendments.
Number of amendments ▶ ___
If "No," submit all prior plan(s) and/or adoption agreement(s). (See instructions.)

c Have interested parties been given the required notification of this application? (See instructions.) Yes ☐ No ☐
d Does the plan have a cash or deferred arrangement (section 401(k))? Yes ☐ No ☐
e Does the plan have matching contributions (section 401(m))? Yes ☐ No ☐
f Does the plan have after-tax employee voluntary contributions (section 401(m))? Yes ☐ No ☐
g Does this plan benefit noncollectively bargained employees or are more than 2% of the employees who are covered under a collective bargaining agreement for professional employees? Yes ☐ No ☐
See Regulations section 1.410(b)-9.
h Does the plan provide for disparity in contributions or benefits that is intended to meet the permitted disparity requirements of section 401(l)? Yes ☐ No ☐

4a Name of plan (Plan name may not exceed 66 characters, including spaces.):

b Enter 3-digit plan number ___/___/___ **d** Enter plan's **original** effective date (MMDDYYYY)
c Enter date plan year ends (MMDD) ___ **e** Enter number of participants (See instructions.)

Under penalties of perjury, I declare that I have examined this application, including accompanying statements and schedules, and to the best of my knowledge and belief, it is true, correct, and complete.

Print Name ▶   Title ▶

Signature ▶   Date ▶

For Paperwork Reduction Act Notice, see separate instructions.   Cat. No. 11740X   Form **5300** (Rev. 9-2001)

Internal Revenue Service, http://www.irs.gov

DETERMINATION LETTER
A letter issued by the IRS in response to an inquiry as to the tax implications of a given situation or transaction.

IN SUMMATION

- Employers may elect to adopt a wide variety of employee benefit plans, including pension plans and welfare benefit plans.
- Qualified plans meet with certain requirements of the Internal Revenue Code and qualify plan sponsors and participants for beneficial tax treatment.
- Tax benefits to the qualified pension plan participants include deferred income tax payments—no income tax is due on the income until benefits are received in the future.
- Qualified welfare benefit plans provide employers with a tax deduction for certain health and welfare benefit plans.
- Qualified plans are subject to the restrictions and requirements of the Employee Retirement Income Security Act of 1974 (ERISA) as that act has been amended and updated by rules adopted for pension plans.
- Summary plan descriptions are used to summarize and communicate important provisions of qualified plans to the plan participants.
- Qualified plans must meet with minimum participation rules and minimum coverage rules set forth in ERISA.
- To ensure that the qualified plan they are adopting will be considered a "qualified plan," plan sponsors may file a Form 5300, Application for Determination for Employee Benefit Plan, with the IRS to receive a letter of determination prior to adoption.

§ 15.3 QUALIFIED PENSION PLANS

ANNUITY
A fixed sum of money, usually paid to a person at fixed times for a fixed time period or for life.

Qualified pension plans are designed to provide retirement income to participants. Benefits may be paid in a lump sum or in the form of an **annuity**. Disbursements from qualified pension plans are typically not made until the participant retires, reaches retirement age, becomes disabled, or terminates employment with the sponsoring employer.

Contributions made to the qualified pension plan are held in a trust where the funds are managed until they are fully distributed.

Qualified pension plans generally fall into one of two broad categories: the defined benefit plan or the defined contribution plan.

CONTRIBUTIONS

QUALIFIED PLAN CONTRIBUTIONS
Contributions made to a qualified plan by the sponsor, participants, or third parties. Limitations on the amount of contributions are set forth in the Internal Revenue Code.

Qualified plan contributions are made to the plan by the plan sponsor, the plan participant, or both. The amount of the contribution is established in accordance with the provisions of the plan and is subject to several different limitations imposed by law, including limitations based on the total amount of the contribution per employee and the total amount of compensation of each employee that may be considered when calculating the contribution. Contributions to qualified pension plans must be made in accordance with special rules that prohibit discrimination in favor of highly compensated employees.

THE TRUST

Contributions made to a qualified plan are generally held in a **qualified plan trust** that is managed by trustees who are appointed by the plan sponsors in the plan document or a supplement thereto. The contributions will be invested by the trustees or others who are designated to manage the trust assets. As long as the pension plan remains "qualified," the trust will pay no income tax on the income of its assets.

QUALIFIED PLAN TRUST
Trust managed by trustees who are appointed by the qualified plan sponsors to manage the assets of the qualified plan.

BENEFITS

In addition to meeting certain requirements concerning the pension plan participation, pension plans must be designed to provide certain minimum benefits to employees. Qualified pension plan benefits must not exceed certain limitations and discriminate in favor of highly compensated employees, and all pension plans must meet certain accrued benefit rules and minimum vesting standards for all employees.

The term **accrued benefits** refers to the amount of benefit each participant has accumulated or has been allocated in his or her name as of a particular point in time. With a few exceptions, a participant's accrued benefits under a qualified pension plan may not be reduced or eliminated by plan amendment.

ACCRUED BENEFIT
The amount of benefit a participant has accumulated or that has been allocated to him or her as of a particular point in time.

Vesting

Qualified plans must provide that participants become **vested** in their benefits in accordance with certain requirements set forth in ERISA 203 and the Pension Protection Act of 2006. Vesting refers to the participant's nonforfeitable right to receive the benefit.

To comply with minimum vesting standards, qualified plans must:

VESTED
Absolute, accrued, complete, not subject to any conditions that could take it away; not contingent on anything.

1. Provide that the employee's right to normal retirement benefit under the plan is nonforfeitable upon the attainment of normal retirement age;
2. Provide that the employee's right to his or her own contributions to the plan is nonforfeitable;
3. Comply with the minimum vesting provisions set forth in the Pension Protection Act.

Rules that went into effect in 2006 require that any employee who has at least three years of service with the employer has a nonforfeitable right to 100 percent of the employee's accrued benefit derived from employer contributions. In the alternative, a plan may provide for a two- to six-year phased vesting period that vests 20 percent for each year of service beginning with the participant's second year of service and ending with 100 percent after six years of service.

Top-Heavy Plans

If a plan primarily favors officers, directors, stockholders, partners, or other key employees, it is considered to be "top-heavy." Top-heavy plans must comply with certain vesting, benefits, and contribution rules for nonkey employees that are prescribed specifically for top-heavy plans.

DISTRIBUTIONS

QUALIFIED PLAN DISTRIBUTIONS

Distributions made to qualified plan participants or their beneficiaries from a qualified retirement plan trust, usually on the retirement, death, or termination of employment of the plan participant.

Distributions are made from the qualified plan trust to the plan participants or their beneficiaries in accordance with the terms and provisions of the plan. **Qualified plan distributions** are usually made at the time of the participant's retirement, death, or termination from the plan sponsor's employment.

DEFINED BENEFIT PLANS

DEFINED BENEFIT PLANS

Retirement plans in which the benefit payable to the participant is definitely determinable from a benefit formula set forth in the plan.

ACTUARY

A person skilled in mathematical calculations to determine insurance risks, premiums, and so on; a statistician.

As the name implies, **defined benefit plans** are those in which the benefit payable to the participant or the participant's beneficiaries is determined by a benefit formula defined in the plan. Contributions to defined benefit plans are based on the amount that will eventually be paid out to the participant, not on the income or profits of the corporation. Benefits are generally calculated by a formula that takes into consideration the employees' years of service and their salaries.

Most defined benefit pension plans provide for the payment of benefits to employees over a period of years, usually for life, after retirement.[5] Pension plan contributions may be made by employers, employees, and third parties. The actual contribution to be made to the plan is typically calculated by an **actuary** or by use of actuarial tables. The basis for contributions to qualified pension plans must be established in the plan, and the contributions must meet the funding requirements of ERISA and the Pension Protection Act, which are designed to ensure that funds in the pension plan trust will be adequate to meet the plan's obligation to pay benefits as defined in the pension plan.

The amount of investment income generated by the pension trust's assets will not affect the benefit payable to the participant of a defined benefit pension plan. The amount of investment income (or loss) may, however, affect the amount of the contribution required each year to maintain adequate assets in the pension trust.

The pension plan's provisions determine when a participant's benefits commence. A qualified pension plan must provide retirement benefits to its participants, but the plan determines when payment of those retirement benefits will commence, within certain limitations set forth by law. Distributions from a qualified pension plan may be either in a lump sum or by distribution of an **annuity policy**.

ANNUITY POLICY

An insurance policy that may be purchased to provide an annuity.

Annuity Plans

ANNUITY PLAN

Type of qualified plan that does not involve a qualified plan trust. Contributions to an annuity plan are used to buy annuity policies directly from an insurance company.

An **annuity plan** is a type of defined benefit pension plan with no trust. When annuity plans are used, contributions to the pension plan are used to purchase retirement annuities directly from an insurance company. Although annuity contracts are not "trusts," annuity contracts held by an insurance company are treated as qualified trusts, and the person holding the contract is treated as the trustee.

DEFINED CONTRIBUTION PLANS

Defined contribution plans establish an individual account for each participant and provide benefits based solely on the amount contributed to the participant's account. They are often designed to allow the plan participants, and beneficiaries of the participants, to share in the profits of the corporation.

Contributions to participants' accounts, which may be made by the employer, the employee, or a third party, are defined by a formula prescribed in the plan, which may be based on any or all of the following: the corporation's profits, the salary of the participant, and/or the contributions made to the plan by the participant. Each participant's account is credited with the participant's share of the contribution pursuant to the terms of the plan. See Exhibit 15-2.

Plan contributions are retained in a qualified plan trust and income earned through investment of the plan assets is credited to each account, generally in the same proportion as plan contributions. The benefit payable to the participant or the participant's beneficiaries is calculated based upon contributions to the participant's account and any income, expenses, gains, losses, and forfeitures attributable to the participant's account.

Contributions made by the employer to the plan will be vested pursuant to a schedule set forth in the plan, which must comply with the minimum vesting standards of ERISA and the Pension Protection Act. Contributions made by employees are 100 percent vested as of the date of the contribution.

Distributions are made from the defined contribution plan pursuant to plan provisions and the provisions of ERISA 206(a).

DEFINED CONTRIBUTION PLAN

Retirement plan that establishes individual accounts for each plan participant and provides benefits based solely on the amount contributed to the participants' accounts.

EXHIBIT 15-2	DEFINED BENEFIT PLANS COMPARED TO DEFINED CONTRIBUTION PLANS
Defined Benefit Plan	**Defined Contribution Plan**
Contributions are calculated based upon a formula to provide a certain benefit at a designated point in time.	Contributions are defined by a formula prescribed by the plan, based upon the corporation's profits, the salary of the participant, and contributions made to the plan by the participant.
Benefits payable to the participant or participant's beneficiaries are defined by a formula within the plan. The amount of the future benefit can be calculated by the terms of the plan.	Benefits are based on the contributions made to the plan on the participant's behalf and the income earned by those contributions.

Profit-Sharing Plans

The **profit-sharing plan** is the most common type of qualified defined contribution plan. The profit-sharing plan is a type of deferred compensation plan whereby contributions are made to the accounts of the individual participants based on the profits of the corporation for the previous fiscal year. Employer contributions are often calculated as a percentage of the corporation's profits. However, the plan may provide that the board of directors has the discretion to set the annual contribution. The employer's contribution is generally credited to the account of each profit-sharing plan participant based on a formula that takes into consideration each participant's income as a fraction of the total income of all participants.

A profit-sharing plan offers the employer the flexibility to reduce or omit contributions to the plan during years of adversity. At the same time, it can increase employee motivation by giving employees an added benefit when the corporation does well.

401(k) Provisions and Plans

IRC 401(k) provides that employees may elect to defer a certain percentage of their compensation each year to provide for their own retirement benefits. Salary deferrals are considered to be employer contributions and are not taxable to employees until distributed. 401(k) provisions are often found within profit-sharing plans that provide for matching contributions by the employer (as permitted by IRC 401[m]) and discretionary profit-sharing contributions (also by the employer). Participants are always 100 percent vested in their plan benefits to the extent that those benefits are attributed to salary deferrals. Plans that contain only 401(k) provisions are sometimes referred to as **401(k) plans**. To receive favorable tax treatment, 401(k) plans must not discriminate in favor of highly compensated individuals with regard either to eligibility to participate in the plan or to the actual deferrals made. To encourage saving for retirement years, under new provisions of the Pension Protection Act, employers may automatically enroll employees in 401(k) plans and set default contribution levels starting at 3 percent of the employee's gross income. Employees who do not wish to participate must opt out of the plan.

Money Purchase Pension Plans

The **money purchase pension plan** is a defined contribution pension plan whereby the employer contributes a fixed amount based on a formula set forth in the plan that is based on the employee's salary. The money purchase pension plan is a defined contribution plan, because the employer's contribution is allocated to individual accounts on behalf of the employees and because the benefit received depends on the amount contributed to each account. However, it also resembles a defined benefit plan, because the employer is obligated to contribute to the plan each year and the amount of the contribution is not discretionary, and because the amount of the contributions to the plan each year is not dependent on any profits made by the corporation.

Benefit payments under a money purchase pension plan generally commence with the employee's retirement, as defined in the plan, or at age 70½.

Target Benefit Plan

Similar to the money purchase pension plan, the **target benefit plan** is a defined contribution plan that has many features in common with the defined benefit plan. Like a defined benefit plan, contributions to the target benefit plan are based on the amount of the fixed retirement benefit for each participant. However, like most defined contribution plans, the actual amount distributed to the participant of a target benefit plan depends on the value of the assets of the participant's account at the time of retirement.

TARGET BENEFIT PLAN
Type of qualified plan that has many characteristics of both a defined benefit plan and a defined contribution plan.

Stock Bonus Plans

The **stock bonus plan** is similar to the profit-sharing plan in design. As with the profit-sharing plan, the employer has the discretion to set the amount of the plan contribution each year. However, unlike the profit-sharing plan, the main investment of the stock bonus plan is in the employer's stock. Contributions to the plan may be in the form of cash or the corporation's stock, and distributions to the retiring or terminating employee are in the form of the corporation's stock. If the stock being distributed is not publicly traded, the plan participant is granted the option of receiving cash instead of shares of stock, at a fair price according to a formula established in the plan. Stock bonus plans allow plan participants to own equity in the corporation without committing the corporation to a large cash outlay each year for plan contributions. However, as seen in recent years, participants in these plans run the risk of receiving no retirement benefits from the plans if the corportion's stock loses its value before the employee retires.

STOCK BONUS PLAN
Type of defined contribution plan, similar to the profit-sharing plan, in which the main investment is in the employer's stock.

Employee Stock Ownership Plans

An **employee stock ownership plan (ESOP)** is designed to give partial ownership of the corporation to the employees of the corporation. ESOPs are generally established by completing the following steps (see Exhibit 15-3):

EMPLOYEE STOCK OWNERSHIP PLAN (ESOP)
Qualified plan designed to give partial ownership of the corporation to the employees.

1. A contribution is made to the employee stock ownership trust (ESOT). This contribution may be either profits from the corporation, or it may be in the form of a loan. Lenders and borrowers involved in loan transactions may enjoy beneficial tax treatment.
2. The money in the ESOT is used to purchase stock of the corporation. This stock may be newly issued shares of the corporation, or it may be the shares of major stockholders of the corporation who wish to sell some of those shares to the company's employees.
3. Stock (or the cash equivalent of the shares of stock held in the name of each employee) is distributed to the employees upon their termination, retirement, or other event specified in the plan.

ESOPs offer many unique advantages to both the employer and the plan participant. Instead of being a drain on the cash reserves of the corporation, the ESOP can actually aid the employer in raising cash. This occurs when a corporate employer establishes an ESOP and then borrows money from a bank or other financial

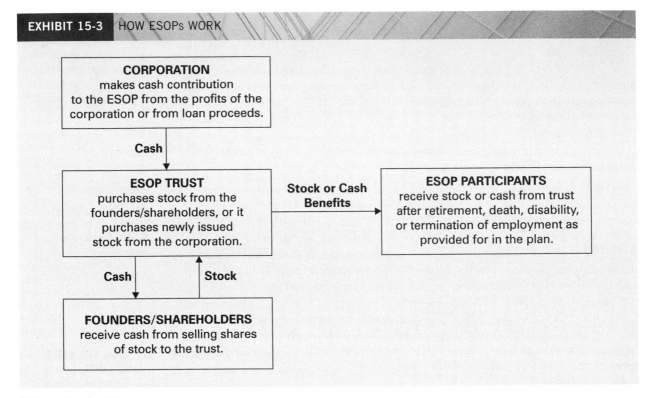

EXHIBIT 15-3 HOW ESOPs WORK

CORPORATION
makes cash contribution
to the ESOP from the profits of the
corporation or from loan proceeds.

Cash

ESOP TRUST
purchases stock from the
founders/shareholders, or it
purchases newly issued
stock from the corporation.

Stock or Cash
Benefits

ESOP PARTICIPANTS
receive stock or cash from trust
after retirement, death, disability,
or termination of employment as
provided for in the plan.

Cash   Stock

FOUNDERS/SHAREHOLDERS
receive cash from selling shares
of stock to the trust.

© Cengage Learning 2013

institution to fund the ESOT. The borrowed cash can then be loaned to the ESOT, and the ESOT in turn invests the cash in newly issued stock of the corporation. The result to the corporation is that it has more issued and outstanding stock and more cash on hand. The result to the plan participants is that they own an equity interest in the corporation that employs them. ESOPs have also been used to thwart hostile takeover attempts by distributing stock to employees of the corporation in an amount sufficient to prevent the aggressor from obtaining a controlling interest. As with the stock bonus plan, plan participants may receive distributions in the form of stock of the corporation, or they may opt to have the corporation purchase their stock for a fair price.

INTEGRATED PLANS

INTEGRATED PLAN

Type of retirement plan that is integrated with the employer's contribution to Social Security on behalf of the participant.

Both defined benefit and defined contribution plans may be integrated with Social Security. **Integrated plans** consider the employer's contribution to Social Security on behalf of a participant or the participant's Social Security benefit when calculating the amount of contribution or the amount of benefit to be received by the participant from the plan.

Qualified plans that are integrated with Social Security benefits may provide benefits favoring highly compensated employees so long as the plan complies with the rules that limit the disparity above and below the integration level and provide for minimum benefits for all employees.[6]

SELF-EMPLOYED PLANS

In general, any employer may adopt a qualified employee benefit plan, including partnerships and self-employed persons, who often adopt qualified **Keogh plans**. Contributions are made to the plan by the employer, the employee, or both. Self-employed plans, or Keogh plans as they are often referred to, are a type of qualified plan available to self-employed individuals. For purposes of the Keogh plan, the self-employed person is considered to be an employer. Self-employed persons and partnerships are usually allowed to adopt the same type of qualified plans available to corporations. However, Keogh plans are subject to special rules regarding coverage, vesting, distribution, limitations on contributions and deductions, and taxation of retirement payouts.

KEOGH PLAN

A tax-free retirement account for persons with self-employment income.

INDIVIDUAL RETIREMENT ACCOUNTS

Individual retirement accounts, or "IRAs" as they are commonly called, are a special type of retirement account that offers tax benefits to self-employed individuals and to employees who are not active participants in a retirement plan maintained by their employer. For 2008, the maximum deductible contribution to an IRA was the lesser of $5,000 or an amount equal to the compensation included in the individual's gross income for a taxable year. That amount is increased to $6,000 for individuals who have attained or are close to age 50. The amount contributed to an IRA is treated as an income tax deduction for federal income tax purposes.

Distributions from an IRA cannot begin before the participant attains the age of 59½, or the tax benefits of the IRA will be lost and the participant will be subject to a tax penalty upon withdrawal of funds from the IRA.

The Roth IRA is a special type of IRA that does not provide tax deductions on contributions, but generally provides for tax-free withdrawals. Income earned on the funds in a Roth IRA is also generally tax-free.

Simplified employee pension plans (SEPs) are an alternative to qualified plans and are often used by small businesses and self-employed individuals. The SEP is an individual retirement account or annuity that must satisfy certain requirements under the IRC. Specifically, the plan must satisfy certain participation requirements; it must not discriminate in favor of key employees; it must permit withdrawals; and contributions must be made pursuant to a written allocation formula. SEPs have the advantage of offering simplified administration and certain tax breaks. Employer contributions to a SEP are deductible to the employer within prescribed limits. An employer may contribute up to 25 percent of an eligible employee's income, providing the contribution does not exceed $46,000.

INDIVIDUAL RETIREMENT ACCOUNT (IRA)

A bank or investment account into which some persons may set aside a certain amount of their earnings each year and have their interest taxed only later when withdrawn.

SIMPLIFIED EMPLOYEE PENSION PLAN (SEP)

An employer's contribution to an employee's IRA (individual retirement account) that meets certain federal requirements. Self-employed persons often use SEPs.

NONQUALIFIED PENSION PLANS

Qualified plans are not the only type of employee benefit plans available. Plan sponsors may determine that their needs would be better met by an unqualified plan—that is, a plan that is not required to comply with all of the rules established for qualified plans. Nonqualified plans often take the form of an agreement between the employer and the employer's executives or otherwise highly compensated individual employees. Nonqualified plans are subject to much less regulation than qualified plans; however, they do not enjoy the same tax benefits as qualified plans.

Plan sponsors who wish to discriminate in favor of highly compensated employees often choose to adopt a nonqualified plan because nonqualified plans are not subject to the nondiscrimination, funding, participation, and vesting requirements of qualified plans.

IN SUMMATION

- Qualified plan contributions are determined by a formula established in the plan and may be made by the plan sponsor, and sometimes the plan participant, to the qualified plan.

- Contributions made to a qualified plan are generally held in a qualified plan trust that invests the funds for the benefit of the plan participants.

- Qualified pension plan benefits must be designed to provide certain minimum benefits to employees and they must not exceed certain limitations and discriminate in favor of highly compensated employees.

- Qualified plans must provide that participants become vested in their benefits in accordance with requirements established by ERISA and the Pension Protection Act.

- If a plan favors officers, directors, and key employees it is considered to be "top heavy."

- Qualified plan distributions are usually made at the time of the plan participant's retirement, death, or termination from employment with the sponsor.

- Defined benefit plans are designed to establish a defined benefit for all participants upon retirement.

- Defined contribution plans establish an individual account for each participant and provide benefits based solely on the amount contributed pursuant to a formula set forth in the plan.

- The profit-sharing plan is a defined contribution plan whereby contributions are made to the accounts of individual plan participants based on the profits of the corporation for the previous fiscal year.

- 401(k) provisions and plans provide that employees may elect to defer a percentage of their compensation each year to provide for their own retirement benefits.

- The money purchase pension plan and target benefit plan are both special types of defined contribution plans.
- The stock bonus plan is similar to a profit-sharing plan except that the employer's main contribution is stock in the corporation.
- An ESOP is a type of qualified plan designed to give partial ownership of the corporation to its employees.
- An integrated plan is a plan that is integrated with the participant's Social Security benefits.
- Self-employed individuals may adopt qualified Keogh or SEP plans.
- Individual retirement accounts (IRAs) offer tax benefits to self-employed individuals and to individuals who are not active participants in an employer's pension plan.
- Agreements between an employer and the employer's executives or otherwise highly compensated employees may be nonqualified plans.

§ 15.4 EMPLOYEE WELFARE BENEFIT PLANS

Employee welfare benefit plans are plans established to provide various benefits to employees, including:

- Medical insurance
- Accident insurance
- Disability insurance
- Life insurance
- Vacation benefits
- Legal services

Welfare benefit plans are subject to most of the same requirements that apply to qualified pension plans under ERISA and the IRC, including coverage requirements and nondiscrimination requirements.

EMPLOYEE WELFARE BENEFIT PLAN

An employee benefit plan that provides participants with welfare benefits such as medical, disability, life insurance, dental, and death benefits. A welfare benefit plan may provide benefits either entirely or partially through insurance coverage.

WELFARE BENEFITS

The most common welfare benefit is health insurance. In addition, welfare plans may offer such benefits as dental insurance, long- and short-term disability benefits, and life insurance.

Section 125 Cafeteria Plans

Cafeteria plans are a special type of welfare benefit plan that offer participants a choice of benefits. This type of plan is designed to cut costs to the employer and offer only the desired benefits to the participant. Benefits offered under cafeteria plans usually include health insurance (possibly more than one option) as well as dependent care reimbursement accounts and medical expense reimbursement accounts.

IN SUMMATION

- Welfare benefit plans provide various employee benefits, including medical insurance, disability and accident insurance, life insurance, vacation benefits, and legal services.
- Welfare benefit plans are subject to many of the same requirements applicable to qualified pension plans under ERISA.
- Section 125 cafeteria plans offer participants a choice of benefits, usually including health insurance.

---

§ 15.5 EMPLOYMENT AGREEMENTS

Most individuals employed in the United States are employees at will. That is, they are hired by an employer for agreed-upon compensation, and they can be dismissed at the employer's discretion, with or without cause. However, many corporations in the United States require at least some of their employees to enter into **employment agreements**. An employment agreement sets forth the rights and obligations of both the employer and employee. Corporations frequently enter into employment agreements with their top executives, but they may also enter into employment agreements with other key employees, especially in the sales and technical areas. Often corporations require entire classes of employees to enter into employment agreements as a condition of employment. Corporations may have simple employment agreements that they require their employees to enter into before commencing work, or the terms may be negotiated with potential key employees prior to hiring. The employment agreement is typically drafted by the attorneys for the employer, often with the assistance of a paralegal.

EMPLOYMENT AGREEMENT

Agreement entered into between an employer and an employee to set forth the rights and obligations of each party with regard to the employee's employment.

SPECIAL CONSIDERATIONS FOR THE EMPLOYER

Some of the benefits to the employer who is a party to an employment agreement are apparent. An employer who enters into an employment agreement with an individual is reasonably assured of hiring and retaining the services of that individual as an employee for a specific period of time. Although the employer cannot compel employees to continue their employment against their will, employees who have entered into employment agreements for a specified time period will probably be reluctant to terminate their employment before the expiration of the agreement's term.

The continued employment of an employee means that the employer will not be forced to search for another individual to fill the position for the duration of the agreement—a task that can be both time consuming and costly. Also, the person being hired will not be working for the competition. This can be a particular benefit to the employer when hiring individuals with unique experience or knowledge in a very competitive business. Although complete certainty can never exist when the human element is involved, employment agreements offer decidedly more certainty than employment at will.

Another benefit to the employer entering into an employment agreement is that the employee's actions, both during the term of employment and after, may be restricted to protect the employer's confidentiality, trade secrets, and work products. Employment agreements may include provisions restricting the future employment and actions of the employee and protecting the trade secrets, patents, and work product of the employer.

The contractual nature of the employment agreement may also result in drawbacks to the employer. For instance, it may be difficult to dismiss an employee who has an employment agreement even if the employee does not work out as well as planned because of lack of performance, personality conflicts, or some other reason. The employer may be considered to be in breach of contract if the employee is terminated before the expiration of the agreement's term. The terms of an employment agreement frequently provide that the employee's employment may be terminated before expiration of the contract only "with cause," and cause for dismissing an employee may be difficult to prove.

Even if the employee performs as expected, the compensation provided for in the employment agreement may result in a hardship to the employer if the employer's business or profits do not meet projections. An employment agreement may require the employer to compensate the employee at a certain level even when the employer's business is performing poorly or losing money.

SPECIAL CONSIDERATIONS FOR THE EMPLOYEE

Although an employment agreement may initially seem to be for the primary benefit of the employer, it also offers several potential benefits to the employee. Most important, it usually assures the employee of continued employment for a definite period of time for definite compensation. This may be a significant benefit when unemployment is high, either in general or in the specific field of the employee's expertise. The employee with an employment agreement that sets a definite term and definite compensation can also usually be assured of receiving that compensation, regardless of the employer's profitability. The employment agreement may also formalize certain benefits, incentives, or rewards that will become a future obligation of the employer to be awarded to the employee upon completion of certain deadlines or the attainment of specific goals.

Disadvantages to the employee include the facts that the employee must typically commit to a position that may not live up to the employee's expectations, and that the employee's obligations may extend beyond the term of the employment. The employee may be required to restrict his or her future employment or actions pursuant to the employment agreement. However, restrictions on future activities must be "reasonable" to be enforceable.

IN SUMMATION

- Most employees in the United States are employees at will—meaning they can be dismissed by the employer with or without cause.

- An employment agreement sets forth the rights and obligations of both the employer and employee.

§ 15.6 DRAFTING THE EMPLOYMENT AGREEMENT

An employment agreement is a binding contract between the employee and the employer, and it must contain all of the elements of a valid contract, including an offer and acceptance, a meeting of minds, and the exchange of consideration. The discussion of employment agreements in this chapter is limited to written employment agreements. This section first discusses the items that must be agreed upon and included in employment agreements. It then examines more closely some of the most important provisions that are commonly included in employment agreements.

A corporation that routinely hires several new employees per year may have a standard employment agreement that each new employee is required to sign before commencing employment. In that event, the attorney for the corporation typically drafts a "master" agreement, and the corporation tailors it as necessary to suit the particular circumstances surrounding the employment of each new employee. A smaller corporation may find it necessary to draft unique employment agreements for its executives and for key personnel.

In any event, certain key elements must be agreed to by both parties and must be included in each employment agreement for the agreement to be enforceable and for it to attain the desired results. The following checklist sets out some of the items that should be agreed to and included in any employment agreement:[7]

- Identification of parties
  - Employer
  - Employee
- Term of agreement
- Place where agreement is to be performed
- Duties of employee
  - Hours of employment
  - Best efforts to be devoted to employment
  - Maintaining outside job or interest
- Working facilities

- Maintaining trade secrets
- Inventions and patents
  — Discovery in course of employment
  — Use of employer's facilities
  — Relation of discovery to employer's business
- Compensation
  — Wages, salary, or commission
  — Overtime work or night differential
  — Pay while unable to work because of illness
  — Effect of termination or noncompletion of employment
- Special compensation plans
  — Deferred compensation
  — Percentage of sales or profits
  — Incentive bonus
  — Profit sharing
  — Stock options
  — Pension and retirement plans
- Expense account
  — Travel
  — Meals
  — Lodging
- Covenant not to compete after leaving employment
  — Length of time
  — Geographical limitations
  — Irreparable harm suffered by employer
  — Hardship not greater than necessary on employee
  — Agreement not injurious to public interest
- Employee benefits
  — Life and disability insurance
  — Medical insurance
  — Dental insurance
  — Workers, compensation
- Termination of employment
- Right of either party to terminate on proper notice
- Discharge of employee for cause

- Remedies for breach
    - — Liquidated damages
- Arbitration of disputes
- Vacations and holidays
- Assignability of contract by employer or employee
- Modification, renewal, or extension of agreement
- Complete agreement in written contract
- Law to govern interpretation of agreement
- Effective date of agreement
- Signatures
- Date(s) of signing

TERM OF THE AGREEMENT

The term of the agreement should be specifically set forth in the agreement. Often a specific time period, such as one year, is set forth, and the agreement is made renewable with the mutual consent of both parties. If the employment agreement does not specify a definite term of employment, the employer may have the discretion to terminate the employee at will. Likewise, the employee may have the option of terminating the agreement at any time.

EXAMPLE: Term of Employment

The term of this agreement shall be a period of _____ years, commencing _____ [date], and terminating _____ [date], subject, however, to prior termination as provided in this agreement. At the expiration date of _____ [date], this agreement shall be considered renewed for regular periods of one year, provided neither party submits a notice of termination.[8]

DESCRIPTION OF DUTIES

The duties and obligations of the employee should be set forth with a certain degree of specificity. Although it would be impossible to set forth every duty and obligation that might possibly be expected of the employee during the term of the employment agreement, the position should be defined well enough to give both the employer and employee a reasonable understanding of the work the employee will be expected to perform and the authority the employee will be granted in accordance with the position. In addition to a description of specific duties, this section of the agreement should include the agreed-upon hours of employment, and a statement that the employee will devote his or her best efforts to the satisfactory performance of the position's duties.

EXAMPLE: Duties of Employee

Employee will serve employer faithfully and to the best of _____ [his or her] ability under the direction of the board of directors of employer. Employee will devote all of _____ [his or her] time, energy, and skill during regular business hours to such employment. Employee shall perform such services and act in such executive capacity as the board of directors of employer shall direct.[9]

EXAMPLE: Best Efforts of Employee

Employee agrees that *[he/she]* will at all times faithfully, industriously, and to the best of *[his/her]* ability, experience, and talents, perform all of the duties that may be required of and from *[him/her]* pursuant to the express and implicit terms of this agreement, to the reasonable satisfaction of employer. Such duties shall be rendered at *[address of employment]*, and at such other place or places as employer shall in good faith require or as the interest, needs, business, or opportunity of employer shall require.[10]

COVENANT NOT TO COMPETE

Covenants not to compete, which restrict the future employment and actions of the employee, are commonly found in employment agreements. The purpose behind these covenants is to prevent the employee from leaving one employer, from which he or she has gained significant experience and knowledge, and taking that experience and knowledge to the employer's competition.

Because covenants not to compete restrict the free actions and future employment of the employee, there are limitations on their enforcement. Under the common law of England, covenants not to compete were considered agreements in restraint of a man's right to exercise his trade or calling, and thus were considered void as against public policy.[11] However, the modern view of the noncompetition clause is that an "anticompetitive covenant supported by consideration and ancillary to a lawful contract is enforceable if reasonable and consistent with public interest."[12]

The test of reasonableness depends on the facts of the case. Generally, an agreement not to compete is considered reasonable if it is restricted to a specific time period and a specific geographical location. For instance, an agreement not to work for the competition for the rest of the employee's life anywhere in the United States would not be enforceable. Although exactly what is considered reasonable will depend on the circumstances of the particular case, the following characteristics are

COVENANTS NOT TO COMPETE

A part of an employee contract, partnership agreement, or agreement to sell a business in which a person promises not to engage in the same business for a certain amount of time after the relationship ends.

often assigned to anticompetition covenants that are considered to be reasonable and enforceable:

1. The covenant is legal in the state in which it is to be executed. (Covenants not to compete may be subject to state statutes that deal specifically with anticompetition covenants.)
2. The covenant is supported by sufficient consideration.
3. The restriction is reasonably necessary to protect some legitimate interest of the employer.
4. The restriction is not contrary to public interests.
5. The covenant applies to only a limited geographical location.
6. The covenant is applicable for only a limited time period.

Another consideration with regard to covenants not to compete is that they are considered unethical, or even illegal in some instances, for certain professionals such as doctors or lawyers. The following example would generally be found to be a reasonable covenant not to compete.

EXAMPLE: Noncompetition with Former Employer

Employee agrees that after termination of employment, for a period of _____ [one year], employee will not engage in the business of _____ [employer's business], within the state of _____, or in any business competitive with employer. For that one-year period after termination, employee will not engage in a competing business as an employee, owner, partner, or agent.

In the *Beckman v. Cox Broadcasting Corporation* case, involving a noncompetition clause in a television weatherman's employment agreement, the agreement was found valid primarily because it was for only a limited time period and a limited geographical location.

CASE
Beckman v. Cox Broadcasting Corporation Supreme Court of Georgia 250 Ga. 127, 296 S.E.2d 566 (1982) October 27, 1982.

From 1962 until June 3, 1982, appellant Beckman was employed by Cox Broadcasting Corporation (Cox) as a meteorologist and "television personality," appearing primarily on Cox's affiliate, WSB-TV. In April 1981, Beckman entered into a five-year contractual agreement with WXIA-TV, a competitor of Cox, to commence working for WXIA as a meteorologist and "television personality" when his contract with Cox expired on July 1, 1982. Cox was made aware of Beckman's plans and in July 1981, Cox filed a petition for declaratory judgment, [Ga.] Code Ann. 110–1101, seeking a determination that the restriction against competition in its employment agreement with Beckman was valid. This restriction provides: "Employee shall not, for a period of one hundred-eighty (180) days after the end of the Term of Employment, allow his/her voice or image to be broadcast 'on air' by any commercial television station whose broadcast transmission tower is located within a radius of thirty-five (35) miles from Company's offices at 1601 West Peachtree Street, N.E., Atlanta, Georgia, unless such broadcast is part of a nationally broadcast program." Following a hearing the trial court dismissed the action finding there was no evidence to conclude either that WXIA-TV would require Beckman to violate the restrictive covenant or that Beckman would violate the covenant. Therefore, the trial court determined, Cox had not presented a justifiable controversy.

On June 16, 1982, Beckman formally demanded to be released from the restrictive covenant in his contract. When Cox refused, Beckman filed this declaratory judgment action to ascertain the validity of the restrictive covenant under Georgia law.

The trial court found that the employment contract with WXIA-TV does not require Beckman to appear "on-air" during the first six months of his employment; that Beckman, under the terms of this agreement, is rendering "substantial duties and services to WXIA-TV" for which he is being compensated; that during the term of Beckman's employment with Cox, WSB-TV spent in excess of a million dollars promoting "Beckman's name, voice and image as an individual television personality and as part of WSB-TV's Action News Team"; that Beckman is one of the most recognized "television personalities" in the Atlanta area; that television viewers select a local newscast, to a certain degree, based on their "appreciation of

the personalities appearing on the newscast"; and that local television personalities "are strongly identified in the minds of television viewers with the stations upon which they appear." The trial court also found that in March 1982, WSB-TV instituted a "transition plan" to reduce the impact Beckman's departure would have on the station's image. As part of this transition plan Beckman was removed from one of the two nightly WSB-TV news programs. Additionally, WSB-TV undertook an extensive promotional campaign, featuring both Beckman and his replacement as members of the "Action News Team." This transition plan contemplated the gradual phasing out of Beckman from the "Action News Team." The station projected that Beckman would then be "off the air" in the Atlanta market for six months, permitting WSB-TV to diminish its association with Beckman in the public's mind and providing the viewing public an opportunity to adjust to Beckman's replacement.

The trial court concluded that to permit Beckman to appear "on air" in the Atlanta area during the first six months of his contract with WXIA-TV would "disrupt the plans and ability of WSB-TV to adjust successfully to the loss of a well-known personality that it has heavily promoted before it must begin competing with that personality in the same marketplace." The trial court also determined that WSB-TV would be injured by allowing a competitor to take advantage of the popularity of a television personality which WSB-TV had expended great sums to promote before WSB-TV had time to compensate for the loss of that personality. The trial court further found that WSB-TV has a legitimate and protectable interest in the image which it projects to the viewing public.

continues

CASE (continued)

Beckman v. Cox Broadcasting Corporation Supreme Court of Georgia 250 Ga. 127, 296 S.E.2d 566 (1982)

While the trial court concluded the damage to WSB-TV would be great if Beckman were permitted to compete against it within the proscribed six months, the court reasoned that Beckman would suffer little harm if the covenant was enforced against him. The trial court found that Beckman is currently employed, without loss of remuneration, and that, based on the testimony of expert witnesses at trial, "Beckman will not suffer substantial damage or loss of recognition and popularity solely as a result of being off the air during the first 180 days of his five-year contract with WXIA-TV."

The trial court ruled that the restrictive covenant is valid under Georgia law as it is reasonable and definite with regard to time and territory and is otherwise reasonable considering the interest of Cox to be protected and the impact on Beckman.

Beckman appeals this decision in Case No. 39176. . .

(1) Case No. 39176. Beckman concedes the covenant not to compete is reasonable with regard to the time and territorial restrictions, but urges that it is otherwise unreasonable in that it is broader than is necessary for Cox's protection. . . .

A covenant not to compete, being in partial restraint of trade, is not favored in the law, and will be upheld only when strictly limited in time, territorial effect, the capacity in which the employee is prohibited from competing and when it is otherwise reasonable. . . In determining whether a covenant is reasonably limited with regard to these factors, the court must balance the interest the employer seeks to protect against the impact the covenant will have on the employee, factoring in the effect of the covenant on the public's interest in promotingcompetition and the freedom of individuals to contract . . . The evidence supports the trial court's finding that WSB-TV has a significant interest in the image of its television station which it has created, in large measure, by promoting those individuals who appear on behalf of the station, whether as newscasters . . . or "television personalities." This interest is entitled to protection. We further agree with the trial court that WSB-TV would be greatly harmed by Beckman's appearance on a competing station prior to the completion of WSB-TV's transition plan.

Beckman argues, however, that the detrimental impact of the restrictive covenant on him outweighs the need to protect the interests of WSB-TV . . . While the evidence is not without conflict, the trial court's finding that a six-month absence from the air will not substantially damage Beckman's popularity or recognition among the public is well-supported by the record.

. . . [W]e conclude that for a limited time and in a narrowly restricted area, WSB-TV is entitled to prevent Beckman from using the popularity and recognition he gained as a result of WSB-TV's investment in the creation of his image so that WSB-TV may protect its interest in its own image by implementing its transition plan. We find that the restrictive covenant in this case is reasonably tailored to that end . . . We agree with the trial court that the restrictive covenant in this case is valid . . .

Judgment affirmed.

INVENTIONS AND PATENTS

Often an employment agreement between an employer and its research or technical staff includes a provision that assigns any inventions of the employee, and subsequent patents on those inventions, to the employer. Unless inventions are assigned to the employer by the employee, or some special circumstances exist, the employer generally has no right to the employee's inventions. Any assignment of inventions must include provisions that define exactly which inventions are covered under the assignment. The assignment may specifically exclude any inventions by the employee during his or her own time that are unrelated to the employee's work for the employer. The employee may also specifically exempt from this assignment prior inventions that he or she brings to the employer.

EXAMPLE: Employer to Have Ownership of Employee's Inventions

All ideas, inventions, and other developments or improvements conceived or reduced to practice by employee, alone or with others, during the term of this employment agreement, whether or not during working hours, that are within the scope of employer's business operations or that relate to any of employer's work or projects, shall be the exclusive property of employer. Employee agrees to assist employer, at its expense, to obtain patents on any such patentable ideas, inventions, and other developments, and agrees to execute all documents necessary to obtain such patents in the name of employer.[13]

In the *Cubic Corporation v. Marty* case, involving a device to train airplane pilots, the court found that an assignment of inventions between the employee and the employer was valid and binding and that the employer was entitled to the patent on the employee's invention.

CASE
Cubic Corporation v. Marty 185 Cal. App. 3d 438, 229 Cal. Rptr. 828 (1996)
August 27, 1986

STANIFORTH, Associate Judge

William B. Marty Jr. appeals a judgment awarding Cubic Corporation $34,102 for Marty's breach of an invention agreement signed when he began his employment with Cubic, awarding the patent to the invention to Cubic and enjoining Marty from exploiting any rights under the patent or using or disclosing Cubic's confidential information to others.

FACTS

When Marty became a Cubic employee in December 1976, he signed an invention and

continues

CASE *(continued)*
Cubic Corporation v. Marty 185 Cal. App. 3d 438, 229 Cal. Rptr. 828 (1996)

secrecy agreement (hereafter the Agreement) which provided in pertinent part that the employee agreed:

"To promptly disclose to Company all ideas, processes, inventions, improvements, developments and discoveries coming within the scope of Company's business or related to Company's products or to any research, design, experimental or production work carried on by Company, or to any problems specifically assigned to Employee, conceived alone or with others during this employment, and whether or not conceived during regular working hours. All such ideas, processes, trademarks, inventions, improvements, developments and discoveries shall be the sole and exclusive property of Company, and Employee assigns and hereby agrees to assign his entire right, title and interest in and to the same to Company."

The agreement also provided the employee would cooperate in obtaining a patent on any such inventions and would not disclose any of Cubic's records, files, drawings, documents or equipment from Cubic without prior written consent. Under the agreement, Cubic promised to pay all expenses in connection with obtaining a patent, pay the employee a $75 cash bonus upon the employee's execution of the patent application and an additional $75 if a patent was obtained.

In mid-May 1977, Marty came up with an idea for an electronic warfare simulator (EWS), a device for training pilots in electronic warfare. Marty's invention had advantages over current training methods which involved the use of very expensive, security-risky, mimic radars. He developed a block diagram in May 1977 and in June 1977 a manuscript describing his invention.

He showed both the diagram and manuscript to Minton Kronkhite of Cubic, representing it might be a new product which Cubic could add to its product for training pilots, the ACMR (air combat maneuvering range) . . . Kronkhite thought Marty's invention was a good idea and passed along the manuscript to Hubert Kohnen, another Cubic employee involved with the ACMR. Kohnen also thought the idea was good. He assumed it was another product for the ACMR since Marty had suggested his invention responded to some of the things Kohnen had been talking about. Kohnen made some technical comments on the manuscript. . . . Cubic funded an internal project to study Marty's invention. Marty used a Cubic computer programmer to help design necessary circuitry. Marty's background in microprocessors was weak.

Based on the developed invention, Cubic submitted a proposal to the Navy for Marty's invention under Kohnen's name. Kohnen told Marty if they got a program from the Navy, Marty would be made the program manager. Cubic did get a government program to study Marty's invention and Marty was made program manager. Marty was also given a more than average raise.

In June 1978, Marty, without telling Cubic, applied for a patent on his invention. The patent was issued in December 1979. Marty's patent attorney forwarded a copy of the patent to Cubic and offered to discuss giving Cubic a license under the patent. Cubic took the position the patent belonged to them under the Agreement Marty had signed. Cubic offered to reimburse Marty's expenses in obtaining the patent if he assigned the patent to Cubic. Marty refused. Cubic told Marty his continued employment at Cubic was contingent

continues

CASE *(continued)*
Cubic Corporation v. Marty 185 Cal. App. 3d 438, 229 Cal. Rptr. 828 (1996)

on his assigning the patent. Marty continued to refuse and was terminated from his employment at Cubic in early 1980.

Cubic filed a complaint against Marty seeking declaratory relief as to ownership of the patent and alleging breach of contract, confidential relationship and trust, interference with prospective economic advantage, and specific enforcement of the secrecy and invention agreement. Marty cross-complained for wrongful discharge, breach of contract, fraudulent misrepresentation, breach of confidential disclosure, copyright infringement, defamation, and injunction.

The trial court awarded the patent to Cubic and $34,102 in damages resulting from a government withhold on a Cubic contract (subject to a credit to Marty if and when the amount was recovered from the government). The court also enjoined Marty from exploiting any rights under the patent and from using or disclosing to others confidential information owned by Cubic in specific documents . . .

Marty contends the Agreement was not specifically enforceable because there was inadequate consideration to support a promise to convey the invention to Cubic.

Civil Code section 3391 provides in pertinent part:

Specific performance cannot be enforced against a party to a contract in any of the following cases:

"1. If he has not received an adequate consideration for the contract;

"2. If it is not, as to him, just and reasonable . . ."

The adequacy of consideration is to be determined in light of the conditions existing at the time a contract is made.

Marty argues the only consideration for the Agreement was a "token" bonus of $150. He argues his employment could not have been the consideration for the Agreement because Cubic hired him before he signed the Agreement.

The evidence shows that on the Monday mornings when new employees were scheduled to begin working at Cubic, they attended an orientation session at which employee benefits were explained. The new hires completed insurance and medical forms as well as the secrecy and invention agreement. Cubic required all new employees to sign the secrecy and invention agreement.

The evidence also shows during the course of his employment, in part because of his invention, Marty was given a substantial raise in salary and made a program manager.

This evidence supports the trial court's conclusion the Agreement was a condition of employment and that the employment was adequate consideration for the Agreement . . .

The judgment is affirmed.

TRADE SECRETS

Another type of restrictive covenant found in employment agreements restricts the divulgence of an employer's trade secrets. A trade secret has been defined as "information, including a formula, pattern, compilation, program device, method, technique, or process, that: (i) derives independent economic value, actual or potential, from not being generally known to, and not being readily ascertainable by proper means by, other persons who can obtain economic value from its disclosure or use, and (ii) is the subject of efforts that are reasonable under the circumstances to maintain its secrecy."[14] This covenant may extend for a period of time beyond the term of the employment agreement, but it must be reasonable to be enforceable, and it generally loses any effect once the covered trade secrets have become common knowledge. The employment agreement usually also covers confidentiality in a general way, preventing the employee from divulging information to the press, the public, or the competition without permission.

EXAMPLE: Trade Secrets

Employee shall not at any time or in any manner, either directly or indirectly, divulge, disclose, or communicate to any person, firm, corporation, or other entity in any manner whatsoever any information concerning any matters affecting or relating to the business of employer, including without limitation, any of its customers, the prices it obtains or has obtained from the sale of, or at which it sells or has sold, its products, or any other information concerning the business of employer, its manner of operation, its plans, processes, or other data without regard to whether all of the above-stated matters will be deemed confidential, material, or important, employer and employee specifically and expressly stipulating that as between them, such matters are important, material, and confidential and gravely affect the effective and successful conduct of the business of employer, and employer's good will, and that any breach of the terms of this section shall be a material breach of this agreement.[15]

EXAMPLE: Trade Secrets after Termination of Employment

All of the terms of this agreement with regard to employer's trade secrets shall remain in full force and effect for a period of _____ years after the termination of employee's employment.

COMPENSATION

Provisions regarding compensation should address the areas of wages, salary, or commission; special incentives; overtime work; night differential; and sick pay.

EXAMPLE: Compensation of Employee

Employer shall pay employee, and employee shall accept from employer, in full payment for employee's services under this agreement, compensation at the rate of _____ dollars ($_____) per _____ [year], payable twice a month on the _____ [number] and _____ [number] days of each month while this agreement shall be in force.

Employer shall reimburse employee for all necessary expenses incurred by employee while traveling pursuant to employer's directions.[16]

EMPLOYEE BENEFITS

Provision should be made in the employment agreement to describe the benefits to which the employee is entitled. This may be done either by describing each benefit in detail, or merely by stating that the employee will be entitled to any employee benefits that the employer maintains for workers in similar positions.

EXAMPLE: Participation in Other Employer Benefits

Employee shall be entitled to and shall receive all other benefits and conditions of employment available generally to other employees of employer employed at the same level and responsibility of employee pursuant to employer plans and programs, including by way of illustration, but not by way of limitation, group health insurance benefits, life insurance benefits, profit-sharing benefits, and pension and retirement benefits.[17]

TERMINATION OF EMPLOYMENT

Termination of the employee's employment prior to expiration of the term of the employment agreement may be grounds for a breach-of-contract action, either on behalf of the employer or the employee, if the agreement is so structured. Employment agreements often include provisions allowing for the employee's termination upon notice given by either party, with or without cause. Although this type of loosely structured agreement affords maximum flexibility to both parties, it provides little certainty of continued employment. As an alternative, the employment agreement may allow the employee to terminate the contract prior to its expiration upon certain specified conditions and allow the employer to terminate the employee only "with cause." Special care must be given to define the causes for which the employee may be terminated.

EXAMPLE: Termination

a. This agreement may be terminated by either party on _____ days' written notice to the other. If employer shall so terminate this agreement, employee shall be entitled to compensation for _____ days.

b. In the event of any violation by employee of any of the terms of this agreement, employer may terminate employment without notice and with compensation to employee only to the date of such termination.

c. It is further agreed that any breach or evasion of any of the terms of this agreement by either party will result in immediate and irreparable injury to the other party and will authorize recourse to injunction and/or specific performance, as well as to all other legal or equitable remedies to which such injured party may be entitled under this agreement.[18]

ARBITRATION OF DISPUTES

Because even the most carefully drafted employment agreement is subject to interpretation, litigation often results when problems arise between the employee and employer. To curb potential legal fees and to resolve disputes expeditiously, both parties to an employment agreement often agree in advance to submit any disputes to binding arbitration.

EXAMPLE: Arbitration

Any differences, claims, or matters in dispute arising between employer and employee out of or connected with this agreement shall be submitted by them to arbitration by the American Arbitration Association or its successor and the determination of the American Arbitration Association or its successor shall be final and absolute. The arbitrator shall be governed by the duly promulgated rules and regulations of the American Arbitration Association or its successor, and the pertinent provisions of the laws of the state of _____, relating to arbitration. The decision of the arbitrator may be entered as a judgment in any court in the state of _____ or elsewhere.[19]

VACATIONS

The employment agreement should include language defining the employer's policy as it pertains to the employee with regard to vacations.

EXAMPLE: Vacations

During the term of this agreement, the employee shall be entitled to _____ days of paid vacation per year. Employer and employee shall mutually agree upon the time for such vacation.

ASSIGNABILITY OF CONTRACT

An employment agreement is typically not an assignable contract, especially on the part of the employee. However, the contract may be assignable by the employer under certain circumstances that involve a merger or acquisition.

EXAMPLE: Assumption and Assignability of Agreement— Employer's Merger, Consolidation, etc.

The rights and duties of employer and employee under this agreement shall not be assignable by either party except that this agreement and all rights under this agreement may be assigned by employer to any corporation or other business entity that succeeds to all or substantially all of the business of employer through merger, consolidation, corporate reorganization, or by acquisition of all or substantially all of the assets of employer and which assumes employer's obligations under this agreement.[20]

AMENDMENT OR RENEWAL OF AGREEMENT

The employment agreement should contain the agreed-upon provisions for amending and renewing the agreement.

EXAMPLE: Modification of Agreement

Any modification or amendment to this agreement shall be binding only if agreed to in a written document signed by each party to the agreement.

DATE AND SIGNATURES

The employment agreement should be dated and signed by both the employee and an authorized representative of the employer prior to the commencement of the employee's employment. Certain employment agreements may require the approval of the employer's board of directors or designated officers.

The sample agreement in Exhibit 15-4 incorporates many of the clauses previously discussed in this chapter. Of course, any actual agreement must be drafted with the needs of the particular situation and client in mind.

EXHIBIT 15-4 SAMPLE EMPLOYMENT AGREEMENT

Employment agreement made *[date of agreement]*, between *[name of employer]*, a corporation organized and existing under the laws of *[state]*, with its principal office located at *[address of employer]* ("employer"), and *[name of employee]*, of *[address of employee]* ("employee").

RECITALS

A. Employer desires to hire employee because of employee's vast business experience and expertise in *[business of employer]*.

B. Employee desires to be employed by employer in the executive capacity described below.

In consideration of the matters described above, and of the mutual benefits and obligations set forth in this agreement, the parties agree as follows:

SECTION ONE.
EMPLOYMENT

Employer employs employee on the terms and conditions stated in this agreement to perform *[description of services employee is to perform]*, and employee agrees to perform such services for employer on the terms and conditions stated in this agreement.

SECTION TWO.
TERM OF EMPLOYMENT

The term of employee's employment shall be *[number]* years commencing *[commencement date]*. Continued employment of employee by employer after *[termination date]* shall be for the term and on the conditions agreed to by the parties prior to the expiration of this agreement.

SECTION THREE.
COMPENSATION

A. Employer shall pay employee an annual salary of $*[dollar amount of annual salary]*, payable monthly, on the *[ordinal number]* day of each month, commencing *[first payment date]*.

B. In addition to the compensation stated in paragraph A of this section, employer shall pay employee on *[first payment date]*, and annually after that date, for the term of this agreement, a sum equal to dividends payable on *[number]* shares of the present authorized *[class]* stock of employer to the extent that dividends are declared for that year. If employer declares a stock dividend, rather than a cash dividend, employee shall receive in cash an amount equal to the fair market value of the stock dividend payable on *[number]* shares. If the stock is not then openly traded, the fair market value of the stock dividends shall be determined by mutual agreement of the parties or, if that

EXHIBIT 15-4 *(continued)*

fails, by arbitration as provided for in Section Eight of this agreement. If there is a stock split, the number of shares on which employee shall receive dividends shall increase on a basis proportionate with the stock split.

SECTION FOUR.
RETIREMENT BENEFITS

If employee remains in the employ of employer until employee reaches the age of *[number]* years, employer shall pay employee or *[his/her]* heirs or designated beneficiary $*[dollar amount of monthly retirement payment]* per month for *[number]* years certain. Employer shall also pay employee, but not a designated beneficiary of employee's heirs or legatees, $*[dollar amount of additional monthly retirement payment]* after the term certain for so long as employee shall live.

SECTION FIVE.
DEATH BENEFITS

If employee remains in the employ of employer continuously until employee's death, employer will pay to employee's designated beneficiary, or in lieu of designated beneficiary, employee's heirs, a monthly income of $*[dollar amount of monthly death benefit]* for *[number]* years.

SECTION SIX.
EMPLOYER'S OBLIGATION ON ITS TERMINATING EMPLOYEE'S EMPLOYMENT

If, during the term of this agreement, employer terminates this agreement for any reason, employer shall nevertheless continue the payments provided for in this agreement for the above-stated term so long as employee does not engage in gainful employment for another employer or enter into self-employment. If employee engages in gainful employment for another employer or enters into self-employment during the remaining term of this employment agreement, employer will pay employee one-half of the monthly payments designated in this agreement.

SECTION SEVEN.
EMPLOYER'S OBLIGATION ON TERMINATION OF EMPLOYMENT BY EMPLOYEE

If, during the term of this agreement, employee should fail or refuse to perform the services contemplated by this agreement, or should be unable to perform such services, or should engage in gainful employment with another employer, employer's obligation to make the payments provided in this agreement shall cease, but employer shall pay the additional compensation based on dividends declared on employer's stock to employee under Section Three of this agreement on a pro rata basis for the number of months employee has been in the employ of employer for which no payment equal to such dividends has been paid.

SECTION EIGHT.
ARBITRATION

Any differences, claims, or matters in dispute arising between employer and employee out of or connected with this agreement shall be submitted by them to arbitration by the American Arbitration Association or its successor and the determination of the American Arbitration Association or its successor shall be final and absolute. The arbitrator shall be governed by the duly promulgated rules and regulations of the American

continues

EXHIBIT 15-4   *(continued)*

Arbitration Association or its successor, and the pertinent provisions of the laws of *[state]*, relating to arbitration. The decision of the arbitrator may be entered as a judgment in any court of *[state]* or elsewhere.

SECTION NINE.
ATTORNEYS' FEES

If any action is filed in relation to this agreement, the unsuccessful party in the action shall pay to the successful party, in addition to all the sums that either party may be called on to pay, a reasonable sum for the successful party's attorneys' fees.

SECTION TEN.
GOVERNING LAW

This agreement shall be governed by, construed, and enforced in accordance with the laws of *[state]*.

SECTION ELEVEN.
ENTIRE AGREEMENT

This agreement shall constitute the entire agreement between the parties and any prior understanding or representation of any kind preceding the date of this agreement shall not be binding upon either party except to the extent incorporated in this agreement.

SECTION TWELVE.
MODIFICATION OF AGREEMENT

Any modification of this agreement or additional obligation assumed by either party in connection with this agreement shall be binding only if evidenced in writing signed by each party or an authorized representative of each party.

SECTION THIRTEEN.
NOTICES

Any notice provided for or concerning this agreement shall be in writing and be deemed sufficiently given when sent by certified or registered mail if sent to the respective address of each party as set forth at the beginning of this agreement.

SECTION FOURTEEN.
SECTION HEADINGS

The titles to the sections and paragraphs of this agreement are solely for the convenience of the parties and shall not be used to explain, modify, simplify, or aid in the interpretation of the provisions of this agreement.

Each party to this agreement has caused it to be executed at [place of execution] on the date indicated below.

[Signatures and date(s) of signing]

IN SUMMATION

- An employment agreement is a binding contract on the employer and employee and must contain all the elements of a valid contract.

- The employee's duties should be described in detail in the employment agreement.

- A covenant not to compete is often found within the employment agreement. To be valid, it must restrict future employment only for a limited time period and/or in a limited geographical area.

- For some employees it is important to establish ownership of any inventions and patents that arise from the employee's position with the employer.

- Employment agreements usually contain strict protections for the employer's trade secrets.

- The employee's compensation and benefits, or a formula for the employee's compensation and benefits, should be set forth in detail in the employment agreement.

- Conditions for the employee's termination should be included in the employment agreement.

- The employment agreement must be signed by both the employer and employee to be valid.

§ 15.7 THE PARALEGAL'S ROLE

Paralegals who work for in-house counsel, as well as those who work for law firms that represent corporate clients, often work on projects that involve executive compensation, employee benefits, and the drafting of employment agreements.

EXECUTIVE COMPENSATION AND EMPLOYEE BENEFITS

Corporate paralegals may be called on to assist with drafting and administering executive compensation plans, including equity compensation plans such as stock option plans. Paralegals also often work with drafting qualified plans and the supplementary documents and in submitting the application for a determination letter to the IRS. They may also be asked to research various legal requirements for employee benefit plans, including pension plans and welfare benefit plans. From time to time, new legislation is passed affecting the requirements for qualified plans. Paralegals are often involved in researching the requirements and seeing to it that qualified plans that have been adopted by corporate clients comply with the new requirements.

EMPLOYMENT AGREEMENTS

Although they may not give legal advice with regard to the employment agreement and other employment matters, paralegals are often involved in every aspect of collecting the information necessary to draft an employment agreement, drafting the agreement, obtaining the signatures, and obtaining approval from the corporation's board of directors when necessary.

When a corporate client requests an attorney to prepare an employment agreement on its behalf, the first step is to collect the pertinent information from the client. The use of an employment agreement worksheet, such as the one shown in Exhibit 15-5, to gather all pertinent information can be very effective. This worksheet illustrates the types of information that must be gathered from the corporate client before drafting an employment agreement. After gathering the pertinent information from the client, the paralegal can draft the employment agreement, under the supervision of an attorney, and see to its proper execution.

Typically, employment agreements entered into with officers or executives of a corporation are approved by a simple resolution of the board of directors, either by a unanimous written consent or at a regular board meeting. The paralegal can also see to it that the employment agreement is properly approved.

EXHIBIT 15-5 EMPLOYMENT AGREEMENT WORKSHEET

Identification of parties

Employer _____

Address _____

_____

Employee _____

Address _____

_____

Term of agreement

Number of years _____

Automatically renewable _____

Position

Title _____

Supervisor _____

EXHIBIT 15-5 *(continued)*

Duties of employee

_____

_____

_____

_____

_____

Hours of employment _____

Compensation

   Salary or commission _____

   Rate of pay _____

   Scheduled pay periods _____

   Overtime compensation _____

   Sick pay _____

Vacations and holidays

_____

Employee benefits _____

   Benefits that the employee is entitled to

_____

_____

_____

_____

_____

_____

   Date on which employee becomes entitled to benefits

_____

Expense account

_____

_____

Covenant not to compete after leaving employment

   Length of time _____

   Geographical location _____

_____

continues

EXHIBIT 15-5 *(continued)*

Termination of employment

  Right of either party to terminate after giving notice

  _____

  _____

  Right of employee to terminate agreement _____

  Conditions _____

  _____

  Right of employer to terminate agreement _____

  Conditions _____

  _____

© Cengage Learning 2013

CORPORATE PARALEGAL PROFILE
Kelly L. Cook

Even with over 25 years of experience and substantial training, I still learn new things every day. The employee benefits area of law is constantly changing and evolving. Keeping up with ERISA statutory, regulatory, and judicial developments is both challenging and exciting.

NAME Kelly L. Cook

LOCATION Syracuse, New York

TITLE CEBS, Manager Employee Benefits Department

SPECIALTY ERISA/Employee Benefits Law

EDUCATION BA Elmira College; Paralegal Certificate in Litigation Management, The Institute of Paralegal Training; Certified Employee Benefit Specialist (CEBS) Designation, International Foundation of Employee Benefit Plans and the Wharton School of the University of Pennsylvania

EXPERIENCE 27 years

Kelly Cook is a paralegal and manager of the employee benefits department of Blitman & King LLP, a Syracuse, New York, law firm dedicated to workplace issues. Blitman & King employs 19 attorneys and 6 paralegals. Kelly reports to the partners in the employee benefits department. After receiving her BA and her paralegal certificate in litigation management, Kelly continued her education to become a Certified Employee Benefit Specialist. As manager of Blitman & King's employee benefits department, Kelly coordinates with the attorneys and other paralegals regarding client assignments and assists with management

CORPORATE PARALEGAL PROFILE
Kelly L. Cook (continued)

of workloads and applicable deadlines. She also assists with training new associates and paralegals in the employee benefits department.

Kelly works with clients who have single-employer and multi-employer pension- and welfare-benefit plans. These clients include sponsors of qualified retirement plans (defined benefit plans, defined contribution plans, 401[k] plans) and non-qualified deferred compensation plans, as well as a variety of self-insured health plans, insured health plans, and apprenticeship and training plans.

While Kelly's position is focused on employee benefits, her job duties are still very diverse. She provides assistance to the attorneys and their clients relative to preparation of plan documents, including trust agreements, summary plan descriptions, annual and periodic notices to participants, service provider agreements, as well as benefit applications and other operational forms. Kelly also assists plan sponsors and coordinates with service providers concerning reporting and disclosure requirements, applications for IRS tax-exempt status, IRS and U.S. Department of Labor audits, and litigation involving employee benefit plans.

Because Blitman & King specializes in employee benefits, changes in the ERISA field can present both opportunities and challenges to the firm's attorneys and paralegals. When new legislation is adopted, they first work to gain an understanding of the changes in the law, then determine what is necessary to implement the changes for all of their affected employee-benefits clients. The final step is management of the document modifications and client informational needs to accomplish timely implementation.

Implementing changes brought on by the new Patient Protection and Affordability Care Act (PPACA) was an "all hands on deck" project for Blitman & King. The health law changes had to be analyzed and the necessary information disseminated to over 30 clients. Benefit plan documents for affected plans had to be appropriately amended with new provisions and procedures designed for the benefit of participants and the necessary participant notices had to be prepared and distributed. Kelly was responsible for overseeing the entire project—from start to finish.

Kelly's advice to new paralegals?

Read everything you possibly can. Every time you read an article or a court decision that refers to a statutory provision or a regulation, look it up and read it as well. Also, create research (topic) folders and file articles of interest related to those topics in them. This will save valuable time later, and it is particularly helpful in the ERISA field where the law is constantly evolving—it's like a giant jigsaw puzzle; the more pieces you can put together, the more clear the picture becomes.

For more information on careers for corporate paralegals, log in to http://www.cengagebrain.com to access the CourseMate website that accompanies this text; then see the Corporate Careers Section.

ETHICAL CONSIDERATION

Attorneys have an ethical duty to represent their clients diligently. According to Rule 1.3 of the American Bar Association's Model Rules of Professional Conduct, "A lawyer shall act with reasonable diligence and promptness in representing a client."

The rules of professional conduct of most states similarly provide that attorneys must always act diligently when representing a client.

Attorneys must carefully track and meet all deadlines associated with a client representation, and they must work to see that the client is kept fully informed of the progress of the attorney's representation.

Paralegals are often invaluable when it comes to tracking important deadlines and in communicating with clients. Therefore, it is important that paralegals provide diligent service too. As a paralegal, you will likely be responsible for keeping a calendar, either electronically or manually, tracking important dates and deadlines. Chances are, you will also be responsible for handling various communications with clients to keep them apprised of the progress on their cases or projects.

You will also assist the attorneys you work for to provide diligent representation by being careful to complete all of your assignments on time to the best of your ability.

Do not set aside the difficult tasks until it is too late. If you need help with any assignments, be sure to ask and ask quickly. Procrastination by a paralegal can have dire consequences when important deadlines are looming.

For more information on ethics for corporate paralegals, including links to the NALA and NFPA codes of ethics, log in to http://www.cengagebrain.com to access the CourseMate website that accompanies this text; then see the Ethics Section.

§ 15.8 RESOURCES

Paralegals working in the executive compensation and employee benefits areas will frequently need to reference the pertinent Internal Revenue Code sections and ERISA. There are several secondary sources that include further explanation of these codes. In addition, federal agencies that deal with pension plans can be very helpful.

FEDERAL LAW

The Employee Retirement Income Security Act of 1974 (ERISA), discussed throughout this chapter, may be found within the United States Code at 29 U.S.C. 1001. Links to ERISA and the federal statutes may be accessed from the CourseMate website.

SECONDARY MATERIALS

Secondary materials that provide explanation of the pertinent federal law, as well as forms and practice tips, can be very useful to paralegals who work with qualified plans. These resources also include several references to form books that may be used in conjunction with these materials. Some of the more popular secondary materials include:

- *Pension Coordinator*, by RIA
- *Pension & Profit Sharing*, by Prentice Hall
- *Pension Plan Guide*, by CCH
- *Pension Reporter*, by BNA

INTERNAL REVENUE SERVICE

The website for the Internal Revenue Service includes several downloadable publications regarding how to comply with the qualified plan provisions of the Internal Revenue Code, as well as a downloadable Form 5300 to apply for a favorable determination letter.

PENSION BENEFIT GUARANTY CORPORATION

The Pension Benefit Guaranty Corporation (PBGC) is a corporation created by the Employee Retirement Income Security Act of 1974 to encourage the continuation and maintenance of private-sector defined benefit pension plans, provide timely and uninterrupted payment of pension benefits, and keep pension insurance premiums at a minimum. Information about pension plans in the the United States can be found on the PBGC website.

SUMMARY

- Employee benefit plans that meet certain requirements of the Internal Revenue Code and qualify for special tax treatment are referred to as qualified plans.
- Employers are allowed a tax deduction for their contributions to qualified plans.
- Investment income earned on contributions to qualified plans is generally tax free until distributed to plan participants.
- Participants of qualified plans can defer their income tax liability on the amount of their contributions until they receive the benefit from the plan in the future, when their income will generally be less.

- Qualified plans are subject to provisions of the Internal Revenue Code and the Employee Retirement Income Security Act of 1974 (ERISA).

- Qualified plans must meet minimum participation rules set forth in the Internal Revenue Code.

- Minimum participation and coverage rules and standards are established to ensure that qualified plans do not discriminate in favor of the corporation's owners or highly compensated employees.

- Qualified plans must meet certain vesting requirements set forth in ERISA.

- Employees are always 100 percent vested in any contribution they make to the qualified plans unless an alternative seven-year incremental vesting plan has been adopted.

- Employee stock ownership plans (ESOPs) are a type of qualified plan that give partial ownership of the corporation to the corporation's employees. Distributions may be made to participants in the form of stock or cash.

- Keoghs are a type of qualified plan available to self-employed individuals.

- Employee welfare benefit plans are plans designed to provide participants and their beneficiaries with medical, dental, disability, and life insurance, and similar benefits.

- Sponsors of employee benefit plans may request favorable determination letters from the IRD to ensure that their plans will be considered qualified plans by the IRS.

- An employment agreement sets forth the rights and obligations of the employer and employee.

- An employment agreement is considered a binding contract on both the employer and employee, and it must include all the elements of a contract.

- A covenant not to compete restricts the future employment and actions of the employee. Covenants not to compete are only enforceable if they are considered reasonable.

- Employees at will are hired by an employer for agreed-upon compensation and they can quit at any time or be dismissed at the employer's discretion, without cause.

▉ REVIEW QUESTIONS _____

1. How can an employer be certain that an employee benefit plan will be considered a qualified plan by the IRS?

2. When is an employee's contribution to a plan considered to be fully vested?

3. What are integrated plans?

4. What unique benefit does an ESOP offer to the employer?

5. If Andrews Electronics wants to adopt an employee benefit plan that will pay its employees a specific amount upon their retirement, what type of plan would the company most likely want to adopt?

6. The owners of Gabrielle Foods, Inc. would like to adopt an employee benefit plan that would encourage their employees to save

money for retirement. They are willing to pay up to a certain amount per employee, per year, provided that the employee invests an equal amount of his or her pretax income. What type of plan might the owners of Gabrielle Foods, Inc. adopt?

7. What is employment "at will"?

8. May the employee's actions be restricted even after termination of employment?

9. Why were covenants not to compete void under the common law of England? What is the modern view toward covenants not to compete?

10. If an employment agreement remains silent on the issue, is the employer necessarily entitled to all inventions of the employee while the employee is working for the employer?

◼ PRACTICAL PROBLEMS

Has the reasonableness of covenants not to compete been defined by the courts of your state? Research the case law in your state to locate a case that discusses the reasonableness of covenants not to compete in employment agreements, and write a brief summary of what the court in that case found to be reasonable (or not reasonable). If you are unable to locate such a case in the courts of your state, locate such a case in a neighboring state.

◼ EXERCISE IN CRITICAL THINKING

Many chief executive officers (CEOs) of publicly held corporations are paid annual salaries that most people would consider excessive—even CEOs of companies that are performing poorly. If shareholders have the salary information available to them and the power to vote on such matters, why do you think they are reluctant to vote against such high salaries for corporate officers?

◼ WORKPLACE SCENARIO

Assume that our fictional clients, the owners of Cutting Edge Computer Repair, Inc., have decided to expand their business by hiring a computer technician. This individual will be a salaried, full-time employee. He will not be an officer or director of the corporation.

Using the following information, and the information in this chapter, prepare a draft of an employment agreement between Cutting Edge Computer Repair, Inc., and its new employee.

Employee's Name: Brian Anderson, 3856 Main Street, Oakdale, (your home state)

Term of Agreement: Indefinite, to terminate on 60 days' notice of either party

Position: Computer Repair Technician

Duties: Those typical of a computer repair technician

Hours of Employment: 9:00 a.m. to 5:00 p.m., Monday through Friday

Compensation $60,000 annual salary: Paid on the 1st and 15th of each month

Vacations: two weeks for the first five years of service; three weeks for 5 to 10 years of service; four weeks after 10 years of service

Employee Benefits: five days sick pay per year; health insurance policy adopted by corporation

Covenant Not to Compete: Brian is not to establish his own computer repair business within a 25-mile radius of Cutting Edge Computer Repair, Inc., for a period of one year after terminating his employment.

Portfolio Reminder:

Save the documents prepared for the Workplace Scenario exercises in each chapter, either in hard copy or electronically, to build a portfolio of documents to be used for job interviews or as sample documents on the job. At this point, your portfolio should include the following:

- Power of attorney
- Application for assumed name
- Application for federal employer identification number
- Application for state employer identification number
- Partnership statement of authority
- Limited partnership certificate
- Limited liability partnership statement of qualification

- Articles of organization
- Subchapter S election by small business corporation, Form 2553
- Articles of incorporation
- Unanimous written consent of shareholders
- Unanimous written consent of the board of directors
- Unanimous written consent of board of directors approving bank loan
- Plan of merger
- Articles of merger
- Application for certificate of authority by a foreign corporation
- Articles of dissolution
- Employment agreement

▣ END NOTES

1. 2010 Trends in CEO Pay, ALF-CIO, http://www.aflcio.org (accessed July 21, 2011).

2. Internal Revenue Code 280G.

3. Internal Revenue Code 4999.

4. Talton, John, "Outrage over CEO pay is so last quarter," *The Seattle Times*, June 21, 2009.

5. 60A Am. Jur. 2d Pensions and Retirement Funds § 15 (May 2011).

6. IRC 401(l).

7. 7B Am. Jur. Legal Forms 2d Employment Contracts 99:4 (May 2011). Reprinted with permission from American Jurisprudence Legal Forms 2d. © 2011 West Group.

8. Id. 99:7. Reprinted with permission from American Jurisprudence Legal Forms 2d. © 2011 West Group.

9. Id. 99:13. Reprinted with permission from American Jurisprudence Legal Forms 2d. © 2011 West Group.

10. Id. 99:7. Reprinted with permission from American Jurisprudence Legal Forms 2d. © 2011 West Group.

11. Annotation, Anticompetitive Covenants, 60 A.L.R.4th 965 (1988).

12. Id.

13. 7B Am. Jur. Legal Forms 2d Employment Contracts 99:231 (May 2011). Reprinted with permission from American Jurisprudence Legal Forms 2d. © 2011 West Group.

14. Uniform Trade Secrets Act as with 1985 amendments.

15. 7B Am. Jur. Legal Forms 2d Employment Contracts 99:7 (May 2011). Reprinted with permission from American Jurisprudence Legal Forms 2d. © 2011 West Group.

16. Id. Reprinted with permission from American Jurisprudence Legal Forms 2d. © 2011 West Group.

17. Id. 99:191. Reprinted with permission from American Jurisprudence Legal Forms 2d. © 2011 West Group.

18. Id. 99:7. Reprinted with permission from American Jurisprudence Legal Forms 2d. © 2011 West Group.

19. Id. 99:12. Reprinted with permission from American Jurisprudence Legal Forms 2d. © 2011 West Group.

20. Id. 99.234. Reprinted with permission from American Jurisprudence Legal Forms 2d. © 2011 West Group.

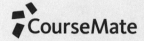

CourseMate

To access additional course materials, including CourseMate, please visit http://www.cengagebrain .com. At the CengageBrain home page, search for the ISBN of your title (from the back cover of your book) using the search box at the top of the page. This will take you to the product page where these resources can be found. The CourseMate resources for this text include Web links, downloadable forms, flash cards, and more.

For links to the websites of the secretary of state offices, log in to http://www.cengagebrain.com to access the CourseMate website that accompanies this text.

Alabama Secretary of State
Corporation Division
P.O. Box 5616
Montgomery, AL 36103-5616
(334) 242-5324

Alaska Department of Commerce and Economic Development
Corporations Section
P.O. Box 110808
Juneau, AK 99811-0808
(907) 465-2530

Arizona Corporation Commission
1300 West Washington
Phoenix, AZ 85007-2929
(602) 542-3026

Arkansas Secretary of State
Corporations Division
State Capitol
Room 256
Little Rock, AR 72201
(501) 682-1010

California Secretary of State
Corporation Filing Division
1500 11th Street
Sacramento, CA 95814
(916) 657-5448

Colorado Secretary of State
Business Division
1700 Broadway, Suite 200
Denver, CO 80290
(303) 894-2200

Connecticut Secretary of State
Division of Corporations
30 Trinity Street
Hartford, CT 06106
(860) 509-6002

Delaware Secretary of State
Division of Corporations
P.O. Box 898
Dover, DE 19903
(302) 739-3073

District of Columbia
Department of Consumer and Regulatory Affairs
941 N. Capitol Street, NE
Washington, DC 20002
(202) 442-4400

Florida Department of State
Division of Corporations
P.O. Box 6327
Tallahassee, FL 32314
(850) 245-6939

Georgia Secretary of State
Business Services and Regulation
2 Martin Luther King Jr. Drive S.E. Suite 315,
West Tower
Atlanta, GA 30334
(404) 656-2817

**Hawaii Department of Commerce
and Consumer Affairs**
Business Registration Division
P.O. Box 40
Honolulu, HI 96810
(808) 586-2727

Idaho Secretary of State
700 W. Jefferson, Room 203
Boise, ID 83720
(208) 334-2301

Illinois Secretary of State
Department of Business Services
213 State Capitol Building
Springfield, IL 62756
(800) 252-6576

Indiana Secretary of State
Corporations Division
302 West Washington Street, Room E-018
Indianapolis, IN 46204
(317) 232-6576

Iowa Secretary of State
Division of Corporations
First Floor, Lucas Building, 321 E. 12th Street
Des Moines, IA 50319
(515) 281-5204

Kansas Secretary of State
120 SW 10th Avenue, Room 100
Topeka, KS 66612
(785) 296-4564

Kentucky Secretary of State
Corporations Department
700 Capital Avenue, Suite 154
Frankfort, KY 40602
(502) 564-2848

Louisiana Secretary of State
Corporate Division
P.O. Box 94125
Baton Rouge, LA 70804-9125
(225) 925-4704

Maine Secretary of State
Bureau of Corporations, Elections
and Commissions
State House Station 101
Augusta, ME 04333-0101
(207) 624-7736

**Maryland State Department of Assessments
and Taxation**
301 West Preston Street, 8th Floor
Baltimore, MD 21201-2395
(410) 767-1340

Massachusetts Secretary of State
Corporations Division
One Ashburton Place
Boston, MA 02108
(617) 727-9640

Michigan Bureau of Commercial Services
P.O. Box 30018
Lansing, MI 48909
(517) 241-6470

Minnesota Secretary of State
Business Services Division
60 Empire Drive, Suite 100
St. Paul, MN 55103
(612) 296-2803

Mississippi Secretary of State
Corporate Division
P.O. Box 136
Jackson, MS 39205
(601) 359-1633

Missouri Secretary of State
Corporation Division
James C. Kirkpatrick State Information Center
P.O. Box 778
Jefferson City, MO 65102
(573) 751-4153

Montana Corporation Bureau
Secretary of State's Office
Room 260, State Capitol
Helena, MT 59620
(406) 444-3665

Nebraska Secretary of State
State Capitol Building, Room 1301
P.O. Box 94608
Lincoln, NE 68509
(402) 471-4079

Nevada Secretary of State
Corporate Division
202 N. Carson Street
Carson City, NV 89710-4201
(775) 684-5708

New Hampshire Secretary of State/Corporations
107 North Main Street
Concord, NH 03301-4989
(603) 271-3246

New Jersey Division of Revenue
P.O. Box 308
Trenton, NJ 08625
(609) 292-9292

New Mexico Public Regulation Commission
Corporation Department
P.O. Box 1269
Santa Fe, NM 87504-1269
(505) 827-4722

New York Department of State
Division of Corporations
One Commerce Plaza
99 Washington Avenue, Suite 600
Albany, NY 12231
(518) 474-1418

North Carolina Secretary of State
Corporations Division
P.O. Box 29622
Raleigh, NC 27626
(919) 807-2225

North Dakota Secretary of State
State Capitol Building
600 East Boulevard Avenue
Bismarck, ND 58505-0500
(701) 328-4284

Ohio Secretary of State
Division of Corporations
180 E. Broad Street, 15th Floor
Columbus, OH 43215
(614) 466-3910

Oklahoma Secretary of State
2300 N. Lincoln Boulevard, Room 101
Oklahoma City, OK 73105
(405) 521-3912

Oregon Secretary of State
Corporation Division
255 Capitol Street NE
Salem, OR 97310
(503) 986-2200

Pennsylvania Department of State
Corporation Bureau
206 North Office Building
Harrisburg, PA 17120
(717) 787-1057

Rhode Island Secretary of State
Corporations Division
148 West River Street
Providence, RI 02904-2615
(401) 222-3040

South Carolina Secretary of State
Corporate Division
P.O. Box 11350
Columbia, SC 29211
(803) 734-2158

South Dakota Secretary of State
Corporate Department
500 East Capitol Street
Pierre, SD 57501
(605) 773-4845

Tennessee Secretary of State
312 Rosa L. Parks Avenue
6th Floor Snodgrass Tower
Nashville, TN 37243
(615) 741-2286

Texas Secretary of State
Corporations Section
1019 Brazos Street
Austin, TX 78701
(512) 463-5555

**Utah Corporations and Commercial
Code Division**
160 E. 300 Street
Salt Lake City, UT 84111
(801) 530-4849

Vermont Secretary of State Corporations
81 River Street
Montpelier, VT 05609
(802) 828-2386

Virginia State Corporation Commission
P.O. Box 1197
Richmond, VA 23218
(804) 371-9733

Washington Secretary of State
Corporations Division
P.O. Box 40234
Olympia, WA 98504-0234
(360) 725-0377

West Virginia Secretary of State
Corporate Division
Building 1, Suite 157-K
Charleston, WV 25305
(304) 558-8000

Wisconsin Secretary of State
Corporation Division
P.O. Box 7846
Madison, WI 53707
(608) 261-7577

Wyoming Secretary of State
State Capitol Building, Room 110
200 West 24th Street
Cheyenne, WY 82002-0200
(307) 777-731

B

Workplace Scenario Data

Workplace Information

Supervising Attorney: Belinda Murphy

Law Firm Employer Name and Address:
   Abrahams & Benson PLLC 4759 Main Street
   Pine City, [Home State] 33221

Law Firm Phone Number: 612-555-2468

B-1
Client Information Sheet

Client Name: Bradley Steven Harris

Home Address: 1753 Oakland Drive
                        Pine City, [Home State] 33221

Telephone: 612-555-1234

County: [Home County]

Business Address: [Home Address]

Social Security Number: 472-84-5544

B-2
Client Information Sheet

Client Name: Cynthia Ann Lund

Home Address: 4827 Willow Drive
                        Kenwood, [Home State] 33221

Telephone: 612-555-5678

County: [Home County]

Business Address: [Home Address]

Social Security Number: 421-94-9576

Partnership Name: Cutting Edge Partners

B-3
Corporate Information Sheet

Corporate Name: Cutting Edge Computer
                        Repair, Inc.

State of Domicile: [Home State]

Corporate Purpose: Computer Repair Business

Corporate Duration: Perpetual

Authorized Shares: 10,000, No Par Value
                        Common Stock

Preemptive Rights: No Preemptive Rights

Cumulative Voting: Not Allowed

Number of Initial Directors: Two

Names and Addresses of Initial Directors:
   Bradley Steven Harris
   1753 Oakland Drive
   Pine City, [Home State] 33221

   Cynthia Lund
   4827 Willow Drive
   Kenwood, [Home State] 33221

Registered Agent: Bradley Steven Harris

Registered Office Address: (principal address as well)
   1753 Oakland Drive
   Pine City, [Home State] 33221

Officers:
Chief Executive Officer: Bradley Steven Harris
Chief Financial Officer: Cynthia Lund
Secretary: Cynthia Lund

Shareholders:
Bradley Steven Harris 2,000 shares
Cynthia Ann Lund 2,000 shares

no other shares purchased

Consideration for Shares: $10.00 per share

B-4
Corporate Information Sheet

Corporate Name:	Kohler's Computers, Inc.
State of Domicile:	[Home State]
Corporate Purpose:	Computer Repair Business
Corporate Duration:	Perpetual
Authorized Shares:	10,000, No Par Value Common Stock

Preemptive Rights: No Preemptive Rights

Cumulative Voting: Not Allowed

Number of Initial Directors: Two

Names and Addresses of Initial Directors:
   Sandra Kohler
   455 Kent Street
   Pine City, [Home State] 33221

   Scott Kohler
   455 Kent Street
   Pine City, [Home State] 33221

Registered Agent: Bradley Steven Harris

Registered Office Address:
   455 Kent Street
   Pine City, [Home State] 33221

Officers:
Chief Executive Officer: Sandra Kohler
Chief Financial Officer: Scott Kohler
Secretary: Sandra Kohler

Shareholders:
Sandra Kohler 2,000 shares
Scott Kohler 2,000 shares

Consideration for Shares: $10.00 per share

Partnership Agreement

[14 AM. JUR. Legal Forms 2d Partnership § 194:18 (May 2011)]

Partnership agreement made on _____ [date], between _____ [A.B.], of _____ [address], _____ [city], _____ County, _____ [state], and _____ [C.D.], of _____ [address], _____ [city], _____ County, _____ [state] ("partners").

RECITALS

A. Partners desire to join together for the pursuit of common business goals.

B. Partners have considered various forms of joint business enterprises for their business activities.

C. Partners desire to enter into a partnership agreement as the most advantageous business form for their mutual purposes.

In consideration of the mutual promises contained in this agreement, partners agree as follows:

ARTICLE ONE NAME, PURPOSE, AND DOMICILE

The name of the partnership shall be _____. The partnership shall be conducted for the purposes of _____. The principal place of business shall be at _____ [address], _____ [city], _____ County, _____ [state], unless relocated by majority consent of the partners.

ARTICLE TWO DURATION OF AGREEMENT

The term of this agreement shall be for _____ years, commencing on _____ [date], and terminating on _____ [date], unless sooner terminated by mutual consent of the parties or by operation of the provisions of this agreement.

ARTICLE THREE CLASSIFICATION AND PERFORMANCE BY PARTNERS

A. Partners shall be classified as active partners, advisory partners, or estate partners.

An active partner may voluntarily become an advisory partner, may be required to become one irrespective of age, and shall automatically become one after attaining the age of _____ years, and in each case shall continue as such for _____ years unless the partner sooner withdraws or dies.

If an active partner dies, the partner's estate will become an estate partner for _____ years. If an advisory partner dies within _____ years of having become an advisory partner, the partner will become an estate partner for the balance of the _____-year period.

Only active partners shall have any vote in any partnership matter.

At the time of the taking effect of this partnership agreement, all the partners shall be active partners except _____ and _____, who shall be advisory partners.

B. An active partner, after attaining the age of _____ years, or prior to that age if the _____ [executive committee or as the case may be] with the approval of _____ [two-thirds or as the case may be] of all the other active partners determines that the reason for the change in status is bad health, may become an advisory partner at the end of any calendar month on giving _____ [number] calendar months' prior notice in writing of the partner's intention to do so. The notice shall be deemed to be sufficient if sent by registered mail addressed to the partnership at its principal office at _____ [address], _____ [city], _____ County, _____ [state] not less than _____ [number] calendar months prior to the date when the change is to become effective.

C. Any active partner may at any age be required to become an advisory partner at any time if the _____ [executive committee or as the case may be] with the approval of _____ [two-thirds or as the case may be] of the other active partners shall decide that the change is for any reason in the best interests of the partnership, provided notice of the decision shall be given in writing to the partner. The notice shall be signed by the _____ [chairman or as the case may be] of the _____ [executive committee or as the case may be] or, in the event of his or her being unable to sign at the time, by another member of the _____ [executive committee or as the case may be]. The notice shall be served personally on the partner required to change his or her status, or mailed by registered mail to the partner's last known address. Change of the partner's status shall become effective as of the date specified in the notice.

D. Every active partner shall automatically and without further act become an advisory partner at the end of the fiscal year in which the partner's _____ birthday occurs.

E. In the event that an active partner becomes an advisory partner or dies, the partner or the partner's estate shall be entitled to the following payments at the following times: _____ [describe].

Each active partner shall apply all of the partner's experience, training, and ability in discharging the partner's assigned functions in the partnership and in the performance of all work that may be necessary or advantageous to further the business interests of the partnership.

ARTICLE FOUR CONTRIBUTION

Each partner shall contribute $_____ on or before _____ [date] to be used by the partnership to establish its capital position. Any additional contribution required of partners shall only be determined and established in accordance with Article Nineteen.

ARTICLE FIVE BUSINESS EXPENSES

The rent of the buildings where the partnership business shall be carried on, and the cost of repairs and alterations, all rates, taxes, payments for insurance, and other expenses in respect to the buildings used by the partnership, and the wages for all persons employed by the partnership are all to become payable on the account of the partnership. All losses incurred shall be paid out of the capital of the partnership or the profits arising from the partnership business, or, if both shall be deficient, by the partners on a pro rata basis, in proportion to their original contributions, as provided in Article Nineteen.

ARTICLE SIX AUTHORITY

No partner shall buy any goods or articles or enter into any contract exceeding the value of $_____ without the prior consent in writing of the other partners. If any partner exceeds this authority, the other partners shall have the option to take the goods or accept the contract on account of the partnership or to let the goods remain the sole property of the partner who shall have obligated himself or herself.

ARTICLE SEVEN SEPARATE DEBTS

No partner shall enter into any bond, or become surety or cosigner, or provide security for any person, partnership, or corporation, or knowingly condone anything by which the partnership property may be attached or taken in execution, without the prior written consent of the other partners.

Each partner shall punctually pay the partner's separate debts and indemnify the other partners and the capital and property of the partnership against the partner's separate debts and all expenses relating to such separate debts.

ARTICLE EIGHT BOOKS AND RECORDS

Books of account shall be maintained by the partners, and proper entries made in the books of all sales, purchases, receipts, payments, transactions, and property of the partnership. The books of account and all records of the partnership shall be retained at the principal place of business as specified in Article One. Each partner shall have free access at all times to all books and records maintained relative to the partnership business.

ARTICLE NINE ACCOUNTING

The fiscal year of the partnership shall be from _____ [month and day] to _____ [month and day] of each year. On the _____ day of _____ [month], commencing in _____ [year], and on the _____ day of _____ [month] in each succeeding year, a general accounting shall be made and taken by the partners of all sales, purchases, receipts, payments, and transactions of the partnership during the preceding fiscal year, and of all the capital property and current liabilities of the partnership. The general accounting shall be written in the partnership account books and signed in each book by each partner immediately after it is completed. After the signature of each partner is entered, each partner shall keep one of the books and shall be bound by every account, except that if any manifest error is found in an account book by any partner and shown to the other partners within _____ months after the error shall have been noted by all of them, the error shall be rectified.

ARTICLE TEN DIVISION OF PROFITS AND LOSSES

Each partner shall be entitled to _____ % of the net profits of the business, and all losses occurring in the course of the business shall be borne in the same proportion, unless the losses are occasioned by the willful neglect or default, and not the mere mistake or error, of any of the partners, in which case the loss so incurred shall be made good by the partner through whose neglect or default the losses shall arise. Distribution of profits shall be made on the _____ day of _____ [month] each year.

ARTICLE ELEVEN ADVANCE DRAWS

Each partner shall be at liberty to draw out of the business in anticipation of the expected profits any sums that may be mutually agreed on, and the sums are to be drawn only after there has been entered in the books of the partnership the terms of agreement, giving the date, the amount to be drawn by the respective partners, the time at which the sums shall be drawn, and any other conditions or matters mutually agreed on. The signatures of each partner shall be affixed on the books of the partnership. The total sum of the advanced draw for each partner shall be deducted from the sum that partner is entitled to under the distribution of profits as provided for in Article Ten.

ARTICLE TWELVE SALARY

No partner shall receive any salary from the partnership, and the only compensation to be paid shall be as provided in Articles Ten and Eleven.

ARTICLE THIRTEEN RETIREMENT

In the event any partner shall desire to retire from the partnership, the partner shall give _____ months' notice in writing to the other partners. The continuing partners shall pay to the retiring partner at the termination of the _____ months' notice the value of the interest of the retiring partner in the partnership. The value shall be determined by a closing of the books and a rendition of the appropriate profit and loss, trial balance, and balance sheet statements. All disputes arising from such determination shall be resolved as provided in Article Twenty.

ARTICLE FOURTEEN RIGHTS OF CONTINUING PARTNERS

On the retirement of any partner, the continuing partners shall be at liberty, if they so desire, to retain all trade names designating the firm name used. Each of the partners shall sign and execute any assignments, instruments, or papers that shall be reasonably required for effectuating an amicable retirement.

ARTICLE FIFTEEN DEATH OF PARTNER

In the event of the death of one partner, the legal representative of the deceased partner shall remain as a partner in the firm, except that the exercise of this right on the part of the representative of the deceased partner shall not continue for a period in excess of _____ months, even though under the terms of this agreement a greater period of time is provided before the termination of this agreement. The original rights of the partners shall accrue to their heirs, executors, or assigns.

ARTICLE SIXTEEN EMPLOYEE MANAGEMENT

No partner shall hire or dismiss any person in the employment of the partnership without the consent of the other partners, except in cases of gross misconduct by the employee.

ARTICLE SEVENTEEN RELEASE OF DEBTS

No partner shall compound, release, or discharge any debt that shall be due or owing to the partnership, without receiving the full amount of the debt, unless that partner obtains the prior written consent of the other partners to the discharge of the indebtedness.

ARTICLE EIGHTEEN COVENANT AGAINST REVEALING TRADE SECRETS

No partner shall, during the continuance of the partnership or for _____ years after its termination by any means, divulge to any person not a member of the firm any trade secret or special information employed in or conducive to the partnership business and which may come to the partner's knowledge in the course of this partnership, without the consent in writing of the other partners, or of the other partners' heirs, administrators, or assigns.

ARTICLE NINETEEN ADDITIONAL CONTRIBUTIONS

The partners shall not have to contribute any additional capital to the partnership to that required under Article Four, except as follows: (1) each partner shall be required to contribute a proportionate share in additional contributions if the fiscal year closes with an insufficiency in the capital account or profits of the partnership to meet current expenses; or (2) the capital account falls below $_____ for a period of _____ months.

ARTICLE TWENTY ARBITRATION

If any differences shall arise between or among the partners as to their rights or liabilities under this agreement, or under any instrument made in furtherance of the partnership business, the difference shall be determined and the instrument shall be settled by _____ [name of arbitrator], acting as arbitrator, and the decision shall be final as to the contents and interpretations of the instrument and as to the proper mode of carrying the provision into effect.

ARTICLE TWENTY-ONE ADDITIONS, ALTERATIONS, OR MODIFICATIONS

Where it shall appear to the partners that this agreement, or any terms and conditions contained in this agreement, are in any way ineffective or deficient, or not expressed as originally intended, and any alteration or addition shall be deemed necessary, the partners will enter into, execute, and perform all further deeds and instruments as their counsel shall advise. Any addition, alteration, or modification shall be in writing, and no oral agreement shall be effective.

The parties have executed this agreement at _____ [designate place of execution] the day and year first above written.

[Signatures]

APPENDIX D

Limited Partnership Agreement

[14A Am. Jur. Legal Forms 2d Partnership §194:664 (May 2011)]

Agreement of limited partnership made on _____ [date], between _____ [A.B.], of _____ [address], _____ [city], _____ County, _____ [state], _____ ("general partner"), and _____ [C.D.], of _____ [address], _____ [city], _____ County, _____ [state], and _____ [E.F.], of _____ [address], _____ [city], _____ County, _____ [state] ("limited partners").

RECITALS

A. General and limited partners desire to enter into the business of _____.

B. General partner desires to manage and operate the business.

C. Limited partners desire to invest in the business and limit their liabilities.

In consideration of the matters described above, and of the mutual benefits and obligations set forth in this agreement, the parties agree as follows:

ARTICLE ONE GENERAL PROVISIONS

The limited partnership is organized pursuant to the provisions of _____ [cite statute] of _____ [state], and the rights and liabilities of the general and limited partners shall be as provided in that statute, except as otherwise stated in this agreement.

ARTICLE TWO NAME OF PARTNERSHIP

The name of the partnership shall be _____ (the "partnership").

ARTICLE THREE BUSINESS OF PARTNERSHIP

The purpose of the partnership is to engage in the business of _____.

ARTICLE FOUR PRINCIPAL PLACE OF BUSINESS

The principal place of business of the partnership shall be at _____ [address], _____ [city], _____ County, _____ [state]. The partnership shall also have other places of business as from time to time shall be determined by general partner.

ARTICLE FIVE CAPITAL CONTRIBUTION OF GENERAL PARTNER

General partner shall contribute $_____ to the original capital of the partnership. The contribution of general partner shall be made on or before _____ [date]. If general partner does not make _____ [his or her] entire contribution to the capital of the partnership on or before that date, this agreement shall be void. Any contributions to the capital of the partnership made at that time shall be returned to the partners who have made the contributions.

ARTICLE SIX CAPITAL CONTRIBUTIONS OF LIMITED PARTNERS

The capital contributions of limited partners shall be as follows:

Name	Amount
_____	$_____
_____	$_____

Receipt of the capital contribution from each limited partner as specified above is acknowledged by the partnership. No limited partner has agreed to contribute any additional cash or property as capital for use of the partnership.

ARTICLE SEVEN DUTIES AND RIGHTS OF PARTNERS

General partner shall diligently and exclusively apply _____ [himself or herself] in and about the business of the partnership to the utmost of _____ [his or her] skill and on a full-time basis.

General partner shall not engage directly or indirectly in any business similar to the business of the partnership at any time during the term of this agreement without obtaining the written approval of all other partners.

General partner shall be entitled to _____ days' vacation and _____ days' sick leave in each calendar year, commencing with the calendar year _____. If general partner uses sick leave or vacation days in a calendar year in excess of the number specified above, the effect on _____ [his or her] capital interest and share of the profits and losses of the partnership for that year shall be determined by a majority vote of limited partners.

No limited partner shall have any right to be active in the conduct of the partnership's business, nor have power to bind the partnership in any contract, agreement, promise, or undertaking.

ARTICLE EIGHT SALARY OF GENERAL PARTNER

General partner shall be entitled to a monthly salary of $_____ for the services rendered by general partner. The salary shall commence on _____ [date], and be payable on the _____ day of each subsequent month. The salary shall be treated as an expense of the operation of the partnership business and shall be payable whether or not the partnership shall operate at a profit.

ARTICLE NINE LIMITATIONS ON DISTRIBUTION OF PROFITS

General partner shall have the right, except as provided below, to determine whether from time to time partnership profits shall be distributed in cash or shall be left in the business, in which event the capital account of all partners shall be increased.

In no event shall any profits be payable for a period of _____ months until _____% of those profits have been deducted to accumulate a reserve fund of $_____ over and above the normal monthly requirements of working capital. This accumulation is to enable the partnership to maintain a sound financial operation.

ARTICLE TEN PROFITS AND LOSSES FOR LIMITED PARTNERS

Limited partners shall be entitled to receive a share of the annual net profits equivalent to their share in the capitalization of the partnership.

Limited partners shall each bear a share of the losses of the partnership equal to the share of profits to which each limited partner is entitled. The share of losses of each limited partner shall be charged against the limited partner's capital contribution.

Limited partners shall at no time become liable for any obligations or losses of the partnership beyond the amounts of their respective capital contributions.

ARTICLE ELEVEN PROFITS AND LOSSES FOR GENERAL PARTNER

After provisions have been made for the shares of profits of limited partners, all remaining profits of the partnership shall be paid to general partner. After giving effect to the share of losses chargeable against the capital contributions of limited partners, the remaining partnership losses shall be borne by general partner.

ARTICLE TWELVE BOOKS OF ACCOUNT

There shall be maintained during the continuance of this partnership an accurate set of books of account of all transactions, assets, and liabilities of the partnership. The books shall be balanced and closed at the end of each year, and at any other time on reasonable request of the general partner. The books are to be kept at the principal place of business of the partnership and are to be open for inspection by any partner at all reasonable times. The profits and losses of the partnership and its books of account shall be maintained on a fiscal year basis, terminating annually on _____ [month and day], unless otherwise determined by general partner.

ARTICLE THIRTEEN SUBSTITUTIONS, ASSIGNMENTS, AND ADMISSION OF ADDITIONAL PARTNERS

General partner shall not substitute a partner in _____ [his or her] place, or sell or assign all or any part of general partner's interest in the partnership business without the written consent of limited partners.

Additional limited partners may be admitted to this partnership on terms that may be agreed on in writing between general partner and the new limited partners. The terms so stipulated shall constitute an amendment to this partnership agreement.

No limited partner may substitute an assignee as a limited partner in _____ [his or her] place; but the person or persons entitled by rule or by intestate laws, as the case may be, shall succeed to all the rights of limited partner as a substituted limited partner.

ARTICLE FOURTEEN TERMINATION OF INTEREST OF LIMITED PARTNER; RETURN OF CAPITAL CONTRIBUTION

The interest of any limited partner may be terminated by (1) dissolution of the partnership for any reason provided in this agreement; (2) the agreement of all partners; or (3) the consent of the personal representative of a deceased limited partner and the partnership.

On the termination of the interest of a limited partner there shall be payable to that limited partner, or the limited partner's estate, as the case may be, a sum to be determined by all partners, which sum shall not be less than _____ times the capital account of the limited partner as shown on the books at the time of the termination, including profits or losses from the last closing of the books of the partnership to the date of the termination, when the interest in profits and losses terminated. The amount payable shall be an obligation payable only out of partnership assets, and at the option of the partnership, may be paid within _____ years after the termination of the interest,

provided that interest at the rate of _____% shall be paid on the unpaid balance.

ARTICLE FIFTEEN BORROWING BY PARTNER

In case of necessity as determined by a majority vote of all partners, a partner may borrow up to $_____ from the partnership. Any such loan shall be repayable at _____ [describe terms of repayment], together with interest at the rate of _____% per year.

ARTICLE SIXTEEN TERM OF PARTNERSHIP AND DISSOLUTION

The partnership term commences on _____ [date], and shall end on (1) the dissolution of the partnership by operation of law; (2) the dissolution of the partnership at any time designated by general partner; or (3) the dissolution of the partnership at the close of the month following the qualification and appointment of the personal representative of deceased general partner.

ARTICLE SEVENTEEN PAYMENT FOR INTEREST OF DECEASED GENERAL PARTNER

In the event of the death of general partner there shall be paid out of the partnership's assets to decedent's personal representative for decedent's interest in the partnership a sum equal to the capital account of decedent as shown on the books at the time of the decedent's death, adjusted to reflect profits or losses from the last closing of the books of the partnership to the day of the decedent's death.

ARTICLE EIGHTEEN AMENDMENTS

This agreement, except with respect to vested rights of partners, may be amended at any time by a majority vote as measured by the interest and the sharing of profits and losses.

ARTICLE NINETEEN BINDING EFFECT OF AGREEMENT

This agreement shall be binding on the parties to the agreement and their respective heirs, executors, administrators, successors, and assigns.

The parties have executed this agreement at _____ [designate place of execution] the day and year first above written.

[Signatures]

Operating Agreement

[12 Am. Jur. Legal Forms 2d Limited Liability Companies § 167A:7 (May 2011)]

This Operating Agreement (this "Agreement") of [name of limited liability company]C], a [name of state] limited liability company (the "Company"), is adopted and entered into on [date of agreement], by and among [name of first member], [name of second member] and [name of third member], as members (the "Members," which term includes any other persons who may become members of the Company in accordance with the terms of this Agreement and the Act) and the Company pursuant to and in accordance with the [name of limited liability company statute] of [name of state], as amended from time to time (the "Act"). Terms used in this Agreement which are not otherwise defined shall have the respective meanings given those terms in the Act.

In consideration of the matters described above, and of the mutual benefits and obligations set forth in this agreement, the parties agree as follows:

ARTICLE ONE
NAME

The name of the limited liability company under which it was formed is [name of limited liability company].

ARTICLE TWO
TERM

_____ [The Company shall dissolve on _____ (date) unless dissolved before such date in accordance with the Act.] or [The Company shall continue until dissolved in accordance with the Act.]

ARTICLE THREE
MANAGEMENT

Management of the Company is vested in its Members, who will manage the Company in accordance with the Act. Any Member exercising management powers or responsibilities will be deemed to be a manager for purposes of applying the provisions of the Act, unless the context otherwise requires, and that Member will have and be subject to all of the duties and liabilities of a manager provided in the Act. The Members will have the power to do any and all acts necessary or convenient to or for the furtherance of the purposes of the Company set forth in this Agreement, including all powers of Members under the Act.

ARTICLE FOUR
PURPOSE

The purpose of the Company is to engage in any lawful act or activity for which limited liability companies may be formed under the Act and to engage in any and all activities necessary or incidental to these acts.

ARTICLE FIVE
MEMBERS

The names and the business, residence, or mailing address of the members are as follows:

Name	Address
_____	_____
_____	_____
_____	_____

ARTICLE SIX
CAPITAL CONTRIBUTIONS

The Members have contributed to the Company the following amounts, in the form of cash, property, or services rendered, or a promissory note or other obligation to contribute cash or property or to render services:

Member	Amount of Capital Contribution
_____	$_____
_____	$_____
_____	$_____

ARTICLE SEVEN
ADDITIONAL CONTRIBUTIONS

No member is required to make any additional capital contribution to the Company.

ARTICLE EIGHT
ALLOCATION OF PROFITS AND LOSSES

The Company's profits and losses will be allocated in proportion to the value of the capital contributions of the Members.

ARTICLE NINE
DISTRIBUTIONS

Distributions shall be made to the Members at the times and in the aggregate amounts determined by the Members. Such distributions shall be allocated among the Members in the same proportion as their then capital account balances.

ARTICLE TEN
WITHDRAWAL OF MEMBER

A Member may withdraw from the Company in accordance with the Act.

ARTICLE ELEVEN
ASSIGNMENTS

A Member may assign in whole or part his or her membership interest in the Company; provided, however, an assignee of a membership interest may not become a Member without the vote or written consent of at least a majority in interest of the Members, other than the Member who assigns or proposes to assign his or her membership interest.

ARTICLE TWELVE
ADMISSION OF ADDITIONAL MEMBERS

One or more additional Members of the Company may be admitted to the Company with the vote or written consent of a majority in interest of the Members (as defined in the Act).

ARTICLE THIRTEEN
LIABILITY OF MEMBERS

The members do not have any liability for the obligations or liabilities of the Company, except to the extent provided in the Act.

ARTICLE FOURTEEN
EXCULPATION OF MEMBER-MANAGERS

A Member exercising management powers or responsibilities for or on behalf of the Company will not have personal liability to the Company or its members for damages for any breach of duty in that capacity, provided that nothing in this Article shall eliminate or limit: (i) the liability of any Member-Manager if a judgment or other final adjudication adverse to him or her establishes that his or her acts or omissions were in bad faith or involved intentional misconduct or a knowing violation of law, or that he or she personally gained in fact a financial profit or other advantage to which he or she was not legally entitled, or that, with respect to a distribution to Members, his or her acts were not performed in accordance with Section [number of section] of the Act; or (ii) the liability of any Member-Manager for any act or omission prior to the date of first inclusion of this paragraph in this Agreement.

ARTICLE FIFTEEN
GOVERNING LAW

This Agreement shall be governed by, and construed in accordance with, the laws of the State of ___, all rights and remedies being governed by those laws.

ARTICLE SIXTEEN
INDEMNIFICATION

To the fullest extent permitted by law, the Company shall indemnify and hold harmless, and may advance expenses to, any Member, manager, or other person, or any testator or intestate of such Member, manager, or other person (collectively, the "Indemnitees"), from and against any and all claims and demands whatsoever; provided, however, that no indemnification may be made to or on behalf of any Indemnitee if a judgment or other final adjudication adverse to such Indemnitee establishes: (i) that his or her acts were committed in bad faith or were the result of active and deliberate dishonesty and were material to the cause of action so adjudicated; or (ii) that he or she

personally gained in fact a financial profit or other advantage to which he or she was not legally entitled. The provisions of this section shall continue to afford protection to each Indemnitee regardless of whether he or she remains a Member, manager, employee, or agent of the Company.

ARTICLE SEVENTEEN
TAX MATTERS

The Members of the Company and the Company intend that the Company be treated as a partnership for all income tax purposes, and will file all necessary and appropriate forms in furtherance of that position.

In witness, the parties have executed this agreement the day and year first above written.

_____
[Name of first member]

_____
[Name of second member]

_____
[Name of third member]
[Name of limited liability company]
By:

_____
[Name of officer of limited liability company]
[Title of officer of limited liability company]

APPENDIX F

Bylaws

[6 Am. Jur. Legal Forms 2d Corporations § 74:632 (May 2011)]

BYLAWS

ARTICLE ONE
OFFICES

The principal office of the corporation shall be located at _____ [address], _____ [city], _____ County, _____ [state]. The board of directors shall have the power and authority to establish and maintain branch or subordinate offices at any other locations _____ [within the same city or within the same state or as the case may be].

ARTICLE TWO
STOCKHOLDERS

A. Annual Meeting. The annual meeting of the stockholders shall be held on the _____ [ordinal number] day in the month of _____ in each year, beginning with the year _____, at _____ [time], for the purpose of electing directors and for the transaction of such other business as may come before the meeting. If the day fixed for the annual meeting shall be a legal holiday in [state] _____, such meeting shall be held on the next succeeding business day. If the election of directors is not held on the day designated in this article for any annual meeting of the shareholders, or at any adjournment of such annual meeting, the board of directors shall cause the election to be held at a special meeting of the stockholders as soon as is convenient.

B. Special Meetings. Special meetings of the stockholders, for any purpose or purposes, unless otherwise prescribed by statute, may be called by the president or by the board of directors, and shall be called by the president at the request of the holders of not less than _____ [number] of all the outstanding shares of the corporation entitled to vote at the meeting.

C. Place of Meeting. The board of directors may designate any place within _____ [if desired, add: or without] [state] _____, as the place of meeting for any annual meeting or for any special meeting called by the board of directors. A waiver of notice signed by all stockholders entitled to vote at a meeting may designate any place, either within or without [state] _____, as the place for the holding of such meeting. If no designation is made, or if a special meeting is otherwise called, the place of meeting shall be the principal office of the corporation in [city] _____, _____ [state].

D. Notice of Meeting. Written or printed notice stating the place, day, and hour of the meeting and, in case of a special meeting, the purpose or purposes for which the meeting is called, shall be delivered not less than _____ nor more than _____ days before the date of the meeting, either personally or by mail, by or at the direction of the president, or the secretary, or the officer or persons calling the meeting, to each shareholder of record entitled to vote at such meeting. If mailed, such notice shall be deemed to be delivered when deposited in the United States mail, addressed to the shareholder at his or her address as it appears on the stock transfer books of the corporation, with postage prepaid. _____ [If appropriate, add: Notice of each meeting shall also be mailed to holders of stock not entitled to vote, as provided in this article, but lack of such notice shall not affect the legality of any meeting otherwise properly called and noticed.]

E. Closing Transfer Books or Fixing Record Date. For the purpose of determining stockholders entitled to notice of, or to vote at, any meeting of stockholders or any adjournment of such a meeting, or stockholders entitled to receive payment of any dividend, or to make a determination of shareholders for any other proper purpose, the board of directors of the corporation may provide that the stock transfer books shall be closed for a stated period, but not to exceed _____ days. If the stock transfer books shall be closed for the purpose of determining stockholders entitled to notice of, or to vote at, a meeting of stockholders, such books shall be closed for at least _____ days immediately preceding such meeting. In lieu of closing the stock transfer books, the board of directors may fix in advance a date as the record date for any such determination of stockholders, such date in any event to be not more than _____ days, and in case of a meeting of stockholders, not less than _____ days prior to the date on which the particular action requiring such determination of stockholders is to be taken.

If the stock transfer books are not closed and no record date is fixed for the determination of stockholders entitled to notice of, or to vote at, a meeting of stockholders, or of stockholders entitled to receive payment of a dividend, the date that notice of the meeting is mailed or the date on which the resolution of the board of directors declaring such dividend is adopted, as the case may be, shall be the record date for such determination of stockholders. When a determination of stockholders entitled to vote at any meeting of stockholders has been made as provided in this paragraph, such determination shall apply to any adjournment of such a meeting except where the determination has been made through the closing of the stock transfer books and the stated period of closing has expired.

F. Quorum. A majority of the outstanding shares of the corporation entitled to vote, represented in person or by proxy, shall constitute a quorum at a meeting of stockholders. If less than a majority of such outstanding shares are represented at a meeting, a majority of the shares so represented may adjourn the meeting from time to time without further notice. At such adjourned meeting at which a quorum is present or represented, any business may be transacted that might have been transacted at the meeting as originally notified. The stockholders present at a duly organized meeting may continue to transact business until adjournment, notwithstanding the withdrawal of enough stockholders to leave less than a quorum.

G. Proxies. At all meetings of stockholders, a stockholder may vote by proxy executed in writing by the stockholder or by his duly authorized attorney in fact. Such proxy shall be filed with the secretary of the corporation before or at the time of the meeting. No proxy shall be valid after _____ months from the date of its execution unless otherwise provided in the proxy.

H. Voting of Shares. Subject to the provisions of any applicable law _____ [if desired, add: or any provision of the _____ (articles or certificate) of incorporation or of these bylaws concerning cumulative voting], each outstanding share entitled to vote shall be entitled to one vote on each matter submitted to a vote at a meeting of stockholders.

ARTICLE THREE
BOARD OF DIRECTORS

A. General Powers. The business and affairs of the corporation shall be managed by its board of directors.

B. Number, Tenure, and Qualifications. The number of directors of the corporation shall be _____. Directors shall be elected at the annual meeting of stockholders, and the term of office of each director shall be until the next annual meeting of stockholders and the election and qualification of his or her successor. Directors need not be residents of [state] _____, _____ [but shall be stockholders of the corporation or and need not be stockholders of the corporation].

C. Regular Meetings. A regular meeting of the board of directors shall be held without notice other than this bylaw immediately after and at the same place as the annual meeting of stockholders. The board of directors may provide, by resolution, the time and place for holding additional regular meetings without other notice than such resolution. Additional regular meetings shall be held at the principal office of the corporation in the absence of any designation in the resolution.

D. Special Meetings. Special meetings of the board of directors may be called by or at the request of the president or any _____ [two] directors, and shall be held at the principal office of the corporation or at such other place as the directors may determine.

E. Notice. Notice of any special meeting shall be given at least _____ [48 hours or as the case may be] before the time fixed for the meeting, by written notice delivered personally or mailed to each director at his or her business address, or by telegram. If mailed, such notice shall be deemed to be delivered when deposited in the United States mail so addressed, with postage prepaid, not less than _____ days prior to the commencement of the above-stated notice period. If notice is given by telegram, such notice shall be deemed to be delivered when the telegram is delivered to the telegraph company. Any director may waive notice of any meeting. The attendance of a director at a meeting shall constitute a waiver of notice of such meeting, except where a director attends a meeting for the express purpose of objecting to the transaction of any business because the meeting is not lawfully called or convened. Neither the business to be transacted at, nor the purpose of, any regular or special meeting of the board of directors need be specified in the notice or waiver of notice of such meeting.

F. Quorum. A majority of the number of directors fixed by these bylaws shall constitute a quorum for the transaction of business at any meeting of the board of directors, but if less than such majority is present at a meeting, a majority of the directors present may adjourn the meeting from time to time without further notice.

G. Board Decisions. The act of the majority of the directors present at a meeting at which a quorum is present shall be the act of the board of directors _____ [except that vote of not less than _____ (fraction) of all the members of the board shall be required for the amendment of or addition to these bylaws or as the case may be].

H. Vacancies. Any vacancy occurring in the board of directors may be filled by the affirmative vote of a majority of the remaining directors though less than a quorum of the board of directors. A director elected to fill a vacancy shall be elected for the unexpired term of his or her predecessor in office. Any directorship to be filled by reason of an increase in the number of directors shall be filled by election at an annual meeting or at a special meeting of stockholders called for that purpose.

I. Compensation. By resolution of the board of directors, the directors may be paid their expenses, if any, of attendance at each meeting of the board of directors, and may be paid a fixed sum for attendance at each meeting of the board of directors or a stated salary as director. No such payment shall preclude any director from serving the corporation in any other capacity and receiving compensation for such service.

J. Presumption of Assent. A director of the corporation who is present at a meeting of the board of directors at which action on any corporate matter is taken shall be presumed to have assented to the action taken unless his or her dissent shall be entered in the minutes of the meeting or unless he or she shall file his or her written dissent to such action with the person acting as the secretary of the meeting before the adjournment of the meeting or shall forward such dissent by registered mail to the secretary of the corporation immediately after the adjournment of the meeting. Such right to dissent shall not apply to a director who voted in favor of such action.

ARTICLE FOUR
OFFICERS

A. Number. The officers of the corporation shall be a president, one or more vice-presidents (the number of which to be determined by the board of directors), a secretary, and a treasurer, each of whom shall be elected by the board of directors. Such other officers and assistant officers as may be deemed necessary may be elected or appointed by the board of directors. Any two or more offices may be held by the same person, except the offices of _____ [president and secretary or as the case may be].

B. Election and Term of Office. The officers of the corporation to be elected by the board of directors shall be elected annually at the first meeting of the board of directors held after each annual meeting of the stockholders. If the election of officers is not held at such meeting, such election shall be held as soon afterward as is convenient. Each officer shall hold office until his or her successor has been duly elected and qualifies or until his or her death or until he or she resigns or is removed in the manner provided below.

C. Removal. Any officer or agent elected or appointed by the board of directors may be removed by the board of directors whenever in its judgment the best interests of the corporation would be served by such removal, but such removal shall be without prejudice to the contract rights, if any, of the person so removed.

D. Vacancies. A vacancy in any office because of death, resignation, removal, disqualification or otherwise, may be filled by the board of directors for the unexpired portion of the term.

E. Powers and Duties. The powers and duties of the several officers shall be as provided from time to time by resolution or other directive of the board of directors. In the absence of such provisions, the respective officers shall have the powers and shall discharge the duties customarily and usually held and performed by like officers of corporations similar in organization and business purposes to this corporation.

F. Salaries. The salaries of the officers shall be fixed from time to time by the board of directors, and no officer shall be prevented from receiving such salary by reason of the fact that he or she is also a director of the corporation.

ARTICLE FIVE
CONTRACTS, LOANS, CHECKS, AND DEPOSITS

A. Contracts. The board of directors may authorize any officer or officers, agent or agents, to enter into any contract or execute and deliver any instrument in the name of and on behalf of the corporation, and such authority may be general or confined to specific instances.

B. Loans. No loans shall be contracted on behalf of the corporation and no evidences of indebtedness

shall be issued in its name unless authorized by a resolution of the board of directors. Such authority may be general or confined to specific instances.

C. Checks, Drafts, or Orders. All checks, drafts, or other orders for the payment of money, notes, or other evidences of indebtedness issued in the name of the corporation shall be signed by such officer or officers, agent or agents of the corporation and in such manner as shall from time to time be determined by resolution of the board of directors.

D. Deposits. All funds of the corporation not otherwise employed shall be deposited from time to time to the credit of the corporation in such banks, trust companies, or other depositaries as the board of directors may select.

ARTICLE SIX
CERTIFICATES FOR SHARES; TRANSFERS

A. Certificates for Shares. Certificates representing shares of the corporation shall be in such form as shall be determined by the board of directors. Such certificates shall be signed by the president or a vice-president and by the secretary or an assistant secretary. All certificates for shares shall be consecutively numbered or otherwise identified. The name and address of the person to whom the shares represented by such certificates are issued, with the number of shares and date of issue, shall be entered on the stock transfer books of the corporation. All certificates surrendered to the corporation for transfer shall be canceled and no new certificate shall be issued until the former certificate for a like number of shares shall have been surrendered and canceled, except that in case of a lost, destroyed, or mutilated certificate a new one may be issued on such terms and indemnity to the corporation as the board of directors may prescribe.

B. Transfer of Shares. Transfer of shares of the corporation shall be made in the manner specified in the _____ [Uniform Commercial Code or as the case may be]. The corporation shall maintain stock transfer books, and any transfer shall be registered on such books only on request and surrender of the stock certificate representing the transferred shares, duly endorsed. The corporation shall have the absolute right to recognize as the owner of any shares of stock issued by it, the person or persons in whose name the certificate representing such shares stands according to the books of the corporation for all proper corporate purposes, including the voting of the shares represented by the certificate at a regular or special meeting of stockholders, and the issuance and payment of dividends on such shares.

ARTICLE SEVEN
FISCAL YEAR

The fiscal year of the corporation shall _____ [be the calendar year or begin on the _____ (ordinal number) day of _____ (month) of each year and end at midnight on the _____ (ordinal number) day of _____ (month) of the following year or as the case may be].

ARTICLE EIGHT
DIVIDENDS

The board of directors may from time to time declare, and the corporation may pay, dividends on its outstanding shares in the manner and on the terms and conditions provided by law and its _____ [articles or certificate] of incorporation.

ARTICLE NINE
SEAL

The board of directors shall provide a corporate seal, which shall be circular in form and shall have inscribed on it the name of the corporation and the state of incorporation and the words "Corporate Seal." The seal shall be stamped or affixed to such documents as may be prescribed by law or custom or by the board of directors.

ARTICLE TEN
WAIVER OF NOTICE

Whenever any notice is required to be given to any stockholder or director of the corporation under the provisions of these bylaws or under the provisions of the _____ [articles or certificate] of incorporation or under the provisions of law, a waiver of such notice in writing, signed by the person or persons entitled to such notice, whether before or after the time stated in the same, shall be deemed equivalent to the giving of such notice.

ARTICLE ELEVEN
AMENDMENTS

These bylaws may be altered, amended, or repealed and new bylaws may be adopted by the board of directors at any regular or special meeting of the board; provided, however, that the number of directors shall not be increased or decreased nor shall the provisions of Article Two, concerning the stockholders, be substantially altered _____ [add other limitations as desired], without the prior approval of the stockholders at a regular or special meeting of the stockholders, or by written consent. _____ [If appropriate, add: Changes in and additions to the bylaws by the board of directors shall be reported to the stockholders at their next regular meeting and shall be subject to the approval or disapproval of the stockholders at such meeting. If no action is then taken by the stockholders on a change in or addition to the bylaws, such change or addition shall be deemed to be fully approved and ratified by the stockholders.]

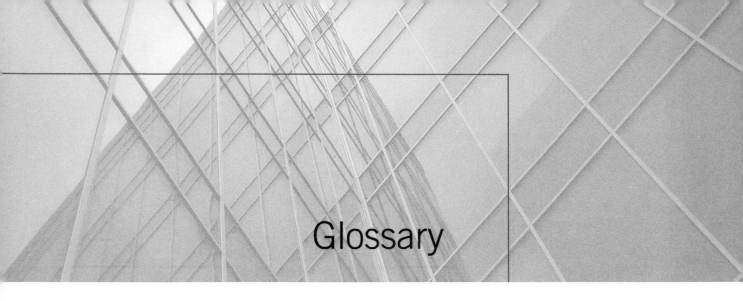

Glossary

10-K report The annual report required by the SEC of publicly held corporations that sell stock.

10-Q report The quarterly report that must be filed with the SEC by all corporations that are required to file 10-K reports.

401(K) plan A type of savings plan, established for the benefit of employees, that allows employees to elect to defer a certain percentage of their compensation to provide for their retirement benefits.

A

accrued benefit The amount of benefit a participant has accumulated or that has been allocated to him or her as of a particular point in time.

actual authority In the law of agency, the right and power to act that a principal (often an employer) intentionally gives to an agent (often an employee), or at least allows the agent to believe he has been given.

actuary A person skilled in mathematical calculations to determine insurance risks, premiums, and so forth; a statistician.

administrative dissolution The dissolution of a corporation by the state of the corporation's domicile, usually for failing to pay income taxes or file annual reports.

affiliate corporations A person or company with an inside business connection to another company. Under bankruptcy, securities, and other laws, if one company owns more than a certain amount of another company's voting stock, or if the companies are under common control, they are affiliates.

agency A relationship in which one person acts for or represents another by the latter's authority.

agency at will An agency relationship that exists at the will of both parties and may be canceled by either the principal or agent at any time.

agent A person authorized (requested or permitted) by another person to act for him or her; a person entrusted with another's business.

aggregate theory A theory regarding partnerships suggesting that a partnership is the totality of the partners rather than a separate entity.

amalgamation A complete joining or blending together of two or more things into one; for example, a consolidation or merger of two or more corporations to create a single company.

annuity A fixed sum of money, usually paid to a person at fixed times for a fixed time period or for life.

annuity plan A type of qualified plan that does not involve a qualified plan trust. Contributions to an annuity plan are used to buy annuity policies directly from an insurance company.

annuity policy An insurance policy that may be purchased to provide an annuity.

antitrust laws Federal and state laws to protect trade from monopoly control and from price fixing and other restraints of trade. The main federal antitrust laws are the Sherman, Clayton, Federal Trade Commission, and Robinson-Patman Acts.

apparent Easily seen; superficially true.

apparent authority The authority an agent seems to have, judged by the words or actions of the person who gave the authority or by the agent's own words or actions.

articles of amendment A document filed with the secretary of state or other appropriate state authority to amend a corporation's articles of incorporation.

articles of dissolution A document filed with the secretary of state or other appropriate state authority to dissolve the corporation.

articles of incorporation A document filed with the secretary of state or other appropriate state authority to form a corporation. Articles of incorporation contain the most basic rules of the corporation and control other corporate rules such as the bylaws.

articles of merger A document filed with the secretary of state or other appropriate authority to effect a merger.

articles of organization A document required to be filed with the proper state authority to form a limited liability company.

articles of share exchange A document filed with the secretary of state or other appropriate state authority to effect a share exchange.

articles of termination A document filed with the secretary of state or other appropriate state authority to dissolve a limited liability company; same as articles of dissolution.

assignment of error Alleged errors of the trial court specified by an appellant in seeking a reversal, vacation, or modification of the trial court's judgment.

assumed name An alias that may be used to transact business; usually requires filing or notification at the state or local level; same as fictitious name.

attorney in fact A person who acts formally for another person. An attorney in fact is usually appointed by a power of attorney.

authorized shares The total number of shares, provided for in the articles or certificate of incorporation, that the corporation is authorized to issue.

B

blue sky law Any state law regulating sales of stock or other investment activities to protect the public from fly-by-night or fraudulent stock deals, or to ensure that an investor gets enough information to make a reasoned purchase of stock or other security.

board of managers A group of individuals elected by the members of a limited liability company to manage the limited liability company; similar to a corporation's board of directors.

bond A document that states a debt owed by a company or a government. The company, government, or government agency promises to pay the owner of the bond a specific amount of interest for a set period of time and to repay the debt on a certain date. A bond, unlike a stock, gives the holder no ownership rights in the company.

business judgment rule The principle that if persons running a corporation make honest, careful decisions within their corporate powers, no court will interfere with these decisions even if the results are bad.

buy-sell agreement An agreement among partners or owners of a company that if one dies or withdraws from the business, his or her share will be bought by the others or disposed of according to a prearranged plan.

bylaws Rules or regulations adopted by an organization such as a corporation, club, or town.

C

capital surplus Property paid into a corporation by the shareholders in excess of capital stock liability.

certificate of assumed name, trade name, or fictitious name A certificate issued by the proper state authority to an individual or an entity that grants the right to use an assumed or fictitious name for the transaction of business in that state.

certificate of authority A certificate issued by the secretary of state, or other appropriate state official, to a foreign business entity to allow that entity to transact business in that state.

certificate of good standing Sometimes referred to as a "certificate of existence." A certificate issued by the secretary of state or other appropriate state authority proving the incorporation and good standing of the corporation in that state.

charter An organization's basic starting document; for example, a corporation's articles of incorporation.

civil law 1. Law that originated from ancient Rome rather than from the common law or from canon law. 2. The law governing private rights and remedies, as opposed to criminal law, military law, international law, natural law, and so on.

Clayton Act (15 U.S.C. 12) A 1914 federal law that extended the Sherman Act's prohibition against monopolies and price discrimination.

clearing agency Any person who acts as an intermediary in making payments or deliveries or both in connection with transactions in securities or who provides facilities for comparison of data respecting the terms of settlement of securities transactions, to reduce the number of settlements of securities transactions, or for the allocation of securities settlement responsibilities.

close corporation A corporation with total ownership in a few hands; also referred to as "closely held corporation."

collateral Money or property subject to a security interest.

commercial paper A negotiable instrument related to business; for example, a bill of exchange. Sometimes, the word is restricted to a company's control.

Commission on Uniform State Laws An organization that, along with the American Law Institute, proposes various model acts and uniform acts for adoption by the states.

common law 1. Judge-made law (based on ancient customs, mores, usages, and principles handed down through the ages) in the absence of controlling statutory or other enacted law. 2. All the statutory and case law of England and the American colonies before the American Revolution.

common stock Shares in a corporation that depend for their value on the value of the company. These shares usually have voting rights (which other types of company stock may lack). Usually, they earn a dividend (profit) only after all other types of the company's obligations have been paid.

conflict of interest Being in a position where your own needs and desires could possibly lead you to violate your duty to a person who has a right to depend on you, or being in a position where you try to serve competing masters or clients.

consideration The reason or main cause for a person to make a contract; something of value received or promised to induce (convince) a person to make a deal.

consolidation Two corporations joining together to form a third, new one.

contract An agreement that affects or creates legal relationships between two or more persons. To be a contract, an agreement must involve: at least one promise, consideration (something of value promised or given), persons legally capable of making binding agreements, and a reasonable certainty about the meaning of the terms.

conversion Any act that deprives an owner of property without that owner's permission and without just cause. For example, it is conversion to refuse to return a borrowed book.

conversion rights Rights, often granted to preferred shareholders with the issuance of preferred stock, that allow the preferred shareholders to convert their shares of preferred stock into common stock at some specific point in time, usually at the shareholder's option.

copyright The right to control the copying, distributing, performing, displaying, and adapting of works (including paintings, music, books, and movies). The right belongs to the creator, or to persons employing the creator, or to persons who buy the right from the creator. The right is created, regulated, and limited by the Federal Copyright Act of 1976 and by the Constitution. The symbol for copyright is ©. The legal life (duration) of a copyright is the author's life plus 50 years, or 75 years from publication date, or 100 years from creation, depending on the circumstances.

corporate compliance program A program established by corporate management to prevent and detect misconduct among officers, directors, and employees of the corporation, and to ensure that corporate activities are conducted legally and ethically.

corporation An organization that is formed under state or federal law and exists, for legal purposes, as a separate being or an "artificial person."

covenants not to compete A part of an employee contract, partnership agreement, or agreement to sell a business in which a person promises not to engage in the same business for a certain amount of time after the relationship ends.

cumulative dividend A type of dividend paid on preferred stock that the corporation is liable for in the next payment period if not satisfied in the current payment period. Cumulative dividends on preferred stock must be paid before any dividends may be paid on common stock.

cumulative voting The type of voting in which each person (or each share of stock, in the case of a corporation) has as many votes as there are positions to be filled. Votes can be either concentrated on one or on a few candidates or spread around.

D

debentures A corporation's obligation to pay money (usually in the form of a note or bond) often unsecured (not backed up) by any specific property; usually refers only to long-term bonds.

debt capital Capital raised with an obligation in terms of interest and principal payments. Debt capital is often raised by issuing bonds.

debt securities Securities that represent loans to the corporation, or other interests that must be repaid.

defined benefit plan A retirement plan in which the benefit payable to the participant is definitely determinable from a benefit formula set forth in the plan.

defined contribution plan A retirement plan that establishes individual accounts for each plan participant and provides benefits based solely on the amount contributed to the participants' accounts.

demurrer A legal pleading that says, in effect, "even if, for the sake of argument, the facts presented by the other side are correct, those facts do not give the other side a legal argument that can possibly stand up in court." The demurrer has been replaced in many courts by a motion to dismiss.

derivative action (corporate) A lawsuit by a stockholder of a corporation against another person (usually an officer of the company) to enforce claims the stockholder thinks the corporation has against that person.

derivative action (limited partnership) With regard to a limited partnership, a derivative action is a lawsuit by a limited partner against another person or entity to enforce claims the limited partner thinks the limited partnership has against that person. Limited partners may bring derivative actions in some states if the general partner(s) refuse to bring the action. Derivative actions by limited partnerships are not allowed in all states.

determination letter A letter issued by the IRS in response to an inquiry as to the tax implications of a given situation or transaction.

direct action A lawsuit by a stockholder to enforce his or her own rights against a corporation or its officers rather than to enforce the corporation's rights in a derivative action.

disgorgement To give up something (usually illegal profits) on demand or by court order.

dissociation The event that occurs when a partner withdraws or otherwise ceases to be associated in the carrying on of the partnership business.

dissolution The termination of a corporation, partnership, or other business entity's existence.

dividend A share of profits or property; usually a payment per share of a corporation's stock.

domicile A person's permanent home, legal home, or main residence. The words "abode," "citizenship," "habitancy," and "residence" sometimes mean the same as "domicile" and sometimes not. A corporate domicile is the corporation's legal home (usually where its headquarters is located); an elected domicile is the place the persons who make a contract specify as their legal homes in the contract.

door-closing statute A state statute providing that a corporation doing business in the state without the necessary authority is precluded from maintaining an action in that state.

downstream merger A merger whereby a parent corporation is merged into a subsidiary.

due diligence Enough care, enough timeliness, or enough investigation to meet legal requirements, to fulfill a duty, or to evaluate the risks of a course of action. Due diligence often refers to a professional investigation of the financial risks of a merger or a securities purchase, or the legal obligation to do the investigation. Due diligence is also used as a synonym for "due care."

durable power of attorney A power of attorney that lasts as long as a person remains incapable of making decisions, usually about health care.

E

EDGAR Electronic Data Gathering, Analysis, and Retrieval system established by the SEC to collect, validate, index, and provide to the public, documents that are required to be filed with the SEC.

Employee Retirement Income Security Act of 1974 (ERISA) (29 U.S.C. 1000) A federal law that established a program to protect employees' pension plans. The law set up a fund to pay pensions when plans go broke and regulates pension plans as to vesting (when a person's pension rights become permanent), nondiversion of benefits to anyone other than those entitled, nondiscrimination against lower-paid employees, and so on.

employee stock ownership plan (ESOP) A qualified plan designed to give partial ownership of the corporation to the employees.

employee welfare benefit plan An employee benefit plan that provides participants with welfare benefits such as medical, disability, life insurance, dental, and death benefits. A welfare benefit plan may provide benefits either entirely or partially through insurance coverage.

employment agreement An agreement entered into between an employer and an employee to set forth the rights and obligations of each party with regard to the employee's employment.

entity at will An entity that may be dissolved at the wish of one or more members or owners.

entity conversion A process whereby a domestic corporation becomes an unincorporated entity or an unincorporated entity becomes a corporation.

entity theory A theory suggesting that a partnership is an entity separate from its partners, much like a corporation.

equity compensation Stock awards, stock options, and other compensation paid to employees and executives in the form of equity of the corporation.

equity securities Securities that represent an ownership interest in the corporation.

estoppel Being stopped by your own prior acts from claiming a right against another person who has legitimately relied on those acts.

exchange An organization set up to buy and sell securities such as stocks.

express Clear, definite, direct, or actual (as opposed to implied); known by explicit words.

express authority Authority delegated to an agent by words that expressly authorize him or her to do a delegable act; authority that is directly granted to or conferred upon an agent in express terms; that authority that principal intentionally confers upon his or her agent by manifestations to him or her.

F

Federal Trade Commission A federal agency created in 1914 to promote free and fair competition and to enforce the provisions of the Federal Trade Commission Act, which prohibits "unfair or deceptive acts or practices in commerce."

Federal Trade Commission Act The federal act passed in 1914, establishing the Federal Trade Commission to curb unfair trade practices.

fictitious name An alias that may be used to transact business; usually requires filing or notification at the state or local level; same as assumed name.

fiduciary 1. A person who manages money or property for another person and in whom that other person has a right to place great trust. 2. A relationship like that in definition no. 1. 3. Any relationship between persons in which one person acts for another in a position of trust; for example, lawyer and client or parent and child.

foreign corporation A corporation incorporated in a state or country other than the state referred to. A corporation is considered a foreign corporation in every state other than its state of incorporation.

foreign limited liability company A limited liability company that is transacting business in any state other than the state of its organization.

Form 8-K A form that must be filed with the SEC by the issuer of registered securities when certain pertinent information contained in the registration statement of the issuer changes.

full shield statutes Laws that provide that obligations of the partnership belong solely to the partnership and that partners are not personally liable for any partnership obligations.

G

general agent One who is authorized to act for his or her principal in all matters concerning a particular business or employment of a particular nature.

general partner 1. Synonymous with partner. A partner in a general partnership, or limited partnership, who typically has unlimited personal liability for the debts and liabilities of the partnership. 2. A member of a general or limited partnership who shares in the profits and losses of the partnership and may participate fully in the management of the partnership. General partners are usually personally liable for the debts and obligations of the partnership.

general partnership A typical partnership in which all partners are general partners. Elements of partnership: association of two or more persons; carry on; co-ownership; business; for profit.

general power of attorney A power of attorney authorizing the attorney in fact to act on behalf of the principal in all matters.

golden parachute An employment contract or termination agreement that gives a top executive a big bonus or other major benefits if the executive loses his or her job (usually due to a change in corporate control).

goodwill The reputation and patronage of a company. The monetary worth of a company's goodwill is roughly what a company would sell for over the value of its physical property, money owed to it, and other assets.

H

Hart-Scott-Rodino act (15 U.S.C. § 18a) A federal law passed in 1976 that strengthens the enforcement powers of the Justice Department. The act requires entities to give notice to the Federal Trade Commission and the Justice Department prior to mergers and acquisitions when the size of the transaction is valued at $50 million or more.

heir A person who inherits property; a person who has a right to inherit property; or a person who has a right to inherit property only if another person dies without leaving a valid, complete will. [pronounce: air]

hostile takeover A corporate takeover that is opposed by the management and board of directors.

I

implied Known indirectly; known by analyzing surrounding circumstances or the actions of the persons involved.

implied authority The authority one person gives to another to do a job, even if the authority is not given directly.

indemnification The act of compensating or promising to compensate a person who has suffered a loss or may suffer a future loss.

independent contractor A person who contracts with an "employer" to do a particular piece of work by his or her own methods and under his or her own control.

individual retirement account (IRA) A bank or investment account into which some persons may set aside a certain amount of their earnings each year and have their interest taxed only later when withdrawn.

inherent Derived from and inseparable from the thing itself.

initial public offering The first offering of a corporation's securities to the public.

insider trading The purchase or sale of securities by corporate insiders based on nonpublic information.

inspectors of election Impartial individuals who are often appointed to oversee the election of directors at the shareholder meetings of large corporations.

integrated plan A type of retirement plan that is integrated with the employer's contribution to Social Security on behalf of the participant.

intellectual property 1. A copyright, patent trademark, trade secret, or similar intangible right in an original tangible or perceivable work. 2. The works themselves in no. 1. 3. The right to obtain a copyright, patent, and so on for the works in no. 1.

investment contract Under federal law, any agreement that involves an investment of money pooled with others' money to gain profits solely from the efforts of others.

involuntary dissolution A dissolution that is not approved by the board of directors or shareholders of a corporation, often initiated by creditors of an insolvent corporation.

issued and outstanding shares The total shares of stock of a corporation that have been authorized by the corporation's articles or certificate of incorporation and issued to shareholders.

J

joint and several Both together and individually. For example, a liability or debt is joint and several if the creditor may sue the debtors either together as a group (with the result that the debtors would have to split the loss) or individually (with the result that one debtor might have to pay the whole thing).

joint venture Sometimes referred to as a "joint adventure"; the relationship created when two or more persons combine jointly in a business enterprise with the understanding that they will share in the profits or losses and that each will have a voice in its management. Although a joint venture is a form of partnership, it customarily involves a single business project rather than an ongoing business relationship.

K

Keogh plan A tax-free retirement account for persons with self-employment income.

L

letter of intent A preliminary written agreement setting forth the intention of the parties to enter into a contract.

limited liability company A cross between a partnership and a corporation owned by members who may manage the company directly or delegate to officers or managers who are similar to a corporation's directors. Governing documents are usually publicly filed articles of organization and a private operating agreement. Members are not usually liable for company debts, and company income and losses are usually divided among and taxed to the members individually according to share.

limited liability limited partnership A type of limited partnership permissible in some states in which the general partners have less than full liability for the actions of other general partners.

limited liability partnership A partnership in which the partners have less than full liability for the actions of other partners, but full liability for their own actions.

limited partner A partner who invests in a limited partnership, but does not assume personal liability for the debts and obligations of the partnership. Limited partners may not participate in the management of the limited partnership in most states.

limited partnership A partnership formed by general partners (who run the business and have liability for all partnership debts) and limited partners (who partly or fully finance the business, take no part in running it, and have no liability for partnership debts beyond the money they put in or promise to put in).

limited partnership certificate A document required for filing at the state level to form a limited partnership.

liquidation Winding up the affairs of a business by identifying assets, converting them into cash, and paying off liabilities (liquidate the company).

long-arm statute A state law that allows the courts of that state to claim jurisdiction over (decide cases directly involving) persons outside the state who have allegedly committed torts or other wrongs inside the state. Even with a long-arm statute, the court will not have jurisdiction unless the person sued has certain minimum contacts with the state.

low-profit limited liability company A subcategory of limited liability company that may be formed in a few states by certain entities that have a charitable or educational purpose.

M

manager-managed limited liability company A limited liability company in which the members have agreed to have the company's affairs managed by one or more managers.

member An owner of a limited liability company.

member-managed limited liability company A limited liability company in which the members have elected to share the managing of the company's affairs.

merger The union of two or more corporations, with one corporation ceasing to exist and becoming a part of the other.

money purchase pension plan A defined contribution pension plan whereby the employer contributes a fixed amount based on a formula set forth in the plan that is based on the employee's salary.

monopoly Control by one or a few companies of the manufacture, sale, distribution, or price of something. A monopoly may be prohibited if, for example, a company deliberately drives out competition.

N

nomenclature Designation, title, or name of something.

novation The substitution by agreement of a new contract for an old one, with all the rights under the old one ended. The new contract is often the same as the old one, except that one or more of the parties is different.

O

operating agreement A document that governs the limited liability company; similar to a corporation's bylaws.

over-the-counter Describes securities, such as stocks and bonds, sold directly from broker to broker or broker to customer rather than through an exchange.

P

par value The nominal value assigned to shares of stock, which is imprinted upon the face of the stock certificate as a dollar value. Most state statutes do not require corporations to assign a par value to their shares of stock.

parent corporation A corporation that fully controls or owns another company.

partial shield statutes Laws designed to protect individual partners from incurring personal liability for partnership debts and obligations arising specifically from the negligence and wrongdoing of other partners.

partnership An association of two or more persons to carry on as co-owners of a business for profit.

partnership at will A partnership formed for an indefinite period of time, without a designated date for termination.

patent An exclusive right granted by the federal government to a person for a limited number of years (usually 20) for the manufacture and sale of something that person has discovered or invented.

perfection To tie down or "make perfect." For example, to perfect title is to record it in the proper place so that your ownership is protected against all persons, not just against the person who sold it to you.

plan administrator An individual or entity responsible for calculating and processing all contributions to and distributions from a qualified plan, and for all other aspects of plan administration.

plan of exchange A document required by statute that sets forth the terms of the agreement between the parties to a statutory share exchange.

plan of merger A document required by state statute that sets forth the terms of the agreement between the two merging parties in detail.

plan of share exchange A document required by statute that sets forth the terms of the agreement between the parties to a statutory share exchange. Also referred to as plan of exchange.

plan participants Employees who meet with certain minimum requirements to participate in a qualified plan.

power of attorney A document authorizing a person to act as attorney in fact for the person signing the document.

preemptive right The right of some stockholders to have the first opportunity to buy any new stock the company issues.

preferred stock A type of stock that is entitled to certain rights and privileges over other outstanding stock of the corporation.

preincorporation agreement An agreement entered into between parties setting forth their intentions with regard to the formation of a corporation.

principal An employer or anyone else who has another person (an agent) do things for him or her.

profit-sharing plan A plan established by an employer to distribute part of the firm's profits to some or all of its employees.

promoter An individual who assists in creating and organizing a corporation, often by bringing interested parties together, obtaining subscriptions for stock of the proposed corporation, and seeing to the actual formation of the corporation.

proxy A person who acts for another person (usually to vote in place of the other person in a meeting the other cannot attend). A document giving that right.

proxy statement The document sent or given to stockholders when their voting proxies are requested for a corporate decision. The SEC has rules for when the statements must be given out and what must be in them.

public corporation A corporation that has shares listed on a national securities exchange or shares that are regularly traded in a market maintained by one or more members of a national securities association. Also referred to as publicly held corporation or publicly traded corporation.

public offering The offering of securities for sale to the public by means of interstate commerce.

punitive damages Extra money given to punish the defendant and to help keep a particular bad act from happening again.

Q

qualified plan A pension plan that meets IRS requirements for the payments to be deducted by the employer and initially tax-free to the employee.

qualified plan contributions Contributions made to a qualified plan by the sponsor, participants, or third parties. Limitations on the amount of contributions are set forth in the Internal Revenue Code.

qualified plan distributions Distributions made to qualified plan participants or their beneficiaries from a qualified retirement plan trust, usually on the retirement, death, or termination of employment of the plan participant.

qualified plan trust A trust managed by trustees who are appointed by the qualified plan sponsors to manage the assets of the qualified plan.

quorum The number of persons who must be present to make the votes and other actions of a group (such as a board) valid. This number is often a majority (over half) of the whole group, but is sometimes much less or much more.

R

ratification The confirmation and acceptance of a previous act done by you or by another person.

red herring prospectus A preliminary prospectus, used during the "waiting period" between filing a registration statement with the SEC and approval of the statement. It has a red "for information only" statement on the front and states that the securities described may not be offered for sale until SEC approval. The red herring must be filed with the SEC before use.

registered agent Individual or organization designated by a corporation as agent to receive service of process for the corporation within the state where the agent is located. A corporation may appoint a registered agent in its state of domicile and an agent in each state where it is authorized to transact business.

registered office Physical office location designated by corporation in articles of incorporation where service of process may be made on the corporation within the state. In addition to the registered office address in the corporation's state of domicile, the corporation must designate a registered office address in each state where it is authorized to transact business.

representative action A lawsuit brought by one stockholder in a corporation to claim rights or to fix wrongs done to many or all stockholders in the company

respondeat superior (Latin) "Let the master answer." Describes the principle that an employer is responsible for most harm caused by an employee acting within the scope of employment. In such a case, the employer is said to have "vicarious liability."

reverse triangle merger A three-way merger whereby a subsidiary corporation is merged into the target corporation. The end result is the survival of the parent corporation and the target corporation, which becomes a new subsidiary.

Revised Uniform Limited Liability Company Act Uniform act adopted by the National Conference of Commissioners on Uniform State Laws in 2006 to address numerous questions that had arisen concerning limited liability company law.

rules of professional conduct American Bar Association rules stating and explaining what lawyers must do, must not do, should do, and should not do. They cover the field of legal ethics (a lawyer's obligations to clients, courts, other lawyers, and the public) and have been adopted in modified forms by most of the states.

S

Sarbanes-Oxley act of 2002 Also referred to as the Public Accounting Reform and Investor Protection Act of 2002. Federal law signed into law effective July 30, 2002, to protect investors by improving the accuracy and reliability of corporate disclosures made pursuant to the securities laws, and for other related purposes.

scrip A piece of paper that is a temporary indication of a right to something valuable. Scrip includes paper money issued for temporary use, partial shares of stock after a stock split, certificates of a deferred stock dividend that can be cashed in later, and so on.

secured transaction A secured deal involving goods or fixtures that is governed by Article 9 of the Uniform Commercial Code.

Securities Act of 1933 A federal securities act requiring the registration of securities that are to be sold to the public and the disclosure of complete information to potential buyers.

Securities and Exchange Commission A federal agency that administers the federal securities acts, primarily by regulating the sale and trading of stocks and other securities.

Securities Exchange Act of 1934 A federal securities act regulating stock exchanges and over-the-counter stock sales.

security A share of stock, a bond, a note, or one of many different kinds of documents showing a share in a company or a debt owed by a company or a government. The U.S. Supreme Court has defined a security as any investment in a common enterprise from which the investor is "led to expect profits solely from the efforts of a promoter or a third party."

security interest Any right in property that is held to make sure money is paid or that something is done.

share exchange A transaction whereby one corporation acquires all of the outstanding shares of one or more classes or series of another corporation by an exchange that is compulsory on the shareholders of the target corporation.

Sherman Act (15 U.S.C. 1) The first antitrust (antimonopoly) law, passed by the federal government in 1890 to break up combinations in restraint of trade.

short-swing profits The profits made by a company insider on the short-term sale of company stock.

simplified employee pension plan (SEP) An employer's contribution to an employee's IRA (individual retirement account) that meets certain federal requirements. Self-employed persons often use SEPs.

sinking fund Money or other assets put aside for a special purpose, such as to pay off bonds and other long-term debts as they come due or to replace, repair, or improve machinery or buildings when they wear out or become outdated.

sister corporations Two (or more) companies with the same or mostly the same owners.

sole proprietor The owner of a sole proprietorship.

sole proprietorship An unincorporated business owned by one person.

special agent One employed to conduct a particular transaction or piece of business for his or her principal or authorized to perform a specified act.

special power of attorney A power of attorney authorizing the attorney in fact to act for the principal with regard to a specific action or a specific transaction.

sponsor In ERISA terms, an employer who adopts a qualified plan for the exclusive benefit of the sponsor's employees and/or their beneficiaries.

stated capital The amount of capital contributed by stockholders; the capital or equity of a corporation as it appears in the balance sheet.

statement of authority A statement filed for public record by the partners of a partnership to expand or limit the agency authority of a partner, to deny the authority or status of a partner, or to give notice of certain events such as the dissociation of a partner or the dissolution of the partnership.

statement of denial A statement filed for public record by a partner or other interested party to contradict the information included in a statement of authority.

statement of qualification With regard to limited liability partnerships, this is the document filed by general partnerships to elect limited liability partnership status. With regard to limited liability limited partnerships, this is the document filed by limited partnerships to elect limited liability limited partnership status.

statutory close corporation A closely held corporation having no more than 50 shareholders that has elected to be treated as a statutory close corporation under the relevant statutes of its state of domicile.

statutory merger A type of merger that is specifically provided for by state statute.

stock bonus plan A type of defined contribution plan, similar to the profit-sharing plan, in which the main investment is in the employer's stock.

stock dividend The profits of stock ownership (dividends) paid out by a corporation in more stock rather than in money. This additional stock reflects the increased worth of the company.

stock options The right to buy a designated stock, at the holder's option, at a specified time for a specified price. Stock options are often granted to executives and key employees as a form of incentive compensation.

stock split A dividing of a company's stock into a greater number of shares without changing each stockholder's proportional ownership.

stock subscription An agreement to purchase a specific number of shares of a corporation.

subsidiary corporation A corporation that is owned by another corporation (the parent corporation).

summary plan description A document required by ERISA to communicate the contents of a qualified plan to plan participants.

T

target benefit plan A type of qualified plan that has many characteristics of both a defined benefit plan and a defined contribution plan.

tenancy in partnership A form of ownership provided for under the Uniform Partnership Act whereby all partners are co-owners with the other partners. Each partner has an equal right to possess the property for partnership purposes, but has no right to possess the property for any other purpose without the consent of the other partners.

tombstone ad A stock (or other securities) or land sales notice that clearly states that it is informational only and not itself an offer to buy or sell. It has a black border that resembles one on a death notice.

tort A civil (as opposed to a criminal) wrong, other than a breach of contract. For an act to be a tort, there must be: a legal duty owed by one person to another; a breach (breaking) of that duty; and harm done as a direct result of the action. Examples of torts are negligence, battery, and libel.

tortious Constituting a tort; a civil (as opposed to a criminal) wrong (tort), other than a breach of contract. For an act to be a tort, there must be: a legal duty owed by one person to another; a breach (breaking) of that duty; and harm done as a direct result of the action. Examples of torts are negligence, battery, and libel.

trade name The name of a business. It will usually be legally protected in the area where the company operates and for the types of products in which it deals.

trademark A distinctive mark, brand name, motto, or symbol used by a company to identify or advertise the products it makes or sells. Trademarks (and service marks) can be federally registered and protected against use by other companies if the marks meet certain criteria. A federally registered mark bears the symbol ®.

transfer agent A person (or an institution such as a bank) who keeps track of who owns a company's stocks and bonds; also called a registrar. A transfer agent sometimes also arranges dividend and interest payments.

transferee A person to whom a transfer is made.

treasury shares Shares of stock that have been rebought by the corporation that issued them.

triangle merger A merger involving three corporations, whereby a corporation forms a subsidiary corporation and funds it with sufficient cash or shares of stock to perform a merger with the target corporation, which is merged into the subsidiary. The parent and subsidiary corporations survive.

U

underwriter With regard to securities offerings, any person or organization that purchases securities from an issuer with a view to distributing them, or any person who offers or sells or participates in the offer or sale for an issuer of any security.

Uniform Limited Liability Company Act Uniform act adopted by the National Conference of Commissioners on Uniform State Laws in 1994 and amended in 1995 to give states guidance when drafting limited liability company statutes.

upstream merger A merger whereby a subsidiary corporation merges into its parent.

V

vested Absolute, accrued, complete, not subject to any conditions that could take it away; not contingent on anything.

voluntary dissolution A dissolution that is approved by the directors and shareholders of the corporation.

voting group All shares of one or more classes that are entitled to vote and be counted together collectively on a certain matter under the corporation's articles of incorporation or the pertinent state statute.

W

watered stock A stock issue that is sold as if fully paid for, but that is not (often because some or all of the shares were given out for less than full price).

white-collar crime A term signifying various types of unlawful, nonviolent conduct committed by corporations and individuals, including theft or fraud and other violations of trust committed in the course of the offender's occupation (e.g., embezzlement, commercial bribery, racketeering, antitrust violations, price fixing, stock manipulation, insider trading). RICO laws are used to prosecute many types of white-collar crimes.

wind up Finish current business, settle accounts, and turn property into cash in order to end a corporation or a partnership and split up the assets.

Index

D

E

G

Galleon Management, 492
General partnerships
    advantages of, 76–78
    agreement, 83–93
    assets of, 86–87
    business continuity in, 80
    capital in, 78, 80, 94–95
    contribution of partners in, 86
    control of, 82–83
    cost of organization of, 77
    death of partners in, 91–92
    definition of, 24, 57
    disadvantages of, 79–82
    dissociation in, 96–104
    dissolution of, 96–104
    financial structure of, 94–95
    income tax benefits in, 77–78
    legal expenses in, 81
    liability in, 79
    limited liability limited *vs.*, 188–189
    limited liability *vs.*, 188–189
    limited *vs.*, 122, 188–189
    losses in, 95
    management in, 76, 79–80, 82–83
    oral agreements for, 84
    organizational expenses in, 81
    profits in, 95
    purchase of, 92
    records in, 95
    regulatory reporting requirements in, 76–77
    returns filed, by industry, 60
    sale of, 92
    tax disadvantages of, 81
    term of, 85
    transfer of interest in, 80
    winding up of, 96–104
    written agreements for, 84–93
Golden parachutes, 640–641
Good standing
    certificate of, 584
    maintenance of, of foreign corporation, 588–591

Goodwill, 40
Grassmueck v. Barnett, 360, 361–363

H

Haberly, Brian, 508–509
Harold Lang Jewelers, Inc. v. Johnson, 578–580
Hart-Scott-Rodino Antitrust Improvements Act,
    530, 551
Heirs, 39
Hostile takeovers, 298, 549–550
Hunter v. Fort Worth Capital Corporation, 620,
    621–622
Hunting v. Elders, 272–276

I

ImClone Systems, Inc., 492
Impossibility of performance, 22
Incapacity, of principal or agent, 22
Income tax. *See* Tax(es)
Incorporation
    articles of incorporation, 264, 310–319,
        559–564
    in Delaware, 298–299
    gathering client information for, 301–302
    organizational meetings for, 319–331
    paralegal role with, 341–345
    preincorporation agreements, 299–300
    promoters and, 303
    stock subscriptions and, 300–301
Incorporators
    definition of, 306
    resolutions, 321
Indemnification
    definition of, 16, 317
    of directors, 364–366
    mandatory, 365
    optional, 365
    prohibited, 365–366
Independent contractor, 3–4

T

U

V